Content Knowledge: A Compendium of Standards and Benchmarks for K–12 Education

by

John S. Kendall   Robert J. Marzano

Mid–continent Regional Educational Laboratory
Aurora, CO

This publication is based on work sponsored wholly, or in part, by the Office of Educational Research and Improvement, Department of Education, under Contract Number RP91002005. The content of this publication does not necessarily reflect the views of OERI or any other agency of the U.S. Government.

McREL
Tim Waters, *Executive Director*
Lou Cicchinelli, *Deputy Director*

A version of this report is currently available on the Internet via Netscape, Mosaic, or other World Wide Web browsers. The Uniform Resource Locator (URL) is:

http://www.mcrel.org/

The standards and benchmarks are linked by hypertext and can be searched.

© Mid-continent Regional Educational Laboratory, Inc. 1996

Mid-continent Regional Educational Laboratory, Inc.
2550 South Parker Road, Suite 500
Aurora, CO 80014

(303) 337-0990 - voice
(303) 337-3005 - fax
info@mcrel.org - E-mail

ASCD Stock No. 396233

Table of Contents

Preface

This report represents the culmination of a series entitled *The Systematic Identification and Articulation of Content Standards and Benchmarks*, which was first published in April 1993 and last updated in March 1995. The first issue provided a treatment of mathematics; with this version all nine subject areas identified in the national goals are addressed, as well as health, physical education, and behavioral studies, in addition to those areas identified as important by the Secretary's Commission on Achieving Necessary Skills.

A study as ambitious as this one is always the product of the hard work and creative insight of a number of individuals. The following individuals had major responsibilities for identifying various standards and benchmarks in this report:

Shelly Wasson shared major responsibility for the identification of standards and benchmarks in science, health, the arts, and foreign language, for additions to the section on life skills, for the verification of standards and benchmarks in geography, and for document preparation.

Jennifer Norford shared major responsibility for the identification of standards and benchmarks in economics and behavioral studies, and for the revision of standards and benchmarks in mathematics.

Lisa Schoch-Roberts shared major responsibility for the identification of standards and benchmarks in physical education and for the revision of standards and benchmarks in United States and world history.

Michael Shea shared major responsibility for the identification of standards and benchmarks in civics.

Therese Sarah shared major responsibility for the initial identification of standards and benchmarks in U.S. history and K–4 history, for draft standards in economics, and assisted in the identification of the geography benchmarks.

Bradley Kennedy shared major responsibility for the initial identification of standards and benchmarks in world history, for draft standards in foreign language, and for the verification of standards in the arts.

Mary Lee Barton shared major responsibility for the revision of standards and benchmarks in the language arts.

Audrey Peralez contributed to the original identification of geography standards in an earlier report.

The contributions that these individuals have made to this study cannot be overstated.

The authors would also like to thank the following individuals for their initial reviews of various national reports and documents: Tom Barlow, Sandy Berger, Jan Birmingham, Linda Brannan, Susan Everson, Joan Grady, Toni Haas, Bob Keller, Fran Mayeski, Barbara McCombs, Joann Sebastian-Morris, Diane Paynter, Sylvia Parker, Jerome Stiller, Jo Sue Whisler, and Terry Young. Carol Loredo provided word-processing support. Thanks also to David Frost, Shae Isaacs, Linda Brannan, Brad Wherry, and Peter Lund who assisted in the production, design, and distribution of this and previous updates in print and electronic media.

Others have also supported this effort through their thoughtful discussions of issues raised in this report. The authors would like to thank C. L. Hutchins, Alice Krueger, Debra Pickering, and Janie Pollock especially, among many other colleagues.

JSK
RJM

November 1995

1. The Call for Standards

Since the publication of *A Nation at Risk* in 1983 (National Commission on Excellence in Education), there has been a growing consensus on what aspects of school reform are critical to the success of our nation's students. It is now understood that in the past, teachers have relied heavily upon textbooks to determine what is important to teach in each discipline, so much so that textbook manufacturers have become the de facto standard-setting group for the content areas. Coincident with this, testing companies, by virtue of the use to which standardized tests are put in school accountability, have provided schools and districts with measures of what students should know and be able to do in order to reach certain minimum standards — in short, testing companies have provided the de facto performance standards for schools. At the same time that the identification of important knowledge, skills, and performances has been relegated to textbook and test publishers, we have entered an age when information grows so rapidly that subject-matter experts are compelled to review their assumptions about the essential knowledge and skills of their disciplines. Clearly there is a need for expert subject-area guidance to determine what students should know and be able to do to prepare themselves for college and the world of work. In short, it is time to establish standards in a rigorous and systematic way.

Although there is national dialogue on the development of standards, there is clearly not a consensus across groups as to what form "standards" should take or how they should be used. The result is that the character, scope, and level of detail provided in standards often vary significantly from one subject area to another. Some subject-area groups have argued that the disciplines are so inherently different that a common approach to standards is not possible (Viadero, 1993); though, as one leading education thinker, Christopher Cross (1993), has said, "In real life, these subjects are not as clearly defined as the experts and advocates in a field might imagine or wish." Regardless of how different the discipline areas might be from one another, they each compete for a common ground: the limited amount of time and resources in the school day. Unless standards and benchmarks are presented in a roughly equivalent and useable format, decisions regarding curriculum or assessment can quickly become problematic. For example, it is difficult for a school or district to articulate a comprehensive set of standards if one subject area describes standards in terms of a performance vignette, as is the case with the work done by the Standards Project for the Language Arts, while another subject area describes standards in terms of specific components of knowledge and skills, as is the case with the mathematics standards developed by the National Council of Teachers of Mathematics. Finally, without a common format for standards, it is not likely that educators can recognize and take advantage of the possibilities for subject-area integration afforded by the commonalities that may be found across subject areas.

The purpose of the project is to address the major issues surrounding content standards, provide a model for their identification, and apply this model to identify standards and benchmarks in the subject areas. This project has been documented in a series of reports and updates (Marzano & Kendall, 1993; Kendall & Marzano, 1994, 1995). This report concludes the project, and reprints, with little or no revision, standards that were earlier identified in the subject areas of geography, the arts, and health. More substantive revisions have been made to standards in mathematics, history, and language arts. Areas that appear for the first time with this report are civics, economics, foreign language, physical education, and behavioral studies (sociology, psychology, and social anthropology). Also included are standards in thinking and reasoning, and an analysis and description of knowledge and skills considered important for the workplace; business and industry have recently identified this area of "workplace basics" as essential in the process of schooling. These standards have been augmented to address basic computer skills and are organized under the heading Life Skills.

The next section of this paper provides an overview of the current efforts toward standards development across subject areas. Section 3 describes in greater detail the types of technical and conceptual differences that have become apparent since the beginning of the standards movement and describes the model of standards and benchmarks adopted for this study. Section 4 presents key questions that should be addressed by schools and districts that are considering a standards-based strategy. Section 5 describes the overall process used in this project to identify standards and benchmarks, and Section 6 lays out the format and citation strategy used in the standards sections. Sections 7 through 19 provide standards and benchmarks for 12 separate areas, each section prefaced by a discussion of the process involved in generating those standards.

2. Work Completed and Work in Progress

Before describing the model of standards and benchmarks that is the basis for this project, it is useful to briefly consider the major efforts that are underway nationally to identify standards and benchmarks. These efforts will, of course, form the data base from which this project draws.

Mathematics

It is certainly no exaggeration to say that the publication of *Curriculum and Evaluation Standards for School Mathematics* in 1989 by the National Council of Teachers of Mathematics (NCTM) ushered in a new era relative to the role of national organizations in the practice of schooling. Through the *Standards* document, NCTM helped to form a new perspective on how national subject-area groups can contribute to the improvement of education when it delineated, for three levels (K–4, 5–8, and 9–12), a consensus on what students should know and be able to do and how that might best be demonstrated in the classroom. Other organizations soon followed NCTM's lead. The influence of the NCTM *Standards* is reflected in another useful resource for the identification of math content: an assessment framework for mathematics developed for the National Assessment of Educational Progress (NAEP)[1]. This document organizes the subject area into five sections, each section provided with up to a dozen statements presented as benchmark indicators; material is identified by the grade at which it should be introduced and when it should be assessed at both informal and formal levels.

In addition, NCTM has recently published *Assessment Standards for School Mathematics* (May 1995), which is organized around six standards that focus on important mathematics, enhanced learning, equity, openness, valid inferences, and coherence. The publication also provides guidelines on the use of assessments for different purposes such as to make instructional decisions, monitor student progress, evaluate student achievement, and evaluate programs.

Science

In science, three recent efforts contribute significantly to the development of standards. The National Committee on Science Education Standards and Assessment (NCSESA) issued the last publicly available draft of the *National Science Education Standards* in November 1994. The final document is scheduled to appear by the end of 1995. Material related directly to content standards fills 200 of the draft's 300-plus pages, while additional chapters address standards for science teaching and professional development, as well as assessment, program, and system standards. In the current draft, the science content standards are written for three levels: science for K–4 is described in 24 standards, grades 5–8 in 28 standards, and grades 9–12 in 34 standards.

The second effort within the field of science comes from the American Association for the

---

[1]NAEP ("the nation's report card"), a nationally representative assessment of student knowledge in various subject areas, is a congressionally mandated project of the National Center for Education Statistics, the U.S. Department of Education; NAEP's policy guidelines are formulated by the National Assessment Governing Board (NAGB).

Advancement of Science (AAAS). Working from the foundation they helped build in *Science for All Americans* (1992), AAAS's Project 2061 provides over 60 "literacy goals" in science as well as mathematics, technology and the social sciences. These goals are well articulated across levels K–2, 3–5, 6–8, and 9–12. This effort, published as *Benchmarks for Science Literacy* (1993), includes a useful discussion and presentation of the research base available to those who worked on the project.

In addition to these efforts, the National Science Teachers Association (NSTA) has published the *Scope, Sequence and Coordination of National Science Education Content Standards* (Aldridge, 1995) as an addendum to *The Content Core: A Guide for Curriculum Designers* (Pearsall, 1993). This supplement is designed to make the *Core* more consistent with the new standards. NSTA has also released *A High School Framework for National Science Education Standards* (Aldridge, 1995), developed under a grant from the National Science Foundation. Like the addendum to the *Core*, this framework builds directly from NCSESA's November 1994 draft of science standards. Essential generalizations in physics, chemistry, biology, Earth and space sciences, and other areas organize the framework. Each generalization is described in some detail with a list of the relevant concepts, empirical laws, and theories or models that students will need in order to acquire a solid grounding in the topic. These subsections are presented in grade sequence (9, 10–12) and include a recommended learning sequence.

The *California Science Framework* (1990) reflects indebtedness to the work done in *Science for All Americans*. Additionally, the *Framework* shows its influence in the standards work from NCSESA. However, since it is a curriculum framework rather than a standards document, it provides considerably more detail than found in the *Benchmarks* or in the NCSESA standards and seems to complement them both. The *Framework* presents the content of the physical, earth, and life sciences at four levels (K–2, 3–5, 6–8, 9–12) through what it calls the "major themes of science": energy, evolution, patterns of change, scale and structure, stability, and systems and interactions.

Finally, additional material on science in the schools is available from the National Assessment of Educational Progress in their *Science Objectives for 1990* and the *Exercise Specifications for 1994 NAEP*.

History

The History Standards Project, under the aegis of the National Center for History in the Schools (NCHS), has published three sets of standards: *National Standards for History K–4, National Standards for United States History,* and *National Standards for World History* (NCHS, 1995). Gary Nash, co-director of NCHS, which heads the history standards project, has indicated the standards may be under revision. Presumably, the efforts to revise the history standards are fueled by the recent controversy over their content ("History Standards," *Education Daily*, January 1995). A panel of historians, practitioners, and public figures, convened by the Council for Basic Education (CBE) to examine the history standards, has found that the "overwhelming majority of criticisms was targeted at the teaching examples in the documents, rather than at the actual standards for student achievement." ("Review panels," CBE, October 1995). In addition to the content standards, the three standards documents from NCHS share a treatment on Historical Thinking, which includes such standards as Chronological Thinking and Historical Comprehension.

Other useful resources are available or under development for the articulation of standards in a history curriculum. *Lessons From History: Essential Understandings and Historical Perspectives Students Should Acquire* (Crabtree, Nash, Gagnon, & Waugh, 1992) is a comprehensive description of K–12 history education; in fact, it was on the basis of this work that NCHS was funded to develop national standards. Another well-received guide, produced by the Bradley Commission on History in the Schools, is *Building a History Curriculum: Guidelines for Teaching History in the Schools* (1988). This document, which also appears as Chapter 2 in *Historical Literacy* (Gagnon, 1989), is more general in scope but does provide a focus on the historical perspective students should acquire in their study of history. A successor to the Bradley commission, The National Council for History Education, is currently developing four booklets with more specific guidelines on building a history curriculum. *Building a U.S. History Curriculum* is currently in draft; companion booklets in western civilization and world history will also appear in 1996, and a guide for history in the early grades will be available in 1997.

In addition to these resources, two documents are available from NAEP: a *Framework for the 1994 National Assessment of Educational Progress U.S. History Assessment* (not dated) and a set of *Provisional Item Specifications for U.S. History* (1992). As in other recent work from NAEP, the framework organizes its subject matter into themes such as: Change and Continuity in American Democracy, The Gathering and Interactions of Peoples, Cultures and Ideas, and The Changing Role of America in the World. The framework recommends some preliminary achievement levels (basic, proficient, and advanced) at 4th, 8th, and 12th grades. The descriptions are at a fairly general level. For example, an 8th-grade student at the basic level should, among other things, "have a beginning understanding of the fundamental political ideas and institutions of American life, and their historical origins" (p. 38). The *Item Specifications*, however, provide a greater level of detail in "defining questions," organized by theme, for students at the 4th, 8th, and 12th grade.

Language Arts
In the language arts, the Standards Project for the English Language Arts (SPELA) was initially funded by FIRST (the Fund for Improvement and Reform of Schools and Teaching) of the Office of Educational Research and Improvement. Beginning in September of 1992, SPELA was designed to be a three-year collaborative effort of the Center for the Study of Reading (CSR), the International Reading Association (IRA), and the National Council of Teachers of English (NCTE). SPELA produced one complete draft of its standards entitled *Incomplete Work of the Task Forces of the Standards Project for the English Language Arts*. That draft contained five strands (Reading/Literature, Writing, Language, Real World Literacy, and Interconnections), each listing two or three standards described at a general level. This draft was to go through a number of iterations until a final document was produced. However on March 18, 1994, the U.S. Department of Education notified SPELA that it would not continue funding for the project. According to NCTE, funding for the project was halted because of a number of "philosophical differences" between

SPELA and the federal agencies. These differences included a disagreement over the inclusion of delivery standards, which was supported by SPELA, and the lack of attention to a specific canon of children's literature, which was not supported by SPELA. However, the primary reason for cessation of funding appears to be the federal government's assertion that SPELA was not attending to the basic task of identifying what students should know and be able to do in the English language arts. As noted by Janice Anderson, interim director of FIRST at the time funding was halted, SPELA had not made "substantial progress toward meeting the objectives" of the project. The proposed standards, she stated, "are vague and often read as opinions and platitudes," focus too much on process rather than content, and lack "a coherent conceptual framework" ("NCTE/ IRA Say Standards Effort Will Continue," *The Council Chronicle*, June 1994). Since then, NCTE and IRA have vowed to complete the project even without federal support. To date, that effort has produced an incomplete draft entitled Standards for the English Language Arts (NCTE, October 1995). That draft articulates eleven very general standards, but does not address benchmarks at different developmental levels. As in the case with the SPELA document, this later effort has met with criticism due to its lack of specificity. According to an article in *Education Daily*, the eleven standards the International Reading Association and the National Council of Teachers of English (NCTE) are drafting "deliberately say little more than that students should be able to read a wide range of texts and write effectively using various strategies... The document elaborates on each standard, but doesn't break down specific competencies students should show at various grade levels, as do standards in other disciplines." (*Education Daily*, October 25, 1995, p.1)

Although its efforts were not designed to produce standards per se, the National Assessment of Educational Progress has produced a number of documents that provide guidance as to the nature and format of English language arts standards. For example, the *Description of Writing Achievement Levels—Setting Process and Proposed Achievement Level Definitions* (NAEP, 1992) provides explicit descriptions of basic, proficient, and advanced performance in writing. These level descriptions can quite easily be translated into expectations about what students should know and be able to do in the area of composition. In the area of reading, the *Assessment and Exercise Specifications: NAEP Reading Consensus Project: 1992 NAEP Reading Assessment* (NAEP, 1990) not only provides a detailed description of what students should know and be able to do at various levels but it also details the types of materials students should be able to read.

Finally, a number of documents, although not very current, have provided implicit descriptions of the knowledge and skills important to the language arts. These include *The English Coalition Conference: Democracy through Language* (NCTE, 1989) and *Essentials of English: A Document for Reflection and Dialogue* (NCTE, 1982).

Geography
The Geography Education Standards Project has published *Geography for Life: National Geography Standards* (1994). The final standards document provides 18 standards articulated for grades K–4, 5–8, and 9–12. The standards are organized under six areas: The World in Spatial Terms, Places and Regions, Physical Systems, Human Systems, Environment and Society, and The Uses of

Geography. At each grade level, a standard is defined by three to six activities, each of which is exemplified by three "learning opportunities," i.e., activities described at a greater level of detail. Certainly the most visually interesting of the standards documents, with numerous high-quality photographs and illustrations on glossy paper, it shows indebtedness to one of the co-developers on the project, the National Geographic Society.

The writing committee of the Standards Project, in addition to the consensus process, relied chiefly upon two sources for their material. The first, *Guidelines for Geographic Education* (Joint Committee on Geographic Education, 1984), provides an instructional framework for teaching and learning geography by structuring content around five themes: Location, Place, Human-Environmental Interaction, Movement, and Regions. The second, NAEP's *Geography Assessment Framework for the 1994 National Assessment of Educational Progress* (1992), uses material from the five themes to develop three content areas for assessment: Space and Place, Environment and Society, and Spatial Dynamics and Connections. The assessment framework recommends the development of questions that measure student cognitive abilities "at a basic Knowing level, a more complex Understanding level, and an Applying level that covers a broad range of thinking skills" (p. 3). This three-tiered approach, together with three content areas, forms a matrix within which essential assessment questions are developed.

In addition to these reports, another source for detailed information on geography comes from NAEP's *Item Specifications* (1992) for the 1994 Assessment. This document provides some detailed descriptions as to the basic, proficient, and advanced levels of achievement in geography. For example, "Eighth grade basic" means that students should be able to, among other things, "...solve fundamental locational questions using latitude and longitude; interpret simple map scales; identify continents, oceans, and selected countries and cities..."(p. 54). The *Item Specifications* provide greater levels of detail in terms of how cells in the NAEP matrix might be developed.

The Arts
Standards for the arts, prepared under a grant from the U.S. Department of Education, the National Endowment for the Arts, and the National Endowment for the Humanities, were published in 1994 by the Consortium of National Arts Education Associations. The design of the final document, *What Every Young American Should Know and Be Able to Do in the Arts*, has been greatly simplified over earlier drafts. Standards for dance, music, theatre, and the visual arts are organized into K–4, 5–8, and 9–12 grade clusters. Each field contains from six to nine content standards, articulated across all grade clusters. Within each grade cluster for a given content standard, several achievement standards are provided. For example, in the visual arts section, a content standard found within each grade range, "Understanding the visual arts in relation to history and cultures," has three achievement standards associated with it for the 5–8 level. One such achievement standard states, "Students know and compare the characteristics of art works in various eras and cultures."

In addition, NAEP, working closely with the authors of the national standards for the arts, has developed an *Arts Education Assessment Framework* (1994). For dance, music, theatre, and the visual arts, the framework describes the learning expected of students in (1) knowledge and understanding about the arts, and (2) perceptual, technical, expressive, and intellectual/reflective skills. The assessment framework is formed of a matrix in which the knowledge and skills for each discipline form one axis and the application of this knowledge and skill forms the other. Application in the arts is defined as students creating, performing, or responding to the arts.

Civics

The Center for Civic Education (CCE) has published *National Standards for Civics and Government* (1994). The standards are presented for K–4, 5–8 and 9–12; major areas organize some 70-plus content standards. Each content standard has associated with it a set of key concepts that students should know in order to meet the standard. The standards are organized into five areas: civic life, politics, and government; the foundations of the U.S. political system; the values and principles of U.S. constitutional democracy; the relationship of U.S. politics to world affairs; and the role of the citizen. Each area is presented as a question, and each of the five outermost questions (e.g., What is government and what should it do?) has more specific questions that organize the content standards beneath them (e.g., What are major ideas about the purposes of government and the role of law in society?). The CCE has also produced a source book of impressive scope and detail, *Civitas: A Framework for Civic Education* (Quigley & Bahmmeller, 1991), which contains more than 600 pages of information about civics.

Economics

The National Council on Economic Education (NCEE) convened a drafting committee on national standards in October 1995; the council reportedly anticipates an additional year before the standards are developed ("Economics group," *Report on Education Research*, October 25, 1995, p. 8). In April 1995, the Education Department determined not to provide grant money to assist the council in standards development, but NCEE continues with funding from private sources. An information packet, "Content Statements for State Standards in Economics," if taken as a model for the final document, indicates the council will provide 21 standards, with a range of five to eighteen elements per standard. Although the draft document does not assign grade levels for concepts, the final work will probably align closely with the structure provided in the most recent work from NCEE, *A Framework for Teaching Basic Economic Concepts with Scope and Sequence Guidelines, K–12* (Saunders & Gilliard, 1995).

Foreign Language

A three-year project funded by a grant from the Department of Education and the National Endowment for the Humanities will result in the development of standards in foreign languages, with a projected completion date of 1996. A joint effort by the American Council on the Teaching of Foreign Languages (ACTFL) and a number of foreign language associations, the effort has thus far resulted in two widely disseminated drafts. The most recently available draft of the *National Standards for Foreign Language Education* (April 1995) organizes standards under five goal areas for students: communicate in languages other than English; gain knowledge and understanding of other cultures; connect with other disciplines and acquire information; develop insight into own language and culture; and participate in multilingual communities. Each goal contains from one to three standards, for a total of ten, which are articulated at three levels: K–4, 5–8, and 9–12. A rationale statement follows each goal and standard. Sample learning scenarios are provided for each goal by level.

Health

The Joint Health Education Standards Committee, funded by the American Cancer Society, recently published *National Health Education Standards: Achieving Health Literacy* (1995). The committee, housed at the Association for the Advancement of Health Education, has developed seven standards, each with rationale statements and "performance indicators" for students at grades K–4, 5–8, and 9–11. The material is organized both by standards and by grade levels. The work includes a set of "opportunity to learn" standards designed to provide direction for the policies, resources, and activities that should facilitate the implementation of the health education standards. In addition, a table is provided that maps the topics covered in the health standards to related adolescent risk behaviors.

Physical Education

The National Association for Sport and Physical Education (NASPE) has recently published *Moving into the Future: National Standards for Physical Education: A Guide to Content and Assessment* (1995). The report lists seven standards with benchmarks at grades K, 2, 4, 6, 8, 10, and 12. These grade-level descriptions of the standards include rationale statements, sample benchmarks, and assessment examples. The assessment examples are quite extensive, providing numerous ideas for student and group projects and student portfolios, all with suggested criteria for assessment. Standards from the self-funded group were based on NASPE's 1992 publication, *Outcomes of Quality Physical Education Programs*.

Social Studies

The National Council for the Social Studies (NCSS) has published *Expectations of Excellence: Curriculum Standards for Social Studies* (1994). As the title indicates, NCSS recognizes a distinction between content and curriculum, specifically, that the role of the social studies is to provide "overall curriculum design and comprehensive student performance expectations, while the individual discipline standards (civics and government, economics, geography, and history) provide focused and enhanced content detail" (p. viii). The document underscores this organizing role of curriculum standards through the elaboration of 10 "thematic strands" such as Culture, Time, Continuity and Change, and Individual Development and Identity. Each theme is provided with a list of student performance expectations and classroom activities appropriate for the early grades, middle grades, and high school. Across all 10 strands, 241 performance expectations are described. A useful appendix provides "essential skills for social studies," organized under the categories of acquiring information, organizing and using information, and interpersonal relationships and social participation. Each area is defined by goal statements and a "suggested strength of instructional effort" toward reaching those goals at levels K–3, 4–6, 7–9, and 10–12.

The World of Work

Progress is also being made in delineating the knowledge and skills students should have to be successful and productive in the world of work. The Secretary's Commission on Achieving Necessary Skills (SCANS) and the report the commission produced, *What Work Requires of Schools* (1991), has helped to focus efforts on standards that address higher-order thinking and reasoning skills, as well as personal traits and interpersonal skills that students should acquire. This document adds a strong voice to the call from other standards groups for greater attention to the development of students' critical thinking skills, their ability to communicate, and their ability to work in groups. The Department of Labor and the National Center for Education Statistics are currently engaged in a project to develop and administer SCANS measures by 1996.

A complementary effort was undertaken by the American Society for Training and Development (ASTD), representing "50,000 practitioners, managers, administrators, educators and researchers in the field of human development" (Carnevale, Gainer, & Meltzer, 1990, p. xiii). An ASTD research team, funded through a grant underwritten by the Department of Labor, reviewed the literature and polled members to determine what skills were most desired by employers. The team identified 16 skill areas, including traditional academic areas such as reading, writing, and computation, as well as nontraditional areas such as interpersonal skills, self-esteem, and negotiation. Their findings were published in *Workplace Basics: The Essential Skills Employers Want* (Carnevale, Gainer & Meltzer, 1990).

As part of the response to this need for clarity in the description of knowledge and skills standards, the United States Departments of Education and Labor have initiated a public-private partnership to develop voluntary skill standards for various industries. In 1992 and 1993 these two departments funded 22 pilot projects (16 by the Department of Education and 6 by the Department of Labor) to develop voluntary skill standards covering 19 major industrial areas. The skill standards were slated for completion in 1995; work still remains to determine how information from these projects might be successfully articulated for K–12 schooling.

State-Level Efforts

Although state departments of education have long been involved in curriculum development efforts, the frameworks produced vary considerably by state in their purpose and intended audience. The authors of a few frameworks, such as those for math and science from California, seem to have anticipated the current standards effort. Recently, however, some states are moving deliberatively toward a standards-based view of curriculum development. In Colorado, for example, legislation for the establishment of standards-based education has resulted in the development and adoption of model standards for K–12 in the areas of reading, writing, mathematics, science, geography and history. Work now continues toward the development of standards for physical education, music, visual arts, civics, economics, and foreign language. Those involved in the process include representatives from business, education agencies, and state K–16 educators, in addition to subject-area specialists.

3. Standards and Standardization

Section 1 alluded to the difficulties created by the wide variety of perspectives taken by various groups on the scope, purpose, and nature of standards. In order to develop an internally consistent model of standards and benchmarks, a number of issues must be reconciled. Here we consider six: (1) whether standards are for subject literacy or subject expertise, (2) whether thinking and reasoning skills can be described independent of content, (3) whether standards should be formed as content or performance standards, (4) whether standards should be content or curriculum standards, (5) how benchmarks are defined, and (6) at what level of generality benchmarks and standards are stated. The model proposed here adopts a perspective on each.

The Literacy versus Expertise Issue

Some groups, such as the National Council of Teachers of Mathematics (NCTM), have developed standards using what might be called a "literacy" model. Such standards serve to ensure that students have a basic understanding of the fundamental knowledge and skills in mathematics that an educated, literate adult should know and be able to make use of. An indication that NCTM makes such a distinction can be seen in the standards the council identifies separately for "the college-intending student." These standards appear to describe knowledge and skills important primarily for those in pursuit of advanced studies in math and science.

For example, in its document *Curriculum and Evaluation Standards for School Mathematics*, NCTM singles out the following as applicable to students seeking to pursue mathematics at a post-secondary level:

- apply the sine and cosine functions to problem situations
- investigate limiting processes by examining infinite sequences, series and areas under a curve
- analyze graphs of polynomial, rational, radical and transcendental functions

A different view is available from the subject area of science. Project 2061 does not provide "expert" standards for students bound for advanced study. In fact, the title of the Project's work, *Benchmarks for Science Literacy*, suggests that a distinction is to be made between knowledge that literate adults should possess and knowledge that is primarily of use to those who plan to do advanced study in the field of science. This accords with another view of science literacy that "...*doing* science is clearly different from *using* science; scientific literacy concerns only the latter." (Hazen & Trefil, 1993) [italics, the authors']. This does not mean, of course, that students should not engage in hands-on science; it merely suggests that there are distinctions that can be made between preparations for understanding science as an educated adult and doing basic science as an adult professional.

The differences between academic and literacy models presented in the various documents do not, on close analysis, constitute an insurmountable problem. At the literacy end of the continuum, standards might be described as the minimum requirements of knowledge and skill students should know and be able to do to function well as adults of the 21st century. At the "expertise" end of the continuum, standards are described in terms of the knowledge and skills that, once acquired, would render students "mini-experts" in every field. In fact, as currently articulated in the documents reviewed for this effort, both positions have strong tendencies toward the middle. That is, those documents that provide what might be characterized as literacy standards commonly include material that goes beyond minimum requirements for basic literacy within a domain. Additionally, those documents that appear to favor the expertise position frequently are structured in such a way that the "expert-level" detail provided beneath a standard does not obscure the basic point of the standard itself, which focuses on information at a literacy level.

If one had to classify the model adopted in this report, it would be most accurately described as a literacy approach to content, in that it is believed that standards and benchmarks should be considered essential for all students, whether they enter the world of work directly from high school or go on to higher education.

The Role of Thinking and Reasoning

Virtually all of the documents reviewed for this study either implicitly or explicitly acknowledged the importance of emphasizing thinking and reasoning in the articulation of standards. This is not surprising given the historical emphasis educators have placed on thinking and reasoning. Over 70 years ago, John Dewey (1916) wrote, "The sole direct path to enduring improvement in the methods of instruction and learning consists of centering upon the conditions which exact, promote and test thinking." Similarly, in 1961, the National Education Association identified the improvement of thinking and reasoning as central to American education:

> ...in the general area of the development of the ability to think, there is a field for new research of the greatest importance. It is essential that those who have responsibility for management and policy determination in education commit themselves to expansion of such research and to the application of the fruits of this research. This is the context in which the significant answers to such issues as educational technology, length of the school year and content of teacher education must be sought and given. (Educational Policies Commission, 1961, pp. 14–15)

More recently, calls for the enhancement of thinking and reasoning in American education have come from the National Science Board Commission on Pre-college Education in Mathematics, Science and Technology (1983), the College Board (1987), the National Education Association (Futrell, 1987), and the American Federation of Teachers (1985).

Although there is agreement as to the importance of enhancing thinking and reasoning, there is not much agreement on the manner in which thinking and reasoning should be articulated in standards. There were three principal ways that thinking and reasoning skills were addressed in the documents reviewed for this report. One approach was to establish a set of standards on generic reasoning. For

Figure 3.1

Basic: Eighth-grade students performing at the basic level should exhibit evidence of conceptual and procedural understanding in the five NAEP content areas [for mathematics]. This level of performance signifies an understanding of arithmetic operations — including estimation on whole numbers, decimals, fractions and percents.

Eighth graders performing at the basic level should complete problems correctly with the help of structural prompts such as diagrams, charts and graphs. They should be able to solve problems in all NAEP content areas through the appropriate selection and use of strategies and technological tools — including calculators, computers, and geometric shapes. Students at this level also should be able to use fundamental algebraic and informal geometric concepts in problem solving.

As they approach the proficient level, students at the basic level should be able to determine which of the available data are necessary and sufficient for correct solutions and use them in problem solving. However, these eighth graders show limited skill in communicating mathematically.

Proficient: Eighth-grade students performing at the proficient level should apply mathematical concepts and procedures consistently to complex problems in the five NAEP content areas.

Eighth graders performing at the proficient level should be able to conjecture, defend their ideas, and five supporting examples. They should understand the connections between fractions, percents, decimals, and other mathematical topics such as algebra and functions. Students at this level are expected to have a thorough understanding of basic level arithmetic operations -- an understanding sufficient for problem solving in practical situations.

Quantity and spatial relationships in problem solving and reasoning should be familiar to them, and they should be able to convey underlying reasoning skills beyond the level of arithmetic. They should be able to compare and contrast mathematical ideas and generate their own examples. These students should make inferences from data and graphs, apply properties of informal geometry, and accurately use the tools of technology. Students at this level should understand the process of gathering and organizing data and be able to calculate, evaluate, and communicate results within the domain of statistics and probability.

Advanced: Eighth-grade students performing at the advanced level should be able to reach beyond the recognition, identification, and application of mathematical rules in order to generalize and synthesize concepts and principals in the five NAEP content areas.

Eighth graders performing at the advanced level should be able to probe examples and counterexamples in order to shape generalizations from which they can develop models. Eighth graders performing at the advanced level should use number sense and geometric awareness to consider the reasonableness of an answer. They are expected to use abstract thinking to create unique problem-solving techniques and explain the reasoning processes underlying their conclusions. (in Shepard, p.35)

These performance levels were then translated into specific items, and a system referred to as the Angoff method was used to determine how many items must be answered correctly to indicate specific levels of performance. In effect, then, the illustrations from NAGB and NAEP represent a continuum of levels of generality for stating performance standards. At one end of the continuum, performance standards are stated in such general terms that they can apply to any and all content areas. At the other end of the continuum, performance standards are articulated in terms of a specific number and type of items that must be answered correctly. Clearly, a great deal of conceptual work remains before the term "performance standard" has a well-articulated meaning. For this reason, we have limited the work of this study to the identification of content standards, all the while recognizing the importance of a complementary set of performance standards.

Another reason for limiting the scope of this study to content standards is the necessary relationship content standards have with performance standards. That is, sound content standards are a necessary but not sufficient condition for sound performance standards. Indeed, the NAEP efforts at setting performance standards have been criticized because they allegedly were not based on sound content standards. As Shepard (1993) notes:

> Current NAEP item pools, particularly at the advanced level, are not sufficiently congruent with emerging national content standards. Therefore, the achievement-level descriptions cannot adequately represent ideal future-oriented standards without departing from the assessment that the students actually took. In addition, some exemplar items were judged by content experts to be less than exemplary. They do not communicate subject-matter standards well. (p. xiii)

In fact, Shepard implies that NAEP should curtail its efforts to set performance standards until content standards are well articulated: "Thus it only makes sense to wait until national content standards are available and then to follow a more coherent process for developing performance standards in conjunction with content standards" (p. xxv). Again, given the developing nature of performance standards and their dependence on well-articulated content standards, we have chosen to focus our efforts on identifying content standards only.

Content Standards or Curriculum Standards?

A distinction that should be made in the types of standards various groups are identifying is that between content standards and curriculum standards. *Content* standards describe what a student should know and be able to do. *Curriculum* standards (sometimes referred to as program standards) are best characterized as descriptions of what should take place in the classroom; as such, they address instructional techniques, recommended activities, and various modes of presentation. The difference between a content and curriculum standard is illustrated by the following two statements from the National Council of Teachers of Mathematics (1989) framework. Within that document, both statements are presented as standards:

a)   recognize when an estimate is appropriate
b)   describe, model, draw and classify shapes

Standard *a* describes a skill or ability a person might use solving a "day-to-day" or academic problem. For example, in day-to-day life, a person might use the skill of estimation to anticipate how much a proposed project might cost; or in a mathematics class, a student might use his estimation skills to determine that a problem can be solved without additional, unnecessary steps. In short, estimation is a skill that is commonly used or applied to solve common day-to-day problems or accomplish goals in academic settings. Standard *b*, "describe, model, draw and classify shapes," does not share this characteristic. That is, it is difficult to imagine many situations that would demand the skill of being able to model, draw, or classify shapes, whether to solve an academic or day-to-day problem. Rather, this kind of activity seems appropriate as an instructional device to help students understand shapes or to provide a way for them to demonstrate their understanding of shapes. Standards like *a* above are referred to as content standards because they describe information or skill that is essential to the practice or application of a content domain. Standards like *b* are referred to as curriculum standards because they identify the instructional or curricular activities that might be used to help students develop skill and ability within a content domain. It might be said that curriculum standards describe the methods designed to help students achieve content standards.

This project has content standards as its focus. There are two overarching reasons for this choice. First, content standards describe the goals for individual student achievement, whereas curriculum standards provide information that is ancillary to reaching those goals.[1] Second, curriculum standards, which usually focus on activities, projects, or techniques, if interpreted rigidly could leave teachers with little or no room for instructional diversity. That is, if teachers or administrators interpret curriculum standards as activities that must be performed, then teaching goals can too easily be equated with the activities performed, and actual student achievement loses its primary focus. When such a prescriptive attitude is taken toward activities, such activities often prove inefficient and time-consuming, leaving little room for experimentation and the refinement of new approaches to teaching.

Given the content (as opposed to curricular) orientation of this project, the standards identified will have the characteristics of content-area knowledge. Specifically, the information that comprises standards identified within this project will generally fall into three broad categories representing the three general types of knowledge. At a basic level, knowledge within any domain can be organized into the categories exemplified in figure 3.2.

---

[1] The NCTM standards clearly show the value of curriculum standards. It is hoped that similar efforts will be undertaken in the other subject areas, once content standards are made available.

The first column contains examples of knowledge that involves processes. These processes may or may not be performed in a linear fashion. For example, performing long division is a process: you perform one step, then another, and so on. Reading a map also involves certain steps, but these steps, unlike those in long division, do not have to be performed in any set order. You might read the name of the map first, then look at the legend, or you might just as effectively perform these steps in reverse order. Knowledge of this sort is usually called *procedural knowledge*. One might think of such knowledge as composed of the *skills and processes* important to a given content area.

Figure 3.2

Procedural	Declarative	Contextual
reading a map	democracy	know when to use a map instead of a globe
performing long division	a numerator	model numbers using number line
setting up an experiment	an amoeba	classify organisms
shooting a free throw	rules of basketball	know when to use man-to-man vs. zone coverage
editing an essay	conventions of punctuation	use appropriate tone and style for a selected audience

The examples in the second column do not involve a process or a set of steps. Acquiring this type of knowledge involves understanding the component parts. For example, knowledge of the concept of "democracy" includes understanding that decisions are made by the people, that each person has a single vote, that votes are weighted equally, and so on. This type of knowledge is commonly called *declarative knowledge*. One might think of such knowledge as composed of the *information* important to a given content area.

The last column contains items that are not simply declarative or procedural but specify knowledge in context. Column three contains examples of information and/or skills that have particular meaning because of the conditions that form part of their description. "To classify" is a skill; to understand the characteristics of organisms is declarative knowledge, or information; but knowledge of how to classify organisms is knowledge of a particular type: it requires understanding how particular characteristics establish relationships among organisms. Like the declarative/procedural

2. How many standards and benchmarks will be articulated?

In all, this report lists 201 standards and 3,291 benchmarks for implementation in K–12 schooling. Clearly, a school or district could not expect a student to demonstrate competence in all of these (although they may be a part of instruction); sheer numbers would make such a system untenable. Given that there are 180 days in the school year and 13 years of schooling (assuming students go to kindergarten), there are only 2,340 school days available to students. If all benchmarks in this report were addressed, this would mean that students would have to learn and demonstrate mastery in one or more benchmarks every school day, or about seven benchmarks every week.

Thus, a school or district will surely have to select from the standards and benchmarks presented in this report if it wishes to construct a system in which students are to be held accountable for each benchmark. A reasonable number of benchmarks seems to be about 600, distributed in roughly the following way:

Level I:	K–2:	75
Level II:	3–5:	125
Level III:	6–8:	150
Level IV:	9–12:	250

Quite obviously, to implement this 600-benchmarks cap, schools and districts would have to exclude quite a few of the benchmarks identified in this report.

3. Will all selected benchmarks be considered necessary to demonstrate competence in a standard?

One possible way to alleviate the problem of too many benchmarks is to consider benchmarks as exemplars rather than as necessary components of a standard. Using this option, students would be held accountable for demonstrating a mastery of a sample of the benchmarks within a level for a given standard as opposed to all the benchmarks within a given level.

To illustrate, consider the benchmarks in figure 4.1 for the science standard "Understands energy types, sources, and conversions, and their relationship to heat and temperature." A school or district that takes the "exemplar" approach to benchmarks would require students to demonstrate competence in a selected number of benchmarks per level. For example, a school or district might require students to demonstrate competence in two out of the three benchmarks for Level I; three out of five for Level II; five out of seven for Level III; and six out of eight for Level IV. This approach would allow a school or district to meet a larger number of standards without exceeding the recommended limit of 600 benchmarks discussed in the preceding section. It would also allow for more flexibility within the classroom, in that individual teachers would have the option to use those benchmark components which they judged most applicable for their students. However, this approach also results in less continuity of coverage within a content domain since different teachers will no doubt select different benchmark exemplars to illustrate student competence within the levels for a given standard. It is also important to note that this approach may defeat the designed purposes

31

Figure 4.1

Level I (Grades K–2)
- Knows that the Sun applies heat and light to Earth
- Knows that heat can be produced in many ways (e.g., burning, rubbing, mixing chemicals)
- Knows that electricity in circuits can produce light, heat, sound and magnetic effects

Level II (Grades 3–5)
- Knows that things that give off light often also give off heat
- Knows that mechanical and electrical machines give off heat
- Knows that heat can move from one object to another by conduction
- Knows that some materials conduct heat better than others; materials that do not conduct heat well can reduce heat loss
- Knows that electrical circuits require a complete loop through which the electrical current can pass

Level III (Grades 6–8)
- Knows that energy comes in different forms, such as light, heat, chemical, nuclear, mechanical and electrical
- Understands that energy cannot be created or destroyed, but only changed from one form to another
- Knows that the Sun is a major source of energy for changes on the Earth's surface; the Sun's energy arrives as light with a range of wavelengths consisting mainly of visible light with significant amounts of infrared and ultraviolet radiation
- Knows that heat energy moves in predictable ways, flowing from warmer objects to cooler ones until both objects are at the same temperature
- Knows that heat can be transferred through materials by the collisions of atoms or across space by radiation; if the material is fluid, currents will be set up in it that aid the transfer of heat
- Knows that electrical circuits provide a means of converting electrical energy into heat, light, sound, chemical or other forms of energy
- Knows that in most chemical reactions, energy is released or added to the system in the form of heat, light, electrical or mechanical energy

Level IV (Grades 9–12)
- Knows that although energy can be transferred by collisions or waves and converted from one form to another, it can never by created or destroyed, so the total energy of the universe is constant
- Knows that all energy can be considered to be either kinetic energy (energy of motion), potential energy (depends on relative position), or energy contained by a field (electromagnetic waves)
- Knows that heat energy consists of random motion and the vibrations of atoms, molecules, and ions; the higher the temperature, the greater the atomic or molecular motion
- Knows that energy tends to move spontaneously from hotter to cooler objects by conduction, convection or radiation; similarly, any ordered state tends to spontaneously become less ordered over time
- Knows that the energy of waves (electromagnetic and material) can be changed into other forms of energy (e.g., chemical and electrical), just as other forms of energy (chemical and nuclear) can be transformed into wave energy
- Knows that some changes of atomic or molecular configuration require an input of energy, whereas others release energy
- Knows that each kind of atom or molecule can gain or lose energy only in particular discrete amounts and thus can absorb and emit light only at wavelengths corresponding to these amounts; these wavelengths can be used to identify the substance
- Knows that fission is the splitting of a large nucleus into smaller pieces, and fusion is the joining of two nuclei at extremely high temperature and pressure; nuclear reactions convert a fraction of the mass of interacting particles into energy

of some well-articulated standards, such as those developed by Project 2061, where upper-level benchmarks are predicated under the assumption that students are familiar with a logically prior concept addressed at an earlier level. If teachers select without regard to articulation, some of the value of this approach may be lost.

4. Will student performance be reported using course grade or standards?

Currently, most schools and districts report student progress using appropriate grades for broad academic areas organized within courses. However, current research and theory indicate that courses of the same title do not necessarily cover the same content (Yoon, Burstein & Gold, not dated). In other words, two courses of the same name do not necessarily cover the same declarative, procedural, and contextual knowledge. If a school or district wished to use traditional grades but implement a standards-oriented approach, it would ensure that the benchmarks that have been identified would be distributed systematically throughout the various courses within content areas, that is, specific benchmarks would be assigned to courses based upon the elements they cover. Any two courses with the same title would not only cover the same benchmarks but would place the same relative importance on the benchmarks they cover.

For example, assume that two courses of the same title were designed to cover the same seven benchmarks. The school or district could also determine which percentage of the grade each benchmark would command. In such a case, it might be determined that the first two benchmarks each accounted for 25% of the grade and the remaining five benchmarks each accounted for 10% of the grade. Clearly, this would provide more precision for course descriptions and show an equivalence between "identical" courses that is not often found today.

In summary, traditional grading practices and standards-based assessment are not incompatible. A school or district must simply distribute and weight the standards that have been identified across the various courses in a systematic, well-reasoned fashion.

The second reporting option a school or district might adopt is to report student progress by benchmarks. Rather than assign a single grade to a course, a teacher would report progress in some way for each benchmark covered in the course. In effect, for assessment purposes only, each benchmark component would be considered independent of the others covered within the course. When this approach is taken, schools and districts commonly employ rubrics as opposed to grades. A rubric is a description of the levels of understanding or skill for a given benchmark. For example, below is a rubric for the Level II mathematics benchmark "Understands the basic role of place value":

4. Demonstrates a thorough understanding of the role and function of place value and provides insights that are not obvious when using the concept of place value.
3. Demonstrates a complete and accurate understanding of the role and function of place value as it relates to estimating or calculating addition, subtraction, multiplication and division.

2.   Displays an incomplete understanding of the role and function of place value as it relates to estimating or calculating addition, subtraction, multiplication or division.

1.   Has severe misconceptions about the role and function of place value as evidenced by severe place value errors in addition, subtraction, multiplication or division.

Commonly, one of the described levels within a rubric is designated as the targeted level of skill or knowledge. For example, a score of 3 in the reporting rubric above might be selected as the target standard for the Level II mathematics benchmark "Understands the basic role of place value."

Reporting out by benchmarks would, of course, require a record-keeping system that is far different from that currently used in most schools and districts. Each student's score on individual benchmarks would be recorded. Assuming the use of a four-point rubric, individual students would receive a score of 1 through 4 on each benchmark assessed within each standard. These scores could then be averaged to obtain an overall standard score at a given benchmark level.

5. Will all students be required to meet all standards?

A major decision facing a school or district that wishes to emphasize content area standards is whether students will be required to meet a targeted level of knowledge and skills. This approach is reminiscent of the mastery learning approach of the 1970s and early 1980s (see Levine & Associates, 1985) and the more recent outcomes-based approach, or OBE approach (Spady, 1988). In the context of the reporting rubric described previously, a mastery or outcomes-based approach would mean that students would be required to receive a score of 3 on each benchmark. If a student did not meet the targeted level for a benchmark (i.e., did not obtain a score of 3 on the rubric), he or she would be provided with additional instructional opportunities until he or she could meet the required proficiency. Of course, such a system makes extreme demands on resources. In a traditional system, no extra resources need be used if a student does poorly in a course. In a mastery or OBE system, each student who does not meet a standard must be provided with whatever instructional and curriculum resources are necessary to ensure that the student meets the requirements. A variation in the theme of a comprehensive mastery or outcomes-based approach is to require that students meet the performance standards on *some*, but not all, benchmarks. Those benchmarks that are applied to all students would be considered a set of core requirements.

In summary, there are many important decisions a school or district must make regarding the implementation of a standards-oriented approach to schooling. In this section, we have discussed five of the decisions that deal with the nature and function of standards and benchmarks and the extent to which students will be held accountable for them.

6. How the Subject-Area Sections are Structured

As described previously, standards may be procedural or declarative statements or may be statements that describe broader categories; they may be taken directly from draft documents or may have been constructed inductively or extrapolated from an analysis of the documents in the subject area. The benchmarks in this document, however, are all statements of declarative, procedural, and contextual knowledge taken from a wide range of national reports. In most cases, these benchmarks are organized under the standards at four levels:

Level I	=	K–2, or primary
Level II	=	3–5, or upper elementary
Level III	=	6–8, or middle school
Level IV	=	9–12, or high school

However, in some areas, either because of the nature of the content or source materials, the levels are identified somewhat differently. Because of this, the level identifications are best understood as indicators of relative difficulty, rather than strictly equivalent to a range of grades. Attention should be paid to the parentheses following the levels to identify the grade range. For example, in the case of U.S. History, there are three levels identified:

Level II (Grades 5–6)
Level III (Grades 7–8)
Level IV (Grades 9–12)

Whereas in the standards for history at K–4, there are two levels:

Level I (Grades K–2)
Level II (Grades 3–4)

In this example it should be clear that Level II is a relative description, defining grades 3–4 for history in the early grades and grades 5–6 in the U.S. history standards.

The standards are organized and reported in the 13 categories described in the previous section. Each standard within a category is numbered consecutively (the numbering sequence has no significance and was done for ease of reference). The benchmarks are listed immediately under each standard and presented by level (I-IV). A set of codes, called a citation log, appears flush right and just above each benchmark and standard. A key for the log appears at the bottom of each page, so that readers are provided with the following information: the cognitive character of the benchmark (whether it describes declarative, procedural, or contextual knowledge); a page number citation for each instance in which the information was found in reference and supporting documents; the nature of that citation (whether the information was found explicitly stated or could be implied from other statements); and finally, in the case of duplicates, where very similar benchmarks can be found within the same subject area.

To illustrate:

(GE,115)

5. Understands the concept of regions

Level I (Grades K-2)

BD (GE,115;EI,13;NI,35;TI,10;DI,4.1.2)

- Knows areas that can be classified as regions according to physical criteria (e.g., landform regions, soil regions, vegetation regions, climate regions, water basins) and human criteria (e.g., political regions, population regions, economic regions, language regions)

"Understands the concept of regions" appears as the fifth standard in the geography section, and the benchmark shown is from Level I. Just above the benchmark, and flush right, is the abbreviation "BD," followed by the "citation log": (GE,115;EI,13;NI,35;TI,10;DI,4.1.2). A key like the following is provided for each subject area:

Codes (right side of page):	BD= Benchmark, Declarative; BP = Benchmark, Procedural; BC = Benchmark, Contextual
1st letter of each code in parentheses	*2nd letter of code*
G =National Geography Standards	E = Explicitly stated in document
E = Guidelines for Geographic Education	I = Implied in document
N = NAEP: Item Specifications in Geography	
T = K-6 Geography: Themes, Key Ideas	
D = Duplicated in another standard	

Codes (right side of page):
1st letter of each code in parentheses
G =National Geography Standards
E = Guidelines for Geographic Education
N = NAEP: Item Specifications in Geography
T = K-6 Geography: Themes, Key Ideas
D = Duplicated in another standard

BD= Benchmark, Declarative; BP = Benchmark, Procedural; BC = Benchmark, Contextual
2nd letter of code
E = Explicitly stated in document
I = Implied in document

Number
Page number of cited document
or, for duplicates,
Standard number & level of duplicate

The key identifies "BD" as a benchmark that describes declarative knowledge. Within the parentheses that follow "BD," there a number of documents cited, separated by semicolons. The first code, GE,115, indicates that the information described in the benchmark can be found explicitly stated (E) in the National Geography Standards (G) on page 115; the second citation, EI,13, indicates that the same information, although not explicitly stated, is implied in (or, can be inferred from) material on page 13 of the Guidelines for Geographic Education. Similarly, the same information can be inferred from two additional documents, the NAEP item specifications and *K–6 Geography* (full citations for all reports are found in the bibliography). The last piece of information "DI,4.1.2" indicates that another benchmark contains very closely related information. In this case, that particular benchmark is under the standard number 4, at level 1, and is the second bulleted item.

Additionally, when the idea expressed at the standard level has been identified in supporting documents, that information is provided in parentheses, flush right, just above the standard statement. In the example above, the idea that students should have a general understanding of the concept of regions is found (GE,115) in the Geography Standards document on page 115.

7. Mathematics

The following process was used to identify standards and benchmarks in the field of mathematics:

Identification of National Reports

Two basic reports were identified as the primary documents representing the current thinking on standards in mathematics: *Curriculum and Evaluation Standards for School Mathematics* (NCTM, 1989) and the *Mathematics Assessment Framework* (NAEP, 1992). As mentioned in Section 2 of this report, the NCTM document was a major contributor to the national awareness of the benefits of identifying standards in content domains. To prepare for the 1994 NAEP mathematics assessment, the National Assessment Governing Board awarded a contract in the fall of 1991 to the College Board to develop item specifications for the 1994 assessments. Explicit in this project was an alignment with the NCTM standards, inasmuch as they were believed to reflect the most current thinking on what students should know and be able to do in mathematics. The resulting report, entitled *Mathematics Assessment Framework*, provided specific recommendations regarding the content that should be included in the 1994 NAEP assessment, the levels at which students should be assessed regarding specific content, and the proportion of items that should be devoted to specific content at specific levels. A supplemental document was also produced by NAEP entitled *1994 National Assessment of Educational Progress: Mathematics Assessment: Content Specifications* (NAEP, March 26, 1992). This provided additional detail to the *Mathematics Assessment Framework*.

In addition to these three documents which focus solely on mathematics, *Benchmarks for Science Literacy* (Project 2061, 1993 and 1993 draft) contains a section entitled The Mathematical World. This section parallels and details many of the standards found in *Curriculum and Evaluation Standards*(NCTM, 1989). At a much more general level, two documents from the "world of work" contain explicit statements regarding what students should know and be able to do in mathematics: *What Work Requires of Schools: A SCANS Report for America 2000* (The Secretary's Commission on Achieving Necessary Skills, 1991) and *Workplace Basics: The Essential Skills Employers Want* (Carnevale, Gainer & Meltzer, 1990). Finally, the document detailing the national standards in geography, *Geography for Life: National Geography Standards* (Geography Education Standards Project, 1994), contains a number of implicit statements pertinent to mathematics standards.

Selection of the Reference Document

Because of its wide recognition, the NCTM document was selected as the reference report. Additionally, the report had characteristics amenable to the standards/benchmarks model used in this study. Specifically, the report explicitly identifies standards at three developmental levels — grades K–4, 5–8, and 9–12. The latter two levels corresponded well with levels 3 and 4 used in this study. However, the elements identified in the K–4 level of the NCTM document were necessarily reclassified into Level 1 (primary) or Level 2 (upper elementary) for the purposes of this study.

Identification of Standards and Benchmarks and Integration of Information from Other Documents

Close examination of the NCTM levels indicated that in some cases there appeared to be little designed relationship between the content in one developmental level and that in the next. Not infrequently, new types of knowledge and skill were introduced at a superordinate level that seemed to have no developmental relationship to the knowledge and skill identified in the subordinate level. Consequently, many elements within the various NCTM standards and levels were reclassified as more appropriately fitting within another standard. This reclassification process was highly influenced by the NAEP documents. Where the NCTM document identifies 13 standards at Levels 1 and 2 and 14 standards at Level 3, the NAEP document identifies five general categories articulated at three levels roughly equivalent to the three NCTM levels. Our reclassification tended to collapse some of the NCTM standards such that the final set of nine standards (see below) resembled the NAEP classification as much as it did the NCTM classification. In effect, our reclassification tended to erode the original structure of the NCTM document.

Another factor contributing to the erosion of the structure of the NCTM organizational structure was its inclusion of explicit standards regarding mathematics as reasoning and mathematics as communication. For reasons discussed in Section 3 of this report, many of the elements identified within the NCTM standard on mathematics as reasoning were judged to be more appropriately classified under one of the standards within our thinking and reasoning category, and some of the elements within the NCTM standard on mathematics as communication were judged to be more appropriately classified under one of the standards within our language arts category.

Finally, a number of the elements in the NCTM document were identified either as "expert" in nature or curriculum standards, as opposed to content standards, and were not included in the analysis.

For the most part, the information in the documents from the world of work, science and geography was integrated into the standards generated from the NCTM and NAEP reports. The one exception to this general rule was standard 9, Understands the General Nature and Uses of Mathematics. As the title indicates, this standard deals with general awarenesses about mathematics and its relationship to other disciplines, particularly science. This standard was generated solely from the document *Benchmarks for Science Literacy*.

Summary of Standards for Mathematics

1. Effectively uses a variety of strategies in the problem-solving process
2. Understands and applies basic and advanced properties of the concept of numbers
3. Uses basic and advanced procedures while performing the process of computation
4. Understands and applies basic and advanced properties of the concept of measurement
5. Understands and applies basic and advanced properties of the concepts of geometry
6. Understands and applies basic and advanced concepts of data analysis and distributions
7. Understands and applies basic and advanced concepts of probability and statistics
8. Understands and applies basic and advanced properties of functions and algebra
9. Understands the general nature and uses of mathematics

(SE,xviii)

1. Effectively uses a variety of strategies in the problem-solving process

Level I (Grades K-2)

BP (MI,23;C4I,13;PI,27)
- Brainstorms possible approaches to take before starting a problem

BP (MI,23,26;C4E,13;NE,321;PE,34)
- Draws pictures to represent problems

BP (ME,23,26;NE,321)
- Represents problems using physical objects

BP (ME,23,26;NE,321)
- Clarifies problems using discussions with teacher or knowledgeable others

BP (ME,36;2E,290;C4E,5-6;PE,26)
- Makes rough estimates of answers to problems before doing them

BC (ME,26;2E,290;C4I,5;PI,26)
- Explains to others how she or he went about solving a numerical problem

BP (ME,24;C4I,4;PI,25)
- Makes organized lists or tables of information necessary for solving a problem

Level II (Grades 3-5)

BP (MI,75;C4I,5-6;PI,27)
- When appropriate, uses "guess and check" to solve problems

BP (MI,23)
- States problems in his or her own words to better understand them

BP (ME,37;C4E,6;PE,27;WE,122-123)
- Checks the reasonableness of results through estimation

BC (MI,23,32)
- Articulates similarities and differences between basic problem-solving strategies

BP (ME,36;C4E,6;PE,27)
- Makes attempts to verify solutions or results in situations where it is warranted

BP (MI,75,78)
- Constructs physical representations for complex problems

BP (ME,26;C4E,4;PE,25)
- Uses pictographs and graphic representations to model problems

BP (ME,26)
- Clarifies problems using discussions with peers

BD (ME,26;C4I,4;PI,25)
- Understands that some ways of representing a problem are more helpful than others

---

Codes (right side of page):   BD = Benchmark, Declarative; BP = Benchmark, Procedural; BC = Benchmark, Contextual
1st letter of each code in parentheses   *2nd letter of code*   *Number*
M = NCTM: Curric. & Eval. Standards for Math   E = Explicitly stated in document   Page number of cited document
2 = Project 2061: Benchmarks for Science Literacy   I = Implied in document
C4,C8,C12 = NAEP: Math. Content Specs, Grades 4,8,12
G = GESP: National Geography Standards
N = New Standards: Mathematics Draft
P = NAEP: Mathematics Assessment Framework
S = SCANS: Report for America 2000
W = Carnevale: Workplace Basics

MREL

- Uses trial and error and the process of elimination to solve real-world problems
  BP (ME,24,30;C4I,5-6;PI,26-27)

- Writes answers in sentence form
  BP (ME,28;C4I,4;PI,25)

- Identifies a range of possible answers for a given problem situation
  BD (ME,36;C4I,5-6;PE,26-27)

- Distinguishes between pertinent and irrelevant information when solving problems
  BP (ME,30;NE,325)

- Determines appropriate computation method in problem-solving situation (e.g., pencil and paper, mental arithmetic, calculator)
  BC (C4E,5;PE,26)

Level III (Grades 6-8)

- Identifies a similar problem type to solve a problem
  BP (MI,75;PI,27)

- Breaks complex problems into simpler parts
  BP (MI,75;C8I,6-7;NE,325;PI,27)

- Works backwards from the solution to solve a problem
  BP (MI,75;C8I,6-7;PI,27)

- Represents real-world problems using geometric models
  BP (ME,112;C8E,19;PE,34)

- Identifies similarities and differences between a wide variety of problem types and problem-solving strategies
  BC (MI,75,84;C8I,4,27;PI,41)

- Effectively verifies solutions or results in situations where it is warranted
  BP (MI,94;C8E,6-7;PE,27)

- Understands that there is no one right way to solve mathematical problems but that different methods have different advantages and disadvantages
  BD (MI,75;2E,28;C8I,4-5;PI,25)

- Follows a general model for solving real-world problems that includes making some basic assumptions about the problem; constructing a representation of the problem; choosing the appropriate operations or the correct formula or rule; making computations; checking to see if answers make sense; and if answers do not make sense, checking the accuracy of each part of the problem-solving process
  BP (2E,37)

- Selects appropriate computational techniques in problem-solving situations (e.g., paper, pencil, mental, calculator, computer)
  BP (ME,94;C8E,6;PE,26;WE,122-123)

Codes (right side of page):   BD = Benchmark, Declarative; BP = Benchmark, Procedural; BC = Benchmark, Contextual
1st letter of each code in parentheses   *2nd letter of code*   *Number*
M = NCTM: Curric. & Eval. Standards for Math   E = Explicitly stated in document   Page number of cited document
2 = Project 2061: Benchmarks for Science Literacy   I = Implied in document
C4,C8,C12 = NAEP: Math. Content Specs, Grades 4,8,12
G = GESP: National Geography Standards
N = New Standards: Mathematics Draft
P = NAEP: Mathematics Assessment Framework
S = SCANS: Report for America 2000
W = Carnevale: Workplace Basics

MREL

- Determines pertinent information required to solve a problem, methods for obtaining this information, and limits of acceptable solutions BP (ME,76;C8I,6-7;PI,26)

- Writes a number sentence to represent a problem situation BC (MI,91;C8E,4-5;PE,25)

- Uses proportional thinking (e.g., rates, scaling, similarity) to solve problems BC (C8E,8-9;PE,27)

Level IV (Grades 9-12)

- Classifies problem-solving strategies or problem types by underlying general characteristics BC (ME,146;C12I,31;PI,41)

- Constructs and describes simple algorithms for solving problems that take several steps BP (2E,291)

- Constructs direct mathematical proofs when solving problems BP (ME,143)

- Constructs indirect proofs when solving problems BP (ME,143)

- Uses mathematical induction when solving problems BP (ME,143)

- Uses inductive reasoning to make conjectures and tests the conjectures using deductive reasoning to construct either a logical verification or a counterexample BP (ME,143;C12E,31;PE,42-42)

- Provides simple valid arguments as justification for solutions to specific problems and for algorithms constructed for various purposes BP (ME,143;C12E,31;PE,42-42)

- Writes an equation to represent a problem situation BC (C12E,4;PE,25)

2.   Understands and applies basic and advanced properties of the concept of numbers (SE,xviii)

Level I (Grades K-2)

- Has a general understanding that a number is a symbol for how much of something there is BD (MI,38;2I,36;C4I,4;PI,25)

- Uses counting to represent numbers BC (ME,38;C4E,4;PE,25)

Codes (right side of page):   BD = Benchmark, Declarative; BP = Benchmark, Procedural; BC = Benchmark, Contextual
1st letter of each code in parentheses   *2nd letter of code*   *Number*
M = NCTM: Curric. & Eval. Standards for Math   E = Explicitly stated in document   Page number of cited document
2 = Project 2061: Benchmarks for Science Literacy   I = Implied in document
C4,C8,C12 = NAEP: Math. Content Specs, Grades 4,8,12
G = GESP: National Geography Standards
N = New Standards: Mathematics Draft
P = NAEP: Mathematics Assessment Framework
S = SCANS: Report for America 2000
W = Carnevale: Workplace Basics

McREL

- Uses number lines to describe relatively small, whole numbers BC (MI,38;C4E,4;PE,25)

- Orders relatively small sets of numbers BC (ME,91;C4E,4;PE,25)

- Understands that in sharing or measuring things there is sometimes a need to use numbers between whole numbers BD (2E,211)

Level II (Grades 3-5)

- Understands the basic relationship of decimals to whole numbers BD (ME,57,87;C4E,3,6;PE,25,26)

- Understands the basic relationship of fractions to decimals and fractions to whole numbers BD (ME,57,87;C4E,6;PE,26)

- Understands the basic difference between odd and even numbers BD (MI,38;C4E,7;PE,27)

- Understands the basic characteristics of mixed numbers BD (ME,57;C4I,6;PI,26)

- Understands the basic meaning of place value BD (ME,38;C4E,3;PE,25)

- Uses number lines to model a variety of numbers BC (MI,38;C4E,4;PE,25)

- Renames, orders, and compares numbers BC (MI,38;C4E,4;PE,25)

- Understands that "0" can mean none of something or that it can represent a point on a scale BD (2E,212)

- Understands that if "0" and "1" are located on a line, any other number can be depicted as a position on the line BD (2E,223)

- Understands when one form of a number might be more useful than another BD (MI,38;C4E,4;PI,25-26)

- Identifies numbers pictured as shaded regions on two-dimensional or three-dimensional region models BP (ME,88;C4E,4;PI,25)

- Orders numbers presented in nonroutine forms (e.g., 12/6, 10, 4×2, 7 - 2) BP (MI,38;C4E,5;PI,25)

Codes (right side of page):   BD = Benchmark, Declarative; BP = Benchmark, Procedural; BC = Benchmark, Contextual
1st letter of each code in parentheses   *2nd letter of code*   *Number*
M = NCTM: Curric. & Eval. Standards for Math   E = Explicitly stated in document   Page number of cited document
2 = Project 2061: Benchmarks for Science Literacy   I = Implied in document
C4,C8,C12 = NAEP: Math. Content Specs, Grades 4,8,12
G = GESP: National Geography Standards
N = New Standards: Mathematics Draft
P = NAEP: Mathematics Assessment Framework
S = SCANS: Report for America 2000
W = Carnevale: Workplace Basics

MREL

Level III (Grades 6-8)

- Understands the similarities and differences between rational numbers and irrational numbers
  BD (ME,87;C8E,9;PE,27)

- Understands the role of integers in the number system
  BD (ME,87;C8I,4;PI,25)

- Understands the relationship of prime numbers to other numbers
  BD (ME,91;C8E,10;PE,28)

- Understands the basic characteristics of and the relationships among fractions, ratios, proportions, decimals, and percents
  BD (ME,57,87,94;2E,291;C8I,4-5,8;PE,27;WI,122-123)

- Expresses numbers using scientific notation
  BP (ME,87;C8E,3;PI,25)

- Models numbers using two-dimensional regions
  BC (ME,87;C8E,4;PE,25)

- Expresses numbers like 100, 1,000 and 1,000,000 as powers of 10
  BP (2E,291)

- Understands that the Arabic system is not the only system for representing numbers; the numeral system used by the Romans is still used for dates, clock faces, and ordering, and numbers based on 60 are still used for telling time and describing angles
  BP (2E,213)

- Understands that number lines help demonstrate the subtraction of a bigger number from a smaller number and that the results are called negative numbers; number lines are commonly used when measuring something on either side of a reference point (e.g., temperature, altitude below/above sea level)
  BD (2E,213;C8I,4;PI,25)

- Locates, identifies, and orders numbers on a number line, including fractions, decimals, and positive and negative integers
  BC (MI,87;C8E,4;PE,25)

- Understands the role of place value in whole numbers as compared to decimals
  BC (MI,87;C8E,3;PE,25)

- Models operations on a number line
  BC (C8E,4;PI,25)

- Expresses percentages in a variety of equivalent forms or descriptions
  BC (ME,87;C8E,4-5;PE,25)

- Understands rate, proportionality, and percent, and the relationships among them
  BD (C8E,9;PI,27)

Codes (right side of page):   BD = Benchmark, Declarative; BP = Benchmark, Procedural; BC = Benchmark, Contextual

1st letter of each code in parentheses	*2nd letter of code*	*Number*
M = NCTM: Curric. & Eval. Standards for Math	E = Explicitly stated in document	Page number of cited document
2 = Project 2061: Benchmarks for Science Literacy	I = Implied in document	
C4,C8,C12 = NAEP: Math. Content Specs, Grades 4,8,12		
G = GESP: National Geography Standards		
N = New Standards: Mathematics Draft		
P = NAEP: Mathematics Assessment Framework		
S = SCANS: Report for America 2000		
W = Carnevale: Workplace Basics		

McREL

Level IV (Grades 9-12)

- Understands the basic characteristics of the real-number system and its subsystems

  BD (ME,184;C12I,4;PI,42)

- Understands the basic characteristics of roots

  BD (MI,87;C12I,29;PI,42)

- Understands the basic characteristics of exponents

  BD (MI,87;C12I,29;PI,42)

- Models numbers using three-dimensional regions

  BC (ME,87;C12E,4;PE,25)

- Compares and contrasts elements of the real-number system

  BC (ME,184;C12I,4-5;PI,25)

- Demonstrates an understanding of relative magnitude by expressing and comparing very small and very large numbers in scientific notation

  BC (ME,87;2E,214,291;C12E,3-4,7;PE,25)

- Recalls immediately the relations among 10, 100, 1000, 1 million, and 1 billion

  BD (2E,291)

- Understands that numbers can be written in bases other than 10; the simplest base, 2, uses just two symbols ("0" and "1" or "on" and "off")

  BD (2E,214)

- Has a basic understanding of the concept of inequalities

  BD (ME,150;C12E,27-28;PE,41)

3. Uses basic and advanced procedures while performing the process of computation

(SE,xviii)

Level I (Grades K-2)

- Adds and subtracts whole numbers with accuracy

  BP (ME,94;C4E,5;PE,26;WE,122-123)

- Uses common, everyday fractions to count, order, and measure things encountered in everyday experiences

  BC (2E,290)

- Understands that it is useful to estimate quantities without knowing them exactly

  BD (2E,211)

- Solves real-world problems involving addition and subtraction of whole numbers

  BP (ME,41;C4I,5;PI,26;WE,122-123)

- Understands common terms used with estimation (e.g., about, near, closer to, between, a little less than)

  BD (ME,36;C4I,5-6;PI,26)

Codes (right side of page):   BD = Benchmark, Declarative; BP = Benchmark, Procedural; BC = Benchmark, Contextual

1st letter of each code in parentheses	*2nd letter of code*	*Number*
M = NCTM: Curric. & Eval. Standards for Math	E = Explicitly stated in document	Page number of cited document
2 = Project 2061: Benchmarks for Science Literacy	I = Implied in document	

C4,C8,C12 = NAEP: Math. Content Specs, Grades 4,8,12
G = GESP: National Geography Standards
N = New Standards: Mathematics Draft
P = NAEP: Mathematics Assessment Framework
S = SCANS: Report for America 2000
W = Carnevale: Workplace Basics

MREL

BD (ME,36;C4E,5-6;PE,26-27)

- Understands what is meant by an estimate

Level II (Grades 3-5)

BP (ME,94;C4E,5;PI,26;WE,122-123)

- Adds, subtracts, multiplies, and divides whole numbers and decimals with accuracy

BP (MI,36;C4E,6;PE,26)

- Rounds whole numbers

BP (ME,44;C4I,5;PI,26;WE,122-123)

- Mentally adds and subtracts basic combinations of whole numbers with reasonable accuracy

BP (MI,44;C4E,5;PE,26)

- Determines the effects of addition, subtraction, multiplication, and division on size and order of numbers

BP (2E,290;WE,122-123)

- Adds, subtracts, multiplies, and divides whole numbers using a calculator

BP (2E,290;C8I,4-5;PI,26;WE,122-123)

- Accurately translates between decimals and commonly encountered fractions—halves, thirds, fourths, fifths, tenths, and hundredths (but not sixths, sevenths, and so on)

BC (2E,290;C4E,5;PE,26)

- When asked, accurately states the purpose for each step in basic calculations

BP (2E,291;C4I,6-7;PI,27;WE,122-123)

- Calculates what percentage one number is of another

BD (2E,36)

- Understands that choices must be made when determining which operation to use

BD (2E,36;C4I,5-6;PE,27)

- Understands that results of computation must be judged in terms of their usefulness and whether they make sense in the real world

BP (WE,122-123)

- Carries out arithmetic computations involving dollars and cents

BP (ME,41;C4I,5;PI,26;WE,122-123)

- Solves real-world problems involving multiplication and division of whole numbers

BP (ME,57;C4I,5;PI,26;WE,122-123)

- Solves real-world problems involving decimals

BD (ME,36;C4I,5-6;PE,26-27)

- Understands how close an estimate is required in a given problem situation

---

Codes (right side of page):   BD = Benchmark, Declarative; BP = Benchmark, Procedural; BC = Benchmark, Contextual
1st letter of each code in parentheses   *2nd letter of code*   *Number*
M = NCTM: Curric. & Eval. Standards for Math   E = Explicitly stated in document   Page number of cited document
2 = Project 2061: Benchmarks for Science Literacy   I = Implied in document
C4,C8,C12 = NAEP: Math. Content Specs, Grades 4,8,12
G = GESP: National Geography Standards
N = New Standards: Mathematics Draft
P = NAEP: Mathematics Assessment Framework
S = SCANS: Report for America 2000
W = Carnevale: Workplace Basics   50   McREL

Level III (Grades 6-8)

- Adds, subtracts, multiplies, and divides mixed numbers and fractions

  BP (MI,94;C8E,5-6;PI,26;WE,122-123)

- Rounds decimals and fractions

  BP (MI,94;C8E,6;PE,26)

- Mentally multiplies and divides basic combinations of whole numbers with reasonable accuracy

  BP (MI,94;C8I,6;PI,26)

- Uses basic estimation techniques effectively (e.g., overestimate, underestimate, range of estimations)

  BP (ME,94;C8E,6;PE,26)

- Uses order of operations effectively

  BP (ME,91;C8E,28;PE,26)

- Understands the nature of and similarities and differences between multiples and factors

  BD (ME,91;C8I,9;PE,27)

- Uses a calculator to compare amounts proportionally

  BC (2E,294)

- Understands that addition and subtraction are inverses of one another as are multiplication and division; one operation undoes what the other does

  BD (2E,213)

- Understands the three basic meanings of the expression a/b (i.e., a is the number of units each of which has the size $1/b$; a divided by b; and a compared to or in relationship to b)

  BD (2E,213;C8I,8-9;PI,27)

- Converts fractions to decimals, percentages to fractions, fractions to percentages, percentages to decimals, decimals to percentages, common fractions and mixed numbers to decimal fractions, and decimal fractions to common fractions and mixed numbers

  BP (C8E,4-5;PE,25;WE,122-123)

- Solves real-world problems involving fractions

  BP (ME,57,87;2E,291;C8I,6;PI,26;WE,122-123)

- Solves real-world problems involving ratios

  BP (ME,87;2E,291;C8E,8;PE,27)

- Solves real-world problems involving proportions

  BP (ME,94;2E,291;C8E,8;PE,27)

- Solves real-world problems involving percents

  BP (ME,87;2E,291;C8E,8;PE,27)

- Selects and uses appropriate type of estimation (e.g., overestimate, underestimate, range of estimate) to solve real-world problems

  BP (ME,94;C8E,6-7;PE,26)

Codes (right side of page):   BD = Benchmark, Declarative; BP = Benchmark, Procedural; BC = Benchmark, Contextual
1st letter of each code in parentheses   *2nd letter of code*   *Number*
M = NCTM: Curric. & Eval. Standards for Math   E = Explicitly stated in document   Page number of cited document
2 = Project 2061: Benchmarks for Science Literacy   I = Implied in document
C4,C8,C12 = NAEP: Math. Content Specs, Grades 4,8,12
G = GESP: National Geography Standards
N = New Standards: Mathematics Draft
P = NAEP: Mathematics Assessment Framework
S = SCANS: Report for America 2000
W = Carnevale: Workplace Basics

MREL

- Understands and describes the purpose of algorithms (e.g., regrouping with or without manipulatives, partial products, finding the greatest common divisor)
  BD (C8E,5-6;PE,26)

- Solves real-world problems involving decimals
  BP (MI,57,58;2E,291;C8I,4-5;PI,26;WE,122-123)

Level IV (Grades 9-12)

- Adds and subtracts algebraic expressions
  BP (MI,102;C12E,30;PE,42)

- Analyzes rounding errors using a calculator or computer
  BP (MI,94;C12E,6-7;PE,27)

- Identifies the source of any discrepancy between an estimate and a calculated answer
  BP (2E,291;C12I,6;PI,26)

- Understands that the reasonableness of the result of a computation can be estimated from the inputs and operations
  BD (2E,221)

- Solves real-world problems involving roots and exponents
  BP (MI,87;C12I,29-30;PI,42)

4. **Understands and applies basic and advanced properties of the concept of measurement**
(ME,51)

Level I (Grades K-2)

- Understands the relationships between length, width, and height
  BD (ME,51;C4E,8;PE,29)

- Understands the basic characteristics of weight and how it is measured
  BD (ME,51;C4E,8;PE,29)

- Has a basic understanding of the concept of time and how it is measured
  BD (ME,51;C4I,9;PI,29)

- Has a basic understanding of the concept of temperature and how it is measured
  BD (ME,51;C4E,9;PI,29)

- Makes quantitative estimates of familiar lengths, widths, and time intervals and checks them against measurements
  BC (2E,290;C4E,8;PE,29)

- Compares and orders objects according to a given attribute (e.g., weight, length)
  BC(C4E,8;PE,29;PI,29)

Codes (right side of page): BD = Benchmark, Declarative; BP = Benchmark, Procedural; BC = Benchmark, Contextual
1st letter of each code in parentheses   *2nd letter of code*   *Number*
M = NCTM: Curric. & Eval. Standards for Math   E = Explicitly stated in document   Page number of cited document
2 = Project 2061: Benchmarks for Science Literacy   I = Implied in document
C4,C8,C12 = NAEP: Math. Content Specs, Grades 4,8,12
G = GESP: National Geography Standards
N = New Standards: Mathematics Draft
P = NAEP: Mathematics Assessment Framework
S = SCANS: Report for America 2000
W = Carnevale: Workplace Basics

McREL

Level II (Grades 3-5)

- Understands the basic characteristics of area and how it is measured
  BD (ME,51;C4E,9;PE,29,30)

- Understands the basic features of mass
  BD (ME,51;C4E,8;PE,29,30)

- Makes effective use of a ruler, thermometer, and scale for making measurements
  BP (MI,51;C4E,9;PE,29)

- Determines whether measurements of length, area, volume, weight, or time are reasonable by referring to typical values
  BP (2E,290;WI,122-123)

- Uses a calculator to determine the area and volume from linear dimensions
  BP(2E,293)

- Understands the relationships among area, volume, and weight, and between time and cost
  BD (2E,293;C4E,9;PE,29)

- Compares the differences between any two measurements
  BC (2E,293)

- Understands that measurements are likely to give slightly different numbers when measured multiple times
  BD (2E,212)

- Understands that length can be thought of as units of lengths joined together
  BD (2E,223)

- Understands that area can be thought of as a collection of unit squares
  BD (2E,223)

- Understands that volume can be thought of as a collection of unit cubes
  BD (2E,223)

- Approximates the area of irregular shapes using squares, rectangles, and triangles
  BP (2I,223)

- Understands that scale drawings can be used to represent shapes and compare locations of things very different in size
  BD (2E,223)

- Understands the basic characteristics of circumference and how it is measured
  BD (MI,51;C4E,9;PI,29,30)

- Selects and uses appropriate units of measurement, according to type and size of unit
  BP (C4E,9;PE,29)

- Estimates, calculates, and compares perimeter, area, and volume
  BP (C4E,9;PE,30)

- Selects appropriate methods of measurement (i.e., direct or indirect)
  BC (C4E,10;PE,31)

Codes (right side of page):   BD = Benchmark, Declarative; BP = Benchmark, Procedural; BC = Benchmark, Contextual

1st letter of each code in parentheses   *2nd letter of code*   *Number*

M = NCTM: Curric. & Eval. Standards for Math   E = Explicitly stated in document   Page number of cited document

2 = Project 2061: Benchmarks for Science Literacy   I = Implied in document

C4,C8,C12 = NAEP: Math. Content Specs, Grades 4,8,12

G = GESP: National Geography Standards

N = New Standards: Mathematics Draft

P = NAEP: Mathematics Assessment Framework

S = SCANS: Report for America 2000

W = Carnevale: Workplace Basics   53   MREL

Level III (Grades 6-8)

- Has a basic understanding of the concept of rate and how it is measured ^{BD (ME,116;C8E,15;PE,31)}

- Understands the basic characteristics of perimeter and how perimeter is measured ^{BD (ME,116;C8E,12;PE,30)}

- Makes effective use of a meter stick for making measurements ^{BP (MI,116;C8E,11;PE,29)}

- Converts from one measurement to another within the same system, i.e., customary or metric (e.g., feet to miles, minutes to hours) ^{BP (MI,116;C8E,13;PE,30)}

- Determines significant digits in measurement ^{BP (MI,116;C8E,13;PE,31)}

- Determines the level of accuracy needed in measurement situations ^{BP (ME,116;C8E,13-14;PE,30)}

- Identifies and uses appropriate measuring tools for a variety of situations ^{BP (C8E,11;PE,29)}

- Calculates the volumes and surface areas of rectangular solids, cylinders, cones, pyramids, prisms, and combined forms ^{BP (2E,291;C8E,12-13;PE,30)}

- Estimates distances and travel times from maps and the actual size of objects from scale drawings ^{BP (2E,291;C8E,14;PE,31)}

- Expresses answers using appropriate units of measurement (e.g., seconds, square inches, dollars per tankful) ^{BP (2E,291;C8E,12-13;PE,31)}

- Reads analog and digital meters on instruments used to make direct measurements of length, volume, weight, elapsed time, rates and temperature, and chooses appropriate units for reporting various magnitudes ^{BP (2E,294;C8E,11;PE,29-30)}

- Uses measuring devices to determine an object's weight, length, width, or volume in metric units ^{BP (WE,122-123)}

- Performs basic conversions between standard and metric involving weight, distance, and volume ^{BP (WE,122-123)}

- Calculates the perimeter and area of rectangles ^{BP (2E,291;C8E,12;PE,30)}

Codes (right side of page):   BD = Benchmark, Declarative;   BP = Benchmark, Procedural;   BC = Benchmark, Contextual

1st letter of each code in parentheses   *2nd letter of code*   *Number*

M = NCTM: Curric. & Eval. Standards for Math   E = Explicitly stated in document   Page number of cited document

2 = Project 2061: Benchmarks for Science Literacy   I = Implied in document

C4,C8,C12 = NAEP: Math. Content Specs, Grades 4,8,12

G = GESP: National Geography Standards

N = New Standards: Mathematics Draft

P = NAEP: Mathematics Assessment Framework

S = SCANS: Report for America 2000

W = Carnevale: Workplace Basics   54   McREL

- Calculates the perimeter and area of triangles

  BP (2E,291;C8E,12;PE,30)

- Calculates the circumference and area of circles

  BP (2E,291;C8E,12;PE,30)

- Solves real-world problems involving weight, distance, and volume

  BP (ME,116;C8E,12;PE,30;WE,122-123)

- Applies given measurement formulas for perimeter, area, volume, and surface area in problem situations

  BC (C8E,13;PE,30)

- Solves problems involving units of measurement and converts answers to a larger or smaller unit

  BP (C8E,13;PE,30)

- Applies absolute and relative error in problem situations involving area, volume, and surface area

  BP (C8E,14;PE,31)

- Given the dimensions of a shape, creates a scale drawing of the shape

  BC (C8E,14;PE,31)

- Understands that the scale chosen for a graph or drawing makes a big difference in how useful it is

  BD (2E,224;GI,145)

Level IV (Grades 9-12)

- Understands the basic characteristics of the concept of capacity and how it is measured

  BD (MI,116;C12E,11;PE,29)

- Has a basic understanding of the concept of velocity and how it is measured

  BD (MI,116;C12I,11;PI,29)

- Has a basic understanding of the concept of acceleration and how it is measured

  BD (MI,116;C12I,11;PI,29)

- Determines precision and accuracy of measurements

  BP (MI,116;C12E,13;PE,30)

- Analyzes absolute and relative errors in measurement

  BP (MI,116;C12E,13;PE,31)

- Estimates the effects of measurement errors on calculations

  BC (2E,291)

- Understands that a small error in making a measurement can lead to a large error in the result

  BD (2E,214)

- Understands that scale drawings can help one measure distances and angles that are

  BD (2E,225)

Codes (right side of page): BD = Benchmark, Declarative; BP = Benchmark, Procedural; BC = Benchmark, Contextual

1st letter of each code in parentheses *2nd letter of code* *Number*

M = NCTM: Curric. & Eval. Standards for Math E = Explicitly stated in document Page number of cited document

2 = Project 2061: Benchmarks for Science Literacy I = Implied in document

C4,C8,C12 = NAEP: Math. Content Specs, Grades 4,8,12

G = GESP: National Geography Standards

N = New Standards: Mathematics Draft

P = NAEP: Mathematics Assessment Framework

S = SCANS: Report for America 2000

W = Carnevale: Workplace Basics

MREL

inconvenient to measure directly

- Understands the concept of rate and uses it in measurement situations
  BP (C12E,14;PE,31)

5. Understands and applies basic and advanced properties of the concepts of geometry
(ME,48)

Level I (Grades K-2)

- Understands the basic properties of and similarities and differences between circles, squares, and triangles
  BD (MI,48;C4I,11;PI,32)

- Understands the meaning of the concepts inside, outside, between
  BD (MI,48;C4E,12;PE,34)

- Understands that shapes such as circles, squares, and triangles can be found in nature and in things that people make, and that these shapes can be used to describe many things
  BD (2E,26,27,223)

- Understands that patterns can be made by putting different shapes together or taking them apart
  BD (2E,26;C4E,11;PE,33)

- Understands that things can move along straight, curved, circular, back-and-forth, and jagged paths
  BD (2E,26)

Level II (Grades 3-5)

- Understands the basic characteristics of the concept of three dimensions
  BD (MI,48;C4E,11;PI,33)

- Understands the basic characteristics of angles
  BD (ME,51,116;C4I,12;PI,34)

- Predicts and verifies the effects of combining, subdividing, and changing basic shapes
  BC (ME,48;C4E,11;PE,33)

- Compares shapes in terms of such concepts as parallel, perpendicular, congruence, and symmetry
  BC (2E,223;C4E,12;PE,33-35)

- Uses motion geometry (e.g., turns, flips, slides) to investigate concepts of symmetry, similarity, and congruence
  BD (2E,223;C4E,12;PE,33-35)

Codes (right side of page):   BD = Benchmark, Declarative; BP = Benchmark, Procedural; BC = Benchmark, Contextual
1st letter of each code in parentheses   *2nd letter of code*   *Number*
M = NCTM: Curric. & Eval. Standards for Math   E = Explicitly stated in document   Page number of cited document
2 = Project 2061: Benchmarks for Science Literacy   I = Implied in document
C4,C8,C12 = NAEP: Math. Content Specs, Grades 4,8,12
G = GESP: National Geography Standards
N = New Standards: Mathematics Draft
P = NAEP: Mathematics Assessment Framework
S = SCANS: Report for America 2000
W = Carnevale: Workplace Basics   56

MREL

Level III (Grades 6-8)

- Understands the basic characteristics of the concept of symmetry
  BD (MI,112;C8E,16-17;PI,33)

- Understands the basic characteristics of and the relationship between distance and midpoint
  BD (MI,112;C8E,19-20;PE,34)

- Understands the basic characteristics of slope
  BD (MI,112;C8E,19-20;PE,34)

- Compares the basic characteristics of and the similarities and differences between a variety of three-dimensional shapes (e.g., pyramids and prisms, cubes and rectangular prisms)
  BC (MI,112;C8,12;PE,30)

- Predicts and verifies results of combining, subdividing, and changing basic shapes
  BC (C8E,16;PE,33)

- Analyzes effects of basic transformations on geometric shapes
  BC (MI,161;C8E,16-17;PE,33)

- Uses the intersection of two-dimensional figures (e.g., lines, triangles, squares) to derive geometric definitions such as parallel, perpendicular, Pythagorean theorem, and midpoint
  BP (MI,161;C8E,17;PE,33)

- Visualizes geometric figures in various rotations
  BP (ME,112;C8E,15-17;PE,32-33)

- Determines ratios of measures in similar figures using properties of similarity
  BP (C8E,18-19;PE,34)

- Understands that round shapes give the least possible boundary for a given amount of interior area
  BD (2E,224)

- Represents problem situations with geometric models
  BP (C8E,19;PE,34)

- Understands that shapes on a sphere cannot be depicted on a flat surface without some distortion
  BD (2E,224;GE,145)

- Understands that a point can be located on a map given two perpendicular distances from the point, or given an angle and a distance from the point
  BD (2E,224)

- Solves real-world problems involving area of geometric figures
  BP (C8E,19;PE,34)

- Understands the basic properties of and the similarities and differences between a trapezoid, rhombus, and quadrilateral
  BD (MI,48,112;C4I,11;PI,32)

Codes (right side of page):   BD = Benchmark, Declarative; BP = Benchmark, Procedural; BC = Benchmark, Contextual
1st letter of each code in parentheses   *2nd letter of code*   *Number*
M = NCTM: Curric. & Eval. Standards for Math   E = Explicitly stated in document   Page number of cited document
2 = Project 2061: Benchmarks for Science Literacy   I = Implied in document
C4,C8,C12 = NAEP: Math. Content Specs, Grades 4,8,12
G = GESP: National Geography Standards
N = New Standards: Mathematics Draft
P = NAEP: Mathematics Assessment Framework
S = SCANS: Report for America 2000
W = Carnevale: Workplace Basics

MCREL

Level IV (Grades 9-12)

- Understands the relationship between parallel, perpendicular, and oblique lines
  BD (MI,161;2E,24;C12E,19;PE,34)

- Understands the basic characteristics of Pythagorean relationships
  BD (MI,161;C12E,18;PI,34)

- Performs synthetic transformations (e.g., translations, rotations, reflections, dilations) of basic shapes
  BP (MI,157;C12E,16-17;PE,33)

- Understands basic characteristics of vectors
  BP (ME,161;C12E,19;PE,34,35)

- Analyzes the intersection of three-dimensional figures with a plane
  BC (ME,157;C12E,17;PI,33)

- Classifies figures based on congruence and similarity
  BC (ME,157;C12E,17-18;PE,33)

- Describes spatial relationships in geometric terms (e.g., perpendicular, parallel, tangent, similar, congruent, symmetrical)
  BC (2E,297)

- Solves real-world problems involving vectors
  BP (ME,161;C12E,19-20;PE,35)

- Solves real-world problems involving the Pythagorean relationship
  BP (MI,161;C12E,18;PE,34)

- Performs algebraic transformations (e.g., translations, rotations, reflections, dilations) of geometric shapes
  BP (ME,161;C8E,16-17;PE,33)

- Constructs the image of a geometric figure under a given transformation (e.g., subdividing, dilating) and determines the relationship of the areas and perimeters of the two figures
  BC (C12E;PI,33)

- Solves problems involving the Pythagorean theorem
  BP (C12E,18;PE,34)

- Uses geometric models, diagrams, and graphs to solve real-world problems
  BP (MI,157;C12E,19;PE,33)

- Uses coordinates and vectors to represent geometric figures and properties algebraically
  BP (MI,161;C12E,19;PE,33-34)

- Uses properties of lines (e.g., distance, mid-point, slope, parallelism, perpendicularity) to describe figures algebraically
  BP (C12E,19;PE,33-34)

- Knows the characteristics and properties of conic sections
  BD (C12E,19;PE,34)

Codes (right side of page):   BD = Benchmark, Declarative; BP = Benchmark, Procedural; BC = Benchmark, Contextual
1st letter of each code in parentheses   *2nd letter of code*   *Number*
M = NCTM: Curric. & Eval. Standards for Math   E = Explicitly stated in document   Page number of cited document
2 = Project 2061: Benchmarks for Science Literacy   I = Implied in document
C4,C8,C12 = NAEP: Math. Content Specs, Grades 4,8,12
G = GESP: National Geography Standards
N = New Standards: Mathematics Draft
P = NAEP: Mathematics Assessment Framework
S = SCANS: Report for America 2000
W = Carnevale: Workplace Basics

McREL

BP (ME,161;C12E,19;PE,34)

- Uses vectors and simple operations on vectors (e.g., addition, subtraction, scalar multiplication, dot product) to solve real-world problems

BD (2E,225)

- Understands that when the size of a linear shape changes by some factor, its area and volume change disproportionately: area changes in proportion to the square of the factor, and volume changes in proportion to the cube of the factor

BD (2E,225)

- Understands that different ways to map a curved surface onto a flat surface have different advantages and disadvantages

BD (C12E,12-13;PI,30)

- Understands the relationship between surface area and volume for rectangular solids

(ME,54)

6. Understands and applies basic and advanced concepts of data analysis and distributions

Level I (Grades K-2)

BD (ME,54-55;2E,211;C4E,14-15;PE,36-37)

- Understands that observations about objects or events can be organized and displayed in simple graphs

Level II (Grades 3-5)

BC (ME,54;C4E,14-15;PI,36-37)

- Understands that data represents specific pieces of information about real-world objects or activities

BP (ME,54,105;C4E,15;PE,37)

- Collects and organizes simple data sets to answer questions

BD (MI,54;2E,218,223;C4E,14-15;PI,36)

- Understands that tables and graphs can show how the values of one quantity are related to the values of another and that tables and graphs can make it easier to identify patterns

BD (2E,228)

- Understands that spreading data out on a number line helps to see what the extremes are, where the data points pile up, and where the gaps are

BD (2E,228)

- Understands that a summary of data should include where the middle is and how much spread there is around it

---

Codes (right side of page):   BD = Benchmark, Declarative; BP = Benchmark, Procedural; BC = Benchmark, Contextual
1st letter of each code in parentheses   *2nd letter of code*   *Number*
M = NCTM: Curric. & Eval. Standards for Math   E = Explicitly stated in document   Page number of cited document
2 = Project 2061: Benchmarks for Science Literacy   I = Implied in document
C4,C8,C12 = NAEP: Math. Content Specs, Grades 4,8,12
G = GESP: National Geography Standards
N = New Standards: Mathematics Draft
P = NAEP: Mathematics Assessment Framework
S = SCANS: Report for America 2000
W = Carnevale: Workplace Basics

McREL

- Constructs and interprets simple bar graphs, pie charts, and line graphs ^{BP (C4E,15;GE,47;PE,37)}

- Given a table of data, selects the correct graphic representation for the data ^{BC (ME,54-55;C4E,14-15;PE,36-37)}

- Understands that data comes in many different forms and that collecting, organizing, and displaying data can be done in many ways ^{BD (ME,54;C4E,14-15;PE,36-37)}

Level III (Grades 6-8)

- Understands basic characteristics of and calculates measures of central tendency (i.e., mean, median, mode) ^{BD (MI,171;2E,291;C8E,23;GE,51;PE,37;WE,122-123)}

- Understands similarities and differences between tables, bar graphs, and circle graphs ^{BD (ME,105;C8E,21-22;PE,37)}

- Identifies basic trends in tables and graphs including varying rates of change, gaps, and clusters, and uses these trends to make predictions about the phenomena being graphed ^{BC (ME,105;2E,224,297;C8E,21;PE,36)}

- Understands that comparison of data from two groups involves comparing their middles and the spreads around them (i.e., dispersion of data) ^{BD (ME,107;2E,229)}

- Interpolates or extrapolates from data presented in various forms ^{BP (ME,105;C8E,21;PE,36)}

- Constructs, reads, and interprets data in charts, tables, plots (e.g., stem-and-leaf, box-and-whiskers, scatter), and graphs (e.g., bar, circle, line) ^{BP (ME,105-107;C8E,22;PE,37)}

Level IV (Grades 9-12)

- Understands the basic features of data sets (matrices) ^{BD (ME,176;C12E,31;PE,43)}

- Understands the basic measures of dispersion (i.e., standard deviation, variance) ^{BD (MI,171;C12E,22;PE,37)}

- Understands the basic features of outliers and procedures to deal with them ^{BD (ME,169;C12E,21;PE,37)}

- Represents data using stem-and-leaf plots and scatter plots ^{BP (MI,167;C12E,21;PE,37)}

- Understands that the same set of data can be represented using a variety of tables, graphs, ^{BD (ME,169;2E,221)}

Codes (right side of page):   BD = Benchmark, Declarative; BP = Benchmark, Procedural; BC = Benchmark, Contextual
1st letter of each code in parentheses   *2nd letter of code*   *Number*
M = NCTM: Curric. & Eval. Standards for Math   E = Explicitly stated in document   Page number of cited document
2 = Project 2061: Benchmarks for Science Literacy   I = Implied in document
C4,C8,C12 = NAEP: Math. Content Specs, Grades 4,8,12
G = GESP: National Geography Standards
N = New Standards: Mathematics Draft
P = NAEP: Mathematics Assessment Framework
S = SCANS: Report for America 2000
W = Carnevale: Workplace Basics   60   MREL

and symbols and that different modes of representation often convey different messages

BD (2E,230)

- Understands that the middle of a distribution may be misleading under certain circumstances (e.g., when data are not distributed symmetrically, when extreme high or low values exist, when the distribution is not reasonably smooth)

BC (C12E,22;GE,53;PE,37)

- Calculates measures of central tendency (i.e., mean, median, mode) for complex sets of data and analyzes the relative merits of those measures for the various data sets

BP (ME,176;C12E,30;PE,43)

- Solves real-world problems involving data matrices

BD (2E,225)

- Understands basic generalizations about the nature of graphs: the position of any point on a surface can be described by two numbers; a graph represents all the values that satisfy an equation; and the point at which two graphs intersect represents the values that will satisfy the two equations represented by the graphs

(GE,55;SI,xviii)

7. Understands and applies basic and advanced concepts of probability and statistics

Level I (Grades K-2)

BD (2E,227)

- Understands that some events are more likely to happen than others

BD (2E,227)

- Understands that some events can be predicted fairly well but others cannot because we do not always know everything that may affect an event

BD (2E,227)

- Understands that one can find out about a group of things by studying just a few of them

Level II (Grades 3-5)

BD (MI,54)

- Understands that the word "chance" refers to the likelihood of an event

BD (2E,227)

- Understands that when predictions are based on what is known about the past, one must assume that conditions stay the same from the past event to the predicted future event

BD (2E,227)

- Understands that statistical predictions are better for describing what proportion of a group will experience something (e.g., what proportion of automobiles will be involved in

---

Codes (right side of page):   BD = Benchmark, Declarative;   BP = Benchmark, Procedural;   BC = Benchmark, Contextual

1st letter of each code in parentheses   *2nd letter of code*   *Number*

M = NCTM: Curric. & Eval. Standards for Math   E = Explicitly stated in document   Page number of cited document

2 = Project 2061: Benchmarks for Science Literacy   I = Implied in document

C4,C8,C12 = NAEP: Math. Content Specs, Grades 4,8,12

G = GESP: National Geography Standards

N = New Standards: Mathematics Draft

P = NAEP: Mathematics Assessment Framework

S = SCANS: Report for America 2000

W = Carnevale: Workplace Basics

MREL

accidents) rather than which individuals within the group will experience something, and how often events will occur (e.g., how many sunny days will occur over a year) rather than exactly when they will occur

- Understands that summary predictions about large collections of events are usually more accurate than summary predictions about just a few events
  BD (2E,228)

- Understands that even unlikely events may occur fairly often in very large populations
  BD (2E,228)

- Understands that a small part of something may have unique characteristics but not be an accurate representation of the whole, and that how useful a sample is depends on how it is chosen
  BD (2E,228)

- Understands that when choosing a sample, one must guard against choosing only the data that show what is expected
  BD (2E,228)

- Given a sample space for an experiment involving different outcomes, identifies the probabilities associated with each outcome
  BC (C4E,16;PE,38-39)

Level III (Grades 6-8)

- Understands the basic features of a sample and sampling error
  BD (ME,108;2E,250;C8E,22;PE,37)

- Designs a simulation to estimate the probability for given event
  BP (ME,171;C8E,24;PE,38)

- Identifies common errors in the presentation of statistics
  BP (C8E,23;PE,38)

- Estimates probabilities of events in familiar situations using data from the past or by making rough calculations
  BP (2E,229,291;C12E,24-25;PE,38)

- Understands that how probability is estimated depends on what is known about the situation
  BD (2E,229;C8E,25;PI,39)

- Understands that estimates of probability can be based on data from similar situations in the past or on the assumption that all possible situations and events are known
  BD (2E,229;C8E,25;PI,39)

- Understands that data from the past may no longer be applicable to a current problem
  BD (2E,229)

Codes (right side of page):	BD = Benchmark, Declarative; BP = Benchmark, Procedural; BC = Benchmark, Contextual
1st letter of each code in parentheses	*2nd letter of code* · *Number*
M = NCTM: Curric. & Eval. Standards for Math	E = Explicitly stated in document · Page number of cited document
2 = Project 2061: Benchmarks for Science Literacy	I = Implied in document
C4,C8,C12 = NAEP: Math. Content Specs, Grades 4,8,12	
G = GESP: National Geography Standards	
N = New Standards: Mathematics Draft	
P = NAEP: Mathematics Assessment Framework	
S = SCANS: Report for America 2000	
W = Carnevale: Workplace Basics	62

BD (ME,111;2E,229)

- Understands that probabilities are ratios that can be expressed as fractions, percentages, or odds

BD (ME,106;2E,229)

- Understands that the larger a well-chosen sample is, the more likely it is to represent the whole, and that many ways of choosing a sample can make it unrepresentative of the whole

BD (2E,229;C8E,25;PE,39)

- Understands that events can be described in terms of being more or less likely, impossible, or certain

BD (ME,105;C8E,33;PE,37)

- Understands procedures for selecting an unbiased sample

BD (ME,109)

- Understands the relationship between the numerical expression of a probability and the events that produce these numbers (e.g., 3/5 as it relates to the probability of pulling a green chip from a hat)

Level IV (Grades 9-12)

BD (ME,171;C12E,22;PE,37)

- Has a basic understanding of the concept of random variables

BD (MI,171;C12E,25;PI,39)

- Understands the similarities and differences between joint and conditional probability

BD (MI,171;C12E,25;PI,39)

- Understands the concept of independent and dependent events

BD (MI,167;C12I,20-21;PI,37)

- Understands the basic features of a statistic

BP (MI,171;C12E,24;PE,38)

- Determines probabilities using counting procedures, tables, trees, area models, and formulas for permutations and combinations

BP (MI,108;C12I,25;PI,39)

- Compares experimental results with mathematical expectations of probabilities

BP (2E,291)

- Compares data for two groups by representing their averages and spreads graphically

BD (2E,230)

- Understands that when estimating a statistic, one should also estimate how far off he or she may be

BD (2E,230)

- Understands that the larger and more well-chosen a sample of a population is, the better it estimates the population summary statistics; for a well-chosen sample, the size of the sample

Codes (right side of page):   BD = Benchmark, Declarative;   BP = Benchmark, Procedural;   BC = Benchmark, Contextual
1st letter of each code in parentheses   *2nd letter of code*   *Number*
M = NCTM: Curric. & Eval. Standards for Math   E = Explicitly stated in document   Page number of cited document
2 = Project 2061: Benchmarks for Science Literacy   I = Implied in document
C4,C8,C12 = NAEP: Math. Content Specs, Grades 4,8,12
G = GESP: National Geography Standards
N = New Standards: Mathematics Draft
P = NAEP: Mathematics Assessment Framework
S = SCANS: Report for America 2000
W = Carnevale: Workplace Basics   63   McREL

is much more important than the size of the population; to avoid bias, samples are selected by some random system

- Understands that a physical or mathematical model can be used to estimate the probability of real-world events

  BD (2E,230)

- Understands that when comparing percentages and proportions, one must also consider the number of cases on which those percentages are based

  BD (2E,230)

- Designs and carries out statistical experiments

  BP (MI,137;C12E,22;PE,37)

- Solves real-world problems involving conditional probability and joint probability

  BP (MI,171;C12E,25;PE,39)

- Understands the concepts of independent and dependent events and their relationship to compound events and conditional probability

  BP (ME,171;C12E,25;PE,39)

- Determines probability for given independent events

  BP (ME,171;C12E,25;PE,39)

- Determines probability for given dependent events

  BP (ME,171;C12E,25;PE,39)

- Uses the properties of the normal curve to answer questions about sets of data that are assumed to be normally distributed

  BP (ME,171;C12E,22;PE,37)

8. Understands and applies basic and advanced properties of functions and algebra

(ME,102)

Level I (Grades K-2)

- Recognizes basic number patterns

  BP (ME,29;C4E,7,17-18;PE,27)

Level II (Grades 3-5)

- Interpolates simple patterns of numbers

  BP (ME,29,60;C4E,18;PE,41)

- Extrapolates simple patterns of numbers and geometric shapes

  BP (ME,29;C4E,7,18;PE,41)

- Understands that at a very basic level, mathematics is the study of many kinds of patterns,

  BD (ME,29,60;2E,27)

Codes (right side of page):	BD = Benchmark, Declarative; BP = Benchmark, Procedural; BC = Benchmark, Contextual
1st letter of each code in parentheses	*2nd letter of code* — *Number*
M = NCTM: Curric. & Eval. Standards for Math	E = Explicitly stated in document — Page number of cited document
2 = Project 2061: Benchmarks for Science Literacy	I = Implied in document
C4,C8,C12 = NAEP: Math. Content Specs, Grades 4,8,12	
G = GESP: National Geography Standards	
N = New Standards: Mathematics Draft	
P = NAEP: Mathematics Assessment Framework	
S = SCANS: Report for America 2000	
W = Carnevale: Workplace Basics	

64

McREL

including numbers and shapes, and operations applied to them

- Uses patterns and relationships to represent mathematical situations

  BP (ME,29,60;C4E,18-19;PE,41)

- Given general constraints, constructs a pattern and articulates why the pattern works (or, "the rule of the pattern")

  BC (ME,60;C4E,18;PE,40-41)

Level III (Grades 6-8)

- Understands that an algebraic expression contains a variable which is a symbol representing an unknown quantity

  BD (ME,102;C8I,19;PE,41)

- Understands the basic features of coordinates

  BD (MI,102;C8E,27;PE,41)

- Has a basic understanding of the concept of equation

  BD (ME,102;C8E,27;PE,41)

- Understands that a variable can be used as a placeholder for a specific unknown (e.g., $x + 8 = 13$), and as a representative of a range of values (e.g., $4t + 7$)

  BD (ME,102-103;2E,219;C8E,26;PE,41)

- Understands that mathematical statements can be used to describe functional relationships for which one quantity changes when another changes

  BD (ME,98;2E,219;C8E,26;PE,41)

- Computes rates of change from magnitudes and magnitudes from rates of change

  BP (2E,219)

- Understands the common relationships that can exist between two variables and the various ways these relationships will look on a graph (e.g., as one variable increases uniformly, the other variable may do one of the following: always keep the same proportion to the first, increase or decrease steadily, increase or decrease at a faster and faster rate, approach some limiting value, reach some intermediate maximum or minimum, alternately increase and decrease indefinitely, or increase or decrease in steps)

  BD (2E,219;C8E,30-31;PE,43-44)

- Cross-tabulates the occurrence of variables and makes a general determination whether they co-vary

  BP (GE,52)

- Uses substitution within given formulas and expressions with real-world problems

  BP (MI,75;C8E,28;PE,42)

- Solves real-world problems involving rectangular coordinates

  BP (MI,102;C8I,27-28;PI,41)

Codes (right side of page):	BD = Benchmark, Declarative; BP = Benchmark, Procedural; BC = Benchmark, Contextual
1st letter of each code in parentheses	*2nd letter of code* — *Number*

1st letter of each code in parentheses | *2nd letter of code* | *Number*
M = NCTM: Curric. & Eval. Standards for Math | E = Explicitly stated in document | Page number of cited document
2 = Project 2061: Benchmarks for Science Literacy | I = Implied in document
C4,C8,C12 = NAEP: Math. Content Specs, Grades 4,8,12
G = GESP: National Geography Standards
N = New Standards: Mathematics Draft
P = NAEP: Mathematics Assessment Framework
S = SCANS: Report for America 2000
W = Carnevale: Workplace Basics   65   McREL

- Solves real-world problems involving formulas with one variable

  BP (ME,102;C8E,29;PE,42)

- Simplifies algebraic expressions involving numbers and variables

  BP (ME,102;C8E,28-29;PE,42)

- Solves simple systems of equations graphically

  BP (ME,102;C8E,29-30;PE,42)

Level IV (Grades 9-12)

- Uses appropriate terminology and notation to define functions and their properties, including domain, range, function composition, and inverses

  BD (MI,154;C12E,32;PE,43)

- Understands the characteristics and uses of basic trigonometric functions

  BD (ME,163;C12E,33-34;PE,44)

- Investigates the effects of parameter changes on the graphs of functions

  BP (ME,154;C12E,33;PE,43-44)

- Has a basic understanding of polynomial equations

  BD (ME,180;C12E,32;PE,43)

- Has a basic understanding of polar coordinates

  BP (ME,163;C12E,27;PE,41)

- Determines the maximum and minimum points on a graph

  BP (ME,180;C12E,27;PI,41)

- Fits a line or curve to a set of data and uses this line or curve to make predictions

  BP (MI,167;C12E,23-24,26;PE,38)

- Compares and applies the numerical, symbolic, and graphical properties of a variety of functions

  BC (ME,154;C12E,33;PE,43-44)

- Solves systems of equations and inequalities graphically, algebraically, and using matrices

  BP (ME,150;C12E,29-30;PE,42)

- Uses a variety of algebraic and graphical methods to solve polynomial equations with real and complex roots

  BP (C12E,32;PE,43)

- Understands functional relationships for which the rate of change of one variable is dependent on how much there is of another variable (e.g., the rate of change of speed is proportional to the amount of force acting on it)

  BD (2E,220)

- Understands that symbolic statements in mathematics can be manipulated by rules of mathematical logic to produce other statements that preserve the basic relationships but are

  BD (2E,220)

Codes (right side of page):   BD = Benchmark, Declarative; BP = Benchmark, Procedural; BC = Benchmark, Contextual
1st letter of each code in parentheses   *2nd letter of code*   *Number*
M = NCTM: Curric. & Eval. Standards for Math   E = Explicitly stated in document   Page number of cited document
2 = Project 2061: Benchmarks for Science Literacy   I = Implied in document
C4,C8,C12 = NAEP: Math. Content Specs, Grades 4,8,12
G = GESP: National Geography Standards
N = New Standards: Mathematics Draft
P = NAEP: Mathematics Assessment Framework
S = SCANS: Report for America 2000
W = Carnevale: Workplace Basics   66   MREL

more easily interpreted

- Understands that symbolic statements can be combined to look for values of variables that will satisfy all of them at the same time BD (2E,220)

- Understands that any graphic or algebraic mathematical model is limited in how well it represents the world by uncertainties in measurement, neglect of some important influences, or by requiring too much computation BD (2E,220)

- Understands that when a relationship between variables is represented in symbols, numbers can be substituted for all but one of the symbols and the possible value of the remaining symbol computed; sometimes the relationship may be satisfied by one value, sometimes more than one, and sometimes no value satisfies the relationship BD (2E,221)

- Understands that mathematical modeling is a tool that can be used to simulate how a proposed system might behave BD (2E,33)

- Understands that mathematical modeling aids in technological design by simulating how a proposed system would theoretically behave BD (2E,33)

- Understands that the basic process of creating a mathematical model involves the following components: (1) using abstractions to represent things or ideas; (2) manipulating the abstractions according to logical rules; (3) checking to see how well the results match the original thing or idea; and (4) if the match is not a good one, creating a new model BD (2E,38)

- Understands that it may not be easy to determine which mathematical model to use to describe data even when plenty of data is available, and that the mathematical model one chooses may require more computing power than is available BD (2E,230)

- Understands that determining the correlation between two variables involves inspecting their distributions using two-way tables or scatter plots; a correlation between two variables does not mean that one variable causes another (e.g., some other variable may have caused both, or the correlation might simply be due to chance); a true correlation means that differences in one variable imply differences in the other BD (ME,167;2E,230;2I,297;C12E,22;PE,37)

- Uses the technique of spatial sampling to determine the extent to which two variables have a relationship (e.g., placing a transparent grid of squares on a map to determine whether corn BP (GE,53)

Codes (right side of page):   BD = Benchmark, Declarative;   BP = Benchmark, Procedural;   BC = Benchmark, Contextual
1st letter of each code in parentheses   *2nd letter of code*   *Number*
M = NCTM: Curric. & Eval. Standards for Math   E = Explicitly stated in document   Page number of cited document
2 = Project 2061: Benchmarks for Science Literacy   I = Implied in document
C4,C8,C12 = NAEP: Math. Content Specs, Grades 4,8,12
G = GESP: National Geography Standards
N = New Standards: Mathematics Draft
P = NAEP: Mathematics Assessment Framework
S = SCANS: Report for America 2000
W = Carnevale: Workplace Basics   67   MCREL

production and hogs coexist within the same grid cells)

- Constructs scatter plots for data representing two variables and makes a qualitative analysis of the relationship between the two variables
  BC (GE,54)

- Identifies and analyzes linear and nonlinear patterns in data using line graphs
  BC (GE,54)

- Constructs linear mathematical models for real-world phenomena
  BC (ME,154;C12E,28-29;GI,54,55;PE,41-42)

- Constructs nonlinear mathematical models for real-world phenomena
  BC (ME,154;C12E,28-29;GI,54,55;PE,41-42)

- Understands the formal differences between the terms "correlates with" and "causes"
  BD (2I,297)

- Solves real-world problems involving linear programming
  BP (ME,176)

- Represents real-world problems using algebraic functions and graphs of those functions
  BP (MI,150,176)

- Solves real-world problems involving polar coordinates
  BP (ME,163;C12I,28;PE,41)

- Approximates solutions of equations (e.g., bisection, sign changes, successive approximations)
  BP (C12E,32;PE,43)

(2I,34)

9.   Understands the general nature and uses of mathematics

Level I (Grades K-2)

- Not appropriate for this level
  BD (2E,27,32,36)

Level II (Grades 3-5)

- Understands that numbers and the operations performed on them can be used to describe things in the real world and predict what might occur
  BD (2E,36)

- Understands that mathematical ideas and concepts can be represented concretely, graphically, and symbolically
  BD (2E,27)

Codes (right side of page):   BD = Benchmark, Declarative; BP = Benchmark, Procedural; BC = Benchmark, Contextual
1st letter of each code in parentheses   *2nd letter of code*   *Number*
M = NCTM: Curric. & Eval. Standards for Math   E = Explicitly stated in document   Page number of cited document
2 = Project 2061: Benchmarks for Science Literacy   I = Implied in document
C4,C8,C12 = NAEP: Math. Content Specs, Grades 4,8,12
G = GESP: National Geography Standards
N = New Standards: Mathematics Draft
P = NAEP: Mathematics Assessment Framework
S = SCANS: Report for America 2000
W = Carnevale: Workplace Basics   68   MREL

Level III (Grades 6-8)

- Understands that mathematics has been helpful in practical ways for many centuries $\quad$ BD (2E,32)

- Understands that mathematicians often represent real things using abstract ideas like numbers or lines; they then work with these abstractions to learn about the things they represent $\quad$ BD (2E,37)

Level IV (Grades 9-12)

- Understands that mathematics is the study of any pattern or relationship, but natural science is the study of those patterns that are relevant to the observable world $\quad$ BD (2E,29)

- Understands that mathematics began long ago to help solve practical problems; however, it soon focused on abstractions drawn from the world and then on abstract relationships among those abstractions $\quad$ BD (2E,29)

- Understands that in mathematics, as in other sciences, simplicity is one of the highest values; some mathematicians try to identify the smallest set of rules from which many other propositions can be logically derived $\quad$ BD (2E,29)

- Understands that theories in mathematics are greatly influenced by practical issues; real-world problems sometimes result in new mathematical theories and pure mathematical theories sometimes have highly practical applications $\quad$ BD (2E,29)

- Understands that new mathematics continues to be invented even today, along with new connections between various components of mathematics $\quad$ BD (2E,29)

- Understands that science and mathematics operate under common principles: belief in order, ideals of honesty and openness, the importance of review by colleagues, and the importance of imagination $\quad$ BD (2E,33)

- Understands that mathematics provides a precise system to describe objects, events, and relationships and to construct logical arguments $\quad$ BD (2E,33)

- Understands that the development of computers has opened many new doors to mathematics just as other advances in technology can open up new areas to mathematics $\quad$ BD (2E,33)

Codes (right side of page): BD = Benchmark, Declarative; BP = Benchmark, Procedural; BC = Benchmark, Contextual
1st letter of each code in parentheses *2nd letter of code* *Number*
M = NCTM: Curric. & Eval. Standards for Math E = Explicitly stated in document Page number of cited document
2 = Project 2061: Benchmarks for Science Literacy I = Implied in document
C4,C8,C12 = NAEP: Math. Content Specs, Grades 4,8,12
G = GESP: National Geography Standards
N = New Standards: Mathematics Draft
P = NAEP: Mathematics Assessment Framework
S = SCANS: Report for America 2000
W = Carnevale: Workplace Basics

McREL

- Understands that mathematics often stimulates innovations in science and technology [BD (2E,33)]

- Understands that mathematicians commonly operate by choosing an interesting set of rules [BD (2E,38)] and then playing according to those rules; the only limit to those rules is that they should not contradict each other

Codes (right side of page):   BD = Benchmark, Declarative; BP = Benchmark, Procedural; BC = Benchmark, Contextual
1st letter of each code in parentheses   *2nd letter of code*   *Number*
M = NCTM: Curric. & Eval. Standards for Math   E = Explicitly stated in document   Page number of cited document
2 = Project 2061: Benchmarks for Science Literacy   I = Implied in document
C4,C8,C12 = NAEP: Math. Content Specs, Grades 4,8,12
G = GESP: National Geography Standards
N = New Standards: Mathematics Draft
P = NAEP: Mathematics Assessment Framework
S = SCANS: Report for America 2000
W = Carnevale: Workplace Basics

70

McREL

8. Science

The following process was used to identify standards and benchmarks in the field of science:

Identification of National Reports

Three reports were identified as significant for representing current thinking on content standards in science: a draft document available from the National Committee on Science Education Standards and Assessment (NCSESA), *National Science Education Standards* (November, 1994); Project 2061's *Benchmarks for Science Literacy* (1993); and the National Science Teachers Association's (NSTA) *Scope, Sequence, and Coordination of Secondary School Science: The Content Core* (Pearsall, 1993). Additionally, supporting citations were available from the California Department of Education's *Science Framework for California Public Schools* (1991), and from two reports from the National Assessment of Educational Progress, *Science Objectives for 1990* and *Exercise Specifications for 1994 NAEP*.

Selection of the Reference Document

The draft of NCSESA's *National Science Education Standards* was selected as the reference document. This choice required some modification of the standards that were published in our January 1994 update, which had used Project 2061's *Benchmarks for Science Literacy* as the reference. As noted at that time, available drafts from the standard-setting group were not then at a stage of completion that could provide sufficient detail for our purposes.

Identification of Standards and Benchmarks

The content standards from NCSESA, which "outline what students should know, understand, and be able to do in natural science" (p. V-1), are grouped into categories at three grade levels (K-4, 5-8, and 9-12). The number of standards varies by grade level within each of seven categories:

Science as inquiry
Physical science
Life science
Earth and space science
Science and technology
Science in personal and social perspectives
History and nature of science

A final area, "unifying concepts and processes," is not articulated for grade levels, but is intended for development across K-12 science education.

Science information in NCSESA's document is articulated for K-12 at the category level, but not at the standard level. That is, each standard and its associated content appears only once, and at one level (K-4, 5-8, or 9-12). For example, in the physical sciences under the heading "Earth and space science," a standard with the topic "Objects in the sky" appears with two related standards at grades K-4 only; at grades 5-8, three standards are under that category, and a closely related topic is "Earth in the solar system." At grades 9-12, four standards cover the area, and the one nearest in content to "Earth in the solar system" or "Objects in the sky" is the "Origin and evolution of the universe." Thus, the 86 standards are closely related within categories, but are not articulated across the grade ranges by standard. Since our model calls for the articulation of standards across grade levels wherever possible, some reorganization of content was necessary. Although in part the benchmarks were constructed into standards from "the ground up," there was strong guidance provided by the structure of standards available from Project 2061's *Benchmarks for Science Literacy*.

One significant change results from our selection of the NCSESA draft as the new reference document for the identification of standards in science. The reader will find increased emphasis on the nature of scientific knowledge, scientific inquiry, and the design process. In addition, sufficient material and direction from the NCSESA standards document were found to warrant a standard on the relationships of science, technology, and society.

At the benchmark level, Project 2061's *Benchmarks* proved very useful for distinguishing content at the grade ranges selected for this study: K-2, 3-5, 6-8, and 9-12. Material from the reference document, NCSESA's November draft, was added to or revised in four cases: 1) when minor modification of a benchmark statement allowed for additional citation support; 2) when the original statement carried more than one basic idea and was divided into components; 3) when stylistic changes helped the sense of the statement; and 4) when benchmark statements not in the science standards draft were added because the information was found to appear consistently in the other major documents identified for science.

Additionally, there were very few instances of content duplication across standards. In each case that the subject material appeared to be redundant across standards, it was also clear that the same benchmarks within a standard served the purpose of preparing students for more complex, related ideas at later benchmark levels. For this reason, the duplicates were not deleted as would otherwise be done, but cross-referenced in the citation log. (For more detail, see Section 6, How the Subject-Area Sections are Structured.)

Integration of Information from Other Documents

The documents used to integrate information were NSTA's *Content Core*, and the *California Science Framework*. Each was referenced to provide science teachers with ready access to sources via page number citations keyed to the benchmarks. In addition, *Content Core* and Project 2061's *Benchmarks* provided a means for evaluating whether additional benchmarks should be added to the reference document. If information found at the appropriate level in either document could not be found in the reference document (NCSESA's draft standards), then it was identified for possible inclusion as an additional benchmark. A compiled list of this information was then compared against information in the *California Science Framework* and the two documents from NAEP. If the information was found to be present in at least two documents (*Content Core* and/or *Benchmarks*, and one of the three supporting documents), it was integrated with the information from the reference document into a benchmark. Evidence for this process can be found by an examination of the "citation log" found associated with each benchmark: if the benchmark does not show a reference to NCSESA's draft document, then it was added to the information from the reference document using the process just described.

Summary of Standards for Science

Earth and Space
1. Understands basic features of the Earth
2. Understands basic Earth processes
3. Understands essential ideas about the composition and structure of the universe and the Earth's place in it

Life Sciences
4. Knows about the diversity and unity that characterize life
5. Understands the genetic basis for the transfer of biological characteristics from one generation to the next
6. Knows the general structure and functions of cells in organisms
7. Understands how species depend on one another and on the environment for survival
8. Understands the cycling of matter and flow of energy through the living environment
9. Understands the basic concepts of the evolution of species

Physical Sciences
10. Understands basic concepts about the structure and properties of matter
11. Understands energy types, sources, and conversions, and their relationship to heat and temperature
12. Understands motion and the principles that explain it
13. Knows the kinds of forces that exist between objects and within atoms

Science and Technology
14. Understands the nature of scientific knowledge
15. Understands the nature of scientific inquiry
16. Understands the scientific enterprise
17. Understands the nature of technological design
18. Understands the interactions of science, technology, and society

(2E,66)

1. Understands basic features of the Earth

Level I (Grades K-2)

BD (SE,V33;CE,93,99,106;NE,57,58,60)
- Knows that Earth materials consist of solid rocks, soils, liquid water, and the gases of the atmosphere

BD (2E,67;NI,59)
- Knows that water can be a liquid (rain) or a solid (ice) and can be made to go back and forth from one form to the other, but the amount of water stays the same

BD (SI,V34;2E,67;NE,61)
- Knows that weather can change from day to day, but things like temperature and rain (or snow) tend to be high, low, or medium in the same months every year

Level II (Grades 3-5)

BD (2E,68;NE,59)
- Knows that when liquid water disappears, it turns into gas (vapor) in the air and can reappear as a liquid when cooled

BD (CE,101;NE,59;TE,79)
- Knows the major differences between fresh and ocean waters

BD (2E,68;CE,99;NE,60)
- Knows that clouds, like fog or steam from a kettle, are made of tiny droplets of water

BD (2E,68;CE,106)
- Knows that air is a substance that surrounds us, takes up space, and moves around us as wind

BD (2E,68;NE,62-63)
- Knows that the rotation of the Earth on its axis every 24 hours produces the night and day cycle

BD (SE,V34;CI,84;NE,62)
- Knows that the Sun provides the light and heat necessary to maintain the temperature of the Earth

Level III (Grades 6-8)

BD (2E,69;CE,86;NE,74;TE,95)
- Knows that the Earth is the only body in our solar system that appears able to support life

BD (SE,V89;2E,69;CE,90;NE,59,71;TI,79-80)
- Knows that the solid Earth is layered with a thin brittle crust, hot convecting mantle, and dense metallic core; three-fourths of the Earth's surface is covered by a thin layer of water; and the entire planet is surrounded by a blanket of air

---

Codes (right side of page):   BD = Benchmark, Declarative; BP = Benchmark, Procedural; BC = Benchmark, Contextual
1st letter of each code in parentheses   *2nd letter of code*   *Number*
S = NCSESA: National Science Education Standards   E = Explicitly stated in document   Page number of cited document
2 = Project 2061: Benchmarks for Science Literacy   I = Implied in document   *or, for duplicates:*
C = CDE: Science Framework for Calif. Public Schools   Standard number & level of duplicate
N = NAEP: Science Assess./Exercise Specifications
O = NAEP: 1990 Science Objectives
T = NSTA: The Content Core
D = Duplicated in another standard

McREL

- Knows the composition and structure of the Earth's atmosphere

  BD (SE,V90;CE,108;NE,70;TE,80)

- Knows that clouds, which are formed by the condensation of water vapor, affect weather and climate; some do so by reflecting much of the sunlight that reaches Earth from the Sun; others hold heat energy emitted from the Earth's surface

  BD (SE,V90;CI,108;NI,71;TI,80)

- Knows that because of the tilt of the Earth's axis, sunlight and, hence, heat fall more intensely on one part or another of the Earth during its one-year revolution around the Sun; the difference in heating of the Earth's surface produces the planet's seasons and weather patterns

  BD (SE,V91;2E,69;NE,62-63;TE,89)

- Knows that the Earth's climate sometimes changes radically in response to the effects of geological shifts (e.g., the advance or retreat of glaciers over centuries, a series of huge volcanic eruptions in a short time)

  BD (2E,69;NE,68;TE,97)

- Knows that even relatively small changes of atmospheric content or ocean temperature can have widespread effects on climate if the change lasts long enough

  BD (SE,V90;2E,69;NE,69,85;TI,89)

- Knows that the cycling of water in and out of the atmosphere plays an important role in determining climatic patterns; water evaporates from the surface of the Earth, rises and cools, condenses into rain or snow and falls to the surface, where it forms rivers and lakes and collects in porous layers of rock

  BD (SE,V89;2E,69;CE,99;NE,71;TE,82)

- Knows that water is a solvent; as it passes through the water cycle it dissolves minerals and gases and carries them to the oceans

  BD (SE,V89;CE,99;NE,70)

- Knows that the Sun is the major source of energy for phenomena on the Earth's surface, such as winds, ocean currents, the water cycle, and the growth of plants

  BD (SE,V91;CI,108-109;NE,71;TE,84)

Level IV (Grades 9-12)

- Knows that Earth systems have both internal and external sources of energy, both of which create heat; although the Sun is the major external source of energy, the decay of radioactive isotopes and gravitational energy from the Earth's original formation are primary sources of internal heat

  BD (SE,V150)

Codes (right side of page):	BD = Benchmark, Declarative; BP = Benchmark, Procedural; BC = Benchmark, Contextual	
1st letter of each code in parentheses	*2nd letter of code*	*Number*
S = NCSESA: National Science Education Standards	E = Explicitly stated in document	Page number of cited document
2 = Project 2061: Benchmarks for Science Literacy	I = Implied in document	*or, for duplicates:*
C = CDE: Science Framework for Calif. Public Schools		Standard number & level of duplicate
N = NAEP: Science Assess./Exercise Specifications		
O = NAEP: 1990 Science Objectives		
T = NSTA: The Content Core		
D = Duplicated in another standard		

McREL

- Knows that weather (in the short run) and climate (in the long run) involve the transfer of energy in and out of the atmosphere BD (SI,V150;2E,70;NE,84)

- Knows that solar radiation heats the land masses, oceans and air, and that transfer of heat energy at the boundaries (between the atmosphere, the land masses, and the oceans) results in layers at different temperatures and densities in both the ocean and atmosphere; the action of gravitational force on layers of different densities causes them to rise or fall, and such circulation (influenced by the rotation of the Earth) produces winds and ocean currents BD (SE,V150;2E,70;NE,83-85;TI,92)

- Knows how life is adapted to conditions on the Earth, including the force of gravity that enables the planet to retain an adequate atmosphere and the intensity of radiation from the Sun that allows water to cycle between liquid and vapor BD (2E,70;CE,107;NI,78;DE,3.4.4)

2. Understands basic Earth processes

(2E,71)

Level I (Grades K-2)

- Knows that animals and plants sometimes cause changes in their surroundings BD (2E,72;TI,48)

- Knows that chunks of rocks come in all sizes, from boulders to grains of sand and even smaller BD (2E,72;NI,57-58)

Level II (Grades 3-5)

- Knows that smaller rocks come from the breakage and weathering of bedrock and larger rocks BD (2E,72;NI,57)

- Knows that rock is composed of different combinations of minerals BD (2E,72;CE,93;NI,57-58;TE,79)

- Knows that soil is made up of weathered rock and products of plants and animals, and also contains many living organisms BD (SI,V34;2E,72;NE,58)

- Knows that waves, wind, water, and ice constantly change the Earth's land surface by eroding rock and soil in some areas and depositing them in other areas, sometimes in seasonal layers BD (2E,72;NE,57;TI,81)

Codes (right side of page):   BD = Benchmark, Declarative; BP = Benchmark, Procedural; BC = Benchmark, Contextual
1st letter of each code in parentheses   *2nd letter of code*   *Number*
S = NCSESA: National Science Education Standards   E = Explicitly stated in document   Page number of cited document
2 = Project 2061: Benchmarks for Science Literacy   I = Implied in document   *or, for duplicates:*
C = CDE: Science Framework for Calif. Public Schools   Standard number & level of duplicate
N = NAEP: Science Assess./Exercise Specifications
O = NAEP: 1990 Science Objectives
T = NSTA: The Content Core
D = Duplicated in another standard   77   MREL

- Knows that the surface of the Earth changes; some changes are due to slow processes (e.g., erosion, weathering), and some changes are due to rapid processes (e.g., landslides, volcanoes, earthquakes)
  BD (SE,V34;2E,73;NI,57)

- Knows that fossils provide evidence about the plants and animals that lived long ago and the nature of the environment at that time
  BD (SE,V34;CE,95;NE,64)

Level III (Grades 6-8)

- Knows that the composition and texture of the soil and its fertility and resistance to erosion are greatly influenced by plant roots and debris, bacteria, fungi, worms, rodents, and other animals as they break up the soil and add organic material to it
  BD (SE,V89,V90;2E,73;NE,66;TE,85)

- Knows that rock contains evidence of the minerals, temperatures, and forces that created it
  BD (2E,73;NI,66;TI,81)

- Knows that sediments of sand and smaller particles (sometimes containing the remains of organisms) are gradually buried, cemented together by dissolved minerals, and eventually turned into rock again
  BD (SE,V89;2E,73;NE,66;TE,81)

- Knows how land forms are created through a combination of constructive and destructive forces; constructive forces include crustal deformation, volcanoes, and deposition of sediment; destructive forces include weathering and erosion
  BD (SE,V89,V90;2I,73;CE,91;NI,65-66;TI,86-87)

- Knows that thousands of layers of sedimentary rock confirm the long history of the Earth and the long history of changing life forms whose remains are found in successive layers of sedimentary rock; the newest layers may not always be found on top because of the folding, breaking, and uplifting of layers
  BD (2E,73,246;NE,66;TE,80)

- Knows that fossils provide important evidence of how life and environmental conditions have changed on the Earth over time (e.g., changes in atmospheric composition, movement of crustal plates, impact of an asteroid or comet)
  BD (SE,V90;CE,96;NE,77;TE,80)

Level IV (Grades 9-12)

- Knows that the Earth is a system containing a fixed amount of each stable chemical atom or element; each element moves among reservoirs in the solid Earth, oceans, atmosphere, and
  BD (SE,V150-151;2I,74;CI,97;NE,83)

Codes (right side of page):   BD = Benchmark, Declarative;   BP = Benchmark, Procedural;   BC = Benchmark, Contextual
1st letter of each code in parentheses   *2nd letter of code*   *Number*
S = NCSESA: National Science Education Standards   E = Explicitly stated in document   Page number of cited document
2 = Project 2061: Benchmarks for Science Literacy   I = Implied in document   *or, for duplicates:*
C = CDE: Science Framework for Calif. Public Schools   Standard number & level of duplicate
N = NAEP: Science Assess./Exercise Specifications
O = NAEP: 1990 Science Objectives
T = NSTA: The Content Core
D = Duplicated in another standard

78

MREL

living things, as part of geochemical cycles (e.g., carbon cycle, nitrogen cycle)

- BD (2E,74;NE,79;TE,94)
  Knows that the "rock cycle" consists of the formation, weathering, sedimentation, and reformation of rock; in this cycle, the total amount of material stays the same as its form changes

- BD (SE,V150;2E,74,248;NE,80;TE,86,93)
  Knows that the solid crust of the Earth, including both the continents and the ocean basins, consists of separate plates that ride on a denser, hot, gradually deformable layer of the Earth; the crust sections move very slowly, pressing against one another in some places and pulling apart in other places

- BD (SE,V150;2E,74;NI,80;TI,93)
  Knows that the slow movement of material within the Earth results from heat flowing out from the deep interior and from the action of gravitational forces on regions of different density

- BD (SI,V151;2E,74;NI,80;TI,86)
  Knows that earthquakes often occur along the boundaries between colliding plates

- BD (SI,V151;2E,74;NI,80;TI,86)
  Knows that molten rock from below the Earth's surface creates pressure that is released by volcanic eruptions; under the ocean basins, molten rock may well up between separating plates to create new ocean floor; and volcanic activity along the ocean floor may form undersea mountains, which may eventually become islands

- BD (SE,V151;CE,96;NE,89;TE,92-93)
  Knows that geologic time can be estimated by observing rock sequences and using fossils to correlate the sequences at various locations; recent methods use the predictability of decay rates of radioactive isotopes in rock formation to determine geologic time

- BD (SE,V151;2I,74;CE,109;NI,89)
  Knows that evidence for simple, one-celled forms of life such as bacteria and algae, extends back more than 3.5 billion years; the evolution of life resulted in dramatic changes in the composition of the Earth's atmosphere, which did not originally contain oxygen

(2E,61)

3.   Understands essential ideas about the composition and structure of the universe and the Earth's place in it

Level I (Grades K-2)

- BD (SI,V34;2E,62;CI,84)
  Knows that the stars are innumerable, unevenly dispersed, and of unequal brightness

Codes (right side of page):   BD = Benchmark, Declarative; BP = Benchmark, Procedural; BC = Benchmark, Contextual
1st letter of each code in parentheses   *2nd letter of code*   *Number*
S = NCSESA: National Science Education Standards   E = Explicitly stated in document   Page number of cited document
2 = Project 2061: Benchmarks for Science Literacy   I = Implied in document   *or, for duplicates:*
C = CDE: Science Framework for Calif. Public Schools   Standard number & level of duplicate
N = NAEP: Science Assess./Exercise Specifications
O = NAEP: 1990 Science Objectives
T = NSTA: The Content Core
D = Duplicated in another standard   79   MREL

- Knows that the Sun can be seen only in daytime, whereas the Moon is out sometimes at night and sometimes during the day ^BD (SE,V34;2E,62;CE,79;NI,62)

- Knows that the Moon looks a little different every day, but looks the same again about every four weeks ^BD (SI,V34;2E,62;CE,79)

Level II (Grades 3-5)

- Knows that the Earth is one of several planets that orbit the Sun, and the Moon orbits around the Earth ^BD (2E,63;NI,62)

- Knows that over time, planets change their position in the sky relative to the general pattern of stars ^BD (SI,V34;2E,63;CE,80;TE,84)

- Knows that the patterns of stars in the sky stay the same, although they appear to move across the sky nightly, and different stars can be seen in different seasons ^BD (SI,V34;2E,63;CI,80;TE,84)

- Understands that although telescopes magnify distant objects in the sky (such as the Moon and planets) and dramatically increase the number of stars we can see, some objects are so distant, small, or dim that they do not appear in a telescope ^BD (2E,63;CI,84;NE,62)

- Understands that astronomical objects in interstellar space are unimaginably distant from the Earth and each other; stars are like the Sun but are so distant they look like points of light; galaxies, though very large, are so distant they look like a single star ^BD (2E,63;TE,97)

Level III (Grades 6-8)

- Knows that the Sun is a medium-sized star, located at the edge of a disk-shaped galaxy, part of which can be seen on a clear night as a glowing band of light ^BD (2E,64;CI,81;NI,75)

- Knows that nine planets of differing sizes and surface features and with differing compositions move around the Sun in nearly circular orbits; some planets have a variety of moons and rings of particles orbiting around them (e.g., the Earth is orbited by one moon, many artificial satellites, and debris) ^BD (SE,V90;2E,64;CI,81;NE,73-74;TE,90-91)

- Knows that we live on a fairly small planet, the third from the Sun in the only system of ^BD (2E,68;NE,64;TI,95)

Codes (right side of page):   BD = Benchmark, Declarative;   BP = Benchmark, Procedural;   BC = Benchmark, Contextual
1st letter of each code in parentheses   *2nd letter of code*   *Number*
S = NCSESA: National Science Education Standards   E = Explicitly stated in document   Page number of cited document
2 = Project 2061: Benchmarks for Science Literacy   I = Implied in document   *or, for duplicates:*
C = CDE: Science Framework for Calif. Public Schools   Standard number & level of duplicate
N = NAEP: Science Assess./Exercise Specifications
O = NAEP: 1990 Science Objectives
T = NSTA: The Content Core
D = Duplicated in another standard   80   *MREL*

planets definitely known to exist, although other, similar systems might yet be discovered in the universe

BD (SE,V91;2E,95;CE,55;NI,76,78)

- Knows that the Sun's gravitational pull keeps the Earth and other planets in their orbits, just as the gravitational pull of planets keeps their moons in orbit around them

BD (2E,64;CE,81;TE,90)

- Knows that many pieces of rock and ice orbit our Sun; some meet the Earth in its orbit, glow, and disintegrate from friction as they plunge through our atmosphere; other objects have long, off-center orbits that bring them close to the Sun, whose radiation boils off material and pushes it into a long, illuminated tail

BD (SE,V90-V91;2E,69;NE,76;TE,84)

- Knows that the Moon's orbit around the Earth once in some 28 days changes how much of the Moon is lighted by the Sun and how much of that part can be seen from the Earth, resulting in the phases of the Moon

BD (2E,64;CI,81;NE,75)

- Knows that the universe contains many billions of galaxies, each containing many billions of stars

BD (2E,64;CI,86;NI,62)

- Knows that light travels from the Sun to the Earth in a few minutes, from the next nearest star in four years, and from very distant stars in several billion years; the distance light travels in a few years would take the fastest rocket thousands of years to travel

Level IV (Grades 9-12)

BD (SE,V151,V152;2E,65;CE,85;NE,87;TE,98)

- Knows that current theory states that about ten billion years ago, the entire contents of the universe expanded explosively into existence from a single, hot, dense chaotic mass; our solar system formed from a nebular cloud of dust and gas about 4.6 billion years ago

BD (SE,V152;2E,65;CE,85;NE,86-87;TE,96)

- Knows that at the beginning of the universe, stars formed out of clouds of the lightest elements and became hot as the material condensed and began releasing energy from the nuclear fusion of light elements into heavier ones in their extremely hot, dense cores; some stars eventually exploded, producing clouds of material from which other stars and planets would condense; this process of star formation and destruction continues

BD (SI,V152;2E,65;CE,82;TE,97)

- Understands that stars differ from each other in size, temperature, and age, but appear to be made up of the same elements and appear to behave according to the same principles; however, unlike our Sun, most stars are in systems of two or more stars orbiting around a

Codes (right side of page):   BD = Benchmark, Declarative;   BP = Benchmark, Procedural;   BC = Benchmark, Contextual
1st letter of each code in parentheses   *2nd letter of code*   *Number*
S = NCSESA: National Science Education Standards   E = Explicitly stated in document   Page number of cited document
2 = Project 2061: Benchmarks for Science Literacy   I = Implied in document   *or, for duplicates:*
C = CDE: Science Framework for Calif. Public Schools   Standard number & level of duplicate
N = NAEP: Science Assess./Exercise Specifications
O = NAEP: 1990 Science Objectives
T = NSTA: The Content Core
D = Duplicated in another standard   81   *McREL*

common point

- Knows that life is adapted to conditions on Earth, including the strength of gravity to hold an adequate atmosphere and an intensity of radiation from the Sun that allows water to cycle between liquid and vapor BD (2E,70;NI,81;TI,95;DE,1.4.4)

- Knows that the scientific account of the universe comes from studying evidence about its contents and imagining, with the help of mathematical models and computer simulations, how the contents got to be the way they are BD (2E,65;CE,89;NE,74)

4. Knows about the diversity and unity that characterize life

(2E,101)

Level I (Grades K-2)

- Knows that plants and animals have external features that help them thrive in different environments BD (2E,102,123;CE,118;NI,115)

Level II (Grades 3-5)

- Knows that living things can be sorted into groups in many ways using various properties to decide which things belong to which group; features used for grouping depend on the purpose of the grouping BD (2E,103;CI,119;NI,115)

- Knows that plants and animals have life cycles which include birth, growth and development, reproduction, and death; the details of this life cycle are different for different organisms BD (SE,V30;CE,128;NE,118;TE,48)

Level III (Grades 6-8)

- Knows that major categories of living organisms are plants, which get their energy directly from sunlight, and animals, which consume energy-rich foods; some kinds of organisms cannot be neatly classified as either plants or animals BD (2I,104;CE,122;NI,119;TI,53)

- Knows that all organisms, including the human species, are part of and depend on two main global food webs; one global food web starts with microscopic ocean plants and seaweed and includes the animals that feed on them and subsequent animals that feed on the plant- BD (SI,V85;2E,104;CI,139)

Codes (right side of page):   BD = Benchmark, Declarative; BP = Benchmark, Procedural; BC = Benchmark, Contextual
1st letter of each code in parentheses   *2nd letter of code*   *Number*
S = NCSESA: National Science Education Standards   E = Explicitly stated in document   Page number of cited document
2 = Project 2061: Benchmarks for Science Literacy   I = Implied in document   *or, for duplicates:*
C = CDE: Science Framework for Calif. Public Schools   Standard number & level of duplicate
N = NAEP: Science Assess./Exercise Specifications
O = NAEP: 1990 Science Objectives
T = NSTA: The Content Core
D = Duplicated in another standard   82   MREL

eating animals; the other global food web begins with land plants and includes the animals that feed on them and so forth

BD (2E,104;CI,137;NI,118,121,128;TI,47)

- Knows that organisms can be classified according to the function they serve in a food chain (producer, consumer and/or decomposer of organic matter) and by the details of their internal and external features

BD (SE,V83;2E,104;CE,118;NE,116;TE,47)

- Knows that animals and plants have a great variety of body plans and internal structures that contribute to their being able to make or find food and reproduce

BD (2E,104;CE,137)

- Knows that for sexually reproducing organisms, a species comprises all organisms that can mate with one another to produce fertile offspring

BD (SE,V86;CE,118;TI,48)

- Knows that although different species look very different, the unity among organisms becomes apparent from an analysis of internal structures, observation of the similarity of their chemical processes, and the evidence of common ancestry

Level IV (Grades 9-12)

BD (SE,V144;2E,105;CE,120)

- Knows that organisms are classified into a hierarchy of groups and subgroups based on their similarities and reflecting their evolutionary relationships; the similarity of organisms inferred from similarity in their molecular structure closely matches the classification based on anatomical similarities

BD (2E,105;CI,123;TI,53)

- Knows that the variation of organisms within a species increases the likelihood that at least some members of the species will survive under changed environmental conditions, and a great diversity of species increases the chance that at least some living things will survive in the face of large changes in the environment

(2E,106)

5. Understands the genetic basis for the transfer of biological characteristics from one generation to the next

Level I (Grades K-2)

BD (SE,V30;2E,107;CE,128;NI,116)

- Knows that plants and animals closely resemble their parents

---

Codes (right side of page):   BD = Benchmark, Declarative; BP = Benchmark, Procedural; BC = Benchmark, Contextual

1st letter of each code in parentheses	*2nd letter of code*	*Number*
S = NCSESA: National Science Education Standards	E = Explicitly stated in document	Page number of cited document
2 = Project 2061: Benchmarks for Science Literacy	I = Implied in document	*or, for duplicates:*
C = CDE: Science Framework for Calif. Public Schools		Standard number & level of duplicate
N = NAEP: Science Assess./Exercise Specifications		
O = NAEP: 1990 Science Objectives		
T = NSTA: The Content Core		
D = Duplicated in another standard		

McREL

- Knows that there is variation among individuals within a population $^{\text{BD (2E,107;CE,128;NE,115)}}$

Level II (Grades 3-5)

- Knows that many characteristics of an organism are inherited from the parents of the organism (e.g., eye color in human beings, fruit or flower color in plants), but other characteristics result from an individual's interactions with the environment (e.g., people's table manners, ability to play a musical instrument) $^{\text{BD (SE,V30;2E,107;CI,128)}}$

- Knows that for offspring to resemble their parents, there must be a reliable way to transfer information from one generation to the next $^{\text{BD (2E,107;CI,129)}}$

Level III (Grades 6-8)

- Knows that reproduction is a characteristic of all living systems; since no individual organism lives forever, reproduction is essential to the continuation of species $^{\text{BD (SE,V83;CE,118;TE,48)}}$

- Knows that in some kinds of organisms, all the genes come from a single parent, whereas in organisms that have sexes, typically half of the genes come from each parent $^{\text{BD (SE,V83;2E,108;CE,128;NI,124;TE,48,52)}}$

- Knows that in sexual reproduction, an egg from a female unites with a sperm from a male to begin the development of a new individual that has an equal contribution of information from its mother and its father; sexually produced offspring are never identical to either of their parents $^{\text{BD (SE,V83;2E,108;CI,128;NE,132;TI,48)}}$

- Knows that the characteristics of an organism can be described in terms of a combination of traits; some traits are inherited and others result from interactions with the environment $^{\text{BD (SE,V84;CE,128;NE,122)}}$

- Knows that hereditary information is contained in genes, located in the chromosomes of each cell; each gene carries a single unit of information, and an inherited trait of an individual can be determined by either one or many genes $^{\text{BD (SE,V84;2I,108;CE,129;NE,122)}}$

- Knows that selective breeding can cause small differences between parents and offspring to accumulate in successive generations so that descendants are very different from their ancestors; selective breeding for particular traits has resulted in new varieties of cultivated plants and domestic animals $^{\text{BD (2E,108,124;CI,128,131;NI,129-130;TI,52)}}$

Codes (right side of page):   BD = Benchmark, Declarative;   BP = Benchmark, Procedural;   BC = Benchmark, Contextual

1st letter of each code in parentheses   *2nd letter of code*   *Number*

S = NCSESA: National Science Education Standards   E = Explicitly stated in document   Page number of cited document

2 = Project 2061: Benchmarks for Science Literacy   I = Implied in document   *or, for duplicates:*

C = CDE: Science Framework for Calif. Public Schools   Standard number & level of duplicate

N = NAEP: Science Assess./Exercise Specifications

O = NAEP: 1990 Science Objectives

T = NSTA: The Content Core

D = Duplicated in another standard   84   *McREL*

Level IV (Grades 9-12)

- BD (SE,V142;2E,108;CI,129;TI,52)
Knows that in all organisms, the instructions for specifying the characteristics of the organism are carried in DNA; the chemical and structural properties of DNA explain how the genetic information that underlies heredity is both encoded in genes (as a string of molecular "letters") and replicated (by a templating mechanism)

- BD (SI,V143;2E,109;CE,129;NI,128-129;TI,55)
Knows that genes are segments of DNA molecules, and that inserting, deleting, or substituting portions of the DNA can alter genes; changes in DNA (mutations) can also occur when a cell is exposed to certain kinds of radiation or chemical substances

- BD (SI,V143;2E,108;NI,129)
Knows that the sorting and recombination of genes in sexual reproduction results in a great variety of possible gene combinations from the offspring of any two parents

- BD (SE,V143;TI,52)
Knows that most of the cells in a human contain two copies of each of 22 chromosomes; in addition, there is a pair of chromosomes that determines sex: a female contains two X chromosomes and a male contains one X and one Y chromosome

- BD (SE,V143;TI,52)
Knows that the fact that the human body is formed from cells containing two copies of each chromosome (and, therefore, two copies of each gene) explains many features of human heredity, such as how variations that are hidden in one generation can be expressed in the next

(2E,110)

6. Knows the general structure and functions of cells in organisms

Level I (Grades K-2)

- BD (SE,V29;2E,111;CE,116;NE,119;DE,8.1.1)
Knows that animals require air, water, and food; plants require air, water, and light

Level II (Grades 3-5)

- BD (SE,V29;CE,116;NI,116)
Knows that each plant or animal has different structures which serve different functions in growth, survival, and reproduction (e.g., humans have distinct structures of the body for walking, holding, seeing, and talking)

- BD (2E,111;CI,127;NI,124;TI,47)
Knows that microscopes make it possible to see that living things are made mostly of cells; some organisms are made of a collection of similar cells that benefit from cooperating,

---

Codes (right side of page):   BD = Benchmark, Declarative; BP = Benchmark, Procedural; BC = Benchmark, Contextual
1st letter of each code in parentheses   *2nd letter of code*   *Number*
S = NCSESA: National Science Education Standards   E = Explicitly stated in document   Page number of cited document
2 = Project 2061: Benchmarks for Science Literacy   I = Implied in document   *or, for duplicates:*
C = CDE: Science Framework for Calif. Public Schools   Standard number & level of duplicate
N = NAEP: Science Assess./Exercise Specifications
O = NAEP: 1990 Science Objectives
T = NSTA: The Content Core
D = Duplicated in another standard

McREL

whereas other organisms' cells vary greatly in appearance and perform very different roles in the organism

Level III (Grades 6-8)

- Knows that living systems at all levels of organization demonstrate complementarity of structure and function; the major levels of organization for structure and function include cells, tissues, organs, organ systems, whole organisms, and eco-systems
  BD (SE,V82;CE,120;TI,51)

- Knows that all organisms are composed of cells, which are the fundamental units of life; most organisms are single cells, but other organisms (including humans) are multicellular
  BD (SE,V82;2E,112;CE,116;NE,132;TE,47)

- Knows that cells carry on the many functions needed to sustain life and that cells are able to grow and divide; this requires that cells take in nutrients, which they use to power their work and to make the materials that a cell or an organism needs
  BD (SE,V83;2E,112;CI,119;NE,131-132)

- Knows that specialized cells perform specialized functions in multicellular organisms; each type of cell, tissue, and organ has a distinct structure and set of functions that serve the organism as a whole
  BD (SE,V83;2E,112;CI,120;TE,51)

- Knows that disease represents a breakdown in structures or functions of an organism; some diseases are the result of intrinsic failures of the system, whereas others are the result of infection by other organisms
  BD (SE,V83;NI,126)

Level IV (Grades 9-12)

- Knows that every cell is covered by a membrane that separates it from the outside world and controls what molecules can enter and leave the cell; in all but quite primitive cells, a complex network of proteins provides organization and shape and, for animal cells, movement
  BD (SE,V141;2E,113;CE,127;NI,131;TI,51)

- Knows that a concentrated mixture of thousands of different molecules within the cell form a variety of specialized structures that carry out such cell functions as energy production, transport of molecules, waste disposal, synthesis of new molecules, and the storage of genetic material
  BD (SE,V141;2E,113;CE,127;NI,131)

- Knows that initially most cells have the ability to become any kind of cell because they
  BD (SE,V142;CE,128;TI,56)

Codes (right side of page):	BD = Benchmark, Declarative; BP = Benchmark, Procedural; BC = Benchmark, Contextual	
1st letter of each code in parentheses	*2nd letter of code*	*Number*
S = NCSESA: National Science Education Standards	E = Explicitly stated in document	Page number of cited document
2 = Project 2061: Benchmarks for Science Literacy	I = Implied in document	*or, for duplicates:*
C = CDE: Science Framework for Calif. Public Schools		Standard number & level of duplicate
N = NAEP: Science Assess./Exercise Specifications		
O = NAEP: 1990 Science Objectives		
T = NSTA: The Content Core		
D = Duplicated in another standard		

86

McREL

contain the same genetic information; through the process of their growth and development, they differentiate and specialize in structure and function (e.g., to become blood or leaf cells), but they also retain the basic information that allows them to reproduce themselves

- BD (SE,V141,V145;CE,128;NE,131;TI,51)
  Knows that most cell functions involve chemical reactions; food molecules taken into cells are broken down to provide the chemical constituents needed to synthesize other molecules; both breakdown and synthesis are made possible by a large set of protein catalysts called enzymes

- BD (SE,V142;2I,114;CE,128;NI,131)
  Knows that cell functions are regulated; regulation of cells occurs both through changes in the activity of the functions performed by proteins and the selective expression of individual genes, allowing cells to respond to their environment and to control and coordinate the synthesis and breakdown of specific molecules, cell growth, and division

- BD (SE,V141,V145;2E,114;CE,129;NE,131;TE,55)
  Knows that cells store and use information to guide their functions; the genetic information stored in DNA is used to direct the synthesis of the thousands of proteins that each cell requires

- BD (2E,114;CE,129)
  Knows that proteins are long, usually folded chain molecules made from 20 different kinds of smaller amino acid molecules; the function of each molecule depends on the sequence of amino acids in it, and the chain's shape is a consequence of attractions between the chain's parts

- BD (SE,V146;CI,121;NI,133)
  Knows that multicellular animals have nervous systems to generate behavior; nervous systems are formed from specialized cells that conduct signals rapidly through the long cell extensions that make up nerves, and the nerve cells communicate with each other by secreting specific excitatory and inhibitory molecules

(2E,115)

7. Understands how species depend on one another and on the environment for survival

Level I (Grades K-2)

- BD (SE,V29;2E,116;CI,136)
  Knows that living things are found almost everywhere in the world; different types of plants and animals live in different places

---

Codes (right side of page):
1st letter of each code in parentheses
S = NCSESA: National Science Education Standards
2 = Project 2061: Benchmarks for Science Literacy
C = CDE: Science Framework for Calif. Public Schools
N = NAEP: Science Assess./Exercise Specifications
O = NAEP: 1990 Science Objectives
T = NSTA: The Content Core
D = Duplicated in another standard

BD = Benchmark, Declarative; BP = Benchmark, Procedural; BC = Benchmark, Contextual
2nd letter of code
E = Explicitly stated in document
I = Implied in document

Number
Page number of cited document
or, for duplicates:
Standard number & level of duplicate

MREL

Level II (Grades 3-5)

BD (SE,V29-V30;CE,119)
- Knows that the behavior of individual organisms is influenced by internal cues such as hunger and external cues such as environmental change; humans and other organisms have senses that help them detect internal and external cues

BD (SE,V30;2I,116;CE,137;TE,48)
- Knows that an organism's patterns of behavior are related to the nature of that organism's environment, including the kinds and numbers of other organisms present, the availability of food and resources, and the physical characteristics of the environment

BD (SE,V30;2E,116;CE,140)
- Knows that when an environment changes, some plants and animals survive and reproduce and others die or move to new locations

BD (SE,V30,V31;2I,116;CI,140)
- Knows that all organisms (including humans) cause changes in the environment where they live; some of these changes are detrimental to themselves or other organisms, and others are beneficial

Level III (Grades 6-8)

BD (SE,V84;CI,137;TE,48)
- Knows that all organisms must be able to obtain and use resources, grow, reproduce, and maintain a relatively stable internal environment while living in a constantly changing external environment; regulation of an organism's internal environment involves sensing external changes and changing physiological activities to keep within the range required to survive

BD (SE,V84;CI,119;NI,126;TI,48)
- Knows that behavior is one kind of response an organism may make to an internal or environmental stimulus, and may be determined by heredity or from past experience; a behavioral response requires coordination and communication at many levels including cells, organ systems, and whole organisms

BD (SE,V85;2E,117;CE,139;NI,122;TE,54)
- Knows that all species ultimately depend on one another; interactions between two types of organisms include producer/consumer, predator/prey, parasite/host, and relationships that can be mutually beneficial or competitive

BD (SE,V85;2I,117;CE,137;TE,49)
- Knows that populations consist of all individuals of a species that occur together at a given place; all of the populations living together (community) and the physical factors with which they interact compose an ecosystem

---

Codes (right side of page):   BD = Benchmark, Declarative; BP = Benchmark, Procedural; BC = Benchmark, Contextual

1st letter of each code in parentheses   *2nd letter of code*   *Number*

S = NCSESA: National Science Education Standards   E = Explicitly stated in document   Page number of cited document

2 = Project 2061: Benchmarks for Science Literacy   I = Implied in document   *or, for duplicates:*

C = CDE: Science Framework for Calif. Public Schools   Standard number & level of duplicate

N = NAEP: Science Assess./Exercise Specifications

O = NAEP: 1990 Science Objectives

T = NSTA: The Content Core

D = Duplicated in another standard

BD (SE,V85;2E,117;CE,137;TE,49-50)

- Knows that the number and types of organisms an ecosystem can support depend on the resources available and abiotic factors such as quantity of light and water, range of temperatures, and the soil composition; limitations of resources and other factors such as predation and climate limit the growth of populations in specific niches in the ecosystem

Level IV (Grades 9-12)

BD (SE,V144;2E,117;CE,139;NI,126)

- Knows that organisms both cooperate and compete in ecosystems; the interrelationships and interdependencies of these organisms may generate ecosystems that are stable for hundreds or thousands of years

BD (2E,117;CE,139)

- Knows that like many complex systems, ecosystems have cyclic fluctuations around a state of rough equilibrium

BD (SE,V145;2E,117)

- Knows that humans are increasingly modifying ecosystems as a result of population growth, technology, and consumption; human destruction of habitats through direct harvesting, pollution, atmospheric changes, and other factors is threatening global stability, and if not addressed, ecosystems will be irreversibly damaged

(2E,118)

8. Understands the cycling of matter and flow of energy through the living environment

Level I (Grades K-2)

BD (2E,119;CE,116;NE,119;DE,6.1.1)

- Knows that plants and animals both need water, animals need food to eat, and plants need light

BD (2E,119;CE,137)

- Knows that animals eat plants or other animals for food and may also use plants or other animals for shelter and nesting

Level II (Grades 3-5)

BD (2E,119;CE,116;NE,94)

- Knows that some source of "energy" is needed for organisms to live and grow

BD (SE,V30;2I,119;CE,139)

- Knows that all animals depend on plants; some animals eat plants for food while others eat animals that eat the plants

---

Codes (right side of page):   BD = Benchmark, Declarative; BP = Benchmark, Procedural; BC = Benchmark, Contextual
1st letter of each code in parentheses   *2nd letter of code*   *Number*
S = NCSESA: National Science Education Standards   E = Explicitly stated in document   Page number of cited document
2 = Project 2061: Benchmarks for Science Literacy   I = Implied in document   *or, for duplicates:*
C = CDE: Science Framework for Calif. Public Schools   Standard number & level of duplicate
N = NAEP: Science Assess./Exercise Specifications
O = NAEP: 1990 Science Objectives
T = NSTA: The Content Core
D = Duplicated in another standard

- Knows that over the whole Earth, organisms are growing, dying, and decaying, and new organisms are being produced by the old ones

  BD (2E,119;CI,139)

Level III (Grades 6-8)

- Knows that almost all food energy ultimately comes from the Sun as plants convert light into stored chemical energy; energy can change from one form to another in living things; and animals get energy from oxidizing their food, releasing some of its energy as heat

  BD (SE,V85;2E,120;CE,116-118;NE,131;TE,54,65)

- Knows how matter is transferred from one organism to another repeatedly and between organisms and their physical environment; as in all material systems, the total amount of matter remains constant, even though its form and location change

  BD (2E,120;CE,139;NE,135;TI,50)

Level IV (Grades 9-12)

- Knows that as matter and energy flow through different organization levels of living systems (e.g., cells, organs, organisms, communities), and between living systems and the physical environment, chemical elements are transformed and recombined in different ways; each transformation results in storage and dissipation of energy into the environment as heat, and matter and energy are conserved in each transformation

  BD (SE,V144,V146;NI,135;TI,54)

- Knows that because all matter tends toward more disorganized states, living systems require a continuous input of energy to maintain their chemical and physical organizations; the energy for life ultimately derives from the Sun and energy flows through ecosystems in one direction, from photosynthetic organisms to herbivores to carnivores and decomposers

  BD (SE,V144,V145;2E,121;CI,139)

- Knows that plant cells contain chloroplasts, the sites of photosynthesis, which provide the vital connection between the Sun and the energy needs of living systems; plants, and some other organisms, use solar energy to combine molecules of carbon dioxide and water into complex, energy-rich organic compounds

  BD (SE,V142,V145;CE,128;NE,131;TE,51)

- Knows that the complexity and organization of organisms accommodates the need for obtaining, transforming, transporting, releasing, and eliminating the matter and energy used to sustain the organism

  BD (SE,V146;CI,120;NI,133)

- Knows that the amount of life any environment can support is limited by the available

  BD (SE,V146;2E,121;CI,137;TI,54)

Codes (right side of page):   BD = Benchmark, Declarative; BP = Benchmark, Procedural; BC = Benchmark, Contextual
1st letter of each code in parentheses   *2nd letter of code*   *Number*
S = NCSESA: National Science Education Standards   E = Explicitly stated in document   Page number of cited document
2 = Project 2061: Benchmarks for Science Literacy   I = Implied in document   *or, for duplicates:*
C = CDE: Science Framework for Calif. Public Schools   Standard number & level of duplicate
N = NAEP: Science Assess./Exercise Specifications
O = NAEP: 1990 Science Objectives
T = NSTA: The Content Core
D = Duplicated in another standard

McREL

energy, water, oxygen, and materials, and by the ability of ecosystems to recycle the residue of dead organic materials

(2E,122)

9. Understands the basic concepts of the evolution of species

Level I (Grades K-2)

BD (2E,123;CE,121)

- Knows that some things that live today resemble once-living things that have completely disappeared

Level II (Grades 3-5)

BD (2E,123;CI,129)

- Knows that living things of the same kind vary among individuals, and sometimes the differences give individuals an important advantage in surviving and reproducing

BD (2E,123;CE,130;NI,66)

- Knows that fossils provide evidence that some organisms living long ago are now extinct, and fossils can be compared to one another and to living organisms to observe their similarities and differences

Level III (Grades 6-8)

BD (SE,V85-V86;2I,124;CE,135;NI,66)

- Knows how the fossil record, through geologic evidence, documents the appearance, diversification, and extinction of many life forms; millions of species of animals, plants, and micro-organisms living today differ from those that lived in the remote past, and each species lives in a specific and fairly uniform environment

BD (SE,V86)

- Knows that extinction of a species occurs when the environment changes and the adaptive characteristics of a species do not enable it to survive in competition with its neighbors; extinction of species is common—most of the species that have lived on the Earth no longer exist

BD (SE,V84,V86;2I,124;CE,132-133)

- Knows that biological evolution accounts for a diversity of species developed through gradual processes over many generations; species acquire many of their unique characteristics through biological adaptation (e.g., changes in structure, behavior, or physiology that enhance reproductive success), which involves the selection of naturally occurring variations in populations

Codes (right side of page):   BD = Benchmark, Declarative; BP = Benchmark, Procedural; BC = Benchmark, Contextual
1st letter of each code in parentheses   *2nd letter of code*   *Number*
S = NCSESA: National Science Education Standards   E = Explicitly stated in document   Page number of cited document
2 = Project 2061: Benchmarks for Science Literacy   I = Implied in document   *or, for duplicates:*
C = CDE: Science Framework for Calif. Public Schools   Standard number & level of duplicate
N = NAEP: Science Assess./Exercise Specifications
O = NAEP: 1990 Science Objectives
T = NSTA: The Content Core
D = Duplicated in another standard

91

MREL

Level IV (Grades 9-12)

- BD (SE,V143;2E,125;CI,129;NI,129-130)
  Knows that new heritable characteristics can only result from new combinations of existing genes or from mutations of genes in an organism's sex cells; other changes in an organism cannot be passed on

- BD (2E,125;CI,132;NI,129-130)
  Knows that heritable characteristics, which can be biochemical and anatomical, largely determine what capabilities an organism will have, how it will behave and, hence, how likely it is to survive and reproduce

- BD (SE,V143;2I,125;CE,134-135;NI,130;TI,56)
  Knows that the basic idea of evolution is that the Earth's present-day life forms have evolved from earlier, distinctly different species as a consequence of the interactions of (1) the potential for a species to increase its numbers, (2) the genetic variability of offspring due to mutation and recombination of genes, (3) a finite supply of the resources required for life, and (4) the ensuing selection by the environment of those offspring better able to survive and leave offspring

- BD (SI,V144;2E,125;CI,132;NI,77)
  Knows that life on Earth is thought to have begun about four billion years ago as simple, one-celled organisms; during the first two billion years, only microorganisms existed, but once cells with nuclei developed about a billion years ago, increasingly complex multicellular organisms evolved

- BD (SI,V147;2E,125;CE,135;NI,129;TE,56)
  Knows that natural selection leads to organisms that are well suited for survival in particular environments, so that when an environment changes, some inherited characteristics become more or less advantageous or neutral, and chance alone can result in characteristics having no survival or reproductive value

- BD (SE,V144;2E,125;CE,134;NI,130;TI,56-57)
  Knows that natural selection and its evolutionary consequences provide a scientific explanation for the fossil record of ancient life forms, as well as for the striking molecular similarities observed among the diverse species of living organisms; the millions of different species that live on the Earth today are related by descent from common ancestors

(2E,75)

10. Understands basic concepts about the structure and properties of matter

Level I (Grades K-2)

- BD (SE,V25;2E,76;CE,41;NE,91)
  Knows that objects can be described and classified by their composition (wood, metal) and

---

Codes (right side of page):   BD = Benchmark, Declarative; BP = Benchmark, Procedural; BC = Benchmark, Contextual
1st letter of each code in parentheses   *2nd letter of code*   *Number*
S = NCSESA: National Science Education Standards   E = Explicitly stated in document   Page number of cited document
2 = Project 2061: Benchmarks for Science Literacy   I = Implied in document   *or, for duplicates:*
C = CDE: Science Framework for Calif. Public Schools   Standard number & level of duplicate
N = NAEP: Science Assess./Exercise Specifications
O = NAEP: 1990 Science Objectives
T = NSTA: The Content Core
D = Duplicated in another standard   92

MREL

their physical properties (color, size, shape)

- Knows that things can be done to materials to change some of their properties, but not all materials respond the same way to what is done to them

  BD (2E,76;CI,42-43)

Level II (Grades 3-5)

- Knows that things have properties (e.g., magnetism, conductivity, density, solubility) that can be used to tell them apart and to find out which of them are alike

  BD (SE,V25-V26;CI,42;NE,93)

- Knows that materials may be composed of parts that are too small to be seen without magnification

  BD (2E,77;CE,42)

- Knows how an object's properties can be measured using tools such as rulers, balances, and thermometers

  BD (SE,V25;CI,43;NE,99)

- Knows that materials have different states (solid, liquid, gas), and some common materials such as water can be changed from one state to another by heating or cooling

  BD (SE,V26;2I,67,77;CE,42;NI,92-93)

- Knows that the mass of a material is conserved whether it is together, in parts, or in a different state

  BD (2E,77;CE,43;NE,92)

Level III (Grades 6-8)

- Knows that there are more than 100 known elements that combine in numerous ways to produce compounds, which account for the living and nonliving substances that we encounter; chemical elements do not break down by normal laboratory reactions such as heating, electric current, or reaction with acids

  BD (SE,V79;2E,78;CE,45;NE,98)

- Knows that many elements can be grouped according to similar properties, such as highly reactive metals, less-reactive metals, highly reactive nonmetals (chlorine, fluorine, oxygen), and some almost completely nonreactive gases (helium, neon); some elements, such as carbon and hydrogen, do not fit into any of the categories

  BD (SI,V79;2E,78-79;CI,48;TI,61)

- Knows methods used to separate mixtures into their component parts (boiling, filtering, chromatography, screening)

  BD (SE,V78;CE,43;NE,98;TE,61)

Codes (right side of page):	BD = Benchmark, Declarative; BP = Benchmark, Procedural; BC = Benchmark, Contextual	
1st letter of each code in parentheses	*2nd letter of code*	*Number*
S = NCSESA: National Science Education Standards	E = Explicitly stated in document	Page number of cited document
2 = Project 2061: Benchmarks for Science Literacy	I = Implied in document	*or, for duplicates:*
C = CDE: Science Framework for Calif. Public Schools		Standard number & level of duplicate
N = NAEP: Science Assess./Exercise Specifications		
O = NAEP: 1990 Science Objectives		
T = NSTA: The Content Core		
D = Duplicated in another standard		

93

McREL

BD (2E,78;CE,42,43;NE,98;TE,64)

- Knows that different arrangements of atoms into groups compose all substances; atoms are far too small to see directly through a microscope

BD (SI,V78,V79;2E,78;CE,43;NE,99;TE,66)

- Knows that atoms in solids are close together and don't move about easily; in liquids, atoms are close together and stick to each other, but move about easily; atoms in gas are quite far apart and move about freely

BD (2I,78;CE,43;TE,64,66)

- Knows that atoms often combine to form a molecule (or crystal), the smallest particle of a substance that retains its properties

BD (2E,79;CI,50;TE,61)

- Understands that no matter how substances within a closed system interact with one another, or how they combine or break apart, the total weight of the system remains the same; the same number of atoms weighs the same, no matter how the atoms are arranged

BD (2E,78;CI,47;NI,100;TE,62-63)

- Knows that the temperature and acidity of a solution influence reaction rates; many substances dissolve in water, which may greatly facilitate reactions between them

BD (2E,78-79;TE,63)

- Knows that oxidation involves the combining of oxygen with something else—as in burning or rusting

BD (SE,V79;2E,79;CI,43;NI,100)

- Knows that substances react chemically in characteristic ways with other substances to form new substances (compounds) with different characteristic properties; however, in chemical reactions the total mass is conserved

Level IV (Grades 9-12)

BD (SE,V133,V134;2E,80;CI,44;TE,70)

- Knows that an element is composed of a single type of atom; when elements are listed in order according to the number of protons (called the atomic number), repeating patterns of physical and chemical properties identify families of elements with similar properties (as seen in the periodic table)

BD (SE,V134;2I,80;CE,44;TE,71)

- Knows that atoms interact with one another by transferring or sharing electrons that are furthest from the nucleus; these outer electrons govern the chemical properties of the element

BD (SE,V134;2I,80;CE,45-46;TI,71)

- Knows that atoms may be bonded together into molecules or crystalline solids; when two or more kinds of atoms bind together chemically, a compound is formed

---

Codes (right side of page):   BD = Benchmark, Declarative; BP = Benchmark, Procedural; BC = Benchmark, Contextual
1st letter of each code in parentheses   *2nd letter of code*   *Number*
S = NCSESA: National Science Education Standards   E = Explicitly stated in document   Page number of cited document
2 = Project 2061: Benchmarks for Science Literacy   I = Implied in document   *or, for duplicates:*
C = CDE: Science Framework for Calif. Public Schools   Standard number & level of duplicate
N = NAEP: Science Assess./Exercise Specifications
O = NAEP: 1990 Science Objectives
T = NSTA: The Content Core
D = Duplicated in another standard

MREL

- Knows that the properties of a compound reflect the nature of the interactions among its molecules, which are determined by the structure of the molecule (the kinds of atoms and the distances and angles between them)
  BD (SE,V1?4-V135;2I,80;TE,71)

- Knows that atoms consist of negative electrons, which occupy most of the space in the atom, and very tiny nuclei consisting of neutrons and positive protons, each almost two thousand times heavier than an electron; the electric force between the nucleus and electrons holds the atom together
  BD (SE,V133;2E,80,253;CE,43;TI,70,119)

- Knows that the number of electrons usually will equal the number of protons, and the neutron has no electric charge, so the atom, overall, is electrically neutral; but an atom may acquire an unbalanced charge by gaining or losing electrons
  BD (2E,80;CE,45;TI,70)

- Knows that when an element has atoms that differ in the number of neutrons, these atoms are called different isotopes of the element; although neutrons have little effect on how an atom interacts with others, they do affect the mass and stability of the nucleus
  BD (SE,V133;2E,80;CE,46;TE,70)

- Knows that scientists continue to investigate atoms and have discovered even smaller constituents of which electrons, neutrons, and protons are made
  BD (2E,80;CE,44)

- Knows that radioactive isotopes are unstable and undergo spontaneous nuclear reactions, emitting particles and/or wavelike radiation; the decay of any one nucleus cannot be predicted, but a large group of identical nuclei decay at a predictable rate, and this predictability can be used to estimate the age of materials that contain radioactive isotopes
  BD (SE,V134;2E,80;CE,46;TE,119)

- Knows that chemical reactions can take place in time periods ranging from the few femtoseconds required for an atom to move a fraction of a chemical bond distance to geologic time scales; reaction rates depend on how often the reacting atoms and molecules encounter one another, the temperature, and the properties (including shape) of the reacting species
  BD (SE,V136;2E,80;CI,53;TE,69)

- Understands the complete mole concept and ways in which it can be used (e.g., actual mass vs. relative mass; relationship between the mole and the volume of a mole of molecules; relevance of molar volume and Avogadro's hypothesis)
  BD (CE,51;TE,73)

- Knows that catalysts, such as metal surfaces, accelerate chemical reactions; chemical reactions in living systems are often catalyzed by protein molecules called enzymes
  BD (SE,V136;CE,53;TI,74)

Codes (right side of page):   BD = Benchmark, Declarative;   BP = Benchmark, Procedural;   BC = Benchmark, Contextual

1st letter of each code in parentheses	*2nd letter of code*	*Number*
S = NCSESA: National Science Education Standards	E = Explicitly stated in document	Page number of cited document
2 = Project 2061: Benchmarks for Science Literacy	I = Implied in document	*or, for duplicates:*
C = CDE: Science Framework for Calif. Public Schools		Standard number & level of duplicate
N = NAEP: Science Assess./Exercise Specifications		
O = NAEP: 1990 Science Objectives		
T = NSTA: The Content Core		
D = Duplicated in another standard		

McREL

- Knows that carbon atoms can bond to one another in chains, rings, and branching networks to form a variety of structures, including synthetic polymers, oils, and the large molecules essential to life; complex chemical reactions involving carbon-based molecules take place constantly in every cell of our bodies
  BD (SE,V135;NI,110;TI,75)

- Knows that a large number of important reactions involve the transfer of either electrons (oxidation/reduction reactions) or hydrogen ions (acid/base reactions) between reacting ions, molecules or atoms; in other reactions, chemical bonds are broken by heat or light to form very reactive radicals with electrons ready to form new bonds
  BD (SE,V135;TE,73-74)

- Knows that radical reactions control many processes such as the ozone and green house gases in the atmosphere, burning and processing of fossil fuels, formation of polymers, and explosions
  BD (SE,V135;NI,110)

11. Understands energy types, sources, and conversions, and their relationship to heat and temperature
(2I,81)

Level I (Grades K-2)

- Knows that the Sun applies heat and light to Earth
  BD (2E,83;CI,61;NE,95)

- Knows that heat can be produced in many ways (e.g., burning, rubbing, mixing chemicals)
  BD (SE,V26;CE,64)

- Knows that electricity in circuits can produce light, heat, sound, and magnetic effects
  BD (SE,V26;CE,68;NI,95)

Level II (Grades 3-5)

- Knows that things that give off light often also give off heat
  BD (2E,84;CI,73)

- Knows that mechanical and electrical machines give off heat
  BD (2E,84;CI,61;NI,94-95)

- Knows that heat can move from one object to another by conduction
  BD (SE,V26;2E,84;CE,67;TE,65,107)

- Knows that some materials conduct heat better than others; materials that do not conduct heat well can reduce heat loss
  BD (2E,84;CE,65;NI,93)

Codes (right side of page):   BD = Benchmark, Declarative; BP = Benchmark, Procedural; BC = Benchmark, Contextual
1st letter of each code in parentheses   *2nd letter of code*   *Number*
S = NCSESA: National Science Education Standards   E = Explicitly stated in document   Page number of cited document
2 = Project 2061: Benchmarks for Science Literacy   I = Implied in document   *or, for duplicates:*
C = CDE: Science Framework for Calif. Public Schools   Standard number & level of duplicate
N = NAEP: Science Assess./Exercise Specifications
O = NAEP: 1990 Science Objectives
T = NSTA: The Content Core
D = Duplicated in another standard   96   MREL

• Knows that electrical circuits require a complete loop through which the electrical current can pass
BD (SE,V26;CE,68)

Level III (Grades 6-8)

• Knows that energy comes in different forms, such as light, heat, chemical, nuclear, mechanical, and electrical
BD (SE,V79;2E,85;CE,62;NE,100;TI,105)

• Understands that energy cannot be created or destroyed but only changed from one form to another
BD (SE,V79;2E,85;CE,61;NE,101;TI,65)

• Knows that the Sun is a major source of energy for changes on the Earth's surface; the Sun's energy arrives as light with a range of wavelengths consisting mainly of visible light with significant amounts of infrared and ultraviolet radiation
BD (SE,V80;CE,62;TE,65)

• Knows that heat energy moves in predictable ways, flowing from warmer objects to cooler ones until both objects are at the same temperature
BD (SE,V80;2E,84;CE,67;TE,107)

• Knows that heat can be transferred through materials by the collisions of atoms or across space by radiation; if the material is fluid, currents will be set up in it that aid the transfer of heat
BD (2E,85;CI,65)

• Knows that electrical circuits provide a means of converting electrical energy into heat, light, sound, chemical, or other forms of energy
BD (SE,V80;NE,101)

• Knows that in most chemical reactions energy is released or added to the system in the form of heat, light, electrical, or mechanical energy
BD (SE,V80;2I,85;CI,62;TE,64)

Level IV (Grades 9-12)

• Knows that although energy can be transferred by collisions or waves and converted from one form to another, it can never be created or destroyed, so the total energy of the universe is constant
BD (SE,V137;2E,86;CI,61-62;NE,110;TI,65)

• Knows that all energy can be considered to be either kinetic energy (energy of motion), potential energy (depends on relative position), or energy contained by a field
BD (SE,V137;CE,62;TI,114)

Codes (right side of page):   BD = Benchmark, Declarative; BP = Benchmark, Procedural; BC = Benchmark, Contextual

1st letter of each code in parentheses   *2nd letter of code*   *Number*

S = NCSESA: National Science Education Standards   E = Explicitly stated in document   Page number of cited document

2 = Project 2061: Benchmarks for Science Literacy   I = Implied in document   *or, for duplicates:*

C = CDE: Science Framework for Calif. Public Schools   Standard number & level of duplicate

N = NAEP: Science Assess./Exercise Specifications

O = NAEP: 1990 Science Objectives

T = NSTA: The Content Core

D = Duplicated in another standard   97   MREL

(electromagnetic waves)

- Knows that heat energy consists of random motion and the vibrations of atoms, molecules, and ions; the higher the temperature, the greater the atomic or molecular motion
  BD (SE,V137;2E,86;CE,64;TE,121)

- Knows that energy tends to move spontaneously from hotter to cooler objects by conduction, convection, or radiation; similarly, any ordered state tends to spontaneously become less ordered over time
  BD (SE,V137;2E,86;CE,66;NE,110;TI,114)

- Knows that the energy of waves (electromagnetic and material) can be changed into other forms of energy (e.g., chemical and electrical), just as other forms of energy (chemical and nuclear) can be transformed into wave energy
  BD (2E,92;CE,47;NI,109-11)

- Knows that some changes of atomic or molecular configuration require an input of energy, whereas others release energy
  BD (SE,V135;2E,86;CE,47;TI,119,121)

- Knows that each kind of atom or molecule can gain or lose energy only in particular discrete amounts and thus can absorb and emit light only at wavelengths corresponding to these amounts; these wavelengths can be used to identify the substance
  BD (SE,V138;2E,86;CI,75;TE,124)

- Knows that fission is the splitting of a large nucleus into smaller pieces, and fusion is the joining of two nuclei at extremely high temperature and pressure; nuclear reactions convert a fraction of the mass of interacting particles into energy
  BD (SE,V133,V134;2E,86;TE,121)

12.   Understands motion and the principles that explain it
(2E,87)

Level I (Grades K-2)

- Knows that vibrating objects produce sound
  BD (SE,V26;2E,89;CE,75)

- Knows that light travels in a straight line unless it strikes an object
  BD (SE,V26;CI,73;NI,97)

- Knows that the position of an object can be described by locating it relative to another object or the background
  BD (SE,V26;CE,53;NE,96)

- Knows that the varieties of motion include straight line, zigzag, vibrational, or circular
  BD (2E,89;CE,53;NI,97)

Codes (right side of page):   BD = Benchmark, Declarative; BP = Benchmark, Procedural; BC = Benchmark, Contextual
1st letter of each code in parentheses   *2nd letter of code*   *Number*
S = NCSESA: National Science Education Standards   E = Explicitly stated in document   Page number of cited document
2 = Project 2061: Benchmarks for Science Literacy   I = Implied in document   *or, for duplicates:*
C = CDE: Science Framework for Calif. Public Schools   Standard number & level of duplicate
N = NAEP: Science Assess./Exercise Specifications
O = NAEP: 1990 Science Objectives
T = NSTA: The Content Core
D = Duplicated in another standard   98   *MREL*

- Knows that an object's motion can be changed by a push or a pull by people or by other objects

  BD (SE,V26;2E,89;CE,55)

Level II (Grades 3-5)

- Knows that properties of sound such as pitch and loudness can be altered by changing the properties of the sound's source (e.g., by changing the rate of vibration)

  BD (SE,V26;NI,104;TI,110)

- Knows that light can be reflected by a mirror, refracted by a lens, or absorbed by the object

  BD (SE,V26;CE,73-74;NI,97)

- Knows that an object's motion can be described by indicating the change in its position over time

  BD (SE,V26;CE,54;NE,96)

- Knows that when a force is applied to an object, the object either speeds up, slows down, or goes in a different direction

  BD (2E,89;CE,56;NE,96)

- Knows that the greater the force that is applied to an object, the greater the change in motion the object will have; the more massive the object is, the smaller the effect a given force will have

  BD (2E,89;CE,56;NI,104)

Level III (Grades 6-8)

- Knows that vibrations (e.g., sounds, earthquakes) move at different speeds in materials, have different wavelengths, and set up wave-like disturbances that spread away from the source

  BD (2E,90;CE,76;NE,97,104;TI,109)

- Knows that light interacts with matter by transmission (including refraction), absorption, or scattering (including reflection); to see an object, light from that object (emitted by or scattered from it) must enter the eye

  BD (SE,V80;2E,90;CE,74;NE,105;TI,116-117)

- Knows that only a narrow range of wavelengths of electromagnetic radiation can be seen by the human eye; differences of wavelength within that range of visible light are perceived as differences in color

  BD (2E,90;CI,73;NI,97)

- Knows that an object's motion can be described and represented graphically according to its position, direction of motion, and speed

  BD (SE,V79;NI,103;TI,104)

- Knows that the motion of an object is always judged with respect to some other object or

  BD (2E,240;CI,54)

Codes (right side of page):   BD = Benchmark, Declarative; BP = Benchmark, Procedural; BC = Benchmark, Contextual

1st letter of each code in parentheses   *2nd letter of code*   *Number*

S = NCSESA: National Science Education Standards   E = Explicitly stated in document   Page number of cited document

2 = Project 2061: Benchmarks for Science Literacy   I = Implied in document   *or, for duplicates:*

C = CDE: Science Framework for Calif. Public Schools   Standard number & level of duplicate

N = NAEP: Science Assess./Exercise Specifications

O = NAEP: 1990 Science Objectives

T = NSTA: The Content Core

D = Duplicated in another standard   99   *McREL*

point, and so the idea of absolute motion or rest is misleading

BD (2E,90;CE,57;NE,103-104;TE,104-105)

- Knows that whenever an object is seen to speed up, slow down, or change direction, we know that an unbalanced force (e.g., friction) acts on it

BD (SE,V79;CE,57;NE,103-104;TI,105)

- Knows that if more than one force acts on an object, the forces can reinforce or cancel one another depending on their direction and magnitude; unbalanced forces will cause changes in the speed and/or direction of an object's motion

BD (SE,V79;2E,90;CE,57;TE,104-105)

- Knows that an object that is not being subjected to a force will continue to move at a constant speed and in a straight line

Level IV (Grades 9-12)

BD (SE,V138;CE,55;NI,113)

- Knows that waves (e.g., sound, seismic, light, water) carry energy and can interact with matter

BD (SE,V138;2E,92;CE,62;NI,113;TI,121,124)

- Knows that electromagnetic waves include radio waves (the longest wavelength), microwaves, infrared radiation (radiant heat), visible light, ultraviolet radiation, x-rays, and gamma rays; electromagnetic waves result when a charged object is accelerated or decelerated; and each wavelength of light delivers energy in packets whose sizes are inversely proportional to the wavelength

BD (2E,92;CE,78;NE,112;TE,124)

- Knows that apparent changes in wavelength can provide information about changes in motion because the observed wavelength of a wave depends upon the relative motion of the source and the observer; if either the source or observer is moving toward the other, the observed wavelength is shorter; if either is moving away, the wavelength is longer

BD (2E,245;CE,74)

- Knows that the theory of special relativity suggests that in contrast to other moving things, the speed of light is the same for all observers, no matter how they or the light source happen to be moving, and that nothing can travel faster than the speed of light

BD (2E,92;TE,97-98,124)

- Knows that because the light we see from distant galaxies has longer wavelengths than the same light here on Earth, astronomers believe that the whole universe is expanding

BD (SE,V136;2E,92;CE,56;NI,112;TI,120)

- Knows that objects change their motion only when a net force is applied; whenever one object exerts force on another, an equal amount of force is exerted back on the first object

---

Codes (right side of page):   BD = Benchmark, Declarative; BP = Benchmark, Procedural; BC = Benchmark, Contextual
1st letter of each code in parentheses   *2nd letter of code*   *Number*
S = NCSESA: National Science Education Standards   E = Explicitly stated in document   Page number of cited document
2 = Project 2061: Benchmarks for Science Literacy   I = Implied in document   *or, for duplicates:*
C = CDE: Science Framework for Calif. Public Schools   Standard number & level of duplicate
N = NAEP: Science Assess./Exercise Specifications
O = NAEP: 1990 Science Objectives
T = NSTA: The Content Core   100
D = Duplicated in another standard

McREL

BD (SE,V136;2I,91;CE,59;NI,111;TE,112)

- Knows that laws of motion are used to calculate precisely the effects of forces on the motion of objects; the magnitude of the change in motion can be calculated using the relationship $F=ma$

(2E,93)

13. Knows the kinds of forces that exist between objects and within atoms

Level I (Grades K-2)

BD (2E,94;CE,68)

- Knows that magnets can be used to make some things move without being touched

BD (2E,94;CE,55;TE,96)

- Knows that things near the Earth fall to the ground unless something holds them up

Level II (Grades 3-5)

BD (2E,94;CE,68;TE,107)

- Knows that electrically charged material pulls on all other materials and can attract or repel other charged materials

BD (SE,V26;2E,94;CE,68;NI,93)

- Knows that magnets attract and repel each other and certain kinds of metals

BD (2E,94;CE,55;NI,76;TE,96)

- Knows that the Earth's gravity pulls any object toward it without touching it

Level III (Grades 6-8)

BD BD (2I,95;CE,69;NE,100;TE,108,123)

- Knows that just as electric currents can produce magnetic forces, magnets can cause electric currents

BD (2E,95;CE,55)

- Knows that every object exerts gravitational force on every other object; this force depends on the mass of the objects and their distance from one another; gravitational force is hard to detect unless at least one of the objects (e.g., the Earth) has a lot of mass

Level IV (Grades 9-12)

BD (SE,V138;2E,97;CE,48;TE,68,107)

- Knows that different kinds of materials respond differently to electric forces; in some materials, such as metals, electrons flow easily, whereas in insulating materials, such as glass, they hardly flow at all; semiconducting materials have intermediate behavior, and at

---

Codes (right side of page):   BD = Benchmark, Declarative; BP = Benchmark, Procedural; BC = Benchmark, Contextual
1st letter of each code in parentheses   *2nd letter of code*   *Number*
S = NCSESA: National Science Education Standards   E = Explicitly stated in document   Page number of cited document
2 = Project 2061: Benchmarks for Science Literacy   I = Implied in document   *or, for duplicates:*
C = CDE: Science Framework for Calif. Public Schools   Standard number & level of duplicate
N = NAEP: Science Assess./Exercise Specifications
O = NAEP: 1990 Science Objectives
T = NSTA: The Content Core
D = Duplicated in another standard   101   MCREL

low temperatures some materials become superconductors and offer no resistance to the flow of electrons

- Knows that materials contain almost exactly equal proportions of positive and negative charges, making the materials as a whole electrically neutral; a very small excess or deficit of negative charges in a material produces noticeable electric forces

  BD (2E,96;CE,69;TI,107)

- Knows that magnetic forces are very closely related to electric forces and can be thought of as different aspects of a single electromagnetic force; moving electric charges produce magnetic forces and moving magnets produce electric forces; the interplay of these forces is the basis for electric motors, generators, radio, television, and many other modern technologies

  BD (SE,V137;2E,97;CE,70;NI,109;TE,115,121)

- Knows that at the atomic level, electric forces between oppositely charged electrons and protons hold atoms and molecules together and thus are involved in all chemical reactions; on a larger scale, electric forces hold solid and liquid materials together and act between objects when they are in contact

  BD (2E,96;CE,45,48;TI,75,120)

- Knows that electromagnetic forces acting within and between atoms are vastly stronger than the gravitational forces acting between them, and the forces that hold the nucleus of atoms together are much stronger than the electromagnetic force; this explains why great amounts of energy are released from the nuclear reactions in atomic or hydrogen bombs, and in the Sun and other stars

  BD (SE,V133,V137;2E,96,97;CI,52;TI,119)

- Knows that gravity is a universal force that each mass exerts on any other mass; the strength of the gravitational attractive force between two masses is proportional to the masses and inversely proportional to the square of the distance between them

  BD (SE,V136;2E,96;CE,58)

- Knows that the electric force is a universal force that exists between any two charged objects—opposite charges attract whereas like charges repel; as with gravitation, the strength of the force is proportional to the charges and inversely proportional to the square of the distance between them

  BD (SE,V136;CI,58;TI,123)

Codes (right side of page):   BD = Benchmark, Declarative; BP = Benchmark, Procedural; BC = Benchmark, Contextual
1st letter of each code in parentheses   *2nd letter of code*   *Number*
S = NCSESA: National Science Education Standards   E = Explicitly stated in document   Page number of cited document
2 = Project 2061: Benchmarks for Science Literacy   I = Implied in document   *or, for duplicates:*
C = CDE: Science Framework for Calif. Public Schools   Standard number & level of duplicate
N = NAEP: Science Assess./Exercise Specifications
O = NAEP: 1990 Science Objectives
T = NSTA: The Content Core
D = Duplicated in another standard

McREL

(2E,5)

14.   Understands the nature of scientific knowledge

Level I (Grades K-2)

BD (2E,6;OE,26)
● Knows that science experiments normally have reproducible results; that is, science experiments generally work the same way in different places

Level II (Grades 3-5)

BD (2E,6;OE,26)
● Knows that the same scientific investigation often gives slightly different results when it is carried out by different persons, or at different times or places; however, if the results of repeated experiments are very different, something must be wrong with the design of the investigation

Level III (Grades 6-8)

BD (2E,7;OE,26)
● Knows that scientists often repeat an experiment many times before accepting a consistent result as true

BD (SE,V104;2I,7)
● Knows that scientists formulate and test their explanations of nature using observation, experiments, and theoretical and mathematical models; although all scientific ideas are tentative and subject to change or improvement in principle, for most core ideas in the sciences there is much experimental and observational confirmation

BD (SE,V104;2I,7)
● Knows that in areas where active research is being pursued and in which there is not a great deal of experimental or observational evidence and understanding, it is normal for scientists to differ with one another about the evidence or theory being considered; until evidence is available that supports one position over another, scientists acknowledge that a conflict exists

BD (SE,V104;2I,7;OI,23-24)
● Knows that scientists evaluate the results of scientific investigations and the explanations proposed by other scientists by reviewing experimental procedures, examining evidence, identifying faulty reasoning, pointing out statements that go beyond the evidence, and suggesting alternative explanations for the same observations

BD (SE,V104;2I,7;OI,23-24)
● Knows that although scientists may disagree about certain aspects of an investigation or explanation, they do agree that skepticism, questioning, and open communication are

---

Codes (right side of page):   BD = Benchmark, Declarative; BP = Benchmark, Procedural; BC = Benchmark, Contextual
1st letter of each code in parentheses   *2nd letter of code*   *Number*
S = NCSESA: National Science Education Standards   E = Explicitly stated in document   Page number of cited document
2 = Project 2061: Benchmarks for Science Literacy   I = Implied in document   *or, for duplicates:*
C = CDE: Science Framework for Calif. Public Schools   Standard number & level of duplicate
N = NAEP: Science Assess./Exercise Specifications
O = NAEP: 1990 Science Objectives
T = NSTA: The Content Core
D = Duplicated in another standard   103   *McREL*

essential to progress in science

Level IV (Grades 9-12)

- BD (SE,V166)
  Knows that science distinguishes itself from other ways of knowing and from other bodies of knowledge through the use of empirical standards, logical arguments, and skepticism, as scientists strive for certainty of their proposed explanations

- BD (SE,V167;OI,24,26)
  Knows that scientific explanations must meet certain criteria; they must be consistent with experimental and observational evidence about nature; and they must include a logical structure, rules of evidence, openness to criticism, reporting methods and procedures, and a commitment to making knowledge public

- BD (SE,V167;OI,26)
  Knows that because all scientific ideas depend on experimental and observational confirmation, all scientific knowledge is, in principle, subject to change as new evidence becomes available; in areas where data, information, or understanding is incomplete, it is normal for scientific ideas to be incomplete, but this is also where the opportunity for making advances may be greatest

- BD (SE,V168;2E,8;OI,26)
  Knows that from time to time, major shifts occur in the scientific view of how the world works, but usually the changes that take place in the body of scientific knowledge are small modifications of prior knowledge; change and continuity are persistent features of science

- BD (SI,V168;2E,8;OI,26)
  Knows that in science, the testing, revising, and occasional discarding of theories, new and old, never ends; this ongoing process leads to an increasingly better understanding of how things work in the world, but not to absolute truth

(2E,9)

15. Understands the nature of scientific inquiry

Level I (Grades K-2)

- BD (2E,10;OE,26)
  Knows that learning can come from careful observations and simple experiments

- BD (SE,V22;2E,10;OI,20,21)
  Knows that tools like thermometers, magnifiers, rulers, and balances add to information from our senses

---

Codes (right side of page):   BD = Benchmark, Declarative; BP = Benchmark, Procedural; BC = Benchmark, Contextual
1st letter of each code in parentheses   *2nd letter of code*   *Number*
S = NCSESA: National Science Education Standards   E = Explicitly stated in document   Page number of cited document
2 = Project 2061: Benchmarks for Science Literacy   I = Implied in document   *or, for duplicates:*
C = CDE: Science Framework for Calif. Public Schools   Standard number & level of duplicate
N = NAEP: Science Assess./Exercise Specifications
O = NAEP: 1990 Science Objectives
T = NSTA: The Content Core
D = Duplicated in another standard   104   MREL

(2I,48)

17. Understands the nature of technological design

Level I (Grades K-2)

BD (SE,V38;2E,49)

- Knows that some objects occur in nature, whereas others have been designed and made by people to solve human problems

Level II (Grades 3-5)

BC (SE,V38)

- Categorizes items into groups of natural objects and designed objects

BD (SE,V38;2E,49,50)

- Knows that designing a solution to a simple problem may have constraints, such as cost, materials, time, space, and safety

BP (SE,V38)

- Implements proposed solutions using suitable tools, techniques, and quantitative measurements where appropriate

BP (SE,V38-V39)

- Evaluates a product or design based on constraints

Level III (Grades 6-8)

BP (SE,V93;2I,51)

- Identifies appropriate problems for technological design (e.g., identifies a specific need, considers its various aspects, considers criteria for a suitable product)

BD (SE,V93)

- Knows that for some technological needs, the cultural backgrounds and beliefs of different groups can affect the criteria for a suitable product

BP (SE,V93-V94;2I,51)

- Designs a solution or product, taking into account needs and constraints (e.g., cost, time, trade-offs, materials needed)

BP (SE,V94)

- Implements a proposed design (e.g., organizes materials and other resources, plans one's work, makes use of group collaboration, chooses suitable tools and techniques, works with appropriate measurement methods)

BD (SE,V94;2I,51)

- Knows that a technological design should meet criteria established in the original purpose (e.g., developed measures of quality)

Codes (right side of page):   BD = Benchmark, Declarative; BP = Benchmark, Procedural; BC = Benchmark, Contextual
1st letter of each code in parentheses   *2nd letter of code*   *Number*
S = NCSESA: National Science Education Standards   E = Explicitly stated in document   Page number of cited document
2 = Project 2061: Benchmarks for Science Literacy   I = Implied in document   *or, for duplicates:*
C = CDE: Science Framework for Calif. Public Schools   Standard number & level of duplicate
N = NAEP: Science Assess./Exercise Specifications
O = NAEP: 1990 Science Objectives
T = NSTA: The Content Core
D = Duplicated in another standard

McREL

Level IV (Grades 9-12)

- Proposes designs and chooses between alternatives (e.g., models, simulations) BP (SE,V156)

- Implements a proposed solution (e.g., construction of artifacts for intended users or beneficiaries) BP (SE,V156)

- Knows that a solution and its consequences must be tested against the needs or criteria the solution was designed to meet BD (SE,V156;2E,52)

18. Understands the interactions of science, technology, and society (2E,43,53)

Level I (Grades K-2)

- No materials specifically designated for this grade level BD (SE,V39)

Level II (Grades 3-5)

- Knows that scientists and engineers often work in teams with different individuals doing different things that contribute to the results BD (SE,V39;2I,54)

- Knows that tools help scientists make better observations, measurements, and equipment for investigations BD (SE,V39;2E,45)

- Knows that people have always had questions about their world; science is one way of answering questions and explaining the natural world BD (SE,V39)

- Knows that people have always had problems and invented tools and techniques (ways of doing something) to solve problems; trying to determine the effects of various solutions helps people avoid some new problems BD (SE,V39;2E,45,54)

- Knows that people continue inventing new ways of doing things, solving problems, and getting work done; these new ideas and inventions often affect other people—sometimes the effects are good, and sometimes they are bad BD (SE,V44;2I,55)

- Knows that science and technology have improved transportation, health, sanitation, and communication; however, the benefits of science and technology are not available to all BD (SE,V44;2E,54)

Codes (right side of page):   BD = Benchmark, Declarative; BP = Benchmark, Procedural; BC = Benchmark, Contextual
1st letter of each code in parentheses   *2nd letter of code*   *Number*
S = NCSESA: National Science Education Standards   E = Explicitly stated in document   Page number of cited document
2 = Project 2061: Benchmarks for Science Literacy   I = Implied in document   *or, for duplicates:*
C = CDE: Science Framework for Calif. Public Schools   Standard number & level of duplicate
N = NAEP: Science Assess./Exercise Specifications
O = NAEP: 1990 Science Objectives
T = NSTA: The Content Core
D = Duplicated in another standard   110   MCREL

people

Level III (Grades 6-8)

- BD (SE,V94)
Knows that scientific inquiry and technological design have similarities and differences (e.g., scientists propose explanations for questions about the natural world and engineers propose solutions relating to human problems, needs, and aspirations; technological solutions are temporary; technologies exist within nature, and they cannot contravene biological or physical principles; technological solutions have side effects)

- BD (SE,V101,V105;2E,17;DI,16.3.1)
Knows that science and technology have advanced through the contributions of many different people, in different cultures, and at different times in history; science and technology have contributed to the economic growth and productivity of societies and this, in turn, results in social changes with different effects on societies and groups within societies

- BD (SE,V94-95;2I,17)
Knows that a person's gender, race, or national origin should not influence the acceptance or rejection of his or her proposed contributions to science or technology

- BD (SE,V95;2I,46)
Knows that science helps drive technology, providing knowledge for better understanding, instruments, and techniques

- BD (SE,V75,V95;2E,46)
Knows that technology is essential to science because it enables observations of phenomena that are far beyond the capabilities of scientists due to factors such as distance, location, size, and speed

- BD (SE,V95;2I,51)
Knows that technological solutions have trade-offs, such as safety, cost, efficiency, and appearance; engineers often build in back-up systems to provide safety, but risk is part of living in a highly technological world

- BD (SE,V95;2E,51)
Knows that technological designs have constraints; some constraints are unavoidable (e.g., properties of materials, gravity, effects of weather and friction), and other constraints limit choices in the design (e.g., environmental protection, human safety, aesthetics)

- BD (SE,V95;2E,51)
Knows that technological solutions have intended benefits and unintended consequences; some consequences can be predicted, but others cannot

---

Codes (right side of page):   BD = Benchmark, Declarative; BP = Benchmark, Procedural; BC = Benchmark, Contextual

1st letter of each code in parentheses	*2nd letter of code*	*Number*
S = NCSESA: National Science Education Standards	E = Explicitly stated in document	Page number of cited document
2 = Project 2061: Benchmarks for Science Literacy	I = Implied in document	*or, for duplicates:*
C = CDE: Science Framework for Calif. Public Schools		Standard number & level of duplicate
N = NAEP: Science Assess./Exercise Specifications		
O = NAEP: 1990 Science Objectives		
T = NSTA: The Content Core		
D = Duplicated in another standard		

McREL

BD (SE,V100-101;2I,56)

- Knows that scientific knowledge and the procedures used by scientists influence the way many individuals in society think about themselves, others, and the natural environment; societal challenges often inspire questions for scientific research and social priorities often influence research priorities through funding

BD (SE,V101;2I,46,56)

- Knows that technology influences society through its products and processes, and technological changes are often accompanied by social, political, and economic changes that may be beneficial or detrimental to individuals and to society; social needs, attitudes, and values influence the direction of technological development

BD (SE,V101;2E,55)

- Knows that science cannot answer all questions and technology cannot solve all human problems and meet all human needs

Level IV (Grades 9-12)

BD (SE,V129,V157;2E,47)

- Knows that science often advances with the introduction of new technologies and solving technological problems often results in new scientific knowledge; new technologies often extend the current levels of scientific understanding and introduce new arenas of research

BD (SE,V157;2E,47)

- Knows that science and technology are pursued for different purposes; scientific inquiry is driven by the desire to understand the natural world and seeks to answer questions that may or may not directly influence humans; technological design is driven by the need to meet human needs and solve human problems and has a more direct effect on society than science because its purpose is to solve human problems, help humans adapt, and fulfill human aspirations

BD (SE,V164;2I,52)

- Knows that individuals and society must decide on proposals involving new research and technologies; decisions involve assessment of alternatives, risks, costs, and benefits, and consideration of who benefits, who suffers, who pays, who gains, what are the risks, and who bears them

BD (SE,V157-V158;2E,57)

- Knows that technological knowledge is often not made public because of patents and the financial potential of the idea or inventions; scientific knowledge is made public through presentations at professional meetings and publication in scientific journals

---

Codes (right side of page):	BD = Benchmark, Declarative; BP = Benchmark, Procedural; BC = Benchmark, Contextual
1st letter of each code in parentheses	*2nd letter of code* *Number*

Codes (right side of page):
1st letter of each code in parentheses
S = NCSESA: National Science Education Standards
2 = Project 2061: Benchmarks for Science Literacy
C = CDE: Science Framework for Calif. Public Schools
N = NAEP: Science Assess./Exercise Specifications
O = NAEP: 1990 Science Objectives
T = NSTA: The Content Core
D = Duplicated in another standard

BD = Benchmark, Declarative; BP = Benchmark, Procedural; BC = Benchmark, Contextual
2nd letter of code
E = Explicitly stated in document
I = Implied in document

Number
Page number of cited document
or, for duplicates:
Standard number & level of duplicate

McREL

9. History

The following process was used to identify standards in the field of history:

Identification of National Reports

Six reports were identified as important documents representing current thinking on history in the schools. Three reports originate from the National Center for History in the Schools (NCHS) History Standards Project: *National Standards for World History*, *National Standards for U.S. History* and *National Standards for History for Grades K–4* (1994). In addition, NCHS published *Lessons From History: Essential Understandings and Historical Perspectives Students Should Acquire* (1992). Two other significant documents are the *Provisional Item Specifications for the 1994 NAEP in U.S. History* (NAEP, undated) and *Building a History Curriculum: Guidelines for Teaching History in the Schools* (Bradley Commission on History in the Schools, 1988).

Selection of the Reference Document

The NCHS national standards documents were selected as reference documents for World, United States, and K–4 history. The national standards documents were selected because they represent the efforts of a broad group of historians from schools and universities. In addition, they are the only documents available that provide a consistent level of detailed information for both world and U.S. history. The history standards documents also give direction for writing benchmarks at grade level (K–4 history provided information for grades K–2 and K–4; United States and world history covered grades 5–6, 7–8, and 9–12). Such leveling is not within the scope of a work like *Lessons from History*, which deals primarily with what students should know by the end of their schooling.

The standards documents were also used as the reference for standards in Historical Understanding, discussed below. These documents, in turn, show indebtedness to Bradley's *Building a History Curriculum*, which provides supporting material for the "Historical Perspective" standard in this work.

Identification of Standards and Benchmarks

In addition to the content material in history, the national standards documents include standards in Historical Thinking that cover five areas: (1) chronological thinking, (2) historical comprehension, (3) historical analysis and interpretation, (4) historical research capabilities and (5) historical issues-analyses and decision-making. These standards consist of from 4 to 10 statements each. Our analysis showed us that much of this material described general thinking and reasoning abilities or information processing abilities that could be applied to a variety of subject matter, and were not exclusive to history. In accord with our model, then, this material was integrated into the appropriate standards on thinking and reasoning (see Section 17. Life Skills) or the language arts. Two areas, however, appeared to be uniquely related to the study of history, and appear as standards under the category of Historical Understanding: the first treats chronological relationships and patterns, and the second addresses the historical perspective, as outlined first in the Bradley report.

The World and U.S. History standards and benchmarks in this book represent a revision and abridgement of the material that appeared in the last edition (Kendall & Marzano, March 1995).

This revision builds on the previous edition, however, in that it begins from the analysis and synthesis done at that time of the multiple levels and types of information found in the *National Standards* documents.

In order to understand the method used to render material from the source documents it is useful to provide a description of them. There are five levels of organization in the U.S. and world history documents from NCHS. The outermost level is a grouping by historical era. Each era is comprised of two to four statements, which are called standards, and comprise the next, or second level. Each standard is further divided into subheadings, the third level of organization. These subheadings are divided into components designed to help students "demonstrate the integration of historical understanding and thinking." These components, the fourth level, are labeled with grade ranges (5–12, 7–12 and 9–12). Finally, the fifth level is comprised of "examples of student achievement" at grades 5–6, 7–8 and 9–12. It should be noted that in this design it is only at the fifth level, three levels below the standard, that information is found that provides grade appropriate material. For this reason we determined that all levels had to be analyzed to identify grade level benchmarks, in other words, that we otherwise would not have the means for distinguishing benchmark material at 5–6, for example, from information that was more appropriate for grades 7–8, or 9–12.

Thus, in order to compose benchmarks, we analyzed the material in the lowest three organizational levels. These levels were then combined in such a way that the topics found at the lowest levels were kept as a part of the benchmark, but the most detailed level of information was deleted, that is, the information that served to elaborate and extend on the example of student achievement. To take an example almost at random, the following are tasks, or "examples of student achievement," at grades 9–12 of the National Standards for World History:

> Read selections from the philosopher Zhu Xi's conversations with his followers and from the *Schedule for Learning*, and discuss the basic ideas of Neo-Confucianism. Analyze how these ideas affected Chinese society, government, and education

> Read the instructions Zhu Xi gave on rites for honoring ancestors in his Family Rituals, and discuss the relationship between popular rites and Zhu Xi's Neo-Confucian philosophy

> Research how economic changes in China affected society. How mobile was the gentry class? (p. 133)

These activities appear related to the 4th level headings "...major dynastic transition China experienced and the changes in Confucianism in the 10th and 13th centuries" and "...the growth of an economically powerful merchant class in China." The third level heading, that is, the one just beneath the standard level, states that students should be able to: "Demonstrate understanding of China's extensive urbanization and commercial expansion between the 10th and 13th century." Taking this information into account, the following single benchmark was developed to cover the activities cited above at grades 9–12:

- Understands significant religious and economic aspects of Chinese society between the 10th and 13th centuries (e.g., the impact of economic growth on Chinese society and how it affected the gentry class; how Zhu Xi's basic ideas of Neo-Confucianism affected Chinese society, government, and education)

In one sense, the "stuff" of history — the defining facts, events, and episodes — is not amenable to such presentation by developmental levels; and aside from the advantages of introducing information in a chronological sequence, we have not discovered other arguments or research on how this kind of material might be benchmarked. As noted in *Lessons From History*, however, "Historical knowledge must go beyond the factual knowledge implicit in these lists — *important though that knowledge is* — to the explanations of the causes and consequences of these events and the interpretations which can be drawn concerning their enduring significance" (p. 48). What varies from grade level to grade level in the standards documents from NCHS is the sophistication of the "examples of student achievement." These activities are somewhat problematic, in that they mix curriculum and performance with content standards. Additionally, these activities have been recently criticized by a panel convened by the Council for Basic Education (see Section 2, "History") "for undermining principles of scholarship by asking leading questions or by inviting students to make easy moral judgments about historical questions that continue to be debated by scholars" ("Review panels," CBE, October 1995). An analysis of these activities solely for content, however, does indicate some level of distinction between grades, for generally speaking it is often possible to discern between grade levels a difference in the level of detail and depth of understanding demanded from students. Thus, when these activities were examined for their content, and the specific task requirements were removed, they provided useful information for the composition of benchmarks.

A similar, though somewhat simpler, structure is found in the *National History Standards for K–4*, as was found in the U.S. and world history documents, and the kind of analysis described above was applied to that document to generate the standards and benchmarks at the levels K–2 and 3–4.

Integration of Information from Other Documents
Outside of the technical demands of the model employed for the identification and synthesis of content standards and benchmarks, this study applies no other criteria related to the academic content or appropriateness of any standard or benchmark. That is, every effort has been made to provide consistent distinctions between levels and types of content description, but no criteria is applied to determine the value of that content. It is clear, however, that NCHS standards have generated some public discussion on content and, in fact, appear likely to undergo some revision in the near future. In light of this, readers who would like to consult this work in order to inform their own development of history standards might want to acquaint themselves with the citation process used in our model (see section 6. How Subject-area Sections are Structured). To reiterate briefly, every benchmark developed from the standards document is reviewed against the available source documents: in this case, *Lessons from History*, and NAEP's *Provisional Item Specifications*. If the benchmark content is found to be expressed or implied in those documents, the "citation log,"

located flush right and just above the benchmark, will indicate this as well as whether the information was explicitly stated or implied, and the page number on which it was found. Thus, any benchmark can be examined to determine whether it appeared in a source in addition to the National Standards documents. It should be noted, however, that the NAEP's *Specifications* cover only U.S. history, not world history. Additionally, the *Lessons from History* document is written at a more general level of detail than is found at the benchmark level for this document and consequently is not frequently cited.

A Note on the Number of History Standards

The number of standards identified for history in this document might at first appear formidable (see figure 5.1 in section 5. The Process Used in this Report). However, when considered in terms of how these standards are designed for use, the number of standards in U.S. or world history is more nearly comparable to the number of standards found in other subject areas. In history, unlike other areas, each set of benchmarks (at grades 5–6, 7–8, and 9–12) is designed to provide a full description of that standard; in other words, as is the case in most schooling now, material for one historical era is unlikely to be repeated at a different level of schooling. Once a standard is met at particular grade level, the student is no longer required to meet it.

As an example, if a school or district should decide to teach the era on "Civil War and Reconstruction" at the 7–8 grade levels, the standards and benchmarks under that era would not be addressed again at 9–12. For other subject-area standards in this report, by contrast, if a standard has benchmarks listed at more than one grade level, it indicates that the student is expected to meet benchmarks in the other grade levels listed.

Thus, as a hypothetical example, if the standards were implemented fairly evenly across grade levels, each student studying U.S. history would not be responsible for more than 31 standards (91 standards by the 3 years of study recommended by NCHS) at any one time. In world history, the design is only a little more complicated and results in greater flexibility. In addition to the design for implementation found in U.S. History, the authors of the world history have identified material as "core" or "related." Core material is deemed essential for a grounding in world history; "related" material is important, but not critical, and can be omitted if necessary. In this report, each benchmark is designated as either "core" (C) or "related" (R).

Summary of Standards for Historical Understanding

1. Understands and knows how to analyze chronological relationships and patterns
2. Understands the historical perspective

(AE,18;WE,18)
1. Understands and knows how to analyze chronological relationships and patterns

Level I (Grades K-2)

- Knows how to identify the beginning, middle, and end of historical stories, myths and narratives ^BP (KE,19)

- Knows how to develop picture time lines of their own lives or their family's history ^BP (KE,19)

- Understands broad categories of time (e.g., long, long ago; long ago; yesterday; today; tomorrow) ^BD (KE,19)

- Understands calendar time in days, weeks, and months ^BD (KE,19)

- Knows how to identify change and continuity in his or her own life ^BD (KE,19)

Level II (Grades 3-5)

- Understands the broadly defined eras of state and local historical events ^BD (KE,19)

- Understands calendar time in years, decades, and centuries ^BD (KE,19)

- Knows how to construct time lines of significant historical developments that mark at evenly spaced intervals the years, decades, or centuries ^BP (KE,19)

- Knows how to interpret data presented in time lines (e.g., identify the time at which events occurred; the sequence in which events developed; what else was occurring at the time) ^BP (KE,20)

- Knows how to identify patterns of change and continuity in the history of the community, state, and nation, and in the lives of people of various cultures from times long ago until today ^BP (KE,20)

Level III (Grades 6-8)

- Knows how to diagram the temporal structure of events in autobiographies, biographies, literary narratives and historical narratives, and understands the differences between them ^BP (AE,21)

Codes (right side of page):   BD = Benchmark, Declarative; BP = Benchmark, Procedural; BC = Benchmark, Contextual
1st letter of each code in parentheses   *2nd letter of code*   *Number*
B = Bradley Commission on History   E = Explicitly stated in document   Page number of cited document
A = NCHS: National Standards for U.S. History   I = Implied in document
K = NCHS: National Standards for K-4 History
L = Lessons from History
W= NCHS: National Standards for World History

- Knows how to construct and interpret multiple tier time lines (e.g., a time line that contains important social, economic, and political developments in colonial history; a time line that compares developments in the English, French, and Spanish colonies of North America) BP (AE,21)

- Knows how to calculate calendar time B.C (before Christ) or B.C.E (before the Common Era, and A.D. (*Anno Domini*) or C.E. (in the Common Era), determining the onset, duration, and ending dates of historical events or developments BP (AE,21)

- Understands patterns of change and continuity in the historical succession of related events BD (AE,21)

- Knows how to impose temporal structure on their historical narratives (e.g., working backward from some issue, problem, or event to explain its causes that arose from some beginning and developed through subsequent transformations over time) BP (AE,21)

- Knows how to periodize events of the nation into broadly defined eras BP (AE,21)

Level IV (Grades 9-12)

- Knows how to identify the temporal structure and connections disclosed in historical narratives BP (AE,22)

- Understands alternative systems of recording time (e.g., Egyptian, Indian, Mayan, Muslim, Jewish), astronomical systems on which they are based (e.g., solar, lunar, semilunar), their fixed points for measuring time, and their strengths and weaknesses BD (AE,22)

- Understands historical continuity and change related to a particular development or theme (e.g., the Industrial Revolution, the evolution of democracy in the U.S.) BD (AE,22)

- Understands the organizing principles of alternative models of historical periodization BD (AE,22)

- Understands that historical events happen in patterned ways BD (BE,25)

Codes (right side of page):   BD = Benchmark, Declarative; BP = Benchmark, Procedural; BC = Benchmark, Contextual
1st letter of each code in parentheses   *2nd letter of code*   *Number*
B = Bradley Commission on History   E = Explicitly stated in document   Page number of cited document
A = NCHS: National Standards for U.S. History   I = Implied in document
K = NCHS: National Standards for K-4 History
L = Lessons from History
W= NCHS: National Standards for World History

119   *MREL*

2.   Understands the historical perspective

(BE,25;AI,18-19;WI,18-19)

Level II (Grades 5-6)

- Predicts how things might have turned out differently in one's local community if specific individuals or groups had chosen different courses of action

  BP (KE,24;LI,41)

- Understands that specific individuals had a great impact on history

  BD (KE,24;LI,41)

- Understands that specific ideas had an impact on history

  BD (KE,21,24;LI,41)

- Understands that "chance events" had an impact on history

  BD (KE,24;LI,41)

- Understands that specific decisions and events had an impact on history

  BD (KE,24;LI,41)

Level III (Grades 7-8)

- Understands that specific individuals and the values those individuals held had an impact on history

  BD (BE,25;AI,24;WE,24;LI,41)

- Analyzes the influence specific ideas and beliefs had on a period of history

  BP (AI,24;WI,25;LI,41)

- Analyzes the effects that specific "chance events" had on history

  BP (BE,25;AI,24;WI,25;LI,41)

- Analyzes the effects specific decisions had on history

  BP (AI,24;WI,25;LI,41)

- Understands that historical accounts are subject to change based on newly uncovered records and interpretations

  BD (AE,28;WE,28;LI,41)

Level IV (Grades 9-12)

- Analyzes the values held by specific people who influenced history and the role their values played in influencing history

  BP (BE,25;AI,25;WI,25;LI,41)

- Analyzes the influences specific ideas and beliefs had on a period of history and specifies how events might have been different in the absence of those ideas and beliefs

  BP (BE,25;AI,25;WI,25;LI,41)

Codes (right side of page):   BD = Benchmark, Declarative; BP = Benchmark, Procedural; BC = Benchmark, Contextual
1st letter of each code in parentheses   *2nd letter of code*   *Number*
B = Bradley Commission on History   E = Explicitly stated in document   Page number of cited document
A = NCHS: National Standards for U.S. History   I = Implied in document
K = NCHS: National Standards for K-4 History
L = Lessons from History
W= NCHS: National Standards for World History

- Analyzes the effects that specific "chance events" had on history and specifies how things might have been different in the absence of those events
  BP (BE,25;AI,25;WI,25;LI,41)

- Analyzes the effects specific decisions had on history and studies how things might have been different in the absence of those decisions
  BP (AI,28;WI,28;LI,41)

- Understands that the consequences of human intentions are influenced by the means of carrying them out
  BD (BE,25;LI,41)

- Understands that change and continuity are equally probable and natural
  BD (BE,25;LI,41)

- Knows how to avoid seizing upon particular lessons of history as cures for present ills
  BP (BE,25;LI,41)

- Understands that the nonrational, the irrational, and the accidental have affected past events
  BD (BE,25;LI,41)

- Understands the relationship between geography and history as context for events
  BD (BE,25;LI,41)

- Analyzes how specific historical events would be interpreted differently based on newly uncovered records and/or information
  BC (AI,28;WI,28;LI,41)

- Understands how the past affects our private lives and society in general
  BD (BE,25;LI,41)

- Knows how to perceive past events with historical empathy
  BP (BE,25;LI,41)

Codes (right side of page): BD = Benchmark, Declarative; BP = Benchmark, Procedural; BC = Benchmark, Contextual
1st letter of each code in parentheses *2nd letter of code* *Number*
B = Bradley Commission on History E = Explicitly stated in document Page number of cited document
A = NCHS: National Standards for U.S. History I = Implied in document
K = NCHS: National Standards for K-4 History
L = Lessons from History
W= NCHS: National Standards for World History

MREL

Summary of Standards for Grades K–4 History

Topic 1 Living and Working Together in Families and Communities, Now and Long Ago
1.   Understands family life now and in the past, and family life in various places long ago
2.   Understands the history of the local community and how communities in North America varied long ago

Topic 2 The History of Students' Own State or Region
3.   Understands the people, events, problems, and ideas that were significant in creating the history of their state

Topic 3 The History of the United States: Democratic Principles and Values and the People from Many Cultures who Contributed to its Cultural, Economic, and Political Heritage
4.   Understands how democratic values came to be, and how they have been exemplified by people, events, and symbols
5.   Understands the causes and nature of movements of large groups of people into and within the United States, now and long ago
6.   Understands the folklore and other cultural contributions from various regions of the United States and how they helped to form a national heritage

Topic 4 The History of Peoples of Many Cultures Around the World
7.   Understands selected attributes and historical developments of societies in Africa, the Americas, Asia, and Europe
8.   Understands major discoveries in science and technology, some of their social and economic effects, and the major scientists and inventors responsible for them

(KE,32)

1. **Understands family life now and in the past, and family life in various places long ago**

Level I (Grades K-2)

BD (KE,32,33)
- Knows a family history through two generations (e.g., various family members and their connections)

BC (KE,32,33)
- Understands family life today and how it compares with family life in the recent past and family life long ago (in terms of roles, jobs, schooling experiences)

BC (KE,32,33)
- Knows the cultural similarities and differences in clothes, homes, food, communication, technology, and cultural traditions between families now and in the past

BC (KE,32,33)
- Understands family life in a community of the past and life in a community of the present (e.g., roles, jobs, communication, technology, style of homes, transportation, schools, religious observances, cultural traditions)

BD (KE,34)
- Understands personal family or cultural heritage through stories, songs, and celebrations

BD (KE,34)
- Knows ways in which people share family beliefs and values (e.g., oral traditions, literature, songs, art, religion, community celebrations, mementos, food, language)

Level II (Grades 3-4)

BD (KE,34)
- Knows the ways that families long ago expressed and transmitted their beliefs and values through oral tradition, literature, songs, art, religion, community celebrations, mementos, food and language (e.g., celebration of national holidays, religious observances, and ethnic and national traditions; visual arts and crafts; hymns, proverbs, and songs)

BD (KE,34,35)
- Understands the dreams and ideals that people from various groups have sought, some of the problems they encountered in realizing their dreams, and the sources of strength and determination that families drew upon and shared (e.g., families arriving together in America and living together in rural or urban settings, traditions brought from their cultural past)

BD (KE,32,33;NI,17)
- Understands daily life of a farm family from long ago (in terms of work, clothing, tools, food, and food production in the early 1800s)

Codes (right side of page):   BD = Benchmark, Declarative; BP = Benchmark, Procedural; BC = Benchmark, Contextual
1st letter of each code in parentheses   *2nd letter of code*   *Number*
K = NCHS: History for Grades K-4   E = Explicitly stated in document   Page number of cited document
N = NAEP: Provisional Item Specifications   I = Implied in document

McREL

(KE,36)

2. Understands the history of the local community and how communities in North America varied long ago

Level I (Grades K-2)

- Understands changes in community life over time (e.g., changes in goods and services; changes in architecture and landscape; changes in jobs, schooling, transportation, communication, religion, recreation) BD (KE,36)

- Understands the contributions and significance of historical figures of the community BD (KE,36)

- Understands the daily life and values of early Hawaiian or Native American cultures BD (KE,38;NI,3)

- Understands the daily life of a colonial community (e.g., Plymouth, Williamsburg, St. Augustine, San Antonio, Post Vincennes) BD (KE,38;NI,7,8)

- Understands life in a pioneer farming community (e.g., the Old Northwest, the prairies, the Southwest, eastern Canada, the Far West) BD (KE,38;NI,17)

Level II (Grades 3-4)

- Knows the history of the local community since its founding, the people who came, the changes they brought, and significant events over time BD (KE,36,37)

- Knows of problems in the community's past, the different perspectives of those involved, the choices people had, and the solutions they chose BD (KE,36,37)

- Understands changes in land use and economic activities in the local community since its founding (e.g., changes in technology, the work people did, transportation, local resources) BD (KE,36,37)

- Knows the geographical settings, economic activities, food, clothing, homes, crafts, and rituals of Native American societies long ago (e.g., Iroquois, Sioux, Hopi, Nez Perce, Inuit, Cherokee) BD (KE,38;NI,3)

- Understands the historical development and daily life of a colonial community (e.g., Plymouth, Williamsburg, St. Augustine, San Antonio, Post Vincennes) BD (KE,38;NI,7)

- Understands the challenges and difficulties encountered by people in pioneer farming communities (e.g., the Old Northwest, the prairies, the Southwest, eastern Canada, the Far BD (KE,38,39;NI,17)

Codes (right side of page):
1st letter of each code in parentheses
K = NCHS: History for Grades K-4
N = NAEP: Provisional Item Specifications

BD = Benchmark, Declarative; BP = Benchmark, Procedural; BC = Benchmark, Contextual
2nd letter of code
E = Explicitly stated in document
I = Implied in document

Number
Page number of cited document

MREL

West)

BD (KE,38,39)

- Understands how geographical features contributed to the establishment and growth of communities such as mining towns (e.g., Sacramento) and trading settlements (e.g., New Orleans, Vincennes, Astoria)

BD (KE,38,39;NI,24)

- Understands daily life in ethnically diverse urban communities long ago (e.g., a free African American community in Philadelphia, an Italian community in New York, a Chinese community in San Francisco)

(KE,36)

3. Understands the people, events, problems, and ideas that were significant in creating the history of their state

Level I (Grades K-2)

BD (KE,40,41;NI,3)

- Understands through legends, myths, and archaeological evidence the origins and culture of early Native Americans or Hawaiians who lived in the state or region

BD (KE,41)

- Knows ways in which early explorers and settlers adapted to, used, and changed the environment of the state or region

BD (KE,43)

- Understands the reasons different groups came to the state or region

BD (KE,43)

- Understands the different lives, plans, and dreams of the various racial and ethnic groups who lived in the state 100-200 years ago

BD (KE,43,44)

- Understands how symbols, slogans, and mottoes represent the state

BD (KE,46)

- Knows important buildings, statues, and monuments in the state's history

Level II (Grades 3-4)

BC (KE,40,41)

- Understands differences between the lives of Native Americans or Hawaiians today and their lives 100 years ago

BD (KE,41)

- Understands geographic, economic, and religious reasons that brought the first explorers and settlers to the state or region, who they were, and where they settled

BD (KE,41;NI,6,7,15)

- Understands the interactions that occurred between the Native Americans or Hawaiians and

---

Codes (right side of page):   BD = Benchmark, Declarative; BP = Benchmark, Procedural; BC = Benchmark, Contextual
1st letter of each code in parentheses   *2nd letter of code*   *Number*
K = NCHS: History for Grades K-4   E = Explicitly stated in document   Page number of cited document
N = NAEP: Provisional Item Specifications   I = Implied in document

McREL

the first European, African, and Asian-Pacific explorers and settlers in the state or region

- Knows about the first inhabitants who lived in the state or region, each successive group of arrivals and their countries (or origin), and significant changes that developed as a result of each group's arrival

  BD (KE,43,44)

- Understands the reasons recent immigrants came to the state or region, what their lives were like, and their experiences of adjustment (e.g., problems and opportunities experienced in housing, the workplace, and the community)

  BD (KE,43,44)

- Understands patterns and changes in population over a period of time in a city or town in the state or region

  BD (KE,43,44)

- Knows the chronological order of major historical events that are part of the state's history, their significance and impact on people then and now, and their relationship to the history of the nation

  BD (KE,45,46)

- Understands major historical events and developments in the state or region that involved interaction among various groups

  BD (KE,45)

- Understands the influence of geography on the history of the state or region, and issues and approaches to problems (e.g., land use, environmental problems)

  BD (KE,45)

- Understands how the ideas of significant people affected the history of the state

  BD (KE,46;NI,16)

- Understands the unique historical conditions that influenced the formation of the state and how statehood was granted

  BD (KE,46)

- Knows the origin of the names of places, rivers, cities, and counties, and knows the various cultural influences within a particular region

  BD (KE,46)

4. **Understands how democratic values came to be, and how they have been exemplified by people, events, and symbols**

(KE,48)

Level I (Grades K-2)

- Understands the roles and importance of revolutionary leaders (e.g., George Washington, Thomas Jefferson, Benjamin Franklin) as English colonists fought for independence from

  BD (KE,48,49;NE,10,11)

Codes (right side of page):	BD = Benchmark, Declarative; BP = Benchmark, Procedural; BC = Benchmark, Contextual
1st letter of each code in parentheses	*2nd letter of code*	*Number*
K = NCHS: History for Grades K-4	E = Explicitly stated in document	Page number of cited document
N = NAEP: Provisional Item Specifications	I = Implied in document	

126

MREL

England

BD (KE,48,49;NE,31,32)
- Understands how individuals (e.g., Rosa Parks; Martin Luther King Jr.; Sojourner Truth; Cesar Chavez) have worked to achieve the liberties and equality promised in the principles of American democracy and to improve the lives of people from many groups

BD (KE,50)
- Understands the ways in which different people (e.g., those in the local school) have helped by applying such fundamental values as fairness, protection of individual rights, and responsibility for the common good

BD (KE,50)
- Understands how people have helped each other in the past in the community (e.g., the police department, the fire department, senior citizen home, soup kitchen)

BD (KE,50)
- Understands how people have helped newcomers get settled and learn the ways of the new country (e.g., family members, fraternal organizations, houses of worship)

BD (KE,51)
- Understands how important figures reacted to their times and why they were significant to the history of our democracy (e.g., George Washington, Thomas Jefferson; Abraham Lincoln; Sojourner Truth; Susan B. Anthony; Mary McLeod Bethune; Eleanor Roosevelt; Martin Luther King, Jr.)

BD (KE,51)
- Understands the ways in which people in a variety of fields (e.g., Frederick Douglass, Clara Barton, Elizabeth Blackwell, Jackie Robinson, Rosa Parks, Jonas Salk, Cesar Chavez) have advanced the cause of human rights, equality, and the common good

BD (KE,52;NE,32)
- Understands the reasons that Americans celebrate certain national holidays (e.g., Martin Luther King, Jr. Day; the Fourth of July; Memorial Day)

BD (KE,53)
- Knows the history of American symbols (e.g., the eagle, the Liberty Bell, George Washington as the "father of our country," the national flag)

BD (KE,53;NI,24)
- Knows why important buildings, statues, and monuments (e.g., the White House, Lincoln Memorial, Statue of Liberty, Ellis Island, Angel Island, Mt. Rushmore, veterans' memorials) are associated with state and national history

Level II (Grades 3-4)

BD (KE,48,49;NE,10)
- Understands why Americans and those who lead them (e.g., George Washington, Benjamin Franklin, and Thomas Jefferson) went to war to win independence from England

---

Codes (right side of page):	BD = Benchmark, Declarative; BP = Benchmark, Procedural; BC = Benchmark, Contextual
1st letter of each code in parentheses	*2nd letter of code* — *Number*
K = NCHS: History for Grades K-4	E = Explicitly stated in document — Page number of cited document
N = NAEP: Provisional Item Specifications	I = Implied in document

127

McREL

- Understands the basic ideas set forth in the Declaration of Independence and the U.S. Constitution, and the figures responsible for these documents
  BD (KE,49;NE,10,11)

- Understands the basic principles of American democracy: right to life, liberty, and the pursuit of happiness; responsibility for the common good; equality of opportunity and equal protection of the law; freedom of speech and religion; majority rule with protection for minority rights; and limitations on government, with power held by the people and delegated by them to those officials whom they elected to office
  BD (KE,49;NI,10,11)

- Understands how people over the last 200 years (e.g., Sojourner Truth; Harriet Tubman; Frederick Douglass; W.E.B. DuBois; Booker T. Washington; Susan B. Anthony; Martin Luther King, Jr.; Rosa Parks; Cesar Chavez) have continued to struggle to bring to all groups in American society the liberties and equality promised in the basic principles of American democracy
  BD (KE,49;NE,21,31,32)

- Understands the accomplishments of ordinary people in historical situations (e.g., James Armistead, Sybil Ludington, Nathan Beman, Lydia Darragh, Betty Zane) and how each struggled for individual rights or for the common good
  BD (KE,50)

- Understands how people have helped make the community a better place to live (e.g., working to preserve the environment, to help the homeless, to restore houses in low- income areas)
  BD (KE,51)

- Understands how people in the recent past have volunteered to help in unique situations (e.g., during earthquakes, floods, fires)
  BD (KE,51)

- Understands historical figures who believed in the fundamental democratic values (e.g., justice, truth, equality, the rights of the individual, responsibility for the common good, voting rights) and the significance of these people both in their historical context and today
  BD (KE,51,52)

- Understands how historical figures in the U.S. and in other parts of the world have advanced the rights of individuals and promoted the common good, and the character traits that made them successful (e.g., persistence, problem solving, moral responsibility, respect for others)
  BD (KE,51,52)

- Understands the historical events and democratic values commemorated by major national holidays (e.g., Martin Luther King, Jr. Day; President's Day; Memorial Day; the Fourth of July; Labor Day; Veterans Day; Thanksgiving)
  BD (KE,52,53;NE,32)

- Knows the history of events and the historic figures responsible for such historical documents as the Mayflower Compact, the Declaration of Independence, the U.S.
  BD (KE,52,53)

Codes (right side of page):
1st letter of each code in parentheses
K = NCHS: History for Grades K-4
N = NAEP: Provisional Item Specifications

BD = Benchmark, Declarative; BP = Benchmark, Procedural; BC = Benchmark, Contextual
2nd letter of code
E = Explicitly stated in document
I = Implied in document

Number
Page number of cited document

128

MREL

Constitution, the Bill of Rights, and the Emancipation Proclamation

- Understands how ordinary people have worked to contribute money and ideas to create or enhance our national symbols (e.g., French school children who raised money for the Statue of Liberty, Lee Iaccoca's work to restore Ellis Island) BD (KE,54)

- Knows the Pledge of Allegiance and patriotic songs, poems, and sayings that were written long ago, and understands their significance BD (KE,53,54;NI,32)

- Understands how songs, symbols, and slogans demonstrate freedom of expression and the role of protest in a democracy (e.g., the Boston Tea Party, the abolition of slavery, women's suffrage, labor movements, the civil rights movement) BD (KE,53,54)

5. Understands the causes and nature of movements of large groups of people into and within the United States, now and long ago (KE,55)

Level I (Grades K-2)

- Understands the changes that occurred in people's lives when they moved from faraway places to the U.S. BD (KE,55)

- Understands what life was like for children and families "on the trail" when they moved from one part of the U.S. to another BD (KE,55)

Level II (Grades 3-4)

- Knows the various movements (westward, northward, and eastward) of large groups of people in the history of the U.S. BD (KE,55)

- Knows about the forced relocation of Native Americans and how their lives, rights, and territories were affected by European colonization and expansion of the U.S. (e.g., Spanish colonization of the Southwest, Tecumseh's resistance to Indian removal, the Cherokee Trail of Tears, Black Hawk's War, the movement of the Nez Perce) BD (KE,55;NI,15,16,18)

- Understands the experience of immigrant groups (e.g., where they came from, why they left, travel experiences, ports of entry and immigration screening, the opportunities and obstacles they encountered when they arrived) BD (KE,55;NE,17)

- Knows the reasons why various groups (e.g., freed African Americans, Mexican and Puerto Rican migrant workers, Dust Bowl farm families) migrated to different parts of the U.S. BD (KE,55)

Codes (right side of page): BD = Benchmark, Declarative; BP = Benchmark, Procedural; BC = Benchmark, Contextual
1st letter of each code in parentheses *2nd letter of code* *Number*
K = NCHS: History for Grades K-4 E = Explicitly stated in document Page number of cited document
N = NAEP: Provisional Item Specifications I = Implied in document

MREL

- Understands the experiences of those who moved from farm to city during the periods when cities grew BD (KE,55)

6. Understands the folklore and other cultural contributions from various regions of the United States and how they helped to form a national heritage (KE,57)

Level I (Grades K-2)

- Knows regional folk heroes, stories, or songs (e.g., Pecos Bill, Brer Rabbit, Paul Bunyan, Davey Crockett, John Henry, Joe Magarac) that have contributed to the development of the cultural history of the U.S. BD (KE,57;NE,17)

- Knows the differences between the toys and games children played long ago and the toys and games of today BC (KE,57)

Level II (Grades 3-4)

- Understands how regional folk heroes such as frontiersmen (e.g., Daniel Boone), cowboys, mountain men (e.g., Jedediah Smith), American Indian Chiefs (e.g., Geronimo), outlaws (e.g., Billy the Kid), and other popular figures have contributed to the cultural history of the U.S. BD (KE,57,58)

- Understands how stories, legends, songs, ballads, games, and tall tales describe the environment, lifestyles, beliefs, and struggles of people in various regions of the country BD (KE,57,58)

- Understands how art, crafts, music, and language of people from a variety of regions long ago influenced the nation BD (KE,57,58)

7. Understands selected attributes and historical developments of societies in Africa, the Americas, Asia, and Europe (KE,60)

Level I (Grades K-2)

- Understands the main ideas found in folktales, stories of great heroism, fables, legends, and myths from around the world that reflect the beliefs and ways of living of various cultures in times past BD (KE,61)

- Knows the holidays and ceremonies of different societies (e.g., Christmas celebrations in Scandinavia, Germany, or England; Cinco de Mayo; the Chinese New Year; the Japanese tea ceremony; harvest and spring festivals) BD (KE,61)

Codes (right side of page):   BD = Benchmark, Declarative; BP = Benchmark, Procedural; BC = Benchmark, Contextual
1st letter of each code in parentheses   *2nd letter of code*   *Number*
K = NCHS: History for Grades K-4   E = Explicitly stated in document   Page number of cited document
N = NAEP: Provisional Item Specifications   I = Implied in document

- Understands the daily life, history, and beliefs of a country as reflected in dance, music, or the other art forms (such as paintings, sculptures, and masks)
  BD (KE,61)

- Knows the journeys of Marco Polo and Christopher Columbus, the routes they took, and what happened as a result of their travels
  BD (KE,62;NI,2,3,5)

Level II (Grades 3-4)

- Understands how historians learn about the past if there are no written records
  BD (KE,60)

- Knows the effects geography has had on the different aspects of societies (e.g., the development of urban centers, food, clothing, industry, agriculture, shelter, trade)
  BD (KE,60)

- Understands various aspects of family life, structures, and roles in different cultures and in many eras (e.g., medieval families, matrilineal families in Africa, extended families in China)
  BD (KE,60,61;NI,2,3)

- Knows about life in urban areas and communities of various cultures of the world (e.g., Rome, Tenochtitlán, Timbuktu, a medieval European city) at various times in their history
  BD (KE,60,61)

- Knows significant historical achievements of various cultures of the world (e.g., the Hanging Gardens of Babylon, the Taj Mahal in India, pyramids in Egypt, temples in ancient Greece, bridges and aqueducts in ancient Rome)
  BD (KE,60,61)

- Knows about the migrations of large groups in the past and recently (e.g., Native American ancestors across the Bering land bridge; the Bantu migrations in Africa; the movement of Europeans and Africans to the Western Hemisphere; the exodus of Vietnamese boat people, Haitians, and Cubans)
  BD (KE,62;NI,3)

- Knows about the European explorers of the 15th and 16th centuries (e.g., Christopher Columbus, Ferdinand Magellan, Vasco da Gama, Jacques Cartier, Marco Polo, Eric the Red, Zheng He), their reasons for exploring, the information gained from their journeys, and what happened as a result of their travels
  BD (KE,62,63;NI,2,3,5)

- Knows about the various crops, foods, and animals that were transported from the Western Hemisphere (e.g., tomato, corn, cassava, potato) and from the Eastern Hemisphere (e.g., horse, cattle, sugar cane) as a result of the "Columbian Exchange"
  BD (KE,62,63;NI,5)

- Understands the different perspectives and major arguments surrounding the Columbian encounter
  BD (KE,63)

Codes (right side of page):   BD = Benchmark, Declarative; BP = Benchmark, Procedural; BC = Benchmark, Contextual
1st letter of each code in parentheses   *2nd letter of code*   *Number*
K = NCHS: History for Grades K-4   E = Explicitly stated in document   Page number of cited document
N = NAEP: Provisional Item Specifications   I = Implied in document

131   *MREL*

8. Understands major discoveries in science and technology, some of their social and economic effects, and the major scientists and inventors responsible for them $^{(KE,64)}$

Level I (Grades K-2)

- Understands the changes in family life that occurred when the family no longer had to hunt for food, could be supported on smaller amounts of land, and could acquire surplus food for storage and trading $^{BD (KE,64)}$

- Knows the accomplishments of major scientists and inventors (e.g., George Washington Carver, Galileo, Marie Curie, Louis Pasteur, Alexander Graham Bell) $^{BD (KE,64;NE,24,25,26)}$

- Understands differences in the methods of travel from various times in human history and the advantages and disadvantages of each (e.g., the use of animals such as horses, llamas, camels, and elephants; nonmotorized vehicles such as chariots, travoises, bicycles, blimps, hot air balloons, and gliders; motorized vehicles such as railroads, motorcycles, autos, electric rail systems, and airplanes; modern space advancements) $^{BD (KE,66;NI,18,26,35)}$

- Knows basic information about marine transportation (e.g., the technology and activities of people along the Erie Canal) $^{BD (KE,66)}$

- Knows the ways people communicate with each other now and long ago, and the technological developments that facilitated communication (e.g., speaking by gestures, transmitting stories orally, pictographs, hieroglyphics, different alphabets, writing by hand, printing techniques, the invention of the telegraph and telephone, satellite transmission of messages) $^{BD (KE,67;NI,34)}$

- Knows various systems of long-distance communication and their effects (e.g., runners, the "talking drums" of Africa, smoke signals of Native Americans, the pony express, the telegraph, telephones, satellite systems) $^{BD (KE,67)}$

Level II (Grades 3-4)

- Knows about the development of the wheel and its early uses in ancient societies $^{BD (KE,64)}$

- Understands the development and the influence of basic tools on work and behavior $^{BD (NE,64)}$

- Knows various technological developments to control fire, water, wind, and soil and to utilize natural resources (e.g., trees, coal, oil, gas) in order to satisfy basic human needs for food, water, clothing, and shelter $^{BD (KE,64)}$

Codes (right side of page):   BD = Benchmark, Declarative; BP = Benchmark, Procedural; BC = Benchmark, Contextual
1st letter of each code in parentheses   *2nd letter of code*   *Number*
K = NCHS: History for Grades K-4   E = Explicitly stated in document   Page number of cited document
N = NAEP: Provisional Item Specifications   I = Implied in document

McREL

- Knows about technological inventions and developments that evolved during the 19th century and the influence of these changes on the lives of workers
  _BD (KE,64;NE,25,26)_

- Knows the significant scientific and technological achievements of various historical societies (e.g., the invention of paper in China, Mayan calendars, mummification in Egypt, astronomical discoveries in the Moslem world, the invention of the steam engine in England)
  _BD (KE,65)_

- Knows the different forms of transportation and their developments over time
  _BD (KE,66;NI,18,26,35)_

- Understands the developments in marine vessels constructed by people from ancient times until today (e.g., early dugout Phoenician ships, Native American canoes, the Portuguese caravel, the Chinese vessels used by Zheng He, the Arab dhow, the Norse long ships, currachs used in the British Isles, square-riggers, aircraft carriers, submarines, bathyscaphs)
  _BD (KE,66;NI,4)_

- Understands the development of extensive road systems (e.g., the Roman system of roads; the trade routes by camel caravan linking East Asia, Southwest Asia, and Africa during he ancient and early Middle Ages; the network of roads and highways of the Inca in Peru; the interstate highway system), the travel and communication difficulties encountered by people over vast expanses of territory, and the social and economic effects of these developments
  _BD (KE,66,67)_

- Knows the developments in rail transportation beginning in the 19th century and the effects of national systems of railroad transport on the lives of people
  _BD (KE,66;NI,26)_

- Understands the design and development of aircraft and rocketry, and the people involved
  _BD (KE,66;NE,34)_

- Knows about people who have made significant contributions in the field of transportation (e.g., Henry Ford, Amelia Earhart, John Glenn, Sally Ride)
  _BD (KE,66,67;NE,29,34)_

- Understands the origins and changes in methods of writing over time and how the changes made communication between people more effective (e.g., pictographs, cuneiform, hieroglyphics, alphabets)
  _BD (KE,67,68)_

- Understands the significance of the printing press, the computer, and electronic developments in communication and their impact on the spread of ideas
  _BD (KE,67,68)_

- Knows about people who have made significant contributions in the field of communication (e.g., the inventors of the telegraph, telephone, the Braille alphabet, radio, television, the computer, satellite communication)
  _BD (KE,67,68;NE,34,35)_

Codes (right side of page):   BD = Benchmark, Declarative; BP = Benchmark, Procedural; BC = Benchmark, Contextual
1st letter of each code in parentheses   _2nd letter of code_   _Number_
K = NCHS: History for Grades K-4   E = Explicitly stated in document   Page number of cited document
N = NAEP: Provisional Item Specifications   I = Implied in document

Summary of Standards for United States History

Era 1 Three Worlds Meet (Beginnings to 1620)
1. Understands the characteristics of societies in the Americas, Western Europe, and West Africa that increasingly interacted after 1450
2. Understands cultural and ecological interactions resulting from early European exploration and colonization

Era 2 Colonization and Settlement (1585-1763)
3. Understands how the early Europeans and Africans interacted with Native Americans in the Americas
4. Understands how political institutions and religious freedom emerged in the North American colonies
5. Understands how the values and institutions of European economic life took root in the colonies and how slavery reshaped European and African life in the Americas

Era 3 Revolution and the New Nation (1754-1820s)
6. Understands the causes of the American Revolution, the ideas and interests involved in shaping the revolutionary movement, and reasons for the American victory
7. Understands how the American Revolution involved multiple movements among the new nation's many groups to reform American society
8. Understands the institutions and practices of government created during the revolution and how these elements were revised between 1787 and 1815 to create the foundation of the American political system

Era 4 Expansion and Reform (1801-1861)
9. Understands the United States territorial expansion between 1801 and 1861, and how it affected relations with external powers and Native Americans
10. Understands how the industrial revolution, the rapid expansion of slavery, and the westward movement changed American lives and led to regional tensions
11. Understands the extension, restriction, and reorganization of political democracy after 1800
12. Understands the sources and character of reform movements in the antebellum period and what the reforms accomplished or failed to accomplish

Era 5 Civil War and Reconstruction (1850-1877)
13. Understands the causes of the Civil War
14. Understands the course and character of the Civil War and its effects on the American people
15. Understands how various reconstruction plans succeeded or failed

Era 6 The Development of the Industrial United States (1870-1900)
16. Understands how the rise of big business, heavy industry, and mechanized farming transformed American society
17. Understands massive immigration after 1870 and how new social patterns, conflicts, and ideas of national unity developed amid growing cultural diversity

18. Understands the rise of the American labor movement and how political issues reflected social and economic changes
19. Understands federal Indian policy and United States foreign policy after the Civil War

Era 7 The Emergence of Modern America (1890-1930)

20. Understands how progressives and others addressed problems of industrial capitalism, urbanization, and political corruption
21. Understands the changing role of the United States in world affairs through World War I
22. Understands how the United States changed between the post-World War I years and the eve of the Great Depression

Era 8 The Great Depression and World War II (1929-1945)

23. Understands the causes of the Great Depression and how it affected American society
24. Understands how the New Deal addressed the Great Depression, transformed American federalism, and initiated the welfare state
25. Understands the origins and course of World War II, the character of the war at home and abroad, and its reshaping of the U.S. role in world affairs

Era 9 Postwar United States (1945 to early 1970s)

26. Understands the economic boom and social transformation of post-World War II America
27. Understands how the legacy of the New Deal in the post World War II period
28. Understands the Cold War and the Korean and Vietnam conflicts in domestic and international politics
29. Understands the struggle for racial and gender equality and for the extension of civil liberties

Era 10 Contemporary United States (1968 to the present)

30. Understands developments in foreign and domestic policies between the Nixon and Clinton presidencies
31. Understands the major social and economic developments in contemporary America

(AE,35)

1. Understands the characteristics of societies in the Americas, western Europe, and West Africa, and their interactions after 1450

Level II (Grades 5-6)

- Understands Asian migration routes to the Americas (e.g. Bering land bridge) BD (AE,40;LE,55)

- Understands the significance of beliefs held by both Native Americans and Europeans (e.g., Native American beliefs about their origins in America, ideas of land use held by Native Americans and Europeans) BD (AE,40;LE,55;LI,56)

- Understands the economic, social, and cultural influence of location and physical geography on different Native American societies (e.g., Iroquois and Pueblo, Northwest and Southeast societies) BD (AE,40;LE,55-56)

- Understands how the Mohawk, Oneida, Onondaga, Cayuga, and Seneca united to form the Iroquois nation and to solve conflicts peaceably BD (AE,43;LI,55)

- Knows legends of pre-Columbus explorations and the technological, scientific, and geographic factors that led to the age of exploration in the Americas BD (AE,43;LI,55)

- Knows the geographic and social characteristics of major West African political kingdoms (e.g., Mali, Songhai, Benin) and urban centers (e.g., Timbuktu, Jenne) BD (AE,44;LI,56)

Level III (Grades 7-8)

- Understands the migration and settlement patterns of peoples in the Americas (e.g., the archaeological and geological evidence that explains the movement of people from Asia to the Americas, the spread of human societies and the rise of diverse cultures from hunter-gatherers to urban dwellers) BD (AE,41;LE,55;LI,55-56;NI,39)

- Understands the cultural traditions, gender roles, patterns of social organization, trade, and political culture of Native American societies BD (AE,41;LE,55)

- Understands the geographic, technological, and scientific factors that contributed to the European age of exploration and settlement in the Americas BD (AE,43;LE,55)

- Understands European perspectives of different cultures during the period of exploration and early settlement (e.g., European attitudes toward property and the environment) BD (AE,43;LI,56)

Codes (right side of page):   BD = Benchmark, Declarative; BP = Benchmark, Procedural; BC = Benchmark, Contextual
1st letter of each code in parentheses   *2nd letter of code*   *Number*
A = NCHS: National Standards for U.S. History   E = Explicitly stated in document   Page number of cited document
L = Lessons From History   I = Implied in document
N = NAEP: Provisional Item Specifications

- Understands the influence of Islam and Muslim cultures on West African societies and patterns of trade and settlement between West African states and Southwest Asia and Europe before 1450
  BD (AE,44)

Level IV (Grades 9-12)

- Understands different European perceptions of Native American societies during the years of exploration (e.g., John White's vs. Theodore deBry's)
  BD (AE,41;LI,56)

- Understands how values and beliefs in Native American origin stories explain other facets of Native America culture (e.g., migration, settlement, interactions with the environment)
  BD (AE, 40-41;LE,55)

- Understands the differences in the agricultural practices, gender roles, and social development of Native American societies (e.g., Hopi, Zuni, Algonkian, Iroquoian, Moundbuilder, and Mississippian cultures)
  BD (AE,41;LI,55-56)

- Understands the social, economic, and political factors that stimulated overseas exploration and how the spirit of individualism that sparked overseas exploration affected cross-cultural contacts with new peoples
  BD (AE,43)

- Understands social, economic, and cultural characteristics of European society (e.g., the customary European family organization, gender roles, acquisition of private property, relationships to the environment, and ideas about other cultures)
  BD (AE,43;LI,55;NI,84)

- Understands the characteristics of West African society, including Mali, Songhai, and Benin, before 1450 (e.g., how family organization, gender roles, and religion shaped West African societies; the growing influence of Islam in West Africa)
  BD (AE,45;LI,56;NE,85)

2. Understands cultural and ecological interactions resulting from early European exploration and colonization
(AE,46)

Level II (Grades 5-6)

- Knows the features of the major European explorations that took place between the 15th and 17th centuries (e.g., major expeditions, the problems encountered on the high seas; fears and superstitions of the times; what sailors expected to find when they reached their destinations)
  BD (AE,46;LI,56-57;NI,39)

- Understands aspects of the Spanish exploration, conquest, and immigration to the Americas
  BD (AE,48;LI,55-57;NE,41,42)

Codes (right side of page): BD = Benchmark, Declarative; BP = Benchmark, Procedural; BC = Benchmark, Contextual
1st letter of each code in parentheses *2nd letter of code* *Number*
A = NCHS: National Standards for U.S. History E = Explicitly stated in document Page number of cited document
L = Lessons From History I = Implied in document
N = NAEP: Provisional Item Specifications

McREL

in the centuries following Columbus (e.g., the expeditions of Cabeza de Vaca and Francisco Vasquez de Coronado in the American Southwest; Spanish interactions with the Aztec, Inca, and Pueblo, the conquest of Spanish America; motivations for Spanish immigration to the Americas)

Level III (Grades 7-8)

- Understands the immediate and long-term impact of Columbus' voyages on Native populations and on colonization in the Americas (e.g. Columbus' interactions with indigenous peoples, the Columbian Exchange, religious influences) BD (AE,47;LI,56-57;NI,39)

- Understands characteristics of the Spanish exploration and conquest of the Americas (e.g., the social composition of early Spanish settlers of America and their motives for exploration and colonization; methods the Spanish used to conquer the Aztec and Incan empires; societies the Spanish explorers encountered in the Aztec and Incan settlements) BD (AE,48;LI,55-57)

Level IV (Grades 9-12)

- Understands how the religious antagonisms of the Reformation stimulated overseas expansion (e.g., how the Spanish "Black Legend" was used to motivate and justify English colonization of North America; to what extent the "Black Legend" was Protestant propaganda; to what extent it was a valid description of the Spanish conquest) BD (AE,47;LI,55)

- Understands how interpretations of Columbus' voyages and his interactions with indigenous peoples have changed (e.g., between 1892 and 1992) BD (AE,47)

- Understands the long-range social and ecological impact of the Columbian Exchange (e.g. how the horse, the pig, and the dandelion brought about changes in the land; how the sugar trade affected Caribbean slaves, Indian laborers, and European urban proletarians) BD (AE,47;LI,53)

- Understands characteristics of Spanish conquest and settlement in the Americas (e.g., how Cortes and Pizarro were able to conquer the Aztec and Inca; the social composition of early Spanish settlers in the Americas in terms of age, gender, class, and its consequences for Latin America; the role of religious beliefs in perceptions the Aztec and Spanish held of one another; Spanish attempts at justification for their treatment of Native Americans) BD (AE,49; LI, 55-58)

- Understands the economic characteristics of the early Spanish empire in the Americas (e.g., *encomienda* system and the evolution of labor systems within the Spanish empire, the origin BD (AE,49;LI,58;NI,86)

Codes (right side of page):
1st letter of each code in parentheses
A = NCHS: National Standards for U.S. History
L = Lessons From History
N = NAEP: Provisional Item Specifications

BD = Benchmark, Declarative; BP = Benchmark, Procedural; BC = Benchmark, Contextual
2nd letter of code
E = Explicitly stated in document
I = Implied in document

Number
Page number of cited document

McREL

and expansion of the African slave trade in the Americas)

(AE,51)

3.   Understands how the early Europeans and Africans interacted with Native Americans in the Americas

Level II (Grades 5-6)

BD (AE,52;LI,63-66;NE,41,43)
- Understands the routes, goals, motives, and achievements of Spanish, French, Dutch, and English explorers in North America

BD (AE,52;LI,63;NE,43)
- Understands the similarities and differences in backgrounds, motivations, and occupational skills between people in the English settlements and those of the French and Spanish settlements

BD (AE,54)
- Understands how and why family and community life differed in various regions of colonial North America (e.g., Williamsburg, Philadelphia, Boston, New York, French Quebec, Santa Fe)

BD (AE,56;I,62,64;NI,41)
- Understands peaceful and conflictory interaction between English settlers and Native Americans in the New England, Mid-Atlantic, Chesapeake, and Lower South Colonies (e.g., how Native American and European societies influenced one another, differing European and Native American views of the land and its use)

Level III (Grades 7-8)

BD (AE,53;LI,63-64;NE,43)
- Understands how motives and goals differed between the Spanish, French, Dutch, and English colonizers and how motives also differed among English colonizers

BD (AE,53;LE,65,68)
- Understands growth and change in the European colonies during the two centuries following their founding (e.g., the arrival of Africans in the English Colonies in the 17th century, the rapid increase of slave importation in the 18th century)

BD (AE,54)
- Understands how family and gender roles of different regions of colonial America changed across time (1600-1760)

BD (AE,57;LI,62,64;NI,42)
- Understands the cultural and environmental impacts of European settlement in North America (e.g., friendly and conflictory relations between English, French, Spanish, and Dutch settlers and Native Americans; the impact of the fur trade on the environment; how

---

Codes (right side of page):   BD = Benchmark, Declarative; BP = Benchmark, Procedural; BC = Benchmark, Contextual
1st letter of each code in parentheses   *2nd letter of code*   *Number*
A = NCHS: National Standards for U.S. History   E = Explicitly stated in document   Page number of cited document
L = Lessons From History   I = Implied in document
N = NAEP: Provisional Item Specifications

various Native American societies changed as a result of the expanding European settlements and how they influenced European societies)

- Understands the events that culminated in the English victory over the French in the Seven Years War, and why the war and its outcomes were significant $^{BD (AE,57;LI,72-73)}$

Level IV (Grades 9-12)

- Understands the political and religious factors that influenced English, Spanish, French, and Dutch colonization of the Americas $^{BD (AE,53;LE,60,63;NI,89)}$

- Understands social and economic characteristics of European colonization in the 17th and 18th centuries (e.g., changing immigration and settlement patterns of Puritans, Quakers, Germans, and Scots-Irish; the slave trade and chattel slavery in the Spanish, English, and French Caribbean, Louisiana, the Dutch West Indies, and Chesapeake) $^{BD (AE,53;LE,65,68;LI,63,67-68;NI,89)}$

- Understands characteristics of the social structure of colonial America (e.g., different patterns of family life among European settlers and various Native American tribes; different ideals among diverse religious groups, social classes, and cultures; different roles and status of men and women; the property rights of single, married, and widowed women) $^{BD (AE,54;NI,90)}$

- Understands the nature of the interaction between Native Americans and various settlers (e.g., the diversity of Native American interactions with English, French, and Dutch settlers; Native American involvement in the European wars for control between 1675 and 1763) $^{BD (AE,57)}$

- Understands the events and consequences of the Seven Years War (e.g., the significance of the Peace of Paris, options left to Native Americans) $^{BD (AE,57)}$

4. Understands how political institutions and religious freedom emerged in the North American colonies $^{(AE,58)}$

Level II (Grades 5-6)

- Understands how the rise of individualism and the characteristics of colonial self-government such as the right to vote and hold office were reflected in the Mayflower Compact $^{BD (AE,58;NE,42)}$

- Understands Puritanism in colonial America (e.g., why Puritans came to America, how $^{BD (AE,60;LI,61-62)}$

Codes (right side of page):
1st letter of each code in parentheses
A = NCHS: National Standards for U.S. History
L = Lessons From History
N = NAEP: Provisional Item Specifications

BD = Benchmark, Declarative; BP = Benchmark, Procedural; BC = Benchmark, Contextual
2nd letter of code   *Number*
E = Explicitly stated in document   Page number of cited document
I = Implied in document

140

MCREL

Puritanism shaped New England communities, the changes in Puritanism during the 17th century, the Puritan family structure)

BD (AE,60)

- Understands the opposition to King James I

Level III (Grades 7-8)

BD (AE,59;LI,67;NE,42)
- Understands ideas that influenced religious and political aspects of Colonial America (e.g., how Benjamin Franklin's thirteen virtues in his *Autobiography* compare to Puritan ideas and values, how the growth of individualism challenged European ideas of hierarchy and contributed to participatory government)

BD (AE,58;LE,63;NE,42;NI,42)
- Understands the development of colonial governments (e.g., the degree to which colonial society was democratic in practice, how early colonies differed in the way they were established and governed)

BD (AE,58;LI,64)
- Understands the concepts that contributed to the "rights of Englishmen" (e.g., the Magna Carta, English Common law, the English Bill of Rights [1689])

BD (AE,58;LI,64)
- Understands the impact of the English Civil War and the Glorious Revolution on the colonies

BD (AE,60;LI,61-62,67;NE,43,44)
- Understands the role of religion in the English colonies (e.g., treatment of religious dissenters such as Anne Hutchison, the concept of the separation of church and state, the evolution of relgious freedom)

BD (AE,63)
- Understands how political, social, and economic tensions led to violent conflicts between the colonists and their governments (e.g. Bacon's rebellion, the Paxton Boys Massacre)

Level IV (Grades 9-12)

BD (AE,59;LI,64-65)
- Understands influences on the development of government in colonial America (e.g., how different colonies adopted different laws and governmental frameworks, how demography influenced different forms of government in the colonies, how colonial institutions contributed to the growth of representative government)

BD (AE,59;LI,64-65)
- Understands the concept of the "rights of Englishmen" and the impact of the English Civil War, the Glorious Revolution, and Leisler's Rebellion on the colonies

---

Codes (right side of page):	BD = Benchmark, Declarative; BP = Benchmark, Procedural; BC = Benchmark, Contextual	
1st letter of each code in parentheses	*2nd letter of code*	*Number*
A = NCHS: National Standards for U.S. History	E = Explicitly stated in document	Page number of cited document
L = Lessons From History	I = Implied in document	
N = NAEP: Provisional Item Specifications		

MREL

- Understands the similarities and differences in colonial concepts of community (e.g., Puritan's covenant community, Chesapeake colonial emphasis on individualism) ^{BD (AE,59;LI,61-62)}

- Understands how gender, property ownership, religion, and legal status affected political rights (e.g., that women were not allowed to vote even if they held property and met religious requirements) ^{BD (AE,59)}

- Understands factors that challenged European ideas of hierarchy and deference, and contributed to the idea of participatory democracy (e.g., abundance of land, devotion to private property, the growth of individualism, a competitive entrepreneurial spirit) ^{BD (AE,59;LI,65)}

- Understands characteristics of religious development in colonial America (e.g., the major tenets of Puritanism and its legacy in American society, the dissension of Anne Hutchison and Roger Williams, and Puritan objections to their ideas and behavior, the presence of diverse religious groups and their contributions to religious freedom; the political and religious influence of the Great Awakening) ^{BD (AE,61;LI,61-62,67-68;NE,90;NI,90)}

- Understands the elements of ethnic, class, and race relations in conflicts between backwoodsmen and planters of colonial America (e.g., Bacon's Rebellion, Leisler's Rebellion, the Carolina Regulators and Paxton Boys revolts) ^{BD (AE,63)}

- Undertstands political factors that contributed to the development of representative government (e.g., conflict between the lower house of colonial legislatures and the governors; conflicts between legislative and executive branches in Virginia, New York, and Massachusetts government) ^{BD (AE,63)}

5. Understands how the values and institutions of European economic life took root in the colonies and how slavery reshaped European and African life in the Americas ^(AE,64)

Level II (Grades 5-6)

- Understands the factors that shaped the economic system in the colonies and the Americas (e.g., natural resources, relations with other countries and the home country, labor systems) ^{BD (AE,64;NE,45)}

- Understands economic life in the New England, Chesapeake, and southern colonies (e.g., the work people did; environmental conditions; the crops that plantation, yeoman, and family farmers grew) ^{BD (AE,66;LI,65,68;NE,44)}

Codes (right side of page):   BD = Benchmark, Declarative; BP = Benchmark, Procedural; BC = Benchmark, Contextual
1st letter of each code in parentheses   *2nd letter of code*   *Number*
A = NCHS: National Standards for U.S. History   E = Explicitly stated in document   Page number of cited document
L = Lessons From History   I = Implied in document
N = NAEP: Provisional Item Specifications

- Understands the factors that shaped trade patterns and labor in the colonies (e.g., New England merchants' trading triangle, free labor, indentured servitude, slavery) BD (AE,66;LI,65;NE,45)

- Understands elements of African slavery during the colonial period in North America (e.g., chattel slavery, the slave trade, and movement of enslaved Africans to the Caribbean and North America, influence of African heritage on slave life in the colonies) BD (AE,68;LI,65,68)

Level III (Grades 7-8)

- Understands the advantages and disadvantages of mercantilism for the mother country and its colonies; the value of the regions that produced sugar, rice, tobacco, timber, coffee, grains, fish and minerals to the mother country BD (AE,64)

- Understands the environmental and legislative impacts on economic growth in different regions of the English colonies (e.g., the influence of climate, land fertility, water resources, access to markets; the connection between the Navigation Acts and mercantilism) BD (AE,66)

- Understands patterns of indentured servitude and influences on slavery (e.g. why indentured servitude was prevalent in the mid-Atlantic, Chesapeake, and southern colonies; the Virginia and Massachusetts' laws that institutionalized slavery) BD (AE,67;LI,65,68;NE,45)

- Understands the social, cultural, and political events that shaped African slavery in colonial America (e.g., forced relocation of slaves to North America, the introduction of crops by African slaves, African efforts to develop a new culture, incidents of resistance to slavery) BD (AE,68;LE,68;LI,68)

Level IV (Grades 9-12)

- Understands the characteristics of mercantilism in colonial America (e.g., overseas trade and the Navigation Acts, the Atlantic economy and triangular trade, economic development in French, English, and Spanish colonies) BD (AE,64-65)

- Understands factors that influenced economic growth in the North American and West Indian colonies (e.g., land fertility, climate, access to the markets) BD (AE,67)

- Understands elements of slavery in the colonies in the 17th century (e.g., the emergence of chattle slavery in Virginia and Maryland, why free labor and chattel slavery did not provide an alternative for labor in the Chesapeake colonies before 1675) BD (AE,67;LI,65,68)

Codes (right side of page):	BD = Benchmark, Declarative; BP = Benchmark, Procedural; BC = Benchmark, Contextual
1st letter of each code in parentheses	*2nd letter of code* *Number*
A = NCHS: National Standards for U.S. History	E = Explicitly stated in document Page number of cited document
L = Lessons From History	I = Implied in document
N = NAEP: Provisional Item Specifications	

143   MREL

- Understands the contributions of African slaves to economic development in the Americas ^BD (AE,69) (e.g., contributions of rice cultivation and cattle raising in South Carolina) and the transmission of African cultural heritage (e.g., through religious practices, dances, and work songs)

- Understands the conditions of slavery (e.g., "the middle passage") and the response of ^BD (AE,69;LI,68) enslaved Africans (slave resistance in different parts of the Americas)

6. Understands the causes of the American Revolution, the ideas and interests involved ^(AE,72) **in shaping the revolutionary movement, and reasons for the American victory**

Level II (Grades 5-6)

- Understands the major consequences of the Seven Years War (e.g., the English victory, the ^BD (AE,72;LI,72-73) removal of the French as a power in North America, the reduced need of the colonists for the protection of the mother country)

- Understands the events that contributed to the outbreak of the American Revolution and the ^BD (AE,72;LE,73;LI,74;NE,46,51) earliest armed conflict of the Revolutionary War (e.g., the idea of "taxation without representation," the battle at Lexington and Concord)

- Understands the major ideas in the Declaration of Independence and their sources (e.g., ^BD (AE,74;LI,73-74;NE,48,50) major terms, why the document was written, what the signers risked)

- Understands the major developments and chronology of the Revolutionary War, the roles ^BD (AE,76;LE,74,75;NE,46;LI,75-76) of its leaders, and how the war affected the lives of the people

- Understands United States relationships with European countries and their contributions to ^BD (AE,78;LI,74-76,) the outcome of the Revolution (e.g., Ben Franklin's negotiations with the French, consequences of the Treaty of Paris, relations with Holland and Spain)

Level III (Grades 7-8)

- Understands how political and religious ideas joined economic interests to bring about the ^BD (AE,72-73;LE,73;LI,70-71,74;NE,46;NI,46,50) "shot heard 'round the world" (e.g., interests and positions of Loyalists, Patriots, and other groups; resistance to imperial policy; the English tax on the colonists to help pay for the Seven Years War)

Codes (right side of page): BD = Benchmark, Declarative; BP = Benchmark, Procedural; BC = Benchmark, Contextual
1st letter of each code in parentheses *2nd letter of code* *Number*
A = NCHS: National Standards for U.S. History E = Explicitly stated in document Page number of cited document
L = Lessons From History I = Implied in document
N = NAEP: Provisional Item Specifications

144

MREL

- Understands the creation of the Declaration of Independence (e.g., major principles set forth, historical antecedents that contributed to the document, individuals who struggled for independence)

  BD (AE,74;LE,75;LI,73-74;NE,47,NI,46)

- Understands contradictions between the Declaration of Independence and the institution of chattel slavery

  BD (AE,74)

- Understands perspectives of and the roles played in the American Revolution by various groups of people (e.g., Native Americans, African Americans)

  BD (AE,76-77;LI,74-75;NE,49,51)

- Understands the strategic and financial elements of the Revolutionary War (e.g., major military campaigns; American and British military leaders, successes and failures in efforts to finance the war)

  BD (AE,76-77;LI,74-75)

- Understands the impact of European countries and individuals on the American victory (e.g., interest, goals, and actions of France, Holland, and Spain; contributions of European individuals)

  BD (AE,78;LI,74-76)

- Understands the terms of the Treaty of Paris and implications for U.S. relationships with Native Americans and European powers who still held interests and territory in North America

  BD (AE,78;LI,74-76;NI,51)

Level IV (Grades 9-12)

- Understands the social, political, and religious aspects of the American Revolution (e.g., opponents and defenders of England's new imperial policy; decisions leading to crisis of revolution; efforts by Parliament and colonies to prevent revolution; ideas of different religions; economic and social differences of Loyalists, Patriots, and neutrals)

  BD (AE,73;LE,73;LI,71-74)

- Understands how other writings influenced the ideas of the Declaration of Independence and how other government documents compare to it (e.g., influence of John Locke's *Two Treatises on Government* and how it compares to the French Declaration of the Rights of Man and Citizen)

  BD (AE,75;LI,73-74;NI,94)

- Understands the arguments of advocates and opponents of slavery from different regions of the country during the revolutionary period (e.g., how pro-slavery Americans justified their defense of slavery with their espousal of inalienable rights to freedom, how enslaved African Americans employed revolutionary ideals to obtain their freedom)

  BD (AE,75;LI,75)

Codes (right side of page):	BD = Benchmark, Declarative; BP = Benchmark, Procedural; BC = Benchmark, Contextual	
1st letter of each code in parentheses	*2nd letter of code*	*Number*
A = NCHS: National Standards for U.S. History	E = Explicitly stated in document	Page number of cited document
L = Lessons From History	I = Implied in document	
N = NAEP: Provisional Item Specifications		

145

M&REL

- Understands how the principles of the Declaration of Independence justified American independence _{BD (AE,74;LI,73-74;NI,94)}

- Understands the major political and strategic factors that led to the American victory in the Revolutionary War (e.g., leadership of the war, the importance of the Battle of Saratoga, the use of guerilla and conventional warfare, the importance of King's Mountain in defining the war) _{BD (AE,77;LE,75;LI,74;NI,93-94)}

- Understands the social and economic impact of the Revolutionary War (e.g., personal impact and economic hardship on families involved in the war, problems of financing the war, wartime inflation, hoarding and profiteering) _{BD (AE,76;LI,75-76)}

- Understands the military and diplomatic factors that helped produce the Treaty of Paris _{BD (AE,77;LI,74)}

- Understands contributions of European nations during the American Revolution and how their involvement influenced the outcome and aftermath (e.g., the assistance of France and Spain in the war, how self-interests of France and Spain differed from those of the United States after the war, the effect of American diplomatic initiatives and the contributions of the European military leaders on the outcome of the war) _{BD (AE,78-79;LI,74-76)}

- Understands how the Treaty of Paris influenced U.S. relations with other countries and indigenous peoples (e.g., the resulting boundary disputes with Spain; influences on economic and strategic interests of the United States, Native Americans, Spain, England, and France; the impact of the Jay Gardoqui Treaty of 1786) _{B.D. (AE,79;LI,74-76;NI,98)}

7. **Understands how the American Revolution involved multiple movements among the new nation's many groups to reform American society** _(AE,80)

Level II (Grades 5-6)

- Understands the social, political, and economic effects of the American revolutionary victory on different groups (e.g., small farmers, wealthy merchants, women who contributed to the war effort, and Native Americans and newly freed African Americans who had fought on either side of the war) _{BD (AE,80;LI,75-76)}

Codes (right side of page):   BD = Benchmark, Declarative; BP = Benchmark, Procedural; BC = Benchmark, Contextual
1st letter of each code in parentheses   *2nd letter of code*   *Number*
A = NCHS: National Standards for U.S. History   E = Explicitly stated in document   Page number of cited document
L = Lessons From History   I = Implied in document
N = NAEP: Provisional Item Specifications

McREL

Level III (Grades 7-8)

BD (AE,80-81;75-76;NE,49)

- Understands how the ideals of the American Revolution influenced the goals of various groups of people during and after the war (e.g., women, Loyalists, Native Americans, enslaved and free African Americans, abolitionists during and after the war, young people)

Level IV (Grades 9-12)

BD (AE,81;LE,75;LI,75-76;NI,96)

- Understands the goals of different groups of people after the Revolution (e.g., the influence of the American victory in advancing or retarding goals of different groups, the evolution of womens' political rights, the importance of African American leaders and institutions)

(AE,82)

8. Understands the institutions and practices of government created during the revolution and how these elements were revised between 1787 and 1815 to create the foundation of the American political system

Level II (Grades 5-6)

BD (AE,82;LE,76;LI,76,81-82;NE,46)

- Understands the major political issues in the thirteen colonies after their independence from England (e.g., how to govern themselves, how the Articles of Confederation apportioned power to the states and the Continental Congress, the cession of western lands to the government)

BD (AE,84;LI,81-82;NE,46;NI,49)

- Understands the issues and ideas supported and opposed by delegates at the Constitutional Convention (e.g., the Virginia Plan, the New Jersey Plan, the Connecticut Compromise, abolition, the separation of powers, checks and balances)

BD (AE,84;LE,82;NE,48)

- Understands the importance of Shay's Rebellion

BD (AE,86;LI,83)

- Knows some of the guarantees in the Bill of Rights and understands the relevance of the Bill of Rights in today's society

BD (AE,88)

- Understands the issues that impacted the lives of farmers in western Pennsylvania during the Whiskey Rebellion

BD (AE,88;LE,83)

- Understands the differences in leaders (e.g., Alexander Hamilton and Thomas Jefferson) and the social and economic composition of each political party in the 1790s

---

Codes (right side of page):   BD = Benchmark, Declarative; BP = Benchmark, Procedural; BC = Benchmark, Contextual
1st letter of each code in parentheses   *2nd letter of code*   *Number*
A = NCHS: National Standards for U.S. History   E = Explicitly stated in document   Page number of cited document
L = Lessons From History   I = Implied in document
N = NAEP: Provisional Item Specifications

Level III (Grades 7-8)

- Understands land policies developed under the Continental Congress (e.g., sale of western lands, Northwest Ordinance of 1787) BD (AE,82;LE,76;LI,81-82;NE,46)

- Understands events that led to and shaped the Constitutional Convention (e.g., Shay's Rebellion, the accomplishments and failures of the Articles of Confederation, alternative plans, and major compromises considered by delegates) BD (AE,82,84,85;LE,82;LI,81-82;NE,46;NI,48)

- Understands the importance of the guarantees in the Bill of Rights and Anti-Federalist arguments for its inclusion into the Constitution BD (AE,86;LE,80;NI,46)

- Understands the development and impact of the American party system (e.g., social and economic issues of the 1790s, the rise of the Federalist and Democratic-Republican parties, the election of 1800, and the appointment of the "midnight judges") BD (AE,88;LI,78,83-84;NE,47)

- Understands the role of ordinary people in the Whiskey Rebellion and in demonstrations against Jay's Treaty (e.g., the causes of the rebellion, similarities and differences between rebellion against the whiskey tax and British taxation during the revolutionary period, why western farmers objected to Jay's Treaty) BD (AE,88;LI,83-84)

- Understands the establishment of power and significant events in the development of the U.S. Supreme Court (e.g., Article III of the Constitution, Judiciary Act of 1789, *Marbury* v. *Madison*, the role of Chief Justice Marshall in the growth of the court) BD (AE,90;LE,84;LI,84;NE,47,52)

Level IV (Grades 9-12)

- Understands the policies and changes in government organization from the Continental Congress to the Constitutional Convention (e.g., state constitutions reflecting 18th century republicanism, accomplishments and failures of the Continental Congress, the importance of the Northwest Ordinance, arguments over the Articles of Confederation) BD (AE,82,83;LE,76;LI,81-82,84;NE,96)

- Understands ideas the Constitution established, and events that led to the adoption of it (e.g., the ideas of distribution of powers and the system of checks and balances, the role of Shays' Rebellion in calling for a Constitutional Convention, the compromises agreed upon to secure the approval of the Constitution) BD (AE,85;LE,81-82;LI,82,83;NI,93)

- Understands how Federalists and Anti-Federalists differed (e.g., their backgrounds, service during the Revolution, political experience, and their arguments for and against the Constitution of 1787) BD (AE, 85;LI,83)

Codes (right side of page):   BD = Benchmark, Declarative; BP = Benchmark, Procedural; BC = Benchmark, Contextual
1st letter of each code in parentheses   *2nd letter of code*   *Number*
A = NCHS: National Standards for U.S. History   E = Explicitly stated in document   Page number of cited document
L = Lessons From History   I = Implied in document
N = NAEP: Provisional Item Specifications

MREL

- Understands the Bill of Rights and various challenges to it (e.g., specific guarantees of the Bill, arguments by Federalists and Anti-Federalists over the need for a Bill of Rights, the Alien and Sedition Acts) ^{BD (AE,86,87;LE,80,83-84)}

- Understands the factors that led to the development of the two-party system (e.g., Hamilton's financial plan, the emergence of an organized opposition party, social and economic makeup of the Federalist and Democratic-Republican parties of the 1790s) ^{BD (AE,89;LI,83-84)}

- Understands the factors that led to the Whiskey Rebellion (e.g., the extent to which the rebellion was a confrontation between the haves and the have-nots; the government's reaction; similarities and differences between grievances of the Whiskey Rebels and those of the Regulators, the Paxton Boys, and the Shaysites) ^{BD (AE,89;LI,83-84)}

- Understands the significance of Chief Justice Marshall's decisions on the development of the Supreme Court (e.g., *Marbury* v. *Madison* [1803]; *Dartmouth College* v. *Woodward* [1819]; *Gibbons* v. *Ogden* [1824]; *McCulloch* v. *Maryland*) ^{BD (AE,89;NI,93,94)}

- Understands how the stature and significance of the federal judiciary changed during the 1790s and early 19th century, and the influence of the Supreme Court today ^{BD (AE,89;LI,93)}

9. **Understands the United States territorial expansion between 1801 and 1861, and how it affected relations with external powers and Native Americans** ^(AE,94)

Level II (Grades 5-6)

- Understands the factors that led to U.S. territorial expansion in the Western Hemisphere (e.g., expeditions of American explorers and mountain men, the Louisiana Purchase) ^{BD (AE,94;LI,101-102;NI,53)}

- Knows the foreign territorial claims in the Western Hemisphere in 1800 and the impact on American foreign policy (e.g., Spain, France, Britain, and Russia's claims; nations that declared their independence in 1823; how President Monroe dealt with European attempts to reestablish control) ^{BD (AE,94;NI,57)}

- Understands the War of 1812 (e.g., causes, sectional divisions, defining the war) ^{BD (AE,95)}

- Understands the impact of territorial expansion on Native American tribes (e.g., the original lands held by various tribes of the Southeast and those held in the Old Northwest territory, Native American efforts to retain their lands and resist removal policies, the significance of ^{BD (AE,97;LI,100-101,103)}

Codes (right side of page):
1st letter of each code in parentheses
A = NCHS: National Standards for U.S. History
L = Lessons From History
N = NAEP: Provisional Item Specifications

BD = Benchmark, Declarative; BP = Benchmark, Procedural; BC = Benchmark, Contextual
2nd letter of code
E = Explicitly stated in document
I = Implied in document

Number
Page number of cited document

MREL

the Trail of Tears)

- Understands elements of the relationship between Texas and Mexico in the mid-19th century (e.g., American settlement in Mexico's Texas, the Texas Revolution, the American defeat at the Alamo) BD (AE,99;LI,99;NI,57)

- Understands events that led to the Mexican-American War (e.g., U.S. annexation of Texas, the idea of Manifest Destiny, the invasion of Mexico by U.S. troops) BD (AE,99;LI,102;NI,57)

Level III (Grades 7-8)

- Understands the significance of the Lewis and Clark expedition (e.g., its role as a scientific expedition, its contributions to friendly relations with Native Americans) BD (AE,95;LE,102)

- Understands the major events of U.S. domestic and foreign policy during the early 19th century (e.g., the impact of territorial expansion on Native Americans, the Monroe Doctrine, renewed French-English hostilities, the War of 1812) BD (AE,95;LI,84,100-101;NE,53,57)

- Understands the short-term political and long-term cultural impacts of the Louisiana Purchase (e.g., those who opposed and supported the acquisition, the impact on Native Americans between 1801 and 1861) BD (AE,95;LI,93;LE,90,98,100-101;NI,53)

- Understands how early state and federal policy influenced various Native American tribes (e.g., survival strategies by individual Native American leaders, the Cherokee and Choctaw removals, environmental differences between Native American homelands and resettlement areas, the Black Hawk War and removal policies in the Old Northwest) BD (AE,97,98;LI,99,101,103)

- Understands the social and political impact of the idea of Manifest Destiny (e.g., its appeal to 19th century American industrial workers and small farmers, its role in the Mexican-American war; how it was reflected in the Treaty of Guadalupe Hidalgo, how it fueled the controversy over the Oregon territory) BD (AE,99,100;LI,99,102;NI,57)

- Understands the diplomatic and political developments that led to the resolution of conflicts with Britain and Russia in the period 1815-1850 BD (AE,99;LI,102)

Level IV (Grades 9-12)

- Understands the Louisiana Purchase (e.g., factors that led to Napoleon's sale of the Lousiana Territory; how the purchase of the Louisiana Territory was justified; its impact on economic BD (AE,96;LI,102;NI,100)

Codes (right side of page): BD = Benchmark, Declarative; BP = Benchmark, Procedural; BC = Benchmark, Contextual
1st letter of each code in parentheses *2nd letter of code* *Number*
A = NCHS: National Standards for U.S. History E = Explicitly stated in document Page number of cited document
L = Lessons From History I = Implied in document
N = NAEP: Provisional Item Specifications

150 MCREL

development, slavery, politics, and French and Spanish inhabitants)

- Understands political interests and views regarding the War of 1812 (e.g., U.S. responses to shipping harassments prior to the war; reasons for dissent and sectional interests regarding the war; interests of Native American and white settlers of the Northwest Territory during the war; congressional positions for and against the war resolution of June 3, 1812)
  BD (AE,96;LI,84,93,101)

- Understands the major provisions of the Monroe Doctrine (e.g., the extent to which its major purpose was to protect the newly won independence of Latin American states or to serve notice of U.S. expansionist intentions in the hemisphere, why the U.S. and other countries ignored the provisions of the doctrine for so long, its impact today)
  BD (AE,96;NI,104)

- Understands shifts in the U.S. government's policy toward Native Americans in the first half of the 19th century (e.g., from assimilation to removal and isolation after 1825, arguments for and against removal policy, Cherokee resistance to removal and their attempts to retain their cultural heritage)
  BD (AE,98;LI,101,103)

- Understands the initiating factors and outcomes of the Mexican-American War (e.g., the extent to which President Polk bore responsibility for initiating the war, whether the war was justified, arguments for and against the war, the Treaty of Guadalupe Hidalgo, and its impacts on the U.S. and Mexico)
  BD (AE,100;LI,99,102;NI,104)

- Understands Mexican and American perspectives of events leading to the Mexican-American War (e.g., the Alamo, the treatment of Mexicans and Cherokees loyal to the Texas Revolution in the Lone Star Republic prior to 1846)
  BD (AE,100;NI,105)

- Understands the religious, political, and social ideas that contributed to the 19th century belief in Manifest Destiny (e.g., the "City Upon a Hill," Protestant beliefs in building a model Christian community, millennialism and the Great Awakening, Republicanism, the urge to keep foreign enemies from gaining control of adjacent areas and the Pacific Coast, the belief in America's duty to uplift "less civilized" peoples in the West)
  BD (AE,100)

10. Understands how the industrial revolution, the rapid expansion of slavery, and the westward movement changed American lives and led to regional tensions
(AE,101)

Level II (Grades 5-6)

- Understands the major technological developments that influenced transportation, the
  BD (AE,101;LE,90,91;LI,91;NI,56)

Codes (right side of page): BD = Benchmark, Declarative; BP = Benchmark, Procedural; BC = Benchmark, Contextual
1st letter of each code in parentheses *2nd letter of code* *Number*
A = NCHS: National Standards for U.S. History E = Explicitly stated in document Page number of cited document
L = Lessons From History I = Implied in document
N = NAEP: Provisional Item Specifications

151

MREL

economy, international markets, and the environment between 1801 and 1860 (e.g., the importance of the spinning jenny, steam locomotive, and telegraph; the development of the canal system after 1825 and railroad system after 1860)

BD (AE,102,104;LE,91;LI,87,90;NI,56)
- Understands social and economic elements of urban and rural life in the early and mid-19th centuries (e.g., differences in urban and rural childrens' lives, life in New England mill towns in the early 1800s, the impact of the canal and railroad on the locations and size of cities after 1820, why immigrants came to America, city life in the 1840s)

BD (AE,106;LE,110;LI,110-111;NI,55)
- Understands how slavery shaped social and economic life in the South after 1800 (e.g., differences in the lives of poor free black and white families, slaves, and plantation owners; escaped slaves and the Underground Railroad; "King Cotton" and increased demands for slaves)

BD (AE,108;LE,98.100-101,103;LI,102)
- Understands elements of early western migration (e.g., routes taken by settlers of the Western U.S.; motivations of various settlers, including the Mormons; cultural interactions between settlers and Native Americans in the trans-Mississippi West in the first half of the 19th century)

Level III (Grades 7-8)

BD (AE,101-102;LI,90,91-92;NE,56)
- Understands the social and economic impacts of the factory system (e.g., daily life of men, women, and children; child labor in New England mills; its role in developing a labor movement in the antebellum period)

BD (AE,101-102;LI,93)
- Understands the role of government in various areas of public service in the early 1800s (e.g., national and state policies regarding protective tarriffs and a national bank, the controversy over internal improvements)

BD (AE,101;LE,91;LI,90,91)
- Understands how major technological and economic developments influenced various facets of society (e.g., land and water transportation; business owners, farmers, workers in different regions; international markets)

BD (AE,104;LE,91,92)
- Understands influences on urban life in the early and late 19th century (e.g., how rapid urbanization, immigration, and industrialization disrupted the social fabric of cities; individuals who contributed to the development of free black communities in the cities)

BD (AE,106-107;LE,110;LI,110-111;NI,54)
- Understands different economic, cultural, and social characteristics of slavery after 1800 (e.g., impact of the cotton gin on slavery, how slaves forged their own culture in the face of

---

Codes (right side of page):   BD = Benchmark, Declarative; BP = Benchmark, Procedural; BC = Benchmark, Contextual
1st letter of each code in parentheses   *2nd letter of code*   *Number*
A = NCHS: National Standards for U.S. History   E = Explicitly stated in document   Page number of cited document
L = Lessons From History   I = Implied in document
N = NAEP: Provisional Item Specifications

oppression, methods of passive and active resistance to slavery, the experiences of escaped slaves; the role of the plantation system in shaping slaveholders and the enslaved)

- Understands characteristics of life on the western frontier in the 19th century (e.g., how the folklore image of the West differed from the reality of daily life in the West, the cultural interaction between diverse groups, how the Mormons established the Church of Latter Day Saints and their communities) BD (AE,108-109;LE,99,100-101,103;LI,94)

Level IV (Grades 9-12)

- Understands the impact of the Industrial Revolution during the early and later 19th century (e.g., the impact of industrialization on the environment, the growth and spread of the factory system in New England, labor conflicts of the antebellum period) BD (AE,103;LE,90-91;LI,88,92)

- Understands characteristics of economic development during the 19th century (e.g., how early 19th century court cases promoted the market revolution; the causes and results of economic depressions of 1819, 1837, and 1857; how expansion-based economic policies contributed to growing political and sectional differences; the pattern of economic development in different regions of the country during the first half of the 19th century) BD (AE,101,103;LE,91-92,93;LI,85-86,92,93)

- Understands policies affecting regional and national interests during the early 19th century (e.g., a protective tariff; a national bank; internal improvements at federal expense; a cheap price for the sale of western lands to residents of the North, South, and West; Andrew Jackson's veto of the Bank Recharter Bill of 1832) BD (AE,103;LE,88,93)

- Understands popular and high culture in growing urban areas during the 19th century (e.g., novels, theater, minstrel shows, P.T. Barnum's "American Museum") BD (AE,104-105;LI,86,92)

- Understands changes in urban centers during the 19th century (e.g., factors that led to rapid growth in northern, southern, and western cities; factors that contributed to urban conflict and tension from 1830 to 1861) BD (AE,105;LE,92;LI,91)

- Understands the social and cultural influence of former slaves in cities of the North (e.g., their leadership of African American communities, how they advanced the rights and interests of African Americans) BD (AE,105)

- Understands the factors that helped to fuel the slave trade during the antebellum period (e.g., the invention of the cotton gin, opening of new lands in the South and West, why few church leaders and non-slaveholders spoke against the internal slave trade) BD (AE,107;LE,110;NI,103)

Codes (right side of page):   BD = Benchmark, Declarative; BP = Benchmark, Procedural; BC = Benchmark, Contextual
1st letter of each code in parentheses   *2nd letter of code*   *Number*
A = NCHS: National Standards for U.S. History   E = Explicitly stated in document   Page number of cited document
L = Lessons From History   I = Implied in document
N = NAEP: Provisional Item Specifications

McREL

- Understands how slavery influenced economic and social elements of Southern society (e.g., ^{BD (AE,107)} how slavery influenced development of the middle class and hindered the emergence of capitalist institutions, influence of slave revolts on the lifes of slaves and freed slaves)

- Understands significant religious, cultural, and social changes in the American West (e.g., ^{BD (AE,109;LE,101,103;LI,94,103)} cultural conflict between different groups, impact of the Second Great Awakening and religious revivals on Mormon migration to the West, the degree to which political democracy influenced social and political conditions on the frontier, cultural characteristics of diverse groups, the lives of women in the West)

11. Understands the extension, restriction, and reorganization of political democracy after 1800 (AE,110)

Level II (Grades 5-6)

- Understands why the election of Andrew Jackson was considered a victory for the "common ^{BD (AE,110)} man" (e.g., the "spoils system," Jackson's interest in providing the "common man" with opportunities to serve in government)

- Understands divisive issues prior to the Civil War (e.g., the Missouri Compromise and its ^{BD (AE,112;LE,111-112)} role in determining slave and non-slave land areas, the issues that divided the North and the South)

Level III (Grades 7-8)

- Understands elements of suffrage in the antebellum years (e.g., changes in electoral ^{BD (AE,111;LE,92;NI,52)} qualifications for white males, contradictions between the movement for universal white male suffrage and disenfranchisement of free African Americans)

- Understands political influences and views after 1800 (e.g., the influence of the West and ^{BD (AE,111;LE,92,93)} western politcians in supporting equal opportunity in the political process, opposing views of President Jackson's position on the bank recharter and nullification issues)

- Understands political issues that were influenced by slavery (e.g., support and opposition of ^{BD (AE,112;LE,111-112;LI,88)} the Missouri Compromise of 1820, the debate over slavery from the late 1830s to the Compromise of 1850)

Codes (right side of page):   BD = Benchmark, Declarative; BP = Benchmark, Procedural; BC = Benchmark, Contextual
1st letter of each code in parentheses   *2nd letter of code*   *Number*
A = NCHS: National Standards for U.S. History   E = Explicitly stated in document   Page number of cited document
L = Lessons From History   I = Implied in document
N = NAEP: Provisional Item Specifications

MREL

BD (AE,112;LE,93)

- Understands the political positions of Whigs and Democrats on the issues of 1832 (e.g., how tariff policy and state's rights had special appeal to different sections of the country)

Level IV (Grades 9-12)

BD (AE,110,111;LE,92,93)

- Understands elements of politics in the first half of the 19th century (e.g., changes in American politics; factors that affected the vitality of the National Republican, Democratic, Whig, and "Know-Nothing" parties, including President Jackson's actions in the bank war and in the nullification controversy)

BD (AE,113;LE,102;LI,88,111)

- Understands the major events that promoted sectional conflicts and strained national cohesiveness in the antebellum period (e.g., the Missouri controversy, the Mexican War)

BD (AE,113;LE,111-112)

- Understands the positions of northern antislavery advocates and southern proslavery spokesmen on a variety of issues (e.g., race, chattel slavery, the nature of the Union, states' rights)

(AE,114)

12. Understands the sources and character of reform movements in the antebellum period and what the reforms accomplished or failed to accomplish

Level II (Grades 5-6)

BD (AE,114;LE,95;LI,94-95)

- Understands the major characteristics of the abolition movement in the antebellum period (e.g., arguments of those opposed to and those who support slavery, the Underground Railroad, accomplishments and importance of African American and white abolitionist leaders)

BD (AE,116;LE,94)

- Understands the religious revivals that swept the nation in the early 19th century (e.g., the messages of leaders such as Charles Finney and Peter Cartwright, how the Second Great Awakening influenced reform movements)

BD (AE,118;LE,95-96;NE,55)

- Understands the role of women in the reform movements in antebellum America (e.g., the contributions of individuals, the types of reforms women sought, how fashion became a part of the movement for women's rights)

Codes (right side of page):   BD = Benchmark, Declarative; BP = Benchmark, Procedural; BC = Benchmark, Contextual
1st letter of each code in parentheses   *2nd letter of code*   *Number*
A = NCHS: National Standards for U.S. History   E = Explicitly stated in document   Page number of cited document
L = Lessons From History   I = Implied in document
N = NAEP: Provisional Item Specifications

McREL

Level III (Grades 7-8)

- Understands events and perspectives that influenced slavery in the antebellum period (e.g., the influence of the Haitian Revolution on African Americans, arguments used to defend slavery in the 18th and 19th centuries, different viewpoints within the abolitionist movement) BD (AE,114-115;LI,96)

- Understands the significant religious, philosophical, and social movements of the 19th century and their impacts on American society and social reform (e.g., the revivalist spirit of the Second Great Awakening, transcendentalism and its central leaders, utopian communities of the early 19th century) BD (AE,116,117;LE,94;LI,88,93,95)

- Understands how women influenced reform movements and American society during the antebellum period (e.g., changing roles of women of different racial, regional, and social groups; the Seneca Falls "Declaration of Sentiments" of 1848; the leadership role women played in major reform movements) BD (AE,118-119;LE,96;LI,89;NE,54;NI,53)

Level IV (Grades 9-12)

- Understands elements of slavery in both the North and South during the antebellum period (e.g., defense of chattel slavery by slaveholders, growing hostility toward free blacks in the North, how African American leaders fought for rights, similarities and differences between African American and white abolitionists) BD (AE,115;LE,94-95)

- Understands the social impact of the Second Great Awakening (e.g., public education, temperance, women's suffrage, abolitionism) BD (AE,117;LE,95-96;NI,102)

- Understands the ideas of Transcendentalism (e.g., views of Transcendentalists about individualism, society, good and evil, authority, tradition, and reform; similarities and differences between Transcendentalists and evangelical Protestants) BD (AE,117;LI,88,95)

- Understands the development of Utopian communities (e.g., origins, beliefs, size, how their ideas compared to Transcendentalists) BD (AE,117)

- Understands how women influenced the antebellum period in America (e.g., contributions of individual women in reform movements; how gender influenced geographical regions, class, ethnic, racial, and religious lines) BD (AE,119;LE,96)

- Understands the ideas associated with women's rights during the antebellum period (e.g., how the Seneca Falls "Declaration of Sentiments" relates to the ideas of the Declaration of BD (AE,119;LI,89,96)

Codes (right side of page):   BD = Benchmark, Declarative; BP = Benchmark, Procedural; BC = Benchmark, Contextual
1st letter of each code in parentheses   *2nd letter of code*   *Number*
A = NCHS: National Standards for U.S. History   E = Explicitly stated in document   Page number of cited document
L = Lessons From History   I = Implied in document
N = NAEP: Provisional Item Specifications

156

McREL

Independence, the connection between the evangelical movement and the idea of southern woman, how the status of women has evolved since the 19th century)

(AE,122)

13. Understands the causes of the Civil War

Level II (Grades 5-6)

BD (AE,122;LI,90,110)
- Knows the locations of the southern and northern states and their economic resources (e.g., the industries and small family farms of the industrial North, the agricultural economy and slavery of the South)

BD (AE,122;LE,94-95,110,111;NE,58)
- Understands slavery prior to the Civil War (e.g., the growing influence of abolitionists, childrens' roles and family life under slavery, the importance of slavery as a principal cause of the Civil War)

Level III (Grades 7-8)

BD (AE,123;LE,112;LI,111-112;NI,58)
- Understands the development of sectional polarization and secession prior to the Civil War (e.g., how events from the Compromise of 1850 to Harper's Ferry impacted sectional differences, the effectiveness of presidential leadership during secession)

BD (AE,123;LI,110-111;NI,60)
- Understands the impact of social and economic differences between the North and South and how the free labor system of the North differed from that of the South

BD (AE,123;LE,112)
- Understands the extent to which slavery was the primary cause of the Civil War and how other issues contributed to the conflict (e.g., cultural differences, conflicting economic issues, opposing constitutional perspectives)

Level IV (Grades 9-12)

BD (AE,123;LI,112)
- Understands events that fueled the political and sectional conflicts over slavery and ultimately polarized the North and the South (e.g., Missouri Compromise, Wilmot Proviso, Kansas-Nebraska Act, the Dred Scott decision and controversy)

BD (AE,123)
- Understands factors that influenced the secession crisis prior to the Civil War (e.g., southern justification for secession, the presidential leadership of Buchanan and Lincoln during the secession crisis)

Codes (right side of page):   BD = Benchmark, Declarative; BP = Benchmark, Procedural; BC = Benchmark, Contextual
1st letter of each code in parentheses   *2nd letter of code*   *Number*
A = NCHS: National Standards for U.S. History   E = Explicitly stated in document   Page number of cited document
L = Lessons From History   I = Implied in document
N = NAEP: Provisional Item Specifications

McREL

- Understands the reasons for the disruption of the second American party system in the 1850s ^{BD (AE,123)} and how this led to the ascent of the Republican party

14. Understands the course and character of the Civil War and its effects on the American people ^(AE,124)

Level II (Grades 5-6)

- Understands the social and strategic aspects of the Civil War and technological ^{BD (AE,124;LE,113;NI,61)} developments used during that conflict (e.g., conditions, characteristics, armies, leaders of the Confederacy and Union; innovations in military technology; major areas of Civil War combat)

- Understands the Emancipation Proclamation (e.g., reasons Abraham Lincoln issued it, public ^{BD (AE,124;LI,113;NI,59)} reactions to it in the North and the South)

- Understands the impact of the Civil War on social and gender issues (e.g., how it changed ^{BD (AE,126;LE,107,114)} the lives of women, men, and children; the human cost of the war; the roles of women on the home front and on the battlefield)

- Understands motives of different types of soldiers in the Civil War (e.g., Confederate, white, ^{BD (AE,126)} African American Union soldiers)

Level III (Grades 7-8)

- Understands the circumstances that shaped the Civil War and its outcome (e.g., major ^{BD (AE,125;LE,113;NE,59;NI,61)} battles, military technology, the Emancipation Proclamation; differences between the economic, technological, and human resources of both sides)

- Understands how different groups of people shaped the Civil War (e.g., how motives of ^{BD (AE,126-127;LE,114;LI,113;NE,59;NI,61)} Union and Confederate soldiers changed, contributions of African American soldiers, different perspectives on conscription, the role and contributions of women, the effects of divided loyalties)

Level IV (Grades 9-12)

- Understands military events that influenced the outcome of the Civil War (e.g., the ^{BD (AE,125;LE,113)}

Codes (right side of page):   BD = Benchmark, Declarative; BP = Benchmark, Procedural; BC = Benchmark, Contextual
1st letter of each code in parentheses   *2nd letter of code*   *Number*
A = NCHS: National Standards for U.S. History   E = Explicitly stated in document   Page number of cited document
L = Lessons From History   I = Implied in document
N = NAEP: Provisional Item Specifications

MREL

"hammering campaigns" of Generals Grant and Sherman, the wartime leadership of Jefferson Davis and Abraham Lincoln)

- Understands the influence of Abraham Lincoln's ideas on the Civil War (e.g., the Emancipation Proclamation, the Gettysburg Address) BD (AE,125)

- Understands different Native American responses to the Civil War (e.g., how Native Americans in the West were affected by the Civil War, the internal conflicts among the "Five Civilized Tribes" regarding their support for the Union or Confederacy, the long-term consequences for Native Americans) BD (AE,125)

- Understands how the Civil War influenced both military personnel and civilians (e.g., the treatment of African American soldiers in the Union Army and Confederacy, the roles of women at home and on the battlefront, the effects of the Civil War on civilians, and the human cost of the war in the North and South) BD (AE,127;LE,107,114;NI,107)

- Understands how the Civil War influenced Northern and Southern society on the home front (e.g., the New York city draft riots of July 1863, the need for the Union to curb wartime civil liberties, Lincoln's suspension of the writ of habeas corpus during the war) BD (AE,127)

15. Understands how various reconstruction plans succeeded or failed (AE,128)

Level II (Grades 5-6)

- Understands military, political, and social factors affecting the post Civil War period (e.g., demobilization of the Union and Confederate armies; how the leadership of Presidents Lincoln and Johnson affected reconstruction; the basic provisions of the 13th, 14th, and 15th amendments, how the lives of African Americans were changed by them, and the political and social forces that opposed and supported them) BD (AE,128;LE,106,109;LI,113;NE,58;NI,60)

- Understands changes in social relations in the South during Reconstruction (e.g., the impact of emancipation in the South, how former slaves improved their position in society, the role of the Freedmen's Bureau, how people from the North traveled to aid in Reconstruction) BD (AE,130;LE,115;NE,60)

- Understands how economic conditions and family life in the North and South changed over the war years BD (AE,132)

- Understands the lives of African Americans during the Reconstruction era (e.g., individual BD (AE,132)

Codes (right side of page):　　　　　BD = Benchmark, Declarative; BP = Benchmark, Procedural; BC = Benchmark, Contextual
1st letter of each code in parentheses　　　*2nd letter of code*　　　　　*Number*
A = NCHS: National Standards for U.S. History　　E = Explicitly stated in document　　Page number of cited document
L = Lessons From History　　　　　　I = Implied in document
N = NAEP: Provisional Item Specifications

159　　　　　　　　　　　　　　　　MᴄREL

African Americans who served as teachers and political leaders, why some abolition leaders voiced opposition to the 15th amendment)

- Understands the impact of the Reconstruction period on politics in the South ^{BD (AE,132;LI,116)} (e.g., the increase in corruption in the post-Civil War period and the importance of political cartoonists in drawing attention to it)

Level III (Grades 7-8)

- Understands the effect of differing Reconstruction policies and how they were perceived ^{BD (AE,128;LE,114-115;NI,60)} (e.g., plans advocated by President Lincoln, congressional leaders, and President Johnson; the basic principles of the Reconstruction amendments; the Compromise of 1877)

- Understands the factors that led to President Andrew Johnson's impeachment ^{BD (AE,128-129)} (e.g., his resistance to congressional authority, the Tenure of Office Act)

- Understands attempts to improve African American lives during Reconstruction ^{BD (AE,130,131;LI,115;NI,58)} (e.g., the successes and failures of the Freedmen's Bureau, African American attempts to improve their economic position)

- Understands the economic and social problems facing the South and their impact on different ^{BD (AE,130;NI,61)} groups of people at the close of the Civil War

- Understands changes in the political and social structure in different regions during ^{BD (AE,133;LI,115-116;NE,59,NI,60)} Reconstruction (e.g., contributions of African Americans who served in state and national offices, changes in political and economic positions of African Americans in the North, increasing political corruption, changes in gender roles and status in the North and West, personal challenges to Freedmen)

- Understands the differing historical views of Reconstruction ^{BD (AE,133)} (e.g., as a revolution, as having failed because of lack of commitment to carry out its basic goals and pledges)

Level IV (Grades 9-12)

- Understands the elements of different plans for Reconstruction ^{BD (AE,129;LI,114-115)} (e.g., the Lincoln, Johnson, and Radical Republican plans)

- Understands the 14th and 15th amendments to the Constitution ^{BD (AE,129;LI,115;NI,107)} (e.g., how citizenship was included, why the clauses of "equal protection of the laws" and "due process" were included,

---

Codes (right side of page):   BD = Benchmark, Declarative; BP = Benchmark, Procedural; BC = Benchmark, Contextual
1st letter of each code in parentheses   *2nd letter of code*   *Number*
A = NCHS: National Standards for U.S. History   E = Explicitly stated in document   Page number of cited document
L = Lessons From History   I = Implied in document
N = NAEP: Provisional Item Specifications

MREL

why women were excluded in the 15th amendment)

BD (AE,129;LI,115-116)

- Understands events leading to the formation of the Compromise of 1877 (e.g., the role of violence and tactics of the "redeemers" in bringing about the Compromise, the consequences in the South)

BD (AE,129)

- Understands the conflict between President Johnson and Republican legislators and the reasons for and consequences of Johnson's impeachment and trial

BD (AE,131;LI,115-116)

- Understands factors that inhibited and fostered African American attempts to improve their lives during Reconstruction (e.g., how traditional values inhibited the role of the Freedmen's Bureau, the struggle between former masters and former slaves, the role of black churches and schools in providing self-help within the African American community)

BD (AE,134)

- Understands the extent to which social and political issues were influenced by the Civil War and Reconstruction (e.g., gender roles and status, corruption in state and national politics)

BD (AE,133;LI,115-116)

- Understands different perspectives of Reconstuction (e.g., the successes and achievements of "Black Reconstruction," Reconstruction as a revolution)

BD (AE,133)

- Understands social and economic factors during and toward the end of Reconstruction (e.g., the impact of fraud and violence on the end of Reconstruction, how economic expansion and development were influenced by Reconstruction)

(AE, 138)

16. Understands how the rise of big business, heavy industry, and mechanized farming transformed American society

Level II (Grades 5-6)

BD (AE,138;LE,119;LI,119,122;NE,66,67)

- Understands the impact of significant achievements and individuals of the late 19th century (e.g., the effects of major technological, transportation, and communication changes that occurred after 1870, careers of industrial and financial leaders of the late 19th century)

BD (AE,140;LE,124;LI,124;NI,66)

- Understands the economic and social changes that occurred in late 19th century American cities (e.g., where industries and transportation expanded; geographic reasons for building factories, commerical centers, and transportation hubs; living conditions in the growing cities; why different groups moved from the farms to the big cities and how they adjusted)

BD (AE,142;LE,125,126;LI,125,126;NI,66)

- Understands social development and labor patterns in the late 19th century West (e.g., major

---

Codes (right side of page):   BD = Benchmark, Declarative; BP = Benchmark, Procedural; BC = Benchmark, Contextual
1st letter of each code in parentheses   *2nd letter of code*   *Number*
A = NCHS: National Standards for U.S. History   E = Explicitly stated in document   Page number of cited document
L = Lessons From History   I = Implied in document
N = NAEP: Provisional Item Specifications

161

MREL

technological and geographic influences that affected farming, mining, and ranching; life on the Great Plains and the idea of "frontier"; how different people lived and worked in the West during the late 19th century)

- Understands environmental issues of the late 19th century (e.g., efforts of reformers to control pollution and depletion of natural resources; environmental effects of mining and industrial development)   BD (AE,144;LE,131;NI,66,67)

Level III (Grades 7-8)

- Understands influences on social development in 19th century America (e.g., the impact of modern technology, new inventions, and advances in transportation; the concept of the "American Dream")   BD (AE,139;LI,119,122;NE,66)

- Understands influences on business and industry in the 19th century (e.g., how business leaders attempted to limit competition and maximize profits, types of business organizations that affected the economy, the lives of prominent industrial leaders)   BD (AE,139;LE,119,122;LI,122,124;NE,67;NI,66)

- Understands influences on urban development in the late 19th century (e.g., factors that created different kinds of cities in diverse regions of the country, internal migration from farm to city, urban political machines)   BD (AE,140-141;LE,126)

- Understands how urbanization and industrialization affected the division of wealth, living conditions, and economic opportunity in the late 19th century   BD (AE,141;LE,124)

- Understands influences on development and social relations of the labor system in the American West (e.g., influence of geography and technology; conflicts among farmers, ranchers, and miners during settlement; cross-cultural encounters and conflicts among different racial and ethnic groups)   BD (AE,142-143;LE,125-126;LI,126;NI,64,66)

- Understands the daily life of women on the western frontier (e.g., how their experiences differed from those of women in the East and Midwest, the impact of these experiences on expanded women's rights)   BD (AE,143)

- Understands differences in commercial farming in various regions of the United States (e.g., the Northeast, South, Great Plains, West)   BD (AE,142;LI,125)

- Understands various influences on the scenic and urban environment (e.g., industrialization and its impact on natural resources; how rapid industrialization, extractive mining   BD (AE,144;NI,67)

Codes (right side of page):   BD = Benchmark, Declarative; BP = Benchmark, Procedural; BC = Benchmark, Contextual
1st letter of each code in parentheses   *2nd letter of code*   *Number*
A = NCHS: National Standards for U.S. History   E = Explicitly stated in document   Page number of cited document
L = Lessons From History   I = Implied in document
N = NAEP: Provisional Item Specifications

techniques, and the "gridiron pattern" of urban growth influenced the city and countryside)

Level IV (Grades 9-12)

- Understands the development of business in the late 19th century (e.g., changing nature of business enterprise, how business leaders gained dominance in their particular industries) BD (AE,139;LE,122;LI,119,120)

- Understands issues associated with urban growth in the late 19th century (e.g., demographic, economic, and spatial expansion of cities; how city residents dealt with urban problems; how urban bosses gained power) BD (AE,141;LE,124,126)

- Understands the role of class, race, gender, and religion in western communities in the late 19th century (e.g., hardships faced by settlers; racial, ethnic, and gender composition of farmers, miners, and ranchers; how gender and racial roles were defined; role of religion in stabilizing communities) BD (AE,143)

- Understands impacts on economic conditions in various regions of the country (e.g., the extension of railroad lines, increased agricultural productivity and improved transportation facilities on commodity prices, grievances and solutions of farm organizations, the crop lien system in the South, transportation and storage costs for farmers, and the price of staples) BD (AE,143;LI,125,126)

- Understands the factors leading to the conservation movement of the late 19th century (e.g., how emphasis on staple crop production, strip mining, lumbering, ranching, and destruction of western buffalo herds led to massive environmental damage) BD (AE,144-145;NI,115)

- Understands how rapid increase in population and industrial growth in urban areas influenced the environment (e.g., problems with the "gridiron pattern," inefficient urban garbage collection and sewage disposal, how city leaders and residents coped with environmental problems in the city) BD (AE,144-145;NI,115)

17. Understands massive immigration after 1870 and how new social patterns, conflicts, and ideas of national unity developed amid growing cultural diversity (AE,146)

Level II (Grades 5-6)

- Understands patterns of immigrant life after 1870 (e.g., how immigration changed; where people came from, and where they settled; ways in which immigrants learned to live and work in a new country; the obstacles, opportunities, and contributions of different immigrant BD (AE,146;LE,123-124;LI,123;NE,64,65)

Codes (right side of page):
1st letter of each code in parentheses
A = NCHS: National Standards for U.S. History
L = Lessons From History
N = NAEP: Provisional Item Specifications

BD = Benchmark, Declarative; BP = Benchmark, Procedural; BC = Benchmark, Contextual
2nd letter of code
E = Explicitly stated in document
I = Implied in document

Number
Page number of cited document

MREL

groups)

BD (AE,148;LI,123-124,130;NE,64)
- Understands the experiences of diverse groups and minorities in different regions of the country (e.g., the experiences of African Americans, Asian Americans, and Hispanic Americans; Jim Crow laws and the impact on African Americans)

BD (AE,150;NE,64)
- Understands social activities in the late 19th century (e.g., entertainment for children, mass entertainment and leisure activities at different levels of American society, new forms of popular culture and reasons for their development)

Level III (Grades 7-8)

BD (AE,147;LI,123;NE,65)
- Understands the experiences of immigrants of the late 19th century (e.g., how they differed from those of the early 19th century in numbers, motives, origins, ethnic, and religious backgrounds; the attitude toward immigrants; contributions of immigrants to American society; how Catholic and Jewish immigrants responded to discrimination)

BD (AE,148;LE,122-123;NE,64)
- Understands the philosophy of Social Darwinism, its application, and its opponents

BD (AE,148;LE,130;LI,123-124,130;NI,63)
- Understands expressions of and opposition to discrimination in the late 19th century (e.g., racial and ethnic discrimination after 1870, how minority groups worked to obtain equal rights, leadership roles of those who spoke out against discrimination)

BD (AE,150;NI,64)
- Understands changes in American life in the late 19th century (e.g., how regional artists portrayed American life, attitudes, and values; reasons for the appeal of new sports, entertainment, and recreational activities; changes in lifestyles)

Level IV (Grades 9-12)

BD (AE,147;LI,123;NI,113)
- Understands challenges immigrants faced in society in the late 19th century (e.g., experiences of new immigrants from 1870 to 1900, reasons for hositility toward the new immigrants, restrictive measures against immigrants, the tension between American ideals and reality)

BD (AE,149;LI,122-12;NI,112)
- Understands how Social Darwinism affected society in the late 19th century (e.g., arguments of the advocates and opponents, the impact of Social Darwinism on public policy)

BD (AE,148,149;LI,123-124,130)
- Understands the challenges diverse people encountered in late 19th century American society (e.g., political, social, and economic discrimination against African, Asian, and

---

Codes (right side of page):   BD = Benchmark, Declarative; BP = Benchmark, Procedural; BC = Benchmark, Contextual

1st letter of each code in parentheses   *2nd letter of code*   *Number*

A = NCHS: National Standards for U.S. History   E = Explicitly stated in document   Page number of cited document

L = Lessons From History   I = Implied in document

N = NAEP: Provisional Item Specifications

164   *MREL*

Hispanic Americans; arguments and methods by which various minority groups sought to acquire equal rights and opportunities; experiences of African American families who migrated from the South to New York City in the 1890s)

BD (AE,151;LI,119-120)

- Understands how American life of the late 19th century was portrayed in literature (e.g., how social realist writers explored regional topics in their work)

BD (AE,151;LI,124)

- Understands changes in social and class development in late 19th century America (e.g., various forms of leisure activities available to different classes, Victorianism and its impact on manners and morals)

(AE,152)

18. Understands the rise of the American labor movement and how political issues reflected social and economic changes

Level II (Grades 5-6)

BD (AE,152;LE,124;NI,67)

- Understands changes in business and labor practices during the late 19th century (e.g., changes in business operation, working conditions in urban factories, and how workers lives were affected after the Civil War; reasons for child labor and it consequences)

BD (AE,154;NE,66)

- Understands characteristics of the labor conflicts of the late 19th century (e.g., causes and results of labor conflicts, causes and effects of coal mine strikes, and the organizing efforts of Mother Mary Jones)

BD (AE,156;NI,63,67)

- Understands major political issues and events of the late 19th century (e.g., why third parties were established, the importance of Thomas Nast's political cartoons, the lives of important political personalities, the issues and results of the 1896 election)

Level III (Grades 7-8)

BD (AE,152-153;LE,124;LI,124;NI,66,67)

- Understands the conditions affecting employment and labor in the late 19th century (e.g., gender, race, ethnicity, and skill; the rise of big business and change from workshop to factory in different regions; how working conditions changed and how workers responded to deteriorating conditions)

BD (AE,154;LI,124;NE,67;NI,63)

- Understands reactions to developments in labor in late 19th century America (e.g., how management and industry responded to efforts to organize workers, the response of management and government to labor strife in different regions of the country)

Codes (right side of page):   BD = Benchmark, Declarative; BP = Benchmark, Procedural; BC = Benchmark, Contextual
1st letter of each code in parentheses   *2nd letter of code*   *Number*
A = NCHS: National Standards for U.S. History   E = Explicitly stated in document   Page number of cited document
L = Lessons From History   I = Implied in document
N = NAEP: Provisional Item Specifications

- Understands the goals of political parties and individuals in the late 19th century (e.g., the positions of Democratic and Republican parties on issues, importance of individuals in promoting political reform, the goals of the Socialist and Populist parties and their leaders)

  BD (AE,156,157;LI,126;NE,63)

Level IV (Grades 9-12)

- Understands influences on the workforce during the late 19th century (e.g., how big business and the impersonal nature of factory work affected workers, inroads made by women in male-dominated jobs, legal status of women, reasons for increased child labor, the type of work children performed, occupations in which children were employed, dangers they faced during the workday)

  BD (AE,153;NI,113)

- Understands labor issues of the late 19th century (e.g., organizational and agenda differences between reform and trade unions, the extent of radicalism in the labor movements, labor conflicts of 1894 and their effects)

  BD (AE,155;NI,116)

- Understands the appeal of various political parties and the positions they took (e.g., the appeal of the Democratic, Republican, and Greenback Labor parties to different socioeconomic groups; how Democrats and Republicans responded to civil service reform, monetary policy, tariffs, and business regulations)

  BD (AE,156,157;LI,126)

- Understands the development of Populism and the Populist Party (e.g., problems that prompted the establishment of the Populist Party, the sucesses and failures of the Populist movement in meeting the needs of American society)

  BD (AE,157,158;LI,126;NI,112)

- Understands how economic issues influenced American society (e.g., the causes and effects of the depressions of 1873–1879 and 1893–1897, and how government, business, labor, and farmers responded; the reaction of western and southern farmers to the cycle of falling prices, scarce money, and debt)

  BD (AE,156,157)

- Understands the issues and results of the 1896 election (e.g., the extent to which farmers were unable to adjust to the changing industrial scene and the Populist decision to endorse the Democratic nominee, William Jennings Bryan's "Cross of Gold" speech and how it affected the outcome of the election, arguments and strategies used by William McKinley and Mark Hanna, urban women's support of the Republican party, the major components of the "full dinner pail")

  BD (AE,158)

Codes (right side of page):   BD = Benchmark, Declarative; BP = Benchmark, Procedural; BC = Benchmark, Contextual
1st letter of each code in parentheses   *2nd letter of code*   *Number*
A = NCHS: National Standards for U.S. History   E = Explicitly stated in document   Page number of cited document
L = Lessons From History   I = Implied in document
N = NAEP: Provisional Item Specifications

166

MREL

(AE,159)

19. Understands federal Indian policy and United States foreign policy after the Civil War

Level II (Grades 5-6)

BD (AE,159;LE,125;NI,64)

- Understands significant events for Native American tribes in the late 19th century and how they responded (e.g., movement to reservations in western states, the effect of government policies on Native American nations and Native American land holdings between 1870 and 1900, survival strategies of Native American societies)

BD (AE,161;LE,135;NI,68)

- Understands the expansion of U.S. territories in the post-Civil War era (e.g., areas the U.S. annexed and primary interests in these areas)

BD (AE,161;LE,139-140;NE,68)

- Understands critical features of the Spanish-American War (e.g., conditions that led to the war with Spain in 1898, character and objectives of the war, leading personalities of the Spanish-American War)

Level III (Grades 7-8)

BD (AE,159-160;LI,120;NI,64,65)

- Understands interaction between Native Americans and white society (e.g., the attitudes and policies of government officials, the Army, missionaries, settlers, and the general public toward Native Americans; Native American responses to increased white settlement, mining activities, and railroad construction)

BD (AE,161,162;LE,140;NE,68)

- Understands factors that influenced U.S. expansionism in the late 19th century (e.g., geographic, economic, and social factors; arguments used to justify expansion; arguments of opponents to expansion; consequences of the Philippine annexation and Filipino insurrection)

BD (AE,161,162;LE,139,140;NE,63)

- Understands the causes and consequences of the Spanish-American War (e.g., economic and geographic factors, U.S. justifications, impact of the press on the public opinion, the role of the U.S. in Cuba after the war, the war's effects on U.S. involvement in international relations, constitutional issues raised by the acquisition of new territories)

Level IV (Grades 9-12)

BD (AE,160;LE,125;NI,113)

- Understands influences on and perspectives of Native American life in the late 19th century (e.g., the Dawes Severalty Act of 1887; leadership and values of Native American leaders; depiction of Native Americans and whites by 19th century artists)

Codes (right side of page):   BD = Benchmark, Declarative; BP = Benchmark, Procedural; BC = Benchmark, Contextual
1st letter of each code in parentheses   *2nd letter of code*   *Number*
A = NCHS: National Standards for U.S. History   E = Explicitly stated in document   Page number of cited document
L = Lessons From History   I = Implied in document
N = NAEP: Provisional Item Specifications

MREL

- Understands factors in the outbreak and outcome of the Spanish-American War (e.g., President McKinley's reasons for going to war; changing U.S. attitudes toward Emilio Aguinaldo from 1898 to the issue of warrants for his arrest after the Treaty of Paris) ^{BD (AE,162;LE,139-140)}

- Understands elements that contributed to late 19th century expansionist foreign policy (e.g., geopolitics, economic interests, racial ideology, Protestant missionary zeal, nationalism, and domestic tensions) ^{BD (AE,161,162;LE,139;NI,117)}

20. Understands how progressives and others addressed problems of industrial capitalism, urbanization, and political corruption ^(AE,165)

Level II (Grades 5-6)

- Understands the conditions that led the Progressives to far-reaching social and moral reforms (e.g., child labor, urban tenements, slums, poor living conditions) ^{BD (AE,165;LE,131;NI,63)}

- Understands how migrants from rural areas and immigrants from other lands experienced life in growing urban centers and how they coped (e.g., schools, settlement houses, religious groups, philanthropists) ^{BD (AE,165;LI,123-124;NI,63,64)}

- Understands political and legislative elements of the Progressive movement (e.g., the leadership of Presidents Roosevelt, Taft, and Wilson and their ideas for reform; the 16th, 17th, and 18th amendments; the movement for women's suffrage) ^{BD (AE,167;LE,128,133-134;LI,134;NI,63)}

- Understands issues and perspectives of different groups during the Progressive era (e.g., women, Native Americans, African Americans, organized workers) ^{BD (AE,169;LE,130,131;NI,63,65)}

Level III (Grades 7-8)

- Understands the spread of Progressive ideas and the successes of the Progressive movement (e.g., how intellectuals and writers alerted the public to the defects of urban industrial society; how Progressives promoted political change and restored democracy at state and local levels; contributions of governors such as Hiram Johnson, Robert La Follette, and Charles Evans Hughes; Progressive social reforms in education, conservation, and the "Americanization" of immigrants) ^{BD (AE,165-66;LE,123,130-133;NI,63)}

- Understands the influence of events and individuals on the Progressive Movement (e.g., ^{BD (AE,167,168;LE,133-134;LI,134;NI,63)}

Codes (right side of page):   BD = Benchmark, Declarative; BP = Benchmark, Procedural; BC = Benchmark, Contextual
1st letter of each code in parentheses   *2nd letter of code*   *Number*
A = NCHS: National Standards for U.S. History   E = Explicitly stated in document   Page number of cited document
L = Lessons From History   I = Implied in document
N = NAEP: Provisional Item Specifications

168

McREL

major reforms initiated by Presidents Roosevelt, Taft, and Wilson; results of the election of 1912; Progressive amendments to the Constitution and movements that led to the 16th, 17th, and 18th amendments)

BD (AE,167;NI,66)

- Understands the New Nationalism, New Freedom, and Socialist agendas for change

BD (AE,169;LE,130;NI,63,65,66)

- Understands the issues of those groups who supported and rejected the goals of Progressivism (e.g., perspectives of African Americans and their alternate programs, how the goals of the Industrial Workers of the World differed from Progressive programs, why mainstream Progressives abandoned women's issues, and how women responded)

Level IV (Grades 9-12)

BD (AE,166;LE,130,131,132;NI,111,112)

- Understands the origins and impacts of the Progressive movement (e.g., social origins of Progressives and how these contributed to the success and failure of the movement, arguments of Progressive leaders, Progressive reforms pertaining to state and local government and business)

BD (AE,166;LE,123-124;NI,111,113)

- Understands how racial and ethnic events influenced American society during the Progressive era (e.g., racial and ethnic conflicts contributed to delayed statehood for New Mexico and Arizona, the impact of new nativism, the movement to restrict immigration, and influences on African, Native, Asian, and Hispanic Americans)

BD (AE,168;LI,133-134;NI,111,112)

- Understands major social and political issues of the Progressive era (e.g., presidential leadership of Theodore Roosevelt, William Howard Taft, and Woodrow Wilson; the Hetch Hetchy controversy; the election of 1912; Supreme Court cases that affected progressivism)

BD (AE,168;NI,111)

- Understands efforts to achieve women's suffrage in the early twentieth century (e.g., methods used by Carrie Chapman Calt in her leadership of the National Women's Suffrage Association to get the 19th amendment passed and ratified, why President Wilson changed his mind about the amendment, which of Calt's tactics were most successful)

BD (AE,169,170;NI,111,113;LI,131)

- Understands how the Progressive movement influenced different groups in American society (e.g., the founding of the NAACP, how African American women contributed to the movement, how the International Ladies Garment Workers Union provided alternatives, women's issues ignored by mainstream progressives, the changing perception toward Native American assimilation under progressivism; the success of the Progressive movement to groups outside the mainstream)

Codes (right side of page): BD = Benchmark, Declarative; BP = Benchmark, Procedural; BC = Benchmark, Contextual
1st letter of each code in parentheses *2nd letter of code* *Number*
A = NCHS: National Standards for U.S. History E = Explicitly stated in document Page number of cited document
L = Lessons From History I = Implied in document
N = NAEP: Provisional Item Specifications

169 MREL

21.   **Understands the changing role of the United States in world affairs through World War I** (AE,171)

Level II (Grades 5-6)

- Understands various U.S. foreign policies in the early part of the 20th century (e.g., the Open Door policy; places the U.S. claimed, occupied, or protected in the Caribbean after the Spanish-American War; Roosevelt's idea of Big Stick diplomacy; the importance of the Panama Canal) BD (AE,171;LE,135-136,139-140;NI,68,69)

- Understands World War I prior to U.S. intervention (e.g., the causes in 1914, the reasons for the declaration of U.S. neutrality, locations of Allied and Central Powers, the extent of war in Europe and the use of new weapons and technology) BD (AE,173;LE,141;NI,72-74)

- Understands U.S. involvement in World War I (e.g., how the U.S. prepared for the war, Wilson's Fourteen Points, the negotiation of the Versailles Treaty, the national debate over treaty ratification and the League of Nations, how the American Expeditionary Force contributed to the Allied victory) BD (AE,175;LE,136,142;NI,74)

Level III (Grades 7-8)

- Understands different types of U.S. diplomacy in the early 20th century and how they were applied (e.g., American diplomatic initiatives in East Asia; Roosevelt's Big Stick policy in Latin America; the differences between Taft's Dollar Diplomacy, Theodore Roosevelt's Big Stick diplomacy, and Wilson's moral diplomacy) BD (AE,171;LE,139;LI,135-140;NI,68,69)

- Understands the development of World War I (e.g., the system of alliances through which European nations sought to protect their interests; how nationalism and militarism contributed to the outbreak, how the war expanded to become a world war, how technological developments contributed to the war's brutality) BD (AE, 173;LI,141;NI,72)

- Understands the role of the United States in World War I (e.g., the impact of U.S. public opinion on the Wilson administration's evolving foreign policy during the period 1914-1917, Wilson's leadership during the period of neutrality and his reasons for U.S. intervention in World War I) BD (AE,173,174;LI,141;NI,72,73)

- Understands U.S. domestic and foreign policy during World War I (e.g., U.S. military and economic mobilizations for war and the role of labor, women, and African Americans in the war effort; World War I military engagements; the campaigns in which the American BD (AE,175,176;LE,141;NI,73,74)

Codes (right side of page):   BD = Benchmark, Declarative; BP = Benchmark, Procedural; BC = Benchmark, Contextual
1st letter of each code in parentheses   *2nd letter of code*   *Number*
A = NCHS: National Standards for U.S. History   E = Explicitly stated in document   Page number of cited document
L = Lessons From History   I = Implied in document
N = NAEP: Provisional Item Specifications

MREL

Expeditionary force participated; the importance of the U.S. victory and the impact of the war on American troops; Wilson's goals in recommending the establishment of a League of Nations)

BD (AE,175;LI,136;NI,73)

- Understands the significance of the Russian Revolution, its impact on the war and on the foreign policies of the U.S. and allied powers

Level IV (Grades 9-12)

BD (AE,172;LE,140;LI,139-140;NI,117)

- Understands U.S. foreign policy and involvement in foreign countries in the early 20th century (e.g., commercial basis of foreign policy in East Asia, the Roosevelt Corollary and its connection to the Monroe Doctrine, the U.S. role in the Panama Revolution of 1903, U.S. relations with Japan and the "Gentleman's Agreement," Taft's Dollar Diplomacy, Wilson's moral diplomacy)

BD (AE,174;LI,136;NI,123,124)

- Understands the causes, course, and impact of World War I prior to U.S. entry (e.g., motivations of leading world powers, the relative success of nations in mobilizing their resources and populations, the relative success of their propaganda campaigns to influence neutral nations, the successes of military strategies, the general spirit of disillusionment)

BD (AE,174;NI,123)

- Understands various phases of President Wilson's leadership (e.g., his leadership during the period of neutrality, the events of his second term)

BD (AE,176;LI,141;NI,122)

- Understands how the home front influenced and was influenced by U.S. involvement in World War I (e.g., the impact of public opinion and government policies on constitutional interpretation and civil liberties,U.S. military and economic mobilization for war, wartime contributions of labor, and how the war transformed the role and labor of women, the role of African Americans in the war effort)

BD (AE,176,177;LI,136;NI,119,124)

- Understands influences on the outcome of World War I (e.g., how point six of the Fourteen Points dealt specifically with Russia, the effectiveness of the Versailles Treaty, the national debate over the Versailles Treaty ratification and the League of Nations)

Codes (right side of page):   BD = Benchmark, Declarative; BP = Benchmark, Procedural; BC = Benchmark, Contextual
1st letter of each code in parentheses   *2nd letter of code*   *Number*
A = NCHS: National Standards for U.S. History   E = Explicitly stated in document   Page number of cited document
L = Lessons From History   I = Implied in document
N = NAEP: Provisional Item Specifications

McREL

(AE,178)

22. Understands how the United States changed between the post-World War I years and the eve of the Great Depression

Level II (Grades 5-6)

BD (AE,178;LE,144,149;LI,149;NI,70,71)
- Understands efforts to restrict immigrants and diverse groups of people in the post-World War I era (e.g., nativism and anti-immigrant attitudes, the spread of the Ku Klux Klan in different sections of the country in the 1920s)

BD (AE,178)
- Understands how women's lives changed after World War I (e.g., their contributions in schools, hospitals, settlement houses, and social agencies; how the spread of electrification and household appliances improved the life of homemakers)

BD (AE,178)
- Understands elements of Prohibition (e.g., smuggling)

BD (AE,181;LI,144)
- Understands how urban life changed in the 1920s (e.g., new downtowns and suburbs, how improvements in steel construction and elevators contributed to the changes, why people prized home ownership, why people left the cities for the suburbs, changes in transportation that made travel to work easier for people in cities and suburbs)

BD (AE,183;LE,146,149;LI,145,147;NI,64,71)
- Understands the rise of a mass culture in the 1920s (e.g., the media and recreation available in the 1920s; the growth of professional sports facilities, fairgrounds, amusement parks, and recreational areas and their impact on local areas)

BD (AE,183)
- Understands influences on African American culture during the 1920s (e.g., the Harlem Renaissance)

BD (AE,185;LI,96,132,144;NI,63,65)
- Understands the effects of women's suffrage on American society (e.g., the major events of women's suffrage movement from the Senaca Falls Convention of 1848 to the ratification of the 19th amendment)

Level III (Grades 7-8)

BD (AE,179;LE,149;LI,144,149;NI,69,70,71)
- Understands the various social conflicts that took place in the early 1920s (e.g., the "Red Scare," the Palmer raids and the restriction of civil liberties as a reaction to Bolshevism; immigration restrictions after World War I, race relations and increased racial conflict; the clash between traditional moral values and changing ideas as expemplified in the Scopes trial and Prohibition)

Codes (right side of page):   BD = Benchmark, Declarative; BP = Benchmark, Procedural; BC = Benchmark, Contextual
1st letter of each code in parentheses   *2nd letter of code*   *Number*
A = NCHS: National Standards for U.S. History   E = Explicitly stated in document   Page number of cited document
L = Lessons From History   I = Implied in document
N = NAEP: Provisional Item Specifications

McREL

- BD (AE,179)
  Understands changes in women in the post-World War I era (e.g., changing values, new ideas regarding employment opportunities, appearance standards, leisure activities, and political participation)

- BD (AE,181;LI,145;NE,71)
  Understands elements that contributed to the rise of modern capitalist economy (e.g., how new inventions and technologies affected the lives of Americans, and how management techniques changed the methods of production; the impact of advertisement on the desire for new products; changes in the modern corporation of the 1920s, including labor policies and the advent of mass advertising and sales techniques)

- BD (AE,183;LE,146,149;LI,143,145,147;NI,64,71)
  Understands changes in the social and cultural life of American society in the 1920s (e.g., mass culture of the 1920s, the emergence of the Harlem Renaissance and the "Lost Generation," increased leisure time and how Americans used it in the 1920s)

- BD (AE,185;NI,63;LI,150)
  Understands events that shaped the political structure of America in the 1920s (e.g., changes in progressivism during the Harding and Coolidge, administrations; the impact of women's suffrage on American society following the passage of the 19th amendment; U.S. territories and spheres of influence in the 1920s and foreign policy of the Republican administrations of Harding, Coolidge and Hoover)

Level IV (Grades 9-12)

- BD (AE,179-180;LE,149;LI,144,149;NI,113,119,120,121)
  Understands the major social issues of 1920s America (e.g., the "Red Scare," the Sacco and Vanzetti trial, the ethnic composition of immigrants and fears these changes represented, the Garvey Movement, the Scopes trial and its impact, the emergence of the "New Woman" and challenges to Victorian values, the purpose and goals of the "New Klan," the causes and outcome of Prohibition)

- BD (AE,181,182;LI,147)
  Understands factors that contributed to changes in work, production, and the rise of a consumer culture (e.g., new inventions, technologies, and improvements in scientific management; the new paternalism of the modern corporation; new forms of advertising, installment buying, and sales techniques)

- BD (AE,182;LI,147;NI,114)
  Understands influences on urban life in America during the 1920s (e.g., new downtown areas, suburbs, architecture, and the idea of the "civic center")

- BD (AE,184;LI,145,146,149;NI,121)
  Understands the rise of popular culture and its impact on American society in the 1920s (e.g., the impact of radio, high circulation print media, and movies; the emergence of

---

Codes (right side of page):	BD = Benchmark, Declarative; BP = Benchmark, Procedural; BC = Benchmark, Contextual

1st letter of each code in parentheses   *2nd letter of code*   *Number*

A = NCHS: National Standards for U.S. History   E = Explicitly stated in document   Page number of cited document

L = Lessons From History   I = Implied in document

N = NAEP: Provisional Item Specifications

McREL

distinctive American art, literature, and music; the emergence of artists in the postwar period; how increased leisure time in the 1920s promoted the growth of professional sports, amusement parks, and national parks)

BD (AE,186;LI,146,150;NI,111,119)

- Understands how political issues in the 1920s influenced American society (e.g., the Harding and Coolidge administrations and the effects of World War I on progressivism, the effects of women's suffrage on American society, the goals and effectiveness of the Republican party in the 1920s)

(AE,188)

23. Understands the causes of the Great Depression and how it affected American society

Level II (Grades 5-6)

BD (AE,188;LE,155-156;NE,72;NI,72)

- Understands the economic aspects of the Great Depression (e.g., the factors that contributed to the Great Depression and the effects of the depression on farmers, city workers, and military veterans; the consequences of the stock market crash of 1929)

BD (AE,190;LE,156;LI,153-154,156;NI,70-72)

- Understands the environmental and social impact of the Great Depression (e.g., the effects of the Great Depression and Dust Bowl on American farmers, tenants, and sharecroppers; the effects of the depression on diverse groups and on local communities)

Level III (Grades 7-8)

BD (AE,188-189)

- Understands how economic factors influenced American society in the late 1920s (e.g., trickle down economic policies of the Coolidge-Mellon years and their economic impact on wealth distribution, investment, and taxes in the period 1925–29; the factors that contributed to the fluctuation of the stock market, and the causes and consequences of the market crash of 1929)

BD (AE,189;LE,155-156;NE,72)

- Understands various poltical influences on the Great Depression (e.g., the effectiveness of measures the Hoover administration took to stem the tide of the Great Depression, the central political and economic causes of the Great Depression)

BD (AE,190,191;LI,156,158;NE,70,NI,72)

- Understands the social and economic impact of the Great Depression (e.g., the impact of the depression on industry and workers; the response of local and state officials in combating the resulting economic and social crises; the effects of the depression on American families and gender roles; the effect on African, Hispanic, and Native Americans; the victimization of African Americans and white sharecroppers)

Codes (right side of page):   BD = Benchmark, Declarative; BP = Benchmark, Procedural; BC = Benchmark, Contextual
1st letter of each code in parentheses   *2nd letter of code*   *Number*
A = NCHS: National Standards for U.S. History   E = Explicitly stated in document   Page number of cited document
L = Lessons From History   I = Implied in document
N = NAEP: Provisional Item Specifications

174

MREL

Level IV (Grades 9-12)

- Understands influences on the national and global economy in the 1920s and 1930s (e.g., characteristics of the American economy in the 1920s, Hoover's responses to the Great Depression, the reasons for the deepening crisis in the period 1929–1933, the global context of the depression and the reasons for the worldwide economic collapse) ^{BD (AE,189;LE,155;NI,122)}

- Understands how the Great Depression and the Dust Bowl influenced the lives of diverse groups of people (e.g., workers and farmers and their families, African Americans in the North and South, Mexican Americans) ^{BD (AE,191-192;LI,156,158;NI,120,122)}

- Understands how the Great Depression influenced local, state, and charitable resources in the period 1930–1938 ^{BD (AE,191)}

- Understands the impact of the Great Depression on American culture (e.g., how the works of various American artists reflected American conditions in the 1930s and influenced the New Deal; art, literature, and music, and the government's role in promoting artistic expression) ^{BD (AE,190,192;LI,157,158;NI,120,121)}

24. Understands how the New Deal addressed the Great Depression, transformed American federalism, and initiated the welfare state ^(AE,193)

Level II (Grades 5-6)

- Understands the background and leadership styles of depression-era presidents (e.g., Herbert Hoover, Franklin D. Roosevelt) ^{BD (AE,193)}

- Understands influences on and impacts of the New Deal (e.g., how the New Deal affected the lives of local families, how women contributed to New Deal programs) ^{BD (AE,193;LE,159;LI,157-158)}

- Understands the impact of the New Deal on American workers and the labor movement (e.g., the condition of working men and women in the United States in the 1930s) ^{BD (AE,195;LE,157,158,159)}

- Understands the significance and legacy of the New Deal (e.g., support for and opposition to Roosevelt's "court packing" proposal and why he abandoned this proposal, major New Deal programs still in effect today) ^{BD (AE,197;LI,157-158)}

Codes (right side of page):   BD = Benchmark, Declarative; BP = Benchmark, Procedural; BC = Benchmark, Contextual
1st letter of each code in parentheses   *2nd letter of code*   *Number*
A = NCHS: National Standards for U.S. History   E = Explicitly stated in document   Page number of cited document
L = Lessons From History   I = Implied in document
N = NAEP: Provisional Item Specifications

MREL

Level III (Grades 7-8)

BD (AE,193-194;LI,157-158,159;NE,70;NI,70,72)

- Understands the role of the New Deal in American society (e.g., relief, recovery, and reform measures associated with the first and second New Deals; the commitment of Eleanor Roosevelt to improving conditions during the New Deal; the impact of the New Deal on African Americans, Native Americans, Mexican Americans, and women)

BD (AE,193-194;LI,156,157)

- Understands the personal and political reasons for Herbert Hoover's and Franklin D. Roosevelt's responses to the depression

BD (AE,193;LI,134,158)

- Understands the link between progressivism and the early New Deal

BD (AE,195-196;LI,157)

- Understands the labor movement during the New Deal era (e.g., the emergence of labor militancy and the struggle between craft and industrial unions; the commitment of labor unions to organize diverse groups and secure equitable conditions and pay for minorities; the objectives of labor leaders and advocates; how art, photographs, and song lyrics contributed to the emotional appeal to support unions; WPA projects and their impact on local areas)

BD (AE,197;LE,159)

- Understands various challenges to the New Deal (e.g., the controversy between Roosevelt and the Supreme Court, the roots of opposition to Roosevelt's policies, the ideas of the Townsend Plan and the "Share the Wealth" program of Dr. Francis Townsend and Senator Huey Long)

BD (AE, 197;LI,156-159)

- Understands how the New Deal influenced public opinion (e.g., the public's belief in the responsibility of government to deliver public services)

Level IV (Grades 9-12)

BD (AE,194;LI,158;LE,159)

- Understands how the New Deal influenced the civil and political rights of diverse groups (e.g., FDR's commitment to advancing the civil and political rights of African Americans, how African Americans planted the seeds of a civil rights revolution during the 1930s, how the Indian Reorganization Act of 1934 affected Native Americans, and the role of John Collier in securing a "new deal" for Native Americans)

BD (AE,193;LE,156,159)

- Understands the factors contributing to the forging of the Roosevelt coalition in 1936 and its electoral significance in subsequent years

BD (AE,193,194;LI,156,157-158)

- Understands the "first" and "second" New Deals (e.g., the success of the relief, recovery, and reform measures associated with each)

Codes (right side of page):   BD = Benchmark, Declarative; BP = Benchmark, Procedural; BC = Benchmark, Contextual
1st letter of each code in parentheses   *2nd letter of code*   *Number*
A = NCHS: National Standards for U.S. History   E = Explicitly stated in document   Page number of cited document
L = Lessons From History   I = Implied in document
N = NAEP: Provisional Item Specifications

- Understands how the New Deal influenced labor and employment (e.g., factors contributing to the success of the CIO leadership in organizing the rubber, auto, and steel workers in the period 1937–1941; labor's commitment to organizing; causes, strategies, and leadership of major strikes during the New Deal; the impact of the New Deal on non-union workers in the period 1933–1940; the effects of the New Deal agricultural programs on farm laborers)
  BD (AE, 195,196)

- Understands influences on the New Deal (e.g., the Supreme Court cases related to the New Deal and how they affected it; opposition of different groups and their effects; the class basis for support and opposition to the New Deal in the Northeast, South, Midwest, and Far West)
  BD (AE,198;LI,156-157;NI,120)

- Understands the significance and ideology of FDR and the New Deal (e.g., whether the New Deal was able to solve the problems of depression, who the New Deal helped the most and the least; how the New Deal changed the relationship between state and federal government)
  BD (AE,198;LI,158,159)

- Understands the proposals of Upton Sinclair's EPIC campaign in California (e.g., groups that opposed it, why it failed, the reasons for the growth of the American Communist Party during the 1930s, to whom the party most appealed)
  BD (AE,198)

25. **Understands the origins and course of World War II, the character of the war at home and abroad, and its reshaping of the U.S. role in world affairs**
(AE,199)

Level II (Grades 5-6)

- Understands events leading to U.S. involvement in World War II (e.g., global involvement of nations and people before World War II; the location of Pearl Harbor and events that brought the U.S. into the war; the Roosevelt administration's response to aggression in Europe, Africa, and Asia from 1935 to 1941)
  BD (AE,199;LE,161,166;NE,73,74;NI,73)

- Understands significant military aspects of World War II (e.g., Axis and Allied military strategy and the military campaigns of the European and Pacific theaters between 1939 and 1945; the locations of the major theaters of war in North Africa, Europe, and the Pacific; the costs during the war for the Allies and the Axis powers; the diverse contributions of men and women during the war)
  BD (AE,201;LE,163-165;LI,167)

- Understands events on the U.S. home front during World War II (e.g., the internment of Japanese Americans; economic and military mobilization; major developments in aviation, weaponry, communication, and medicine)
  BD (AE,203;LE,167;NE,70;NI,72)

Codes (right side of page):   BD = Benchmark, Declarative; BP = Benchmark, Procedural; BC = Benchmark, Contextual
1st letter of each code in parentheses   *2nd letter of code*   *Number*
A = NCHS: National Standards for U.S. History   E = Explicitly stated in document   Page number of cited document
L = Lessons From History   I = Implied in document
N = NAEP: Provisional Item Specifications

McREL

Level III (Grades 7-8)

- BD (AE,199;LE,161,166;NI,73,74)
Understands the development of new political thinking and forms of government in Europe between World War I and World War II (e.g., the rise of Fascism, German Nazism, and Soviet Communism)

- BD (AE,199,200;LE,166;LI,142,159;NE,73;NI,73)
Understands U.S. international relations prior to its entrance into World War II (e.g., reasons for American isolationist sentiment and its effects on international relations and diplomacy, the events that caused growing tensions between the U.S. and Japan during the period 1900–1941)

- BD (AE,199,200;LI,142,150;NI,73,74)
Understands how the outcome of World War I contributed to the outbreak of World War II (e.g., lack of support for the League of Nations, the breakdown of the Versailles settlement in the 1930s)

- BD (AE, 201,202;LE,166-167)
Understands military strategies used during World War II (e.g., the non-aggression pact between Germany and the USSR in 1939; the "Battle for Britain"; Japanese strategy in East Asia and the Pacific; Roosevelt's strategy for an aggressive war against the Axis powers and a defensive war in Asia; the North Africa, Sicily, and Normandy invasions)

- BD (AE,201,202)
Understands the dimensions of Hitler's "Final Solution" and the Allies' response to the Holocaust (e.g., human costs of Nazi genocide, Roosevelt's immigration policy toward Jewish refugees from Hitler's Germany)

- BD (AE,202;LE,164-165;LI,167;NI,74)
Understands the legacy of World War II (e.g., Truman's decision to use atomic weapons during World War II, the human costs of World War II, the organization and functions of the United Nations)

- BD (AE,203-204;NI,70-72)
Understands how World War II influenced American society (e.g., the effects on gender roles and the American family, the impact on U.S. culture and technology)

- BD (AE,203-204;LE,167;NE,70;NI,72)
Understands how minority groups were affected by World War II (e.g., the contributions of U.S. minorities and the racism and discrimination they faced, the circumstances of the internment of Japanese Americans)

Level IV (Grades 9-12)

- BD (AE,200;NI,123)
Understands events that led to the Japanese attack on Pearl Harbor (e.g., wartime events that affected the U.S. prior to the attack on Pearl Harbor and the official U.S. entry into the war; U.S. interaction with Japan that led to the Japanese attack on Pearl Harbor on December 7,

---

Codes (right side of page):   BD = Benchmark, Declarative; BP = Benchmark, Procedural; BC = Benchmark, Contextual
1st letter of each code in parentheses   *2nd letter of code*   *Number*
A = NCHS: National Standards for U.S. History   E = Explicitly stated in document   Page number of cited document
L = Lessons From History   I = Implied in document
N = NAEP: Provisional Item Specifications

MREL

1941)

BD (AE,200;NI,123)
- Understands the influence of international events on U.S. policies and political developments (e.g., Roosevelt's foreign policy toward Latin America and the reasons for the Good Neighbor Policy; the effect of the Nazi-Soviet Non-Aggression Pact of 1939 on the U.S. Communist Party)

BD (AE,202;LE,167;LI,167)
- Understands characteristics of the end of World War II (e.g., why there was a delay in creating a second front in Europe, the Soviet Union's role in helping to defeat the Axis Powers and the reasons for the success of D-Day, the Allied response to the Holocaust, the factors involved in the decision to use the atomic bomb on Japan)

BD (AE,201,202;LE,168;NI,123)
- Understands President Roosevelt's ideas and policies during World War II (e.g., the ideas presented in Roosevelt's Four Freedoms speech, his administration's wartime diplomacy)

BD (AE,204;LI,162,167;NI,120,122)
- Understands how World War II influenced the home front (e.g., U.S. mobilization during World War II; how African, Mexican, and Native Americans contributed to the war effort and the contradiction between their treatment at home and the goals that they were fighting for in Europe; the effects of the relocation centers on Japanese American families and the restrictions on their civil liberties)

(AE,206)
26. Understands the economic boom and social transformation of post-World War II America

Level II (Grades 5-6)

BD (AE,206;LE,169-170;NI,78)
- Understands how the American economy changed in the post-World War II period (e.g., the reasons for sustained economic growth, why more service sector jobs were available after the war, the difference in standards of living of the urban poor and suburban middle class)

BD (AE,208;NE,77)
- Understands influences on American society during the post-World War II years (e.g., how family life changed after 1945, the influence of popular culture on American society after World War II)

Level III (Grades 7-8)

BD (AE, 206,207)
- Understands the immediate social, political, and economic impacts on America after World War II (e.g., the economic and political effects of demobilization and reconversion; the

---

Codes (right side of page):   BD = Benchmark, Declarative; BP = Benchmark, Procedural; BC = Benchmark, Contextual
1st letter of each code in parentheses   *2nd letter of code*   *Number*
A = NCHS: National Standards for U.S. History   E = Explicitly stated in document   Page number of cited document
L = Lessons From History   I = Implied in document
N = NAEP: Provisional Item Specifications

MREL

growth and impact of opportunities in the service, white collar, and professional sectors in government and business)

- Understands how American society changed once World War II ended (e.g., the effect of the G.I. Bill, reasons for the "return to domesticity" and the effect on gender roles and family life, the role of mass media in homogenizing American culture in the 1950s)

  BD (AE,208,209;LE,170;NI,77)

Level IV (Grades 9-12)

- Understands influences on the American economy after World War II (e.g., increased defense spending; the U.S. economy in relation to Europe and Asian economies, the impact of the Cold War on the economy)

  BD (AE,207;LI,169-170, 173; NI, 129, 130)

- Understands the socioeconomic factors of the post-World War II period in America (e.g., the gap between the "affluent society" and "the other America," and the extent of poverty in post-World War II America)

  BD (AE,206,207)

- Understands social, religious, cultural, and economic changes at the onset of the Cold War era (e.g., how the Cold War influenced the lives and roles of women, the expansion of suburbanization and the impact of the "crabgrass frontier," how artists and writers portrayed the effects of alienation on the individual and society after 1945, the causes and results of new governmental spending on educational programs in the 1950s, the role of religion, the social and economic effects of the G.I. Bill)

  BD(AE,208-209;NI,129)

27. Understands the legacy of the New Deal in the post-World War II period

(AE,210)

Level II (Grades 5-6)

- Understands the civil rights movement during President Truman's presidency (e.g., his support of civil rights, the effect on the Democratic party)

  BD (AE,210;LI,170)

- Understands the impact of the Kennedy and Johnson administrations on domestic affairs (e.g., the domestic accomplishments of the New Frontier, Johnson's presidential leadership and the reforms of the Great Society, how Jacqueline Kennedy developed the Camelot images to depict her husband's presidency)

  BD (AE,212;LI,177;LE,177;NI,79)

Codes (right side of page):   BD = Benchmark, Declarative; BP = Benchmark, Procedural; BC = Benchmark, Contextual
1st letter of each code in parentheses   *2nd letter of code*   *Number*
A = NCHS: National Standards for U.S. History   E = Explicitly stated in document   Page number of cited document
L = Lessons From History   I = Implied in document
N = NAEP: Provisional Item Specifications

180

McREL

Level III (Grades 7-8)

- Understands the domestic policies of Presidents Truman and Eisenhower (e.g., Truman's Fair Deal program for securing fair employment practices, desegregation, civil rights, and race relations; Eisenhower's "Modern Republicanism") BD (AE,210;LI,170)

- Understands the major issues of the 1960 presidential campaign and Kennedy's stance on each (e.g., the central domestic and foreign issues that divided Kennedy and Nixon, the extent to which religion was an issue in the campaign, how Kennedy responded to the Cold War issues) BD (AE,212)

- Understands the legacy of the New Frontier and Great Society domestic programs (e.g., how they differed, the impact of the Kennedy assassination on the passage of reform legislation during the Johnson administration, how Kennedy's and Johnson's leadership styles differed, factors that contributed to greater public support for Great Society legislation, the lasting impact of both programs) BD (AE,212;LI,177;NI,79)

Level IV (Grades 9-12)

- Understands different social and economic elements of the Truman and Eisenhower administrations (e.g., postwar reaction to the labor movement and responses to the Truman and Eisenhower administrations to labor's agenda, civil rights program of the Truman administration, how Eisenhower's domestic and foreign policy priorities contrasted with his predecessors) BD (AE,210,211;LI,170;NI,125)

- Understands characteristics of the Kennedy presidency (e.g., Kennedy's commitment to liberalism and reasons for his election in 1960; Kennedy's ideas about citizenship, rights, and responsibilities; the impact of the New Frontier) BD (AE,212-213;LI,177;NE,127)

- Understands characteristics of the Johnson presidency (e.g., Johnson's presidential leadership and the reforms of the Great Society, how Johnson's presidential leadership contrasted with and was affected by the Kennedy legacy) BD (AE,213; LI,177;NI,127)

Codes (right side of page): BD = Benchmark, Declarative; BP = Benchmark, Procedural; BC = Benchmark, Contextual
1st letter of each code in parentheses *2nd letter of code* *Number*
A = NCHS: National Standards for U.S. History E = Explicitly stated in document Page number of cited document
L = Lessons From History I = Implied in document
N = NAEP: Provisional Item Specifications

MREL

(AE,214)

28. Understands the Cold War and the Korean and Vietnam conflicts in domestic and international politics

Level II (Grades 5-6)

BD (AE,214;LI,169;NI,80)
- Understands influences on international relations after World War II (e.g., the "flawed peace" resulting from World War II, the effectiveness of the United Nations in reducing international tensions and conflict)

BD (AE,214;LI,170)
- Understands the significance of McCarthyism (e.g., its effects, the reasons for its demise, how it changed the lives of individuals who were accused of supporting Communism)

BD (AE,216)
- Understands shifts in international relations after World War II (e.g., the development of nation states in Africa, Asia, Latin America, and the Middle East, and the responses of the Truman and Eisenhower administrations; how the modern state of Israel became an independent country after World War II)

BD (AE,218;LE,179;LI,180)
- Knows the location of the Vietnam War in Southeast Asia, how the war escalated during the 1960s, its effect on Vietnamese combatants, civilians, and on Americans in Vietnam

Level III (Grades 7-8)

BD (AE,214,215;LI,169)
- Understands major events in U.S.foreign policy during the early Cold War period (e.g., the major Soviet-U.S. clashes and the implementation of the containment policy during the Truman and Eisenhower administrations, the circumstances that led to the Marshall Plan and its accomplishments, the factors that led to the Korean conflict and the effects of the police action on U.S. foreign and domestic policy)

BD (AE,214,215;LI,170)
- Understands the role of McCarthyism in the early Cold War period (e.g., the rise of McCarthyism, the effect of McCarthyism on civil liberties, McCarthy's fall from power)

BD (AE,216;LI,178-179;NI,81)
- Understands the differences between the foreign policies of Kennedy and Johnson (e.g., the Kennedy administration's policy toward Cuba, how the Kennedy and Johnson administrations differed in Latin American policy, changes in U.S. foreign policy toward the Soviet Union during the Kennedy and Johnson years and the reasons for these changes)

BD (AE,216;LI,170;NI,80)
- Understands the Truman and Eisenhower doctrines of foreign policy in terms of the international tensions that prompted each

---

Codes (right side of page):   BD = Benchmark, Declarative; BP = Benchmark, Procedural; BC = Benchmark, Contextual
1st letter of each code in parentheses   *2nd letter of code*   *Number*
A = NCHS: National Standards for U.S. History   E = Explicitly stated in document   Page number of cited document
L = Lessons From History   I = Implied in document
N = NAEP: Provisional Item Specifications

McREL

BD (AE,218;LI,170,179-180;NI,75)

- Understands political and social characteristics of the Vietnam War (e.g., early U.S. involvement in Vietnam following World War II and the policies of the Truman and Eisenhower administrations; growing disillusionment with the Vietnam War and the impact of the War on American society; the Vietnam policies of the Kennedy, Johnson, and Nixon administrations and consequences of the war's escalation)

Level IV (Grades 9-12)

BD (AE,214-215;LE,169;NE,131)

- Understands the origins of the Cold War and the advent of nuclear politics (e.g., the mutual suspicions and divisions fragmenting the Grand Alliance at the end of World War II, U.S. support for "self-determination" and the U.S.S.R's desire for security in Eastern Europe, the practice of "atomic diplomacy")

BD (AE,215;LI,170)

- Understands the various anti-communist movements after World War II (e.g., causes and consequences of the second "Red Scare" that emerged after World War II, the emergence of McCarthyism and its impact on civil liberties)

BD (AE,216-217;LI,169,178-179;NI,131,132)

- Understands U.S. foreign policy from the Truman adminstration to the Johnson administration (e.g., U.S. policy regarding the British mandate over Palestine and the establishment of the state of Israel, the major arguments supporting and opposing the "containment" policy, Kennedy's response to the Bay of Pigs and the Cuban Missile crises, the Kennedy-Johnson response to anti-colonial movements in Africa, U.S. responses to "wars of liberation" in Africa and Asia in the 1960s, how the Korean War affected the premises of U.S. foreign policy)

BD (AE,218,219;LI,179-180;NI,132)

- Understands the political elements of the Vietnam War (e.g., U.S. foreign policy related to Vietnam in the 1960s, the provisions of the Paris Peace Treaty of 1973 and Nixon's accomplishments, the constitutional issues involved in the Vietnam War)

BD (AE,218,219;LI,179-180)

- Understands the social issues that resulted from U.S. involvement in the Vietnam War (e.g., why the Vietnam War contributed to a generational conflict and concomitant lack of respect for traditional authority figures, the impact of class and race on war-time mobilization)

Codes (right side of page):   BD = Benchmark, Declarative; BP = Benchmark, Procedural; BC = Benchmark, Contextual
1st letter of each code in parentheses   *2nd letter of code*   *Number*
A = NCHS: National Standards for U.S. History   E = Explicitly stated in document   Page number of cited document
L = Lessons From History   I = Implied in document
N = NAEP: Provisional Item Specifications

McREL

29. Understands the struggle for racial and gender equality and for the extension of civil liberties (AE,220)

Level II (Grades 5-6)

- Understands the development of the Civil Rights Movement (e.g., how the "freedom ride," "civil disobedience," and "non-violent resistance" were important to the civil rights movement; how civil rights were resisted in the South between 1954 and 1965; Martin Luther King Jr.'s "I Have a Dream" speech in the context of major events; the goals and accomplishments of individuals and groups in the movement; the Supreme court case *Brown* v. *Board of Education* and its significance in advancing civil rights) BD (AE,220;LE,177-178;NI,75;NE,75)

- Understands the involvement of diverse groups in the civil rights movement (e.g., regional issues important to diverse groups and their efforts to attain equality and civil rights after World War II; the grievances, goals, accomplishments, and failures of Asian, Mexican, and Native Americans in advancing the movement for civil and equal rights) BD (AE,222;LI,178)

- Understands the development of the post-World War II women's movement (e.g., the major issues affecting women, the conflicts these issues engendered, and the emergence of the National Organization for women; post-World War II attitudes toward women) BD (AE,224;LI,178;NI,75)

- Understands the Warren Court's interpretation of freedom of religion (e.g., the importance of the separation of church and state, and freedom of religion in contemporary American society, local and regional issues regarding religious freedom) BD (AE,226;NI,75)

Level III (Grades 7-8)

- Understands individual and institutional influences on the civil rights movement (e.g., important milestones in the civil rights movement between 1954 and 1965; the effects of white resistance in the South; the roles and ideologies of Martin Luther King, Jr. and Malcolm X; the effects of the constitutional steps taken in the executive, judicial, and legislative branches of government; Eisenhower's reasons for dispatching federal troops to Little Rock in 1957) BD (AE,220,221;LI,175,177-178; NI,75,LE,170)

- Understands the role of diverse groups in the movement to advance civil and equal rights after World War II (e.g., the development of movements and the principle grievances of Mexican, Asian, and Native Americans in the post-World War II period, and the means by which they worked to improve their civil and equal rights and their status in modern American society) BD (AE,222,223;LI,178)

Codes (right side of page):   BD = Benchmark, Declarative; BP = Benchmark, Procedural; BC = Benchmark, Contextual
1st letter of each code in parentheses   *2nd letter of code*   *Number*
A = NCHS: National Standards for U.S. History   E = Explicitly stated in document   Page number of cited document
L = Lessons From History   I = Implied in document
N = NAEP: Provisional Item Specifications

- Understands factors that shaped the women's rights movement after World War II (e.g., the _{BD (AE,224;LI,178)} evolution of the movement for women's rights in the 20th century, the factors that contributed to modern feminism and the movement's accomplishments and setbacks, conflicts originating from within and outside of the women's movement, conflicting perspectives over the Equal Rights Amendment)

BD (AE,224;LI,178)

- Understands conflicts raised by the Warren Court decisions (e.g., "due process of law" and the Warren Court's stand on the extension of due process rights for the accused; the decision *Engel* v. *Vitale* and why the decision provoked widespread opposition)

BD (AE,226;NE,75)

Level IV (Grades 9-12)

BD (AE,221;LE,177;NI,126,127)
- Understands how legislation and the Supreme Court influenced the civil rights movement (e.g., the social and constitutional issues involved in *Plessy* v. *Ferguson* (1896) and *Brown* v. *Board of Education* (1954) court cases; the connection between legislative acts, Supreme Court decisions, and the civil rights movement)

BD (AE,220,221;LE,177;NI,126,127)
- Understands significant influences on the civil rights movement (e.g., the leadership of Martin Luther King, Jr.; the role of women in the civil rights movement and in shaping the struggle for civil rights)

BD (AE,220)
- Understands how the focus shifted from *de jure* segregation to the nationwide assault on *de facto* segregation

BD (AE,222,223;LI,178)
- Understands how diverse groups united during the civil rights movement (e.g., the development of the Asian Civil Rights Movement and the Native American Civil Rights Movement, the issues and goals of the farm labor movement and La Raza Unida, the escalation from civil disobedience to "Brown Power" and "Red Power")

BD (AE,226,227;NI,126,127)
- Understands how various Warren Court decisions influenced society (e.g., the Warren Court's extension of due process rights for the accused; the Warren Court's reasoning in establishing the "one man, one vote" principle; the Warren Court's interpretation of the First Amendment guarantee of freedom of religion)

Codes (right side of page):   BD = Benchmark, Declarative; BP = Benchmark, Procedural; BC = Benchmark, Contextual
1st letter of each code in parentheses   *2nd letter of code*   *Number*
A = NCHS: National Standards for U.S. History   E = Explicitly stated in document   Page number of cited document
L = Lessons From History   I = Implied in document
N = NAEP: Provisional Item Specifications

(AE,229)

30. **Understands developments in foreign and domestic policies between the Nixon and Clinton presidencies**

Level II (Grades 5-6)

BD (AE,229)
- Understands the ideas and major events of the Nixon administration years (e.g., how "law and order," the "Silent Majority," and the "New Federalism" were used by the Nixon administration; the Nixon administration's involvement in Watergate, and the role of the media in exposing the scandal)

BD (AE,231;LI,183;LE,183)
- Understands characteristics of America's economic problems of the 1970s (e.g., the Republican and Democratic administrations' attempts to deal with economic "stagflation," the OPEC countries and how they controlled oil prices in the 1970s)

BD (AE,231;LI,183;NI,79)
- Understands elements of both the Reagan and Bush presidencies (e.g., the reasons for Reagan's popularity, the major domestic problems facing Presidents Reagan and Bush, and how their administrations dealt with these issues)

BD (AE,234;LI,184,185;NI,80)
- Understands the events that influenced U.S. foreign policy from the Carter to the Bush administrations (e.g., the crisis areas around the world and some of the major peace initiatives made during the Carter administration; the countries that made up the Soviet Union and the geographic changes after the fall of the U.S.S.R and communist states in eastern Europe; places in the Middle East, Central America, the Caribbean, Africa, and Asia where U.S. advisers and military forces were involved during the Reagan and Bush years)

Level III (Grades 7-8)

BD (AE,229;LI,182)
- Understands the impact of the Nixon administration's ideas and policies on American society (e.g., the "Silent Majority" and factors that caused so many Americans to support Nixon and his "law and order" stance; the ways in which Nixon initiated and changed social and environmental programs)

BD (AE,230;LI,182)
- Understands how Watergate influenced American society (e.g., the events of Watergate; the effects of Watergate on public opinion with regard to the presidency, the federal government, and the system of checks and balances)

BD (AE,231)
- Understands key domestic issues of the post-Nixon years (e.g., President Ford's pardon of Richard Nixon; the successes and failures of the Carter administration)

Codes (right side of page):   BD = Benchmark, Declarative; BP = Benchmark, Procedural; BC = Benchmark, Contextual
1st letter of each code in parentheses   *2nd letter of code*   *Number*
A = NCHS: National Standards for U.S. History   E = Explicitly stated in document   Page number of cited document
L = Lessons From History   I = Implied in document
N = NAEP: Provisional Item Specifications

MREL

- Understands how the Reagan presidency influenced American perceptions of government BD (AE,231,232;LI,182-183;NI,81) (e.g., the impact of the "Reagan Revolution" on federalism and public perceptions of the role of government, Reagan's environmental program and the views of its supporters and opponents, the Iran-Contra affair and the role of individuals involved in it)

- Understands the domestic problems facing President Bush and the programs his BD (AE,232) administration presented to deal with these issues (e.g., the effectiveness of the administration in dealing with the recession, the effectiveness of the Republican administration in dealing with the Democratic congress)

- Understands the principal issues and legislation affecting organized labor in the post-World BD (AE,232) War II era (e.g., terms such as "open shop," "closed shop," "featherbedding," "right to work" laws; how the general public has perceived labor unions; the extent to which economic conditions have affected membership in labor unions; the relationship between the Reagan-Bush administrations and organized labor)

- Understands the major foreign policy events and how they influenced public opinion of the BD (AE,234,235;LI,184,185;NI,80,81) administrations from Nixon to Clinton (e.g., Nixon's foreign policy toward the Soviet Union, the People's Republic of China, and the Middle East; President Carter's role in the Camp David Accords; the Iranian hostage crisis; the foreign policy of the Reagan administration and domestic and foreign reactions to it; reasons for the collapse of Communist governments in Eastern Europe and the U.S.S.R; foreign policy goals of the Bush and Clinton administrations and their effectiveness)

Level IV (Grades 9-12)

- Understands the social and political impact of Nixon's domestic policies (e.g., the policy of BD (AE,229,330;LE,182;NI,127) "law and order," the political significance of Nixon's administration's "southern strategy," Nixon's support of "New Federalism," the Nixon administration's policy for dealing with the twin problems of recession and inflation)

- Understands the events and legacy of the Watergate break-in (e.g., the involvement of the BD (AE,229,230;LI,182) Nixon administration in the cover-up, the constitutional issues raised by the affair, and the role of the media in exposing the scandal)

- Understands how the Ford and Carter administrations dealt with major domestic issues of BD (AE,232;LI,183) the 1970s (e.g., how the Ford and Carter administrations handled the economic situation of the 1970s, how Presidents Ford and Carter addressed the concept of the "imperial

---

Codes (right side of page):   BD = Benchmark, Declarative; BP = Benchmark, Procedural; BC = Benchmark, Contextual
1st letter of each code in parentheses   *2nd letter of code*   *Number*
A = NCHS: National Standards for U.S. History   E = Explicitly stated in document   Page number of cited document
L = Lessons From History   I = Implied in document
N = NAEP: Provisional Item Specifications

187

McREL

presidency" after Watergate and attempted to restore credibility to the presidency, Carter's program for dealing with the energy crisis)

BD (AE,231,232,233;LI,182-183;NI,132)

- Understands the impact of the Reagan presidency on relations with other countries (e.g., Reagan's view of the Soviet Union as an "evil empire" and how that shaped defense policy, the issues raised in the Iran-Contra affair)

BD (AE,231,233;LI,183)

- Understands the major economic issues from the Reagan through the Clinton presidencies (e.g., the impact of Reagan's tax policies on the national economy; why labor unions declined in the Reagan-Bush era, the impact of recession and the growing national debt on the Bush and Clinton administration's domestic agendas)

BD (AE,235,236;LI,184;NI,131)

- Understands how U.S. foreign policy shaped international relations from the Nixon administration to the Carter years (e.g., Nixon's foreign policy during the Cold War, U.S. goals and objectives in the Middle East)

BD (AE,234,236;LI,185;NI,132,133)

- Understands the influence of U.S. foreign policy on international events during the Reagan and Bush administrations (e.g., the pros and cons of U.S. intervention in the Persian Gulf under Reagan and Bush, the Reagan administration's policy toward South Africa, the reasons for the collapse of communism in Eastern Europe and the Soviet Union)

BD (AE,234,NE,132)

- Understands influences on U.S. foreign policy (e.g., how human rights has been used in American foreign policy; the interconnections between the U.S.'s role as superpower with the evolving political struggles in the Middle East, Africa, Asia, and Latin America)

(AE,237)

31. Understands the major social and economic developments in contemporary America

Level II (Grades 5-6)

BD (AE,237;NI,75)

- Understands contemporary issues concerning the economy, gender, and ethnicity (e.g., issues involving justice and common welfare; how interest groups attempted to achieve their goals of equality and justice; the changing goals of the women's movement and the issues currently dividing women; how African, Asian, Hispanic, and Native Americans have shaped American life and retained their cultural heritage)

BD (AE,240;LI,181;NI,78)

- Understands the factors that prompted the new immigration in contemporary American society (e.g., areas of the world from which most immigrants have come)

Codes (right side of page): BD = Benchmark, Declarative; BP = Benchmark, Procedural; BC = Benchmark, Contextual
1st letter of each code in parentheses   *2nd letter of code*   *Number*
A = NCHS: National Standards for U.S. History   E = Explicitly stated in document   Page number of cited document
L = Lessons From History   I = Implied in document
N = NAEP: Provisional Item Specifications

- Understands influences on religion in contemporary society (e.g., issues related to religious belief, how changing immigration patterns affected religious diversity)

  BD (AE,242;LI,181;LE,181;NI,77,78)

- Understands changes in the contemporary workplace (e.g., how scientific and technological changes affected the workplace and productivity, the impact of trade and overseas competition on the economy, kinds of education and skills required for available jobs)

  BD (AE,244;LI,183,184;NI,79,80)

- Understands aspects of contemporary American culture (e.g., the effects of ethnic diversity on popular culture, sports and entertainment figures who advertise specific products)

  BD (AE,245;LI,176;NI,77)

Level III (Grades 7-8)

- Understands how different groups attempted to achieve their goals (e.g., issues important to the women's movement and the different methods for achieving those goals; the grievances of African, Asian, Hispanic, and Native Americans and the steps they have taken to rectify past injustices; local community efforts to adapt facilities for the physically challenged)

  BD (AE,238;NI,75)

- Understands the influences on recent immigration patterns (e.g., reasons for internal migrations from the "Rustbelt" to the "Sunbelt" and its impact on politics; reasons for the decisions of new immigrants to move to a new land and the challenges they faced; how the immigration acts of 1965, 1986, and 1991 changed immigration patterns)

  BD (AE,240;LI,181;NI,77,78)

- Understands the growth of religious issues in contemporary society (e.g., issues regarding the guarantee of no establishment of religion and the free exercise clauses of the First Amendment, the growth of religious fundamentalism and the appeal of television evangelists, the significance of religious groups in local communities and their approaches to social issues, the position of major religious groups on political and social issues)

  BD (AE,242;LI,181)

- Understands changes in the workplace and the economy in contemporary America (e.g., the changing composition of the American workforce; ways in which computers and accessories such as modems and CD-ROM drives increase worker productivity and efficiency; how new technologies and increased global competition affect the contemporary U.S. economy)

  BD (AE,244;LI,183,184;NI,79)

- Understands various influences on American culture (e.g., the influence of the media on contemporary American culture; how ethnic art, food, music, and clothing are incorporated into mainstream culture and society)

  BD (AE,245;NI,77,78)

Codes (right side of page):   BD = Benchmark, Declarative; BP = Benchmark, Procedural; BC = Benchmark, Contextual
1st letter of each code in parentheses   *2nd letter of code*   *Number*
A = NCHS: National Standards for U.S. History   E = Explicitly stated in document   Page number of cited document
L = Lessons From History   I = Implied in document
N = NAEP: Provisional Item Specifications

McREL

Level IV (Grades 9-12)

BD (AE,237,238,239;NI,125-126;NE,128)
- Understands major contemporary social issues and the groups involved (e.g., arguments for and against affirmative action and its effects on women and minorities; issues raised by African, Asian, Hispanic, and Native Americans and how they have organized to address grievances; the evolution of government support for the rights of the physically and emotionally challenged; the emergence of the Gay Liberation Movement and civil rights of gay Americans; contributions of diverse peoples and cultures to American society; how the modern feminist movement has been both a success and a failure)

BD (AE,240,241;NI,77,128,129;LI,181)
- Understands how recent immigration and migration patterns impacted social and political issues (e.g., how new immigration raised issues concerning intergroup relations and governmental responsibilities, demographic, and resident mobility since 1970 and the effect of migration from the "Rustbelt" to the "Sunbelt" on representation in Congress, demographic changes resulting from the Immigration Act of 1965)

BD (AE,242,243;LI,181)
- Understands how the rise of religious groups and movements influenced political issues in contemporary American society (e.g., the causes and significance of religious evangelism and its effect on American political and religious culture in the 1980s; the position of major religious groups on such issues as abortion, gay rights, women in the clergy, and educational issues; how Supreme Court decisions since 1968 have affected the meaning and practice of religious freedom)

BD (AE,244;LI,183,184;NI,129,130)
- Understands how changes in the national and global economy have influenced the workplace (e.g., the impact of the "post-industrial" economy on the nature of work and job creation, the influence of new technology on education and learning, the advantages and disadvantages of increased global trade and competition on the U.S. economy)

BD (AE,245,LE,186)
- Understands the influence of social change and the entertainment industry in shaping views on art, gender, and culture (e.g., how social change affected artisitic expression in contemporary American society, increased commercialization of professional sports and popular culture, the reflection of values in popular TV shows, the effects of women's participation in sports on gender roles and career choices)

Codes (right side of page):   BD = Benchmark, Declarative; BP = Benchmark, Procedural; BC = Benchmark, Contextual
1st letter of each code in parentheses   *2nd letter of code*   *Number*
A = NCHS: National Standards for U.S. History   E = Explicitly stated in document   Page number of cited document
L = Lessons From History   I = Implied in document
N = NAEP: Provisional Item Specifications

190

MREL

Summary of Standards for World History

Era 1   The Beginnings of Human Society
1. Understands the biological and cultural processes that shaped the earliest human communities
2. Understands the processes that contributed to the emergence of agricultural societies around the world

Era 2   Early Civilizations and the Rise of Pastoral Peoples, 4000-1000 BCE
3. Understands the major characteristics of civilization and the development of civilizations in Mesopotamia, Egypt, and the Indus Valley
4. Understands how agrarian societies spread and new states emerged in the third and second millennium BCE
5. Understands the political, social, and cultural consequences of population movements and militarization in Eurasia in the second millennium BCE

Era 3   Classical Traditions, Major Religions, and Giant Empires, 1000 BCE-300 CE
6. Understands technological and cultural innovation and change from 1000 to 600 BCE
7. Understands how Aegean civilization emerged and how interrelations developed among peoples of the eastern Mediterranean and Southwest Asia from 600 to 200 BCE
8. Understands how major religious and large-scale empires arose in the Mediterranean basin, China, and India from 500 BCE to 300 CE
9. Understands how early agrarian civilizations arose in Mesoamerica

Era 4   Expanding Zones of Exchange and Encounter, 300-1000 CE
10. Understands the Imperial crises and their aftermath in various regions from 300 to 700 CE
11. Understands the causes and consequences of the development of Islamic civilization between the 7th and 10th centuries
12. Understands major developments in East Asia in the era of the Tang Dynasty from 600 to 900 CE
13. Understands the political, social, and cultural redefinitions in Europe from 500 to 1000 CE
14. Understands state-building in the Northeast and West Africa, and the southward migrations of Bantu-speaking peoples
15. Understands the rise of centers of civilization in Mesoamerica and Andean South America in the first millennium CE

Era 5   Intensified Hemispheric Interactions 1000-1500 CE
16. Understands the maturation of an interregional system of communication, trade, and cultural exchange during a period of Chinese economic power and Islamic expansion
17. Understands the redefinition of European society and culture from 1000 to 1300 CE
18. Understands the rise of the Mongol empire and its consequences for Eurasian peoples from 1200 to 1350
19. Understands the growth of states, towns, and trade in Sub-Saharan Africa between the 11th

and 15th centuries

20. Understands patterns of crisis and recovery in Afro-Eurasia between 1300 and 1450

21. Understands the expansion of states and civilizations in the Americas between 1000 and 1500

Era 6 Global Expansion and Encounter, 1450-1770

22. Understands how the transoceanic interlinking of all major regions of the world between 1450 and 1600 led to global transformations

23. Understands how European society experienced political, economic, and cultural transformations in an age of global intercommunication between 1450 and 1750

24. Understands how large territorial empires dominated much of Eurasia between the 16th and 18th centuries

25. Understands the economic, political, and cultural interrelations among peoples of Africa, Europe, and the Americas between 1500 and 1750

26. Understands transformations in Asian societies in the era of European expansion

27. Understands major global trends from 1450 to 1770

Era 7 An Age of Revolutions, 1750-1914

28. Understands the causes and consequences of political revolutions in the late 18th and early 19th centuries

29. Understands the causes and consequences of the agricultural and industrial revolutions from 1700 to 1850

30. Understands how Eurasian societies were transformed in an era of global trade and the emergence of European power from 1750 to 1850

31. Understands patterns of nationalism, state-building, and social reform in Europe and the Americas from 1830 to 1914

32. Understands patterns of global change in the era of Western military and economic domination from 1850 to 1914

33. Understands major global trends from 1750 to 1914

Era 8 The 20th Century

34. Understands global and economic trends in the high period of Western dominance

35. Understands the causes and global consequences of World War I

36. Understands the search for peace and stability throughout the world in the 1920s and 1930s

37. Understands the causes and global consequences of World War II

38. Understands how new international power relations took shape in the context of the Cold War and how colonial empires broke up

39. Understands the promises and paradoxes of the second half of the 20th century

1. Understands the biological and cultural processes that shaped the earliest human communities ^(WE,41)

Level II (Grades 5-6)

- Understands scientific evidence regarding early hominid evolution in Africa (e.g., daily life of individuals and communities in early hunter-gatherer populations; major anthropological discoveries, their locations, and their discoverers; how scientists use archaeological evidence to reconstruct early human evolution and cultural development) ^{BD (R;WE,41;LI,197;NI,41)}

- Understands the social and cultural characteristics of hunter-gatherer communities in various continental regions (e.g., similarities and differences between hunter-gatherer communities in Africa, Eurasia, and the Americas; how local environments affected the lifestyles of early Cro-Magnon and other communities; location and composition of archaeological discoveries and what understanding these bring to Neanderthal culture and community life) ^{BD (C;WE,43)}

Level III (Grades 7-8)

- Understands scientific methods used to determine the dates and evolution of different human communities (e.g., different types of evidence dating techniques; different methods employed by archaeologists, geologists, and anthropologists to study hominid evolution; how human remains can be used to construct possible chronological sequences of human evolution) ^{BD (R;WE,41,42)}

- Understands the role of the environment in the development of different human communities (e.g., how the nomadic life of early hunter-gatherer groups such as the Cro-Magnons was a response to local environments; current and past theories regarding the emergence of Homo sapiens sapiens and the processes by which human groups populated the major world regions; how environmental conditions in the last Ice Age possibly affected change in the economy, culture, and organization of human communities) ^{BD (C;WE,43,44;LE,197)}

- Understands how different human communities expressed their beliefs (e.g., possible social, cultural, and/or religious meanings inferred from late paleolithic cave paintings found in Spain and France; theories about the ways in which hunter-gatherers may have communicated, maintained memory of past events, and expressed religious feelings) ^{BD (C;WE,44)}

Level IV (Grades 9-12)

- Understands physical, social, and cultural characteristics of different human communities ^{BD (R;WE,42;LE,197)}

Codes (right side of page):   BD = Benchmark, Declarative; BP = Benchmark, Procedural; BC = Benchmark, Contextual
1st letter of each code in parentheses   *2nd letter of code*   *Number*
W = NCHS: World History Standards   E = Explicitly stated in document   Page number of cited document
L = Lessons from History   I = Implied in document
C = Core material
R = Related material

McREL

(e.g., the possible types of early hominid communities; characteristics of skeletal remains of non-hominid, primate, hominid, and Homo sapiens and how to classify them chronologically; the approximate chronology, sequence, and territorial range of Australopithecine, Homo erectus, Neanderthal, and early Homo sapiens sapiens)

BD (R;WE,42)
- Understands methods by which early human communities are studied and what these studies reveal (e.g., the way in which newly discovered sites and investigative techniques used to examine them affect the study and understanding of human evolution, how common refuse can be studied to make inferences about earlier communities)

BD (C;WE,44)
- Understands how different kinds of evidence are used to determine the cultural characteristics of early human communities (e.g., how non-verbal evidence such as burials, carvings, and paintings can indicate the presence of religion; how archaeological evidence demonstrates the influences of climate, geographic location, and economic specialization on everyday life)

BD (C;WE,44)
- Understands environmental, biological, and cultural influences on early human communities (e.g., the proposition that Mesolithic peoples were the first to take advantage of a changing climate; biological and cultural relationships between Neanderthal and Homo sapiens sapiens; why language developed as a way for humans to communicate and how it helped early humans hunt, establish roles, rules, and structure within communities)

(WE,45)
2. **Understands the processes that contributed to the emergence of agricultural societies around the world**

Level II (Grades 5-6)

BD (C;WE,45)
- Understands the role of agriculture in early settled communities (e.g., differences between wild and domestic plants and animals; how patterns of settlement were influenced by agricultural practices; how archaeological evidence explains the technology, social organization, and cultural life of settled farming communities in Southwest Asia)

BD (R;WE,47;LE,198)
- Understands the development of early agricultural communities in different regions of the world (e.g., differences between hunter-gatherer, fishing, and agrarian communities; social, cultural, and economic characteristics of large agricultural settlements and their unique problems; the development of tropical agriculture in Southeast Asia)

Codes (right side of page):   BD = Benchmark, Declarative; BP = Benchmark, Procedural; BC = Benchmark, Contextual
1st letter of each code in parentheses   *2nd letter of code*   *Number*
W = NCHS: World History Standards   E = Explicitly stated in document   Page number of cited document
L = Lessons from History   I = Implied in document
C = Core material
R = Related material   194   MᴄREL

Level III (Grades 7-8)

- Understands inherent disadvantages and advantages of hunter-gatherer and early farming styles ^{BD (C;WE,45;LE,198)}

- Understands immediate and long-term impacts and influences of early agricultural communities (e.g., the effect of new tools and other objects on early farming settlements, how human communities might have inadvertently domesticated wheat, whether fishing was considered a nomadic or agricultural way of life) ^{BD (C;WE,45,46;LI,198)}

- Understands what archaeological evidence reveals about the social and cultural conditions of agricultural societies (e.g., the emergence of social class divisions, occupational specialization, differences in gender roles; long distance trade routes in Southwest Asia and the importance of obsidian to this trade) ^{BD (R;WE,47;LE,198;LI,199)}

- Understands influences on the spread of agricultural communities (e.g., how local needs and conditions affected food plant domestication and world-wide patterns of settlement) ^{BD (R;WE,47)}

- Understands the bases for the argument that agricultural life was an advance in human social development ^{BD (R;WE,48;LI,198)}

Level IV (Grades 9-12)

- Understands how agricultural communities maintained their produce and livestock (e.g., the importance of controlling food supplies and storing them in the "Neolithic revolution," how and why human groups domesticated wild grains and animals after the last Ice Age) ^{BD (C;WE,45,46)}

- Understands social and cultural factors that define agricultural communities (e.g., archaeological evidence that distinguishes hunter-gatherer from agricultural sites, the relationship between agricultural production and cultural change) ^{BD (C;WE,46)}

- Understands the role of geography in the development of certain agricultural communities (e.g., the location and beneficial characteristics of areas in Southwest Asia and the Nile Valley where early farming first appeared) ^{BD (C;WE,45)}

- Understands what environmental and architectural evidence reveals about different types of large agricultural communities (e.g., the differences between hunter-gatherer and agricultural sites; the locations of different types of communities between 10,000 and 4,000 BCE; how patterns of layout, fortification, and standardization in large settlements helped transform human culture) ^{BD (R;WE,47,48;LI,198)}

Codes (right side of page):   BD = Benchmark, Declarative; BP = Benchmark, Procedural; BC = Benchmark, Contextual
1st letter of each code in parentheses   *2nd letter of code*   *Number*
W = NCHS: World History Standards   E = Explicitly stated in document   Page number of cited document
L = Lessons from History   I = Implied in document
C = Core material
R = Related material

McREL

BD (R;WE,47)

- Understands what archaeological evidence has revealed about the cultural beliefs of early agricultural societies (e.g., the emergence of complete belief systems, including female deity worship)

BD (R;WE,48)

- Understands why some groups developed and accepted complete sedentary agriculture and other retained earlier subsistence methods

(WE,52)

3. Understands the major characteristics of civilization and the development of civilizations in Mesopotamia, Egypt, and the Indus Valley

Level II (Grades 5-6)

BD (C;WE,52)

- Understands the concept of "civilization" (e.g., the various criteria used to define "civilization" and fundamental differences between civilizations and other forms of social organization)

BD (C;WE,52;LI,199,207)

- Understands influences on the development of various civilizations in the 4th and 3rd millennia BCE (e.g., how the natural environment of the Tigris-Euphrates, Nile, and Indus Valleys shaped the early development of civilization; different characteristics of urban development in Mesopotamia, Egypt, and the Indus Valley)

BD (C;WE,52;LE,200,205,207)

- Understands the characteristics of writing forms in Mesopotamia, Egypt, and the Indus Valley and how written records shaped political, legal, religious, and cultural life

BD (R;WE,54;LE,199,206)

- Understands how economic, political, and environmental factors influenced the civilizations of Mesopotamia, Egypt, and the Indus Valley (e.g., the impact of trade networks connecting various regions of Southwest Asia on Mesopotamian civilization; the importance of commercial, cultural, and political connections between Egypt and peoples of Nubia along the upper Nile; how geography and climate affected trade in the Nile Valley)

Level III (Grades 7-8)

BD (C;WE,53;LE,199,203)

- Understands environmental and cultural factors that shaped the development of Mesopotamia, Egypt and the Indus Valley (e.g., demands of the natural environment; development of religious and ethical belief systems and how they legitimized political and social order; different characteristics of urban development; how written records such as the Epic of Gilgamesh reflected and shaped the political, religious, and cultural life of Mesopotamia)

Codes (right side of page):   BD = Benchmark, Declarative; BP = Benchmark, Procedural; BC = Benchmark, Contextual
1st letter of each code in parentheses   *2nd letter of code*   *Number*
W = NCHS: World History Standards   E = Explicitly stated in document   Page number of cited document
L = Lessons from History   I = Implied in document
C = Core material
R = Related material   196   MREL

- Understands how Mohenjo-Daro meets criteria for defining civilization, and differences with ^BD (C;WE,53) other forms of social organization such as hunter-gatherer bands and Neolithic agricultural societies

- Understands the role of economics in shaping the development of Mesopotamia, Egypt, and ^BD (R;WE,54) the Indus Valley (e.g., the commercial trade routes between the three civilizations; the economic and cultural significance of the trade routes between Egypt, India, and Mesopotamia in the 3rd millennium)

Level IV (Grades 9-12)

- Understands influences on the social and economic framework of Mesopotamia, Egypt, and ^BD (C;WE,52,53;LE,199,200,207) the Indus Valley (e.g., the characteristics of government and military in Egypt and Mesopotamia and the ways in which central authorities commanded labor and taxes from peasant farmers; how architectural, artistic, technological, and scientific achievements of these civilizations affected the economics of daily life)

- Understands how written codes and stories reflect social conditions in Mesopotamia, Egypt, ^BD (C;WE,53) and the Indus Valley (e.g., aspects of ethical values, social hierarchy and attitudes, and roles of women in Mesopotamia as illustrated in the code of Hammurabi; how the biblical account of Genesis and the Enuma Elish from Babylon reflect contrasting beliefs)

- Understands features of trading networks in Mesopotamia, Egypt, and the Indus Valley (e.g., ^BD (R;WE,55;LI,202,208) geographical characteristics that encouraged Mesopotamia to engage in trade and those which made trade difficult, shifting political relationships between trading partners in the 1st and 2nd millennia BCE and sources of conflict between them, technology and the breadth of the Indus trade network, evidence and importance of cultural connections between trading partners)

4. **Understands how agrarian societies spread and new states emerged in the 3rd and 2nd** ^(WE,56) **millennium BCE**

Level II (Grades 5-6)

- Understands significant aspects of early Chinese society and religion (e.g., early Chinese ^BD (C;WE,56;LE,208,209;LI,208) urban societies and how they compare to those of Mesopotamia and the Indus Valley, the influence of the natural environment on Huang He [Yellow River] civilization, the nature of Shang ancestor worship and what it illustrates about concepts of life and death in Shang

---

Codes (right side of page):   BD = Benchmark, Declarative; BP = Benchmark, Procedural; BC = Benchmark, Contextual
1st letter of each code in parentheses   *2nd letter of code*   *Number*
W = NCHS: World History Standards   E = Explicitly stated in document   Page number of cited document
L = Lessons from History   I = Implied in document
C = Core material
R = Related material

McREL

society)

- Understands how the development of different types of tools influenced Chinese civilization ^{BD (C;WE,56)} (e.g., the fundamentals of bronze-making technology, and the uses and significance of bronze tools, weapons, and luxury goods in the 3rd and 2nd millennia BCE; the unique nature of Chinese writing tools, surfaces, and styles in the 2nd millennium BCE)

- Understands how technology influenced different regions of the world (e.g., changes for ^{BD (R;WE,58;LE,198)} humankind and civilization brought on by the bow and arrow and by pottery; how the advent of the plow influenced new agrarian societies in Southwest Asia, the Mediterrean basin, and temperate Europe; what physical evidence indicated about the characteristics of the agrarian society of ancient Egypt and the life of the Pharaoh)

Level III (Grades 7-8)

- Understands how the natural environment shaped Huang He civilization (e.g., how changes ^{BD (C;WE,56;LE,208;LI,208)} in the course of the Huang He river challenged citizens and government; how the influence in the Huang He civilization compared to the environment's impact on Mesopotamia, Egypt, and the Indus Valley)

- Understands what archaeological evidence (e.g., oracle bone inscriptions, bronze vessels) ^{BD (C;WE,57;LI,208)} reveals about Chinese history during the Shang Dynasty

- Understands the rise of urban and complex agrarian societies in the 3rd and 2nd millennium ^{BD (R;WE,58)} BCE (e.g., how the Minoan civilization emerged on Crete and significant cultural achievements; the origins and possible purpose of Stonehenge and the effort made to create it)

- Understands the significance of advancements in tool and weapon technology (e.g., the ^{BD (R;WE,58)} technology of bronze casting and why bronze weapons were superior to those made of stone; how the development of the plow, bow and arrow, and pottery affected early man and led to changes in gender roles)

Level IV (Grades 9-12)

- Understands the social, cultural, and political characteristics of the Shang Dynasty (e.g., the ^{BD (C;WE,57)} development of royal, military-religious leadership, and government under the Shang Dynasty and the development of social hierarchy, religious institutions, and writing; the role that Chinese peasants played in sustaining the wealth and power of the Shang political

---

Codes (right side of page):   BD = Benchmark, Declarative; BP = Benchmark, Procedural; BC = Benchmark, Contextual
1st letter of each code in parentheses   *2nd letter of code*   *Number*
W = NCHS: World History Standards   E = Explicitly stated in document   Page number of cited document
L = Lessons from History   I = Implied in document
C = Core material
R = Related material

centers)

- Understands evidence of social and cultural development of Chinese civilization in the 3rd ^BD (C;WE,57) and 2nd millenium BCE (e.g., evidence that the Chinese had developed urbanization, sophisticated social cooperation, and written language before 1700 BCE; the physical evidence that highlights possible cultural contact between China and other centers of civilization in antiquity)

- Understands how environmental conditions influenced civilizations in the Tigris, Nile, and ^BD (C;WE,57;LI,208) Huang He valleys (e.g., the prevailing wind, current, and flooding patterns)

- Understands influences on the cultural and economic conditions of Minoan and Egyptian ^BD (R;WE,58) civilizations (e.g., the nature and extent of cultural contact between Minoan and Egyptian civilizations, the extent of Minoan trade and its impact on the development of Minoan civilization)

- Understands how different agrarian societies developed (e.g., what archaeological evidence ^BD (R;WE,58) suggests about the growth of agricultural societies in West Africa and Southeast Asia, the origins of domesticated rice in Southeast Asia and the routes of its spread throughout the rest of Asia)

- Understands the impact of various technologies (e.g., the wheel, pottery, the sail, weaving, ^BD (R;WE,58) bronze casting, the plow) upon social organization and the political and economic power of the groups that used them

- Understands interaction between urban centers of Southwest Asia, Egypt, and the Aegean ^BD (R;WE,58,59) Basin, and the Eastern Mediterranean coast (e.g., the important urban centers of Southwest Asia, Egypt, and the Aegean basin; the role of cities along the Mediterranean coast as commercial bridges between the trading networks of Southwest Asia, Egypt, and the Mediterranean)

5. **Understands the political, social, and cultural consequences of population movements** ^(WE,60) **and militarization in Eurasia in the second millennium BCE**

Level II (Grades 5-6)

- Understands how the rise of pastoral societies was linked to the climate and geography of ^BD (C;WE,60) the Central Asian steppes, and how kinship-based pastoral society differed from the social organization of agrarian states

---

Codes (right side of page):   BD = Benchmark, Declarative; BP = Benchmark, Procedural; BC = Benchmark, Contextual
1st letter of each code in parentheses   *2nd letter of code*   *Number*
W = NCHS: World History Standards   E = Explicitly stated in document   Page number of cited document
L = Lessons from History   I = Implied in document
C = Core material
R = Related material   199   MREL

- Understands how the invention of the chariot affected Southwest Asian societies (e.g., how the chariot changed transportation, the development of chariot warfare and the chariot's effective and ineffective qualities as a weapon of war, how the chariot contributed to the spread of new ideas and technology) ^{BD (C;WE,62)}

- Understands characteristics of Mycenaean Greek society and culture (e.g., the political and social organization of the Mycenaean Greeks as revealed in archaeological and written records, how geography influenced the development of Mycenaean society, the significance of the story of the siege of Troy) ^{BD (R;WE,64)}

- Understands why some cities disappeared during the 2nd millennium BCE (e.g., possible causes for the disappearance of cities such as Mohenjo-Daro in history, the role environmental changes played in the fall of Indus cities) ^{BD (R;WE,65)}

Level III (Grades 7-8)

- Understands the development of Indo-European language (e.g., the probable geographic homeland of speakers of early Indo-European languages and the spread of the language to other parts of Eurasia, languages which developed from the Indo-European root language) ^{BD (C;WE,60,61)}

- Understands the hypothesis that animal breeding enabled successful human adaptation to the climate and geography of the Central Asian steppe ^{BD (C;WE,61)}

- Understands significant individuals and events in Egyptian civilization (e.g., major political and cultural achievements of Thutmose III, Ramses II, and Queen Hatshepsut in Egypt; the extent of Egyptian expansion during the Old, Middle, and New Kingdoms, and some of the factors that made this expansion possible) ^{BD (C;WE,62)}

- Understands the origins of the Hittite people, their empire in Anatolia, and major culture and political achievements for this society ^{BD (C;WE,62)}

- Understands significant events in the development of Mycenaean culture (e.g., the cultural influences of Egypt, Minoan Crete, and Southwest Asian civilizations on the Mycenaeans; the story of the Trojan war through different sources) ^{BD (R;WE,64)}

- Understands characteristics of Aryan culture (e.g., the reasons for the migration of Indo-Aryan and Mycenaean-speaking peoples into India, the Eastern Mediterranean, and the Iranian Plateau; the belief system embraced by the Aryan people; odes from the Vedas that praise major Vedic gods and what they illustrate about Aryan values; potential conflict and ^{BD (R;WE,65)}

Codes (right side of page):   BD = Benchmark, Declarative; BP = Benchmark, Procedural; BC = Benchmark, Contextual
1st letter of each code in parentheses   *2nd letter of code*   *Number*
W = NCHS: World History Standards   E = Explicitly stated in document   Page number of cited document
L = Lessons from History   I = Implied in document
C = Core material
R = Related material

McREL

tension among Aryan tribes as they began to settle down in the Indo-Gangetic plain)

- Understands potential sources for the decline in trade, the overcrowding, and eventual collapse of cities such as Mohenjo-Daro ^{BD (R;WE,65,65)}

Level IV (Grades 9-12)

- Understands characteristics of pastoral and agrarian societies (e.g., economy, social relations, and political authority among pastoral peoples; women's social equality with men in pastoral societies as opposed to agrarian societies; why relations between pastoral peoples and agrarian societies have tended to involve both conflict and mutual dependence) ^{BD (C;WE,60,61)}

- Understands the probable geographic homeland of Indo-European language speakers and the approximate dates of their arrivals in new locations ^{BD (C;WE,61)}

- Understands the emergence of new kingdoms and their militarization (e.g., the boundaries of major states in Southwest Asia, Egypt, and the Eastern Mediterranean in the later part of the 2nd millennium BCE and why wars and diplomatic relations among these states may have represented the first era of "internationalism" in world history; what visual and written sources suggest about the impact of chariot warfare on the battlefield) ^{BD (C;WE,63)}

- Understands the beliefs and accomplishments of Mesopotamian and Egyptian rulers (e.g., the accomplishments of Sargon and Akenaton [Amenhotep IV]; the religious ideas of Akenaton [Amenhotep IV] and the viewpoint that Atonism was an early form of monotheism) ^{BD (C;WE,63)}

- Understands characteristics of Mycenaean society (e.g., the impact of Mycenaean expansion and city-building on commerce and political life in the Eastern Mediterranean; society, trade, and government in Mycenae; comparisons of Mycenaean and Minoan societies from archaeological remains) ^{BD (R;WE,64)}

- Understands cultural elements of the Aryan civilization (e.g., beliefs expressed in the Vedic hymns; the root of the word "Aryan," those people who came to be called Indo-Aryan; Aryan culture in India as denoted in linguistic, literary, and archaeological materials) ^{BD (R;WE,66)}

- Understands possible causes of the decline and collapse of Indus Valley civilization (e.g., technical inferiority, disease, famine, environment) ^{BD (R;WE,65)}

- Understands the reliability of epics as historic sources and the aspects of these works ^{BD (R;WE,65;LE,223)}

Codes (right side of page):   BD = Benchmark, Declarative; BP = Benchmark, Procedural; BC = Benchmark, Contextual
1st letter of each code in parentheses   *2nd letter of code*   *Number*
W = NCHS: World History Standards   E = Explicitly stated in document   Page number of cited document
L = Lessons from History   I = Implied in document
C = Core material
R = Related material   201   M∘REL

historians have determined actually reflect contemporary or later culture (e.g., the Iliad, the Odyssey, the Mahabarata, and the Ramayana)

(WE,70)

6. Understands technological and cultural innovation and change from 1000 to 600 BCE

Level II (Grades 5-6)

- Knows locations, dominant trade routes, and traded goods of major Phoenician port cities such as Carthage
  BD (C;WE,70)

- Understands the development of Greek city-states (e.g., how geography influenced the location and development of Greek city-states, common features of Greek city-states in the Aegean region)
  BD (C;WE,70)

- Understands elements of Judaism and how it compares to other religions (e.g., the ethical teachings of Judaism illustrated in stories from the Hebrew Scriptures, the differences between Jewish monotheism and the polytheism of Southwest Asia, the major events in the early history of Judaism through the Babylonian Captivity)
  BD (C;WE,72;LE,201;LI,201)

- Understands geographical and architectural features of Egypt and Kush (e.g., the locations of Egypt and Kush on the African continent and the geographic features that either assisted or hampered communication between these two kingdoms, what architectural evidence suggests about the relationship between Egypt and Kush)
  BD (R;WE,74)

- Understands major technological, military, and political events in the development of Kushite society (e.g., how iron was used in Kushite society and which uses were most important to the kingdom, the impact and significance of the Kushite invasion of Egypt for both sides, the importance of Nile Valley trade as a factor in the rise of the Kushite state in the 1st millennium BCE)
  BD (R;WE,74)

- Understands characteristics of pastoral nomadic societies (e.g., the location and range of nomadic peoples in the 1st millennium BCE and how they moved their herds and belongings; the importance of the horse to the pastoral nomadic peoples of Central Asia; reasons for conflict and economic interdependence between pastoral nomadic peoples of Central Asia, and major agrarian states of Eurasia)
  BD (R;WE,76)

Codes (right side of page): BD = Benchmark, Declarative; BP = Benchmark, Procedural; BC = Benchmark, Contextual
1st letter of each code in parentheses *2nd letter of code* *Number*
W = NCHS: World History Standards E = Explicitly stated in document Page number of cited document
L = Lessons from History I = Implied in document
C = Core material
R = Related material   202   MREL

Level III (Grades 7-8)

- Understands the role of technology in societies of Southwest Asia and the Mediterranean region (e.g., the fundamentals of iron-making technology and consequences of iron tools and weapons to those societies) ^{BD (C;WE,71)}

- Knows the locations of significant Greek city-states and colonies in the Black Sea, Northern Africa, and the Western Mediterranean basin and reasons for their establishment ^{BD (C;WE,71)}

- Understands characteristics of the Assyrian and Babylonian Empires (e.g., the geographic extent of the Assyrian and Babylonian Empires and the significance of geographic features to the success of these empires, what Assyrian art indicates about Assyrian culture and society) ^{BD (C;WE,70,71)}

- Understands social development and religious beliefs of Jewish civilization (e.g., the course of development of the Jewish Kingdoms and the Jews' maintenance of religious and cultural traditions despite destruction of these kingdoms, the significance of the Torah in Judaism) ^{BD (C;WE,72;LI,201)}

- Understands cultural elements of Kush society and their interaction with Egyptian civilization (e.g., the linguistic, architectural, and artistic achievements of Kush in the Meroitic period; the social and political consequences of economic contacts between Kush and Egypt; how Assyrian and Kushite invasions affected Egyptian society) ^{BD (R;WE,74;LE,206;LI,206)}

- Understands elements of different pastoral nomadic peoples in Central Asia (e.g., what archaeological and other evidence has revealed about Scythian and Xiongnu society and culture; the geography of arid lands of the Eastern Hemisphere, aspects of social relations between peoples of these desert and steppe lands, and how individual communities adapted to the land; how the use of the horse with the chariot changed the life of nomadic peoples on the steppes) ^{BD (R;WE,76)}

Level IV (Grades 9-12)

- Understands how the implementation of laws and the spread of language influenced societies of the Mediterranean Basin and Southwest Asia (e.g., social sources of and differences in laws created by early lawmakers, the social and cultural effects of the spread of alphabetic writing in Southwest Asia and the Mediterranean Basin) ^{BD (C;WE,70;LE,216)}

- Understands events that led to the spread of Judaism (e.g., the significance of the Babylonian captivity for the subsequent history and survival of Judaism, the significance of the Jewish diaspora for the transmission of Judaism in the Mediterranean region and Southwest Asia) ^{BD (C;WE,73)}

Codes (right side of page): BD = Benchmark, Declarative; BP = Benchmark, Procedural; BC = Benchmark, Contextual
1st letter of each code in parentheses *2nd letter of code* *Number*
W = NCHS: World History Standards E = Explicitly stated in document Page number of cited document
L = Lessons from History I = Implied in document
C = Core material
R = Related material

MREL

● Understands how Judaism compares to other beliefs (e.g., the fundamental teachings and
practices of Judaism and how they relate to ethical prescriptions for personal behavior; the
differences between Jewish monotheism and the polytheistic religions of Southwest Asia) _{BD (C;WE,73;LE,201)}

● Understands the influence of metal technology in Sub-Saharan and West Africa (e.g.,
theories about the spread of iron technology in Sub-Saharan African; whether this
technology was brought to West Africa, and how; whether it developed in this region
independently; what archaeological evidence such as Nok terra cotta figures and metal
implements illustrate about the society and culture of their West African creators) _{BD (R;WE,75)}

● Understands how Kush culture interacted with or reflected characteristics of other
civilizations (e.g., how Kush could be viewed as a cultural satellite of Egypt, or its own
distinctive civilization or both, and the evidence used to support such arguments; the
importance of political, commercial, and cultural relations between Egypt and Kush; how
Kushite achievements during the Meroitic period might have been seen by contemporaries
in the Nile Delta, Sub-Saharan Africa, and Assyria) _{BD (R;WE,75)}

● Understands the interaction between pastoral nomadic societies, warrior states, and agrarian
states in Central Asia (e.g., how the Scythian and Xiongnu warrior states arose among the
pastoral nomadic peoples on the Central Asian steppes; the circumstances and trade that led
to interdependence and conflict between pastoral nomadic and agrarian societies such as
Xiongnu and China; aspects of Scythian or Xiongnu society and culture as inferred from
basic evidence) _{BD (R;WE,76,77)}

**7. Understands how Aegean civilization emerged and how interrelations developed among
peoples of the Eastern Mediterranean and Southwest Asia from 600 to 200 BCE** _(WE,78)

Level II (Grades 5-6)

● Understands the social and political characteristics of Greek city-states (e.g., significant
similarities and differences between Athenian democracy and Spartan military aristocracy,
class division in Greek societies and the political and social roles of the classes, how
women's roles and social positions varied between Sparta and Athens, the location and
political structure of the major Greek city-states) _{BD (C;WE,78;LE,216,217)}

● Understands the major cultural elements of Greek society (e.g., characteristics of Classical
Greek art and architecture and how they are reflected in modern art and architecture; the
major characteristics of Hellenic sculpture and pottery, and how they reflected social values _{BD (R;WE,80;LE,216)}

Codes (right side of page):   BD = Benchmark, Declarative; BP = Benchmark, Procedural; BC = Benchmark, Contextual
1st letter of each code in parentheses   *2nd letter of code*   *Number*
W = NCHS: World History Standards   E = Explicitly stated in document   Page number of cited document
L = Lessons from History   I = Implied in document
C = Core material
R = Related material

and culture; Socrates' values and ideas as reflected in his trial; how Greek gods and goddesses represent non-human entities, and how gods, goddesses, and humans interact in Greek myths)

BD (R;WE,82)
- Understands Persian religious beliefs (e.g., the basic teachings of Zoroastrianism)

BD (R;WE,82)
- Understands the characteristics of Persian expansion (e.g., the growth of and geographic influences on the Persian Empire, from the reign of Cyrus I though the wars with Greece; sources of the conflict between the Greeks and the Persians; the four major battles of the Persian wars)

BD (C;WE,84;LE,218)
- Knows the campaigns, battles, and cities founded in Alexander's imperial conquests

BD (C;WE,84)
- Understands major scientific and artistic achievements of Hellenistic society (e.g., Hellenistic achievements in astronomy and measurement of the earth, Hellenistic contributions to ancient architecture), and knows the Seven Wonders of the Ancient World

Level III (Grades 7-8)

BD (C;WE,79;LE,216)
- Understands the evolution, inherent advantages, and disadvantages of major governmental systems in Greek city-states in the 6th and 5th centuries BCE

BD (C;WE,79)
- Understands the political framework of Athenian society (e.g., political ideals of Athenian society in the 5th century BCE; major changes made to the Athenian political organization between the initial monarchy and the governments of Solon and Cleisthenes; the role of women in Athenian society, their rights under the law, and possible reasons why Athenian democracy was limited solely to males)

BD (R;WE,80;LE,216)
- Understands the role of art and literature in Greek society (e.g., major works of Greek drama and how they reveal ancient moral values and civic culture, how the arts and literature reflected cultural traditions in ancient Greece)

BD (R;WE,80;LE,216)
- Understands comparisons of the creation myths of Sumer, Babylon, Egypt, Greece, and nationalized China and the similarities and differences in world view they suggest

BD (R;WE,82)
- Understands comparisons between Zoroastrianism and the belief systems of the Greeks, Hebrews, and Sumerians (e.g., religion's association with the political structure, inclusiveness)

Codes (right side of page):   BD = Benchmark, Declarative; BP = Benchmark, Procedural; BC = Benchmark, Contextual
1st letter of each code in parentheses   *2nd letter of code*   *Number*
W = NCHS: World History Standards   E = Explicitly stated in document   Page number of cited document
L = Lessons from History   I = Implied in document
C = Core material
R = Related material

McREL

- Understands significant political and military developments of the Persian Empire (e.g., BD (R;WE,82) major events of the wars between Persia and the Greek city-states; reasons for Persia's failure to conquer the Aegean region; the political structure of Persia under Darius the Great, and how the Persian Empire ruled diverse ethnic populations; the leadership organization of Darius I, and why his "chain of command" was so effective; the effects of the Persian Wars upon the daily lives of the people of Persia and Greece)

- Understands elements of Alexander of Macedon's legacy (e.g., his rise to power, methods BD (C;WE,84;LE,218) used to unite the empire, reasons for the disintegration of the empire into smaller areas after his rule)

- Understands the impact and achievements of the Hellenistic period (e.g., the impact of BD (C;WE,84,85) Hellenism on Indian art; major lasting achievements of Hellenistic mathematics, science, and philosophy; how architecture in West Asia after the conquests of Alexander reflected Greek and Macedonian influence)

Level IV (Grades 9-12)

- Understands the legacy of Greek thought and government (e.g., essential ideas in Plato's BD (C;WE,78,79;LE,216) Republic and the influence of this work on modern political thought; the importance of participatory government in Greek city-states for the development of Western political thought and institutions; Athenian ideas and practices related to political freedom, national security, and justice; how the maturing democratic institutions in Greece resulted in greater restrictions on the rights and freedoms of women)

- Understands different forms and methods of social stratification in Greek city-states such as BD (C;WE,79) Athens, Corinth, Sparta, and Thebes

- Understands how Sumerian, Egyptian, and Greek societies saw themselves in relation to BD (R;WE,81) their gods and how attitudes towards women are indicated in representations of their goddesses

- Knows significant Greek writings and literature (e.g., the prominent ideas of Greek BD (R;WE,80,81;LE,216,218;LI,216) philosophers; the significance and major works of Greek historians; significant Greek tragedies and comedies, and the values and lessons they transmitted; aspects of daily life in Greece between 600 and 200 BCE as they are represented by playwrights of the time)

- Understands the major events and the significance of the Persian Wars (e.g., the long-term BD (R;WE,83) effects of the Persian Wars upon Greece, how the internal political and military structure of

Codes (right side of page):   BD = Benchmark, Declarative; BP = Benchmark, Procedural; BC = Benchmark, Contextual
1st letter of each code in parentheses   *2nd letter of code*   *Number*
W = NCHS: World History Standards   E = Explicitly stated in document   Page number of cited document
L = Lessons from History   I = Implied in document
C = Core material
R = Related material

206

MREL

the two antagonists in the Persian Wars dictated their strategies, how the Greek city-states were able to defeat the "monolithic" Persian armies and navies, Herodotus' version of the key events of the Persian Wars and how reliable this account might be)

- Understands the relationship between religion and politics in Persian society and the place BD (R;WE,83) of Zoroastrianism within the various levels of Persian society

- Understands how conquest influenced cultural life during the Hellenistic era (e.g., the BD (C;WE,84,85;LI,221) cultural diffusion of Greek, Egyptian, Persian, and Indian art and architecture through assimilation, conquest, migration, and trade; the benefits and costs of Alexander's conquests on numerous cultures, and the extent to which these conquests brought about cultural mixing and exchange)

- Understands the characteristics of religion, gender, and philosophy in the Hellenistic era BD (C;WE,84,85;LI,221) (e.g., the significance of the interaction of Greek and Jewish traditions for the emergence of Rabbinic Judaism and early Christianity; the changes in the status of women during the Hellenistic era, their new opportunities, and greater restrictions; what different Greek philosophers considered to be a "good life")

8. **Understands how major religious and large-scale empires arose in the Mediterranean** (WE,86) **Basin, China, and India from 500 BCE to 300 CE**

Level II (Grades 5-6)

- Understands the origins and social framework of Roman society (e.g., how legends of the BD (C;WE,86,87;LE,218,219;LI,220) founding of Rome describe ancient Rome and reflect the beliefs and values of its citizens, the geographic location of different ethnic groups on the Italian peninsula in the late 6th century BCE and their influences on early Roman society and culture, what life was like for the common people living in Rome and Pompeii)

- Understands shifts in the political and social framework of Roman society (e.g., political and BD (C;WE, 86;LE,219) social institutions of the Roman Republic and reasons for its transformation from Republic to Empire; how values changed from the early Republic to the last years of the Empire as reflected through the lives of such Romans as Cincinnatus, Scipio Africanus, Tiberius Gracchus, Cicero, Julius Caesar, Augustus, Nero, Marcus Aurelius, and Constantine)

- Understands the significance of Jesus of Nazareth (e.g., the story of the life of Jesus, the BD (C;WE,88) messages of Jesus' prominent parables)

Codes (right side of page):   BD = Benchmark, Declarative; BP = Benchmark, Procedural; BC = Benchmark, Contextual
1st letter of each code in parentheses   *2nd letter of code*   *Number*
W = NCHS: World History Standards   E = Explicitly stated in document   Page number of cited document
L = Lessons from History   I = Implied in document
C = Core material
R = Related material   207

M∕REL

- Understands events in the rise of Christianity (e.g., the life of Paul the Apostle and his contribution to the spread of Christian beliefs, how the New Testament illustrates early Christian beliefs) BD (C;WE,88;LE,221)

- Understands the fundamental elements of Chinese society under the early imperial dynasties (e.g., policies and achievements of the Qin emperor Shi Huangdi, the concept of the Mandate of Heaven and the idea of virtuous rule, the fundamentals of Chinese values and belief systems, what life was like for ordinary people in ancient China as illustrated in Chinese folktales) BD (C;WE,90;LE,225)

- Understands the commercial and cultural significance of the trans-Eurasian "silk roads" to the Roman and Chinese Empires and the peoples of Central Asia BD (C;WE,90;LE,222)

- Understands the origins of Buddhism and fundamental Buddhist beliefs (e.g., the life story of Buddha and his essential teachings; how the Buddhist teachings were a response to the Brahamanic system; the contributions of the emperor Ashoka to the expansion of Buddhism in India; how Indian epic stories reflect social values, and how the Jakata tales reveal Buddhist teachings) BD (C;WE,92;LE,223,224)

Level III (Grades 7-8)

- Understands the significant individuals and achievements of Roman society (e.g., the accomplishments of different, famous Roman citizens [Cincinnatus, the Gracchi, Cicero, Constantine, Nero, Marcus Auraleus]; the major legal, artistic, architectural, technological, and literary achievements of the Roman Republic) BD (C;WE,86,87)

- Understands events that shaped the political framework of Roman society (e.g., the history of the Punic Wars and the consequences of the wars for Rome; the major phases of Roman expansion, including the Roman occupation of Britain) BD (C;WE,87;LE,219,220)

- Understands the status and role of women in Roman society BD (C;WE,87)

- Understands the influence of Christian beliefs on political, social, and cultural aspects of society (e.g., how Jesus' moral teachings utilized and expanded upon the prohibitions of the Ten Commandments in the Hebrew Torah, the extent of the spread of Christianity by the end of the 4th century and the locations of centers of the Christian church, the impact of Christianity upon the Roman Empire, the values and stories expressed in early Christian religious art) BD (C;WE,88;LE,221)

Codes (right side of page):   BD = Benchmark, Declarative; BP = Benchmark, Procedural; BC = Benchmark, Contextual

1st letter of each code in parentheses   *2nd letter of code*   *Number*

W = NCHS: World History Standards   E = Explicitly stated in document   Page number of cited document

L = Lessons from History   I = Implied in document

C = Core material

R = Related material   208   MREL

- Understands fundamental social, political, and cultural characteristics of Chinese society under early imperial dynasties (e.g., comparisons between the Shang, Zhou, Quin, and Han Empires in areas controlled and methods of government; the importance of the "Mandate of Heaven" to the success of the Zhou Dynasty and its development of imperial rule; the literary and artistic achievements of early imperial dynasties; the development and consequences of iron technology and the family division of labor system; the composition and stratification of Chinese society, and factors that gave individuals status; imperial attitudes and actions toward nomadic peoples along the borders of the kingdom) BD (C;WE,91;LE,226;LI,225)

- Understands the major religious beliefs and social framework in India during the Gangetic states and the Mauryan Empire (e.g., the major beliefs and practices of Brahmanism in India; how Buddhism spread in India, Ceylon, and Central Asia; aspects of social structure of India during the Mauryan Empire; what advice the animal stories of the Panchantantra offer to people with little power, how this advice was used by Chandragupta; how the teachings of Shvetaketu from the Chandogya Upanishad compare to the Buddhist idea of nirvana) BD (C;WE,92;LI,223)

Level IV (Grades 9-12)

- Understands shifts in the political framework of Roman society (e.g., how innovations in ancient military technology affected patterns of warfare and empire building; how imperial rule over a vast area transformed Roman society, economy, and culture; the causes and consequences of the transition from Republic to Empire under Augustus in Rome; how Rome governed its provinces from the late Republic to the Empire) BD (C;WE,86,87;LE,219;LI,219)

- Understands cultural influences on Roman society (e.g., Latin and Greek as universal languages of the Roman Empire and the political, commercial, and cultural purpose of each; the influence and diffusion of Hellenistic art and architecture upon the Romans) BD (C;WE,87)

- Understands the political legacy of Roman society (e.g., influences of the Roman Constitution on the modern U.S. political system) BD (C;WE,87)

- Understands the spread of Christianity and how it related to other belief systems (e.g., comparisons between Jewish and Christian approaches to monotheism; the extent and consequences of Christian expansion in Asia, Africa, and Europe to the 4th century, and the events and circumstances, including the role of the martyr, that helped this expansion; the influence of other faiths upon the development of Christianity and those teachings that are distinctive to Christianity; the fundamental teachings of Christianity as set forth by Jesus and Paul) BD (C;WE,89;LI,221)

Codes (right side of page): BD = Benchmark, Declarative; BP = Benchmark, Procedural; BC = Benchmark, Contextual
1st letter of each code in parentheses *2nd letter of code* *Number*
W = NCHS: World History Standards E = Explicitly stated in document Page number of cited document
L = Lessons from History I = Implied in document
C = Core material
R = Related material 209 M*REL

- Understands the political and cultural characteristics of the Han Dynasty (e.g., the political and ideological contributions of the Han to the development of the imperial bureaucratic state and imperial expansion, how art reflects the history and philosophy of China through the end of the Han Dynasty) BD (C;WE,91;LE,226;LI,225)

- Understands elements of Confucianism (e.g., the role of status of women in the Confucian tradition, the essential moral teachings of Confucianism and how they compare to other beliefs) BD (C;WE,91;LE,225;LI,225)

- Understands how Buddhism and Brahmanism influenced one another and Indian society (e.g., how Buddhist teachings challenged the Brahmanic social system and contributed to the spread of Buddhism within and beyond India, how Ashoka's support for Buddhism affected the spread of religious beliefs, how the Upinshads reflected Brahmanic teachings and how these compared with Buddhist teachings) BD (C;WE,92,93;LE,223)

- Understands how art and literature reflect different aspects of Indian society (e.g., how literature such as the Ramayana can reflect the status and role of women in ancient cultures, how Indian art reflects a Persian or Greek influence) BD (C;WE,93)

- Understands the growth of the Mauryan Empire in the context of rivalries among Indian states BD (C;WE,92)

9. Understands how early agrarian civilizations arose in Mesoamerica (WE,94)

Level II (Grades 5-6)

- Understands the major characteristics and contributions of Olmec civilization (e.g, the achievements of Olmec civilization circa 1200 to 400 BCE, how geography influenced the development of Olmec civilization, the essential aspects of the Olmec civilization, how maize cultivation influenced the development of the Olmec civilization, the major contributions of Olmec civilization to Mesopotamian civilization) BD (C;WE,94;LE,209;LI,209)

Level III (Grades 7-8)

- Understands characteristics of Olmec agriculture (e.g., the social and environmental impacts, and the methods of Olmec agriculture; the importance of maize to the Olmec civilization and how farming in Mesoamerica differed from that of other agrarian societies in the ancient world) BD (C;WE,95)

Codes (right side of page): BD = Benchmark, Declarative; BP = Benchmark, Procedural; BC = Benchmark, Contextual
1st letter of each code in parentheses *2nd letter of code* *Number*
W = NCHS: World History Standards E = Explicitly stated in document Page number of cited document
L = Lessons from History I = Implied in document
C = Core material
R = Related material   210   MᴄREL

- Understands methods used to study Olmec civilization (e.g., what archaeological evidence indicates about the development of Olmec civilization in the 2nd millennium BCE, clues about political and economic structure found in the monumental Olmec stone heads) _{BD (C;WE,95)}

Level IV (Grades 9-12)

- Understands the framework of Olmec society and the influence of Olmec civilization on other civilizations (e.g., the cultural influence of the Olmecs on the development of Zapotec and Mayan civilizations, and the role of trade in the diffusion of this culture; the political, economic, and social structure of Olmec society and Olmec beliefs, and how this knowledge has been acquired in spite of undeciphered written records) _{BD (C;WE,95;LE,209;LI,209)}

10. **Understands the Imperial crises and their aftermath in various regions from 300 to 700 CE** _(WE,100)

Level II (Grades 5-6)

- Understands possible reasons for the decline of the Roman and Han Empires (e.g., the chronological order of significant historical events for Rome from the late Empire through the reign of Justinian, how differences in architecture can illustrate unity and alienation between the Eastern and Western halves of the Roman Empire, possible factors that motivated nomadic peoples to move into the Roman Empire and China, common patterns of decline and fall in the Roman and Han Empires) _{BD (C;WE,100)}

- Understands various characteristics of Christianity and Buddhism (e.g., possible aspects of Christianity and Buddhism which appealed to people living between the 3rd and 5th centuries CE; the importance of missions to Christianity and Buddhism in their first millennia and methods used to spread the two religions to new areas and people; the approximate geographical realms of Buddhism, Christianity, Hinduism, and Confucianism until the 5th century CE) _{BD (C;WE,102;LE,222,223;LI,224)}

- Understands fundamental Hindu beliefs (e.g., how the concept of dharma reflects a social value for the ideal king, husband and wife, brother and friend; the concepts of Brahma, dharma, and karma, the caste system, ritual sacrifice, and reincarnation) _{BD (C;WE,104)}

- Understands significant religious and cultural features of the Gupta era (e.g., the relationship among various religions in India during Gupta times; significant Gupta achievements in art, literature, and mathematics) _{BD (C;WE,104;LE,224;LI,224)}

Codes (right side of page):   BD = Benchmark, Declarative; BP = Benchmark, Procedural; BC = Benchmark, Contextual
1st letter of each code in parentheses   *2nd letter of code*   *Number*
W = NCHS: World History Standards   E = Explicitly stated in document   Page number of cited document
L = Lessons from History   I = Implied in document
C = Core material
R = Related material   211   MREL

- Understands the influence of Hinduism and Buddhism in East and Southeast Asia (e.g., the BD (R;WE,106) geographical limits of Hindu and Buddhist influence, and the role of trade in spreading these religions; the presence and influence of Hinduism and Buddhism in India, Malaysia, and Southeast Asia, how Malayo-Polynesian peoples of East and Southeast Asia origin settled the Pacific islands and New Zealand; how ocean currents affected cultural contact between India and Southeast Asia, and the evidence for this contact)

Level III (Grades 7-8)

- Understands political events that may have contributed to the decline of the Roman and Han BD (C;WE,101;LI,220) Empires (e.g., the nomadic invasions of the Roman Empire as described in the accounts of Orosius, Ammianus Marcellinus, Priscus, and secondary sources; significant battles, internal divisions, political changes, and invasions between the 3rd and 7th centuries CE that led to the fall of the Roman and Han Empires; the relative strengths and weaknesses of the Roman, Byzantine, and Han Empires)

- Understands how the spread of Buddhism and Christianity influenced different regions (e.g., BD (C;WE,102) the locations of new centers of Buddhism and Christianity and the major routes used to spread the faith beyond these centers; the efforts and successes of Ashoka and Constantine to legitimize Buddhism and Christianity and spread them throughout India and Europe respectively; the causal connections between the collapse of the Roman and Han Empires, the spread of Buddhism and Christianity, and the importance of universal salvation to the early history of these two religions)

- Understands the changing status of women in early Christian and Buddhist societies BD (C;WE,103)

- Understands the caste system in Gupta, India (e.g., the social and legal position of women BD (C;WE,104,105) during the Gupta era, restrictions upon them, and their place within the caste system; different social perspectives on the advantages and disadvantages of the caste system in Gupta India)

- Understands political events that shaped the Guptan Empire (e.g., possible reasons for the BD (C;WE,105) alliance of the Gupta Empire with Brahmanism and the fall of the Mauryan-Buddhist power, how and why Guptan kings promoted Hinduism while simultaneously fostering Buddhist culture and integrating marginal groups into the political system)

- Understands achievements of the Gupta period (e.g., technology, mathematics, astronomy, BD (C;WE,105;LE,224) medicine)

Codes (right side of page):   BD = Benchmark, Declarative; BP = Benchmark, Procedural; BC = Benchmark, Contextual
1st letter of each code in parentheses   *2nd letter of code*   *Number*
W = NCHS: World History Standards   E = Explicitly stated in document   Page number of cited document
L = Lessons from History   I = Implied in document
C = Core material
R = Related material

McREL

- Understands common features of the cultures of the Southeast Asia, the Pacific Islands of Polynesia, and New Zealand and possible links between these cultures (e.g., through ocean-borne migration) ^{BD (R;WE,106)}

- Understands how the spread of trade and religion influenced Southeast Asia and Polynesian areas (e.g., the function of Hindu and Buddhist clerics in the spread of their religions and trade to Southeast Asia and Malayo Polynesia by the end of the 1st millennium BCE; the locations and geographic challenges of potential and actual trade routes in the Southeast Asian and Polynesian areas, the nature of monumental religious architecture as evidence for the spread of Buddhist and Hindu belief and practice in Southeast Asia) ^{BD (R;WE,106,107)}

Level IV (Grades 9-12)

- Understands political and social elements during the decline of the Roman and Han Empires and the rise of the Byzantine Empire (e.g., the links between military, social, and economic causes for the decline in the Han and Roman Empires; the life of Germanic peoples and society including the status and role of women; the impact of barbarian movements on the regions of Europe, China, and India by the end of the 7th century CE; the strengths and weaknesses of the Eastern and Western Roman Empires, and what factors enabled the Byzantine Empire to continue as Rome fell; how Constantine selectively supported aspects of Western rule with Eastern institutions to create a new, independent, Byzantine state in the 4th century CE) ^{BD (C;WE,101)}

- Understands how the spread of different religions influenced political and social conditions in various regions (e.g., the Apostle Paul's views and their influence on the spread of Christianity, the spread of religious Daoism and Buddhism in China, possible causal relationships between the spread of Christianity and Buddhism, and the expansion of international trade, royal patronage of religion and the desires of a growing middle class for "peace" to enable commercial expansion) ^{BD (C;WE,103)}

- Understands shifts in the status of women from pagan Roman society to Christian society (e.g., the shifting importance of social class, marital status) ^{BD (C;WE,103)}

- Understands the significant social, political, and cultural characteristics of Gupta society (e.g., achievements in art, literature, and mathematics under Chandragupta II; centers of learning in India in the 4th and 5th centuries CE, and the role of Buddhist monks in education and higher learning; types of evidence available for understanding Gupta India; the route of the Hun invasion of India, and the revival of the golden age of the Guptas) ^{BD (C;WE,105,108;LE,224;LI,224)}

Codes (right side of page):   BD = Benchmark, Declarative; BP = Benchmark, Procedural; BC = Benchmark, Contextual
1st letter of each code in parentheses   *2nd letter of code*   *Number*
W = NCHS: World History Standards   E = Explicitly stated in document   Page number of cited document
L = Lessons from History   I = Implied in document
C = Core material
R = Related material

McREL

- Understands the resurgence of Hinduism in India and its spread to South India (e.g., as reflected in the growth of temple towns and the development of South Indian temple architecture such as the temple of Maduri) BD (C;WE,105)

- Understands Indian contributions to Southeast Asia (e.g., how art and architecture revealed the spread of Indian influence in Southeast Asia, the adaptation of Buddhist-Hindu culture in Southeast Asia, the Indian concept of ideal kingship and its introduction and spread throughout the emerging states of Southeast Asia) BD (R;WE,107)

- Understands the significance of Pandyas and Pallavas (e.g., the history of Pandyas and Pallavas in South India; trade relationships with West Asia, Greece, Rome, and Southeast Asia; how Pallavas helped spread Hindu and Buddhist thought to Southeast Asia) BD (R;WE,107)

11. Understands the causes and consequences of the development of Islamic civilization between the 7th and 10th centuries (WE,108)

Level II (Grades 5-6)

- Understands the effect of geography on different groups and their trade practices (e.g., nomads, town-dwellers, trade practices on the Arabian peninsula; the goods traded between them and the origins of these goods) BD (C;WE,108)

- Understands the spread of Islam in Southwest Asia and the Mediterranean region (e.g., the life of Muhammad, his devotion to God, and the basic beliefs and values he preached; the importance to Islam of the Hegira [Hirjah], the Ka'abah, the Qur'an, the Sunnah, the Hajj, the daily prayer [Salat], the poor due [Zakat] and Ramadan; how Islam spread in Southwest Asia and the Mediterranean and evidence for its influence) BD (C;WE,108;LE,233,234)

- Understands the significance of Baghdad (e.g., the trade network and goods traded, its role as a center of commerce in the 8th to 10th centuries CE) BD (C;WE,110;LE,235)

- Understands the impact of the invention of paper on various cultures (e.g., Chinese, Muslim, later European culture; its route from its source through Muslim lands to Europe) BD (C;WE,110)

- Understands the influence of Islamic ideas and practices on other cultures and social behavior (e.g., the possible appeal of Islam to culturally diverse non-Muslims across Afro-Eurasia in the Abbasid era; the origin and development of Islamic law; the influence of Islamic law and Muslim practice on family life, morals, marriage, women's status, BD (C;WE,110;LE,234)

Codes (right side of page):   BD = Benchmark, Declarative; BP = Benchmark, Procedural; BC = Benchmark, Contextual
1st letter of each code in parentheses   *2nd letter of code*   *Number*
W = NCHS: World History Standards   E = Explicitly stated in document   Page number of cited document
L = Lessons from History   I = Implied in document
C = Core material
R = Related material   214   MᴄREL

inheritance, justice, and slavery)

- Understands how the Byzantine state withstood attacks between the 8th and 10th centuries ^{BD (R;WE,112)} (e.g., military technology and the successful defense of Byzantium against Arab Muslim attacks)

- Understands where and how Orthodox Christianity spread in Eastern Europe in the 9th to ^{BD (R;WE,112;LI,239)} 11th centuries

Level III (Grades 7-8)

- Understands how the Muslims spread Islamic beliefs and established their empire (e.g., how ^{BD (C;WE,108,109;LE,234;LI,234)} Islam attracted new converts; Arab Muslim success in founding an empire stretching from Western Europe to India and China; the diverse religious, cultural, and geographic factors that influenced the ability of the Muslim government to rule)

- Understands elements of Islamic civilization (e.g., the emergence of Islamic civilization in ^{BD (C;WE,110)} Iberia and it economic and cultural achievements, how family life and gender relations were prescribed in Islamic society)

- Understands elements of Abbasid culture (e.g., how the Abbasids promoted and preserved ^{BD (C;WE,110;LE,236)} Greek learning and contributed to science, mathematics, and medicine; the contributions of specific individuals to the Abbasid advancement of scientific knowledge; why the Abbasid state became a center of Afro-Eurasian commercial exchange)

- Understands how the Byzantine Empire defended itself against various invaders (e.g., ^{BD (R;WE,112)} variations in maritime technology and ship design in the 9th century and the role of the navy in Byzantine defense against Arab Muslim attacks; weapons, fortification, and military preparedness of the Byzantine Empire and explanations for its successful defense against Bulgar and Arab invaders)

- Understands the Byzantine role in preserving and transmitting ancient Greek learning ^{BD (R;WE,112)}

Level IV (Grades 9-12)

- Understands challenges to Muslim civilization (e.g., the significance of the Battle of Tours ^{BD (C;WE,109)} of 733 as interpreted by Muslim and Christian sources and changing historiographical views of the event; the transformation of the Arab Caliphate into a Southwest Asian and Mediterranean Empire under the Umyyad Dynasty, and why the Muslim community divided

---

Codes (right side of page):   BD = Benchmark, Declarative; BP = Benchmark, Procedural; BC = Benchmark, Contextual
1st letter of each code in parentheses   *2nd letter of code*   *Number*
W = NCHS: World History Standards   E = Explicitly stated in document   Page number of cited document
L = Lessons from History   I = Implied in document
C = Core material
R = Related material

McREL

into Sunni and Shi'ite factions)

- Understands significant social and cultural changes during the Islamic centuries (e.g., the changing position of women in the new Islamic, how Muslim mosque architecture physically reflects the relationship between people, spiritual leaders, and God in Islam; the process through which Arabic became a common language in the early Islamic centuries; what branches of scholarship developed out of the efforts of Muslim leaders and scholars to record the Qur'an and Hadith) BD (C;WE,109;LE,234,235)

- Understands the political, social, and religious problems confronting the Byzantine and Sassanid Persian Empires in the 7th century and the commercial role of Arabia in the Southwest Asian economy BD (C;WE,109)

- Understands the social structure of the Abbasid Empire (e.g., the lives of prominent women and factors that facilitated and mitigated their rise to prominence; the role and status of royal bureaucrats, landowning nobles, peasants, urban artisans, and slaves; what Islamic conversion and adherence meant for social status; the treatment and legal status of non-Muslims and their contributions to society) BD (C;WE,111;LE,235)

- Understands the strengths and weaknesses of the Abbasid, Byzantine, and Sassanid Persian governments and military institutions BD (C;WE,111)

- Understands how the spread of Greek Orthodox Christianity affected different regions (e.g., the patterns of the spread of Greek Orthodox Christianity into the Balkans, Ukraine, and Russia between the 9th and 11th centuries; explanations for the preference of Greek over Latin Christianity in the Slavic world; the story of Vladirmir of Kiev in the Russian Chronicle, and the nature of the church/state relationship in Kievan Russia) BD (R;WE,113)

- Understands possible motivations behind the Byzantine preservation of ancient Greek and Hellenistic scholastic works BD (R;WE,112)

- Understands patterns of economic, political, and military power in the manufacturing and trading centers of Constantinople and Baghdad BD (R;WE,112)

Codes (right side of page):   BD = Benchmark, Declarative; BP = Benchmark, Procedural; BC = Benchmark, Contextual
1st letter of each code in parentheses   *2nd letter of code*   *Number*
W = NCHS: World History Standards   E = Explicitly stated in document   Page number of cited document
L = Lessons from History   I = Implied in document
C = Core material
R = Related material   216

McREL

12. **Understands major developments in East Asia in the era of the Tang Dynasty from 600 to 900 CE** ^(WE,114)

Level II (Grades 5-6)

- Understands geographic and political features of Tang China (e.g., major geographical features of the area incorporated by the Tang Dynasty, the location of the network of canals, and how the Great Canal changed life in China; features of government and administration of Tang China and the territorial expansion of the empire to Southeast and Central Asia; the locations of major cities in Tang China and their attraction for diverse people of differing religions) ^{BD (C;WE,114;LE,243)}

- Understands characteristics of Japanese society through the imperial period (e.g., how the geography of Japan affected its development and its relations with China and Korea; the political, social, and cultural role of women and their contributions to the court of Heian, Japan; aspects of the indigenous development of Japanese society until the 7th century CE; the establishment of the imperial state in Japan and the role of the emperor in government) ^{BD (R;WE,116;LI,244)}

Level III (Grades 7-8)

- Understands the culture and technological achievements of Tang China (e.g., the system of roads and canals in Tang China; the extent of the Tang Empire, the trade routes used by the empire, and the products exchanged; the ideals and values of everyday life expressed in the poetry, landscape, painting, and pottery of the Tang Dynasty; major technologies developed under the Tang Dynasty, how these technologies influenced Tang society, and spread to other regions) ^{BD (C;WE,114,115;LE,243)}

- Understands how Buddhism was introduced from China to Korea and Japan and why the Korean emperor encouraged Japan to adopt this religion ^{BD (C;WE,114)}

- Understands events that shaped Japanese culture (e.g., major contributions and developments of early cultures of Japan from 10,000 BCE to circa 200 CE; the influence of Buddhism on Japan between the 8th and 9th centuries, how it changed Japanese society, and reasons for its restriction by the emperor in Heian; the influence of Chinese culture on Japanese society from the 7th to the 11th century and use of Chinese as the lingua franca in East Asia in the late 1st millennium) ^{BD (R;WE,116,117;LE,244)}

- Understands basic beliefs in Japanese culture (e.g., the legends of creation of Japan and what these legends reveal about Japanese history, the basic beliefs of Shinto and how art and ^{BD (R;WE,116,117)}

Codes (right side of page): BD = Benchmark, Declarative; BP = Benchmark, Procedural; BC = Benchmark, Contextual
1st letter of each code in parentheses *2nd letter of code* *Number*
W = NCHS: World History Standards E = Explicitly stated in document Page number of cited document
L = Lessons from History I = Implied in document
C = Core material
R = Related material

217

MℝEL

literature reflect Shinto's impact, courtly life and ideals in Heian)

- Understands China's influence on other cultures (e.g., relations with pastoral peoples of Inner Asia in the Tang period and long-term patterns of interaction along China's grassland frontier) BD (R;WE,117)

Level IV (Grades 9-12)

- Understands features of cultural life in various regions of China (e.g., differences between the lifestyles and living conditions in rural areas and urban communities during the Tang Dynasty, and how urban centers influenced growth in the arts; the significance of Chinese popular culture from the Tang Dynasty onward; the place of poetry and painting in the lives of scholar-officials in China, the values of the Chinese elite, and attitudes of poets toward the common people) BD (C;WE,115)

- Understands social and political characteristics of the reunification of China (e.g., the roles of women and family, the process of political centralization and economic reforms that marked China's reunification under the Sui and Tang dynasties) BD (C;WE,115)

- Understands the influence of Chinese culture on different countries (e.g., the political and cultural influence of Tang China in East Asian countries such as Korea, Vietnam, and Japan; the uniqueness of the Chinese writing system and how Japan adapted this system to fit the spoken language of Japan) BD (R;WE,117)

- Understands the role of women in Heian (e.g., women of the Japanese court of the Heian period, the courtly roles and values reflected in works by female authors such as the *Diary of Muraski Shikibu* and *The Pillow Book* by Sei Shonagon) BD (R;WE,117;LE,245)

- Understands the importance of the commercial state of Srivijava in Southeast Asia as a trade link between India and China and how the monsoon winds and geography of the Strait of Malacca contributed to its wealth and power BD (R;WE,117)

13. Understands the political, social, and cultural redefinitions in Europe from 500 to 1000 CE (WE,118)

Level II (Grades 5-6)

- Understands the influence of the monastery in European development (e.g., how the BD (C;WE,118;LI,242)

Codes (right side of page):   BD = Benchmark, Declarative; BP = Benchmark, Procedural; BC = Benchmark, Contextual
1st letter of each code in parentheses   *2nd letter of code*   *Number*
W = NCHS: World History Standards   E = Explicitly stated in document   Page number of cited document
L = Lessons from History   I = Implied in document
C = Core material
R = Related material   218   *MREL*

monastery in early Medieval Europe served as centers of preservation of ancient learning or missions, the individual duties of monks and nuns in this society, the importance of monasteries and missionaries from Britain and Ireland in the Christianizing of Western and Central Europe)

- Understands the significance of Charlemagne (e.g., his government, laws, conquests, personal values) BD (C;WE,118;LI,240)

- Understands the significance of Norse migrations and invasions (e.g., locations of Norse settlements, including routes to North America, Russia, Western Europe, and the Black Sea; how Norse explorations stimulated the emergence of independent lords and the knightly class) BD (R;WE,120)

- Knows the life story and major achievements of King Alfred of England, and understands how he earned the title "Alfred the Great" BD (R;WE,120)

Level III (Grades 7-8)

- Understands the influence of the Carolingian Empire on the development of European civilization (e.g., extent and causes of the Carolingian influence in Europe and reasons for its decline; how the Rules of St. Benedict shaped Medieval Europe; how Charlemagne's royal court and monasteries preserved Greco-Roman and early Christian learning and contributed to the emergence of European civilization; changing political relations between the papacy and the secular rulers of Europe, and how secular leaders such as Charlemagne influenced political order within Europe) BD (C;WE,118-119;LE,242;LI,240)

- Understands the significance of Clovis (e.g., the major conquests of Clovis, how his conversion to Christianity was influenced by his wife, Clothilde; how his conversion affected the Frankish and Saxon peoples) BD (C;WE,119)

- Understands the role of Norse peoples in the development of Europe (e.g., Nordic contributions to long-distance trade and exploration, the failure of Norse settlements in Newfoundland and Greenland) BD (R;WE,120)

- Understands social class and gender roles in Medieval Europe (e.g., the responsibilities of women with different social status; the changes in the legal, social, and economic status of peasants in the 9th and 10th centuries; how the political fragmentation of Europe after Charlemagne affected their lives) BD (R;WE,120;LE,241,242)

Codes (right side of page):   BD = Benchmark, Declarative; BP = Benchmark, Procedural; BC = Benchmark, Contextual
1st letter of each code in parentheses   *2nd letter of code*   *Number*
W = NCHS: World History Standards   E = Explicitly stated in document   Page number of cited document
L = Lessons from History   I = Implied in document
C = Core material
R = Related material

McREL

Level IV (Grades 9-12)

- Understands significant religious events that shaped medieval society (e.g., similarities and differences in governance and worship in the Latin Catholic and Byzantine churches; the successes of the Latin Catholic and Byzantine churches in introducing Christianity and Christian culture to Eastern Europe; how the Anglo-Saxon Boniface was an exemplar for other missionaries, and how he represented the "romanization of Europe") ^BD (C;WE,119)

- Understands the significance of different empires in Europe (e.g., the extent of the Frankish Empire under Clovis, the eventual division of imperial territory among his four sons, and the consequences of this division; the degree of success enjoyed by the Merovingian and Carolingian Empires at maintaining public order and local defense in Western Europe) ^BD (C;WE,119)

- Understands central and peripheral reasons for the failure of the Carolingian Empire to endure after the death of Charlemagne (e.g., independent power of nobles, Viking, and Magyar; how successful invasions stimulated the development of feudalism and feudal institutions) ^BD (C;WE,121)

- Understands shifts in political power during 9th and 10th century Europe (e.g., how royal officials such as counts and dukes transformed delegated powers into hereditary, autonomous power over land and people) ^BD (R;WE,121)

- Understands the role of technology in the development of feudalism (e.g., the advantage of the Magyar cavalry and Viking longboat, and how successful invasions stimulated the development of feudalism and feudal institutions) ^BD (R;WE,121)

14. Understands state-building in the Northeast and West Africa, and the southward migrations of Bantu-speaking peoples ^(WE,122)

Level II (Grades 5-6)

- Understands influences on the development of different African civilizations (e.g., the location of the Jenné-jeno civilization and the influence of the natural environment on the agriculture, settlement patterns, and trade of this settlement; the process by which Christianity was introduced to Ethiopia in the 4th century) ^BD (C;WE,122;LI,246)

Level III (Grades 7-8)

- Understands the role of oral history in understanding West African history (e.g.,the griot ^BD (C;WE,122,123)

Codes (right side of page):   BD = Benchmark, Declarative; BP = Benchmark, Procedural; BC = Benchmark, Contextual
1st letter of each code in parentheses   *2nd letter of code*   *Number*
W = NCHS: World History Standards   E = Explicitly stated in document   Page number of cited document
L = Lessons from History   I = Implied in document
C = Core material
R = Related material

MREL

"keeper of tales" and other sources used to understand history)

- Understands influences on the development of the Ghana Empire (e.g., how Islam, the gold BD (C;WE,122,123) and salt production, and the trans-Saharan camel trade promoted urbanization in West Africa and the growth of the Ghana Empire; the governing system of the royal court in Ghana, and how the effectiveness of imperial efforts was aided by a belief in the king's divinity)

Level IV (Grades 9-12)

- Understands economic, social, and religious influences on Ghana society (e.g., the BD (C;WE,123) agriculture, trade, standard of living, expansionary tendencies and role of religious ideas in Ghana; what archaeological evidence indicates about the development of Ghana into a large scale empire, and the development of Jenné-jeno and Kumbi-Saleh into important early commercial cities)

- Understands settlement patterns in different regions of Africa (e.g., how the natural BD (C;WE,122;LE,246,247) environments of West Africa defined agricultural production, settlement patterns, and trade; causes and consequences of the settling of East, Central, and Southern Africa by Bantu-speaking farmers and cattle herders until 1000 CE)

- Understands the importance of maritime trade to the kingdom of Askum until the latter part BD (C;WE,122) of the 1st millennium CE, the goods traded in this kingdom, and the situation that enabled Askum to play a role in long-distance trade

15. Understands the rise of centers of civilization in Mesoamerica and Andean South America in the 1st millennium CE (WE,124)

Level II (Grades 5-6)

- Understands the significant features of Mayan civilization (e.g., locations of Mayan city-states, road systems, and sea routes in Mesoamerica and the influence of the environment on these developments; the importance of religion in Mayan society; the structure and purpose of Mayan pyramids; the role and status of women in Mayan society as indicated by their portrayal in Mayan monumental architecture; ceremonial games among the Mayans) BD (C;WE,124)

- Understands methods used to study Zapotec, Teotihuacán, and Moche civilizations (e.g., BD (R;WE,126) locations of these communities and their major archaeological remains, what archaeological evidence such as clay pottery and figures reveal about Moche civilization, what remains of

---

Codes (right side of page):   BD = Benchmark, Declarative; BP = Benchmark, Procedural; BC = Benchmark, Contextual
1st letter of each code in parentheses   *2nd letter of code*   *Number*
W = NCHS: World History Standards   E = Explicitly stated in document   Page number of cited document
L = Lessons from History   I = Implied in document
C = Core material
R = Related material

MREL

planned cities reveal about the structure of Zapotec and Teotihuacán civilization)

- Understands different farming methods of Teotihuacán and Moche civilization (e.g., ^{BD (R;WE,126)} agricultural methods, water utilization, herding methods used by the Teotihuacán and Moche peoples, and how the natural environment of the Andes helped to influence these methods)

Level III (Grades 7-8)

- Understands the economic and agricultural elements of Mayan society (e.g., the extent, ^{BD (C;WE,125;LI,249)} importance, and composition of Mayan trade; the adaptability and importance of Mayan agricultural techniques and their connection to the rise of Mayan city-states; the importance of astronomy and mathematics to everyday life in Mayan society and the importance of mathematical innovations and the calendar to farmers)

- Understands social features of Mayan culture (e.g., ways that Mayan myths reflect social ^{BD (C;WE,124,125)} values and daily survival skills, differing views concerning the causes for the decline of Mayan civilization)

- Understands what art and architecture reveal about early Mesoamerica and Andean societies ^{BD (R;WE,126,127)} (e.g., what murals infer about Mayan and Teothuacán societies; what art and artifacts indicate about the interests, occupations, and religious concerns of the Moche people; what art and architecture reflects about the character of Zapotec state in the valley of Oaxaca)

- Understands social features of Andean societies (e.g., different agriculture practices in the ^{BD (R;WE,127)} Moche/Andean region; kinship groups, regulated family and community life in Andean societies)

Level IV (Grades 9-12)

- Understands the role of art and architecture in Mayan culture (e.g., the Mayan cosmic world ^{BD (C;WE,125;LI,249)} and the role of Mayan deities as revealed in art and architecture, the place of archaeological evidence such as the "Long Count" calendar in the interpretation of Mayan history, the descriptions of social and religious life inferred in Mayan [Bonampak] glyphs and murals)

- Understands urban planning in Mayan culture (e.g., patterns and significance of architectural ^{BD (C;WE,125;LI,249)} planning and city planning in Mayan culture and the religious factors that affected these layouts)

- Understands ways in which Mayan beliefs were portrayed (e.g., what the Popul Vuh tells ^{BD (C;WE,125)}

Codes (right side of page): BD = Benchmark, Declarative; BP = Benchmark, Procedural; BC = Benchmark, Contextual
1st letter of each code in parentheses *2nd letter of code* *Number*
W = NCHS: World History Standards E = Explicitly stated in document Page number of cited document
L = Lessons from History I = Implied in document
C = Core material
R = Related material 222 *MREL*

about the Mayan world view and creation myth and its reliability as an account of the Mayan world view)

- Understands relationships between Mesoamerican and Andean societies (e.g., comparisons between Mayan, Moche, and Teotihuacán religions and rituals; the basic structure, economy, and ritual of Andean societies such as the Moche, Tihuanaco, and Chimu; the basic construction and variations of Mesoamerican calendars; possible methods of contact between Mesoamerican and Andean societies and the cultural diffusion seen in areas such as agriculture, societal structure, and artisan crafts; the growth of urban society centered on Teotihuacán and the importance of this city as a transmitter of Mesoamerican cultural traditions to later societies) BD (R;WE,127)

16. Understands the maturation of an interregional system of communication, trade, and cultural exchange during a period of Chinese economic power and Islamic expansion (WE,132)

Level II (Grades 5-6)

- Understands how technological and economic features influenced Chinese society between the 10th and 13th centuries (e.g., major technological and scientific inventions in the Song era and how they might have impacted the lives of the Chinese, where the Chinese engaged in trade and how this trade affected them internally) BD (C;WE,132)

- Understands different elements of Japanese feudal society (e.g., the rise of the warrior class in feudal Japan and the values it prescribed; how the Japanese successfully defended themselves against Mongol invasions in the 13th century; how art and aesthetic values were cherished in the warrior culture in Japan and what this art reveals about Japanese values; the type of government in Japan during the Kamakura and Ashikaga periods, and whether it was feudalism; how the economic and social status of women and peasants changed in feudal Japanese society) BD (R;WE,134;LE,245)

- Understands the cultural characteristics of Islamic society (e.g., the importance of scientific, literary, and artistic contributions made by the Islamic civilization between the 11th and 13th centuries and how these contributions helped communication between different Islamic peoples; the diverse, multiethnic character of the Islamic state) BD (C;WE,136;LE,235)

- Understands features of trade routes in Asia, Europe, and Africa (e.g., how goods traveled from East Asia to Europe and the importance of the Indian Ocean to the societies of Asia, East Africa, and Europe; where camels were used in trade and the usefulness of the camel BD (R;WE,138;LE,247;LI,247)

Codes (right side of page):   BD = Benchmark, Declarative; BP = Benchmark, Procedural; BC = Benchmark, Contextual
1st letter of each code in parentheses   *2nd letter of code*   *Number*
W = NCHS: World History Standards   E = Explicitly stated in document   Page number of cited document
L = Lessons from History   I = Implied in document
C = Core material
R = Related material

223

McREL

in desert transportation and trade)

Level III (Grades 7-8)

- Understands the social and economic elements of Song China (e.g., how increased trade helped cities and the merchant class grow in Song China and the traditional social attitudes of China toward merchants and commercial activity, significant achievements and developments of the Song Dynasty, the rigors and class restrictions of the civil service examination in Song China) _{BD (C;WE,133)}

- Understands how Confucianism changed between the 10th and 13th centuries (e.g., the synthesis of Confucianism, Buddhism, and Daoism created by Zhu Xi to form neo-Confucianism) _{BD (C;WE,133)}

- Understands the emergence of different social classes in China (e.g., how an economically powerful merchant class emerged in China, the importance of women of gentry families in preserving and transmitting Chinese cultural values) _{BD (C;WE,132,133)}

- Understands government and politics of the Kamakura period (e.g., development of feudalism in Japan in Kamakura and Ashikaga periods, significant political events in the history of the Kamakura period) _{BD (R;WE,133,134;LE,240,245)}

- Understands influences on the development of Buddhist sects in Japan (e.g., the impact of the warrior culture on the lives of common people and the development of Buddhist sects; how unique forms of Buddhism [sects] developed under the influence of social, political, and religious forces) _{BD (R;WE,134,135;LI,245)}

- Understands the development of Southeast Asian states (e.g., Champa, Angkor, and Dai Vet and how they accumulated power and wealth; the influence of Confucianism, Buddhism, and Hinduism on these states) _{BD (R;WE,134)}

- Understands the expansion of Islam and daily life in Islamic regions (e.g., how Cairo became an international center of commerce and Islamic culture in the age of the Fatamids what life in Egypt was like for Jewish and Christian communities, how Turkic migration from Turkestan into Southwest Asia and India helped Islam expand and forced the retreat of Byzantium and Greek Christian civilization, what student life was like in Islamic regions) _{BD (C;WE,136;LE,236)}

- Understands elements of trade in different regions (e.g., the importance to individual societies of goods traded between Asia, Africa, and Europe; the consequences placed on this _{BD (R;WE,138;LI,248)}

Codes (right side of page):   BD = Benchmark, Declarative; BP = Benchmark, Procedural; BC = Benchmark, Contextual
1st letter of each code in parentheses   *2nd letter of code*   *Number*
W = NCHS: World History Standards   E = Explicitly stated in document   Page number of cited document
L = Lessons from History   I = Implied in document
C = Core material
R = Related material   224   MCREL

maritime trade by the seasonal monsoon winds in the Indian Ocean; features and functions of caravansaries and khans in Central Asian and Middle Eastern cities; which ships were most successfully used for trade in the Indian Ocean and why; how the spread of Islam is connected to trade in Central Asia, East Africa, West Africa, the coasts of India, and Southeast Asia)

Level IV (Grades 9-12)

- Understands significant religious and economic aspects of Chinese society between the 10th and 13th centuries (e.g., the impact of economic growth on Chinese society and how it affected the gentry class; how Zhu Xi's basic ideas of Neo-Confucianism affected Chinese society, government, and education) ^{BD (C;WE,133)}

- Understands religious, social, and political aspects of the Song Dynasty (e.g., the values of Confucianism, Taoism, and Buddhism as reflected in Song art; changes in the social and moral status of women as reflected in the practice of foot binding; the attitudes of typical Chinese gentlemen toward women, family, servants, tenants, and social inferiors; the debate during the Song Dynasty about how the government should respond to rapid social and economic change; Chinese advancements in alchemy, astronomy, and medicine) ^{BD (C;WE,133)}

- Understands different social classes and gender roles in Japanese society (e.g., the role of social class, area, time, and age in determining women's experiences; the development of Buddhist sects in Japanese society and their influence on the samurai class) ^{BD (R;WE,135)}

- Understands the significance of art and philosophy in Japanese and Cambodian society (e.g., philosophical values and traditions presented in Noh drama, how diverse Japanese art forms from the Kamakura and Ashikaga periods reflect Shinto and Buddhist philosophy, Indian and Southeast Asian influences on the architecture of the 12th-century temple of Angkor Wat in Cambodia, what art and literature reveal about the lives of people in Japan in the Kamakura and Ashikaga periods) ^{BD (R;WE,135;LI,246)}

- Understands how the wars with the Mongols influenced Japanese society (e.g., the defeat of the Mongols, the samurai revolt against the Kamakura shogunate and the negative economic impact of these conflicts) ^{BD (R;WE,135)}

- Understands cultural and political aspects of the Turkic Empires (e.g., the way of life of Turkic peoples such as the Seljuks, the origins and growth of the militaristic Seljuk and Ghazanavid Empires) ^{BD (C;WE,136,137;LI,237)}

Codes (right side of page):   BD = Benchmark, Declarative; BP = Benchmark, Procedural; BC = Benchmark, Contextual
1st letter of each code in parentheses   *2nd letter of code*   *Number*
W = NCHS: World History Standards   E = Explicitly stated in document   Page number of cited document
L = Lessons from History   I = Implied in document
C = Core material
R = Related material

McREL

- Understands how different religious movements influenced various cultures between the 11th and 13th centuries (e.g., the impact of Christian campaigns of the Crusades on the societies and Muslim populations of Cairo, Damascus, and Sicily; the origins of the North African Islamic reform movements) BD (C;WE,137;LE,249;LI,237)

- Understands the significance of Sufism (e.g., the basic beliefs of Sufism and Sufism's role in the spread of Islam, how society and Sufi ideas are described and exemplified in Islamic literature, the roles and social position of Sufi orders in rural and urban areas) BD (C;WE,137;LI,236)

- Understands how interregional trade and communication affected Eurasia and Africa (e.g., how international trade was broadened through the spread of Islam, encouraged the rise of city-states along the East African coast, and helped end the isolation of African societies below the Saharan desert; the impact of economic and commercial expansion of Song China on communication and trade in Eurasia; the influence of the direction of trade across the Indian Ocean for communication between Asia, East Africa, and Europe) BD (R;WE,139;LI,248)

17. Understands the redefinition of European society and culture from 1000 to 1300 CE (WE,140)

Level II (Grades 5-6)

- Understands the systems of feudalism and manorialism (e.g., the principles of feudalism and manorialism and their widespread use in parts of Europe in the 11th century; the legal, social, and economic position of serfs in the manorial/feudal system) BD (C;WE,140;LI,241)

- Understands the significance of William the Conqueror in English society (e.g., why William invaded England; how he won control of England after the Battle of Hastings; what changes he made in governing England) BD (C;WE, 140)

- Understands the influence of Christianity in Medieval Europe (e.g., the reasons for and consequences of the European Crusades against Syria and Palestine, how successful the Christian states were in overthrowing Muslim powers in Central and Southern Iberia between the 11th and 13th centuries) BD (C;WE,142;LE,241;LI,241)

- Understands the lives of peasants and serfs in Medieval Europe (e.g., how their lives differed, how their lives were affected by the manors and castles) BD (C;WE,142)

- Understands the lives of different groups of people in Medieval Europe (e.g., life in Jewish communities and what Jews added to the cultural and economic development of Europe; BD (R;WE,144;LE,242)

Codes (right side of page):   BD = Benchmark, Declarative; BP = Benchmark, Procedural; BC = Benchmark, Contextual
1st letter of each code in parentheses   *2nd letter of code*   *Number*
W = NCHS: World History Standards   E = Explicitly stated in document   Page number of cited document
L = Lessons from History   I = Implied in document
C = Core material
R = Related material   226   MREL

between the 14th and 15th centuries, the impact of the plague on young people)

- Understands causes for changes in social, political, and religious events in Europe after the 14th century (e.g., how the population decreased after the Great Plague; increased wage levels and what governments did to discourage these increases; causes for the Hundred Years War; the effect of the crises in the Catholic Church on its organization, prestige, and power)

  BD (C;WE,156)

- Understands the "humanism" that emerged in Italy in the 14th and 15th centuries, and how new studies (e.g., Greco-Roman antiquity, critical text analysis) encouraged new forms of literature, philosophy, and education

  BD (C;WE,156;LE,256)

- Understands the significance of Timur the Lame (Tamerlane) (e.g., the impact of conquests in Southwest Asia, India, and Central Asia; how Timur's rule encouraged a flourishing of cultural life in Samarkand and the role his government played in the support of arts and sciences)

  BD (R;WE,158)

Level IV (Grades 9-12)

- Understands perceptions of the Black Death from diverse, contemporaneous sources (e.g., from Boccaccio in Europe and Ibn Battuta in Egypt and Syria)

  BD (C;WE,155)

- Understands events and consequences of Jewish scapegoating in Europe during the Great Plague (e.g., the cremation of Strasbourg Jews, pogroms in the Holy Roman Empire, Jewish flight to Poland and Russia) and the attitudes and values these events represent

  BD (C;WE,155;LE,242)

- Understands immediate and long-term consequences of the plague on European society (e.g., the medical, administrative, and psychological measures taken to cope with the plague in the 14th century; long-term consequences of recurrent pandemics in the 14th and 15th centuries on Europe society)

  BD (C;WE,155;LE,242)

- Knows ways in which long-term climatic change contributed to Europe's economic and social crisis in the 14th century

  BD (C;WE,154)

- Understands how economic conditions influenced the political and social climate in post-14th- century Europe (e.g., the impact of climatic change on the European agricultural system and the social and political consequences; how decreasing revenues led to competition between nobles for other sources of income, which increased the occurrence of Civil Wars; the relationship between economic changes and population decline in the 14th and 15th centuries)

  BD (C;WE,157;LI,242)

Codes (right side of page):   BD = Benchmark, Declarative; BP = Benchmark, Procedural; BC = Benchmark, Contextual
1st letter of each code in parentheses   *2nd letter of code*   *Number*
W = NCHS: World History Standards   E = Explicitly stated in document   Page number of cited document
L = Lessons from History   I = Implied in document
C = Core material
R = Related material

MREL

- BD (C;WE,156,157;LE,243)
  Understands religious and political changes in post-14th century Europe (e.g., the elements and consequences of the "Great Western Schism," the resurgence of centralized monarchies and economically powerful city-states in Western Europe in the 15th century)

- BD (C;WE,157;LE,256)
  Understands the characteristics of 15th century Italian humanism (e.g., how its emphasis on Greco-Roman texts and critical analysis of texts fostered new forms of literature, philosophy, and education; which social populations it most significantly affected)

- BD (C;WE,157)
  Understands the significance of Joan of Arc (e.g., her role in the Hundred Years War; her subsequent trial and execution; the Church's review of her trial 25 years later, and her revered image as a patron saint of France)

- BD (R;WE,158;LE,244)
  Understands shifts in the leadership and political climate in China (e.g., the events that led to the collapse of Mongol rule in China; economic and political reforms and other achievements of the Hongwu emperor in China, and how these reforms restored for the Ming Dynasty continuity with pre-Yuan Empires; the reconstitution of the Mongol Empire under the Chinese Ming Dynasty)

- BD (R;WE,159)
  Understands Timur the Lame's patronage of scholars, artists, and scientists at Samarkand; the extent to which the "Republic of Letters" was a widespread phenomenon; and evidence of cross-cultural communication among scholars and artists

- BD (R;WE,159;LE,237)
  Knows the chronology of the Ottoman Empire from its beginning to the sack of Constantinople, and understands what accounts for the success of the empire

(WE,160)
21. Understands the expansion of states and civilizations in the Americas between 1000 and 1500

Level II (Grades 5-6)

- BD (C;WE,160)
  Understands what archeaological, artistic, and written sources can illustrate about pre-European life in the Americas

- BD (C;WE,160;LE,249)
  Understands how the Aztec Empire arose in the 14th century (e.g., through the construction of Tenochtitlán, the "Foundation of Heaven")

- BD (C;WE,162)
  Understands social and political elements of Incan society (e.g., daily life for different people in Incan society, the food plants that formed the basis of Incan as compared with

---

Codes (right side of page):   BD = Benchmark, Declarative; BP = Benchmark, Procedural; BC = Benchmark, Contextual
1st letter of each code in parentheses   *2nd letter of code*   *Number*
W = NCHS: World History Standards   E = Explicitly stated in document   Page number of cited document
L = Lessons from History   I = Implied in document
C = Core material
R = Related material

McREL

Aztec agriculture, Incan methods for expansion and unification of their empire)

Level III (Grades 7-8)

- Understands how the natural environment affected the organization of developing societies of the North American plains, Southwestern deserts, and the tropical forests of the Yucatan
  BD (C;WE,160)

- Understands social and cultural features of Aztec society (e.g., the characteristics of Tenochtitlán that made it a unique city, gender roles in Aztec society and what these indicate about Aztec culture)
  BD (C;WE,160;LE,250)

- Understands cultural and economic elements of North American and Mesoamerican civilizations (e.g., the major characteristics of Toltecs, Anasazi, Pueblo, and North American mound-building peoples; patterns of long-distance trade centered in Mesoamerica)
  BD (C;WE,160)

- Understands major political and social features of Incan society (e.g., the chronology of Incan imperial expansion from 1230 to 1525 and the difficulties posed by its geographically and climatically diverse territories, the development of Incan social and political institutions, the location and major features of Machu Picchu and what this site reveals about Incan civilization)
  BD (C;WE,162;LE,250;LI,250)

- Understands the similarities and differences between Incan and Aztec society (e.g., how Incan and Aztec art and architecture reveal cultural achievements in their societies; the essential differences between Aztec and Incan government, economy, religion, and social organization)
  BD (C;WE,162;LE,250)

Level IV (Grades 9-12)

- Understands political, social, and economic features of Aztec society (e.g., the locations and geographic limits of different phases of the Aztec Empire, the role and status of women in Aztec society and how this compares to the Incan and Mayan societies, the complex structure and features of the Aztec city of Tenochtitlán)
  BD (C;WE,161;LI,249)

- Understands the significance of the mound centers located in the Mississippi valley, such as the mound center at Cahokia in Illinois
  BD (C;WE,161,162)

- Understands gender roles in Caribbean, Mesoamerican, and Andean societies and how these are reflected in images, myths, and individual qualities of their gods
  BD (C;WE,162)

Codes (right side of page): BD = Benchmark, Declarative; BP = Benchmark, Procedural; BC = Benchmark, Contextual
1st letter of each code in parentheses   *2nd letter of code*   *Number*
W = NCHS: World History Standards   E = Explicitly stated in document   Page number of cited document
L = Lessons from History   I = Implied in document
C = Core material
R = Related material

McREL

- BD (C;WE,163;LE,250)
Knows the technology (e.g., engineering of roads, bridges, irrigation systems) and urbanism of the Incas (in Cuzco), the Aztecs (in Tenochtitlán), and of North American mound-builders

- BD (C;WE,163;LE,250)
Understands the cause of Inca conquest and expansion and how Incan rulers successfully governed a geographically diverse group of territories

(WE,168)
22. Understands how the transoceanic interlinking of all major regions of the world between 1450 and 1600 led to global transformations

Level II (Grades 5-6)

- BD (C;WE,168)
Understands what contributed to increasing oceanic travel in the 15th and 16th centuries (e.g., trade routes of prominent Asian and European explorers and how prevailing wind currents influenced these routes; navigational inventions such as the compass, astrolabe, and quadrant; major Spanish and Portuguese technological innovations in shipbuilding, navigation, and naval warfare; the features of Chinese and Arab sailing vessels that made long-distance travel easier)

- BD (C;WE,168)
Knows the major accomplishments of Columbus (e.g., his voyages off the coast of Africa and to North America)

- BD (C;WE,168)
Understands the interregional trading system that linked peoples of Africa, Asia, and Europe on the eve of the European overseas voyages

- BD (C;WE,170;LI,258)
Understands the character and impact of Portuguese maritime expansion to Africa, India, and Southeast Asia upon local populations (e.g., relations between King Affonso II of the Kongo and Portuguese, why Bartholomew de las Casas was considered the "defender of the Indians")

- BD (C;WE,170;LI,258)
Understands features of Spanish exploration and conquest (e.g., interaction between the Spanish and indigenous populations such as the Inca and the Aztec; different perspectives on Cortés' journey into Mexico; why the Spanish wanted to invade the Incan and Aztec Empires, and why these empires collapsed after the conflict with the Spanish)

- BD (R;WE,172;LI,258)
Understands the cultural and biological exchange between the Americas and Afro-Eurasia in the late 15th and 16th centuries (e.g., the roots of "cowboy" culture in the Americas; the spread of disease throughout the world, and how new disease microorganisms in the Americas devastated indigenous populations; the exchange of animals between the Americas

Codes (right side of page):   BD = Benchmark, Declarative; BP = Benchmark, Procedural; BC = Benchmark, Contextual
1st letter of each code in parentheses   *2nd letter of code*   *Number*
W = NCHS: World History Standards   E = Explicitly stated in document   Page number of cited document
L = Lessons from History   I = Implied in document
C = Core material
R = Related material

236   MREL

and Afro-Eurasia; how the exchange of plants between the Americas and other countries affected societies and commerce)

Level III (Grades 7-8)

- Understands the impact of the exploratory and commercial expeditions in the 15th and 16th BD (C;WE,169)
centuries (e.g., technologies that advanced international, seaborne trade in the latter part of the century; the connotations of the words "conquest," "exchange," and "discovery" used to describe Columbus' travels to North America and his encounters with indigenous populations; the motives and short-term significance of the Portuguese and Spanish military and commercial expeditions to Sub-Saharan Africa, Asia, and the Americas)

- Understands the significance and cultural impact of migrations of the Muslims and Jews BD (C;WE,169)
after their expulsion from Spain

- Understands cultural interaction between various societies in the late 15th and 16th centuries BD (C;WE,170,171;LI,258)
(e.g., reasons for the fall of the Incan Empire to Pizarro; how the Portuguese dominated seaborne trade in the Indian Ocean basin in the 16th century; the relations between pilgrims and indigenous populations in North and South America, and the role different religious sects played in these relations; how the Church helped administer Spanish and Portuguese colonies in the Americas; how the presence of Spanish conquerors affected the daily lives of Aztec, Maya, and Inca peoples)

- Understands how the Ottoman, Indian, Chinese, and Japanese powers restricted European BD (C;WE,170)
commercial, military, and political penetration in the 16th century

- Understands the impact of the exchange of flora, fauna, and pathogens on the Americas and BD (R;WE,173,LI,258)
the global population (e.g., population decline in parts of the Americas within the context of global population trends and growth in Europe and East Asia in the 16th and 17th centuries, origins and routes of flora and fauna exchanged across the globe, the physical and psychological effects of disease on indigenous populations in the Americas)

- Knows which crops in Spanish and Portuguese regions of the Americas were domestic and BD (R;WE,173)
which were commercial, and knows what resources commercial crops demanded

Level IV (Grades 9-12)

- Knows the extent of Chinese naval and commercial activities in the Indian Ocean in the 15th BD (C;WE,169)
century, and understands what these activities reveal about Chinese wealth, technology, and

Codes (right side of page):   BD = Benchmark, Declarative; BP = Benchmark, Procedural; BC = Benchmark, Contextual
1st letter of each code in parentheses   *2nd letter of code*   *Number*
W = NCHS: World History Standards   E = Explicitly stated in document   Page number of cited document
L = Lessons from History   I = Implied in document
C = Core material
R = Related material   237   MREL

its use of tributes as a means of trade

- Understands measures that restricted Muslims and Jews in the 15th and 16th centuries (e.g., the moral and religious justifications used by the Spanish for the expulsion of Jews and Muslims from Spain, and possible consequences of the Spanish conquest of Grenada in 1492; how the organization of overseas trades in the Iberian states prohibited Mudehar Muslims, converts, and Jews from settling in the Americas)
  BD (C;WE,169)

- Understands features of Portuguese overseas trade and exploration (e.g., the goals of the Portuguese trading policy as established by King João II, and his reasons for refusing to finance Columbus' expedition west; the impact of maritime technologies on the quality of Portuguese sailing in the 15th century)
  BD (C;WE,169;LI,257)

- Understands significant social, economic, political, and cultural features of European society (particularly Spain and Portugal) that stimulated exploration and conquest overseas
  BD (C;WE,168;LE,257)

- Understands how various cultures responded to European presence in the 15th and 16th centuries (e.g., how practitioners of free trade along the northern rim of the Indian Ocean responded to European penetration; the role of the church and church missionaries in the colonization of Africa, Asia, and the Americas, and relations between the church and native populations; Asian responses to European naval encroachments)
  BD (C;WE,171;LI,258)

- Understands the consequences of Portuguese military conflicts and interaction with other cultures (e.g., the origins and consequences of Ottoman-Portuguese military conflicts in the Red Sea, Arabian Sea, and Ethiopia in the early 16th century; the political and economic impact of Portuguese presence on the peoples of West and East Africa in the late 15th and 16th centuries)
  BD (C;WE,171;LI,258)

- Knows the dynamics of the encomienda system of colonial government and labor, and how this compares to European manorial systems
  BD (C;WE,171;LI,258)

- Knows the routes of exchange of specific flora and fauna (e.g., corn, cassava, sugar; horses, cattle, pigs) throughout the world between the 15th and 18th centuries, and the impact of these exchanges on the world economy
  BD (R;WE,173)

- Understands the consequences of the spread of disease globally and regionally (e.g., which diseases spread through colonization and exploration in the 16th and 17th centuries, how they were spread, and the effects of these diseases on individual societies, world trade, political expansion, and political control; the demographic changes wrought by disease on specific indigenous populations; fundamental plantation systems brought to the New World
  BD (R;WE,173;LE,258)

Codes (right side of page):   BD = Benchmark, Declarative; BP = Benchmark, Procedural; BC = Benchmark, Contextual
1st letter of each code in parentheses   *2nd letter of code*   *Number*
W = NCHS: World History Standards   E = Explicitly stated in document   Page number of cited document
L = Lessons from History   I = Implied in document
C = Core material
R = Related material

238

MREL

and how these may be connected to the spread of disease on the continents)

- BD (R;WE,173;LE,258)
Understands the effects that knowledge of the peoples, geography, and natural environments of the Americas had on European religious and intellectual life (e.g., through such ideas as the romanticized "noble savage," systems of human classification, natural history, and cartography)

(WE,174)
23. Understands how European society experienced political, economic, and cultural transformations in an age of global intercommunication between 1450 and 1750

Level II (Grades 5-6)

- BD (C;WE,174;LI,258)
Understands the social characteristics of European society from 1450 to 1750 (e.g., changes in the social status of women, how lifestyles were different among varied social classes in early modern Europe)

- BD (C;WE,176;LE,256;LI,258)
Understands significant contributions of the Renaissance and Reformation to European society (e.g., how the printing press increased the spread of knowledge in Europe; the life and accomplishments of select figures from the Renaissance to the Reformation; major achievements in literature, music, painting, sculpture, and architecture in 16th-century Europe)

- BD (C;WE,176;LI,258,259)
Understands origins of the Reformation and Catholic Reformation (e.g., why many Europeans were unhappy with the late medieval Catholic Church, and how the beliefs and ideas of leading Protestant reformers reflected this discontent; what the Catholic Reformation sought to achieve, and the effect of religious reforms and divisions on Europeans)

- BD (C;WE,178)
Understands the role of gunpowder in changing European warfare (e.g., through the necessary redesign of fortifications)

- BD (C;WE,178;LE,260)
Understands the emergence of absolutist monarchy in various European regions (e.g., the concept of absolutist monarchy and how it was practiced differently across Europe; the growth of the Russian monarchy and the success of Russian expansion in the Caucasus, Central Asia, and Siberia)

- BD (C;WE,178;LE,260)
Understands the English civil war and the Revolution of 1688, and how these events impacted government, religion, economy, and society in England (e.g., new freedoms granted to the English people after 1688)

Codes (right side of page):   BD = Benchmark, Declarative; BP = Benchmark, Procedural; BC = Benchmark, Contextual
1st letter of each code in parentheses   *2nd letter of code*   *Number*
W = NCHS: World History Standards   E = Explicitly stated in document   Page number of cited document
L = Lessons from History   I = Implied in document
C = Core material
R = Related material   239   MREL

- Understands the significance of the Scientific Revolution and the Age of Enlightenment (e.g., the word "revolution" and what is meant by the term "Scientific Revolution"; the lives and achievements of significant figures of the Scientific Revolution; how Diderot's encyclopedia contributed to the Age of Enlightenment; the importance of discoveries in mathematics, physics, biology, and chemistry to 17th-and 18th-century Europe; the impact of astronomical discoveries from Copernicus to Newton) BD (C;WE,180;LE,261;LI,261)

Level III (Grades 7-8)

- Understands the effects on world trade of the Spanish silver trade from America BD (C;WE,174)

- Understands changes in urban and rural Europe between the 15th and 18th centuries (e.g., the growth pattern of European cities between the 17th and 18th centuries, and the major urban centers of this period; causes and effects of the "agrarian revolution" on Western and Eastern European society; social and economic consequences of population growth and urbanization in Europe between the 15th and 18th centuries) BD (C;WE,174;LE,257;LI,257)

- Understands significant social and cultural changes that took place during the Renaissance (e.g., advances in printing press technology, positive and negative changes in the status of women during the Renaissance and Reformation, the legacy of Renaissance architecture, changes in European art and architecture between the Middle Ages and the High Renaissance, the connections between the Italian Renaissance and the development of Humanist ideals in Europe north of the Alps) BD (C;WE,176,177;LE,256,257)

- Understands the patterns of religious affiliation in Europe in the early 17th century and factors that led some populations to embrace the Protestant Reformation while others rejected it BD (C;WE,177;LE,257,259)

- Understands the emergence of strong individual leaders and monarchies in Europe between the 16th and 18th centuries (e.g., the reign of Elizabeth I and her efficacy as a leader and builder of a strong nation-state; the governmental policies of Peter the Great and Catherine the Great, and how they made St. Petersburg the "window on the West"; the nature and development of strong monarchies in the 16th century such as that of James I) BD (C;WE,178;LE,260;LI,260)

- Understands the role of gunpowder in the development of strong European leadership (e.g., how gunpowder came to Europe from China, and how it helped establish and maintain the power of state leaders in Europe) BD (C;WE,178)

- Understands the significance of the "Glorious" revolution (e.g., the long and short-term BD (C;WE,179;LE,260)

Codes (right side of page): BD = Benchmark, Declarative; BP = Benchmark, Procedural; BC = Benchmark, Contextual
1st letter of each code in parentheses   *2nd letter of code*   *Number*
W = NCHS: World History Standards   E = Explicitly stated in document   Page number of cited document
L = Lessons from History   I = Implied in document
C = Core material
R = Related material

240

M*REL

causes of the "Glorious" revolution of 1688 and how it earned this title; the consequences of its ideals on the development of self-government in the American colonies)

- Understands the coexistence of the new scientific rationalism in 17th-and 18th-century Europe with traditional learning and rituals (e.g., factors that prevented widespread acceptance of Scientific Method; principles of the scientific method advanced by Francis Bacon and René Descartes; the trial of Galileo and arguments and evidence used to prove him "innocent" or "guilty"; 16th and 17th century attitudes toward witches, superstition, and astrology, and consequences of these beliefs; the major features of the scientific revolution in major fields of endeavor; ways in which scientific and philosophic knowledge was communicated throughout Europe)

BD (C;WE,180,181;LE,261;LI,261)

Level IV (Grades 9-12)

- Understands shifts in the European economy, trade, and labor systems in the 16th century (e.g., aspects of manufacturing and production in the 16th century's emerging capitalist economy, trends in worldwide trade in the 16th century, how the Dutch and English merchant classes established a significant presence in the world market, developments that affected men's and women's work options in this period)

BD (C;WE,175;LE,258)

- Understands significant individuals and ideologies that emerged during the Renaissance and Reformation (e.g., the basic arguments in *The Prince* by Machiavelli; works of Renaissance writers and elements of Humanism in these works; individuals and factors that contributed to the revival of Classical, Greco-Roman art, architecture, and scholarship; different ideas on women's roles in the Protestant household; social oppression and conflict in Europe during the Renaissance, as contrasted with humanist principles of the time)

BD (C;WE,177;LE,256,259;LI,256)

- Understands causes and the major political, social, and economic consequences of the religious wars in Europe in the 16th and 17th centuries, and the legacy of these wars in modern Europe

BD (C;WE,177;LI,259)

- Understands sources of military buildup of the 17th and 18th centuries (e.g., how they compare with the advice of Machiavelli on the use of mercenaries)

BD (C;WE,179)

- Understands the complaints, goals, and issues of the Cavaliers and Roundheads in the English Civil War

BD (C;WE,179)

- Understands the accomplishments of significant European leaders between the 16th and 18th centuries (e.g., the life and achievements of Louis XIV, and elements of absolutist power

BD (C;WE,179;LE,260)

Codes (right side of page): BD = Benchmark, Declarative; BP = Benchmark, Procedural; BC = Benchmark, Contextual
1st letter of each code in parentheses *2nd letter of code* *Number*
W = NCHS: World History Standards E = Explicitly stated in document Page number of cited document
L = Lessons from History I = Implied in document
C = Core material
R = Related material

241

MREL

during this period; how Peter the Great and Catherine the Great expanded Russian territory during this period; major achievements in the reigns of Frederick the Great, Catherine the Great, and Joseph II, and which of these leaders displayed the features of an "Enlightened Despot")

- Understands factors that influenced the economic and political development of the Dutch Republic, England, and France (e.g., characteristics of the Dutch Republic that affected commerce and religion, and enabled Amsterdam to gain commercial supremacy over the northern Italian city-states in the late 16th century; factors that led England to develop a Parliamentary government and led to absolutism in France under Louis XIV) ^{BD (C;WE,179;LE,260)}

- Understands features of the conflict between religious beliefs and scientific thought during the Scientific Revolution (e.g., Galileo's ideas about the solar system, and why he hesitated to apply scriptural passages to science-related problems; the fundamental ideas of Descarte's *Discourse on Method,* and the methods he used to ascertain the "truth") ^{BD (C;WE,181;LI,261)}

- Understands influences on the spread of Enlightenment thought (e.g., how the salons of aristocratic and bourgeois Parisian women influenced French political affairs and the spread of Enlightenment thought, and why men eventually created their own salons; how Chinese humanist philosophy influenced the ideas of major Enlightenment writers and thinkers) ^{BD (C;WE,181)}

- Understands the role of the Enlightenment in shaping European society (e.g., the connection between the Enlightenment and the Scientific Revolution, and arguments supporting the notion that one was dependent upon the other; how Enlightenment-era thought contributed to the reform of church and state) ^{BD (C;WE,181;LE,261;LI,261)}

24. Understands how large territorial empires dominated much of Eurasia between the 16th and 18th centuries ^(WE,182)

Level II (Grades 5-6)

- Understands how China viewed its role in the world during the Ming Dynasty (e.g., why China's attitude toward external political and commercial relations changed after the Zheng He voyages from 1405 to 1433, the Chinese view of itself as the "Middle Kingdom" and its belief that other countries had a tributary relationship to the celestial empire) ^{BD (C;WE,182)}

- Understands the power and limit of imperial absolutism under the Ming Dynasty (e.g., variations in control over society and the bureaucracy) ^{BD (C;WE,182)}

Codes (right side of page):   BD = Benchmark, Declarative; BP = Benchmark, Procedural; BC = Benchmark, Contextual
1st letter of each code in parentheses   *2nd letter of code*   *Number*
W = NCHS: World History Standards   E = Explicitly stated in document   Page number of cited document
L = Lessons from History   I = Implied in document
C = Core material
R = Related material

McREL

- Understands political and cultural achievements of the Ottoman Empire (e.g., achievements BD (C;WE,184) of Sulieman the Magnificent; the extent of the Byzantine and Ottoman Empires in the 14th and 15th centuries; the significance of the capture of Constantinople for Christians and Ottomans; how the Ottoman military succeeded against various enemies; artistic, architectural, and literary achievements of the Ottoman Empire in the 15th and 16th centuries)

- Understands political achievements of the Safavid and Mughal Empires (e.g., how Persia BD (R;WE,186) was unified by the Turkic Safavids, the political and cultural achievements of the Safavid Golden Age under Shah Abbas I, the Mughal conquest of India and how the Turkic warrior class united diverse peoples of the Indian continent)

- Understands the network of Afro-Eurasian trade in the 16th and 17th centuries (e.g., the BD (R;WE,186) importance of Indian textiles, spices, and other products in the trade; how spices brought to Europe by Vasco da Gama initiated the spice trade between India and Europe)

Level III (Grades 7-8)

- Understands features of class structure and sources of social change in China (e.g., the BD (C;WE,182,183) stratification of Chinese society under Ming rule; the effects of American crops and silver on demographic, economic, and social change in China)

- Understands changes in the political structure of the Ming Dynasty (e.g., how the power of BD (C;WE,182,183) the Ming emperor changed over time, the source of political threat to the Ming Empire and the role of defense in their military strategy)

- Understands cultural, political, and economic factors that influenced the development of the BD (C;WE,184,185) Ottoman Empire (e.g., the development of the Ottoman Empire among diverse religious and ethnic groups, the Christian European view of the Ottoman seizure of Constantinople in 1453, trade and trade routes within the Ottoman Empire and how this trade was affected by the development of a sea route around Africa)

- Understands factors that influenced the development and expansion of the Safavid Empire BD (R;WE,186,187) (e.g., key urban areas of the empire, and factors that contributed to the success of Safavid rule; how the city of Isfahan developed under the reign of Shah Abbas I)

- Knows how the popularity of Indian textiles in Europe undermined the efforts of the East BD (R;WE,187) India Company to sell more British goods in India than it imported

---

Codes (right side of page):   BD = Benchmark, Declarative; BP = Benchmark, Procedural; BC = Benchmark, Contextual
1st letter of each code in parentheses   *2nd letter of code*   *Number*
W = NCHS: World History Standards   E = Explicitly stated in document   Page number of cited document
L = Lessons from History   I = Implied in document
C = Core material
R = Related material

McREL

- Understands political and religious influences on the development of the Mughal Empire ^{BD (R;WE,187;LE,269)} (e.g., the effectiveness of Akbar's governing methods and religious ideas in comparison to other Mughal emperors, relations between Muslims and Hindus in the empire)

Level IV (Grades 9-12)

- Understands significant cultural and social features of the Ming Dynasty (e.g., how the Ming ^{BD (C;WE,183;LI,266)} Dynasty brought cultural unity to China; the imperial examination system in China established under Ming rule; the role of Neo-Confucianism, Buddhism, and Daoism in Ming government and society)

- Understands influences on the Chinese economy and social structure (e.g., the impact of the ^{BD (C;WE,183;LE,267)} massive silver trade between the Americas and China from the 16th to the early 19th centuries; how the Chinese central government controlled various aspects of peoples' lives; the effects of commercialization on social relations among gentry elites, urban merchants, and peasants)

- Understands major political events in the rise and decline of the Ottoman Empire (e.g., the ^{BD (C;WE,185;LE,269)} emergence of the Ottomans as a regional and world power between 1450 and 1650, the Ottoman Empire in the context of the Byzantine and Roman Empires, Austrian and Russian responses to Ottoman aggression, significant events in the expansion and recession of the Ottoman Empire from the 15th to the 17th centuries)

- Understands the social, economic, and cultural features of the Ottoman Empire (e.g., the role ^{BD (C;WE,185;LE,269)} and legal status of women within the Ottoman Empire, sources of revenue and patterns in state spending in the Ottoman Empire, the ethnic and religious diversity of people within the Ottoman Empire and the effect of Ottoman governance on these peoples)

- Understands the origins and development of the Safavid Empire (e.g., how Ismail created ^{BD (R;WE,187)} the Safavid Empire with the support of Qizilbash nomadic tribesmen; the evolution of Safavid social and political system from the nomadic-warrior years of Ismail to the golden age of Shah Abbas I)

- Understands cultural and religious influences on Mughal social and cultural conditions (e.g., ^{BD (R;WE,187;LE,269)} how Akbar unified diverse cultures and encouraged religious tolerance within his Mughal Empire; the synthesis of Muslim and Hindu influences in art of the Mughal Empire; the Indian, Persian, and European influences in Mughal artistic, architectural, literary, and scientific achievements)

Codes (right side of page):   BD = Benchmark, Declarative; BP = Benchmark, Procedural; BC = Benchmark, Contextual
1st letter of each code in parentheses   *2nd letter of code*   *Number*
W = NCHS: World History Standards   E = Explicitly stated in document   Page number of cited document
L = Lessons from History   I = Implied in document
C = Core material
R = Related material   244   M?REL

BD (R;WE,187;LE,269)

- Knows similarities and differences between major empires and leaders (e.g., comparisons between the Ottoman, Safavid, and Mughal Empires; differences and similarities in government, military, and religious patterns of the six major Mughal emperors)

(WE,188)
25. Understands the economic, political, and cultural interrelations among peoples of Africa, Europe, and the Americas between 1500 and 1750

Level II (Grades 5-6)

BD (C;WE,188)
- Understands the European influence in the Americas between the 16th and 18th centuries (e.g., the locations of the British and French in the Americas, and their interest in trade there; the concept of mercantilism and its advantages and disadvantages for the colonies and the mother country; the four major types of European activity and control in the Americas; how Holland, England, and France became naval, commercial, and political powers in the Atlantic basin in the 16th and 17th centuries)

BD (C;WE,190;LI,262)
- Understands elements of the trans-Atlantic African slave trade (e.g., how slaves were transported to the Americas via the "middle passage"; how European firms and governments organized and financed the slave trade; conditions of slave life on plantations in the Caribbean, Brazil, and British North America)

BD (C;WE,190;LI,262)
- Understands features of the labor system and economy in the Americas (e.g., different jobs performed by indigenous peoples in the Americas; why sugar, tobacco, coffee, tea, and other crops grown in the colonies became so important in the world economy)

BD (R;WE,192;LE,262;LI,262)
- Understands elements of the slave trade in Africa (e.g., what narratives reveal about the experience of Africans sold into slavery; how the slave trade affected population, economic systems, family life, and relations between men and women in West and Central Africa)

Level III (Grades 7-8)

BD (C;WE,188,189)
- Understands the differences in the demands and purposes of European colonies in different areas of the Western Hemisphere (e.g., how European colonies in Peru differed from those in the Great Lakes region, Barbados, or Massachusetts)

BD (C;WE,188,189;LI,263)
- Understands the consequences of European interaction with indigenous populations of the Americas (e.g., the Seven Years War and its consequences for Britain, France, Spain, and the indigenous peoples of the American colonial territories; the political relationships

---

Codes (right side of page):   BD = Benchmark, Declarative; BP = Benchmark, Procedural; BC = Benchmark, Contextual
1st letter of each code in parentheses   *2nd letter of code*   *Number*
W = NCHS: World History Standards   E = Explicitly stated in document   Page number of cited document
L = Lessons from History   I = Implied in document
C = Core material
R = Related material

McREL

between American Indian nations and Holland, France, and England; the moral, political, and cultural role of Catholic and Protestant Christianity in the European colonies in America)

- Understands features of and participants in the African slave trade (e.g., European exploitation of American Indian labor and the use of African slave labor for commercial agriculture; treatment of slaves and forms of resistance used in the "middle passage"; the treatment of slaves in the Western Hemisphere as opposed to those in the Islamic lands, Christian Europe, and West Africa; the organization of long-distance trade in West and Central Africa and circumstances under which African governments, elites, and merchants participated in the sale of slaves to Europeans)

  BD (C;WE,191;LE,262;LI,262,265)

- Understands factors that contributed to the development of various African societies (e.g., different forms of slave resistance and the founding of Maroon societies; the importance of trade, slavery, and an expanding world economy to the development of such African states as Ashanti, Dahomey, and Oyo; how Ashanti concepts of monarchical power compare to those of Europeans; the development, characteristics, and decline of the Songhay Empire in the 16th century)

  BD (R;WE,192)

- Knows the causes and consequences of encounters among Koisan groups, Bantu-speaking peoples, and European settlers in South Africa in the 17th and 18th centuries

  BD (R;WE,192)

Level IV (Grades 9-12)

- Understands economic and political features of various European colonies between the 16th and 18th centuries (e.g., the fundamental ideas of mercantilism and differences in how it was practiced by Holland, France, and England; diversity in colonial governments, economies, the military, and social organization in European colonies; the administrative system of the Spanish viceroyalties of Peru and Mexico, and the importance of Indian agriculture and silver production to Spanish colonial economy)

  BD (C;WE,189;LE,264,265;LI,264)

- Understands events in the development of European colonies in the Americas (e.g., the appeal of the Americas for European colonists in the 16th and 17th centuries, why Europeans were able to establish large colonies on these continents, and why they did not assert this type of control in Africa and Asia; the short-and long-term effects of the Seven Years' War and the American Revolution upon Native American populations)

  BD (C;WE,189;LE,264)

- Understands possible reasons why Catholics were generally more successful than Protestants in converting non-Europeans between the 16th and 18th centuries

  BD (C;WE,189)

Codes (right side of page):   BD = Benchmark, Declarative; BP = Benchmark, Procedural; BC = Benchmark, Contextual
1st letter of each code in parentheses   *2nd letter of code*   *Number*
W = NCHS: World History Standards   E = Explicitly stated in document   Page number of cited document
L = Lessons from History   I = Implied in document
C = Core material
R = Related material

MREL

- Understands the development of different colonial labor systems and their impact on ^{BD (C;WE,191;LE,264)} indigenous populations (e.g., the evolution of labor systems — from the encomienda to the hacienda — in North and South America from the 16th to the 17th centuries, the impact of the encomienda system on indigenous peoples and how it compares to slavery, the variety of ways in which Europeans exploited American Indian labor)

- Understands the "Black Legend," how it helped build opposition toward Spain, and how it illustrates Spain's unique dealings with aboriginal populations

- Understands how slavery was defined by different groups of people (e.g., key differences between the understanding of "slavery" by Africans and by European settlers in the Americas, the character of the Atlantic slave trade and how it compared to bondage practices in other regions)

- Knows reasons for the emergence of social hierarchies based on race in both the Iberian Empire and the British colonies in the Americas

- Understands how the African slave trade influenced the lives of slaves in both Africa and the Western Hemisphere (e.g., how the slave trade affected family life and gender roles in West and Central Africa; the institutions, beliefs, and practices of slaves working on plantations in the Western Hemisphere, and how they preserved their African heritage; the history of open slave rebellion and resistance in the Western Hemisphere; how the English and Spanish subdued slave rebellion in their colonies)

- Understands the development of different African societies (e.g., the history of the African kingdom of Palmares in Brazil, the regional and international circumstances under which large new states such as Lunda and Bugunda emerged in East and Central Africa)

26.   **Understands transformations in Asian societies in the era of European expansion**

Level II (Grades 5-6)

- Understands the impact of European military and commercial involvement in Asia (e.g., how Holland, England, and France became naval and commercial powers in the Indian Ocean basin in the 17th and 18th centuries; why Asian trade was so important within the British economic and political structure; the impact of British and French commercial and military penetration on politics, economy, and society in India; why the Dutch wanted military and commercial influence in Indonesia and how this imperialism affected the region's economy

---

Codes (right side of page):   BD = Benchmark, Declarative; BP = Benchmark, Procedural; BC = Benchmark, Contextual
1st letter of each code in parentheses   *2nd letter of code*   *Number*
W = NCHS: World History Standards   E = Explicitly stated in document   Page number of cited document
L = Lessons from History   I = Implied in document
C = Core material
R = Related material   247   MCREL

and society)

- Understands significant economic and political shifts in Chinese society (e.g., trade relationships between China and European powers; how the Manchus overthrew the Ming Dynasty and the consequences of this event) ^{BD (C;WE,196;LE,270)}

- Understands major causes for the decline of the Mughal Empire and the rise of regional powers such as the Marathas and Sikhs ^{BD (C;WE,196;LE,270)}

- Understands social and political features of Japanese society under the Tokugawa shogunate (e.g., centralized feudalism in Japan and how Japan achieved political stability, economic growth, and cultural dynamism; the nature of the relationship between Japan and European powers between the 16th and 18th centuries) ^{BD (C;WE,196;LE,267,268)}

- Understands the role of art in conveying ideas in China and Japan (e.g., how nature is portrayed in Chinese and Japanese brush paintings) ^{BD (R;WE,198)}

- Knows what groups of people in India most frequently converted to Islam between the 16th and 18th centuries, and the major vehicle for conversion ^{BD (R;WE,198)}

Level III (Grades 7-8)

- Understands trade patterns and relations between Europe and China (e.g., trade routes and major port cities used by the Europeans in their trade with China, why Gangzhou [Canton] was central in this trade, and how the Chinese controlled European activities in this city; the trade relationship between Britain and China in the 18th century) ^{BD (C;WE,194,195)}

- Understands the effects of European commercial and military interests in the Indian ocean (British, French, and Dutch naval buildup in the Indian Ocean between 1600 and 1700; the importance of forced labor for the prosperity of the Dutch in Indonesia) ^{BD (C;WE,195)}

- Understands cultural, economic, and social aspects of Chinese society during the era of European expansion (e.g., cultural and economic achievements of the Chinese during the reigns of the Kangzi and Qianlong emperors; demands and consequences of increasing population growth, agricultural output, commerce, and European trading networks in the Manchu Empire; treatment and opportunities open to women in 17th-and 18th-century China) ^{BD (C;WE,196)}

- Understands features in the development of Korean and Japanese culture (e.g., why Korea ^{BD (C;WE,197;LE,268)}

Codes (right side of page):   BD = Benchmark, Declarative; BP = Benchmark, Procedural; BC = Benchmark, Contextual
1st letter of each code in parentheses   *2nd letter of code*   *Number*
W = NCHS: World History Standards   E = Explicitly stated in document   Page number of cited document
L = Lessons from History   I = Implied in document
C = Core material
R = Related material

MREL

was called the "Hermit Kingdom" before 1800, the role and status of women in Tokugawa Japan, the roots and development of 17th-century Japanese art forms)

- Understands the spread of Confucianism in various Asian cultures (e.g., how the rising popularity of Confucianism among the elites in Korea and Japan contributed to changes in the roles of women; how Confucianism was influenced by government and society in China, Korea, Japan, and Vietnam; the extent of the influence of new currents in both Confucianism and Chinese art, architecture, and literary styles on cultural life in Korea, Vietnam, and Japan)
  BD (R;WE,198)

- Understands how the spread of different religions affected various Asian countries (e.g., the varieties of Buddhism and Hindu practice and teaching that developed in Asia and their influence on social and cultural life; how and why Islam continued to expand in India, Southeast Asia, and China)
  BD (R;WE,198)

- Understands the evolution, recurring themes, and foreign influence in Japanese art and artists (e.g., Nikko and Katsuru rikyu, Sotabu screens, brush painting, works of Shiba Kokan) and how they reflected society
  BD (R;WE,198)

Level IV (Grades 9-12)

- Understands the economic and cultural consequences of European involvement in other countries (e.g., Joseph Francois Dupleix's theory of "divide and rule" in South India for the French, and how this policy affected relations between the British East India Company and Indian peasants; how the French, Dutch, and British attempted to remedy unfavorable trade balances in Asia between 1500 and 1800; the significance of Christian missionary activity in India, the East Indies, and the Philippines, and how people of other religions — Buddhism, Hinduism, and Islam — responded to these efforts; how well the Chinese government was able to control European trade within its borders and the extent of European commercial penetration)
  BD (C;WE,195;LE,270;LI,270)

- Understands Mughal responses to the expansion of European commercial and maritime power in Asia (e.g., Mughal efforts to control the expansion and influence of European trading centers in India, and how these compared to similar efforts by the Chinese and Japanese to regulate foreign trade and influence within their borders; the catalysts behind the military buildup of Emperor Aurazngzeb in 1700 and how he responded to growing maritime strength of the British and French)
  BD (C;WE,195;LI,270)

- Understands the impact of the Seven Years War on the relative power of Britain and France
  BD (C;WE,194)

Codes (right side of page):   BD = Benchmark, Declarative; BP = Benchmark, Procedural; BC = Benchmark, Contextual

1st letter of each code in parentheses	*2nd letter of code*	*Number*
W = NCHS: World History Standards	E = Explicitly stated in document	Page number of cited document
L = Lessons from History	I = Implied in document	
C = Core material		
R = Related material		

McREL

in Asia

- Knows the events that led to the demise of centralized control by the imperial Mughals and the ascent of Maratha and Sikh power in India ^BD (C;WE,197;LE,270)

- Understands foreign influences on Japanese and Chinese economies (e.g., the impact of American silver upon the Japanese and Chinese economies between the 16th and 18th centuries; Japanese and Chinese attitudes regarding trade with foreign states, the role the Portuguese and Dutch played in Japanese trade, and why Japan limited trade to the West but not to Asia) ^BD (C; WE,197;DE,63.4)

- Understands the economic and social structure of China during the period of European commercial expansion (e.g., the major differences in the trading policies of the Ming and Manchu, the factors that contributed to these changes, and European products desired by the Chinese; aspects of life of the elite in China; the family and its role in Chinese society) ^BD (C;WE,197)

- Understands how the unification of Japan and the centralization of feudalism under Tokugawa rule compared to the rise of nation states in early modern Europe ^BD (C;WE,197;LE,267)

- Understands the spread of different religions throughout the world (e.g., major world religions in the mid-18th century, their relative sizes, and their degrees of success at winning new converts; how the development of Buddhism in Japan compared to that in China) ^BD (R;WE,199)

- Understands how art, literature, and architecture reflect features of different cultures and religions (e.g., the Chinese influence on the art, architecture, and literature of Korea and Vietnam in the 17th and 18th centuries; the role of women in the Bhati movement of the 16th century, as reflected in the poetry of Mirabai; the Islamic and Hindu influences in the poetry of Kabir) ^BD (R;WE,199)

27. Understands major global trends from 1450 to 1770 (WE,200)

Level II (Grades 5-6)

- Understands the major changes in world political boundaries that took place between 1450 and 1770, and how far European nations had extended political and military influence in Africa, Asia, and the Americas until the mid-18th century ^BD (R;WE,200)

- Understands major shifts in world demography and urbanization between 1450 and 1770 and reasons for these changes ^BD (R;WE,200)

Codes (right side of page):   BD = Benchmark, Declarative; BP = Benchmark, Procedural; BC = Benchmark, Contextual
1st letter of each code in parentheses   *2nd letter of code*   *Number*
W = NCHS: World History Standards   E = Explicitly stated in document   Page number of cited document
L = Lessons from History   I = Implied in document
C = Core material
R = Related material   250   McREL

- Understands how the acceleration of scientific and technological innovations in this era affected social, economic, and cultural life in various parts of the world (e.g., the broad effects of navigational and ship-building innovations such as astrolabe and lateen sails) BD (R;WE,200)

Level III (Grades 7-8)

- Understands major urbanization between 1450 and 1750, and why certain cities grew faster than others BD (R;WE,201)

- Knows the spread of Buddhism, Islam, and Christianity between 1450 and 1750 (e.g., the location and geographical area of influence, the rate of growth of practitioners, reasons for growth) BD (R;WE,201)

- Understands the influence of technological advancements on society (e.g., major technological innovations in navigation and military technology between 1500 and 1770, and what changes they affected; how innovations in military technology and tactics changed the balance of naval military power and affected empire building around the globe) BD (R;WE,201)

- Understands patterns of social and cultural continuity in various societies, and understands ways in which peoples maintained traditions and resisted external challenges in the context of a rapidly changing world BD (R;WE,200)

- Knows ways in which expanding capitalistic enterprise and commercialization affected relations among states and contributed to changing class relations BD (R;WE,200)

Level IV (Grades 9-12)

- Understands the catalysts behind the shift of economic power from the Mediterranean basin to Northern Europe during the 16th century BD (R;WE,201)

- Understands the emergence of capitalism in India and Europe (e.g., the expanding capitalist system, the rise of the middle class, and changes in the textile industry in India after 1700; why modern capitalism successfully developed in England, Holland, and France but failed to take root in Italy, Spain, or Portugal; the rise of Western European capitalism and its effects on the rest of the world) BD (R;WE,201)

- Understands how the Ming and Qing rulers viewed the European merchants, Christian missionaries, and military personnel who sought trading privileges in China BD (R;WE,201)

Codes (right side of page):   BD = Benchmark, Declarative; BP = Benchmark, Procedural; BC = Benchmark, Contextual
1st letter of each code in parentheses   *2nd letter of code*   *Number*
W = NCHS: World History Standards   E = Explicitly stated in document   Page number of cited document
L = Lessons from History   I = Implied in document
C = Core material
R = Related material   251   *McREL*

- Understands how traditional Puritan and Confucian attitudes toward profit making affected commerce and trading practices in China and the early New England colonies
  BD (R;WE,201)

- Knows changes in boundaries and understands shifts of political power in Europe, Asia, Africa, and the Western Hemisphere between 1500 and 1800
  BD (R;WE,201)

28. Understands the causes and consequences of political revolutions in the late 18th and early 19th centuries (WE,206)

Level II (Grades 5-6)

- Understands the ideas and events that shaped the Revolution in France (e.g., the meaning of the revolutionary slogan in France, "Liberty, Equality, Fraternity," and the social ideals it embodied; how the wars of the revolutionary and Napoleonic periods changed Europe and Napolean's effects on the aims and outcomes of the revolution; the unique character of the American Revolution and its effect on Europe)
  BD (C;WE,206;LE,275)

- Understands connections between political events in the Americas and Western Europe between 1770 and 1815
  BD (C;WE,206)

- Understands the origins and development of Latin American independence movements (e.g., how the colonial powers and independent countries of Latin America changed between 1790 and 1828; the role of geography in the outcome of the Latin American independence movements; the political and ideological objectives, and the success of the independence movements between 1808 and 1830; how the American, French, and Haitian revolutions and South American rebellions influenced the development of independence movements in Latin America)
  BD (C;WE,208;LI,276,277)

Level III (Grades 7-8)

- Understands events and ideas that influenced the course of the French Revolution (e.g., the organization of the Estates-General and its merits and limitations; central ideas and origins of the Declaration of Rights of Man and Citizen)
  BD (C;WE,207)

- Knows the leading figures and issues of the Congress of Vienna
  BD (C;WE,207)

- Understands how the French Revolution changed social conditions in France (e.g., how territorial changes were made in Europe between 1789 and 1815 and their consequences for
  BD (C;WE,206,207)

Codes (right side of page):   BD = Benchmark, Declarative; BP = Benchmark, Procedural; BC = Benchmark, Contextual
1st letter of each code in parentheses   *2nd letter of code*   *Number*
W = NCHS: World History Standards   E = Explicitly stated in document   Page number of cited document
L = Lessons from History   I = Implied in document
C = Core material
R = Related material   252   *MREL*

diverse social groups such as clergy, nobility, peasantry, bourgeoisie, and sans-culottes; how the revolution changed political and religious institutions, social relations, education, family life, and the status of women in French society)

- Understands the diverse factors (e.g., the Seven Years War, Enlightenment-era thought, escalating internal economic crisis) that affected social and political conditions in Old Regime France
  BD (C;WE,206)

- Understands the political and ideological objectives of Latin American independence movements (e.g., knows who supported Father Miguel Hidalgo, his role in the Mexican Revolution of 1810; knows the role of Agustín de Iturbide in the Creole-dominated revolt of 1821)
  BD (C;WE,208)

- Knows the consequences of Napoleon's invasions (e.g., the events surrounding Napoleon's invasion of Portugal, the flight of the Portuguese court to Brazil; the impact of Napoleon's invasion of Iberia together with growing British power in the Atlantic basin on the independence movements in Latin America)
  BD (C;WE,208)

- Understands elements of the Haitian revolution (e.g., the role of Touissant L'Overture, Haiti's social and economic conditions under French rule, the effect of events in France on the revolution)
  BD (C;WE,208)

Level IV (Grades 9-12)

- Understands the political beliefs and writings that emerged during the French Revolution (e.g., characteristics and actions of radical, liberal, moderate, conservative, and reactionary thinking; the ideas in Olympe de Gouge's "Declaration of the Rights of Women and the Female Citizen" and the "Declaration of the Rights of Man and the Citizen"; the implications of the "Code Napoleon" for Protestant and Catholic Clergy, property owners, workers, and women)
  BD (C;WE,207;LI,276)

- Understands the impact of the Haitian Revolution (e.g., connections between the French and Haitian Revolutions, the impact of this event on race relations and slavery in the Americas and the French Empire)
  BD (C;WE,207;LI,277)

- Understands the ideas and issues during and after the Latin American independence movement (e.g., issues that concerned New Granada after independence; the provisions of and Latin American response to the Monroe Doctrine; the ideological grounding of Latin American independence movements, their political objectives, and how the Brazilian
  BD (C;WE,209;LE,276,277)

Codes (right side of page):   BD = Benchmark, Declarative; BP = Benchmark, Procedural; BC = Benchmark, Contextual
1st letter of each code in parentheses   *2nd letter of code*   *Number*
W = NCHS: World History Standards   E = Explicitly stated in document   Page number of cited document
L = Lessons from History   I = Implied in document
C = Core material
R = Related material   253   McREL

independence movement different from the rest)

- Understands the status of women and other social classes during and following the Latin American independence movements (e.g., how independence changed the status of women in Latin America and affected mestizo, mulatto, and Indian populations; social and racial divisions in most of Latin American during and following the independence movements; roles played by prominent women before the wars of independence in Latin America) BD (C;WE,209)

- Understands comparisons between the Latin American revolutions and those in America, France, and Haiti (e.g., pre-independence social and political conditions, opposed regimes/policies, justifications of the revolutionaries, class representation, extent of revolution) BD (C;WE,209;LE,276,277)

29. Understands the causes and consequences of the agricultural and industrial revolutions from 1700 to 1850 (WE,210)

Level II (Grades 5-6)

- Understands the emergence of and impact of industrialism in 18th-century England (e.g., how agricultural inventions influenced the industrial as well as agricultural revolutions; how the industrial revolution affected population shifts; how the industrial revolution in the textile industry changed the way people worked; how figures such as John Kay, James Hargreaves, James Watt, Edmund Cartwright, or Richard Arkwright contributed to industrialization in England) BD (C;WE,210)

- Understands how the industrial revolution affected social class and gender roles (e.g., the daily life of the working class in Britain during the industrial revolution; the effects of urbanization on the development of class distinctions, family life, and the political and economic status of women) BD (C;WE,212)

- Understands shifts in society during the industrial revolution (e.g., advances made in communication and transportation; connections between population growth, industrialization, and urbanization; connections between industrialization, labor unions, and movements for political and social reform in England, Western Europe, and the United States) BD (C;WE,212;LE,277-278)

- Understands aspects of the abolition movement in the 18th and 19th centuries (e.g., why and how the slave trade continued after it had been outlawed; major accomplishments of the American abolitionist Frederick Douglass; the organization and arguments of movements BD (R;WE,214)

Codes (right side of page): BD = Benchmark, Declarative; BP = Benchmark, Procedural; BC = Benchmark, Contextual
1st letter of each code in parentheses   *2nd letter of code*   *Number*
W = NCHS: World History Standards   E = Explicitly stated in document   Page number of cited document
L = Lessons from History   I = Implied in document
C = Core material
R = Related material

MREL

in Europe and the Americas that sought to end slavery, and how the trans-Atlantic slave trade was suppressed)

Level III (Grades 7-8)

- Understands why industrialization flourished in Britain (e.g., Britain's unique combination of geography, location, natural resources, economy, technology, and political tendencies; Britain's commercial connections with foreign markets in the early industrial revolution) BD (C;WE,211;LI,277)

- Understands the importance and consequences of new technologies (e.g., seed drill, crop rotation, stock breeding, three piece iron) in the agricultural revolution BD (C;WE,211)

- Understands the impact of new technology that emerged during the industrial revolution (e.g., technological innovations that propelled the textile industry to the forefront of the industrial revolution; the roles of interchangeable parts and mass production in the industrial revolution) BD (C;WE,211)

- Understands the effect of the industrial revolution on social and political conditions in various regions (e.g., the pace and extent of industrialization in Great Britain and the United States in the latter half of the 19th century; Robert Owen's New Lanark System and its role in dealing with societal problems caused by the industrial revolution; the impact of industrialization on working conditions and urban conditions; changes affected by the "Great Reform" bill of 1832, and how it addressed problems of the industrial revolution; connections between industrialization and the rise of new types of labor organizations and mobilization) BD (C;WE,212;LI,278)

- Knows new patterns in world manufacturing production that developed among the nations of Great Britain, United States, Germany, France, Russia, and Italy between 1800 and 1900 BD (C;WE,212)

- Understands the discourse surrounding the abolition of slavery (e.g., the debate over abolition of slavery in the context of the French Revolution, the different strategies to resist slavery employed by peoples in the Americas) BD (C;WE,214)

- Understands significant individuals in the abolition movement (e.g., prominent women from the abolitionist movement in America and their major accomplishments, including Harriet Tubman, Sojourner Truth, the Grimké sisters, Lucretia Mott; the story of Olaudah Equiana [Gustavus Vasa], his experience during the "middle passage," and his efforts to bring an end to the slave trade) BD (R;WE,214)

Codes (right side of page): BD = Benchmark, Declarative; BP = Benchmark, Procedural; BC = Benchmark, Contextual
1st letter of each code in parentheses *2nd letter of code* *Number*
W = NCHS: World History Standards E = Explicitly stated in document Page number of cited document
L = Lessons from History I = Implied in document
C = Core material
R = Related material

255

MREL

- Understands the status of slavery and slaves throughout the 19th century (e.g., locations of BD (R;WE,214) legal slavery around the world in 1800, 1830, and 1880, and how changes in the legal status could be linked to revolution ideology and economics; how contract labor migration and other forms of coerced labor compare with slavery as methods of organizing commercial agriculture in the Americas in the later 19th century; the degree to which emancipated slaves and their descendants achieved social equality and economic advancement in various countries of the Western Hemisphere)

Level IV (Grades 9-12)

- Understands the realities and romanticized visions of pre-industrial England (e.g., as BD (C;WE,211;LE,278) reflected in the paintings of Constable and Turner)

- Understands the effect of economic conditions on the development of industrialization (e.g., BD (C;WE,211) knows differences between mercantilist and free market economies and the effect of new economic theories on industrial policies and practices, the relationship between the expanding global market of the 16th to 18th century and the development of industrialization)

- Understands the relationship between improvements in agriculture, population increase, the BD (C;WE,211) rise of the textile industry, the enclosure movement, urbanization, and industrialization in 18th century England

- Knows the strengths and weaknesses of Adam Smith's analysis of capitalism in the *The* BD (C;WE,213) *Wealth of Nations* (e.g., his principle of "Invisible Hand," the role of free enterprise, the profit motive, and competition; his "pin" story)

- Understands how and why industrialization developed differently in Britain than it did on BD (C;WE,213;LI,277) the continent

- Understands how industrialization shaped social class and labor methods (e.g., what 19th- BD (C;WE,213) century literature reveals about the emergence and conditions of new social classes during the industrial period; conditions for children employed by 19th-century England before and after major legislation passed in 1833, 1842, and 1847; how the industrial revolution affected the family structure; the wide variety of organizations created by working-class peoples in England, Western Europe, and the United States in response to the conditions of industrial labor)

- Understands different perspectives regarding the nature of the African slave trade (e.g., how BD (R;WE,215)

Codes (right side of page):   BD = Benchmark, Declarative; BP = Benchmark, Procedural; BC = Benchmark, Contextual
1st letter of each code in parentheses   *2nd letter of code*   *Number*
W = NCHS: World History Standards   E = Explicitly stated in document   Page number of cited document
L = Lessons from History   I = Implied in document
C = Core material
R = Related material   256   MREL

the African slave trade might be compared to the migration of Chinese workers to North and South America, and Indian workers to the Caribbean in the 19th century; the significance of the book *The Interesting Narrative of the Life of Olaudah Equiano or Gustavus Vasa, Written by Himself* about the slave trade)

- Understands reasons why various countries abolished slavery (e.g., evangelical arguments against slavery, and the economic, evangelical, and "Enlightened" reasons for Britain's abolition of slavery; why Brazil was the last nation to abolish slavery and the slave trade; the consequences of the Haitian Revolution for the slave trade; the importance of Enlightenment thought, Christian piety, democratic revolutions, slave resistance, and changes in the world economy in bringing about the abolition of the slave trade and emancipation of the slaves in the Americas) BD (R;WE,215)

- Knows the extent of slave imports to Brazil, Spanish America, the British West Indies, the French West Indies, British North America, and the U.S. and how the influx of slaves differed in the periods 1701 to 1810 and 1811 to 1871 BD (R;WE,214)

30. Understands how Eurasian societies were transformed in an era of global trade and the emergence of European power from 1750 to 1850 (WE,216)

Level II (Grades 5-6)

- Understands changes in social and political elements of the Ottoman Empire during the 18th and 19th centuries (e.g., the lives of different members of Ottoman society such as the janissary, attendees of the Palace School, the role of women; the Western style reforms made to the Ottoman Empire under the reign Selim III; reasons for the empire's retreat from the Balkans and Black Sea region) BD (C;WE,216)

- Understands political characteristics of Egypt (e.g., the reign and major accomplishments of Muhammad Ali of Egypt and why he was known as the "father of modern Egypt," the impact of the French invasion of Egypt in 1798) BD (C;WE,216)

- Understands aspects of Russian expansion and settlement in the late 18th and 19th centuries (e.g., why and how Russia expanded across Asia into Alaska, and along the California coast; what archaeological evidence reveals about daily life in the Russian settlements at Sitka and Bogeda Bay) BD (R;WE,218)

- Understands the emergence of European trading companies and their impact on Indian culture (e.g., how and where goods were traded between China, India, and Europe, and the BD (C;WE,220;LE,282)

Codes (right side of page):   BD = Benchmark, Declarative; BP = Benchmark, Procedural; BC = Benchmark, Contextual
1st letter of each code in parentheses   *2nd letter of code*   *Number*
W = NCHS: World History Standards   E = Explicitly stated in document   Page number of cited document
L = Lessons from History   I = Implied in document
C = Core material
R = Related material

McREL

impact of this trade on Indian agriculture and industry; the origins of both the French and British East India companies, what their charters enabled them to do, and how the home countries viewed the role of these companies in India; the trading relationship between the East India companies and Indian rulers)

- Understands the advance of British power in India up to 1850, its social and economic impact, and the efforts of Indians to resist European conquest and achieve cultural renewal

  BD (C;WE,220;LI,282)

- Understands Chinese policies toward foreign trade and immigration to other countries (e.g., why China resisted political contact and trade with Europeans, and how the opium trade contributed to European penetration of Chinese markets; motivations behind the Chinese trading policy and China's desire to keep out foreigners; motivations behind Chinese immigration to the U.S. and Southeast Asia)

  BD (C;WE,222;LI,286)

- Understands events and ideas that led to the modernization of Japan (e.g., what Commodore Matthew Perry accomplished in Japan in the 1850s and what his voyage meant for the Japanese; the goals and policies of the Meiji state, and the impact of these upon Japan's modernization; the impact of Western ideas and the role of Confucianism and Shinto traditional values on Japan in the Meiji period)

  BD (C;WE,224;LE,285)

Level III (Grades 7-8)

- Understands the decline of the Ottoman Empire in the 19th century (e.g., sources of weakness of the Ottoman Empire in the late 19th century; the military training and equipment of the Janissary Corps; how and when territory of the Ottoman Empire changed during the first half of the 19th century; causes of the Crimean War, the main events, nations involved, and forms of warfare employed; the defensive reform programs of Selim III and Mahmud II, and the challenges they faced in resolving the empire's political and economic crisis)

  BD (C;WE,216)

- Understands political conditions in Russia during the reign of Catherine the Great (e.g., the extent of Russian expansion into Eastern Europe and Central Asia, how Poland was partitioned in 1772, 1793, and 1795, and the location and significance of Russian ports on the White and Black Seas and the Baltic; the characteristics of Russian absolutism and reasons for the emergence of movements to reform or oppose the czarist regime)

  BD (R;WE,218)

- Understands the general political, social, and economic structure of Russia in the 1800s, including the relationship between landowners and peasants

  BD (R;WE,218)

Codes (right side of page):   BD = Benchmark, Declarative; BP = Benchmark, Procedural; BC = Benchmark, Contextual
1st letter of each code in parentheses   *2nd letter of code*   *Number*
W = NCHS: World History Standards   E = Explicitly stated in document   Page number of cited document
L = Lessons from History   I = Implied in document
C = Core material
R = Related material   258   *MREL*

- Understands significant cultural and political changes in India in the 18th and 19th centuries ^{BD (C;WE,220)} (e.g., changing linguistic and religious diversity in India between the early 18th and late 19th centuries, the significant changes in political control and boundaries in India between 1798 and 1850)

- Understands the impact of foreign trade and politics on Indian culture (e.g., the competitive ^{BD (C;WE,220,221)} policies of the British and the French in India, and why the British East India Company was able to prevail; the locations of major trade routes that linked India with China and Europe, the goods imported to and exported from India, and the effect of world trade on Indian agriculture, industry, and resources; the decline of the Mughal Empire and the rise of British political and military influence in India between 1750 and 1858)

- Understands Dutch involvement in various regions (e.g., changes in Dutch influence and ^{BD (C;WE,220,221)} control in South Asia between 1815 and 1850, how the Dutch ruled their colonies in the East Indies and what types of goods were traded by the Dutch in this region)

- Understands causes of political and social turmoil in China in the 18th and 19th centuries ^{BD (C;WE,222;LI,286)} (e.g., causes of governmental breakdown, political conflict, and social disintegration and conflict in China in the late 18th and 19th centuries; the main events surrounding the Boxer Rebellion and the Opium War; causes and consequences of the mid-19th century Taiping rebellion)

- Understands the economic and social consequences of rapid population growth in China ^{BD (C;WE,222)} between the 17th and 19th centuries

- Understands the origins of Japanese modernization and Japan's changing policies toward ^{BD (C;WE,224;LI,285)} Western influences (e.g., internal and external causes of the Meiji Restoration and the position of the samurai; how Japan's relations with China and the Western powers changed from the 1850s to the 1890s)

Level IV (Grades 9-12)

- Understands the social structure of the Ottoman Empire in the early and middle 19th century ^{BD (C;WE,217;LI,284)} (e.g., the roles of janissaries and Jewish and Christian merchant and landowners changed by the middle of the 19th century; the relative presence and the location of diverse religious and ethnic groups within the Ottoman Empire in 1800, and the prevailing Ottoman policy toward religion; the effects of population growth and European commercial penetration on Ottoman society and government)

Codes (right side of page):   BD = Benchmark, Declarative; BP = Benchmark, Procedural; BC = Benchmark, Contextual
1st letter of each code in parentheses   *2nd letter of code*   *Number*
W = NCHS: World History Standards   E = Explicitly stated in document   Page number of cited document
L = Lessons from History   I = Implied in document
C = Core material
R = Related material

259

MREL

- Knows the different attempts at reform by Ottoman leaders (e.g., the success and reception of the reforms of 1856 in the Hatt-I-Humayun issued by Abdul-Mejid; the political, military, and economic problems faced by Selim III in his rule, the reforms he instituted to deal with these problems, and their consequences) _{BD (C;WE,217)}

- Knows the events of the French invasion of Egypt in 1798, and understands the positive and negative impact of the French upon Egyptian culture (e.g., as viewed by the Egyptian chronicler of the invasion, al-Jabarti) _{BD (C;WE,217)}

- Knows the individual motivations and relative military strength of the English, French, and Ottomans in the Crimean War, as well as the significance of the outcome of the war for each of these participants _{BD (C;WE,217)}

- Understands events that shaped the social structure of Russia in the 19th century (e.g., the czarist reform movements of the 1820s and how they appealed to different social sectors; Czar Nicholas I's positions on the creation of a constitution, freedom of the press, the Decembrist uprising, the Polish rebellion, and the process of Russification) _{BD (R;WE,218,219)}

- Understands events that shaped the expansion and development of Russia in the 19th century and early 20th century (e.g., the causes of the Crimean War and its consequences for Russia, the Ottoman Empire, Britain, and France; the limits of Russian expansion eastward across Siberia and southward beyond the Caspian Sea; why Russia invaded the Ottoman territory in the early 1850s; how the Crimean War led to political and social reform for Russia; how Pan-Slavism affected Russian foreign policy in the late 19th century; what the Trans-Siberian and other railroad routes tell about Russian development and expansion from 1801 to 1914) _{BD (R;WE,219;LE,284)}

- Understands how Western culture influenced Indian society (e.g., how Western culture influenced the lives of elite groups living in India and Indonesia, and aspects of indigenous cultures that were embraced by Europeans; the major accomplishments of Ram Mohan Roy and his central ideas regarding Western influence in India) _{BD (C;WE,221)}

- Understands how the British presence and British policies shaped Indian society (e.g., the attitude of Muslim and upper-class Hindus toward the British presence in India; Britain's "modernizing" policies in India under the administration of Lord Dalhousie, and the social and political impact of the railroad on India; the central issues surrounding the supposition that the British "unified" India; comparisons between British policies in India and the Dutch colonial practices in the East Indies) _{BD (C;WE,221;LE,282)}

Codes (right side of page):   BD = Benchmark, Declarative; BP = Benchmark, Procedural; BC = Benchmark, Contextual
1st letter of each code in parentheses   *2nd letter of code*   *Number*
W = NCHS: World History Standards   E = Explicitly stated in document   Page number of cited document
L = Lessons from History   I = Implied in document
C = Core material
R = Related material   MREL

BD (C;WE,223;LE,286)

- Understand how Christianity, rural class relations, and rural poverty contributed to the Taiping rebellion

BD (C;WE,223)

- Understands China's relations with Western countries (e.g., the Chinese and British positions on opium sales and trade within China; prominent Chinese views on China's relations with the West and challenges presented to the West; reasons for the Chinese diaspora in Southeast Asia and the Americas)

BD (C;WE,223;LI,286)

- Understands how the Treaties of Nanking (1842) and Shimonoseki (1895) illustrate the advent of late 19th-century Chinese imperialism

BD (C;WE,224,225;LI,285-286)

- Understands social conditions and change in Meiji Japan (e.g., the nature of living conditions for factory workers, aspects of education and social change, comparisons between the Meiji restoration and the French and American revolutions, the meaning and significance of various Meiji slogans)

BD (C;WE,224;LE,285)

- Understands Japan's political and social transformation in the 19th century (e.g., the goals of the new imperial government, as outlined in the Charter Oath of 1868; reasons for Japan's rapid industrialization and its response to Western commerce; aspects of Western society that appealed to 19th-century Japanese; Japan's transformation from a hereditary social system to a middle-class society, and who benefitted and suffered in the initial decades of industrialization and nation building)

(WE,226)

31. Understands patterns of nationalism, state-building, and social reform in Europe and the Americas from 1830 to 1914

Level II (Grades 5-6)

BD (C;WE,226;LI,279)

- Understands the emergence of nationalist movements in Italy and Germany (e.g., the appeal of Garibaldi's nationalist Redshirts to Italians; the major leaders of unification and nationalism in Italy and Germany, and why these movements succeeded)

BD (C;WE,228)

- Understand causes of large-scale population movements from rural areas to cities in continental Europe

BD (C;WE,228;LI,278)

- Understands movements and ideas that contributed to social change in 19th-century North America and Europe (e.g., the origins of women's suffrage in North America and Europe, leading figures on both continents, and their success until World War I; the leading ideas of

---

Codes (right side of page):   BD = Benchmark, Declarative; BP = Benchmark, Procedural; BC = Benchmark, Contextual
1st letter of each code in parentheses   *2nd letter of code*   *Number*
W = NCHS: World History Standards   E = Explicitly stated in document   Page number of cited document
L = Lessons from History   I = Implied in document
C = Core material
R = Related material

261

MREL

Marxism, other forms of socialism, and myriad labor movements, and how they contributed to social and political change in Europe)

- Understands aspects of education in 19th-century Europe (e.g., aspects of the basic school day for male and female students in the 19th century; how significantly education, or lack thereof, affected the lives and prospects of 19th century Europeans; differences in the daily lives of children from working, middle class, and upper class families) ^{BD (R;WE,230)}

- Understands the impact of inventions and cultural achievements on 19th-century Europe and America (e.g., significant inventions and inventors in 19th-century Europe and America and the social, economic, and cultural impact of these new inventions; the social significance of the work of 19th-century scientists such as Maxwell, Darwin, Pasteur, and Curie; movements in literature, music, and the visual arts, and ways in which they shaped or reflected social and cultural values) ^{BD (R;WE,230;LI,278)}

- Understands the political and social changes in 19th-century Latin America (e.g., how geography possibly influenced nation-building in Latin America, where democracy failed and succeeded in Latin American nations after independence was achieved, the class system in Latin America and its racial core) ^{BD (R;WE,232)}

- Understands how major events in the United States affected the rest of the hemisphere ^{BD (R;WE,232)}

- Understands the degree of progress in race relations and the status of women made in the 19th century ^{BD (R;WE,232)}

Level III (Grades 7-8)

- Understands how the revolutions of 1848 affected various countries (e.g., knows where revolutions occurred in 1848, how they were a chain reaction, and the goals and motivating spirit of each; knows the major accomplishments of prominent figures in the revolutionary era; the chronology of significant events in the unifications of Italy and Germany; the purpose of Bismarck's "Blood and Iron" speech, and previous attempts at unification to which he refers) ^{BD (C;WE,226,227;LI,279)}

- Understands the ideas that influenced the nationalist movements (e.g., major characteristics of 19th-century European nationalism, and connections between nationalist ideology, the French Revolution, Romanticism, and liberal reform movements; the extent to which Garibaldi reflected 19th-century Romanticism) ^{BD (C;WE,227)}

Codes (right side of page):   BD = Benchmark, Declarative; BP = Benchmark, Procedural; BC = Benchmark, Contextual
1st letter of each code in parentheses   *2nd letter of code*   *Number*
W = NCHS: World History Standards   E = Explicitly stated in document   Page number of cited document
L = Lessons from History   I = Implied in document
C = Core material
R = Related material   262

McREL

- Understands causes for major demographic changes (e.g., rural-urban populations shifts) in 19th-century Europe, as well as trends in immigration within and out of Europe in the same period ^{BD (C;WE,228)}

BD (C;WE,228)

- Understands the status of different groups in 19th-century Europe (e.g., the leaders and development of the woman's suffrage movement in Britain, and their major accomplishments until the end of the 19th century; changing roles and status of European Jews and the rise of new forms of anti-Semitism)

BD (R;WE,230,231;LI,278)

- Understands technological and cultural achievements in 19th-century Europe (e.g., the major figures and discoveries in 19th-century science; the social, economic, and cultural impact of the railroad; how leisure activity and popular culture changed throughout the 19th century; major movements in the arts during the 19th century and how these movements reflected social change)

BD (R;WE,230;LI,278)

- Understands social change and the emergence new social class culture in 19th-century Europe (e.g., how the average standard of living changed in Europe in the 19th century and the factors that accounted for this change; broad-ranging benefits and disadvantages of attending school for children from peasant, middle class, craft, and urban factory-working families; the elements of the distinctive middle-class and working class culture that developed in industrial Europe)

BD (R;WE,232)

- Understands influences on the government structure in Latin America and Mexico (e.g., the advent of the caudillo ruler in Latin America, his supporters, and the methods by which he maintained power; the effects of foreign intervention and liberal government policies on social and economic change in Mexico)

BD (R;WE,232)

- Understands expansion and nation-building in the United States and Canada in the 19th century (e.g., the territorial expansions of the United States in the 19th century, how new territories were acquired, and from whom; the factors that contributed to nation-building in Canada)

Level IV (Grades 9-12)

BD (C;WE,227)

- Understands the chronology, major events, and outcomes of the Franco-Prussian War (e.g., how it impacted the British, Bavarians, and French; how the French were agitated into war by the edited Ems telegram)

BD (C;WE,227)

- Understands the definition of realpolitik and how Cavour and Bismarck exemplified this

---

Codes (right side of page):   BD = Benchmark, Declarative; BP = Benchmark, Procedural; BC = Benchmark, Contextual
1st letter of each code in parentheses   *2nd letter of code*   *Number*
W = NCHS: World History Standards   E = Explicitly stated in document   Page number of cited document
L = Lessons from History   I = Implied in document
C = Core material
R = Related material

263

MREL

political philosophy

- Understands the role of nationalism in conflicts within different nations (e.g., the importance ^{BD (C;WE,227)} of Greek nationalists' and Europeans' roles in the struggle for Greek independence from the Ottomans; how nationalism fostered tension and conflict in the Austro-Hungarian and Ottoman Empires)

- Understands how different movements and ideas influenced society in the 19th century (e.g., ^{BD (C;WE,229)} the effect of the continental revolutions on the Chartist movement in England, and how the ruling classes reacted to Chartist demands; the essential ideas outlined in Marx and Engel's *Communist Manifesto* and their meaning in the context of late 19th-century economic, political, and social conditions)

- Understands factors that influenced the women's movement in the 19th century (e.g., the ^{BD (C;WE,229)} goals of the women's movement in the 19th century, and the essential ideas outlined by Mary Wollstonecraft in *Vindication of the Rights of Women*; support for and opposition to women's suffrage in the late 19th century)

- Understands factors that led to social and political change in 19th-century Europe (e.g., the ^{BD (C;WE,228,229)} broad beneficial and detrimental effects of the industrial revolution on specific European countries; the influence of industrialization, democratization, and nationalism on popular 19th-century reform movements; the extent to which Britain, France, and Italy become broadly liberal and democratic societies in the 19th century)

- Knows the events and issues of the Dreyfus affair in France (e.g., why the French military ^{BD (C;WE,229)} establishment refused to pardon Dreyfus in the face of overwhelming evidence proving his innocence, how this affair became a political conflict between conservatives and progressives)

- Understands the status of education in 19th-century Europe (e.g., what countries enacted ^{BD (R;WE,231)} compulsory education by the end of the 19th century, and how school attendance figures were affected by the industrial age; how expanded educational opportunities and literacy contributed to changes in European society and cultural life)

- Understands the emergence of new scientific and social thought in the 19th century (e.g., ^{BD (R;WE,231)} ways in which trends in philosophy and the new social sciences challenged and reshaped traditional patterns of thought, religious understanding, and understanding of social organization; the major new scientific thinkers of the 19th century and how they built upon or rejected each other's theories)

Codes (right side of page):   BD = Benchmark, Declarative; BP = Benchmark, Procedural; BC = Benchmark, Contextual
1st letter of each code in parentheses   *2nd letter of code*   *Number*
W = NCHS: World History Standards   E = Explicitly stated in document   Page number of cited document
L = Lessons from History   I = Implied in document
C = Core material
R = Related material

McREL

- Understands sources that illustrate social conditions and cultural identity in 19th-century ^{BD (R;WE,231)} Europe (e.g., how primary sources such as diaries reflect the life experiences of middle and working class men and women in 19th-century Europe; the characteristics of popular, diverse 19th-century art styles, such as Romanticism, Realism, and Impressionism; how Europeans shaped their identity through their view of "other" peoples and cultures)

- Understands how political and economic change influenced Latin American society in the ^{BD (R;WE,232,233)} 19th century (e.g., the roles and perspectives of the caudillo, military official, landowner, urban bourgeoisie, or church official in post-independence Latin America; attitudes toward nationalism and cultural identity in 19th-century Latin America; the consequences of economic development, elite domination, and the abolition of slavery for peasants, indigenous populations, and immigrant laborers in Latin America; Latin America's growing dependence on the global market economy, as well as the effects of international trade and investment on the power of landowners and the urban middle class)

32. Understands patterns of global change in the era of Western military and economic ^(WE,234) **domination from 1850 to 1914**

Level II (Grades 5-6)

- Understands trends in the population of Europe for the last three and a half centuries, and ^{BD (R;WE,234)} at what time Europe had the greatest number of inhabitants

- Understands the experiences and motivations of European migrants and immigrants in the ^{BD (R;WE,234)} 18th and 19th centuries (e.g., why migrants left Europe in large numbers in the 18th century and in what regions of the world they settled; the consequences of encounters between European migrants and indigenous peoples in such regions as the United States, Canada, South Africa, Australia, and Siberia; the general appeal of Canada to European immigrants in the second half of the 19th century)

- Understands factors that contributed to European imperialist expansion between 1850 and ^{BD (C;WE,236;LI,280)} 1914 (e.g., how motives for European imperialist expansion into Africa, Southeast Asia, and China varied with the region where expansion took place; advances in transportation, medicine, and weaponry that helped the European imperial expansion in the late 19th century)

- Knows the causes, course, and consequences of the Boxer Rebellion ^{BD (C;WE,238;LI,286;DI,30.3.7)}

Codes (right side of page):   BD = Benchmark, Declarative; BP = Benchmark, Procedural; BC = Benchmark, Contextual
1st letter of each code in parentheses   *2nd letter of code*   *Number*
W = NCHS: World History Standards   E = Explicitly stated in document   Page number of cited document
L = Lessons from History   I = Implied in document
C = Core material
R = Related material

BD (C;WE,238;DI, .30.2.6)

- Understands political and economic changes in Japanese society in the 19th and 20th centuries (e.g., the death of the Meiji emperor in 1912 and the main achievements of Meiji Japan; Japan's rapid industrialization, technological advancement, and national integration in the late 19th and 20th centuries)

BD (C;WE,240;LE,281)

- Understands events that shaped African relations with other countries (e.g., how the discovery of gold and diamonds in South Africa affected British investors; the relationship between European and African merchants and the types of products traded between the two in the period after slavery ended)

BD (C;WE,240)

- Understands major changes in the political geography of Africa between 1880 and 1914

Level III (Grades 7-8)

BD (R;WE,234)

- Understands influences on European migration, immigration, and emigration patterns throughout the world between 1846 and 1932 (e.g., possible connections of the rise of the Zulu Empire in South Africa to European settlements in the Cape Region; relations between migrating European and African peoples that laid the foundation for the apartheid system in the 20th century; the geographical, political, economic, and epidemiological factors that contributed to the success of European colonial settlements in various regions; how technology such as the steamship and the railroad facilitated emigration)

BD (R;WE,235)

- Understands the diverse factors (e.g., variations in birth and death rates, infant mortality rates) that contributed to the peaking and then leveling off of European population growth from the 17th to the 20th centuries

BD (C;WE,236;LI,279)

- Understands European motives and ideology that justified extending imperial power into African and Asian countries (e.g., achievements of Cecil Rhodes and his motives and goals in the "scramble for Africa"; the motives that impelled several European powers to undertake imperial expansion against peoples of Africa, Southeast Asia, and China between the 1850s and 1914; the ideas of Social Darwinism and pseudoscientific racism in 19th-century Europe and how these encouraged European imperial expansion in Africa and Asia)

BD (C;WE,236)

- Understands events that led to Japan's emergence as a world power (e.g., the causes, events, and outcome of the Russo-Japanese War; Japan's imperial expansion in Korea and Manchuria, and Japan's rise to world power status)

BD (C;WE,236)

- Knows the causes and course of the Spanish-American War, and how this related to U.S. participation in Western imperial expansion

---

Codes (right side of page):   BD = Benchmark, Declarative; BP = Benchmark, Procedural; BC = Benchmark, Contextual

1st letter of each code in parentheses	*2nd letter of code*	*Number*
W = NCHS: World History Standards	E = Explicitly stated in document	Page number of cited document
L = Lessons from History	I = Implied in document	
C = Core material		
R = Related material		

MREL

- Understands the geographic location of European interests in South, Southeast, and East Asia in the late 19th century BD (C;WE,238)

- Understands the extent of British rule in India, and British reaction to Indian nationalism (e.g., the social, economic, and intellectual sources of Indian nationalism, the causes of the Uprising of 1857, and the British reaction to Indian nationalism; the economic and political impact of British rule on India in the 19th century) BD (C;WE,238;LI,282-283)

- Understands political and social elements of Chinese society in the late 19th and early 20th centuries (e.g., how the Chinese reacted to the presence and activities of foreigners in their country in the late 1890s; Chinese efforts to reform government and society after 1895, as well as related causes for revolution in 1911) BD (C;WE,238)

- Understands the accomplishments and goals of specific African resistance movements (e.g., Abd al-Qadir in Algeria, Samori Ture in West Africa, the Mahdist state in the Sudan, Memelik II in Ethiopia, the Zulus in South Africa) BD (C;WE,240;LI,281)

- Understands the role of trade in shaping political and social conditions in various regions (e.g., the location of the Suez Canal, how and why it was created, and what it did for world trade and political alliances; how trade helped make empire-builders such as Tippu Tip, and the effect trade had on resistance to European imperialism; how West African economies changed after the end of the trans-Atlantic slave trade) BD (C;WE,240)

Level IV (Grades 9-12)

- Understands the debate on the westward movement in North America in the 19th century: whether this movement was unique, or simply part of a larger pattern of European overseas settlement, and what consequences the expansion had for indigenous peoples BD (R;WE,235)

- Understands influences on and consequences of European immigration and settlement (e.g., general global patterns of European settlement, and how they affected the politics and economy of the local regions, as well as resources, labor, the flow of goods, and markets; the diverse motivations behind resettlement for specific groups of immigrants; the impact of new immigrants upon the environment and indigenous populations of Australia; how substantial European immigration in the 19th century had economic consequences for cities in the United States) BD (R;WE,235)

- Understands the influence of European imperial expansion on political and social facets of African and Indian society (e.g., the major chain of events in Europe and Africa that led to BD (C;WE,237)

Codes (right side of page):   BD = Benchmark, Declarative; BP = Benchmark, Procedural; BC = Benchmark, Contextual
1st letter of each code in parentheses   *2nd letter of code*   *Number*
W = NCHS: World History Standards   E = Explicitly stated in document   Page number of cited document
L = Lessons from History   I = Implied in document
C = Core material
R = Related material

MREL

the "scramble" for African territory, and the role of particular African governments or peoples in the partition of Africa by the Europeans; the impact of European expansion on legal, familial, and gender relations in Indian and African village life)

- Understands the advantages and disadvantages of imperialism (e.g., the chief benefits and costs of the introduction of new political institutions, and advances in communication, technology, and medicine to countries under European imperialist rule; how medical advances, steam power, and military technology were used in European imperialism)

  BD (C;WE,237;LE,280)

- Knows the locations, history, and source of funding of major national and international rail lines in Africa and Eurasia constructed in the late 19th and early 20th centuries, and understands the benefits they provided to imperial powers and indigenous economies

  BD (C;WE,237)

- Understands the effects of the Sino-Japanese War, the Russo-Japanese War, and the colonization of Korea on Japan's status as a world power, and how Japan justified its imperial expansion

  BD (C;WE,236-237)

- Understands the European intellectual justifications for imperialism (e.g., the French notion of mission civilisatrice, the German concept of Kultur, and British imperialism as reflected Rudyard Kipling's *White Man's Burden)*

  BD (C;WE,237;LE,280)

- Knows the causes of the Indian Uprising of 1857 (e.g., British imposed religious policies, the participants in the uprising, the varied reactions to the revolt on the part of Sikhs, Hindus, Muslims, and Indian royalty who had made alliances with the East India Company)

  BD (C;WE,238;LI,282)

- Understands significant political events in 20th-century China (e.g., reasons for initial Chinese imperial support for the Boxer Rebellion, the major achievements of Sun Yatsen, the role overseas Chinese played in the 1911 revolution)

  BD (C;WE,238)

- Understands Western influence on Japanese society in the 19th century (e.g., the chronology of major social, economic, and technological changes derived from the West in 19th-century Japan; the political and symbolic role of the emperor of Meiji Japan and how that role compared to those of British and other Western monarchs of the time)

  BD (C;WE,239;LI,285)

- Knows where the British and French expanded into mainland Southeast Asia, how their colonial policies differed, and how Thailand avoided colonization

  BD (C;WE,239)

- Understands economic, social, and religious influences on African society (e.g., how and why slavery and the slave trade flourished in both West and East Africa even after the end of the trans-Atlantic slave trade; the relative strengths of Islam and Christianity in Africa at

  BD (C;WE,241)

Codes (right side of page): BD = Benchmark, Declarative; BP = Benchmark, Procedural; BC = Benchmark, Contextual
1st letter of each code in parentheses   *2nd letter of code*   *Number*
W = NCHS: World History Standards   E = Explicitly stated in document   Page number of cited document
L = Lessons from History   I = Implied in document
C = Core material
R = Related material

McREL

the beginning of the 20th century, types of rivalries among Christian denominations, and the links between both of these and the interests of the government)

- Understands African resistance movements against the British during the period of European imperial expansion (e.g., the successes and failures of prominent African resistance movements in West Africa, Sudan, Ethiopia, and South Africa; the nature of the Sudanese resistance to the British, as well as the general success of Mahdi Muhammad Ahmed and the Mahdi uprising against British imperialism)

BD (C;WE,241;LI,281)

33. Understands major global trends from 1750 to 1914

(WE,242)

Level II (Grades 5-6)

- Understands the experiences of immigrants to North and South America in the 19th century

BD (R;WE,242)

- Understands major patterns of long-distance migration of Europeans, Africans, and Asians, as well as causes and consequences of these movements (e.g., migrations from Asia and Africa between 1750 and 1900)

BD (R;WE,242)

- Understands major shifts in world population and urbanization in this era and how factors such as industrialization, migration, changing diets, and scientific and medical advances affected worldwide demographic trends (e.g., understands the changes large cities around the world went through during this period, such as Guangzhou [Canton], Cairo, Tokyo, Buenos Aires, Bombay, San Francisco, or London)

BD (R;WE,242)

Level III (Grades 7-8)

- Understands trends in world population between 1500 and 1900, where the greatest increases occurred, and possible factors for this growth

BD (R;WE,243)

- Understands where Christianity and Islam grew in this era, and understands the causes of 19th-century reform movements or renewal in Buddhism, Christianity, Hinduism, Islam, and Judaism

BD (R;WE,243)

- Understands the diverse processes through which industrialization occurred in Great Britain, France, Germany, the United States, Russia, Japan, and other countries, and how industrialization affected class relations and social positions (e.g., conditions for rural families, the roles of women and children)

BD (R;WE,243)

Codes (right side of page):   BD = Benchmark, Declarative; BP = Benchmark, Procedural; BC = Benchmark, Contextual
1st letter of each code in parentheses   *2nd letter of code*   *Number*
W = NCHS: World History Standards   E = Explicitly stated in document   Page number of cited document
L = Lessons from History   I = Implied in document
C = Core material
R = Related material   269   M*REL*

- Understands how daily lives of working class men and women differed in the industrial era $^{BD\ (R;WE,243)}$

- Understands the reform movements in specific world religions in the 19th century, including Buddhism, Islam, Christianity, Hinduism, and Judaism, and knows what degree of success these movements met $^{BD\ (R;WE,243)}$

- Understands the importance of ideas associated with republicanism, liberalism, socialism, and constitutionalism on 19th-century political life in such states as Great Britain, Germany, Russia, Mexico, Argentina, the Ottoman Empire, China, or Japan (e.g., how these movements were tied to new or old-class interests) $^{BD\ (R;WE,243)}$

- Understands patterns of social and cultural continuity in various societies, and how people maintained and resisted external changes in an era of expanding Western hegemony and rapid industrial and urban change (e.g., the efforts of people such as Jamal al-Din, al-Afghani, Rashid Rida, and Muhammad Abdul) $^{BD\ (R;WE,243)}$

- Understands the process of educational reform in various Muslim regions during the 19th century (e.g., the new institutions that were established, the effect of this reform on women, those areas that wholly embraced Western values, and those that rejected them) $^{BD\ (R;WE,243)}$

34. Understands global and economic trends in the high period of Western dominance $^{(WE,248)}$

- Understands factors that transformed American and European society in the early 20th century (e.g., major scientific, medical, and technological advances in Europe and the United States at the turn of the century; popular attitudes regarding material progress and the West's global leadership; how industrial development affected standards of living and lifestyles of middle and working class people in the United States and Europe) $^{BD\ (C;WE,248;LI,293)}$

- Understands the consequences of the significant revolutions of the early 20th century (e.g., the causes, events, and consequences of the Russian Rebellion of 1905; the prominent figures in the Mexican Revolution and the significance of that revolution as the first 20th century movement in which peasants played a prominent role) $^{BD\ (R;WE,250;LE,303;LI,295,310)}$

- Understands why Dr. Sun Yatsen is considered an important figure in the history of modern China $^{BD\ (R;WE,250;LE,303)}$

- Understands the industrial power of Great Britain, France, Germany, Japan, and the United States in the early 20th century (e.g., how the nations compare statistically), and understands $^{BD\ (C;WE,255;LI,293)}$

Codes (right side of page):   BD = Benchmark, Declarative; BP = Benchmark, Procedural; BC = Benchmark, Contextual
1st letter of each code in parentheses   *2nd letter of code*   *Number*
W = NCHS: World History Standards   E = Explicitly stated in document   Page number of cited document
L = Lessons from History   I = Implied in document
C = Core material
R = Related material   270   McREL

the importance and potential of industrialization

- Understands prominent features and ideas of liberalism, social reformism, conservatism, and socialism in the early part of this century (e.g., the "welfare state" promoted by liberal ideals; the influential ideas of leading Europeans such as Stanley Baldwin, Ramsay MacDonald, Emmeline Pankhurst, Jean Jaurés, Raymond Poncaré, Peter Stolypin, Alfred Krupp, or Rosa Luxemborg)
  BD (C;WE,255;LI,293)

- Understands the consequences of shifts in Japan's political conditions in the early 20th century (e.g., Japan's economic development, national integration, and political ideologies around the turn of the century; how Japanese territorial expansion affected the industrialization and economic development of Japan)
  BD (C;WE,248,249;LI,302)

- Understands events that led to revolutions in the early 20th century (e.g., causes, events, and consequences of the Russian "Bloody Sunday" in 1905, and the ensuing revolution; what the peasantry and middle class fought for and against in the Mexican Revolution; the promises of China's 1911 republican revolution and the New Culture movement and why they failed to address China's political, economic, and social problems; the causes, course, and consequences of the South African [Anglo-Boer] War; the efforts of the Young Turks to reform Ottoman government and society)
  BD (R;WE,250;LI,295,303)

Level IV (Grades 9-12)

- Understands how government programs and technological development influenced the industrial nations of the Northern Hemisphere in the early 20th century (e.g., government programs that included social legislation such as Social Security, minimum wage laws, and compulsory free public education; the broad effects of technological developments in labor, capital investment, and industrial production)
  BD (C;WE,248,249;LE,293)

- Understands the diverse factors that contributed to the industrialization of Japan (e.g., land ownership policy, new technology, government subsidies)
  BD (C;WE,249)

- Understands why European colonial territories and Latin American countries continued to maintain largely agricultural economies in the early 20th century (e.g., restrictive policies of the European countries regarding industrialization in the colonies)
  BD (C;WE,249)

- Understands the diverse events that led to and resulted from the Russian Revolution of 1905 (e.g., the Russo-Japanese War, "Bloody Sunday," the October Manifesto) and knows which groups were agitating for political reform and which for radical changes
  BD (R;WE,257)

Codes (right side of page):   BD = Benchmark, Declarative; BP = Benchmark, Procedural; BC = Benchmark, Contextual
1st letter of each code in parentheses   *2nd letter of code*   *Number*
W = NCHS: World History Standards   E = Explicitly stated in document   Page number of cited document
L = Lessons from History   I = Implied in document
C = Core material
R = Related material

MREL

- Understands the role of the peasantry in the Mexican Revolution (e.g., the aspects of nationalism expressed in the works of the Mexican Revolution by muralists José Clemente Orozco, David Siquieros, and Diego Riviera, and how these murals fostered support for the Revolution among the peasantry; the impact of the Mexican Revolution on the peasantry) BD (R;WE,257;LI,310)

- Understands events and ideas that led to China's revolutionary movements in the early 20th century (e.g., social and cultural conditions in China that led to the New Culture, or May Fourth movement; the four points of Sun Yatsen's *Manifesto for the Revolutionary Alliance* [Tong Meng Hui] and to whom these revolutionary goals appealed) BD (R;WE,257;LI,303)

- Understands the reforms advocated by the Young Turk movement, its origins, and possible reasons for its success BD (R;WE,257)

- Understands the attitude of the British toward non-British people and colonial troops at the time of the Boer War, and the consequences of the war for Boers, British, and African populations BD (R;WE,257)

35. Understands the causes and global consequences of World War I (WE,252)

Level II (Grades 5-6)

- Understands the origins and significant features of World War I (e.g., the precipitating causes of the war; which countries joined each of the two alliances — the Allied Powers and the Central Powers — and the advantages and disadvantages for the formation of alliances; major areas of combat in Europe and Southwest Asia and the factors that led to military stalemate in some of these areas) BD (C;WE,252;LE,293,294)

- Understands the immediate and long-term consequences of World War I (e.g., the principal theaters of conflict in World War I and major turning points in the war; the hardships of trench warfare; the short-term demographic, social, economic, and environmental consequences of the war's violence and destruction) BD (C;WE,254)

- Understands how the homefront contributed to World War I (e.g., how nationalism and propaganda helped mobilize civilian populations to support "total war"; how massive industrial production and innovations in military technology affected strategy and tactics, and the scale, duration, brutality, and efficiency of the war) BD (C;WE,254)

- Understands the roles of significant individuals, and the events that led to the Russian BD (C;WE,256;LE,295)

Codes (right side of page):   BD = Benchmark, Declarative; BP = Benchmark, Procedural; BC = Benchmark, Contextual
1st letter of each code in parentheses   *2nd letter of code*   *Number*
W = NCHS: World History Standards   E = Explicitly stated in document   Page number of cited document
L = Lessons from History   I = Implied in document
C = Core material
R = Related material   272   M°REL

Revolution of 1917 (e.g., causes of the Russian Revolution of 1917 and how the revolutionary government progressed from moderate to radical; the historical importance of Russian leaders such as Tsar Nicholas II, Rasputin, and Lenin)

BD (C;WE,256;LE,295)
- Understands the rise of Joseph Stalin, and his impact on the Soviet Union (e.g., how Joseph Stalin came to and maintained power in the Soviet Union, and how his projects [collectivization, the first Five Year Plan] disrupted and transformed Soviet society in the 1920s and 1930s; what life was like for common people under Stalin's rule)

Level III (Grades 7-8)

BD (C;WE,252)
- Understands events that contributed to the outbreak of World War I (e.g., how nationalism threatened the balance of power among the Great Powers in Europe, and why it was considered one of the causes of World War I; diverse long-range causes of World War I, such as political and economic rivalries, ethnic and ideological conflicts, militarism, imperialism, and nationalism)

BD (C;WE,252)
- Understands ways in which popular faith in science, technology, and material progress affected attitudes toward the possibility of war among European states

BD (C;WE,252,253;LI,294;LE,294)
- Understands how different countries were aligned during World War I (e.g., the systems of alliances through which Europe organized itself into World War I, the role militarism played in these alliances, and the reasons for the war's expansion beyond European boundaries to become a world war; immediate causes for the entry of different nations into World War I)

BD (C;WE,253;LE,294)
- Understands the nature of the war in Europe, and how technological innovations contributed to the brutality of the "Great War"

BD (C;WE,254,255;LE,294)
- Understands the role of the U.S. and other countries in World War I (e.g., how the Russian Revolution and the entry of the United States affected the course and outcome of the war, motivations behind the entrance of the U.S. into the war)

BD (C;WE,255;LI,294)
- Understands the extent to which different sources supported the war effort (e.g., ways in which colonial peoples contributed to the war effort of the Allies and the Central Powers by providing military forces and supplies, and what this effort might have meant to colonial subjects; how propaganda posters helped mobilize civilian populations to support the war; how and why original support and enthusiasm to support the war deteriorated)

BD (C;WE,255)
- Knows the principal theaters of battle, including Europe, Southeast Asia, Sub-Saharan Africa, East Asia, and the South Pacific, the major turning points of the war, and the impact

Codes (right side of page):   BD = Benchmark, Declarative; BP = Benchmark, Procedural; BC = Benchmark, Contextual
1st letter of each code in parentheses   *2nd letter of code*   *Number*
W = NCHS: World History Standards   E = Explicitly stated in document   Page number of cited document
L = Lessons from History   I = Implied in document
C = Core material
R = Related material

273

MREL

of geography on the outcome of the battles

- Understands the role of Tsar Nicholas II and Rasputin prior to and during the Russian Revolution of 1917 (e.g., the biography of Tsar Nicholas III and his family, including how they died; the role the monk Rasputin played in determining Russian policy, and his influence on the royal court) BD (C;WE,256)

- Understands the influence of Lenin and Stalin on the government, economy, and social conditions in Russia and the Soviet Union after the Revolution of 1917 (e.g., the effects of Lenin's New Economic Policy on Soviet society, economy, and government; why and how Stalin changed Lenin's policy and forced collectivization, and the consequences of resistance to this policy for the kulaks; how people who were persecuted survived during Stalin's purges) BD (C;WE,257;LE,295;LI,295)

Level IV (Grades 9-12)

- Understands arguments and theories regarding the causes of World War I (e.g., how primary and secondary sources illustrate the arguments presented by leaders on the eve of the Great War; why and how political leaders in European nations felt aggressive foreign policy, and the advocation of war, would help subdue domestic discontent and disorder; the arguments for and against war used by diverse political groups and figures in European countries; how belief in technology, science, and a better quality of life earlier in the century encouraged Europeans to think that a massive war was inconceivable; the role of nationalism, militarism, imperialism, and social and class conflict leading to World War I) BD (C;WE,253;LI,293,294)

- Understands the Schlieffen Plan and whether it contributed to a military stalemate BD (C;WE,253)

- Understands the effectiveness of propaganda for both the Allies and Central Powers to galvanize the war effort, gain support in colonies, and gain support from neutral nations BD (C;WE,253)

- Understands the strategies of the Allied and Central Powers at the beginning of the war, when these changed, and how BD (C;WE,255)

- Understands the human cost and social impact of World War I (e.g., what sources, such as letters and books illustrate about the mental and physical costs of the war to soldiers around the world; how the casualty figures for World War I compare to other wars, and reasons for the high casualty rate; the changes in women's roles during the Great War) BD (C;WE,255)

- Understands Lenin's ideology and policies and their impact on Russia after the Revolution of 1917 (e.g., the platforms and promises of Kerenksy and Lenin in 1917, the impact of war BD (C;WE,257;LI,295)

Codes (right side of page):   BD = Benchmark, Declarative; BP = Benchmark, Procedural; BC = Benchmark, Contextual
1st letter of each code in parentheses   *2nd letter of code*   *Number*
W = NCHS: World History Standards   E = Explicitly stated in document   Page number of cited document
L = Lessons from History   I = Implied in document
C = Core material
R = Related material   274   MℜEL

upon Kerensky's program, and the importance of Lenin's promise, "land, bread, peace"; Lenin's political ideology and how the Bolsheviks adapted Marxist ideas to conditions particular to Russia, and why Lenin declined to follow Marxist economic philosophy; how statistics on women in the labor force and education contradict Lenin's statements concerning women's equality)

- Understands different views of the Russian Revolution from the Red Russians, the White BD (C;WE,257) Russians, the British, French, and Japanese

- Understands the role of Stalin in the emerging Soviet Union (e.g., to what degree Stalin was BD (C;WE,257) able to accomplish his goal of bringing the USSR to industrial parity with the West, the unique problems in industrialization Stalin faced, and how this model differed from those of Western nations; what primary sources reveal about the human cost of Stalinist totalitarianism in the USSR in the 1920s and 1930s)

36. Understands the search for peace and stability throughout the world in the 1920s and 1930s (WE,258)

Level II (Grades 5-6)

- Understands treaties and other efforts to achieve peace and recovery from World War I (e.g., BD (C;WE,258;LE,294) changes made to political boundaries after the peace treaties ending World War I, and what countries were winners or losers; the conflicting aims and aspirations of the conferees at Versailles, and how the major powers responded to the terms of the settlement; why and how the League of Nations was founded, its initial goals, its limitations, and the nations that were and were not invited to participate)

- Knows the major advocates and goals of the women's suffrage movement around the world BD (C;WE,258)

- Understands how the settlements of World War I influenced the Middle East, Africa, Asia, BD (C;WE,260) and Latin America (e.g., the mandate system created by the League of Nations and how it changed European rule in the Middle East and Africa, how World War I settlements contributed to the rise of both Pan-Arabism and nationalist struggles for the independence in the Middle East, how the readjustment of national borders in Africa after World War I affected people in East and West Africa)

- Understands the emergence of a new mass and popular culture between 1900 and 1940 (e.g., BD (R;WE,262;LE,301) the new approaches to visual art respresented by the works of Pablo Picasso and Henri Matisse; how the new media — newspapers, magazines, commercial advertising, film, and

Codes (right side of page):   BD = Benchmark, Declarative; BP = Benchmark, Procedural; BC = Benchmark, Contextual
1st letter of each code in parentheses   *2nd letter of code*   *Number*
W = NCHS: World History Standards   E = Explicitly stated in document   Page number of cited document
L = Lessons from History   I = Implied in document
C = Core material
R = Related material   275   MʁEL

radio — contributed to the rise of mass culture around the world; the types of leisure activity and sports people enjoyed; changes in clothing fashions for men and women, and how they reflected changes in social attitudes and values)

BD (R;WE,262)

- Knows the major contributions to society of such scientists as Thomas Edison, Marie Curie, Albert Einstein, and Guglielmo Marconi

BD (R;WE,264)

- Understands the economic and social impact of the Great Depression (e.g., how the Great Depression affected industrialized economies and societies around the world, the human cost of the depression)

Level III (Grades 7-8)

BD (C;WE,259;LI,294)

- Understands the immediate and long-term political and social effects of World War I (e.g., the agreements on reparation payments made at the Conference of Versailles and how these agreements corresponded to Woodrow Wilson's Fourteen Points, the causes and effects of the U.S. isolationist policies on world politics and international relations in the 1920s, the objectives and achievements of the women's movements in the context of World War I and its aftermath)

BD (C;WE,259;LI,294)

- Understands how the collapse of the German, Hapsburg, and Ottoman Empires and the creation of new states affected international relations in Europe and the Middle East

BD (C;WE,260)

- Understands internal shifts in the political conditions of China and Japan in the 1920s and 1930s (e.g., the factors that influenced the struggle for dominance in China between the Guomindang and the Communist Party, how militarism and fascism derailed parliamentary democracy in Japan)

BD (C;WE,260)

- Understands the goals and policies of European colonial rule in India, Africa, and Southeast Asia, and how these policies affected indigenous societies and economies (e.g., the response to the Moroccan resistance movement against the Spanish led by Abd al Quadir)

BD (C;WE,261)

- Understands the causes as well as immediate and long-term consequences of U.S. intervention in the Caribbean in the first two decades of the century

BD (R;WE,262)

- Understands influences on art and culture in Europe and around the world in the early 20th century (e.g., the impact and aftermath of World War I on literature, art, and intellectual life in Europe; the impact of innovative movements in Western art and literature on other regions of the world; the influence of African and Asian art forms in Europe; the rise of mass culture

Codes (right side of page):   BD = Benchmark, Declarative; BP = Benchmark, Procedural; BC = Benchmark, Contextual
1st letter of each code in parentheses   *2nd letter of code*   *Number*
W = NCHS: World History Standards   E = Explicitly stated in document   Page number of cited document
L = Lessons from History   I = Implied in document
C = Core material
R = Related material   276   MᴙEL

around the world)

- Understands major discoveries in science and medicine in the first half of the 20th century (e.g., those made by Einstein, Freud) and how they affected the quality of life and traditional views of nature and the universe ^BD (R;WE,263,LI,301)

- Understands how the Great Depression affected economies and systems of government globally (e.g., how the depression contributed to the growth of communist, fascist, and socialist movements, and how it affected capitalist economic theory and practice among leading Western industrial powers; how the depression affected countries dependent on foreign markets and foreign capital investment) ^BD (R;WE,264)

- Understands the reflections of Depression-era hunger and poverty in the works of such artists as Käthe Kollwitz, José Clemente Orozco, and Dorothea Lange, and their impact upon society ^BD (R;WE,264)

Level IV (Grades 9-12)

- Understands how the treaties ending World War I and the League of Nations addressed different groups of people (e.g., how treaties ending World War I accorded with Woodrow Wilson's Fourteen Points and the processes by which the treaties were established, the varied reactions of the Chinese to the provisions of the Versailles Peace Treaty, the goals and failures of the "racial equality clause" in the preamble to the Covenant of the League of Nations) ^BD (C;WE,259)

- Understands how World War I influenced demographics and the international economy (e.g., significant refugee populations created as a result of World War I, and their movements and dispersion; the impact of the war on the international economy and the effects of industrial conversion from war to peace in Britain, France, Italy, and Germany) ^BD (C;WE,257,258,259)

- Understands post-World War I shifts in geographic and political borders in Europe and the Middle East (e.g., how the postwar borders in Southern Europe and the Middle East were created, including influence of local opinion, prewar "spheres of influence," long-and short-term interests; how Ataturk worked to modernize Turkey, how Turkish society and international society responded) ^BD (WE,259;LE,305)

- Understands reasons for the shifts in the political conditions in nations around the world after World War I (e.g., how Japan's domestic democracy may have fallen victim to its imperialist foreign policy; the successes and failures of democratic government in Latin America in the

---

Codes (right side of page):   BD = Benchmark, Declarative; BP = Benchmark, Procedural; BC = Benchmark, Contextual
1st letter of each code in parentheses   *2nd letter of code*   *Number*
W = NCHS: World History Standards   E = Explicitly stated in document   Page number of cited document
L = Lessons from History   I = Implied in document
C = Core material
R = Related material

McREL

context of class divisions, economic dependency, and U.S. intervention; how social and economic conditions of colonial rule, and ideals of liberal democracy and national autonomy contributed to the rise of nationalist movements in India, Africa, and Southeast Asia)

BD (C;WE,261)

- Understands elements of social and political change in China in the early 20th century (e.g., which populations supported the Guomindang and the Chinese Communist Party, and how the Japanese invasion of China in the 1930s changed viewpoints regarding these two parties; how Mao Zedong adapted Marxism to Chinese needs and how he viewed the peasantry as a revolutionary force; the goals and outcomes of the three major revolutions in China in the first half of the century)

BD (R;WE,261)

- Understands the conditions of the Hussein-McMahon correspondence and the Sykes-Picot agreement, how they differed with conditions of the treaties of Versailles and San Remo, and what each party sought to gain from these efforts

BD (R;WE,262,263;LE,301)

- Understands how the emergence of new art, literature, music, and scientific theories influenced society in the early 20th century (e.g., the impact of innovative movements in art, architecture, and literature, such as Cubism, Surrealism, Expressionism, Futurism, and Socialist Realism; reflections of war in such movements as Dadaism, and the literary works of Remarque, Spender, Brooke, and Hemingway; the major themes of writers of the "Lost Generation" in the post-World War I era; prominent musicians and composers of the first half of the century and the cultural impact of their music around the world; how Freud's psychoanalytic method and theories of the unconscious changed views of human motives and human nature)

BD (R;WE,264,265)

- Understands the causes of the Great Depression and its immediate and long-term consequences for the world (e.g., the financial, economic, and social causes of the Great Depression, and its global impact; how the depression affected colonial peoples of Africa and Asia, and how it contributed to the growth of nationalist movements; how the Great Depression affected the Middle East under British and French mandates; to what degree Britain, Germany, Japan, the Soviet Union, and the United States employed the military-industrial complex to stimulate recovery from the Great Depression)

BD (R;WE,265)

- Understands the origins and consequences for international trade of the U.S. Smoot-Hawley Tariff (e.g., how international trade was affected by the depression, how other nations reacted to the tariff)

Codes (right side of page):   BD = Benchmark, Declarative; BP = Benchmark, Procedural; BC = Benchmark, Contextual
1st letter of each code in parentheses   *2nd letter of code*   *Number*
W = NCHS: World History Standards   E = Explicitly stated in document   Page number of cited document
L = Lessons from History   I = Implied in document
C = Core material
R = Related material

MREL

(WE,266)

37. Understands the causes and global consequences of World War II

Level II (Grades 5-6)

BD (C;WE,266;LE,296)

- Understands the rise of fascism and Nazism in Europe (e.g., the ideologies of fascism and Nazism, and how fascist regimes seized power in Germany, Italy, and Spain; how Hitler, Franco, and Mussolini rose to power; the causes of the Spanish Civil War and how this war coincided with the rise of fascism in Europe; what Nazi oppression in Germany was like)

BD (C;WE,268;LI,296,297)

- Understands the major turning points in the war, and knows the principal theaters of conflict in Western Europe, Eastern Europe, the Soviet Union, North Africa, Asia, and the Pacific

BD (C;WE,268;LI,296)

- Understands the human costs of World War II (e.g., how and why the Nazi regime forged a "war against the Jews," and the devastation suffered by Jews and other groups in the Nazi Holocaust; the human consequences of war and resulting social problems)

Level III (Grades 7-8)

BD (C;WE,267;LI,296,302)

- Understands events that led to the outbreak of World War II (e.g., how Hitler capitalized on the despair of the German people to rise to power; the German, Italian, and Japanese drives for empire in the 1930s and their attempts to influence or annex new territories; the precipitating causes of the war and the reasons for early German and Japanese victories between 1939 and 1942)

BD (C;WE,267;LI,297)

- Understands the positions of the major powers —Britain, France, the U.S., and the Soviet Union — on fascist aggression, and the consequences of their failure to take forceful measures to stop this aggression

BD (C;WE,267)

- Understands motives and consequences of the Soviet nonaggression pacts with Germany and Japan

BD (C;WE,269)

- Understands the impact of World War II on civilian populations and soldiers (e.g., the roles of women and children during the war and how they differed in Allied and Axis countries, the hardships of the war on soldiers from both sides)

BD (C;WE,269;LI,298)

- Understands the influence of Nazism on European society and Jewish culture (e.g., European and Jewish resistance movements to the Nazis and their policies, discrepancies between Nazi public announcements concerning Jews and the actual experiences of Jews between 1941 and 1944)

Codes (right side of page):   BD = Benchmark, Declarative; BP = Benchmark, Procedural; BC = Benchmark, Contextual
1st letter of each code in parentheses   *2nd letter of code*   *Number*
W = NCHS: World History Standards   E = Explicitly stated in document   Page number of cited document
L = Lessons from History   I = Implied in document
C = Core material
R = Related material

McREL

- Understands the overall effect of World War II on various facets of society (e.g., the impact on industrial production, communication, transportation, technological innovations, science, and medicine, and how these in turn made an impact upon war strategies, tactics, and levels of destruction; the consequences of World War II as a "total war") BD (C;WE,269)

Level IV (Grades 9-12)

- Understands the rise of Nazism and how it was received by society (e.g., the essence and elements of Nazi ideology as represented in *Mein Kampf* and the Nazi party platform, and their use of terror against "enemies of the state"; the propaganda techniques employed by the Nazis to promote their ideas; political debate and opposition to the Nazi and Fascist movements in Germany and Italy in the 1920s and 1930s) BD (C;WE,267;LE,296)

- Understands the exceptional violence of the Spanish Civil War (e.g., as described in works by George Orwell and Ernest Hemingway) and understands how foreign intervention affected the outcome of this war BD (C;WE,267)

- Understands the argument that the severity of the Treaty of Versailles caused unavoidable revolt against the nations that imposed it BD (C;WE,267)

- Understands Japan's "greater East Asia co-prosperity" sphere and the support of this idea in European colonies in East Asia BD (C;WE,267;LI,297)

- Understands the Munich Agreement in 1938, what it meant for Stalin, and how it lead to the Nazi-Soviet Non-Aggression Pact of 1939 BD (C;WE,267;LI,297)

- Understands the Holocaust and its impact on Jewish culture and European society (e.g., the chronology of the Nazi "war on the Jews," and the geography and scale of Jewish deaths resulting from this policy; personal reasons for resistance to or compliance with Nazi policies and orders; the brutality of Nazi genocide in the Holocaust as revealed in personal stories of the victims) BD (C;WE,269;LE,296)

- Understands the climax and moral implications of World War II (e.g., what battles were turning points in the Atlantic and Pacific theaters and why, the moral implications of military technologies and techniques used in the war, statistics of population displacement caused by the war, debates surrounding the use of the atomic bomb to end the war with Japan) BD (C;WE,269;LI,297)

Codes (right side of page):   BD = Benchmark, Declarative; BP = Benchmark, Procedural; BC = Benchmark, Contextual
1st letter of each code in parentheses   *2nd letter of code*   *Number*
W = NCHS: World History Standards   E = Explicitly stated in document   Page number of cited document
L = Lessons from History   I = Implied in document
C = Core material
R = Related material   280   M2REL

(WE,270)

38. Understands how new international power relations took shape in the context of the Cold War and how colonial empires broke up

Level II (Grades 5-6)

BD (C;WE,277;LE,298,300;LI,298)

- Understands the shift in political conditions after World War II (e.g., the definition of the term "Cold War" and how the United States and the Soviet Union competed for power and influence in Europe; how the Marshall Plan helped Western European countries achieve rapid economic recovery after the war; why and how the United Nations was established, where it has been active in the world, and how successful it has been as a peacekeeper)

BD (C;WE,227;LI,303)

- Understands aspects of social and political conflict in China in the period following the war

BD (C;WE,272;LI,307)

- Understands political and social change in the developing countries of the Middle East, Africa, and Asia after World War II (e.g., how Israel was created, and why persistent conflict developed between Israel and both Arab Palestinians and neighboring states; the African experience under European colonial rule; major social and economic forces that compelled many Vietnamese to seek refuge in foreign countries)

BD (C;WE,272)

- Understands the position of women in developing countries (e.g., as compared to their position in industrialized countries, how change has occurred in different societies)

Level III (Grades 7-8)

BD (C;WE,270,271;LE,298;LI,298)

- Understands factors that brought about the political transformation of Western and Eastern Europe after World War II (e.g., the impact of Soviet domination in Eastern Europe; the Marshall plan and how it helped Western European nations achieve rapid economic recovery after the war; the formations of the Warsaw Pact and the North Atlantic Treaty Organization after the war, and which countries have participated in each of these pacts; why Germany and Berlin were divided after the 1948 crisis, and the resulting problems)

BD (C;WE,270)

- Understands the rise of the Communist Party in China between 1936 and 1949, the factors leading to Mao's programs (i.e., the Great Leap Forward, the Cultural Revolution) and their results (e.g., effects on economic development, human suffering)

BD (C;WE,270;LI,298-300)

- Knows the significance of international crises such as the Berlin blockade, the Korean War, the Hungarian revolt, and the Cuban missile crisis on international politics

BD (C;WE,272;LI,308,309)

- Understands nationalist movements and other attempts by colonial countries to achieve

---

Codes (right side of page): BD = Benchmark, Declarative; BP = Benchmark, Procedural; BC = Benchmark, Contextual
1st letter of each code in parentheses   *2nd letter of code*   *Number*
W = NCHS: World History Standards   E = Explicitly stated in document   Page number of cited document
L = Lessons from History   I = Implied in document
C = Core material
R = Related material

MᴄREL

independence after World War II (e.g., how World War II and postwar global politics affected the mass nationalist movements in colonial Africa and Southeast Asia; the methods used by Indians to achieve independence from British rule and the effects of Mohandas Ghandi's call for nonviolent action; the rise of independent nations out of Western colonial rule in Southeast Asia; factors that enabled some African and Asian countries to achieve independence through constitutional devolution of power, while others used armed revolution)

- Understands political conditions in Africa after World War II (e.g., the moral, social, political, and economic implications of apartheid; the diverse leadership and governing styles of African regimes through the second half of the 20th century) BD (C;WE,272)

- Understands important events in the struggle between Israelis and Palestinians since 1948 and the argument on each side for rights to the disputed land BD (C;WE,273;LI,308)

Level IV (Grades 9-12)

- Understands relations between the United States and the Soviet Union during the Cold War (e.g., causes and consequences of United States and Soviet competition for influence or dominance around the world; the "superpower" characteristics of the U.S. and U.S.S.R., how they gained these characteristics, and how the space race defined the competition between them) BD (C;WE,270,271)

- Understands the strategic role of the Muslim countries during the Cold War (e.g., the importance of geography, economy, and population) and the change in the region's role since the breakup of the Soviet Union BD (C;WE,271)

- Understands factors that influenced political conditions in China after World War II (e.g., how much of the Communist success in the Chinese civil war was the result of Mao Zedong's leadership or Jiang Jieshi's lack of leadership, why rifts developed in the relationships between the U.S.S.R. and China in spite of the common bond of Communist-led government) BD (C;WE,271)

- Understands the impact of independence movements in various countries and whether they were successful (e.g., the connections between the rise of independence movements in Africa and Southeast Asia and social transformations such as accelerated population growth, urbanization, and new Western-educated elites; the chronology of the Algerian struggle for independence, the role of domestic and international public opinion in the actions of the government, and how the French presence influenced the outcome; how diverse independence movements in Asia and Africa succeeded) BD (C;WE,272)

Codes (right side of page): BD = Benchmark, Declarative; BP = Benchmark, Procedural; BC = Benchmark, Contextual
1st letter of each code in parentheses *2nd letter of code* *Number*
W = NCHS: World History Standards E = Explicitly stated in document Page number of cited document
L = Lessons from History I = Implied in document
C = Core material
R = Related material

McREL

- Understands reasons for the shift in government in Africa and how Africans responded (e.g., reasons for the replacement of parliamentary-style governments with military regimes and one-party states in much of Africa, how Africans survived and resisted apartheid)

  BD (C;WE,272)

- Understands reasons for the division of the Indian subcontinent (e.g.,events that led to the dispute over Kashmir and the resulting partition of the Indian subcontinent, and the role of the United Nations in the mediation of the dispute; how the withdrawal of the British and the divison between Muslims and Hindus affected the division of the Indian subcontinent into two nations)

  BD (C;WE,273;LI,309)

- Understands similarities between the stance of Buddhist priests against the Diem regime in Vietnam and the Muslim stance against the Kukarn regime in Indonesia

  BD (C;WE,273)

- Understands how the Balfour Declaration affected British policy toward Palestine and the political goals of the Arab League and the Zionist Movement, and how the White Paper Reports affected Jewish and Arab inhabitants of Palestine

  BD (C;WE,273;LE,305,306)

39. Understands the promises and paradoxes of the second half of the 20th century

(WE,274)

Level II (Grades 5-6)

- Understands different influences on living standards (e.g., why scientific, technological, and medical advances have improved living standards but have failed to eradicate hunger, poverty, and epidemic disease; how urbanization has affected family life and standards of living worldwide)

  BD (C;WE,274,283)

- Understands global influences on the environment (e.g., how population growth, urbanization, industrialization, warfare, and the global market economy have contributed to environmental alterations; how effective governments and citizens' groups have been at protecting the global natural environment)

  BD (C;WE,274)

- Understands how global trends have affected world economy (e.g., the effects of new transport and communications technology on patterns of world trade and finance; the impact of major scientific, technological, and medical breakthroughs of the postwar decades on systems of production, global trade, and standards of living)

  BD (C;WE,276)

- Understands how global communications and changing international labor demands have shaped new patterns of world migration since World War II

  BD (C;WE,276)

Codes (right side of page):   BD = Benchmark, Declarative; BP = Benchmark, Procedural; BC = Benchmark, Contextual
1st letter of each code in parentheses   *2nd letter of code*   *Number*
W = NCHS: World History Standards   E = Explicitly stated in document   Page number of cited document
L = Lessons from History   I = Implied in document
C = Core material
R = Related material

McREL

- BD (C;WE,278;LI,300)

  Understands events that have improved political and social conditions around the world (e.g., the origins of the U.N. Declaration of Human Rights in 1948, and how the tenets of this document have and have not been followed in specific countries around the globe; how the apartheid system was dismantled in South Africa and the black majority won voting rights)

- BD (C;WE,278)

  Understands the extent of women's progress in both industrialized and developing countries, in social equality and economic opportunity, since the end of World War II

- BD (C;WE,278;LE,300)

  Understands the consequences of ethnic conflict in specific countries around the globe

- BD (R;WE,280;LI,304)

  Understands sources of conflict in specific countries and around the world (e.g., the changes continuing urban protest and reformist economic policies have caused in post-Mao China under authoritarian rule; "terrorism" and why terrorist movements have proliferated, affecting policies and society in countries around the world)

- BD (R;WE,282)

  Understands the emergence of a global culture (e.g., how rapid developments in communication, information technology, and mass marketing techniques have contributed to the acceleration of social change and the rise of a "global culture"; how contemporary art and architecture reflect local and global culture)

- BD (R;WE,282)

  Understands comparisons between the "consumer societies" of industrialized nations and those in predominantly agrarian nations

- BD (R;WE,282;LI,306)

  Understands how the world's religions have responded to recent changes and uncertainties in society and the world

Level III (Grades 7-8)

- BD (C;WE,274;LI,306)

  Understands the causes and effects of population growth and urbanization (e.g., why the population growth rate is accelerating around the world, and why this growth has hindered economic and social development in many countries; the global proliferation of cities and the rise of the megalopolis, as well as the impact of urbanization on family life, standards of living, class relations, and ethnic identity; how the specific factors of population growth, urbanization, warfare, and the global market economy have contributed to the alteration and degradation of the environment)

- BD (C;WE,275)

  Understands the importance or meaning of the natural environment for societies around the world

---

Codes (right side of page):   BD = Benchmark, Declarative; BP = Benchmark, Procedural; BC = Benchmark, Contextual
1st letter of each code in parentheses   *2nd letter of code*   *Number*
W = NCHS: World History Standards   E = Explicitly stated in document   Page number of cited document
L = Lessons from History   I = Implied in document
C = Core material
R = Related material

McREL

BD (C;WE,276;LI,299,305)

- Understands factors that contributed to the rise of a global economy (e.g., why economic disparities between industrialized nations have persisted or increased, and problems that have hindered industrialization in developing countries; events that have affected world oil prices since 1950, and how these events reflect the extent and complexity of global economic interdependence; why and how economic partnerships such as the European Economic Community [EEC] have been created)

BD (C;WE,285)

- Understands the role and difficulties of the present day migrant worker (e.g., the Southeast Asian domestic in the Persian Gulf, the American oil executive in Saudi Arabia, the Moraccan factory worker in France)

BD (C;WE,278,279;LE,300)

- Understands events that led to an easing of Cold War tensions from the 1970s to the early 1990s (e.g., why the Cold War eased in the 1970s and how the growing global influence of China, Japan, Western Europe, and the oil producing states resulted in a world of multipolar power; the collapse of the government of the Soviet Union and other communist governments around the world in the late 1980s and 1990s; the internal and external forces that led to changes within the USSR and in its relations with Eastern European countries)

BD (C;WE,279)

- Understands the motivations, moral imperatives, and goals of specific separatist movements around the globe and the potential impact on the affected populations

BD (C;WE,278)

- Understands why the United Nations Declaration of Human Rights was created in 1948, and the progress made on human rights around the world

BD (C;WE,279)

- Understands how pressure placed on the government of South Africa led to a change in the system of apartheid

BD (R;WE,280;LI,306)

- Understands instances of political conflict and terrorism in modern society (e.g., the progress made since the 1970s in resolving conflict between Israel and neighboring states; possible factors in modern society that facilitate politically motivated terrorism and random forms of violence; world events that gave rise to the 1989 movement in China and led to the Tiannamen Square protest, the government response to this movement, and the international reaction)

BD (R;WE,281)

- Understands the definition of "fundamentalism," and the political objectives of religious fundamentalism in various countries of the world, as well as the social and political factors that contribute to the growth of these movements

BD (R;WE,280)

- Understands the impact of population pressure, poverty, and environmental degradation on

---

Codes (right side of page):   BD = Benchmark, Declarative; BP = Benchmark, Procedural; BC = Benchmark, Contextual
1st letter of each code in parentheses   *2nd letter of code*   *Number*
W = NCHS: World History Standards   E = Explicitly stated in document   Page number of cited document
L = Lessons from History   I = Implied in document
C = Core material
R = Related material

McREL

the breakdown of state authority in various countries in the 1980s and 1990s, and international reaction to the deterioration of these states

- Understands how social change has been expressed, and what has accelerated this social change (e.g., how modern arts have expressed and reflected social transformations, political changes, and how they have been internationalized; how global communication, information technology, and global mass marketing have contributed to accelerated social change) BD (R;WE,282,283;LE,301,308)

- Understands the effects of modern communication on consumer tastes and demands in different parts of the world BD (R;WE,283)

Level IV (Grades 9-12)

- Understands influences on population growth, and efforts to control such growth in modern society (e.g., how statistics from specific, diverse nations illustrate the relationship between scientific, medical, and technological advancements and population growth; China's population growth from the 1700s to 1990, why the population growth increased dramatically, and the effects of the "one-child" policy of the 1990s; issues and objections raised at the 1994 Cairo Conference on World Population and the difficulty of arriving at a consensus document on population growth) BD (C;WE,275;LI,304)

- Understands the effectiveness of United Nations programs in improving health and welfare (e.g., whether UN programs have been cost-effective; whether programs fulfilled the purpose for which they were created) BD (C;WE,275)

- Understands rates of economic development, and the emergence of different economic systems around the globe (e.g., systems of economic management in communist and capitalist countries, as well as the global impact of multinational corporations; patterns of inward, outward, and internal migration in the Middle East and North Africa, types of jobs involved, and the impact of the patterns upon national economies; the rapid economic development of East Asian countries in the late 20th century, and the relatively slow development of Sub-Saharan African countries) BD (C;WE,276,277)

- Understands major reasons for the great disparities between industrialized and developing nations, and possible programs and measures to help equalize these disparities (e.g., disparities in resources, production, captial investment, labor, or trade) BD (C;WE,276)

- Understands the relationships between U.S. domestic energy policy and foreign policy in oil producing regions since 1970 BD (C;WE,276)

Codes (right side of page):   BD = Benchmark, Declarative; BP = Benchmark, Procedural; BC = Benchmark, Contextual
1st letter of each code in parentheses   *2nd letter of code*   *Number*
W = NCHS: World History Standards   E = Explicitly stated in document   Page number of cited document
L = Lessons from History   I = Implied in document
C = Core material
R = Related material

286

MCREL

- Understands the role of political ideology, religion, and ethnicity in shaping modern governments (e.g., how successful democratic reform movements have been in challenging authoritarian governments in Africa, Asia, and Latin America; the implications of ethnic, religious, and border conflicts on state-building in the newly independent republics of Africa; the difficulties of multi-ethnic formation in former colonies; significant differences among nationalist movements in Eastern Europe that have developed in the 20th century, how resulting conflicts have been resolved, and the outcomes of these conflicts)
  BD (C;WE,279)

- Understands common arguments of opposition groups in various countries around the world, common solutions they offer, and the position of these ideas with regard to Western economic and strategic interests
  BD (C;WE,279)

- Understands gender roles across the globe (e.g., conflicts in the perception of gender roles in various religions, especially the role of women; how the legal status of women varies around the world in Muslim societies, and how the status of women from different classes has changed in the past century)
  BD (C;WE,279;LI,307)

- Understands the role of ethnic and cultural identity and religious beliefs in shaping economic and political conflicts across the globe (e.g., the tensions and contradictions between globalizing trends of the world economy and assertions of traditional cultural identity and distinctiveness, including the challenges to the role of religion in contemporary society; reasons for economic and arms embargoes sponsored by U.N. resolutions and the political and economic consequences for the sanctioned countries; the meaning of jihad and other Islamic beliefs that are relevant to military activity, how these compare to the Geneva Accords, and how such laws and principles apply to terrorist acts)
  BD (R;WE,280,281)

- Understands how trends in science and art have influenced society (e.g., the impact of space exploration, biotechnology, the new physics, and medical advances on human society and ecology; how the space program has helped advance scientific and medical research and how modern technology has affected our ability to deal with health-related issues; how art can reflect the cultural values of a particular society and time)
  BD (R;WE,283;LE,301)

- Understands how global political change has altered the world economy (e.g., what participation in the world economy can mean for different countries; the relationship between demands for democratic reform and the trend toward privatization and economic liberalization in developing economies and former communist states, and how multilateral aid organizations and multinational corporations have supported or challenged these trends)
  BD (R;WE,290)

- Understands how specific countries have implemented social and cultural changes (e.g., the
  BD (R;WE,290;LE,304)

Codes (right side of page):   BD = Benchmark, Declarative; BP = Benchmark, Procedural; BC = Benchmark, Contextual
1st letter of each code in parentheses   *2nd letter of code*   *Number*
W = NCHS: World History Standards   E = Explicitly stated in document   Page number of cited document
L = Lessons from History   I = Implied in document
C = Core material
R = Related material   287   MREL

different manifestations of China's contingency quest for a "new culture" throughout the 20th century, and what the Cultural Revolution meant for Chinese people in the late 1960s; models for family life, the economy, and social and political institutions suggested by modern Muslim intellectuals)

- Understands "liberation theology" and the ideological conflicts that have surrounded this philosophy

  BD (R;WE,283)

Codes (right side of page):   BD = Benchmark, Declarative; BP = Benchmark, Procedural; BC = Benchmark, Contextual
1st letter of each code in parentheses   *2nd letter of code*   *Number*
W = NCHS: World History Standards   E = Explicitly stated in document   Page number of cited document
L = Lessons from History   I = Implied in document
C = Core material
R = Related material   288   McREL

10. Language Arts

The following process was used to identify standards and benchmarks for the language arts:

Identification of National Reports
This category deals with basic knowledge and skill in reading, writing, and language. Unfortunately, as described in Chapter 2, the federally funded efforts to develop language arts standards have come to a stop. Specifically, federal funding halted for the Standards Projects for the English Language Arts (SPELA) as of March 1994. One complete draft document has survived from that effort, the *Incomplete Work of the Task Forces of the Standards Project for English Language Arts* (1994). It identifies standards in five broad areas referred to as strands. The five strands are (1) Reading/Literature, (2) Writing, (3) Language, (4) Real World Literacy, and (5) Interconnections. The document was the product of a joint effort of the Center for the Study of Reading (CSR) at the University of Illinois, the International Reading Association (IRA), and the National Council of Teachers of English (NCTE). When funding for SPELA was halted in 1994, NCTE and IRA continued their joint effort to produce language arts standards. In October 1995 a draft document entitled *Standards for the English Language Arts* (NCTE, IRA, 1995) was distributed for review. It articulated eleven standards primarily dealing with reading and writing. However, it has been criticized for its lack of specificity as was the SPELA document.

Fortunately, a number of other documents contain explicit and implicit descriptions of language arts standards; they provided a rather comprehensive source of information for identifying standards in the English language arts. The most explicit of these are documents produced by the National Assessment of Educational Progress (NAEP) as a part of its 1992 assessment efforts. In the area of writing, NAEP has produced the *Description of Writing Achievement Levels—Setting Process and Proposed Achievement Level Definitions* (1992). This document provides descriptions of basic, proficient, and advanced levels of performance at three levels: grade 4, grade 8, and grade 12. The performance levels represent fairly straightforward descriptions of what students should know and be able to do in writing. In reading, NAEP has produced the *Assessment and Exercise Specifications: NAEP Reading Consensus Project: 1992 NAEP Reading Assessment* (1990). This document provides explicit statements of what students should know and be able to do relative to the process of reading and identifies the types of materials students should be able to read at various levels. Other sources of explicit descriptions of knowledge and skills students should acquire within the language arts include documents from the Edison Project (1994a, 1994b, 1994c), selected language arts frameworks from the state of California (California State Department of Education, 1993, 1994b, 1994c), the language arts framework from New York State (New York State Education Department, 1994), the language arts standards framework from Australia (Australian Education Council, 1994), and the draft document from the New Standards Project (New Standards, June 1995). At a more implicit level, *The English Coalition Conference: Democracy through Language* (NCTE, 1989) provides very general descriptions of the knowledge and skills important to the language arts at the elementary and secondary levels.

One area of interest to the language arts not addressed in previous versions of this project is literature. To obtain a comprehensive view of the various perspectives regarding the literature with which students should be familiar, a number of sources were consulted. These included: selected lists of recommended readings from the National Council of Teacher of English (Committee on the Junior High and Middle School Booklist of the National Council of Teachers of English and Nilsen, 1991; Committee on the Senior High School Booklist of the National Council of Teachers of English and Wurth, 1992); a list of recommended readings from the New England Association of Teachers of English (Stotsky, Anderson, and Beierl, 1989); recommended readings from the California State Department of Education (California State Department of Education, 1989); lists of "best books" by Gillespie (1991a, 1991b); and recommended literature by Ravitch and Finn (1987), E.D. Hirsch (Hirsch, 1987, 1993a, 1993b, 1993c, 1993d, 1993e, 1993f), and the Edison Project (1994a, 1994b, 1994c).

In addition to documents that have a specific focus on the language arts, there are a number of reports from other content areas that have explicit and implicit standards that deal with reading and writing. Among these are *Expectations of Excellence: Curriculum Standards for Social Studies* (NCSS, 1994); *National Standards for World History, National Standards for U.S. History* and *National Standards for History for Grades K–4* (NCHS, 1994); *Geography for Life: National Geography Standards* (Geography Education Standards Project, 1994); and *Curriculum and Evaluation Standards for School Mathematics* (National Council of Teachers of Mathematics, 1989).

Finally, what might be termed "the world of work" has produced documents that contain both implicit and explicit statements of what students should know and be able to do in reading and writing. These include *What Work Requires of Schools: A SCANS Report for America 2000* (The Secretary's Commission on Achieving Necessary Skills, 1991) and *Workplace Basics: The Essential Skills Employers Want* (Carnevale, Gainer & Meltzer, 1990).

Selection of Reference Documents and Identification of Standards

If the federally funded effort to identify English language arts standards had not ceased, the latest draft document of the SPELA effort would have been the most logical choice as the reference report. Additionally, the "unfunded" effort by NCTE and IRA has produced a document that is far too general to satisfy the level of detail necessary for this project. Given the absence of a single official "source" of standards, different reference documents were identified for different aspects of the English language arts. Two NAEP documents were identified as reference documents for reading and writing since they contained the most explicit statements of standards. Specifically, the reference document selected for the general area of writing was the *Description of Writing Achievement Levels—Setting Process and Proposed Achievement Level Definitions*. The reference document selected for the general area of reading was *Assessment and Exercise Specifications: NAEP Reading Consensus Project: 1992 NAEP Reading Assessment*. Both of these documents contain a level of detail sufficient to provide a strong basis for identifying standards in the areas of writing and reading. The reference document identified for the area of listening and speaking was the standards framework developed by the Australian Education Council, *English: A Curriculum Profile for Australian Schools* (Australian Education Council, 1994). Although listening and speaking were addressed to some extent within other sources (e.g., the New Standards Project), the

Australian Framework was deemed the most comprehensive treatment of this area.

No single source was used as the reference document for the area of literature. Rather, the literature cited in the various sources mentioned previously was organized into fairly traditional categories (e.g., nursery rhymes, fairy tales, folk tales, fiction, Greek and Roman mythology).

The final area addressed in the language arts standards is language. This area has traditionally been considered important to English language arts teachers as evidenced by its inclusion in the five strands identified in the SPELA effort. Consequently, the *Incomplete Work of the Task Forces of the Standards Project for English Language Arts* was considered the reference document for this area.

Analysis of the SPELA document, however, proved problematic because of its format. Rather than identify what students should know and be able to do within each strand, the document authors chose to provide vignettes at one or more of three levels: early school, middle school, and high school. In simple terms, a vignette is a description of what might occur in a classroom that exemplifies a specific standard. At the end of each vignette is a list of student "accomplishments" exemplified in the vignette. Some of the accomplishments listed after vignettes approached explicit statements of knowledge and skill. For example, the following are the accomplishments listed for the early-school vignette for the Reading/Literature Standard "Students will read, discuss and write about literature so that they can learn about themselves and their values, assumptions and beliefs":

* see their lives reflected in literature
* clarify assumptions about others as they read
* respect the uniqueness and diversity of individuals
* relate literature to their own lives

Given the very specific nature of standards and their related benchmarks as defined in this study, we analyzed the vignettes and the list of accomplishments following each vignette for implied and (occasionally) explicit statements of declarative, procedural, and contextual knowledge. In effect, we were obliged to extract implied statements of declarative, procedural and contextual knowledge based on a close reading of the activities and dialogues described in the vignettes.

In keeping with the fact that multiple reference documents were identified for the English language arts, the standards in this section are organized into five categories: writing, reading, speaking and listening, literature, and language. Four standards are identified in writing, six standards are identified in reading, one standard is identified in speaking and listening, one in literature, and one in language.

Integration of Information from Other Documents

The implicit and explicit information found in the other documents identified as pertinent to this area were integrated into the standards extracted from the reference documents. For the three history documents—*National Standards for History for Grades K–4, National Standards for U.S. History,* and *National Standards for World History* (NCHS, 1994)—this information came from the sections of those documents entitled Standards in Historical Thinking. These sections deal with thinking about and communicating about history. In the social studies document, *Expectations of Excellence: Curriculum Standards for Social Studies* (NCSS, 1994), the information used to supplement the language arts standards was taken from the sections entitled Reading and Reference and Information-Search Skills. In the geography document, *Geography for Life: National Geography Standards* (GESP, 1994), the information was taken from the chapter entitled Geographic Skills and Perspectives, which deals with analyzing geographic issues and communicating about those issues. In the mathematics document, *Curriculum and Evaluation Standards for School Mathematics* (NCTM, 1989), the information was taken primarily from the standard that deals with communicating mathematically.

Finally, within the *SCANS Report* and *Workplace Basics*, reading and writing skills are addressed explicitly. This information was used to supplement the standards within those areas.

Summary of Standards for Language Arts

Writing

1. Demonstrates competence in the general skills and strategies of the writing process
2. Demonstrates competence in the stylistic and rhetorical aspects of writing
3. Writes with a command of the grammatical and mechanical conventions of composition
4. Effectively gathers and uses information for research purposes

Reading

5. Demonstrates competence in the general skills and strategies of the reading process
6. Demonstrates competence in general skills and strategies for reading literature
7. Demonstrates competence in the general skills and strategies for reading information
8. Demonstrates competence in applying the reading process to specific types of literary texts
9. Demonstrates competence in applying the reading process to specific types of informational texts
10. Demonstrates competence in using different information sources, including those of a technical nature, to accomplish specific tasks

Listening and Speaking

11. Demonstrates competence in speaking and listening as tools for learning

Language

12. Demonstrates an understanding of the nature and function of the English language

Literature

13. Demonstrates a familiarity with selected literary works of enduring quality

1 .   Demonstrates competence in the general skills and strategies of the writing process ^(E2,3,19;SE,xviii;WI,90)

Level I (Grades K-2)

- Dictates or writes stories or essays, based on one's own experience, with a sequence of events that make sense ^{BP (E1I,25;NWI,23)}

- Dictates or writes stories or essays that have some evidence of a beginning, middle, and ending ^{BP (NWI,23)}

- Writes detailed descriptions of familiar persons, places, or objects ^{BP (E1E,25;AE,38)}

- Revises writing by improving sequence, providing more descriptive detail, or adding more variety of sentence types ^{BP (E1E,25)}

- Makes an attempt to help edit classmates' writing ^{BP (E1E,25)}

Level II (Grades 3-5)

- Makes some attempt to identify strengths and weaknesses in own writing ^{BP (LI,33;EI,4;E2I,36)}

- Seeks help from others to improve writing ^{BP (LE,67;E2E,36)}

- Writes stories or essays that show an awareness of an intended audience ^{BP (E2E,36;E2,4;NWE,23)}

- Writes stories or essays that show an awareness of an intended purpose ^{BP (E2,4;NWE,23;E2I,36)}

- Demonstrates competence in expository writing (e.g., attempts to identify and stay on the topic, and to develop the topic with simple facts, details, examples, and explanations) ^{BP (NWI,23;E2E,36;C8E,10,11)}

- Demonstrates competence in persuasive writing (e.g., states a clear position, elaborates on this position with reasons, examples, information, and other evidence that is organized and generally relevant to the writer's purpose) ^{BP (NWI,23,25;C4E,130)}

- Demonstrates competence in writing essays that speculate on causes and effects (e.g., ^{BP (NWI,23,25;E2E,36;C8E,191)}

Codes (right side of page):   BD = Benchmark, Declarative; BP = Benchmark, Procedural; BC = Benchmark, Contextual
1st letter(s) of each code in parentheses   *2nd letter of code*   *Number*
A = Australian Education Council   E = Explicitly stated in document   Page number of cited document
C4,8: CDE: Elementary, Middle Perf. Assessments   I = Implied in document
C12 = CDE: Calif. Writing Assess. Handbook
E = NCTE: Democracy Through Language
E1,2,3: Edison Proj: Primary,Elementary,Junior Acad.   NW = NAEP: Writing Achieve. Levels-Setting Proc.
G = GESP: National Geography Standards   NY = NY Draft Framework for Eng. Lang. Arts
L = SPELA: Standards Proj. for English/Lang. Arts   S = SCANS: Report for America 2000
NR = NAEP: 1992 Reading Assessment   SS = NCSS: Curric. Standards for Social Studies
NS = NSP: Draft Standards for Eng. Lang. Arts   U = NCHS: National Standards for U.S. History
                                                       W = Carnevale: Workplace Basics

MREL

attempts to describe the situation to be speculated about, to establish the connection between the situation and the postulated causes or effects, and to offer simple persuasive evidence for the validity of the proposed causes or effects)

BP (NWI,23,25;C4E,85,86)
- Demonstrates competence in expressive writing (e.g., attempts to express ideas, observations, and memories by using narrative strategies, relevant details, and ideas that enable the reader to imagine the world of the event/experience, and an individual, authentic voice)

BP (E2E,36;C8E,134,135)
- Demonstrates competence in autobiographical writing (e.g., makes an attempt to relate a single incident, to provide a context within which the incident occurs, to use simple narrative strategies, and to provide some insight into why this incident is memorable)

BP (AE,38;NS,290)
- Demonstrates competence in narrative writing (e.g., engages the reader by establishing a context, creating a point of view, and otherwise developing reader interest; establishes a situation, plot, point of view, setting, and conflict; creates an organizing structure that balances and unifies all narrative aspects of the story; includes sensory details and concrete language to develop plot and character; uses a range of appropriate strategies such as dialogue and tension or suspense)

Level III (Grades 6-8)

BP (LI,39)
- Uses direct feedback from peers to revise content of a composition

BP (EI,20;E3E,35;AE,61)
- Drafts, revises, edits, and proofreads written work

BP (LI,32;E2,20;NWE,25)
- Writes for public and private audiences

BP (C8E,10)
- Demonstrates competence in expository writing (e.g., presents useful, specific, and well-developed information; is knowledgeable about the topic of the report; organizes and presents information in a logical manner)

BP (NS,303;AE,82)
- Demonstrates competence in writing persuasive essays (e.g., engages the reader by establishing a context, creating a persona, and otherwise developing reader interest; develops a controlling idea that makes a clear and knowledgeable judgment; creates and organizes a

Codes (right side of page):	BD = Benchmark, Declarative; BP = Benchmark, Procedural; BC = Benchmark, Contextual	
1st letter(s) of each code in parentheses	*2nd letter of code*	*Number*
A = Australian Education Council	E = Explicitly stated in document	Page number of cited document
C4,8: CDE: Elementary, Middle Perf. Assessments	I = Implied in document	
C12 = CDE: Calif. Writing Assess. Handbook		
E = NCTE: Democracy Through Language	NW = NAEP: Writing Achieve. Levels-Setting Proc.	
E1,2,3: Edison Proj: Primary,Elementary,Junior Acad.	NY = NY Draft Framework for Eng. Lang. Arts	
G = GESP: National Geography Standards	S = SCANS: Report for America 2000	
L = SPELA: Standards Proj. for English/Lang. Arts	SS = NCSS: Curric. Standards for Social Studies	
NR = NAEP: 1992 Reading Assessment	U = NCHS: National Standards for U.S. History	
NS = NSP: Draft Standards for Eng. Lang. Arts	W = Carnevale: Workplace Basics	

295

McREL

structure appropriate in terms of the needs, values, and interests of a specified audience, arranging details, reasons, examples, and/or anecdotes effectively and persuasively; includes appropriate information and arguments and excludes information and arguments that are irrelevant; anticipates and addresses reader concerns and counter-arguments; supports arguments with detailed evidence, citing sources of information as appropriate)

- Demonstrates competence in writing essays that speculate on problem/solutions (e.g., identifies and defines the problem in a way appropriate to the intended audience, describes at least one solution clearly and convincingly, presents logical and well-supported reasons) BP (C8E,124;E3I,34)

- Demonstrates competence in writing essays that speculate on causes and effects (e.g., presents the situation clearly, establishes a convincing connection between the situation and the postulated causes or effects, includes relevant and convincing evidence, reveals an awareness of the audience) BP (C8E,190;E3I,34)

- Demonstrates competence in writing essays about autobiographical incidents (e.g., relates a clear, coherent incident; may treat the incident as a springboard for an exploration of its significance; locates the incident by using some well-chosen details; reveals the writer's attitude and the impact of the incident; presents details in a coherent and logical manner) BP (NWI,23,25;SSI,149;C8E,134;E3I,34)

- Demonstrates competence in writing biographical sketches (e.g., chooses and employs narrative and descriptive strategies such as relevant dialogue, specific action, physical description, background description, and comparison or contrast to other people that support the characterization; reveals the significance of the subject to the writer; presents details in a coherent and logical manner) BP (NWI,23;C8E,332;E3I,34)

- Demonstrates competence in writing narrative accounts (e.g., engages the reader by establishing a context, creating a point of view or persona, and otherwise developing reader interest through techniques like suspense; establishes a situation, plot, point of view, setting, and conflict; creates an organizing structure that balances and unifies all narrative aspects of the story; includes sensory details and concrete language to develop plot and character; excludes extraneous details and inconsistencies; develops complex characters; uses a range of appropriate strategies such as dialogue, tension or suspense, naming, and specific narrative action such as movement, gestures, and expressions) BP (NS,302;AE,60,82)

Codes (right side of page):   BD = Benchmark, Declarative; BP = Benchmark, Procedural; BC = Benchmark, Contextual
1st letter(s) of each code in parentheses   *2nd letter of code*   *Number*
A = Australian Education Council   E = Explicitly stated in document   Page number of cited document
C4,8: CDE: Elementary, Middle Perf. Assessments   I = Implied in document
C12 = CDE: Calif. Writing Assess. Handbook
E = NCTE: Democracy Through Language   NW = NAEP: Writing Achieve. Levels-Setting Proc.
E1,2,3: Edison Proj: Primary,Elementary,Junior Acad.   NY = NY Draft Framework for Eng. Lang. Arts
G = GESP: National Geography Standards   S = SCANS: Report for America 2000
L = SPELA: Standards Proj. for English/Lang. Arts   SS = NCSS: Curric. Standards for Social Studies
NR = NAEP: 1992 Reading Assessment   U = NCHS: National Standards for U.S. History
NS = NSP: Draft Standards for Eng. Lang. Arts   W = Carnevale: Workplace Basics

McREL

●   Understands the form and use of footnotes when writing research papers   ^{BP (E3E,35)}

Level IV (Grades 9-12)

●   Uses personal response to text as a basis for writing   ^{BP (LE,32)}

●   Writes compositions that are clearly focused for different audiences including those informed about the topic, those uninformed about the topic, those that are highly public, and those that are not   ^{BP (LI,32;E2,20;NWI,26)}

●   Writes compositions that clearly fulfill different purposes, including to entertain and to stimulate emotion   ^{BP (LI,32;E2,20;NWE,26)}

●   Uses a range of strategies for drafting, revising, editing, and proofreading written work (e.g., plans writing through discussion with others and by making notes, lists, or diagrams; attempts to rearrange sections of text to improve organization of ideas; uses a checklist to guide proofreading; redrafts for readability and needs of readers; reviews writing to ensure that content and linguistic structures and features are consistent with purpose)   ^{BP (AE,83,107)}

●   Demonstrates competence in writing expository essays (i.e., synthesizes and organizes information from first- and second-hand sources, including books, magazines, computer data banks, and the community; selects appropriate techniques to develop the main idea [e.g., names, describes or differentiates parts; compares or contrasts subject with something; examines the history of a subject; cites an anecdote to provide an example; illustrates through a scenario; provides interesting facts about the subject])   ^{BP (C12I,133,183)}

●   Demonstrates competence in writing persuasive essays, including evaluation, interpretation, and speculation about problem/solution and causes and effects (i.e., clearly articulates a position through the use of a thesis statement; anticipates and deals with counter arguments; backs up assertions using criteria commonly accepted in the field or through the use of specific rhetorical devices [e.g., via an appeal to logic through reasoning; via an appeal to emotion through connotative language or through figurative language that engages the emotion; by an appeal to ethical beliefs; by rhetorical question; by personal anecdote, case study, analogy, or domino effect]; and develops arguments using a variety of methods such   ^{BP (C12E,61,62,83,106,210-211;AE,82)}

Codes (right side of page):   BD = Benchmark, Declarative;   BP = Benchmark, Procedural;   BC = Benchmark, Contextual

1st letter(s) of each code in parentheses	*2nd letter of code*	*Number*
A = Australian Education Council	E = Explicitly stated in document	Page number of cited document
C4,8: CDE: Elementary, Middle Perf. Assessments	I = Implied in document	
C12 = CDE: Calif. Writing Assess. Handbook		
E = NCTE: Democracy Through Language	NW = NAEP: Writing Achieve. Levels-Setting Proc.	
E1,2,3: Edison Proj: Primary,Elementary,Junior Acad.	NY = NY Draft Framework for Eng. Lang. Arts	
G = GESP: National Geography Standards	S = SCANS: Report for America 2000	
L = SPELA: Standards Proj. for English/Lang. Arts	SS = NCSS: Curric. Standards for Social Studies	
NR = NAEP: 1992 Reading Assessment	U = NCHS: National Standards for U.S. History	
NS = NSP: Draft Standards for Eng. Lang. Arts	W = Carnevale: Workplace Basics	

MREL

as examples and details, commonly accepted beliefs, expert opinion, quotations of lines or passages from literature, cause and effect reasoning, comparison-contrast reasoning, hypothetical situations, and logical syllogisms)

- Demonstrates competence in writing descriptive essays (i.e., provides clear perspective on the object being described [e.g., near/far, top/bottom]; clearly establishes his/her relationship with the object [e.g., objective, partially involved, very involved]; makes effective use of supporting detail [e.g., factual descriptions of appearance, concrete images, shifting perspectives and vantage points, and sensory detail]) BP (C12E,133)

- Demonstrates competence in writing fictional, biographical, autobiographical, and observational narrative essays (i.e., clearly narrates a sequence of events; evaluates the significance of the incident; locates scenes and incidents in specific places; provides supporting descriptive detail [e.g., specific names for people, objects, places; visual details of scenes, objects, or places; descriptions of sounds, smells, specific actions, movements, and gestures; the interior monologue or feelings of the characters]; effectively paces the actions to accommodate time or mood changes) BP (C12E,29,30,133-134;AE,82;NS,310)

- Demonstrates competence in writing reflective essays (i.e., uses personal experience as a basis for reflection on some aspect of life, draws abstract comparisons between the specific incident and abstract concepts, maintains a balance between describing the incident and relating it to more general abstract ideas that illustrate the writer's important beliefs, moves from specific examples to generalizations about life) BP (C12E,160,161;AI,82;NS,311)

- Writes compositions that have a strong overall sense of cohesion BP (E2,20;NWI,26,27;C12I,84,133,183)

- Writes compositions that exhibit a clear personal style and voice BP (E2,20;NWI,25-27)

- Understands personal writing strengths and weaknesses and uses strategies to enhance strengths and overcome weaknesses BP (EI,20)

Codes (right side of page):   BD = Benchmark, Declarative; BP = Benchmark, Procedural; BC = Benchmark, Contextual

1st letter(s) of each code in parentheses   *2nd letter of code*   *Number*

A = Australian Education Council   E = Explicitly stated in document   Page number of cited document
C4,8: CDE: Elementary, Middle Perf. Assessments   I = Implied in document
C12 = CDE: Calif. Writing Assess. Handbook
E = NCTE: Democracy Through Language
E1,2,3: Edison Proj: Primary,Elementary,Junior Acad.   NW = NAEP: Writing Achieve. Levels-Setting Proc.
G = GESP: National Geography Standards   NY = NY Draft Framework for Eng. Lang. Arts
L = SPELA: Standards Proj. for English/Lang. Arts   S = SCANS: Report for America 2000
NR = NAEP: 1992 Reading Assessment   SS = NCSS: Curric. Standards for Social Studies
NS = NSP: Draft Standards for Eng. Lang. Arts   U = NCHS: National Standards for U.S. History
    W = Carnevale: Workplace Basics

MREL

(EI,21;SE,xviii;WI,90)
2. Demonstrates competence in the stylistic and rhetorical aspects of writing

Level I (Grades K-2)

BP (NWI,23)
- Writes compositions that make effective use of very general, frequently used words to convey basic ideas

Level II (Grades 3-5)

BP (NWE,23)
- Writes compositions that show some attempt to use descriptive language that clarifies and enhances ideas

Level III (Grades 6-8)

BP (NWI,25;E3I,34)
- Writes compositions that show clear evidence of descriptive language that clarifies and enhances ideas

BP (NWE,25)
- Writes compositions that have some explicit transitional devices

BP (NWE,25)
- Writes compositions that use a variety of sentence structures

BP (MI,78,140,150;WI,106-107)
- Makes limited but appropriate use of technical terms and notations in writing

Level IV (Grades 9-12)

BP (NWI,26)
- Writes compositions that demonstrate effective use of descriptive language that clarifies and enhances ideas

BP (NWI,26)
- Writes compositions that use a variety of transitional devices (e.g., phrases, sentences, paragraphs)

BP (NWI,26,27;AE,107)
- Writes compositions with a variety of sentence structures and lengths

BP (NWI,26)
- Makes effective use of a variety of techniques for providing supportive detail (e.g.,

---

Codes (right side of page):   BD = Benchmark, Declarative; BP = Benchmark, Procedural; BC = Benchmark, Contextual
1st letter(s) of each code in parentheses   *2nd letter of code*   *Number*
A = Australian Education Council   E = Explicitly stated in document   Page number of cited document
C4,8: CDE: Elementary, Middle Perf. Assessments   I = Implied in document
C12 = CDE: Calif. Writing Assess. Handbook
E = NCTE: Democracy Through Language   NW = NAEP: Writing Achieve. Levels-Setting Proc.
E1,2,3: Edison Proj: Primary,Elementary,Junior Acad.   NY = NY Draft Framework for Eng. Lang. Arts
G = GESP: National Geography Standards   S = SCANS: Report for America 2000
L = SPELA: Standards Proj. for English/Lang. Arts   SS = NCSS: Curric. Standards for Social Studies
NR = NAEP: 1992 Reading Assessment   U = NCHS: National Standards for U.S. History
NS = NSP: Draft Standards for Eng. Lang. Arts   W = Carnevale: Workplace Basics

MREL

analogies, anecdotes, restatements, paraphrases, examples, comparisons)

- Uses vocabulary that stimulates the imagination of the reader $\quad$ BP (NWI,26,27)

- Makes effective use of technical terms and notations in writing $\quad$ BP (MI,78,140,150;WI,106-107)

3. $\quad$ **Writes with a command of the grammatical and mechanical conventions of composition** $\quad$ (E2,21;SE,xviii;WI,90)

Level I (Grades K-2)

- Writes compositions that contain complete sentences $\quad$ BP (NWI,23)

- Writes compositions that show some attention to the proper use of pronouns $\quad$ BP (NWI,23;)

- Writes compositions that show some attention to the proper use of adjectives $\quad$ BP (NWI,23)

- Writes compositions that show some attention to the proper use of adverbial forms $\quad$ BP (NWI,23)

- Writes compositions that show some attention to the proper use of coordinating conjunctions $\quad$ BP (NWI,23)

- Writes compositions that show some evidence of correctly spelling common, frequently used words $\quad$ BP (NWI,23;E1E,25)

- Writes compositions that have few significant errors in the capitalization of words that begin sentences and shows some attention to the capitalization of proper nouns $\quad$ BP (NWI,23)

- Writes compositions that have few significant errors in the use of a period as the end punctuation mark and shows some attention to the use of the question mark $\quad$ BP (NWI,23)

- Writes compositions that have few significant errors in the formation of verb tenses and plurals $\quad$ BP (E1E,25)

- Writes compositions that have few significant errors in the use of commas in a series of words $\quad$ BP (E1E,25)

Codes (right side of page): $\quad$ BD = Benchmark, Declarative; BP = Benchmark, Procedural; BC = Benchmark, Contextual

1st letter(s) of each code in parentheses	*2nd letter of code*	*Number*
A = Australian Education Council	E = Explicitly stated in document	Page number of cited document
C4,8: CDE: Elementary, Middle Perf. Assessments	I = Implied in document	
C12 = CDE: Calif. Writing Assess. Handbook		
E = NCTE: Democracy Through Language	NW = NAEP: Writing Achieve. Levels-Setting Proc.	
E1,2,3: Edison Proj: Primary,Elementary,Junior Acad.	NY = NY Draft Framework for Eng. Lang. Arts	
G = GESP: National Geography Standards	S = SCANS: Report for America 2000	
L = SPELA: Standards Proj. for English/Lang. Arts	SS = NCSS: Curric. Standards for Social Studies	
NR = NAEP: 1992 Reading Assessment	U = NCHS: National Standards for U.S. History	
NS = NSP: Draft Standards for Eng. Lang. Arts	W = Carnevale: Workplace Basics	

McREL

Level II (Grades 3-5)

- Writes legibly   BP (LE,67)

- Writes compositions that have few significant errors in the use of personal, relative, and demonstrative pronouns   BP (NWI,24;E2I,36)

- Writes compositions that have few significant errors in the use of indefinite, numerical, and pronominal adjectives   BP (NWI,24;E2I,36)

- Writes compositions that have few significant errors in the use of adverbial forms   BP (NWI,24; E2I,36)

- Writes compositions that have few significant errors in the use of coordinating conjunctions and shows some attention to the proper use of subordinating conjunctions   BP (NWI,24;E2I,36)

- Writes compositions that have few significant errors in the spelling of common, frequently used words   BP (NWI,24;E2E,36)

- Writes compositions that have no significant errors in the capitalization of words that begin sentences and few significant errors in the capitalization of proper nouns and titles   BP (NWI,24;E2I,36)

- Writes compositions that have no significant errors in the use of ending punctuation marks (e.g., periods and quotation marks) and shows some attention to the common uses of commas   BP (NWI,24;E2I,36)

- Writes compositions that show some attention to the proper use of commonly confused terms (e.g., *affect* and *effect*)   BP (NWI,24;E2I,36)

Level III (Grades 6-8)

- Writes compositions that have no significant errors in the use of personal, relative, and demonstrative pronouns, and few significant errors in the use of reflexive pronouns, indefinite pronouns, and collective nouns   BP (NWI,25;E3I,34)

- Writes compositions that have no significant errors in the use of indefinite, numerical, and pronominal adjectives, and few significant errors in the use of descriptive adjective forms   BP (NWI,25;E3I,34)

Codes (right side of page):	BD = Benchmark, Declarative; BP = Benchmark, Procedural; BC = Benchmark, Contextual	
1st letter(s) of each code in parentheses	*2nd letter of code*	*Number*
A = Australian Education Council	E = Explicitly stated in document	Page number of cited document
C4,8: CDE: Elementary, Middle Perf. Assessments	I = Implied in document	
C12 = CDE: Calif. Writing Assess. Handbook		
E = NCTE: Democracy Through Language	NW = NAEP: Writing Achieve. Levels-Setting Proc.	
E1,2,3: Edison Proj: Primary,Elementary,Junior Acad.	NY = NY Draft Framework for Eng. Lang. Arts	
G = GESP: National Geography Standards	S = SCANS: Report for America 2000	
L = SPELA: Standards Proj. for English/Lang. Arts	SS = NCSS: Curric. Standards for Social Studies	
NR = NAEP: 1992 Reading Assessment	U = NCHS: National Standards for U.S. History	
NS = NSP: Draft Standards for Eng. Lang. Arts	W = Carnevale: Workplace Basics	

MREL

(e.g., comparative, superlative)

- Writes compositions that have no significant errors in the use of adverbial forms [BP (NWI,25;E3I,34)]

- Writes compositions that have no significant errors in the use of coordinating conjunctions and few significant errors in the use of subordinating conjunctions [BP (NWI,25;E3I,34)]

- Writes compositions that have no significant errors in the spelling of frequently used words and shows some attention to the correct spelling of commonly misspelled words and less common words [BP (NWI,25;E3I,34;AE,61)]

- Writes compositions that have no significant errors in the common conventions of capitalization (i.e., words that begin sentences, proper nouns, names, titles) and shows some attention to the less common capitalization conventions (e.g., capitalizing the names of nationalities) [BP (NWI,25;E3I,34)]

- Writes compositions that have no significant errors in the use of ending punctuation marks (e.g., periods and quotation marks), few significant errors in the common uses of commas, and shows some attention to the proper use of the colon, semicolon, hyphen, dash, apostrophe, and quotation marks [BP (NWI,25;E3I,34)]

- Writes compositions that have few significant errors in the proper use of commonly confused terms (e.g., *affect* and *effect*) and shows some attention to the proper use of clichés [BP (NWI,25;E3I,34)]

- Writes compositions that show some attention to the proper use of italics, marginal notes, and footnotes [BP (SSI,148;E3I,35)]

Level IV (Grades 9-12)

- Writes compositions that have no significant errors in the use of personal, relative, demonstrative, reflexive, and indefinite pronouns and collective nouns [BP (NWI,26)]

- Writes compositions that have no significant errors in the use of indefinite, pronominal, descriptive, and other adjectival forms [BP (NWI,26)]

Codes (right side of page):	BD = Benchmark, Declarative; BP = Benchmark, Procedural; BC = Benchmark, Contextual	
1st letter(s) of each code in parentheses	*2nd letter of code*	*Number*
A = Australian Education Council	E = Explicitly stated in document	Page number of cited document
C4,8: CDE: Elementary, Middle Perf. Assessments	I = Implied in document	
C12 = CDE: Calif. Writing Assess. Handbook		
E = NCTE: Democracy Through Language	NW = NAEP: Writing Achieve. Levels-Setting Proc.	
E1,2,3: Edison Proj: Primary,Elementary,Junior Acad.	NY = NY Draft Framework for Eng. Lang. Arts	
G = GESP: National Geography Standards	S = SCANS: Report for America 2000	
L = SPELA: Standards Proj. for English/Lang. Arts	SS = NCSS: Curric. Standards for Social Studies	
NR = NAEP: 1992 Reading Assessment	U = NCHS: National Standards for U.S. History	
NS = NSP: Draft Standards for Eng. Lang. Arts	W = Carnevale: Workplace Basics	

McREL

- Writes compositions that have no significant errors in the use of adverbial forms ^{BP (NWI,26)}

- Writes compositions that have no significant errors in the use of coordinating and subordinating conjunctions ^{BP (NWI,26)}

- Writes compositions that have no significant errors in the spelling of frequently used words and few significant errors in the spelling of commonly misspelled and rare words ^{BP (NWI,26;AI,83)}

- Writes compositions that have no significant errors in the common conventions of capitalization (i.e., words that begin sentences, proper nouns, names, titles) and few significant errors in the less common capitalization conventions (e.g., capitalizing the names of nationalities) ^{BP (NWI,26)}

- Writes compositions that have no significant errors in the use of ending punctuation marks (e.g., periods and quotation marks) and common uses of commas, and few significant errors in the common use of the colon, semicolon, hyphen, dash, apostrophe, and quotation marks ^{BP (NWI,26)}

- Writes compositions that have no significant errors in the proper use of commonly confused terms (e.g., *affect* and *effect*) and few significant errors in the proper use of cliches ^{BP (NWI,26)}

- Writes compositions that have few significant errors in the use of italics, marginal notes, and footnotes ^{BP (SSI,148)}

- Understands that language usage may be correct or incorrect, depending on the situation in which it is used ^{BD (E2,20)}

4. Effectively gathers and uses information for research purposes [SSE,149;WE,106]

Level I (Grades K-2)

- Formulates questions about family or background that would require consulting family artifacts and other family records of the past ^{BC (GE,46)}

Codes (right side of page):	BD = Benchmark, Declarative; BP = Benchmark, Procedural; BC = Benchmark, Contextual
1st letter(s) of each code in parentheses	*2nd letter of code* *Number*
A = Australian Education Council	E = Explicitly stated in document Page number of cited document
C4,8: CDE: Elementary, Middle Perf. Assessments	I = Implied in document
C12 = CDE: Calif. Writing Assess. Handbook	
E = NCTE: Democracy Through Language	NW = NAEP: Writing Achieve. Levels-Setting Proc.
E1,2,3: Edison Proj: Primary,Elementary,Junior Acad.	NY = NY Draft Framework for Eng. Lang. Arts
G = GESP: National Geography Standards	S = SCANS: Report for America 2000
L = SPELA: Standards Proj. for English/Lang. Arts	SS = NCSS: Curric. Standards for Social Studies
NR = NAEP: 1992 Reading Assessment	U = NCHS: National Standards for U.S. History
NS = NSP: Draft Standards for Eng. Lang. Arts	W = Carnevale: Workplace Basics

MREL

Level II (Grades 3-5)

- Asks and seeks to answer questions regarding the characteristics of various places outside the local community and the people who live in those places
  BC (GE,46)

- Asks and seeks to answer questions about people and places in one's local community (e.g., school, neighborhood)
  BC (GI,46)

- Uses encyclopedias to gather information for research topics
  BP (SSE,148)

- Uses dictionaries to gather information for research topics
  BP (SSE,148)

- Uses key words, indexes, cross references, and letters on volumes to find information for research topics
  BP (SSE,148)

- Uses multiple representations of information (e.g., maps, charts, photos) to find information for research topics
  BP (GI,48)

- Has a basic understanding of the concept of a primary source
  BD (GE,48)

Level III (Grades 6-8)

- Gathers and synthesizes data for research topics from interviews and field surveys
  BP (LI,45;GE,49,50;C4I,36)

- Gathers information for research topics using note taking
  BP (LI,32,45;GE,49,50;C4E,36)

- Separates information gathered for a research topic into major components based on appropriate criteria
  BP (GI,49;SSE,149;C4E,36)

- Examines critical relationships between and among elements of a research topic
  BP (GI,49;SSE,149;C4I,36)

- Uses the card catalogue to locate books for research reports
  BP (GI,49;SSE,148;C4I,36)

- Uses the *Reader's Guide to Periodical Literature* and other indexes to gather information for research topics
  BP (GI,49;SSE,148;C4I,36)

Codes (right side of page): BD = Benchmark, Declarative; BP = Benchmark, Procedural; BC = Benchmark, Contextual

1st letter(s) of each code in parentheses	*2nd letter of code*	*Number*
A = Australian Education Council	E = Explicitly stated in document	Page number of cited document
C4,8: CDE: Elementary, Middle Perf. Assessments	I = Implied in document	
C12 = CDE: Calif. Writing Assess. Handbook		
E = NCTE: Democracy Through Language	NW = NAEP: Writing Achieve. Levels-Setting Proc.	
E1,2,3: Edison Proj: Primary,Elementary,Junior Acad.	NY = NY Draft Framework for Eng. Lang. Arts	
G = GESP: National Geography Standards	S = SCANS: Report for America 2000	
L = SPELA: Standards Proj. for English/Lang. Arts	SS = NCSS: Curric. Standards for Social Studies	
NR = NAEP: 1992 Reading Assessment	U = NCHS: National Standards for U.S. History	
NS = NSP: Draft Standards for Eng. Lang. Arts	W = Carnevale: Workplace Basics	

McREL

- Uses a computer catalog to gather information for research topics ^BP (SSE,148;C4I,36)

- Uses magazines, newspapers, dictionaries, schedules, and journals to gather information for research topics ^BP (GE,49;SSE,148;C4I,36)

- Makes limited but effective use of primary sources when researching topics ^BP (GI,49;UI,25;C4E,35)

- Considers the importance of primary sources from the perspective of the validity and reliability of the information ^BP (UE,25,27)

- Understands the concept of a "likely informant" for obtaining information about a specific topic ^BC (GE,49)

- Takes photographs or makes short videos or sketches as a way of collecting field data for a research project ^BP (GE,50)

Level IV (Grades 9-12)

- Creates bibliographies for research topics ^BP (GI,53;SSE,148)

- Uses cross referencing while gathering information for a research topic ^BP (GI,53,54;WE,64,90)

- Writes basic descriptions of events to record information for research purposes ^BP (GI,53,54;WE,106)

- Summarizes dialogues for the purpose of collecting information for research purposes ^BP (GI,53,54;WE,106)

- Uses almanacs to gather information for research purposes ^BP (GI,53,54;SSE,148)

- Uses government publications to gather information for research purposes ^BP (GI,53,54;SSE,148)

- Uses microfiche to gather information for research purposes ^BP (GI,53,54;SSE,148)

- Uses a variety of news sources to gather information for research purposes (e.g., newspapers, news magazines, TV, radio, videotapes, artifacts) ^BP (GI,53,54;SSE,148)

Codes (right side of page): BD = Benchmark, Declarative; BP = Benchmark, Procedural; BC = Benchmark, Contextual
1st letter(s) of each code in parentheses — *2nd letter of code* — *Number*
A = Australian Education Council — E = Explicitly stated in document — Page number of cited document
C4,8: CDE: Elementary, Middle Perf. Assessments — I = Implied in document
C12 = CDE: Calif. Writing Assess. Handbook
E = NCTE: Democracy Through Language — NW = NAEP: Writing Achieve. Levels-Setting Proc.
E1,2,3: Edison Proj: Primary,Elementary,Junior Acad. — NY = NY Draft Framework for Eng. Lang. Arts
G = GESP: National Geography Standards — S = SCANS: Report for America 2000
L = SPELA: Standards Proj. for English/Lang. Arts — SS = NCSS: Curric. Standards for Social Studies
NR = NAEP: 1992 Reading Assessment — U = NCHS: National Standards for U.S. History
NS = NSP: Draft Standards for Eng. Lang. Arts — W = Carnevale: Workplace Basics

- Uses public library telephone information services to gather information for research purposes ^{BP (GI,53,54;SSI,148)}

- Synthesizes a variety of types of visual information including pictures and symbols when researching a topic ^{BP (GI,53,54;SE,xviii;WI,90)}

- Makes extensive use of primary sources when researching a topic and makes careful consideration of the motives and perspectives of the authors of those sources ^{BP (GI,53,54;UI,27,28)}

- Makes in-depth analyses of the validity and reliability of primary source information and uses information accordingly in reporting on a research topic ^{BP (GI,53,54;UE,27)}

- Identifies and uses "likely informants" to gather information for a research topic ^{BP (GI,54)}

- Conducts research using data from in-depth field studies ^{BP (GI,54)}

- Synthesizes information from multiple research studies to draw conclusions that go beyond those found in any of the individual studies ^{BP (GE,55)}

- Identifies and defends research questions and topics that will be important in the future ^{BP (GI,56)}

5. Demonstrates competence in the general skills and strategies of the reading process ^(E2,3,20;SE,xviii;SSE,148;WI,90)

Level I (Grades K-2)

- Understands that reading is a way of gaining information about the world ^{BD (LI,62)}

- Creates mental pictures for concrete information one has read ^{BP (SI,xviii;WI,90)}

- Uses picture clues and picture captions as an aid to comprehension ^{BP (SSE,148)}

- Decodes unknown words using basic elements of phonetic analysis (e.g., common letter/sound relationships) and structural analysis (e.g., syllables, basic prefixes, and suffixes) ^{BP (SSE,148)}

Codes (right side of page):   BD = Benchmark, Declarative;   BP = Benchmark, Procedural;   BC = Benchmark, Contextual

1st letter(s) of each code in parentheses	*2nd letter of code*	*Number*
A = Australian Education Council	E = Explicitly stated in document	Page number of cited document
C4,8: CDE: Elementary, Middle Perf. Assessments	I = Implied in document	
C12 = CDE: Calif. Writing Assess. Handbook		
E = NCTE: Democracy Through Language	NW = NAEP: Writing Achieve. Levels-Setting Proc.	
E1,2,3: Edison Proj: Primary,Elementary,Junior Acad.	NY = NY Draft Framework for Eng. Lang. Arts	
G = GESP: National Geography Standards	S = SCANS: Report for America 2000	
L = SPELA: Standards Proj. for English/Lang. Arts	SS = NCSS: Curric. Standards for Social Studies	
NR = NAEP: 1992 Reading Assessment	U = NCHS: National Standards for U.S. History	
NS = NSP: Draft Standards for Eng. Lang. Arts	W = Carnevale: Workplace Basics	

MREL

Level II (Grades 3-5)

- Makes and confirms simple predictions about what will be found in a text ^BP (LI,54;SSI,148)

- Effectively decodes unknown words using a variety of context clues ^BP (E2,4;SSE,148;WI,90-91)

- Determines the meaning of unknown words using a glossary and dictionary ^BP (E2,19;SSE,148)

- Adjusts speed of reading to suit purpose and difficulty of the material ^BP (SSE,148)

- Recognizes when a text is primarily intended to persuade ^BP (NRI,17)

- Decodes words not recognized immediately by using phonetic and structural analysis techniques, the syntactic structure in which the word appears, and the semantic context surrounding the word ^BP (NRI,39)

- Recognizes when she or he is confused by a section of text ^BP (NRI,32,33)

- Represents concrete information (e.g., persons, places, things, events) as explicit mental pictures ^BP (MI,81;NRI,4;SI,xvii;WI,90)

Level III (Grades 6-8)

- Generates interesting questions to be answered while reading ^BP (LI,54)

- Reflects on what has been learned after reading ^BP (LI,54)

- Identifies specific devices an author is using to persuade readers ^BP (NRI,17,18)

- Uses specific strategies to clear up confusing parts of a text (e.g., rereads the text, consults another source, asks for help) ^BP (NRI,32,33)

- Represents abstract information (e.g., concepts, generalizations) as explicit mental pictures ^BP (NRI,4,16)

- Understands stories and expository texts from the perspective of the attitudes and values of the time period in which they were written ^BP (UI,25)

Codes (right side of page):   BD = Benchmark, Declarative;   BP = Benchmark, Procedural;   BC = Benchmark, Contextual

1st letter(s) of each code in parentheses	*2nd letter of code*	*Number*
A = Australian Education Council	E = Explicitly stated in document	Page number of cited document
C4,8: CDE: Elementary, Middle Perf. Assessments	I = Implied in document	
C12 = CDE: Calif. Writing Assess. Handbook		
E = NCTE: Democracy Through Language	NW = NAEP: Writing Achieve. Levels-Setting Proc.	
E1,2,3: Edison Proj: Primary,Elementary,Junior Acad.	NY = NY Draft Framework for Eng. Lang. Arts	
G = GESP: National Geography Standards	S = SCANS: Report for America 2000	
L = SPELA: Standards Proj. for English/Lang. Arts	SS = NCSS: Curric. Standards for Social Studies	
NR = NAEP: 1992 Reading Assessment	U = NCHS: National Standards for U.S. History	
NS = NSP: Draft Standards for Eng. Lang. Arts	W = Carnevale: Workplace Basics	

McREL

- Accurately identifies author's purpose

  BP (NRI,17;UI,21,27,28)

- Accurately identifies author's point of view

  BP (NRI,17;UI,21,27,28)

Level IV (Grades 9-12)

- Determines figurative, idiomatic, and technical meanings of terms through context

  BP (WE,90)

- Determines the meaning of abbreviations and acronyms from context

  BP (WE,90)

- Understands that reading is a gradual process of constructing meaning and making revisions of initial understandings

  BD (LI,31)

- Represents key ideas and supporting details in outline or graph form

  BC (LI,53;WE,106-17)

- Recognizes when and why one is responding to the text

  BP (LI,30)

- Understands that reactions to a text will change throughout the course of reading the text

  BD (LI,30)

- Accurately identifies author's purpose and analyzes the effects of that purpose on the text

  BP (NRI,17,18;UI,21,27,28)

- Accurately identifies the author's point of view and analyzes the effects of that point of view on the text

  BP (NRI,17,18;UI,21,27,28)

- Understands that a single text will elicit a wide variety of responses, each of which is valid from a personal, subjective perspective

  BD (LE,32)

- Understands that readers have the right and even the responsibility to bring their own values to bear as they respond to a text

  BD (LE,32)

- Identifies the devices an author is using to persuade readers, and critiques the effectiveness of the use of those devices

  BP (NRI,17,19)

- Understands relatively uncommon technical terms used in informational texts

  BD (NRI,5)

Codes (right side of page):   BD = Benchmark, Declarative; BP = Benchmark, Procedural; BC = Benchmark, Contextual
1st letter(s) of each code in parentheses   *2nd letter of code*   *Number*
A = Australian Education Council   E = Explicitly stated in document   Page number of cited document
C4,8: CDE: Elementary, Middle Perf. Assessments   I = Implied in document
C12 = CDE: Calif. Writing Assess. Handbook
E = NCTE: Democracy Through Language
E1,2,3: Edison Proj: Primary,Elementary,Junior Acad.   NW = NAEP: Writing Achieve. Levels-Setting Proc.
G = GESP: National Geography Standards   NY = NY Draft Framework for Eng. Lang. Arts
L = SPELA: Standards Proj. for English/Lang. Arts   S = SCANS: Report for America 2000
NR = NAEP: 1992 Reading Assessment   SS = NCSS: Curric. Standards for Social Studies
NS = NSP: Draft Standards for Eng. Lang. Arts   U = NCHS: National Standards for U.S. History
    W = Carnevale: Workplace Basics

MREL

- Analyzes the overall effectiveness of one's own reading
  BP (NRI,32,33)

- Identifies and analyzes the philosophical assumptions and basic beliefs underlying an author's work
  BP (NRI,4,16)

- Analyzes the effects on the text of the attitudes and values of the time period in which a text was written
  BP (UI,25)

- Determines the meaning of codes and symbols from context
  BP (WE,90)

6. Demonstrates competence in general skills and strategies for reading literature
(E2,3,20;SE,xviii;SSE,148;WI,90)

Level I (Grades K-2)

- Comprehends the basic plot of simple stories
  BP (LI,34-37,54;E2,4)

- Makes simple inferences regarding "what will happen next" or "how things could have turned out differently"
  BP (NSE,296)

Level II (Grades 3-5)

- Is aware of the geographic information important to the stories one reads
  BP (GE,46)

- Uses specific aspects of a piece of literature to better understand the actions of others in one's life
  BP (LI,14-17)

- Shares responses to literature with peers
  BC (LI,26)

- Identifies the main characters in works containing only a few basic characters
  BP (NRI,4,14)

- Explains how characters or simple events in a work are like people or events in one's own life
  BC (LI,14-17;NRI,15)

- Understands simple dialogues and how they relate to a story
  BP (NRI,4)

Codes (right side of page):   BD = Benchmark, Declarative; BP = Benchmark, Procedural; BC = Benchmark, Contextual

1st letter(s) of each code in parentheses	*2nd letter of code*	*Number*
A = Australian Education Council	E = Explicitly stated in document	Page number of cited document
C4,8: CDE: Elementary, Middle Perf. Assessments	I = Implied in document	
C12 = CDE: Calif. Writing Assess. Handbook		
E = NCTE: Democracy Through Language	NW = NAEP: Writing Achieve. Levels-Setting Proc.	
E1,2,3: Edison Proj: Primary,Elementary,Junior Acad.	NY = NY Draft Framework for Eng. Lang. Arts	
G = GESP: National Geography Standards	S = SCANS: Report for America 2000	
L = SPELA: Standards Proj. for English/Lang. Arts	SS = NCSS: Curric. Standards for Social Studies	
NR = NAEP: 1992 Reading Assessment	U = NCHS: National Standards for U.S. History	
NS = NSP: Draft Standards for Eng. Lang. Arts	W = Carnevale: Workplace Basics	

MREL

- Recognizes basic elements of a plot

  BP (LI,34-37,54;NRI,4)

- Makes inferences regarding the motives of characters and the consequences of their actions

  BP (AE,36)

Level III (Grades 6-8)

- Understands that people respond differently to literature

  BD (LE,17-21)

- Identifies specific questions of personal importance and seeks to answer them through literature

  BP (LI,24)

- Identifies specific interests and the literature that will satisfy those interests

  BP (LE,26)

- Identifies the main and subordinate characters in works containing complex character structures

  BP (NRI,4,14)

- Explains how the motives of characters or the causes for complex events in texts are similar to and different from those in one's own life

  BC (NRI,15)

- Understands complex, extended dialogues and how they relate to a story

  BP (NRI,4)

- Recognizes the use of specific literary devices (e.g., foreshadowing, flashback, progressive time, digressive time)

  BP (NRI,4)

- Recognizes complex elements of plot (e.g., setting, major events, problems, conflicts, resolutions)

  BP (NRI,24)

Level IV (Grades 9-12)

- Relates personal response to the text with that intended by the author

  BP (LI,27)

- Identifies the simple and complex actions (e.g., internal/external conflicts) between main and subordinate characters in texts containing complex character structures

  BP (NRI,4,14,24)

Codes (right side of page): BD = Benchmark, Declarative; BP = Benchmark, Procedural; BC = Benchmark, Contextual
1st letter(s) of each code in parentheses *2nd letter of code* *Number*
A = Australian Education Council E = Explicitly stated in document Page number of cited document
C4,8: CDE: Elementary, Middle Perf. Assessments I = Implied in document
C12 = CDE: Calif. Writing Assess. Handbook
E = NCTE: Democracy Through Language NW = NAEP: Writing Achieve. Levels-Setting Proc.
E1,2,3: Edison Proj: Primary,Elementary,Junior Acad. NY = NY Draft Framework for Eng. Lang. Arts
G = GESP: National Geography Standards S = SCANS: Report for America 2000
L = SPELA: Standards Proj. for English/Lang. Arts SS = NCSS: Curric. Standards for Social Studies
NR = NAEP: 1992 Reading Assessment U = NCHS: National Standards for U.S. History
NS = NSP: Draft Standards for Eng. Lang. Arts W = Carnevale: Workplace Basics

MREL

- Makes abstract connections between one's own life and the characters, events, motives, and causes of conflict in texts $\quad$ BC (NRI,15)

- Understands complex dialogues and analyzes the stylistic effect of those dialogues on a story $\quad$ BP (NRI,4,16)

- Analyzes the effects of complex literary devices on the overall quality of a work (e.g., foreshadowing, flashbacks, progressive time, digressive time) $\quad$ BP (NRI,4,16,19)

- Analyzes the effectiveness of complex elements of plot (e.g., setting, major events, problems, conflicts, resolutions) $\quad$ BP (NRI,16,29,24)

7. Demonstrates competence in the general skills and strategies for reading information $\quad$ (NRI,4)

Level I (Grades K-2)

- Comprehends the main idea of simple expository information $\quad$ BC (LI,34-37,54;E2,3)

Level II (Grades 3-5)

- Uses chapter and section headings, topic sentences, and summary sentences to construct the main ideas $\quad$ BP (SSE,148)

- Understands the uses of the various parts of a book (index, table of contents, glossary, appendix) $\quad$ BD (SSE,148)

- Attempts to identify the author's purpose when reading expository information $\quad$ BP (NRI,5)

- Attempts to identify the author's point of view when reading expository information $\quad$ BP (NRI,5)

- Identifies simple hierarchic structures in informational texts (e.g., one main idea or concept with supporting or illustrative detail) $\quad$ BP (LI,34-37,54;E2,4;NRI,5,18;SSE,148)

- Recognizes when a text is primarily intended to persuade $\quad$ BP (NRI,17)

Codes (right side of page):   BD = Benchmark, Declarative;   BP = Benchmark, Procedural;   BC = Benchmark, Contextual

1st letter(s) of each code in parentheses   *2nd letter of code*   *Number*

A = Australian Education Council   E = Explicitly stated in document   Page number of cited document

C4,8: CDE: Elementary, Middle Perf. Assessments   I = Implied in document

C12 = CDE: Calif. Writing Assess. Handbook

E = NCTE: Democracy Through Language   NW = NAEP: Writing Achieve. Levels-Setting Proc.

E1,2,3: Edison Proj: Primary,Elementary,Junior Acad.   NY = NY Draft Framework for Eng. Lang. Arts

G = GESP: National Geography Standards   S = SCANS: Report for America 2000

L = SPELA: Standards Proj. for English/Lang. Arts   SS = NCSS: Curric. Standards for Social Studies

NR = NAEP: 1992 Reading Assessment   U = NCHS: National Standards for U.S. History

NS = NSP: Draft Standards for Eng. Lang. Arts   W = Carnevale: Workplace Basics

MREL

- Understands commonly used technical terms in informational texts $\qquad$ BD (NRI,5)

- Recognizes when information presented in a text is new knowledge $\qquad$ BP (NRI,18)

Level III (Grades 6-8)

- Seeks peer help to understand information $\qquad$ BC (LI,58)

- Identifies information-organizing strategies that are personally most useful $\qquad$ BD (LE,56)

- Reads for a variety of purposes including to answer a specific question, to form an opinion, to skim for facts $\qquad$ BP (LE,56;SSE,148)

- Identifies complex, explicit hierarchic structures in informational texts (e.g., two or more explicit main ideas or concepts with supporting or illustrative detail) $\qquad$ BP (NRI,5,18,19)

- Generates implied generalizations from informational texts along with the specific information that supports these generalizations $\qquad$ BP (NRI,18)

- Recognizes when information presented in a text is new knowledge and describes how it can be used $\qquad$ BP (NRI,18,19)

- Understands somewhat common technical terms used in informational texts $\qquad$ BD (NRI,5)

- Uses the various parts of a text (index, table of contents, glossary) to locate specific information $\qquad$ BP (SSE,148)

Level IV (Grades 9-12)

- Scans a passage to determine whether a text contains relevant information $\qquad$ BP (WE,90-91)

- Uses discussions with peers as a way of understanding information $\qquad$ BP (LI,32)

- Identifies complex, implicit hierarchic structures in informational texts and the relationships $\qquad$ BP (NRI,5,18,19)

Codes (right side of page):   BD = Benchmark, Declarative; BP = Benchmark, Procedural; BC = Benchmark, Contextual
1st letter(s) of each code in parentheses   *2nd letter of code*   *Number*
A = Australian Education Council   E = Explicitly stated in document   Page number of cited document
C4,8: CDE: Elementary, Middle Perf. Assessments   I = Implied in document
C12 = CDE: Calif. Writing Assess. Handbook
E = NCTE: Democracy Through Language   NW = NAEP: Writing Achieve. Levels-Setting Proc.
E1,2,3: Edison Proj: Primary,Elementary,Junior Acad.   NY = NY Draft Framework for Eng. Lang. Arts
G = GESP: National Geography Standards   S = SCANS: Report for America 2000
L = SPELA: Standards Proj. for English/Lang. Arts   SS = NCSS: Curric. Standards for Social Studies
NR = NAEP: 1992 Reading Assessment   U = NCHS: National Standards for U.S. History
NS = NSP: Draft Standards for Eng. Lang. Arts   W = Carnevale: Workplace Basics

McREL

between the concepts and details in those structures

- Reorganizes the concepts and details in informational texts in new ways and describes the advantages and disadvantages of the new organization ^{BC (NRI,18,19)}

- Recognizes how the new information gleaned from a text has changed one's personal knowledge base ^{BP (NRI,18,19)}

- Effectively uses indexes, appendixes, glossaries, and tables of contents ^{BP (SSE,148;WE,90)}

- Understands mathematical notations presented in writing ^{BD (MI,140)}

8. Demonstrates competence in applying the reading process to specific types of literary texts ^(SE,xviii;WE,90)

Level I (Grades K-2)

- Not appropriate for this level ^{BP (NRE,3)}

Level II (Grades 3-5)

- Independently applies the reading process and strategies to passages from fantasies, fables, and fairy tales that are relatively short (i.e., 400 to 800 words in length); developmentally appropriate with regard to complexity of character, plot, theme, and dialogue; and appropriately sophisticated with regard to literary devices, point of view, and style ^{BP (NRE,3)}

- Understands the defining features and structure of fantasies, fables and fairy tales at this developmental level ^{BD (NRE,3)}

- Independently applies the reading process and strategies to passages from mysteries, realistic fiction, adventure stories, and humorous stories that are relatively short (i.e., 400 to 800 words in length); developmentally appropriate with regard to complexity of character, plot, theme, and dialogue; and appropriately sophisticated with regard to literary devices, point of view, and style ^{BP (NRE,3)}

Codes (right side of page):   BD = Benchmark, Declarative; BP = Benchmark, Procedural; BC = Benchmark, Contextual

1st letter(s) of each code in parentheses	*2nd letter of code*	*Number*
A = Australian Education Council	E = Explicitly stated in document	Page number of cited document
C4,8: CDE: Elementary, Middle Perf. Assessments	I = Implied in document	
C12 = CDE: Calif. Writing Assess. Handbook		
E = NCTE: Democracy Through Language	NW = NAEP: Writing Achieve. Levels-Setting Proc.	
E1,2,3: Edison Proj: Primary,Elementary,Junior Acad.	NY = NY Draft Framework for Eng. Lang. Arts	
G = GESP: National Geography Standards	S = SCANS: Report for America 2000	
L = SPELA: Standards Proj. for English/Lang. Arts	SS = NCSS: Curric. Standards for Social Studies	
NR = NAEP: 1992 Reading Assessment	U = NCHS: National Standards for U.S. History	
NS = NSP: Draft Standards for Eng. Lang. Arts	W = Carnevale: Workplace Basics	

MREL

- Understands the defining features and structure of mysteries, realistic fiction, adventure stories and humorous stories at this developmental level ^BD NRE,3)

- Independently applies the reading process and strategies to passages from myths and historical fiction that are relatively short (i.e., 400 to 800 words in length); developmentally appropriate with regard to complexity of character, plot, theme, and dialogue; and appropriately sophisticated with regard to literary devices, point of view, and style ^BP (NRE,3;UI,21,27,28,30)

- Understands the defining features and structure of myths and historical fiction at this developmental level ^BD (NRE,3;UI,21,27,28,30)

- Independently applies the reading process and strategies to biographic and autobiographic passages that are relatively short (i.e., 400 to 800 words in length); developmentally appropriate with regard to complexity of character, plot, theme, and dialogue; and appropriately sophisticated with regard to literary devices, point of view, and style ^BP (NRE,3;UI,21,27,28,30)

- Understands the defining features and structure of biographies and autobiographies at this developmental level ^BD (NRE,3;UI,21,27,28,30)

- Independently applies the reading process and strategies to letters and diary passages that are relatively short (i.e., 250 to 800 words in length); developmentally appropriate with regard to number and complexity of character and theme(s); and appropriately sophisticated with regard to literary devices, point of view, and style ^BP (NRE,4;UI,21,27,28,30)

- Understands the defining features and structure of letters and diary passages at this developmental level ^BD (NRE,4;UI,21,27,28,30)

Level III (Grades 6-8)

- Independently applies the reading process and strategies to passages about myths that are of moderate length (i.e., at least 1,000 words in length); developmentally appropriate with regard to complexity of character, plot, theme, and dialogue; and appropriately sophisticated with regard to literary devices, point of view, and style ^BP (NRE,3;UI,21,27,28,30)

Codes (right side of page):   BD = Benchmark, Declarative; BP = Benchmark, Procedural; BC = Benchmark, Contextual

1st letter(s) of each code in parentheses	*2nd letter of code*	*Number*
A = Australian Education Council	E = Explicitly stated in document	Page number of cited document
C4,8: CDE: Elementary, Middle Perf. Assessments	I = Implied in document	
C12 = CDE: Calif. Writing Assess. Handbook		
E = NCTE: Democracy Through Language	NW = NAEP: Writing Achieve. Levels-Setting Proc.	
E1,2,3: Edison Proj: Primary,Elementary,Junior Acad.	NY = NY Draft Framework for Eng. Lang. Arts	
G = GESP: National Geography Standards	S = SCANS: Report for America 2000	
L = SPELA: Standards Proj. for English/Lang. Arts	SS = NCSS: Curric. Standards for Social Studies	
NR = NAEP: 1992 Reading Assessment	U = NCHS: National Standards for U.S. History	
NS = NSP: Draft Standards for Eng. Lang. Arts	W = Carnevale: Workplace Basics	

MREL

- Understands the defining features and structure of myths at this developmental level   BD (NRE,3;UI,21,27,28,30)

- Independently applies the reading process and strategies to passages about mysteries, realistic fiction, adventure stories, and humorous passages that are of moderate length (i.e., at least 1000 words in length); developmentally appropriate with regard to complexity of character, plot, theme, and dialogue; and appropriately sophisticated with regard to literary devices, point of view, and style BP (NRE,3)

- Understands the defining features and structure of mysteries, realistic fiction, adventure stories, and humorous pieces at this developmental level BD (NRE,3)

- Independently applies the reading process and strategies to biographical and autobiographical passages that are of moderate length (i.e., at least 1,000 words in length); developmentally appropriate with regard to complexity of character, plot, theme, and dialogue; and appropriately sophisticated with regard to literary devices, point of view, and style BP (NRE,3;UI,21,27,28,30)

- Understands the defining features and structure of biographies and autobiographies at this developmental level BD (NRE,3;UI,21,27,28,30)

- Independently applies the reading process and strategies to passages about science fiction, fantasies, tall tales, and supernatural tales that are of moderate length (i.e., at least 1,000 words in length); developmentally appropriate with regard to complexity of character, plot, theme, and dialogue; and appropriately sophisticated with regard to literary devices, point of view, and style BP (NRE,3)

- Understands the defining features and structure of science fiction, fantasies, tall tales, and supernatural tales at this developmental level BD (NRE,3)

- Independently applies the reading process and strategies to poems that are about 1,000 words in length; developmentally appropriate with regard to complexity of theme(s); and appropriately sophisticated with regard to literary devices, point of view, and style BP (NRE,3)

- Understands the defining features and structure of poems at this developmental level BD (NRE,3)

Codes (right side of page): | BD = Benchmark, Declarative; BP = Benchmark, Procedural; BC = Benchmark, Contextual

1st letter(s) of each code in parentheses | *2nd letter of code* | *Number*
A = Australian Education Council | E = Explicitly stated in document | Page number of cited document
C4,8: CDE: Elementary, Middle Perf. Assessments | I = Implied in document
C12 = CDE: Calif. Writing Assess. Handbook
E = NCTE: Democracy Through Language | NW = NAEP: Writing Achieve. Levels-Setting Proc.
E1,2,3: Edison Proj: Primary,Elementary,Junior Acad. | NY = NY Draft Framework for Eng. Lang. Arts
G = GESP: National Geography Standards | S = SCANS: Report for America 2000
L = SPELA: Standards Proj. for English/Lang. Arts | SS = NCSS: Curric. Standards for Social Studies
NR = NAEP: 1992 Reading Assessment | U = NCHS: National Standards for U.S. History
NS = NSP: Draft Standards for Eng. Lang. Arts | W = Carnevale: Workplace Basics

MREL

- Independently applies the reading process and strategies to letters and diaries that are about 1,000 words in length; developmentally appropriate with regard to number and complexity of character and theme(s); and appropriately sophisticated with regard to literary devices, point of view and style

  BP (NRE,5;UI,21,27,28,30)

- Understands the defining features and structure of letters and diaries at this developmental level

  BD (NRE,5;UI,21,27,28,30)

Level IV (Grades 9-12)

- Independently applies the reading process and strategies to myths that are of substantial length (i.e., 1,500 words to book length); developmentally appropriate with regard to complexity of character, plot, theme, and dialogue; and appropriately sophisticated with regard to literary devices, point of view, and style

  BP (NRE,4;UI,21,27,28,30)

- Understands the defining features and structure of myths at this developmental level

  BD (NRE,4;UI,21,27,28,30)

- Independently applies the reading process and strategies to fiction (mysteries, fantasies, humorous passages) that are of substantial length (i.e., 1,500 words to book length); developmentally appropriate with regard to complexity of character, plot, theme, and dialogue; and appropriately sophisticated with regard to literary devices, point of view, and style

  BP (NRE,4)

- Understands the defining features and structure of fiction (mysteries, fantasies, humorous pieces) at this developmental level

  BP (NRE,4)

- Independently applies the reading process and strategies to biographies and autobiographies that are of substantial length (i.e., 1,500 words to book length); developmentally appropriate with regard to complexity of character, plot, theme, and dialogue; and appropriately sophisticated with regard to literary devices, point of view, and style

  BP (NRE,4;UI,21,27,28,30)

- Understands the defining features and structure of biographies and autobiographies at this developmental level

  BD (NRE,4;UI,21,27,28,30)

Codes (right side of page):   BD = Benchmark, Declarative;   BP = Benchmark, Procedural;   BC = Benchmark, Contextual

1st letter(s) of each code in parentheses	*2nd letter of code*	*Number*
A = Australian Education Council	E = Explicitly stated in document	Page number of cited document
C4,8: CDE: Elementary, Middle Perf. Assessments	I = Implied in document	
C12 = CDE: Calif. Writing Assess. Handbook		
E = NCTE: Democracy Through Language	NW = NAEP: Writing Achieve. Levels-Setting Proc.	
E1,2,3: Edison Proj: Primary,Elementary,Junior Acad.	NY = NY Draft Framework for Eng. Lang. Arts	
G = GESP: National Geography Standards	S = SCANS: Report for America 2000	
L = SPELA: Standards Proj. for English/Lang. Arts	SS = NCSS: Curric. Standards for Social Studies	
NR = NAEP: 1992 Reading Assessment	U = NCHS: National Standards for U.S. History	
NS = NSP: Draft Standards for Eng. Lang. Arts	W = Carnevale: Workplace Basics	

MREL

- Independently applies the reading process and strategies to science fiction and supernatural tales that are substantial in length (i.e., 1,500 words to book length); developmentally appropriate with regard to complexity of character, plot, theme, and dialogue; and appropriately sophisticated with regard to literary devices, point of view, and style ^BP (NRE,4)

- Understands the defining features and structure of science fiction and supernatural tales at this developmental level ^BD (NRE,4)

- Independently applies the reading process and strategies to poems that are about 1,500 words in length; developmentally appropriate with regard to complexity of theme(s); and appropriately sophisticated with regard to literary devices, point of view, and style ^BP (NRE,4)

- Understands the defining features and structure of poems at this developmental level ^BP (NRE,4)

- Independently applies the reading process and strategies to satires and parodies that are of substantial length (i.e., 1,500 words to book length); developmentally appropriate with regard to complexity of character, plot, theme, and dialogue; and appropriately sophisticated with regard to literary devices, point of view, and style ^BP (NRE,4)

- Understands the defining features and structure of satires and parodies at this developmental level ^BD (NRE,4)

- Independently applies the reading process and strategies to one-act plays that are of substantial length (i.e., 1,500 words to book length); developmentally appropriate with regard to complexity of character, plot, theme, and dialogue; and appropriately sophisticated with regard to literary devices, point of view, and style ^BP (NRE,4)

- Understands the defining features and structure of one act-plays at this developmental level ^BD (NRE,4)

- Independently applies the reading process and strategies to letters and diaries that are about 1,500 words in length; developmentally appropriate with regard to number and complexity of character and theme(s); and appropriately sophisticated with regard to literary devices, point of view, and style ^BP (NRE,5;UI,21,27,28,30)

- Understands the defining features and structure of letters and diaries at this developmental ^BD (NRE,5;UI,21,27,28,30)

Codes (right side of page):   BD = Benchmark, Declarative; BP = Benchmark, Procedural; BC = Benchmark, Contextual
1st letter(s) of each code in parentheses   2nd letter of code   Number
A = Australian Education Council   E = Explicitly stated in document   Page number of cited document
C4,8: CDE: Elementary, Middle Perf. Assessments   I = Implied in document
C12 = CDE: Calif. Writing Assess. Handbook
E = NCTE: Democracy Through Language   NW = NAEP: Writing Achieve. Levels-Setting Proc.
E1,2,3: Edison Proj: Primary,Elementary,Junior Acad.   NY = NY Draft Framework for Eng. Lang. Arts
G = GESP: National Geography Standards   S = SCANS: Report for America 2000
L = SPELA: Standards Proj. for English/Lang. Arts   SS = NCSS: Curric. Standards for Social Studies
NR = NAEP: 1992 Reading Assessment   U = NCHS: National Standards for U.S. History
NS = NSP: Draft Standards for Eng. Lang. Arts   W = Carnevale: Workplace Basics

level

(SE,xviii;WE,90)

9. Demonstrates competence in applying the reading process to specific types of informational texts

Level I (Grades K-2)

BP (NRE,4)

- No material specifically designated for this level

Level II (Grades 3-5)

BP (NRE,4;UI,21,27,28,30)

- Independently applies the reading process and strategies to passages about social studies that are relatively short (i.e., 250 to 800 words in length), developmentally appropriate with regard to complexity of topic(s) and hierarchical structure (e.g., chronology, problem/solution), and conceptually appropriate (in terms of number of concepts, familiarity, level of abstraction)

BD (NRE,4;UI,21,27,28,30)

- Understands the defining features and structure of social studies texts at this developmental level

BP (NRE,4)

- Independently applies the reading process and strategies to passages about general science that are relatively short (i.e., 250 to 800 words in length), developmentally appropriate with regard to complexity of topic(s) and hierarchical structure (e.g., chronology, problem/solution), and conceptually appropriate (in terms of number of concepts, familiarity, level of abstraction)

BD (NRE,4)

- Understands the defining features and structure of general science texts at this developmental level

BP (NRE,4)

- Independently applies the reading process and strategies to passages about sports that are relatively short (i.e., 250 to 800 words in length), developmentally appropriate with regard to complexity of topic(s) and hierarchical structure (e.g., chronology, problem/solution), and conceptually appropriate (in terms of number of concepts, familiarity, level of abstraction)

Codes (right side of page):   BD = Benchmark, Declarative; BP = Benchmark, Procedural; BC = Benchmark, Contextual
1st letter(s) of each code in parentheses   *2nd letter of code*   *Number*
A = Australian Education Council   E = Explicitly stated in document   Page number of cited document
C4,8: CDE: Elementary, Middle Perf. Assessments   I = Implied in document
C12 = CDE: Calif. Writing Assess. Handbook
E = NCTE: Democracy Through Language   NW = NAEP: Writing Achieve. Levels-Setting Proc.
E1,2,3: Edison Proj: Primary,Elementary,Junior Acad.   NY = NY Draft Framework for Eng. Lang. Arts
G = GESP: National Geography Standards   S = SCANS: Report for America 2000
L = SPELA: Standards Proj. for English/Lang. Arts   SS = NCSS: Curric. Standards for Social Studies
NR = NAEP: 1992 Reading Assessment   U = NCHS: National Standards for U.S. History
NS = NSP: Draft Standards for Eng. Lang. Arts   W = Carnevale: Workplace Basics

McREL

- Understands the defining features and structure of sports texts at this developmental level ^{BD (NRE,4)}

Level III (Grades 6-8)

- Independently applies the reading process and strategies to passages about social studies that are of moderate length (i.e., at least 1,000 words in length), developmentally appropriate with regard to complexity of topic(s) and hierarchical structure (e.g., chronology, problem/solution), and conceptually appropriate (in terms of number of concepts, familiarity, level of abstraction) ^{BP (NRE,5;UI,21,27,28,30)}

- Understands the defining features and structure of social studies texts at this developmental level ^{BD (NRE,5;UI,21,27,28,30)}

- Independently applies the reading process and strategies to passages about history that are of moderate length (i.e., at least 1,000 words in length); developmentally appropriate with regard to complexity of topic(s) and hierarchical structure (e.g., chronology, problem/solution), and conceptually appropriate (in terms of number of concepts, familiarity, level of abstraction) ^{BP (NRE,5;UI,21,27,28,30)}

- Understands the defining features and structure of history texts at this developmental level ^{BD (NRE,5;UI,21,27,28,30)}

- Independently applies the reading process and strategies to passages about geography that are of moderate length (i.e., at least 1,000 words in length), developmentally appropriate with regard to complexity of topic(s) and hierarchical structure (e.g., chronology, problem/solution), and conceptually appropriate (in terms of number of concepts, familiarity, level of abstraction) ^{BP (NRE,5)}

- Understands the defining features and structure of geography texts at this developmental level ^{BD (NRE,5)}

- Independently applies the reading process and strategies to passages about the sciences (general, earth, physical and life sciences) that are of moderate length (i.e., at least 1,000 words in length), developmentally appropriate with regard to complexity of topic(s) and hierarchical structure (e.g., chronology, problem/solution), and conceptually appropriate (in ^{BP (NRE,5)}

Codes (right side of page):   BD = Benchmark, Declarative;   BP = Benchmark, Procedural;   BC = Benchmark, Contextual

1st letter(s) of each code in parentheses	*2nd letter of code*	*Number*
A = Australian Education Council	E = Explicitly stated in document	Page number of cited document
C4,8: CDE: Elementary, Middle Perf. Assessments	I = Implied in document	
C12 = CDE: Calif. Writing Assess. Handbook		
E = NCTE: Democracy Through Language	NW = NAEP: Writing Achieve. Levels-Setting Proc.	
E1,2,3: Edison Proj: Primary,Elementary,Junior Acad.	NY = NY Draft Framework for Eng. Lang. Arts	
G = GESP: National Geography Standards	S = SCANS: Report for America 2000	
L = SPELA: Standards Proj. for English/Lang. Arts	SS = NCSS: Curric. Standards for Social Studies	
NR = NAEP: 1992 Reading Assessment	U = NCHS: National Standards for U.S. History	
NS = NSP: Draft Standards for Eng. Lang. Arts	W = Carnevale: Workplace Basics	

319

McREL

terms of number of concepts, familiarity, level of abstraction)

- BD (NRE,5)

  Understands the defining features and structure of science texts (general, earth, physical, life) at this developmental level

- BP (NRE,5)

  Independently applies the reading process and strategies to passages about nutrition that are of moderate length (i.e., at least 1,000 words in length), developmentally appropriate with regard to complexity of topic(s) and hierarchical structure (e.g., chronology, problem/solution), and conceptually appropriate (in terms of number of concepts, familiarity, level of abstraction)

- BD (NRE,5)

  Understands the defining features and structure of nutrition texts at this developmental level

- BP (NRE,5)

  Independently applies the reading process and strategies to essays that are of moderate length (i.e., at least 1000 words in length); developmentally appropriate with regard to complexity of topic(s) and hierarchical structure (e.g., chronology, problem/solution); and conceptually appropriate (in terms of number of concepts, familiarity, level of abstraction)

- BD (NRE,5)

  Understands the defining features and structure of essays at this developmental level

- BP (NRE,5;UI,21,27,28,30)

  Independently applies the reading process and strategies to primary source historical documents that are of moderate length (i.e., at least 1,000 words in length) developmentally appropriate with regard to complexity of topic(s) and hierarchical structure (e.g., chronology, problem/solution), and conceptually appropriate (in terms of number of concepts, familiarity, level of abstraction)

- BD (NRE,5;UI,21,27,28,30)

  Understands the defining features and structure of primary source historical documents at this developmental level

- BP (NRE,5)

  Independently applies the reading process and strategies to editorials that are about 1000 words in length, developmentally appropriate with regard to complexity of topic(s) and hierarchical structure (e.g., chronology, problem/solution), and conceptually appropriate (in terms of number of concepts, familiarity, level of abstraction)

- BD (NRE,5)

  Understands the defining features and structure of editorials at this developmental level

Codes (right side of page):   BD = Benchmark, Declarative; BP = Benchmark, Procedural; BC = Benchmark, Contextual
1st letter(s) of each code in parentheses   *2nd letter of code*   *Number*
A = Australian Education Council   E = Explicitly stated in document   Page number of cited document
C4,8: CDE: Elementary, Middle Perf. Assessments   I = Implied in document
C12 = CDE: Calif. Writing Assess. Handbook
E = NCTE: Democracy Through Language   NW = NAEP: Writing Achieve. Levels-Setting Proc.
E1,2,3: Edison Proj: Primary,Elementary,Junior Acad.   NY = NY Draft Framework for Eng. Lang. Arts
G = GESP: National Geography Standards   S = SCANS: Report for America 2000
L = SPELA: Standards Proj. for English/Lang. Arts   SS = NCSS: Curric. Standards for Social Studies
NR = NAEP: 1992 Reading Assessment   U = NCHS: National Standards for U.S. History
NS = NSP: Draft Standards for Eng. Lang. Arts   W = Carnevale: Workplace Basics

- Independently applies the reading process and strategies to news stories that are about 1,000 words in length, developmentally appropriate with regard to complexity of topic(s) and hierarchical structure (e.g., chronology, problem/solution), and conceptually appropriate (in terms of number of concepts, familiarity, level of abstraction) ^{BP (NRE,5)}

- Understands the defining features and structure of news stories at this developmental level ^{BD (NRE,5)}

Level IV (Grades 9-12)

- Independently applies the reading process and strategies to essays that are of substantial length (i.e., 1,500 words to book length), developmentally appropriate with regard to complexity of topic(s) and hierarchical structure (e.g., chronology, problem/solution), and conceptually appropriate (in terms of number of concepts, familiarity, level of abstraction) ^{BP (NRE,4)}

- Understands the defining features and structure of essays at this developmental level ^{BD (NRE,4)}

- Independently applies the reading process and strategies to social studies texts that are of substantial length (i.e., 1,500 words to book length), developmentally appropriate with regard to complexity of topic(s) and hierarchical structure (e.g., chronology, problem/solution); and conceptually appropriate (in terms of number of concepts, familiarity, level of abstraction) ^{BP (NRE,5;UI,21,27,28,30)}

- Understands the defining features and structure of social studies texts at this developmental level ^{BD (NRE,5;UI,21,27,28,30)}

- Independently applies the reading process and strategies to history texts that are of substantial length (i.e., 1,500 words to book length), developmentally appropriate with regard to complexity of topic(s) and hierarchical structure (e.g., chronology, problem/solution), and conceptually appropriate (in terms of number of concepts, familiarity, level of abstraction) ^{BP (NRE,5;UI,21,27,28,30)}

- Understands the defining features and structure of history texts at this developmental level ^{BD (NRE,5;UI,21,27,28,30)}

- Independently applies the reading process and strategies to economics texts that are of ^{BP (NRE,5)}

Codes (right side of page):   BD = Benchmark, Declarative;   BP = Benchmark, Procedural;   BC = Benchmark, Contextual

1st letter(s) of each code in parentheses   *2nd letter of code*   *Number*

A = Australian Education Council   E = Explicitly stated in document   Page number of cited document

C4,8: CDE: Elementary, Middle Perf. Assessments   I = Implied in document

C12 = CDE: Calif. Writing Assess. Handbook

E = NCTE: Democracy Through Language   NW = NAEP: Writing Achieve. Levels-Setting Proc.

E1,2,3: Edison Proj: Primary,Elementary,Junior Acad.   NY = NY Draft Framework for Eng. Lang. Arts

G = GESP: National Geography Standards   S = SCANS: Report for America 2000

L = SPELA: Standards Proj. for English/Lang. Arts   SS = NCSS: Curric. Standards for Social Studies

NR = NAEP: 1992 Reading Assessment   U = NCHS: National Standards for U.S. History

NS = NSP: Draft Standards for Eng. Lang. Arts   W = Carnevale: Workplace Basics

McREL

substantial length (i.e., 1,500 words to book length), developmentally appropriate with regard to complexity of topic(s) and hierarchical structure (e.g., chronology, problem/solution), and conceptually appropriate (in terms of number of concepts, familiarity, level of abstraction)

- Understands the defining features and structure of economics texts at this developmental level ^BD (NRE,5)

- Independently applies the reading process and strategies to science texts (biology texts, general science, earth science, physical science, environmental science) that are of substantial length (i.e., 1,500 words to book length), developmentally appropriate with regard to complexity of topic(s) and hierarchical structure (e.g., chronology, problem/solution), and conceptually appropriate (in terms of number of concepts, familiarity, level of abstraction) ^BP (NRE,5)

- Understands the defining features and structure of science texts (biology, general science, earth science, environmental science) at this developmental level ^BD (NRE,5)

- Independently applies the reading process and strategies to texts about nutrition and fitness that are of substantial length (i.e., 1,500 words to book length), developmentally appropriate with regard to complexity of topic(s) and hierarchical structure (e.g., chronology, problem/solution), and conceptually appropriate (in terms of number of concepts, familiarity, level of abstraction) ^BP (NRE,5)

- Understands the defining features and structure of nutrition and fitness texts at this developmental level ^BD (NRE,5)

- Independently applies the reading process and strategies to consumer economics texts that are of substantial length (i.e., 1,500 words to book length), developmentally appropriate with regard to complexity of topic(s) and hierarchical structure (e.g., chronology, problem/solution), and conceptually appropriate (in terms of number of concepts, familiarity, level of abstraction) ^BP (NRE,5)

- Understands the defining features and structure of consumer economics texts at this developmental level ^BD (NRE,5)

Codes (right side of page):   BD = Benchmark, Declarative; BP = Benchmark, Procedural; BC = Benchmark, Contextual
1st letter(s) of each code in parentheses   *2nd letter of code*   *Number*
A = Australian Education Council   E = Explicitly stated in document   Page number of cited document
C4,8: CDE: Elementary, Middle Perf. Assessments   I = Implied in document
C12 = CDE: Calif. Writing Assess. Handbook
E = NCTE: Democracy Through Language   NW = NAEP: Writing Achieve. Levels-Setting Proc.
E1,2,3: Edison Proj: Primary,Elementary,Junior Acad.   NY = NY Draft Framework for Eng. Lang. Arts
G = GESP: National Geography Standards   S = SCANS: Report for America 2000
L = SPELA: Standards Proj. for English/Lang. Arts   SS = NCSS: Curric. Standards for Social Studies
NR = NAEP: 1992 Reading Assessment   U = NCHS: National Standards for U.S. History
NS = NSP: Draft Standards for Eng. Lang. Arts   W = Carnevale: Workplace Basics

NREL

- Independently applies the reading process and strategies to primary source historical documents that are of substantial length (i.e., about 1,500 words to book length), developmentally appropriate with regard to complexity of topic(s) and hierarchical structure (e.g., chronology, problem/solution), and conceptually appropriate (in terms of number of concepts, familiarity, level of abstraction) BP (NRE,5;UI,21,27,28,30)

- Understands the defining features and structure of primary source historical documents at this developmental level BD (NRE,5;UI,21,27,28,30)

- Independently applies the reading process and strategies to essays that are of substantial length (i.e., 1,500 words to book length), developmentally appropriate with regard to complexity of topic(s) and hierarchical structure (e.g., chronology, problem/solution), and conceptually appropriate (in terms of number of concepts, familiarity, level of abstraction) BP (NRE,5)

- Understands the defining features and structure of essays at this developmental level BD (NRE,5)

- Independently applies the reading process and strategies to editorials that are at least 1500 words in length, developmentally appropriate with regard to complexity of topic(s) and hierarchical structure (e.g., chronology, problem/solution), and conceptually appropriate (in terms of number of concepts, familiarity, level of abstraction) BP (NRE,5)

- Understands the defining features and structure of editorials at this developmental level BD (NRE,5)

- Independently applies the reading process and strategies to news stories that are at least 1,500 words in length, developmentally appropriate with regard to complexity of topic(s) and hierarchical structure (e.g., chronology, problem/solution), and conceptually appropriate (in terms of number of concepts, familiarity, level of abstraction) BP (NRE,5)

- Understands the defining features and structure of news stories at this developmental level BD (NRE,5)

Codes (right side of page):   BD = Benchmark, Declarative;   BP = Benchmark, Procedural;   BC = Benchmark, Contextual

1st letter(s) of each code in parentheses   *2nd letter of code*   *Number*
A = Australian Education Council   E = Explicitly stated in document   Page number of cited document
C4,8: CDE: Elementary, Middle Perf. Assessments   I = Implied in document
C12 = CDE: Calif. Writing Assess. Handbook
E = NCTE: Democracy Through Language   NW = NAEP: Writing Achieve. Levels-Setting Proc.
E1,2,3: Edison Proj: Primary,Elementary,Junior Acad.   NY = NY Draft Framework for Eng. Lang. Arts
G = GESP: National Geography Standards   S = SCANS: Report for America 2000
L = SPELA: Standards Proj. for English/Lang. Arts   SS = NCSS: Curric. Standards for Social Studies
NR = NAEP: 1992 Reading Assessment   U = NCHS: National Standards for U.S. History
NS = NSP: Draft Standards for Eng. Lang. Arts   W = Carnevale: Workplace Basics

323   *NREL*

(SI,xviii;WI,90)

10 . Demonstrates competence in using different information sources, including those of a technical nature, to accomplish specific tasks

Level I (Grades K-2)

BP (NRE,6)

- Not appropriate for this level

Level II (Grades 3-5)

BP (NRE,6)

- Applies the reading process and strategies to directions or procedures (e.g., for school activities, camping or scouting procedures, recipes, games, hobbies) that are relatively short (i.e., about one page in length) and developmentally appropriate with regard to the number of categories of information or directions and the familiarity of concepts and vocabulary

Level III (Grades 6-8)

BP (EI,3;SSE,148)

- Interprets political and social messages of political cartoons

BP (NRE,5)

- Applies the reading process and strategies to directions or procedures (e.g., for school activities, camping or scouting procedures, recipes, games, or hobbies) that are of medium length (i.e., about 1,000 words in length) and developmentally appropriate with regard to the number of categories of information or directions and the familiarity of concepts and vocabulary

BP (NRE,6)

- Applies the reading process and strategies to bus routes and catalogues that are of medium length (i.e., about three pages in length)

Level IV (Grades 9-12)

BP (WE,90)

- Accurately interprets information from and detects inconsistencies in a data matrix

BP (WE,90-91)

- Follows basic linear paths in organizational charts

BP (WE,90)

- Identifies major sections in schematic diagrams

Codes (right side of page):	BD = Benchmark, Declarative; BP = Benchmark, Procedural; BC = Benchmark, Contextual

1st letter(s) of each code in parentheses   *2nd letter of code*   *Number*

A = Australian Education Council   E = Explicitly stated in document   Page number of cited document
C4,8: CDE: Elementary, Middle Perf. Assessments   I = Implied in document
C12 = CDE: Calif. Writing Assess. Handbook
E = NCTE: Democracy Through Language   NW = NAEP: Writing Achieve. Levels-Setting Proc.
E1,2,3: Edison Proj: Primary,Elementary,Junior Acad.   NY = NY Draft Framework for Eng. Lang. Arts
G = GESP: National Geography Standards   S = SCANS: Report for America 2000
L = SPELA: Standards Proj. for English/Lang. Arts   SS = NCSS: Curric. Standards for Social Studies
NR = NAEP: 1992 Reading Assessment   U = NCHS: National Standards for U.S. History
NS = NSP: Draft Standards for Eng. Lang. Arts   W = Carnevale: Workplace Basics

MREL

- Uses the linear path of a flowchart to provide visual and textual directions to a procedure ^{BP (WE,90-91)}

- Isolates a problem component in a schematic diagram and traces it to the cause of the problem ^{BP (WE,90-91)}

- Interprets symbols in a flowchart to indicate flow of direction, test points, components, and diagrammatic decision points ^{BP (WE,90-91)}

- Interprets a drawing of a cross section for assembly or disassembly ^{BP (WE,90-91)}

- Obtains a factor specification from a two-column chart to find information ^{BP (WE,90-91)}

- Obtains a factor specification from an intersection of row by column in a table or chart ^{BP (WE,90-91)}

- Uses a table or chart to identify a malfunction in a mechanism ^{BP (WE,90-91)}

- Applies the reading process and strategies to catalogue or catalogue sections that are of substantial length (i.e., at least 1,500 words in length) and developmentally appropriate with regard to the number of categories of information and the familiarity of concepts and vocabulary ^{BP (NRE,5)}

- Applies the reading process and strategies to directions and procedures (e.g., for school activities, camping or scouting procedures, recipes, games or hobbies) that are of substantial length (i.e., at least five pages in length) and developmentally appropriate with regard to the number of directions and the familiarity of concepts and vocabulary ^{BP (NRE,6)}

- Applies the reading process and strategies to directions for home or auto repairs that are of substantial length (i.e., at least five pages in length) and developmentally appropriate with regard to the number of directions and the familarity of concepts and vocabulary ^{BP (NRE,6)}

- Applies the reading process and strategies to schedules (e.g., of classes, for buses, trains or planes) that are of substantial length (i.e., at least five pages in length) and developmentally appropriate with regard to the number of categories of information or directions and the familarity of concepts and vocabulary ^{BP (NRE,6)}

Codes (right side of page):   BD = Benchmark, Declarative;   BP = Benchmark, Procedural;   BC = Benchmark, Contextual

1st letter(s) of each code in parentheses   *2nd letter of code*   *Number*

A = Australian Education Council   E = Explicitly stated in document   Page number of cited document

C4,8: CDE: Elementary, Middle Perf. Assessments   I = Implied in document

C12 = CDE: Calif. Writing Assess. Handbook

E = NCTE: Democracy Through Language   NW = NAEP: Writing Achieve. Levels-Setting Proc.

E1,2,3: Edison Proj: Primary,Elementary,Junior Acad.   NY = NY Draft Framework for Eng. Lang. Arts

G = GESP: National Geography Standards   S = SCANS: Report for America 2000

L = SPELA: Standards Proj. for English/Lang. Arts   SS = NCSS: Curric. Standards for Social Studies

NR = NAEP: 1992 Reading Assessment   U = NCHS: National Standards for U.S. History

NS = NSP: Draft Standards for Eng. Lang. Arts   W = Carnevale: Workplace Basics

McREL

- Correctly enters information into basic forms

  BP (WE,106)

- Interprets a drawing for assembly or disassembly

  BP (WE,90)

(AI, 6,7;NSI,291;NYE,16)
11. Demonstrates competence in speaking and listening as tools for learning

Level I (Grades K-2)

- When prompted, makes relevant contributions in class and group discussions

  BP (AE,18;NYE,17)

- Asks questions to help clear up personal confusion about a topic

  BP (AI,18;NSE,295)

- When prompted, recounts personal experiences or reports on personal knowledge about a topic

  BP (AE,18)

Level II (Grades 3-5)

- Actively contributes to group discussions

  BP (AE,34;NSE,295;NYI,17)

- Asks questions in class when he or she is confused

  BP (AE,35;NSE,295;NYI,32)

- Listens to classmates and adults without interrupting

  BP (AE,35;NSE,295;NYI,32)

- Makes some effort to have a clear main point when speaking to others

  BP (AE,35;NYI,17,18)

- Reads compositions to the class

  BP (AI,34;NYI,27)

- Makes eye contact while giving oral presentations

  BP (AI,34;NSE,295)

Level III (Grades 6-8)

- Plays a variety of roles in group discussions (e.g., active listener, discussion leader,

  BP (AI,56,57;NSE,304;NYI,32)

Codes (right side of page):   BD = Benchmark, Declarative; BP = Benchmark, Procedural; BC = Benchmark, Contextual

1st letter(s) of each code in parentheses	*2nd letter of code*	*Number*
A = Australian Education Council	E = Explicitly stated in document	Page number of cited document
C4,8: CDE: Elementary, Middle Perf. Assessments	I = Implied in document	
C12 = CDE: Calif. Writing Assess. Handbook		
E = NCTE: Democracy Through Language	NW = NAEP: Writing Achieve. Levels-Setting Proc.	
E1,2,3: Edison Proj: Primary,Elementary,Junior Acad.	NY = NY Draft Framework for Eng. Lang. Arts	
G = GESP: National Geography Standards	S = SCANS: Report for America 2000	
L = SPELA: Standards Proj. for English/Lang. Arts	SS = NCSS: Curric. Standards for Social Studies	
NR = NAEP: 1992 Reading Assessment	U = NCHS: National Standards for U.S. History	
NS = NSP: Draft Standards for Eng. Lang. Arts	W = Carnevale: Workplace Basics	

326

MREL

facilitator)

- Asks questions to help clear up personal confusion while exhibiting sensitivity to the effects of those questions on the learning and well-being of others <small>BP (AI,57;NSE,303;NYI,28)</small>

- Makes an effort to understand what others are saying and stays on the topic being discussed <small>BP (AE,56,57;NYI,18)</small>

- Has a clear main point when speaking to others <small>BP (AE,78;NYE,19)</small>

- Presents simple prepared reports to the class <small>BP (AE,56;NSI,303,304;NYE,19)</small>

- Makes eye contact while giving oral presentations and begins to use explicit techniques for effective presentations (e.g., modulation of voice, inflection, tempo, enunciation, physical gestures) <small>BP (AE,779;NSE,303;NYI,19)</small>

Level IV (Grades 9-12)

- Evaluates personal effectiveness in group discussions and makes corrections as necessary <small>BC (AE,119;NSI,312;NYE,30)</small>

- Asks questions as a way to broaden and enrich classroom discussions <small>BP (NSE,312;NYI,30)</small>

- Has a clear main point when speaking to others and adjusts the message wording and delivery to the particular audience and context <small>BP (AI,118;NSE,312;NYI,33)</small>

- Makes well-informed and well-organized formal presentations to the class <small>BP (AE,118;NSE,312;NYE,29)</small>

- Makes explicit use of various techniques for effective presentations (e.g., modulation of voice, inflection, tempo, enunciation, physical gestures) and demonstrates poise and self-control while presenting <small>BP (AI,119;NSE,312;NYE,25)</small>

Codes (right side of page): BD = Benchmark, Declarative; BP = Benchmark, Procedural; BC = Benchmark, Contextual

1st letter(s) of each code in parentheses	*2nd letter of code*	*Number*
A = Australian Education Council	E = Explicitly stated in document	Page number of cited document
C4,8: CDE: Elementary, Middle Perf. Assessments	I = Implied in document	
C12 = CDE: Calif. Writing Assess. Handbook		
E = NCTE: Democracy Through Language	NW = NAEP: Writing Achieve. Levels-Setting Proc.	
E1,2,3: Edison Proj: Primary,Elementary,Junior Acad.	NY = NY Draft Framework for Eng. Lang. Arts	
G = GESP: National Geography Standards	S = SCANS: Report for America 2000	
L = SPELA: Standards Proj. for English/Lang. Arts	SS = NCSS: Curric. Standards for Social Studies	
NR = NAEP: 1992 Reading Assessment	U = NCHS: National Standards for U.S. History	
NS = NSP: Draft Standards for Eng. Lang. Arts	W = Carnevale: Workplace Basics	

M-REL

(LI,42)

12. Demonstrates an understanding of the nature and function of the English language

Level I (Grades K-2)

- Recognizes characteristic sounds and rhythms of language

  BD (LI,58;E2,4)

- Makes valid observations about the use of words

  BC (LI,58;EI,4)

- Makes valid observations about the use of language at home as opposed to the use of language in school

  BC (LI,60;EI,4)

Level II (Grades 3-5)

- Identifies specific ways in which language varies across situations in one's personal life

  BD (LI,42;EI,4)

- Identifies the social context of conversations and its effect on the language used in conversations

  BD (LI,43;EI,4)

- Identifies the use of nonverbal cues used in conversation

  BD (LI,43;EI,4)

- Makes observations about language in real-life situations

  BC (LI,43;EI,4)

- Identifies appropriate and inappropriate uses of language in different settings including school and home

  BD (LI,44;EI,4)

- Compares the ways in which language is used in a variety of contexts

  BC (LI,44;EI,4)

- Makes observations about specific uses of own language

  BC (LI,45;EI,4)

- Compares the uses of language in the home, community, and school

  BC (LI,45;EI,4)

Codes (right side of page):   BD = Benchmark, Declarative; BP = Benchmark, Procedural; BC = Benchmark, Contextual
1st letter(s) of each code in parentheses   *2nd letter of code*   *Number*
A = Australian Education Council   E = Explicitly stated in document   Page number of cited document
C4,8: CDE: Elementary, Middle Perf. Assessments   I = Implied in document
C12 = CDE: Calif. Writing Assess. Handbook
E = NCTE: Democracy Through Language   NW = NAEP: Writing Achieve. Levels-Setting Proc.
E1,2,3: Edison Proj: Primary,Elementary,Junior Acad.   NY = NY Draft Framework for Eng. Lang. Arts
G = GESP: National Geography Standards   S = SCANS: Report for America 2000
L = SPELA: Standards Proj. for English/Lang. Arts   SS = NCSS: Curric. Standards for Social Studies
NR = NAEP: 1992 Reading Assessment   U = NCHS: National Standards for U.S. History
NS = NSP: Draft Standards for Eng. Lang. Arts   W = Carnevale: Workplace Basics

Level III (Grades 6-8)

- Forms explicit conclusions regarding language use based on observation

  BP (LI,49;E2,19)

- Understands those factors that commonly affect the use of language

  BD (LE,49;EI,19)

- Communicates effectively in more than one language or dialect

  BP (LI,49)

Level IV (Grades 9-12)

- Understands the influence of gender on language use

  BD (LI,50;EI,20)

- Carries out investigations of unanswered questions regarding language

  BP (LI,50;EI,20)

- Engages in public speaking around issues of personal concern

  BP (LI,64;EI,20)

- Has a general understanding of the history of the English language

  BD (E2,20)

- Compares form, meaning, and value of different kinds of language

  BC (LE,51;EI,20)

- Understands the political implications of using different forms of language

  BD (LI,52;EI,20)

Codes (right side of page):   BD = Benchmark, Declarative;   BP = Benchmark, Procedural;   BC = Benchmark, Contextual

1st letter(s) of each code in parentheses	*2nd letter of code*	*Number*
A = Australian Education Council	E = Explicitly stated in document	Page number of cited document
C4,8: CDE: Elementary, Middle Perf. Assessments	I = Implied in document	
C12 = CDE: Calif. Writing Assess. Handbook		
E = NCTE: Democracy Through Language	NW = NAEP: Writing Achieve. Levels-Setting Proc.	
E1,2,3: Edison Proj: Primary,Elementary,Junior Acad.	NY = NY Draft Framework for Eng. Lang. Arts	
G = GESP: National Geography Standards	S = SCANS: Report for America 2000	
L = SPELA: Standards Proj. for English/Lang. Arts	SS = NCSS: Curric. Standards for Social Studies	
NR = NAEP: 1992 Reading Assessment	U = NCHS: National Standards for U.S. History	
NS = NSP: Draft Standards for Eng. Lang. Arts	W = Carnevale: Workplace Basics	

(HI,146;E1E,21;E3I,36;NSI,308)

13 . Demonstrates a familiarity with selected literary works of enduring quality

Level I (Grades K-2)

BP (AP,332)
- When prompted by the teacher recites the texts of a variety of familiar rhymes

BD (AP,332-334)
- Demonstrates a knowledge of the plots and major characters of selected classic fairy tales, folktales, legends, and fables from around the world

BP (AP,334)
- Identifies the characters and simple story lines in selected classical myths (i.e., Greek and Roman mythology)

BD (AP,335)
- Demonstrates a basic familiarity with selected fiction and poetry

BD (AP,335)
- Demonstrates a basic familiarity with selected works of nonfiction

Level II (Grades 3-5)

BD (AP,336)
- Demonstrates a basic familiarity with the characters and plots in selected classical mythology (e.g., Norse mythology, the Arthurian legend, and classical Greek mythology)

BD (AP,337-341)
- Demonstrates a familiarity with a variety of selected classic fiction, folktales, and poetry

BD (AP,341-342)
- Demonstrates a familiarity with a variety of selected nonfiction

Level III (Grades 6-8)

BD (AP,343-345)
- Identifies the defining characteristics of classic literature

BD (AP,343)
- Demonstrates a familiarity with the plots and characters from selected classical Greek and Roman mythology

BD (AP,343-345,347-348)
- Demonstrates an understanding of selected works of classic fiction, drama, and nonfiction

BD (AP,345-347)
- Demonstrates an understanding of a variety of selected contemporary fiction

BD (AP,347)
- Demonstrates a familiarity with selected poets and classic poetry

Codes (right side of page):   BD = Benchmark, Declarative; BP = Benchmark, Procedural; BC = Benchmark, Contextual
AP   *Number*
See appendix immediately following the Language Arts Standards   Page number of appendix

330

MREL

Level IV (Grades 9-12)

- Demonstrates an understanding of why certain literary works may be considered classics or works of enduring quality and substance ^BD (AP,349-360)

- Demonstrates a familiarity with a variety of classic American, British, and world literature and their authors (e.g., through literary allusions and literary criticism) ^BD (AP,349-350,354-360)

- Identifies the plots, characters, and significance of selected works of ancient literature, including selected works of Greek philosophers, poets, and dramatists ^BP (AP,359)

- Demonstrates an understanding of the Bible as literature ^BD (AP,359-360)

Codes (right side of page):   BD = Benchmark, Declarative; BP = Benchmark, Procedural; BC = Benchmark, Contextual
AP   *Number*
See appendix immediately following the Language Arts Standards   Page number of appendix

331

MᴄREL

Appendix for Language Arts Standard 13: Level I (Primary)

Nursery Rhymes

"A Diller, A Dollar" (H1,17)
"Baa, Baa, Black Sheep" (H1,17)
"Chinese Mother Goose Rhymes" by
     Robert Wyndham (CS,15)
"Diddle, Diddle, Dumpling" (H1,17)
"Early to Bed" (H1,17)
"Georgie Porgie" (H1,18)
"Here We Go Round the Mulberry Bush"
     (H1,19)
"Hey, Diddle, Diddle" (H1,18)
"Hickory, Dickory, Dock" (H1,18)
"Hot Cross Buns!" (H1,18)
"Humpty Dumpty" (H1,19)
"Jack Sprat" (H,181;H1,17)
"Jack, Be Nimble" (H,181;H1,19)
"Jack and Jill" (H,181;H1,18)
"Ladybug, Ladybug"(H1,17)
"Little Bo Peep" (H,184;H1,21)
"Little Miss Muffett" (H,184;H1,20)
"Little Jack Horner" (H,184;H1,21)
"Little Boy Blue" (H,184;H1,19)
"London Bridge Is Falling Down" (H1,19)
"Mary Had a Little Lamb" (H1,20)
"Mary, Mary, Quite Contrary" (H1,20)
"Old King Cole" (H,193;H1,20)
"Old Mother Hubbard" (H,193;H1,23)

"One, Two, Buckle My Shoe" (H1,21)
"Pat-a-Cake" (H1,21)
"Rain, Rain, Go Away" (H1,24)
"Ride a Cock Horse" (H,200;H1,23)
"Ring Around the Rosey" (Hl,21)
"Rock-a-bye, Baby" (H1,23)
"Roses are Red" (H1,24)
"Rub-a-dub-dub" (H1,24)
"See-Saw, Margery Daw" (H1,23)
"Simple Simon" (H,204;H1,25)
"Sing a Song of Sixpence" (H1,24)
"Star Light, Star Bright" (H1,23)
"The Owl and the Pussycat" (H1,22)
"There Was an Old Woman Who Lived in a
     Shoe" (H1,26)
"There Was A Little Girl" (H1,25)
"This Little Pig Went to Market" (H1,26)
"Three Blind Mice" (H1,25)
"Tom, Tom, the Piper's Son" (H1,23)
Tortillitas para mama; And Other Spanish
     Nursery Rhymes by Griego, Margot
     C., and others (CS,11)
"Twinkle, Twinkle, Little Star" (H1,25)
"Wynken, Blynken, and Nod"
     (H,215;H1,18)

Fairy Tales

Andersen, Hans Christian (H,154)
     "Cinderella" (CS,9;RF,270;H1,29)
     "Princess and the Pea" (H,197;H1,43)
     "The Emperor's New Clothes" (H,170)
"Beauty and the Beast" (H,157;H2,18)
"Chicken Little" (CS,10;H1,28)
"Goldilocks and The Three Bears" (H,209;H1,31)
Grimm brothers (H,176)
     "Hansel and Gretel" (H,176;H2,29)

C = California Recommended Readings, K-8
CS = California Recommended Literature, 9-12
E1 = The Edison Project: Primary
E2 = The Edison Project: Elementary Academy
E3 = The Edison Project: Junior Academy
GJ = Gillespie: Best Books for Junior High Readers

GS = Gillespie: Best Books for Senior High Readers
H = Hirsch: Cultural Literacy
H1 - H6 = Hirsch: Core Knowledge Series, Grades 1-6
NE = New England Association of Teachers of English
NS = NCTE: Books for You
RF = Ravitch & Finn: What Do Our 17-Year-Olds Know?

MREL

"Snow White" (H,204;H1,52)
The Bremen Town Musicians (CS,12)
The Shoemaker and the Elves (CS,12)
"Jack and the Beanstalk" (CS,11;E1,19;H,181;H1,32)
"Red Riding Hood" (H,184)
"Pied Piper of Hamelin" (H,195;H1,40)
"Pinocchio" (H,195;H1,42)
"Puss-in-Boots" (H,199;H1,44)
"Rumpelstiltskin" (H1,46)
"Rupunzel" (H1,46)
"Sleeping Beauty" (H,204;H1,50)
"The Little Red Hen" (CS,10;H,184;H1,34)
"The Three Little Pigs" (H,209;H1,54)
"The Emperor's New Clothes" (H2,27)
"The Three Billy Goats Gruff" (CS,11;H1,65)
"The Ugly Duckling" (H1,55)
The Three Bears (CS,11)

Folktales and Legends

Aardema, Verna *Why Mosquitoes Buzz in People's Ears: A West African Tale* (CS,8)
Aardema, Verna *Bringing the Rain to Kapiti Plain* (CS,8)
"Aladdin and the Wonderful Lamp" (H,53)
"Anansi" (E1,19;H1,27)
Brown, Marica *Once a Mouse* (CS,9)
Carpenter, Frances *Tales of a Korean Grandmother* (CS,9)
DePoala, Tomie *Strega Nona* (CS,10)
"El Pajaro Cu" (H2,25)
"From Tiger to Anansi" (H2,48)
Gerson, Mary-Joan "Why the Sky is Far Away: A Nigerian Folktale" (E1,18)
Haley, Gail E. *A Story, a Story* (CS,12)
Hodges, Margaret *The Wave* (CS,12)
Hogrogian, Nonny "One Fine Day" (CS,13;E1,18)
Hong, Lily "How the Ox Star Fell From Heaven" (E1,18)
"Inktomi Lost His Eyes" (H2,31)
Leaf, Munro "The Story of Ferdinand" (E1,18)
Lindgren, Aastrid "The Tomten" (E1,18)
Lobel, Arnold "Frog and Toad are Friends" (E1,18)

C = California Recommended Readings, K-8	GS = Gillespie: Best Books for Senior High Readers
CS = California Recommended Literature, 9-12	H = Hirsch: Cultural Literacy
E1 = The Edison Project: Primary	H1 - H6 = Hirsch: Core Knowledge Series, Grades 1-6
E2 = The Edison Project: Elementary Academy	NE = New England Association of Teachers of English
E3 = The Edison Project: Junior Academy	NS = NCTE: Books for You
GJ = Gillespie: Best Books for Junior High Readers	RF = Ravitch & Finn: What Do Our 17-Year-Olds Know?

333   *McREL*

"Medio Pollito" (H1,37)
"One-Inch Fellow" (H2,36)
"Peter Pan" (H2,43)
Roland, Donna *Grandfather's Stories - Cambodia* (CS,14)
Roland, Donna *More of Grandfather's Stories* (CS,14)
"St. George and the Dragon" (H,202)
Steptoe, John "Mufaro's Beautiful Daughters: An African Tale" (E1,18)
"The Blind Men and the Elephant" (H2,20)
"The Fable of Brer Rabbit and the Tar Baby" (H1,68)
"The Tiger and the Brahmin" (E1,19)
Uchida, Yoshiko *The Magic Listening Cap: More Folktales from Japan* (CS,15)
Van Allsburg, Chris "Jumanji" (E1,18)
"Why the Owl Has Big Eyes" (H1,56)
Wolkstein, Dian *The Banza* (CS,15)
Yashima, Taro *Umbrella* (CS,16)
Young, Ed "Lon Po Po: A Red Riding Hood Story from China" (E1,18)

Fables and Myth
Aesop's fables (RF,272; E1,18;H,152)
     "The Boy Who Cried Wolf" (H,159;H1,59)
     "Tortoise and Hare" (RF,271;H,176;H1,62)
     "The Dog in the Manger" (H1,60)
     "The Wolf in Sheep's Clothing" (H1,60)
     "The Maid and the Milk Pail" (H1,61)
     "The Fox and the Grapes" (H1,62)
     "The Goose and the Golden Eggs" (H1,63)
     "King Midas" (E1,19)
Mythology--Introducing Some Gods and Goddesses (i.e., Zeus, Hera, Apollo, Poseidon,
     Aphrodite and Eros, Ares, Hermes, Hephaestos, Athena, Hades) (H2,52-55)
     "Demeter and Persephone" (H2,56)
     "Prometheus and Pandora" (H2,58)
     "The Quest of the Golden Fleece" (H2,59)
     "Sailing with the Argonauts" (H2,60)
     "Finding the Fleece" (H2,61)
"The Legend of Oedipus and the Sphinx" (H1,66)
"The Legend of the Minotaur, Daedalus, and Icarus" (H1,67)

C = California Recommended Readings, K-8
CS = California Recommended Literature, 9-12
E1 = The Edison Project: Primary
E2 = The Edison Project: Elementary Academy
E3 = The Edison Project: Junior Academy
GJ = Gillespie: Best Books for Junior High Readers

GS = Gillespie: Best Books for Senior High Readers
H = Hirsch: Cultural Literacy
H1 - H6 = Hirsch: Core Knowledge Series, Grades 1-6
NE = New England Association of Teachers of English
NS = NCTE: Books for You
RF = Ravitch & Finn: What Do Our 17-Year-Olds Know?

MREL

Novels

Dickens, Charles *A Christmas Carol* (H2,22)

Hahn, Jae Hyun, and Han Hahn *Special Korean Birthday* (CS,32)

Lionni, Leo *Alexander and the Wind-up Mouse* (CS,19)

Lobel, Arnold *Frog and Toad Are Friends* (CS,20)

Milne, A. A. *Winnie the Pooh* (H,214)

Peet, Bill *Big Bad Bruce* (CS,20)

Potter, Beatrix *Peter Rabbit* (E1,18; H1,38)

Seuss, Dr. *And to Think That I Saw It on Mulberry Street* (CS,21)

Steig, William *Sylvester and the Magic Pebble* (CS,21)

Yashima, Mitsu and Taro *Momo's Kitten* (CS,22;E1,18)

Zolotow, Charlotte *Mr. Rabbit and the Lovely Present* (CS,22)

Poetry

Adoff, Arnold *Outside-Inside Poems* (CS,23)

Livingston, Myra C., ed. *Listen, Children, Listen: An Anthology of Poems for the Very Young* (CS,26)

Blake, William "Spring" (E1,18)

Chippewa Indians, North America *The Approach of the Storm* (E1,18)

De Reniers, Beatrice Schenk *Keep a Poem in Your Pocket* (E1,18)

Farjean, Eleanor *Eleanor Farjeon's Poems for Children* (E1,18)

Giovanni, Nikki "Because" (E1,18)

Hopkins, Lee Bennett "Poetry Time" (E1,18)

Surprises (CS,28)

Koriyama, Naoshi *"Unfolding Bud"* (E1,18)

Kuskin, Karla *"Take a Word like a Cat"* and *"Honey, I Love You"* (E1,18)

Longfellow, Henry Wadsworth *"Paul Revere's Ride"* (H2,38;RF,273)

Moore, Clement C. *"'Twas the Night Before Christmas"* (H2,33)

Nonfiction

Baylor, Byrd *The Desert Is Theirs* (CS,41)

Boynton, Sandra *A is for Angry: An Animal and Adjective Alphabet* (E1,18)

Lauber, Patricia *Seeds: Pop Stick Glide* and *What's Hatching Out of That Egg* (CS,41)

Price, Christine *Dancing Masks of Africa* (CS,44)

C = California Recommended Readings, K-8	GS = Gillespie: Best Books for Senior High Readers
CS = California Recommended Literature, 9-12	H = Hirsch: Cultural Literacy
E1 = The Edison Project: Primary	H1 - H6 = Hirsch: Core Knowledge Series, Grades 1-6
E2 = The Edison Project: Elementary Academy	NE = New England Association of Teachers of English
E3 = The Edison Project: Junior Academy	NS = NCTE: Books for You
GJ = Gillespie: Best Books for Junior High Readers	RF = Ravitch & Finn: What Do Our 17-Year-Olds Know?

McREL

Appendix for Language Arts Standard 13: Level II (Upper Elementary)

Mythology from Around the World
Norse Mythology
    "Balder and Loki" (H3,46)
    "How the Norse Gods Lived" (H3,44)
    "How the Days of the Week Got Their Names" (H3,42)
    "How the Gods' Home, Asgard, Was Built" (H3,45)
    "The Enemies of the Gods" (H3,44)
    "Why the Universe Doesn't Fall Down" (H3,47)

Myths from Medieval England
    "Guinevere" (H4,59)
    "How Arthur Became King: the Sword in the Stone" (H4,56)
    "Merlin and the Lady of the Lake" (H4,61)
    "Sir Launcelot" (H4,62)
    "The Sword Excalibur and the Lady of the Lake" (H4,58)
    "The Legend of King Arthur and the Knights of the Round Table" (H4,55)

Classical Greek Mythology
    Background information on *The Iliad* and *The Odyssey* (H5,28)
    D'Aulaire, Ingri, and Edgar P. D'Aulaire *D'aulaires' Book of Greek Myths* (CS,10)
    from *The Iliad*
        "Epilogue to the Iliad" (H5,39)
        "Hector and Andromache" (H5,34)
        "The Arming of Achilles" (H5,36)
        "The Combat Between Menelaus and Paris" (H5,35)
        "The Death of Hector" (H5,38)
        "The Judgment of Paris" (H5,28)
        "The Quarrel Between Agamemnon and Achilles" (H5,31)
    from *The Odyssey*
        Background to T*he Odyssey* (H5,40)
        "Odysseus and the Cyclops" (H5,41)

Adaptations from the Classics
"A Voyage to Lilliput" (H4,3)
"Adventures of Sherlock Homes: The Red-Headed League" (H5,14)
"Aladdin and the Wonderful Lamp" (H3,12)
"Ali Baba and the Forty Thieves" (H3,15)

C = California Recommended Readings, K-8
CS = California Recommended Literature, 9-12
E1 = The Edison Project: Primary
E2 = The Edison Project: Elementary Academy
E3 = The Edison Project: Junior Academy
GJ = Gillespie: Best Books for Junior High Readers

GS = Gillespie: Best Books for Senior High Readers
H = Hirsch: Cultural Literacy
H1 - H6 = Hirsch: Core Knowledge Series, Grades 1-6
NE = New England Association of Teachers of English
NS = NCTE: Books for You
RF = Ravitch & Finn: What Do Our 17-Year-Olds Know?

336

McREL

"Alice's Adventures in Wonderland" (H3,17)

Andersen, Hans Christian *The Ugly Duckling* Retold by Lorinda B. Cauley (CS,17)

Beauty and the Beast Retold by Marianna Mayer (CS,9)

"Dr. Jekyll and Mr. Hyde" (H5,23)

"Julius Caesar" (H5,8)

"On Thin Ice" from *Little Women* (H4,13)

"Pollyanna" (H3,25;E2,37)

"Rip Van Winkle" (H4,17;RF,270)

"Robinson Crusoe" (H4,8)

"The Adventures of Don Quixote" (H5,19)

"The Adventures of Tom Sawyer" (H5,5;RF,272)

"The Glittering Cloud" from *On the Banks of Plum Creek* (H4,37)

"The Legend of Sleepy Hollow" (H4,21)

"Treasure Island" (H4,30)

Folktales

Aesop *Aesop's Fables* (CS,8)

Asbjornsen, Peter Christian, and Jorgen E. Moe *East of the Sun and West of the Moon and Other Tales* (CS,8)

Blair, Walter *Tall Tale America* (CS,9)

Brown, Marcia *Once a Mouse* (CS,9)

Chase, Richard *The Jack Tales* (CS,10)

"Coyote Goes to the Land of the Dead" (H5,2)

Dayrell, Elphinstone *Why the Sun and Moon Live in the Sky* (CS,10)

DePaola, Tomie *Strega Nona* (CS,10)

Fleischman, Sid *Humbug Mountain* (CS,11)

Gag, Wanda *Tales from Grimm* (CS,11)

Granfa' Grig Had a Pig and Other Rhymes Without Reason from Mother Goose (CS,11)

Grimm, Jacob, and Wilhelm Grimm *Little Red Riding Hood* (CS,12)

Rapunzel (CS,12)

Snow-White and the Seven Dwarfs (CS,12)

Jaquith, Priscilla *Bo Rabbit Smart for True: Folktales from the Gullah* (CS,13)

Keats, Ezra Jack *John Henry: An American Legend* (CS,13)

Louie, Ai-Lang *Yeh Shen: A Cinderella Story from China* (CS,13)

Luenn, Nancy *The Dragon Kite* (CS,13)

North American Legends Virginia Havland, ed. (CS,14)

Paul Bunyan Retold by Steven Kellogg (CS,14)

C = California Recommended Readings, K-8	GS = Gillespie: Best Books for Senior High Readers
CS = California Recommended Literature, 9-12	H = Hirsch: Cultural Literacy
E1 = The Edison Project: Primary	H1 - H6 = Hirsch: Core Knowledge Series, Grades 1-6
E2 = The Edison Project: Elementary Academy	NE = New England Association of Teachers of English
E3 = The Edison Project: Junior Academy	NS = NCTE: Books for You
GJ = Gillespie: Best Books for Junior High Readers	RF = Ravitch & Finn: What Do Our 17-Year-Olds Know?

McREL

Steptoe, John *The Story of Jumping Mouse, a Native American Legend* (CS,15)
"Talk" (H3,36)
"The People Could Fly" (H3,24)
The Sleeping Beauty by the Brothers Grimm (CS,15)
"The Quillwork Girl and Her Seven Brothers" (H3,32)
"The Sun Dance" (H4,25)
"The Tongue-cut Sparrow" (H4,6)
"Three Words of Wisdom" (H3,34)
Two Brothers and Their Magic Gourds Edward B. Adams, ed. (CS,15)
Yagawa, Sumiko *The Crane Wife* (CS,16)

Unabridged Fiction
Andersen, Hans Christian *The Nightingale* (CS,17)
Atkinson, Mary *Maria Teresa* (CS,29)
Baylor, Byrd *Amigo* (E2,36)
Bernstein, Margery and Janet Kobrin *Coyote Goes Hunting for Fire: A California Indian Myth* (E2,37)
Brenner, Barbara *Wagon Wheels* (CS,36)
Bryan, Ashley *Beat the Story Drum, Pum-Pum* (CS,9;E2,37)
Cameron, Eleanor *The Court of the Stone Children* (CS,18)
Cleary, Beverly *Ramona and Her Father* (CS,30)
Clifton, Lucille *The Boy Who Didn't Believe in Spring* (E2,36)
Dahl, Roald *James and the Giant Peach* (CS,18)
Dalgliesh, Alice *The Courage of Sarah Noble* (CS,36)
DeClements, Barthe *Nothing's Fair in Fifth Grade* (E2,36)
DePaola, Tomie *Nana Upstairs and Nana Downstairs* (CS,30)
DuBois, William P. *Lion* (CS,18)
Estes, Eleanor *The Hundred Dresses* (CS,30)
Galbraith, Claire K. *Victor* (CS,31)
Gates, Doris *Blue Willow* (CS,31)
Grahame, Kenneth *Wind in the Willows* (E2,37)
Greene, Bette *Philip Hall Likes Me, I Reckon Maybe* (CS,31)
Hahn, Jae, Hyun *Seven Korean Sisters* (CS,31;E2,37)
Haley, Gail *Jack Jouett's Ride* (CS,37)
Hall, Donald *The Ox-Cart Man* (CS,37)
Hamilton, Virginia *Zeely* (CS,32)
Han, Mieko *Turtle Power - Vietnamese* (CS,18)

C = California Recommended Readings, K-8
CS = California Recommended Literature, 9-12
E1 = The Edison Project: Primary
E2 = The Edison Project: Elementary Academy
E3 = The Edison Project: Junior Academy
GJ = Gillespie: Best Books for Junior High Readers
GS = Gillespie: Best Books for Senior High Readers
H = Hirsch: Cultural Literacy
H1 - H6 = Hirsch: Core Knowledge Series, Grades 1-6
NE = New England Association of Teachers of English
NS = NCTE: Books for You
RF = Ravitch & Finn: What Do Our 17-Year-Olds Know?

Konigsburg, E. L. *From the Mixed-Up Files of Mrs. Basil E. Frankweiler* (CS,32)
Lasker, Joe *He's My Brother* (E2,36)
Lawson, Robert *Ben and Me* (CS,19)
L'Engle, Madeliene *A Wrinkle in Time* (CS,19;E2,37)
Lewis, Thomas P. *Hill of Fire* (CS,37)
Lobel, Arnold *Fables* (CS,20)
Lord, Bette B. *In the Year of the Boar and Jackie Robinson* (CS,37)
Lowry, Lois *Anastasia Krupnik* (CS,33)
MacLachlan, Patricia *Arthur, for the Very First Time* (CS,33)
                 Sarah, Plain and Tall (CS,38)
Maury, Inex *My Mother the Mail Carrier* (CS,33)
Meadowcroft, Enid *By Secret Railway* (CS,38)
Miles, Miska *Annie and the Old One* (CS,33)
Milne, A.A. *Winnie-the-Pooh* (CS,20)
Monjo, F. N. *The Drinking Gourd* (CS,38)
Ness, Evaline *Sam, Bangs, and Moonshine* (CS,33)
O'Brien, Robert C. *Mrs. Frisby and the Rats of NIMH* (E2,36)
Robinson, Marc *Cock-a-Doodle-Doo! What Does It Sound Like to You?* (E2,36)
Sendak, Maurice *Where the Wild Things Are* (CS,21)
Seuss, Dr. *Five Hundred Hats of Bartholomew Cubbins* (CS,21)
Shub, Elizabeth *The White Stallion* (CS,39)
Speare, Elizabeth G. *The Sign of the Beaver* (CS,39;E2,36)
Sperry, Armstrong *Call It Courage* (CS,39;E2,36)
Steig, William *Abel's Island* (CS,21)
Steptoe, John *Stevie* (CS,34)
Spyri, Johanna *Heidi* (E2,36)
Turkle, Brinton *Do Not Open* (CS,21)
Turner, Ann *Nettie's Trip South* (E2,36)
Uchida, Yoshiko *Journey to Topaz* (CS,39)
Van Allsburg, Chris *Jumanji* (CS,21)
Williams, Margery *The Velveteen Rabbit* (CS,22)
Williams, Vera B. *A Chair for My Mother* (CS,34;E2,36)
White, E. B. *Charlotte's Web* (CS,22)
Wilder, Laura I. *Little House in the Big Woods* (CS,40)
Yashima, Taro *Crow Boy* (CS,34)

C = California Recommended Readings, K-8	GS = Gillespie: Best Books for Senior High Readers
CS = California Recommended Literature, 9-12	H = Hirsch: Cultural Literacy
E1 = The Edison Project: Primary	H1 - H6 = Hirsch: Core Knowledge Series, Grades 1-6
E2 = The Edison Project: Elementary Academy	NE = New England Association of Teachers of English
E3 = The Edison Project: Junior Academy	NS = NCTE: Books for You
GJ = Gillespie: Best Books for Junior High Readers	RF = Ravitch & Finn: What Do Our 17-Year-Olds Know?

339

M?REL

Poetry

A Book of Animal Poems Selected by William Cole (CS,24)

Amon, Aline *The Earth is Sore: Native Amricans on Nature* (CS,24)

Angelou, Maya "Life Doesn't Frighten Me" (H4,50)

Anonymous "Monday's Child Is Fair of Face" (H4,43)

Anonymous "Solomon Grundy" (H4,43)

Baylor, Byrd *When Clay Sings* (CS,24)

Cricket Songs: Japanese Haiku Translated by Harry Behn (CS,24)

Belloc, Hilaire "The Frog" (H4,44)

Benet, Rosemary, and Stephen Vincent Benet *A Book of Americans* (CS,24)

Blake, William "The Tiger" (E2,37;H5,50;RF,277)

Brooks, Gwendolyn "Narcissa" (H5,58)

Burgess, Gelett "The Purple Cow" (H4,47)

Carroll, Lewis "Jabberwocky" (H5,53)

Carroll, Lewis "The Crocodile" (H4,45)

Crazy to Be Alive in Such a Strange World Edited by Nancy Larrick (CS,24)

Cullen, Countee "Incident" (H5,59)

Dickinson, Emily "A Bird Came Down the Walk" (H5,48)

Fisher, Aileen *Out in the Dark and Daylight* (CS,25)

Froman, Robert *Seeing Things: A Book of Poems* (CS,25)

Greenfield, Eloise "Things" (H4,52)

How to Eat a Poem and Other Morsels Selected by Rose Agree (CS,25)

Howard, Coralie *The Firt Book of Short Verse* (CS,25)

Howe, Julia Ward "Battle Hymn of the Republic" (H5,54)

Hughes, Langston "Dreams" (E2,37;H4,46)

Hughes, Langston "I, Too" (H5,57)

Hughes, Langston *The Dream Keeper* (E2,37)

Kilmer, Sergeant Joyce "Trees" (H5,49)

Knock on a Star: A Child's Introduction to Poetry Edited by X.J. Kennedy and Dorothy Kennedy (CS,26)

Lear, Edward *How Pleasant to Know Mr. Lear!* (CS,26)

Lear, Edward "The Pobble Who Has No Toes" (H4,49)

Livingston, Myra C. *Circle of Seasons* (CS,26)

Longfellow, Henry Wadsworth "The Arrow and the Song" (H5,58)

McCord, David *One at a Time* (CS,26)

Merriam, Eve *There is No Rhyme for Silver* (CS,26)

Millay, Edna St. Vincent "Afternoon on a Hill" (E2,37;H4,53)

Moore, Lilian *Something New Begins* (CS,26)

C = California Recommended Readings, K-8	GS = Gillespie: Best Books for Senior High Readers
CS = California Recommended Literature, 9-12	H = Hirsch: Cultural Literacy
E1 = The Edison Project: Primary	H1 - H6 = Hirsch: Core Knowledge Series, Grades 1-6
E2 = The Edison Project: Elementary Academy	NE = New England Association of Teachers of English
E3 = The Edison Project: Junior Academy	NS = NCTE: Books for You
GJ = Gillespie: Best Books for Junior High Readers	RF = Ravitch & Finn: What Do Our 17-Year-Olds Know?

McREL

My Song Is A Piece of Jade: Poems of Ancient Mexico in English and Spanish Edited by Toni de Gerez (CS,26)

My Tang's Tungled and Other Ridiculous Situations Compiled by Sara Brewton (CS,26)

Nash, Ogden "The Rhinoceros" (H4,44)

O'Neill, Mary *Hailstones and Halibut Bones* (CS, 27)

Perkins, Useni Eugene "Ballad of John Henry" (H5,54)

Piping Down the Valleys Wild Edited by Nancy Larrick (CS,27)

Poem Stew Edited by William Cole (CS,27)

Richards, Edward Hersey "A Wise, Old Owl" (H5,50)

Sandburg, Carl "Fog" (H5,48)

Silverstein, Shel "Clarence" (H4,48)

Stuckey, Elma "Humanity" (H4,46)

Sutherland, Zena, and Myra Livingston *The Scott, Foresman Anthology of Children's Literature* (CS,28)

Tennyson, Alfred "The Eagle" (H5,51)

Thackeray, William Makepeace "The Tragic Story" (H4,47)

Thayer, Ernest Lawrence "Casey at the Bat" (H5,51)

Whitman, Walt "I Hear America Singing" (E2,37;H5,56)

Whitman, Walt "O Captain! My Captain!" (H5,56)

Wilbur, Richard "Some Opposites" (H5,59)

Nonfiction - Information

Aliki *Corn is Maize: The Gift of the Indians* and *The Story of Johnny Appleseed* (C,40)

Ancona, George *Bananas: From Manolo to Margie* (C,41)

Baylor, Byrd *The Way to Start a Day* (C,41)

Charlip, Remy, and Marybeth *Handtalk: An ABC of Finger Spelling and Sign Language* (C,42)

Chief Joseph "I Will Fight No More Forever" (H5,45)

DePaola, Tomie *The Quicksand Book* (C,42)

"Give Me Liberty or Give Me Death!" (H3,40)

Isenbart, Hans-Heinrich *A Duckling is Born* (C,42)

Kohl, Herbert and Judith *The View from the Oak* (C,42)

Krementz, Jill *A Very Young Rider* (C,43)

Kuskin, Karla *The Philharmonic Gets Dressed* (C,43)

Lincoln, Abraham *Gettysburg Address* (H5,46)

Meyers, Susan *Pearson, a Harbor Seal Pup* (C,43)

Patterson, Francine *Koko's Kitten* (C,44)

Price, Christine *Dancing Masks of Africa* (C,44)

C = California Recommended Readings, K-8

CS = California Recommended Literature, 9-12

E1 = The Edison Project: Primary

E2 = The Edison Project: Elementary Academy

E3 = The Edison Project: Junior Academy

GJ = Gillespie: Best Books for Junior High Readers

GS = Gillespie: Best Books for Senior High Readers

H = Hirsch: Cultural Literacy

H1 - H6 = Hirsch: Core Knowledge Series, Grades 1-6

NE = New England Association of Teachers of English

NS = NCTE: Books for You

RF = Ravitch & Finn: What Do Our 17-Year-Olds Know?

Rockwell, Anne *The Toolbox* (C,44)

Selsam, Millicent E. *Cotton* and *The Maple Tree* and *See Through the Forest* (C,44,45)

Truth, Sojourner "Ain't I a Woman" (H4,40)

Nonfiction - Biography

Aliki *A Weed Is a Flower: The Life of George Washington Carver* (C,46)

Barnard, Jacqueline *Voices from the Southwest: Antonio Jose Martinez, Elfego Baca, and Reies Lopez Tijerina* (C,46)

Fritz, Jean *And Then What Happened, Paul Revere?* and *What's the Big Idea, Ben Franklin?* and *Where Was Patrick Henry on the 29th of May?* (C,47,48)

Meltzer, Milton *Dorothea Lange: A Photographer's Life* (C,49)

Monjo, Ferdinand N. *Me and Willie an Pa* and *The One Bad Thing About Father* (C,49)

Provensen, Alice, and Martin *The Glorious Flight Across the Channel with Louis Bleriot* (C,49)

Tobias, Tobi *Isamu Noguchi: The Life of a Sculptor* (C,50)

C = California Recommended Readings, K-8
CS = California Recommended Literature, 9-12
E1 = The Edison Project: Primary
E2 = The Edison Project: Elementary Academy
E3 = The Edison Project: Junior Academy
GJ = Gillespie: Best Books for Junior High Readers

GS = Gillespie: Best Books for Senior High Readers
H = Hirsch: Cultural Literacy
H1 - H6 = Hirsch: Core Knowledge Series, Grades 1-6
NE = New England Association of Teachers of English
NS = NCTE: Books for You
RF = Ravitch & Finn: What Do Our 17-Year-Olds Know?

Appendix for Language Arts Standard 13: Level III (Middle School)

Greek and Roman Mythology

Aphrodite/Venus (H,154;RF,271)
"Apollo and Daphne" (H6,52)
Apollo/Mars (H,154;RF,273)
Artemis/Diana (H,155)
Athena/Minerva (H,155)
Atlas (RF,272)
Cupid/Eros (H,165)
"Cupid and Psyche" (H6,58)
Dionysus/Bacchus (H,167)
"Echo and Narcissus" (H6,55)
Elysian Fields (H,169)
Eros/Cupid (H,170)
Furies (H,173)
Hera/Juno (H,177)
Hercules (H,177)

Hermes/Mercury (H,177)
Janus (H,181)
Lord of the Sky: Zeus by Doris Gates (CS,11)
Medusa (H,187)
"Orpheus and Eurydice" (H6,53)
Pandora's box (RF,272)
Posieden/Neptune (H,197)
Prometheus (RF,275)
Pygmalion (H6,57)
Romulus and Remus (H,201)
Sirens (H,204)
Styx (H,206)

Classic American Literature

Alcott, Louisa May *Little Women* (H,153;GJ,17)
Cooper, James Fennimore *The Last of the Mohicans* (GJ,17;H,164)
Crane, Stephen *The Red Badge of Courage* (GJ,17)
Hale, E. E. *The Man Without a Country and Other Stories* (GJ,17)
Henry, O. "The Gift of the Magi" (GJ,17)
Irving, Washington *The Legend of Sleepy Hollow and Other Selections* (GJ,18)
London, Jack (E3,38;RF,272)
      Call of the Wild (NE,6)
      "To Build a Fire" (NE,6)
      Sea Wolf (GJ,18)
      White Fang (GJ, 18)
Poe, Edgar Allan (GJ,18)
      "The Black Cat" (NE,10)
      The Complete Tales and Poems of Edgar Allan Poe (GJ,18)
      Tales of Terror (GJ,18)
Twain, Mark (E3,38;GJ,18)
      The Adventures of Tom Sawyer (NE,6;GJ,18)
      The Adventures of Huckleberry Finn (NE,10;GJ,18)
      A Connecticut Yankee in King Arthur's Court (GJ,18)

C = California Recommended Readings, K-8
CS = California Recommended Literature, 9-12
E1 = The Edison Project: Primary
E2 = The Edison Project: Elementary Academy
E3 = The Edison Project: Junior Academy
GJ = Gillespie: Best Books for Junior High Readers

GS = Gillespie: Best Books for Senior High Readers
H = Hirsch: Cultural Literacy
H1 - H6 = Hirsch: Core Knowledge Series, Grades 1-6
NE = New England Association of Teachers of English
NS = NCTE: Books for You
RF = Ravitch & Finn: What Do Our 17-Year-Olds Know?

McREL

  The Prince and the Pauper (GJ,18)
  Pudd'nhead Wilson (GJ,18)
  Tom Sawyer Abroad (GJ,18)
  Tom Sawyer, Detective (GJ,18)
Steinbeck, John *Of Mice and Men* (NE,6)
  The Pearl (NE,6)
  The Red Pony (NE,6)
Hemingway, Ernest *The Old Man and the Sea* (NE,6)
Wilder, Thornton *Our Town* (NE,10)

Classic British Literature

Barrie, J. M. *Peter Pan* (GJ,16)
Shelley, Mary W. *Frankenstein* (GJ,17)
Stevenson, Robert Louis *Dr. Jeckyl and Mr. Hyde* (GJ,17)
Swift, Jonathan *Gulliver's Travels* (GJ,17)
Orwell, George *Animal Farm* (H6,20;NE,6)
Burnett, Frances H. *The Secret Garden* (GJ,16)
Defoe, Daniel *Robinson Crusoe* (GJ,16)
Dickens, Charles (GJ,16-17)
  David Copperfield (GJ,16)
  Oliver Twist (GJ,16)
  A Christmas Carol (NE,6)
  Great Expectations (NE,10)
  A Tale of Two Cities (NE,10)
Eliot, George *Silas Marner* (GJ,17)
Doyle, Arthur Conan *Sherlock Holmes: The Complete Novels and Stories* (GJ,17)
Kipling, Rudyard *Captains Courageous, Kim* (GJ,17)
Tennyson, Alfred (GJ,17)
Wilde, Oscar *The Canterville Ghost* (GJ,17)
Bronte, Charlotte *Jane Eyre* (GJ,16)
Bronte, Emily *Wuthering Heights* (GJ,16)
Shakespeare, William *The Taming of the Shrew* (NE,6)
  Romeo and Juliet (NE,6)
  Julius Caesar (NE,10)
  A Midsummer Night's Dream (NE,10)

C = California Recommended Readings, K-8
CS = California Recommended Literature, 9-12
E1 = The Edison Project: Primary
E2 = The Edison Project: Elementary Academy
E3 = The Edison Project: Junior Academy
GJ = Gillespie: Best Books for Junior High Readers

GS = Gillespie: Best Books for Senior High Readers
H = Hirsch: Cultural Literacy
H1 - H6 = Hirsch: Core Knowledge Series, Grades 1-6
NE = New England Association of Teachers of English
NS = NCTE: Books for You
RF = Ravitch & Finn: What Do Our 17-Year-Olds Know?

M·REL

Classic World Literature

Cervantes, Miguel de *The Adventures of Don Quixote de la Mancha* (GJ,16)

Dumas, Alexandre *The Count of Monte Cristo, The Three Musketeers* (GJ,16)

Frank, Anne *The Diary of a Young Girl* (H6,25;NE,6)

Maupassant, Guy de *Best Short Stories* (GJ,16)

Verne, Jules *Around the World in Eighty Days* (GJ, 16)
      Journey to the Center of the Earth (GJ,16)
      Twenty Thousand Leagues Under the Sea (GJ,16)

Wyss, Johann *The Swiss Family Robinson* (GJ,16)

Adapted/Retold and Exerpted Literature

Angelou, Maya *I Know Why the Caged Bird Sings* (H6,27)

Oliver Twist (H6,7)

Romeo and Juliet (H6,2)

The Secret Garden (H6,12)

Modern/Contemporary Fiction

Hien, Nguyen Thai Duc *Doi song moi/Tren dat moi: A New Life in a New Land* (CS,12)

Adams, Edward B., ed. *Two Brothers and Their Magic Gourds* (CS,15)

Armstrong, William H. *Sounder* (NE,10;GJ,18)

Borland, Hal *When the Legends Die* (NE,10)

Bradbury, Ray *Fahrenheit 451* (NE,10)

Bradbury, Ray *All Summer in a Day* (NE,10)

Buck, Pearl S. *The Good Earth* (E3,79)

Burch, Robert *Queenie Peavy* (CS,29)

Byers, Betsy *The Summer of Swans* (CS,30)

Clapp, Patricia *I'm Deborah Sampson: A Soldier in the War of the Revolution* (CS,36)

Cleary, Beverly *Dear Mr. Henshaw* (CS,30)

Cormier, Robert *8+1* (NE,10)

Cormier, Robert *I Am the Cheese* (NE,10)

Cormier, Robert *The Chocolate War* (NE,6)

Craven, Margaret *I Heard the Owl Call My Name* (NE,10)

Dorris, Michael *Morning Girl* (E3,39)

Fletcher, Lucille *Sorry, Wrong Number* (NE,10)

Forbes, Esther *Johnny Tremain* (NE,6)

Fox, Paula *One-Eyed Cat* (CS,31)

C = California Recommended Readings, K-8
CS = California Recommended Literature, 9-12
E1 = The Edison Project: Primary
E2 = The Edison Project: Elementary Academy
E3 = The Edison Project: Junior Academy
GJ = Gillespie: Best Books for Junior High Readers

GS = Gillespie: Best Books for Senior High Readers
H = Hirsch: Cultural Literacy
H1 - H6 = Hirsch: Core Knowledge Series, Grades 1-6
NE = New England Association of Teachers of English
NS = NCTE: Books for You
RF = Ravitch & Finn: What Do Our 17-Year-Olds Know?

345

MREL

George, Jean Craighead *Julie of the Wolves* (E3,39;NE,10;NJ,95,141)
Gibson, William *The Miracle Worker* (E3,39;NE,10)
Gipson, Fred *Old Yeller* (NE,6)
Golding, William *Lord of the Flies* (NE,6)
Hamilton, Virginia *The House of Dies Drear*
Hansberry , Lorraine *A Raisen in the Sun* (NE,6)
Hautzig, Esther *A Gift for Mama* (CS,37)
Hinton, S. E. *Tex* (NE,10)
Hinton, S. E. *The Outsiders* (NE,6)
Keyes, Daniel *Flowers for Algernon* (NE,6)
Knowles, John *A Separate Peace* (NE,6)
Kroeber, Theodora *Ishi, Last of His Tribe* (E3,39)
Lawrence, Jerome and Robert Lee *Inherit the Wind* (NE,10)
Lee, Harper *To Kill a Mockingbird* (NE,6)
L'Engle, Madeleine *A Wrinkle in Time* (CS,19)
Lewis, C. S. *The Lion, the Witch and the Wardrobe* (CS,19)
Mathis, Sharon B. *The Hundred Penny Box* (CS,33)
O'Dell, Scott *Island of the Blue Dolphins* (CS,38)
Orgel, Doris *Ariadne, Awake!* (E3,39;NJ,42)
Orlev, Uri *The Island on Bird Street* (CS,38)
Paulsen, Gary *The River* (E3,39;NJ,8,54,78,132)
Paterson, Katherine *Bridge to Terabithia* (CS,33)
Peck, Robert Newton *A Day No Pigs Would Die* (NE,6)
Rawlings, Marjorie Kinnan *The Yearling* (NE,10)
Rawls, Wilson *Where the Red Fern Grows* (CS,34;E3,39;NE,6)
Richter, Conrad *The Light in the Forest* (NE,10)
Rose, Reginald *Twelve Angry Men* (NE, 10)
Saint-Exupery, Antoine de *The Little Prince* (CS,30)
Salinger, J. D. *Catcher in the Rye* (NE,6)
Saroyan, Willliam *The Human Comedy* (NE,10)
Schaeffer, Jack *Shane* (NE,6)
Soto, Gary *Local News* (E3,39;NJ,220)
Speare, Elizabeth *The Witch of Blackbird Pond* (CS,39;NE,6)
Taylor, Theodore *The Cay* (NE,10)
Taylor, Mildred D. *Roll of Thunder, Hear My Cry* (CS,39;E3,39;NE,6;NJ,79)
Thurber, James "The Secret Life of Walter Mitty" (RF,275;H,203)
Tolkien, J. R. R. *The Hobbit* (NE,7)
Uchida, Yoshiko *A Jar of Dreams* (E3,39)

C = California Recommended Readings, K-8
CS = California Recommended Literature, 9-12
E1 = The Edison Project: Primary
E2 = The Edison Project: Elementary Academy
E3 = The Edison Project: Junior Academy
GJ = Gillespie: Best Books for Junior High Readers

GS = Gillespie: Best Books for Senior High Readers
H = Hirsch: Cultural Literacy
H1 - H6 = Hirsch: Core Knowledge Series, Grades 1-6
NE = New England Association of Teachers of English
NS = NCTE: Books for You
RF = Ravitch & Finn: What Do Our 17-Year-Olds Know?

346

MREL

White, T.H. *The Once and Future King* (E3,38)
Yep, Laurence *Dragonwings* (E3,39;NJ,201)
Yep, Laurence *Child of the Owl* (CS,35)
Zindel, Paul *The Pigman* (NE,6)

Poetry and Poets
Angelou, Maya "Caged Bird", "Woman Work" (H6,47, 49)
Austin, Mary, translator "A Song of Greatness" a Chippewa song (H6,38)
Brewton, Sara, and John Brewton, eds. *America Forever New: A Book of Poems* (CS,23)
Brooks, Gwendolyn "The Bean Eaters" (E3,39)
Carroll, Lewis "Father William" (H6,41)
Dickinson, Emily "I Like to See It Lap the Miles" (H6,41)
Dunbar, Paul Laurence "Sympathy" (H6,47)
Dunning, Stephen, ed. *Reflections on a Gift of Watermelon Pickle* (NE,6)
Frost, Robert "Stopping by the Woods on a Snowy Evening," "The Road Not Taken"
     (H6,39,50)
Hughes, Langston *Don't You Turn Back* (CS,25)
              "Harlem," "Life is Fine," "The Negro Speaks of Rivers" (H6,35,50,51)
Johnson, James Weldon "Lift Ev'ry Voice and Sing" (H6,38)
Longfellow, Henry Wadsworth "A Psalm of Life" (H6,36)
              "Song of Hiawatha" (H,166)
Ortiz, Simon "My Father's Song" (E3,39)
Plotz, Helen, ed. *The Gift Outright: America to Her Poets* (CS,25)
Poe, Edgar Allan "Annabel Lee," "The Raven" (H6,43;RF,271)
Sandburg, Carl (GJ,18)
Shakespeare, William "All the World's a Stage" from *As You Like It* (H6,40)
Tennyson, Alfred "The Lady of Shallot" (GJ,17)
Williams, William Carlos "This is Just to Say" (H6,42)

Nonfiction - Information
Beatty, Patricia *Lupita Mañana* (C,41)
Brenner, Barbara *On the Frontier with Mr. Audubon* (C,41)
De Garza, Patricia *Chicanos: The Story of Mexican-Americans* (C,41)
Demuth, Patricia *Joel: Growing Up on Farm Man* (C,41)
Kennedy, John. F. Inaugural Address (H6,30)
King, Martin Luther, Jr. "I Have a Dream" (H6,32)

C = California Recommended Readings, K-8
CS = California Recommended Literature, 9-12
E1 = The Edison Project: Primary
E2 = The Edison Project: Elementary Academy
E3 = The Edison Project: Junior Academy
GJ = Gillespie: Best Books for Junior High Readers

GS = Gillespie: Best Books for Senior High Readers
H = Hirsch: Cultural Literacy
H1 - H6 = Hirsch: Core Knowledge Series, Grades 1-6
NE = New England Association of Teachers of English
NS = NCTE: Books for You
RF = Ravitch & Finn: What Do Our 17-Year-Olds Know?

MREL

St. George, Judith *The Brooklyn Bridge: They Said It Couldn't Be Built* (C,45)

Nonfiction - Biography

Franchere, Ruth *Cesar Chaves* (C,47)

Greenfield, Howard *Marc Chagall: An Introduction* (C,48)

Hunter, Edith Fisher *Child of the Silent Night: The Story of Laura Bridgman* (C,48)

Jackson, Jesse *Make a Joyful Noise Unto the Lord: The Life of Mahalia Jackson, Queen of Gospel Singers* (C,48)

Kohn, Bernice *Talking Leaves: The Story of Sequoyah* (C,48)

Kroeber, Theodora *Ishi, Last of His Tribe* (C,48)

McCunn, Ruthanne L. *Thousand Pieces of Gold: A Biographical Novel* (C,48)

McGovern, Ann *The Secret Soldier: The Story of Deborah Sampson* (C,49)

Nhuong, Huynh Quang *Land I Lost* (C,49)

Reiss, Johanna *The Upstairs Room* (C,50)

C = California Recommended Readings, K-8
CS = California Recommended Literature, 9-12
E1 = The Edison Project: Primary
E2 = The Edison Project: Elementary Academy
E3 = The Edison Project: Junior Academy
GJ = Gillespie: Best Books for Junior High Readers

GS = Gillespie: Best Books for Senior High Readers
H = Hirsch: Cultural Literacy
H1 - H6 = Hirsch: Core Knowledge Series, Grades 1-6
NE = New England Association of Teachers of English
NS = NCTE: Books for You
RF = Ravitch & Finn: What Do Our 17-Year-Olds Know?

McREL

Appendix for Language Arts Standard 13: Level IV (High School)

Classic American Literature

Poetry
Dickenson, Emily (H,167;RF,271)
Whitman, Walt *Leaves of Grass* (H,183;RF,275)

Fiction
Alcott, Louisa May *Little Women* (GS,21)
Alger, Horatio (H,153)
Anderson, Sherwood *Winesburg, Ohio* (GS,21)
Cather, Willa (GS,21;H,161)
    My Antonia (CS,23;NE,4;RF,276)
    O Pioneers! (RF,276)
    Death Comes for the Archbishop (RF,276)
Chopin, Kate *The Awakening* (NE,5)
Cooper, James Fennimore *The Last of the Mohicans* (GS,21)
Crane, Stephen
    Red Badge of Courage (CS,24;GS,21;H,199;NE,4;RF,272)
    Maggie: A Girl of the Streets (NE,5)
Harte, Bret "Outcasts of Poker Flat" (CS,44;GS,22;H,176)
Hawthorne, Nathanial (GS,22;H,176)
    "Rappucini's Daughter" (RF,274)
    The House of Seven Gables (GS,22)
    "The Minister's Black Veil" (RF,274)
    The Scarlet Letter (CS,25;H,202;NE,4;RF,272)
    "Young Goodman Brown" (CS,44;RF,274)
Henry, O. "Gift of the Magi" (GS,22)
Holmes, Oliver Wendell (H,177)
Irving, Washington "The Devil and Tom Walker" (CS,44;GS,22)
James, Henry (GS,22;H,181)
    Daisy Miller (RF,276)
    Portrait of a Lady (GS,22;RF,276)
    The Turn of the Screw (CS,26)
Lewis, Sinclair *Babbitt* (CS,27;H,155)
London, Jack *Call of the Wild* (CS,27;GS,22)
Melville, Herman (GS,22,25)
    "Bartleby" (RF,275)

C = California Recommended Readings, K-8
CS = California Recommended Literature, 9-12
E1 = The Edison Project: Primary
E2 = The Edison Project: Elementary Academy
E3 = The Edison Project: Junior Academy
GJ = Gillespie: Best Books for Junior High Readers

GS = Gillespie: Best Books for Senior High Readers
H = Hirsch: Cultural Literacy
H1 - H6 = Hirsch: Core Knowledge Series, Grades 1-6
NE = New England Association of Teachers of English
NS = NCTE: Books for You
RF = Ravitch & Finn: What Do Our 17-Year-Olds Know?

349

MREL

"Benito Cereno" (NE,5;RF,275)
"Billy Budd" (CS,27;NE,7;RF,275)
Moby Dick (H,153;NE,4;RF,272,275)
Norris, Frank *McTeague* (GS,22;NE,9)
Poe, Edgar Allan (H,196;RF,270)
  "Fall of the House of Usher" (GS,22;H,171;RF,270)
  "Pit and Pendulum" (RF,270)
Stowe, Harriet Beecher *Uncle Tom's Cabin* (H,206;RF,271)
Twain, Mark (RF,270)
  Huckleberry Finn (CS,30;GS,22;H,178;NE,4;RF,270)
  Pudd'nhead Wilson (NE,9)
  The Prince and the Pauper (NE,10)
Wharton, Edith *Ethan Frome* (CS,30;H,213;NE,4)

Nonfiction

Declaration of Independence (RF,271;H,166)
Douglass, Frederick *Narrative of the Life of Frederick Douglass* (NE,8)
Edwards, Jonathan (H,169)
Emerson, Ralph Waldo (H,170)
Franklin, Ben *Poor Richard's Almanack* (H,196;RF,274)
Lincoln, Abraham (H,184)
  Gettysburg Address (RF,271)
  "With malice toward none..." (RF,274)
The Constitution, Preamble (RF,272)
Thoreau, Henry David *Walden* (H,209;NE,5;RF,274)

MODERN/CONTEMPORARY AMERICAN LITERATURE

Poetry

cummings, e.e. (H,165)
Frost, Robert "The Road Not Taken" (H6,39,173;NE,8;RF,272)
Hughes, Langston (RF,275)
Sandburg, Carl (CL,202;NS,200)

C = California Recommended Readings, K-8
CS = California Recommended Literature, 9-12
E1 = The Edison Project: Primary
E2 = The Edison Project: Elementary Academy
E3 = The Edison Project: Junior Academy
GJ = Gillespie: Best Books for Junior High Readers

GS = Gillespie: Best Books for Senior High Readers
H = Hirsch: Cultural Literacy
H1 - H6 = Hirsch: Core Knowledge Series, Grades 1-6
NE = New England Association of Teachers of English
NS = NCTE: Books for You
RF = Ravitch & Finn: What Do Our 17-Year-Olds Know?

M*REL

Fiction

Anaya, Rudolfo A. *Bless Me, Ultima* (CS,22)

Baldwin, James *Go Tell It on the Mountain* (CS,22)

Borland, Hal *When the Legends Die* (CS,22)

Bradbury, Ray *Fahrenheit 451* and *The Martian Chronicles* (CS,23;NE,7,8)

Bryant, Dorothy *Miss Giardino* (CS,23)

Buck, Pearl *The Good Earth* (CS,23)

Cisneros, Sandra *The House on Mango Street* (CS,23)

Clark, Walter Van Tilburg *Ox-bow Incident* (CS,23)

Clavell, James *The Children's Story* (NE,10)

Cormier, Robert *After the First Death, I Am the Cheese, The Chocolate War* (CS,23;NE,5,7)

Craven, Margaret *I Heard the Owl Call My Name* (CS,24)

Dos Passos, John (GS,21;H,168)

Ellison, Ralph *Invisible Man* (CS,24;NE,4;H,169;RF,276)

Faulkner, William *The Light in August, The Bear* (CS,24;H,171;NE,8;RF,276)

Fitzgerald, F. Scott *The Great Gatsby* (CS,24;H,175;NE,4;RF,273)

Gaines, Ernest J. *The Autobiography of Miss Jane Pittman* (CS,24)

Gardner, John *Grendel* (NE,5)

Gibson, William *The Miracle Worker* (NE,4)

Guest, Judith *Ordinary People* (NE,8)

Hailey, Alex *Roots* (H,214)

Hale, E. E. (GS,22)

Hemingway, Ernest (H,176;GS,22)

     A Farewell to Arms (NE,4)

     For Whom the Bell Tolls (RF,272)

     The Sun Also Rises (H,207;NE,8;RF,272)

     The Old Man and the Sea (CS,25;NE,4;RF,274)

     In Our Time (NE,8)

     "In Another Country" (RF,276)

     "The Short Happy Life of Francis Macomber" (RF,276)

     "The Killers" (RF,276)

Heller, Joseph *Catch 22* (CS,25;NE,5)

Hersey, John *Hiroshima* (NE,5,7)

Hinton, S. E. *The Outsiders* (CS,25;NE,8)

Hurston, Zora Neale *Their Eyes Were Watching God* (CS,25;NE,5)

Kesey, Ken *One Flew Over the Cuckoo's Nest* (NE,4)

Keyes, Daniel *Flowers for Algernon* (CS,26)

Kim, Richard *Martyred* (CS,26)

C = California Recommended Readings, K-8	GS = Gillespie: Best Books for Senior High Readers
CS = California Recommended Literature, 9-12	H = Hirsch: Cultural Literacy
E1 = The Edison Project: Primary	H1 - H6 = Hirsch: Core Knowledge Series, Grades 1-6
E2 = The Edison Project: Elementary Academy	NE = New England Association of Teachers of English
E3 = The Edison Project: Junior Academy	NS = NCTE: Books for You
GJ = Gillespie: Best Books for Junior High Readers	RF = Ravitch & Finn: What Do Our 17-Year-Olds Know?

Kincaid, Jamaica *Annie John* (CS,26)

Knowles, John *A Separate Peace* (CS,26;NE,4)

Lee, Harper *To Kill a Mockingbird* (CS,26;NE,5;RF,273)

Malamud, Bernard *The Assistant* (NE,8)

Marshall, Paule *Brown Girl, Brownstones* (CS,27)

McCullers, Carson *The Heart is a Lonely Hunter, The Ballad of the Sad Cafe: The Novels and Stories of Carson McCullers* (CS,27;GS,58)

Mitchell, Margaret *Gone with the Wind* (H,175)

Momaday, N. Scott *House Made of Dawn* (CS,27)

Morrison, Toni *Beloved, Song of Solomon, Sula, The Bluest Eye* (CS,27;NE,5)

Naylor, Gloria *The Women of Brewster Place* (NE,5)

Neihardt, John *Black Elk Speaks* (NE,8)

O'Connor, Flannery (RF,277)

Okada, John *No-No Boy* (CS,28)

Peck, Richard *Remembering the Good Times* (CS,28)

Peck, Robert Newton *A Day No Pigs Would Die* (CS,28;NE,5)

Plath, Sylvia *The Bell Jar* (NE,8)

Porter, Katherine Anne *Noon Wine* (CS,28)

Potok, Chaim *The Chosen* (CS,28;NE,5)

Rawlings, Marjorie Kinnan *The Yearling* (CS,28)

Richter, Conrad *Light in the Forest* (CS,28)

Rivera, Tomas *And the Earth Did Not Part* (CS,29)

Ronyoung, Kim *Clay Walls* (CS,29)

Salinger, J. D. *Catcher in the Rye* (CS,29;H,161;NE,4;RF,276)

Saroyan, William *The Human Comedy* (CS,29)

Schaeffer, Jack *Shane* (NE,8)

Steinbeck, John (GS,22;H,175)

    The Grapes of Wrath (NE,4;RF,275)

    Of Mice and Men (CS,29;NE,4)

    The Pearl (NE,4)

Uchida, Yoshiko *Picture Bride* (CS,30)

Updike, John *Centaur* (CS,30)

Vonnegut, Kurt *Slaughterhouse Five, Cat's Cradle* (NE,8)

Walker, Alice *The Color Purple* (NE,5,7)

Warren, Robert Penn *All the King's Men* (NE,5)

Welty, Eudora (RF,277)

Wiesel, Elie *Night* (NE,5)

Wright, Richard *Native Son* and *Black Boy* (CS,30;H,158,191;NE,4,8;RF,276)

C = California Recommended Readings, K-8

CS = California Recommended Literature, 9-12

E1 = The Edison Project: Primary

E2 = The Edison Project: Elementary Academy

E3 = The Edison Project: Junior Academy

GJ = Gillespie: Best Books for Junior High Readers

GS = Gillespie: Best Books for Senior High Readers

H = Hirsch: Cultural Literacy

H1 - H6 = Hirsch: Core Knowledge Series, Grades 1-6

NE = New England Association of Teachers of English

NS = NCTE: Books for You

RF = Ravitch & Finn: What Do Our 17-Year-Olds Know?

Zindel, Paul *The Pigman* (CS,30;NE,8)

Drama

Agee, James *Death in the Family* (CS,10)

Albee, Edward *American Dream, Zoo Story, Who's Afraid of Virginia Woolf*
    (CS,7;GS,151;NE,8)

Anderson, Robert *I Never Sang for My Father* (CS,7)

Chin, Frank *The Chickencoop Chinaman and The Year of the Dragon: Two Plays* (CS,8)

Elder, Lonne *Ceremonies in Dark Old Men* (CS,8)

Fugard, Athol *Master Harold and the Boys* (CS,8;NE,5)

Goodrich, Frances, and Albert Hackett *Diary of Anne Frank* (CS,8)

Gibson, William *The Miracle Worker* (CS,8;GS,151)

Hansberry, Lorraine *A Raisin in the Sun* (CS,8;NE,4;RF,273)

Hellman, Lillian *The Little Foxes* (CS,8)

Laurents, Arthur *West Side Story* (NE,8)

Lawrence, Jerome and Robert E. Lee
        Inherit the Wind, The Night Thoreau Spent in Jail (CS,9;GS,152;NE,4,9)

Lum, Wing Tek *Oranges are Lucky* (CS,9)

McCullers, Carson *The Member of the Wedding* (CS,9)

Medoff, Mark *Children of a Lesser God* (CS,9)

Miller, Arthur *Death of a Salesman, The Crucible* (CS,9;GS,153;H,166;NE,4;RF,273)

O'Neill, Eugene *Anna Christie, The Emperor Jones, The Hairy Ape, The Iceman Cometh, Long*
        Day's Journey Into Night (CS,9;GS,153;H,192)

Rose, Reginald *Twelve Angry Men* (CS,9)

Sakamoto, Edward *In the Alley* (CS,9)

Simon, Neil *Barefoot in the Park, Brighton Beach Memoirs, Broadway Bound, The Odd Couple,*
        They're Playing Our Song (GS,154)

Valdez, Luis *Zoot Suit* (CS,10)

Vidal, Gore *A Visit to a Small Planet* (CS,10)

Wilder, Thornton *Our Town* (CS,10;H,193;NE,4;NE,9;RF,272)

Williams, Tennessee *A Streetcar Named Desire, The Glass Menagerie, Cat on a Hot Tin Roof*
    (CS,10;GS,154;H,20;NE4,5;RF,276)

Wilson, August *Fences* (CS,10)

C = California Recommended Readings, K-8	GS = Gillespie: Best Books for Senior High Readers
CS = California Recommended Literature, 9-12	H = Hirsch: Cultural Literacy
E1 = The Edison Project: Primary	H1 - H6 = Hirsch: Core Knowledge Series, Grades 1-6
E2 = The Edison Project: Elementary Academy	NE = New England Association of Teachers of English
E3 = The Edison Project: Junior Academy	NS = NCTE: Books for You
GJ = Gillespie: Best Books for Junior High Readers	RF = Ravitch & Finn: What Do Our 17-Year-Olds Know?

Nonfiction

Angelou, Maya *I Know Why the Caged Bird Sings* (NE,4)

Capote, Truman *In Cold Blood* (NE,7)

Friedan, Betty (H,173)

King, Martin Luther, Jr. "I Have a Dream" (RF,270)

Menken, H.L. (H,188)

Roosevelt, Franklin D. "The only thing we have to fear is fear itself" and "Yesterday, Dec. 7, 1941,--a date which will live in infamy" (RF,273)

Turkel, Studs *Working* (NE,9)

BRITISH LITERATURE

Poetry

Auden, W. H. *Collected Poems* (GS,158)

Browning, Elizabeth Barrett *The Poetical Works of Elizabeth Barrett Browning* and *Sonnets from the Portuguese* (GS,158)

Browning, Robert *Robert Browning's Poetry: Authoritative Texts, Criticism* (GS,158;H,159)

Burns, Robert *The Poetical Works of Burns* (GS,158;H,160)

Byron, George Gordon "Don Juan" (GS,158;H,168;RF,274)

Chaucer, Geoffrey *Canterbury Tales* (GS,19;H,160;NE,4;RF,275)

Coleridge, Samuel Taylor *The Rime of the Ancient Mariner* (H,162;NE,8)

Donne, John *The Complete Works of John Donne* (GS,160;H,168)

Eliot, T. S. "The Hollow Men," "The Love Song of J. Alfred Prufrock," *The Waste Land* (H,169,213;RF,274)

Gray, Thomas "Elegy Written in a Country Churchyard" (H,169)

Hardy, Thomas *The Complete Poems of Thomas Hardy* (GS,159)

Hopkins, Gerard Manley *The Complete Poems of Gerard Manley Hopkins* (GS,159)

Houseman, A. E. *The Complete Poems of A. E. Houseman* (GS,159)

Joyce, James "Araby" and "Eveline" (RF,277)

Keats, John "Ode on a Grecian Urn" (GS,159;H,192;RF,274)

Kipling, Rudyard "Gunga Din" (H,176)

Milton, John *Paradise Lost* (GS,160;H,193;RF,275)

Pope, Alexander (H,196)

Shakespeare, William *Sonnets* (RF,273;GS,160)

Shelley, Percy Bysshe *The Poetical Works of Shelley* (GS,16;H,204)

Spender, S. *Collected Poems* (GS,160)

Tennyson, Alfred "Charge of the Light Brigade" (GS,160;H,162)

C = California Recommended Readings, K-8	GS = Gillespie: Best Books for Senior High Readers
CS = California Recommended Literature, 9-12	H = Hirsch: Cultural Literacy
E1 = The Edison Project: Primary	H1 - H6 = Hirsch: Core Knowledge Series, Grades 1-6
E2 = The Edison Project: Elementary Academy	NE = New England Association of Teachers of English
E3 = The Edison Project: Junior Academy	NS = NCTE: Books for You
GJ = Gillespie: Best Books for Junior High Readers	RF = Ravitch & Finn: What Do Our 17-Year-Olds Know?

354

McREL

Thomas, Dylan *The Poems of Dylan Thomas* (GS,160)
Wordsworth, William *The Poetical Works of Wordsworth* (GS,160;H,214;RF,274)
Yeats, William Butler "The Second Coming" (H,215;RF,275)

Fiction

Austen, Jane *Pride and Prejudice* (CS,22;GS,18;H,156;NE,4;RF,275)
Bennett, Arnold *The Old Wives' Tale* (GS,19)
Blackmore, R. D. *Lorna Doone* (GS,19)
Bronte, Charlotte *Jane Eyre* (CS,23;GS,19;H,159;NE,4)
Bronte, Emily *Wuthering Heights* (CS,23;H,159;NE,4;RF,275)
Bunyan, John *Pilgrim's Progress* (GS,19;H,1915;RF,277)
Butler, Samuel *The Way of All Flesh* (GS,19)
Carroll, Lewis *Alice in Wonderland* (CS,23)
Christie, Agatha (H,162)
Clarke, Arthur C. *Childhood's End* (CS,23)
Collins, Wilkie *The Moonstone, The Woman in White* (GS,19)
Conrad, Joseph (GS,19;H,164;RF,276)
      The Heart of Darkness (CS,23;GS,19;NE,4)
      Lord Jim (GS,19;RF,275)
Defoe, Daniel *Robinson Crusoe* (GS,19)
Dickens, Charles (GS,19;H,167)
      Oliver Twist (H,193;NE,8;RF,271)
      A Tale of Two Cities (CS,24;NE,4;RF,273)
      Great Expectations (H,175;NE,4)
      Hard Times (NE,7;RF,271)
      David Copperfield (H,166)
Doyle, Sir Arthur Conan *Hound of the Baskervilles* (GS,20;H,164;RF,271)
Eliot, George *The Mill on the Floss* and *Silas Marner* (GS,20;NE,4)
Fielding, Henry *Tom Jones* (GS,20;H,172)
Forster, E.M. *Passage to India* (CS,24)
Golding, William *Lord of the Flies* (CS,24;NE,4;RF,275)
Greene, Graham *The Power and the Glory* (CS,25;NE,9)
Hardy, Thomas (RF,276)
      Jude the Obscure (GS,20)
      Return of the Native (GS,20;NE,8;RF,276)
      Tess of the D'Urbervilles (GS,20;NE,8;RF,276)
      The Mayor of Casterbridge (CS,25;GS,20;NE,8;RF,276)

C = California Recommended Readings, K-8	GS = Gillespie: Best Books for Senior High Readers
CS = California Recommended Literature, 9-12	H = Hirsch: Cultural Literacy
E1 = The Edison Project: Primary	H1 - H6 = Hirsch: Core Knowledge Series, Grades 1-6
E2 = The Edison Project: Elementary Academy	NE = New England Association of Teachers of English
E3 = The Edison Project: Junior Academy	NS = NCTE: Books for You
GJ = Gillespie: Best Books for Junior High Readers	RF = Ravitch & Finn: What Do Our 17-Year-Olds Know?

MREL

Huxley, Aldous *Brave New World* (CS,25;H,178;NE,7)
Joyce, James (H,182)
> *Ulysses, A Portrait of the Artist As a Young Man* (CS,26;RF,277)

Kipling, Rudyard *Captains Courageous, Kim,* and *The Man Who Would Be King* (GS,20)
Lawrence, D.H. "The Rocking Horse Winner" and *Sons and Lovers* (CS,26;GS,20;RF,276)
Munro, H. H. *The Complete Works of Saki* (GS,21)
Orwell, George *1984* and *Animal Farm* (CS,28;H,193;NE,4;RF,275)
Shelley, Mary *Frankenstein* (GS,20;NE,7;RF,271)
Sillitoe, Alan *Loneliness of the Long Distance Runner* (NE,8)
Sterne, Laurence *Tristam Shandy* (GS,21)
Stevenson, Robert Louis *The Strange Case of Dr. Jekyll and Mr. Hyde, The Black Arrow,* and
> *Kidnapped* (GS,21;H,168)

Swift, Jonathan *Gulliver's Travels* and "A Modest Proposal"
> (CS,29;GS,21;H,176,188,207;NE,7;RF,272)

Thackeray, William M. *Vanity Fair* (GS,21)
Tolkien, J.R.R. *The Hobbit* (NE,7)
Trollope, Anthony *Barchester Towers* (CS,30;GS,21)
White, T. H. *The Once and Future King* (NE,8)
Wilde, Oscar *The Picture of Dorian Gray* (GS,21)
Woolf, Virginia (H,214)

Drama

Bolt, Robert *A Man for All Seasons* (CS,7)
Congreve, William *The Way of the World* (GS,149)
Coward, Noel *Blithe Spirit, Hay Fever, Private Lives* (GS,149)
Eliot, T. S. *Murder in the Cathedral, The Family Reunion, The Cocktail Party* (GS,149)
Marlowe, Christopher *Doctor Faustus* (GS,149)
Shakespeare, William (CS,9;GS,150)
> *Romeo and Juliet* (GS,151;H,201;NE,4;RF,270)
> *Hamlet* (GS,150;H,176;NE,4;RF,270)
> *Julius Caesar* (H,170;NE,4;RF,271,274)
> *Macbeth* (GS,150H,185;NE,4;RF,274)
> *Antony and Cleopatra* (H,154)
> *The Tempest* (GS,150;H,208)
> *Othello* (GS,151;H,193)
> *King Lear* (GS,150;H,182;NE,8)
> *Merchant of Venice* (H,189;NE,8)

C = California Recommended Readings, K-8
CS = California Recommended Literature, 9-12
E1 = The Edison Project: Primary
E2 = The Edison Project: Elementary Academy
E3 = The Edison Project: Junior Academy
GJ = Gillespie: Best Books for Junior High Readers

GS = Gillespie: Best Books for Senior High Readers
H = Hirsch: Cultural Literacy
H1 - H6 = Hirsch: Core Knowledge Series, Grades 1-6
NE = New England Association of Teachers of English
NS = NCTE: Books for You
RF = Ravitch & Finn: What Do Our 17-Year-Olds Know?

MREL

The Taming of the Shrew (GS,150;NE,8)
Twelfth Night (GS,150)
A Midsummer Night's Dream (GS,151)
Shaw, George Bernard *Androcles and the Lion, Arms and the Man, Caesar and Cleopatra,*
    Major Barbara, Pygmalian, Saint Joan (CS,10;GS,150;RF,275)
Sheridan, Richard B. *The Rivals* and *The School for Scandal* (GS,150)
Thomas, Dylan *Under Milkwood: A Play for Voices* (CS,10)
Wilde, Oscar *The Importance of Being Earnest* (GS,150;H,214;NE,5)

Nonfiction

Churchill, Winston "Blood, toil, tears, and sweat" speech and "From Stettin in the Baltic to
    Trieste in the Adriatic, an Iron Curtain has descended across the continent" (RF,273)

WORLD LITERATURE

Achebe, Chinua *Things Fall Apart* (NE,5)
Alain-Fournier, Henri *The Wanderer* (GS,17)
Anouilh, Jean *Antigone* (CS,7)
Azuela, Mariano *The Underdogs* (CS,22)
Balzac, Honore de *Old Goriot* (GS,17)
Beckett, Samuel *Waiting for Godot* (CS,7)
Beowulf (RF,274;NE,7)
Brecht, Bertold *Mother Courage and Her Children* (CS,7;G,158)
Camus, Albert *The Stranger, The Plague* (CS,23;NE,4,8)
Cervantes *Don Quixote* (GS,17;RF,274)
Chekov, Anton *The Cherry Orchard* (CS,7;GS17,148;H,162)
Confucius (H,164)
Dante *The Divine Comedy* (H,167;RF,276)
Descartes (H,167)
Dostoevsky, F. *The Brothers Karamazov, Crime and Punishment, The Idiot*
    (CS,24;GS,17;H,165;NE,4;RF,277)
Dumas,Alexandre *The Count of Monte Cristo, The Man in the Iron Mask, The Three Musketeers*
    (GS,17,18)
Everyman (NE,7)
Flaubert, Gustave *Madame Bovary* (CS,24;GS,17)
Frankl, Victor *Man's Search for Meaning* (NE,9)

C = California Recommended Readings, K-8	GS = Gillespie: Best Books for Senior High Readers
CS = California Recommended Literature, 9-12	H = Hirsch: Cultural Literacy
E1 = The Edison Project: Primary	H1 - H6 = Hirsch: Core Knowledge Series, Grades 1-6
E2 = The Edison Project: Elementary Academy	NE = New England Association of Teachers of English
E3 = The Edison Project: Junior Academy	NS = NCTE: Books for You
GJ = Gillespie: Best Books for Junior High Readers	RF = Ravitch & Finn: What Do Our 17-Year-Olds Know?

357

McREL

Garcia Lorca, Federico *Blood Wedding* (CS,8)

Garcia Marques, Gabriel *Love in the Time of Cholera* (CS,24)

Giraudoux, Jean *The Madwoman of Chaillot* (GS,148)

Goethe, Johann Wolfgang von *Faust* (H,171)

Hesse, Hermann *Siddhartha, Beneath the Wheel* (CS,25;NE,8)

Hitler, Adolph *Mein Kampf* (H,187)

Hugo, Victor *The Hunchback of Notre Dame, Les Miserables* (CS,25;GS,18;H,178)

Ibsen, Henrik *A Doll's House, An Enemy of the People, Hedda Gabler, The Master Builder, The Wild Duck* (CS,8;GS,148;H,168;NE,7;RF,276)

Ionesco, Eugene *Rhinoceros* (CS,8)

Kafka, Franz (H,182) *Metamorphosis* (NE,8)

Kawabata, Yasunari *Snow Country* (CS,26)

Khayyam, Omar *The Rubaiyat* (H,192)

Machiavelli *The Prince* (H,197)

Mansfield, Katherine *Miss Brill* (NE,8)

Maupassant, Guy de *Selected Short Stories* (GS,17)

Mishima, Yukio *The Sound of Waves* (CS,27)

Mo, Timothy *Sour Sweet* (CS,27)

Moliere, Jean *The Misanthrope and Other Plays* (GS,148)

Montaigne (H,188)

O Yong-Jin and others *Wedding day and Other Korean Plays* (CS,9)

Paton, Alan *Cry, the Beloved Country* (CS,28;NE,5)

Proust, Marcel (H,108)

Rabelais (H,199)

Racine, Jean Baptiste *Phaedra* (GS,149)

Remarque, Erich Maria *All Quiet on the Western Front* (CS,28;NE,4)

Rostand, Edmond *Cyrano de Bergerac* (CS,9;GS,149)

Rousseau, Jean Jacques *Confessions* (H,164)

Saint-Exupery, Antoine de *The Little Prince* (CS,29)

Sartre, Jean-Paul *No Exit* (GS,149;H,202)

Solzhenitsyn, Alexander *One Day in the Life of Ivan Denisovich* (CS,29;NE,8)

St. Augustine's *Confessions* (H,164)

Tocqueville, Count Alexis de *Democracy in America* (RF,277)

Tolstoy, A. *Anna Karenina, The Death of Ivan Ilyich, War and Peace* (CS,29;GS,18;H,209)

Turgenev, Ivan *Fathers and Sons* (GS,18)

Verne, Jules *Around the World in Eighty Days, 20,000 Leagues under the Sea* (GS,18;H,212)

Voltaire *Candide* (GS,18;H,160)

Zola, Emile (H,215)

C = California Recommended Readings, K-8
CS = California Recommended Literature, 9-12
E1 = The Edison Project: Primary
E2 = The Edison Project: Elementary Academy
E3 = The Edison Project: Junior Academy
GJ = Gillespie: Best Books for Junior High Readers

GS = Gillespie: Best Books for Senior High Readers
H = Hirsch: Cultural Literacy
H1 - H6 = Hirsch: Core Knowledge Series, Grades 1-6
NE = New England Association of Teachers of English
NS = NCTE: Books for You
RF = Ravitch & Finn: What Do Our 17-Year-Olds Know?

CLASSICAL/ANCIENT LITERATURE

Aeschylus *Oresteian Trilogy* (CS,7)
Aristophanes *Lysistrata* (GS,148)
Aristotle *Nichomachean Ethics* (H,155)
Cicero (H,162)
Euripedes *Medea* (CS,8;H,170;NE,8)
Homer *The Iliad* and *The Odyssey* (GS,158;NE,4;RF,271,274)
Horace (H,178)
Ovid *Metamorphoses* (GS,158;H,193)
Plato *The Republic, The Last Days of Socrates* [*Euthyphro, The Apology, Crito, Phaedo*]
    (GS,158;RF,270)
Sophocles *Antigone, Oedipus at Colonus, Oedipus Rex*
    (CS,10;GS,149;H,154;NE,4;RF,273,275)
Virgil *Aeneid* (GS,158;H,152)

THE BIBLE AS LITERATURE

23rd Psalm, "The Lord is my Shepherd..." 3 lines (RF,270)
Abraham and Isaac (H,152)
Beatitudes (H,157)
Cain and Abel (RF,271)
Daniel in the Lion's Den (H,166)
David and Goliath (H,166;RF,270)
Exodus (H,171)
Gospel according to St. Matthew (G,187)
Gospel according to St. Luke (H,185)
Gospel according to St. John (H,181)
Jacob and Esau (H,181)
Jeremiah (H,181)
Jesus betrayed for 30 pieces of silver (H,209;RF,271)
Job (H,181;RF,275)
King Solomon's wisdom (RF,272)
Lucifer (as another name for Satan) (RF,271)
Moses, the Ten Commandments (RF,270)
Noah, the ark (RF,270)
Revelations (H,200)

C = California Recommended Readings, K-8
CS = California Recommended Literature, 9-12
E1 = The Edison Project: Primary
E2 = The Edison Project: Elementary Academy
E3 = The Edison Project: Junior Academy
GJ = Gillespie: Best Books for Junior High Readers

GS = Gillespie: Best Books for Senior High Readers
H = Hirsch: Cultural Literacy
H1 - H6 = Hirsch: Core Knowledge Series, Grades 1-6
NE = New England Association of Teachers of English
NS = NCTE: Books for You
RF = Ravitch & Finn: What Do Our 17-Year-Olds Know?

MREL

Salome (H,202)
Samson and Delilah (H,202;RF,271)
Sermon on the Mount (H,203)
Sodom and Gomorrah (H,205;RF,276)
The Garden of Eden (H,169)
The Crucifixion (H,165)
The Second Coming (H,203)
The Prodigal Son (RF,273)
The story of Creation in Genesis (H,174;RF,270)
Tower of Babel (H,210)
"To every thing there is a season..." (RF,274)

C = California Recommended Readings, K-8
CS = California Recommended Literature, 9-12
E1 = The Edison Project: Primary
E2 = The Edison Project: Elementary Academy
E3 = The Edison Project: Junior Academy
GJ = Gillespie: Best Books for Junior High Readers

GS = Gillespie: Best Books for Senior High Readers
H = Hirsch: Cultural Literacy
H1 - H6 = Hirsch: Core Knowledge Series, Grades 1-6
NE = New England Association of Teachers of English
NS = NCTE: Books for You
RF = Ravitch & Finn: What Do Our 17-Year-Olds Know?

11. Geography

The following process was used to identify standards and benchmarks in the field of geography:

Identification of National Reports

Four reports were identified as important documents representing current thinking on standards in geography: *National Geography Standards* (1994) from the Geography Education Standards Project; *Item Specifications: 1994 National Assessment of Educational Progress in Geography* (1992) from the NAEP Geography Consensus Project; *Guidelines for Geographic Education* (1984) from the Joint Committee on Geographic Education; and *K–6 Geography: Themes, Key Ideas, and Learning Opportunities* (1987) from the Geographic Education National Implementation Project.

Selection of the Reference Document

The Geography Education Standards Project's *National Geography Standards* (1994) was selected as the central document. The project has broad-based representation and was brought together for the express purpose of composing standards for geography. The project also makes use of the other important documents in the field (for further details, see the geography discussion under Section 2).

Identification of Standards and Benchmarks

The *Standards* work shares several aspects with our model for standards development. First, the standards statements in the document are expressed at a level of generality that fits our model for articulated standards. In addition, beneath each standard are provided descriptions of the knowledge and skills students should acquire in geography and in a range of closely related subjects.

There are a number of areas, however, in which the document is not directly compatible with our approach. For example, under each standard, student knowledge and skill are couched in terms of activities or tasks rather than in statements of declarative or procedural knowledge. For the most part it was possible, from a close analysis of the task, to discern what the authors considered to be the essential geographic knowledge or skill. Each activity, then, was studied to determine the knowledge or skill that might be presumed from a successful completion of the task. This analysis allowed us to generate benchmarks that describe declarative, procedural, and contextual content knowledge.

Another area of divergence between our model and the reference document concerns the range and number of benchmark levels. The standards document specifies three benchmark levels: K–4, 5–8, and 9–12. Our model recommends four, roughly corresponding to primary, upper elementary, middle, and high school. In this case, then, completion of our benchmark levels depended upon an analysis of supplementary materials that could provide us with further benchmark information, especially at the primary grades (discussed below).

Integration of Information from Other Documents

During the next stage of the process, the supplementary documents were reviewed, both to integrate information into the main document and to confirm our analysis of the reference document. That analysis, as described above, required us to deduce, from descriptions of tasks and activities, the knowledge and skills the authors believed the student should have. *Item Specifications: 1994 National Assessment of Educational Progress in Geography* provided us with an independent means to check the accuracy of our analysis. This document provides detailed descriptions as to the basic, proficient, and advanced levels of achievement in geography. For example, "Eighth grade basic" means that students should be able to, among other things, "...solve fundamental locational questions using latitude and longitude; interpret simple map scales; identify continents, oceans, and selected countries and cities..."(p. 54).

Another document used to support benchmark statements was *K–6 Geography: Themes, Key Ideas, and Learning Opportunities*. This guide for curriculum development also provided useful information for the elaboration of benchmarks at the primary level. This information was important because the reference document, as noted above, does not identify the knowledge and skills that might be especially suitable for the early (K–2) grades. Additionally, *Guidelines for Geographic Education*, which provides an instructional framework for teaching and learning geography by structuring content around five themes (Location, Place, Human-Environmental Interaction, Movement, and Regions), was analyzed and cited wherever appropriate at the benchmark level. Since page citations are provided for both these documents wherever appropriate, users are afforded easy reference to supporting material.

Summary of Standards for Geography

The World in Spatial Terms
1. Understands the characteristics and uses of maps, globes, and other geographic tools and technologies
2. Knows the location of places, geographic features, and patterns of the environment
3. Understands the characteristics and uses of spatial organization of Earth's surface

Places and Regions
4. Understands the physical and human characteristics of place
5. Understands the concept of regions
6. Understands that culture and experience influence people's perceptions of places and regions

Physical Systems
7. Knows the physical processes that shape patterns on Earth's surface
8. Understands the characteristics of ecosystems on Earth's surface

Human Systems
9. Understands the nature, distribution, and migration of human populations on Earth's surface
10. Understands the nature and complexity of Earth's cultural mosaics
11. Understands the patterns and networks of economic interdependence on Earth's surface
12. Understands the patterns of human settlement and their causes
13. Understands the forces of cooperation and conflict that shape the divisions of Earth's surface

Environment and Society
14. Understands how human actions modify the physical environment
15. Understands how physical systems affect human systems
16. Understands the changes that occur in the meaning, use, distribution, and importance of resources

Uses of Geography
17. Understands how geography is used to interpret the past
18. Understands global development and environmental issues

(GE,106)

1. Understands the characteristics and uses of maps, globes and other geographic tools and technologies

Level I (Grades K-2)

BD (GE,106)

- No material specifically designated for this level

Level II (Grades 3-5)

BD (GE,106;EE,12;NE,35;TE,35)

- Knows the basic elements of maps and globes (e.g., title, legend, cardinal and intermediate directions, scale, grid, principal parallels, meridians, projection)

BP (GE,106;EI,14;NI,34;TE,28)

- Interprets aerial photos and maps (topography)

BP (GE,107;EI,13;NE,36;TE,27)

- Uses map grids (e.g., latitude and longitude or alphanumeric system) to plot absolute location

Level III (Grades 6-8)

BC (GE,144,145;NE,52-53)

- Knows the purposes and distinguishing characteristics of different map projections, including distortion on flat-map projections

BP (GE,144;NE,52-53)

- Uses thematic maps (e.g., patterns of population, disease, economic features, rainfall, vegetation)

BD (GE,145;NE,37)

- Understands concepts such as axis, major parallels, seasons, rotation, revolution, and principal lines of latitude and longitude (Earth-Sun relations)

BC (GE,145;NE,53)

- Knows the advantages and disadvantages of maps, globes, and other geographic tools to illustrate a data set (e.g., data on population distribution, language-use patterns, energy consumption at different times of the year)

BD (GE,145;NE,52-53)

- Knows the characteristics and uses of cartograms

BD (GE,145;NI,53)

- Knows how maps help to find patterns of movement in space and time (e.g., mapping hurricane tracks over several seasons; mapping the spread of influenza throughout the world)

BD (GE,144;NI,53)

- Knows the characteristics and purposes of geographic databases (e.g., databases containing

---

Codes (right side of page):   BD = Benchmark, Declarative; BP = Benchmark, Procedural; BC = Benchmark, Contextual
1st letter of each code in parentheses   *2nd letter of code*   *Number*
G = GESP: National Geography Standards   E = Explicitly stated in document   Page number of cited document
E = JCGE: Guidelines for Geographic Education   I = Implied in document   *or, for duplicates,*
N = NAEP: Item Specifications in Geography   Standard number & level of duplicate
T = GENIP: K-6 Geography: Themes, Key Ideas
D = Duplicated in another standard   364   McREL

census data, land-use data, topographic information)

Level IV (Grades 9-12)

- Understands the advantages and disadvantages of using maps from different sources and different points of view (e.g., maps developed by the media, business, government, industry, and military to show how a recently closed military installation can be utilized for civilian purposes) ^{BC (GE,185;NI,71-72)}

- Knows the characteristics and uses of geographic technologies (e.g., geographic information systems (GIS) and satellite-produced imagery) ^{BD (GE,185;NE,71-72)}

- Transforms primary data into maps, graphs and charts (e.g., charts developed from recent census data ranking selected information on various topics; cartograms depicting the relative sizes of Latin American countries based on their urban populations) ^{BP (GE,184)}

2. Knows the location of places, geographic features, and patterns of the environment ^(GI,108)

Level I (Grades K-2)

- Knows the location of school, home, neighborhood, community, state, and country ^{BD (GI,108;EE,11,12;NI,36;TE,11,15,21)}

Level II (Grades 3-5)

- Knows major physical and human features of places as they are represented on maps and globes (e.g., shopping areas, fast-food restaurants, fire stations, largest cities, rivers, lakes, wetlands, recreation areas, historic sites, landforms, locations of places discussed in history, language arts, science, and other school subjects) ^{BD (GE,108,109;EE,14;NE,34-36;TE,27)}

- Knows the location of major cities in North America ^{BD (GI,109;EI,15;NE,34;TE,27)}

- Knows the approximate location of major mountain ranges on Earth ^{BD (GE,109;EE,16;NE,34;TI,28)}

Level III (Grades 6-8)

- Knows the location of physical and human features on maps and globes (e.g., culture hearths such as Mesopotamia, Huang Ho, the Yucatan Peninsula, the Nile Valley; major ocean ^{BD (GE,146;NI,52)}

Codes (right side of page):   BD = Benchmark, Declarative; BP = Benchmark, Procedural; BC = Benchmark, Contextual

1st letter of each code in parentheses   *2nd letter of code*   *Number*

G = GESP: National Geography Standards   E = Explicitly stated in document   Page number of cited document

E = JCGE: Guidelines for Geographic Education   I = Implied in document   *or, for duplicates,*

N = NAEP: Item Specifications in Geography   Standard number & level of duplicate

T = GENIP: K-6 Geography: Themes, Key Ideas

D = Duplicated in another standard   365   MREL

currents; wind patterns; land forms; climate regions)

- Knows how mental maps of place location affect spatial associations (e.g., how to get from Paris to Moscow, from Cairo to Nairobi, from Rio de Janeiro to Lima)

  BD (GE,146;NI,52)

- Knows the relative location of, size of, and distances between places (e.g., major urban centers in the United States)

  BD (GE,147;NI,52)

- Knows the factors that influence spatial perception (e.g., culture, education, age, gender, occupation, experience)

  BD (GE,147;NI,52)

Level IV (Grades 9-12)

- Knows the approximate locations of major political or economic cultures

  BD (GE,186;NE,71)

- Knows the spatial dynamics of various contemporary and historical events (e.g., the spread of radiation from the Chernobyl nuclear accident; how physical features have deterred migrations and invasions; trade and transportation in the contemporary world; the diffusion of contagious diseases such as the bubonic plague in 14th-century Europe or AIDS in the present-day world)

  BD (GE,186;NI,71)

- Knows the ways in which mental maps influence human decisions about location, settlement, and public policy (e.g., locating houses in areas with scenic views; decisions to migrate based on newspaper and magazine advertisements, or television programs and movies)

  BD (GE,186-187;NI,71)

- Knows the common factors that affect people's mental maps (e.g., how differences in life experiences, age, and gender influence people's housing preferences or their view of public transportation in a city; Eurocentric, Americentric, or Sinocentric mental maps of the world)

  BD (GE,187)

3. Understands the characteristics and uses of spatial organization of Earth's surface

(GE,110)

Level I (Grades K-2)

- Identifies physical and human features in terms of the four spatial elements (e.g., locations [point], transportation and communication routes [line], regions [area], lakes filled with water [volume])

  BC (GE,110;EI,11,12;NI,36,38)

Codes (right side of page):   BD = Benchmark, Declarative; BP = Benchmark, Procedural; BC = Benchmark, Contextual

1st letter of each code in parentheses   *2nd letter of code*   *Number*
G = GESP: National Geography Standards   E = Explicitly stated in document   Page number of cited document
E = JCGE: Guidelines for Geographic Education   I = Implied in document   *or, for duplicates,*
N = NAEP: Item Specifications in Geography   Standard number & level of duplicate
T = GENIP: K-6 Geography: Themes, Key Ideas
D = Duplicated in another standard   366   McREL

- Knows the absolute and relative location of a community and places within it (e.g., parks, stores, landmarks) ^{BD (GI,110-111;EI,11-12;NI,35;TE,15)}

Level II (Grades 3-5)

- Knows patterns on the landscape produced by physical processes (e.g., the drainage basin of a river system, the ridge-and-valley pattern of the Appalachians, vegetation on the windward and leeward sides of a mountain range) ^{BD (GE,112;EI,13-14;NE,34;TI,32;DI,7.3.1)}

- Understands the spatial organization of places through such concepts as location, distance, direction, scale, movement, and region ^{BD (GE,110-111;EI,14;NE,45;TI,35)}

- Understands how changing transportation and communication technology have affected relationships between locations ^{BD (GI,112;EI,14;NE,45-48;TE,38-39;DI,11.2.3)}

- Knows different methods used to measure distance (e.g., miles, kilometers, time, cost, perception) ^{BD (GE,111;EI,13;NE,36;TE,25)}

Level III (Grades 6-8)

- Understands distributions of physical and human occurrences with respect to spatial patterns, arrangements, and associations (why some areas are more densely settled than others; relationships and patterns in the kind and number of links between settlements) ^{BD (GE,148;NE,54-57)}

- Understands patterns of land use in urban, suburban, and rural areas (land uses that are frequently nearby and others not frequently adjacent to one another; dominant land-use patterns in city centers and peripheral areas) ^{BD (GE,148-149;NE,66)}

- Understands the different ways in which places are connected and how these connections demonstrate interdependence and accessibility (e.g., where classmates were born and now live; where sports teams travel to play; the role of changing transportation and communication technology; regions and countries Americans depend on for imported resources and manufactured goods) ^{BD (GE,149;NI,45)}

- Understands the patterns and processes of migration and diffusion (spread of language, religion, and customs from one culture to another; spread of a contagious disease through a population; global migration patterns of plants and animals) ^{BD (GE,149;NE,68)}

Codes (right side of page):   BD = Benchmark, Declarative; BP = Benchmark, Procedural; BC = Benchmark, Contextual
1st letter of each code in parentheses   *2nd letter of code*   *Number*
G = GESP: National Geography Standards   E = Explicitly stated in document   Page number of cited document
E = JCGE: Guidelines for Geographic Education   I = Implied in document   *or, for duplicates,*
N = NAEP: Item Specifications in Geography   Standard number & level of duplicate
T = GENIP: K-6 Geography: Themes, Key Ideas
D = Duplicated in another standard

McREL

Level IV (Grades 9-12)

- BD (GE,188;NE,82)
Understands how concepts of spatial interaction (e.g., complementarity, intervening opportunity, distance decay, connections) account for patterns of movement in space (e.g., transportation routes, trade and migration patterns, commodity flows)

- BD (GE,188-189;NE,82)
Understands relationships in and between places (e.g., differences in threshold population or demand needed to support retail activities in a place; why there are many small central places and few large central places; law of retail gravitation)

- BD (GE,189)
Understands how characteristics such as age, sex, employment, and income level affect the way people perceive and use space (e.g., school-age children travelling to and from school, employed people commuting by public transit, high-income people travelling long distances for vacations)

- BD (GE,93-94;NE,83)
Understands principles of location (e.g., optimum plant-location decisions based on labor costs, transportation costs, market locations, climate; advantages for retailers to locate in malls rather than in dispersed locations)

(GE,113)
4. Understands the physical and human characteristics of place

Level I (Grades K-2)

- BD (GE,113;EE,13;NE,45;TE,22)
Knows the physical and human characteristics of the local community (e.g., neighborhoods, schools, parks, creeks, shopping areas, airports, museums, sports stadiums, hospitals)

- BD (GI,114;EI,14;NE,42;TE,22;DI,5.1.1)
Knows that places can be defined in terms of their predominant human and physical characteristics (e.g., rural, urban, forest, desert; or by types of landforms, vegetation, water bodies, climate)

Level II (Grades 3-5)

- BD (GE,114;NE,37,38;TE,28,29)
Knows how the characteristics of places are shaped by physical and human processes (e.g., effects of agriculture in changing land use and vegetation; effects of settlement on the building of roads; relationship of population distribution to landforms, climate, vegetation, or resources)

Codes (right side of page):   BD = Benchmark, Declarative; BP = Benchmark, Procedural; BC = Benchmark, Contextual
1st letter of each code in parentheses   *2nd letter of code*   *Number*
G = GESP: National Geography Standards   E = Explicitly stated in document   Page number of cited document
E = JCGE: Guidelines for Geographic Education   I = Implied in document   *or, for duplicates,*
N = NAEP: Item Specifications in Geography   Standard number & level of duplicate
T = GENIP: K-6 Geography: Themes, Key Ideas
D = Duplicated in another standard   368   McREL

Level III (Grades 6-8)

- Knows the human characteristics of places (e.g., cultural characteristics such as religion, language, politics, technology, family structure, gender; population characteristics; land uses; levels of development) BD (GE,150;NE,56-57)

- Knows the physical characteristics of places (e.g., soils, landforms, vegetation, wildlife, climate, natural hazards) BD (GE,150;NE,61)

- Knows how technology shapes the human and physical characteristics of places (e.g., satellite dishes, computers, road construction) BD (GE,151;NI,61-62)

- Knows the causes and effects of changes in a place over time (e.g., physical changes such as forest cover, water distribution, temperature fluctuations; human changes such as urban growth, the clearing of forests, development of transportation systems) BD (GE,150-151;NI,56,57)

Level IV (Grades 9-12)

- Knows how social, cultural, and economic processes shape the features of places (e.g., resource use, belief systems, modes of transportation and communication, major technological changes such as the agricultural and industrial revolutions, population growth and urbanization) BD (GE,191;NI,75)

- Understands why places have specific physical and human characteristics in different parts of the world (e.g., the effects of climatic and tectonic processes, settlement and migration patterns, site and situation components) BD (GE,190;NI,72,75)

- Knows the locational advantages and disadvantages of using places for different activities based on their physical characteristics (e.g., flood plain, forest, tundra, earthquake zone, river crossing, coastal flood zone) BD (GE,191;NI,83)

5. Understands the concept of regions (GE,115)

Level I (Grades K-2)

- Knows areas that can be classified as regions according to physical criteria (e.g., landform regions, soil regions, vegetation regions, climate regions, water basins) and human criteria (e.g., political regions, population regions, economic regions, language regions) BD (GE,115;EI,13;NI,35;TI,10;DI,4.1.2)

Codes (right side of page):   BD = Benchmark, Declarative; BP = Benchmark, Procedural; BC = Benchmark, Contextual
1st letter of each code in parentheses   *2nd letter of code*   *Number*
G = GESP: National Geography Standards   E = Explicitly stated in document   Page number of cited document
E = JCGE: Guidelines for Geographic Education   I = Implied in document   *or, for duplicates,*
N = NAEP: Item Specifications in Geography   Standard number & level of duplicate
T = GENIP: K-6 Geography: Themes, Key Ideas
D = Duplicated in another standard   369   *M:REL*

Level II (Grades 3-5)

BD (GI,115;EE,13;NE,38;TE,32)

- Knows the characteristics of a variety of regions (landform, climate, vegetation, shopping, housing, manufacturing, religion, language)

BD (GE,116;EE,14;NI,38;TE,26)

- Understands how regions change over time and the consequences of these changes (e.g., changes in population size or ethnic composition; construction of a new shopping center, a regional hospital, or a new manufacturing plant; changes in transportation; changes in environmental conditions)

BD (GE,115;EE,13;NI,35;TE,20)

- Knows how regions are similar and different in form and function (e.g., local neighborhoods versus Central Business District)

Level III (Grades 6-8)

BD (GE,152;NI,45)

- Knows regions at various spatial scales (e.g., hemispheres, regions within continents, countries, cities)

BD (GE,152;NI,56-57)

- Understands criteria that give a region identity (e.g., its central focus, such as Amsterdam as a transportation center; relationships between physical and cultural characteristics, such as the Sunbelt's warm climate and popularity with retired people)

BD (GE,152)

- Knows types of regions such as formal regions (e.g., school districts, circuit-court districts, states of the United States), functional regions (e.g., the marketing area of a local newspaper, the "fanshed" of a professional sports team), and perceptual regions (e.g., the Bible Belt in the United States, the Riviera in southern France, the Great American Desert)

BD (GE,153;NE,64-65)

- Knows factors that contribute to changing regional characteristics (e.g., economic development, accessibility, migration, media image)

BD (GE,153;NI,56-57)

- Understands the influences and effects of particular regional labels and images (e.g., Twin Peaks in San Francisco; Capitol Hill in Washington, D.C.; the South; the rust belt; "developed" vs. "less-developed" regions)

BD (GE,153;NI,56-57)

- Understands ways regional systems are interconnected (e.g., watersheds and river systems, regional connections through trade, cultural ties between regions)

Codes (right side of page): BD = Benchmark, Declarative; BP = Benchmark, Procedural; BC = Benchmark, Contextual
1st letter of each code in parentheses *2nd letter of code* *Number*
G = GESP: National Geography Standards E = Explicitly stated in document Page number of cited document
E = JCGE: Guidelines for Geographic Education I = Implied in document *or, for duplicates,*
N = NAEP: Item Specifications in Geography Standard number & level of duplicate
T = GENIP: K-6 Geography: Themes, Key Ideas
D = Duplicated in another standard 370 MREL

Level IV (Grades 9-12)

- Understands how regional boundaries change (e.g., changes resulting from shifts in population, environmental degradation, shifts in production and market patterns, wars) _{BD (GE,193;NE,64)}

- Knows factors that contribute to the dynamic nature of regions (e.g., human influences such as migration, technology, and capital investment; physical influences such as long-term climate shifts and seismic activity) _{BD (GE,193;NI,82)}

- Understands connections within and among the parts of a regional system (e.g., links involving neighborhoods within a city, municipalities within a metropolitan area or power blocs within a defense or economic alliance) _{BD (GE,194;NI,82)}

- Understands how changing conditions can result in a region taking on a new structure (e.g., the reshaping of South Africa resulting from the economic and political realignments that followed the end of European colonialism; the Caribbean Basin's transition from a major sugarcane and hemp producer to a center for tourism) _{BD (GE,192;NI,82)}

- Knows ways in which the concept of a region can be used to simplify the complexity of Earth's space (e.g., by arranging an area into sections to help understand a particular topic or problem) _{BD (GE,193)}

- Understands the different ways in which regional systems are structured (e.g., precinct, ward, county, state, and national levels of a political party hierarchy; hub-and-spoke airline operations; postal-service zip codes; assignment of Social Security numbers by region) _{BD (GE,194;NI,82)}

6. Understands that culture and experience influence people's perceptions of places and regions _(GE,117)

Level I (Grades K-2)

- No material specifically designated for this grade level _{BD (GE,117)}

Level II (Grades 3-5)

- Understands ways in which people view and relate to places and regions differently (e.g., how children, mothers, joggers, and city park workers view a park) _{BD (GE,117;EI,14;NE,44;TE,29)}

Codes (right side of page):   BD = Benchmark, Declarative;   BP = Benchmark, Procedural;   BC = Benchmark, Contextual
1st letter of each code in parentheses   *2nd letter of code*   *Number*
G = GESP: National Geography Standards   E = Explicitly stated in document   Page number of cited document
E = JCGE: Guidelines for Geographic Education   I = Implied in document   *or, for duplicates,*
N = NAEP: Item Specifications in Geography   Standard number & level of duplicate
T = GENIP: K-6 Geography: Themes, Key Ideas
D = Duplicated in another standard   371   MREL

Level III (Grades 6-8)

BD (GE,155;NI,56-57)

- Knows how places and regions serve as cultural symbols (e.g. Golden Gate Bridge in San Francisco; Opera House in Sydney, Australia; the Gateway Arch in St. Louis; Tower Bridge in London)

BD (GE,154NI,56-57)

- Knows how technology affects the ways in which culture groups perceive and use places and regions (e.g., impact of technology such as air conditioning and irrigation on the human use of arid lands; changes in perception of environment by culture groups, such as the snowmobile's impact on the lives of Inuit people or the swamp buggy's impact on tourist travel in the Everglades)

BD (GE,154-155;NI,56-57)

- Knows the ways in which culture influences the perception of places and regions (e.g., religion and other belief systems, language, and tradition; perceptions of "beautiful" or "valuable")

Level IV (Grades 9-12)

BD (GE,195;NI,79-80)

- Understands why places and regions are important to individual human identity and as symbols for unifying or fragmenting society (e.g., sense of belonging, attachment, or rootedness; symbolic meaning of places such as Jerusalem as a holy city for Muslims, Christians, and Jews)

BD (GE,195-196;NI,79-80)

- Understands how individuals view places and regions on the basis of their stage of life, sex, social class, ethnicity, values, and belief systems (e.g., perceptions of distance, impressions about what makes a place secure, views of public housing or wealthy urban neighborhoods)

BD (GE,196)

- Knows ways in which people's changing views of places and regions reflect cultural change (e.g., rural settings becoming attractive as recreation areas to people living in densely populated cities, old mining ghost towns becoming tourist and gambling centers)

(GE,118)

7.   Knows the physical processes that shape patterns on Earth's surface

Level I (Grades K-2)

BD (GE,118)

- No material specifically designated for this grade level

Codes (right side of page):   BD = Benchmark, Declarative; BP = Benchmark, Procedural; BC = Benchmark, Contextual
1st letter of each code in parentheses   *2nd letter of code*   *Number*
G = GESP: National Geography Standards   E = Explicitly stated in document   Page number of cited document
E = JCGE: Guidelines for Geographic Education   I = Implied in document   *or, for duplicates,*
N = NAEP: Item Specifications in Geography   Standard number & level of duplicate
T = GENIP: K-6 Geography: Themes, Key Ideas
D = Duplicated in another standard   372   McREL

Level II (Grades 3-5)

- Knows the physical components of Earth's atmosphere (e.g., weather and climate), lithosphere (e.g., landforms such as mountains, hills, plateaus, plains), hydrosphere (e.g., oceans, lakes, rivers), and biosphere (e.g., vegetation and biomes) BD (GE,118;EI,16;NE,37;TI,28)

- Understands how physical processes help to shape features and patterns on Earth's surface (e.g., the effects of climate and weather on vegetation, erosion and deposition on landforms, mud slides on hills) BD (GE,118;EI,16;NE,37;TI,28)

- Knows how Earth's position relative to the Sun affects events and conditions on Earth (e.g., how the tilt of the Earth in relation to the Sun explains seasons in different locations on Earth; how the length of day influences human activity in different regions of the world) BD (GE,119;EI,11-12;NI,37;TI,16)

Level III (Grades 6-8)

- Knows the major processes that shape patterns in the physical environment (e.g., the erosional agents such as water and ice, earthquake zones and volcanic activity, the ocean circulation system) BD (GE,156,190;NE,55-56;DI,3.2.1)

- Knows the processes that produce renewable and nonrenewable resources (e.g., fossil fuels, hydroelectric power, soil fertility) BD (GE,157;NI,55-56)

- Knows the consequences of a specific physical process operating on Earth's surface (e.g., effects of an extreme weather phenomenon such as a hurricane's impact on a coastal ecosystem; effects of heavy rainfall on hillslopes; effects of the continued movement of Earth's tectonic plates) BD (GE,157;NI,55-56)

Level IV (Grades 9-12)

- Understands the distribution of different types of climate (e.g., marine or continental climate) that is produced by such processes as air-mass circulation, temperature, and moisture BD (GE,197;NE,73-74)

- Understands the effects of different physical cycles (e.g., world atmospheric circulation, ocean circulation) on the physical environment of Earth BD (GE,198;NE,73-74)

- Understands how physical systems are dynamic and interactive (e.g., the relationships between changes in landforms and the effects of climate such as the erosion of hill slopes by precipitation, deposition of sediments by floods, shaping of land surfaces by wind) BD (GE,198;NI,73-74)

Codes (right side of page): BD = Benchmark, Declarative; BP = Benchmark, Procedural; BC = Benchmark, Contextual
1st letter of each code in parentheses   *2nd letter of code*   *Number*
G = GESP: National Geography Standards   E = Explicitly stated in document   Page number of cited document
E = JCGE: Guidelines for Geographic Education   I = Implied in document   *or, for duplicates,*
N = NAEP: Item Specifications in Geography   Standard number & level of duplicate
T = GENIP: K-6 Geography: Themes, Key Ideas
D = Duplicated in another standard   373   MREL

BD (GE,197;NE,73-74)
- Understands how physical processes affect different regions of the United States and the world (e.g., effects of hurricanes in the Caribbean Basin and the eastern United States or of earthquakes in Turkey, Japan, and Nicaragua; effects of desertification and soil degradation, flash floods, dust storms, sand movement, soil erosion, and salt accumulation in dry environments)

(GE,120)

8. Understands the characteristics of ecosystems on Earth's surface

Level I (Grades K-2)

BD (GE,120)
- No material specifically designated for this grade level

Level II (Grades 3-5)

BD (GE,120;EI,13;NI,37;TI,41)
- Knows the components of ecosystems at a variety of scales (e.g., fungi, insects, plants, and animals in a food chain or food web; fish and marine vegetation in coastal zones; grasses, birds, and insects in grassland areas)

BD (GE,121;EI,14;NI,60;TE,42;DI,14.2.1)
- Knows ways in which humans can change ecosystems (e.g., clearing forests, widening channels of waterways, draining wetlands, wetting or suppressing fires)

BD (GE,120;NI,37;TE,33)
- Knows plants and animals associated with various vegetation and climatic regions on Earth (e.g., the plant and animal life supported in a midlatitude forest in North America, the kinds of plants and animals found in a tropical rain forest in Africa, animals and trees that thrive in cities)

Level III (Grades 6-8)

BD (GE,158;NI,54,55)
- Understands the distribution of ecosystems from local to global scales (e.g., the consequences of differences in soils, climates, and human and natural disturbances)

BD (GE,158;NI,59,60)
- Understands the functions and dynamics of ecosystems (e.g., interdependence of flora and fauna, the flow of energy and the cycling of energy, feeding levels and location of elements in the food chain)

BD (GE,159;NI,56)
- Understands ecosystems in terms of their characteristics and ability to withstand stress

---

Codes (right side of page):   BD = Benchmark, Declarative; BP = Benchmark, Procedural; BC = Benchmark, Contextual
1st letter of each code in parentheses   *2nd letter of code*   *Number*
G = GESP: National Geography Standards   E = Explicitly stated in document   Page number of cited document
E = JCGE: Guidelines for Geographic Education   I = Implied in document   *or, for duplicates,*
N = NAEP: Item Specifications in Geography   Standard number & level of duplicate
T = GENIP: K-6 Geography: Themes, Key Ideas
D = Duplicated in another standard   374   MREL

caused by physical events (e.g., a river system adjusting to the arrival of introduced plant species such as hydrilla; regrowth of a forest after a forest fire; effects of disease on specific populations)

- Knows changes that have occurred over time in ecosystems in the local region (e.g., natural wetlands on a floodplain being replaced by farms, farmlands on a floodplain being replaced by housing developments)

  BD (GE,159;NI,54-55)

- Knows the potential impact of human activities within a given ecosystem on the carbon, nitrogen, and oxygen cycles (e.g., the role of air pollution in atmospheric warming or the growing of peas and other legumes, which supply their own nitrogen and do not deplete the soil)

  BD (GE,159;NI,54-55)

- Understands the life cycle of a lake ecosystem from birth to death (including the process of eutrophication)

  BD (GE,159;NI,54-55)

Level IV (Grades 9-12)

- Understands how relationships between soil, climate, and plant and animal life affect the distribution of ecosystems (e.g., effects of solar energy and water supply on the nature of plant communities)

  BD (GE,199;NE,73)

- Knows ecosystems in terms of their biodiversity and productivity (e.g., the low productivity of deserts and the high productivity of midlatitude forests and tropical forests) and their potential value to all living things (e.g., as a source of oxygen for life forms, as a source of food for indigenous peoples, as a source of raw materials for international trade)

  BD (GE,200;NI,72-73)

- Knows the effects of biological magnification in ecosystems (e.g., the increase in contaminants in succeeding levels of the food chain and the consequences for different life forms)

  BD (GE,200;NI,72-73)

- Knows the effects of both physical and human changes in ecosystems (e.g., the disruption of energy flows and chemical cycles and the reduction of species diversity; how acid rain resulting from air pollution affects water bodies and forests and how depletion of the atmosphere's ozone layer through the use of chemicals may affect the health of humans)

  BD (GE,200;NI,78-79)

Codes (right side of page):   BD = Benchmark, Declarative; BP = Benchmark, Procedural; BC = Benchmark, Contextual

1st letter of each code in parentheses	*2nd letter of code*	*Number*
G = GESP: National Geography Standards	E = Explicitly stated in document	Page number of cited document
E = JCGE: Guidelines for Geographic Education	I = Implied in document	*or, for duplicates,*
N = NAEP: Item Specifications in Geography		Standard number & level of duplicate
T = GENIP: K-6 Geography: Themes, Key Ideas		
D = Duplicated in another standard	375	M*REL

(GE,122)

9. Understands the nature, distribution, and migration of human populations on Earth's surface

Level I (Grades K-2)

BD (GE,122)

● No material specifically designated for this grade level

Level II (Grades 3-5)

BD (GE,122-123;EE,13-14;NI,38;TE,22)

● Understands the characteristics of populations at a variety of scales (e.g., ethnicity, age distribution, number of families and single households, number of employed and unemployed, males and females, life expectancy, infant mortality)

BD (GE,122;EI,17;NI,34-45;TI,28-29)

● Knows the spatial distribution of population (e.g., that population density is higher east of the Mississippi River than west of it; population density is higher on the East Coast and West Coast than in the mountains and deserts of the western part of the country; few people live where it is very dry or very cold)

BD (GE,123;EI,16;NE,49-50;TI,43)

● Understands voluntary and involuntary migration

BD (GE,123;EI,16;NI,49-50;TI,43)

● Knows the causes and effects of human migration (e.g., European colonists and African slaves to America; movement of people from drought areas in Africa; movement of people from East Asia to North America; effects of physical geography on national and international migration; cultural factors)

Level III (Grades 6-8)

BD (GE,160;NE,74-75)

● Understands demographic concepts and how they are related to population characteristics of a country or region (e.g., rates of natural increase, crude birth and death rates, infant mortality, population growth rates, doubling time, life expectancy, average family size)

BD (GE,161;NE,68-69)

● Knows the factors that influence patterns of rural-urban migration (e.g., urban commuting; effects of technology on transportation, communication, and people's mobility; barriers that impede the flow of people, goods, and ideas)

BD (GE,161;EI,15-16;NI,68-69;TE,32)

● Knows the ways in which human movement and migration influence the character of a place (e.g., New Delhi before and after the partition of the Indian subcontinent in the 1940s and the massive realignment of the Hindu and Muslim populations; Boston before and after the

---

Codes (right side of page):   BD = Benchmark, Declarative;   BP = Benchmark, Procedural;   BC = Benchmark, Contextual
1st letter of each code in parentheses   *2nd letter of code*   *Number*
G = GESP: National Geography Standards   E = Explicitly stated in document   Page number of cited document
E = JCGE: Guidelines for Geographic Education   I = Implied in document   *or, for duplicates,*
N = NAEP: Item Specifications in Geography   Standard number & level of duplicate
T = GENIP: K-6 Geography: Themes, Key Ideas
D = Duplicated in another standard   376

MREL

large-scale influx of Irish immigrants in the mid-nineteenth century; the impact of Indians settling in South Africa, Algerians settling in France, or Vietnamese settling in the United States)

Level IV (Grades 9-12)

- Understands population issues (e.g., the ongoing policies to limit population growth; the policy in the former Soviet Union to encourage ethnic Russians to have large families; economic considerations such as a country's need for more or fewer workers) BD (GE,201;NI,74-75)

- Knows how human mobility and city/region interdependence can be increased and regional integration can be facilitated by improved transportation systems (e.g., the national interstate highway system in the United States, the network of global air routes) BD (GE,202;NE,68-69)

- Knows how international migrations are shaped by push and pull factors (e.g., political conditions, economic incentives, religious values, family ties) BD (GE,202;NE,68-69)

- Understands the impact of human migration on physical and human systems (e.g., the impact of European settlers on the High Plains of North America in the nineteenth century; impact of rural-to-urban migration on suburban development and the resulting lack of adequate housing and stress on infrastructure; effects of population gains or losses on socioeconomic conditions) BD (GE,202;NI,87)

10. Understands the nature and complexity of Earth's cultural mosaics

(GE,124)

Level I (Grades K-2)

- Knows the basic components of culture (e.g., language, social organization, beliefs and customs, forms of shelter, economic activities, education systems) BD (GE,124;EI,12;NI,46;TI,22)

Level II (Grades 3-5)

- Knows the similarities and differences in characteristics of culture in different regions (e.g., in terms of environment and resources, technology, food, shelter, social organization, beliefs and customs, schooling, what girls and boys are allowed to do) BD (GE,124;EI,14;NI,38-39;TI,29)

- Understands how different people living in the same region maintain different ways of life BD (GE,124,172;EI,14;NE,44;TI,13)

Codes (right side of page):   BD = Benchmark, Declarative; BP = Benchmark, Procedural; BC = Benchmark, Contextual
1st letter of each code in parentheses   *2nd letter of code*   *Number*
G = GESP: National Geography Standards   E = Explicitly stated in document   Page number of cited document
E = JCGE: Guidelines for Geographic Education   I = Implied in document   *or, for duplicates,*
N = NAEP: Item Specifications in Geography   Standard number & level of duplicate
T = GENIP: K-6 Geography: Themes, Key Ideas
D = Duplicated in another standard   377

McREL

(e.g., the cultural differences between Native Americans and Europeans living along the eastern seaboard in the 17th century; differences among Sikhs, Hindus, and Muslims living in India today)

BD (GE,125;EI,14;NI,61;TE,30)

- Understands how cultures differ in their use of similar environments and resources (e.g., by comparing how people live in Phoenix, Arizona with how people live in Riyadh, Saudi Arabia)

BD (GE,125;EI,16;NI,46)

- Understands cultural change (in terms of, e.g., the role of women in society, the role of children in society, clothing styles, modes of transportation, food preferences, types of housing, attitudes toward the environment and resources)

Level III (Grades 6-8)

BD (GE,162;NI,56-57)

- Knows the distinctive cultural landscapes associated with migrant populations (e.g., Chinatowns in the Western world, European enclaves in Japan and China in the 19th century, Little Italy sections of American cities from the beginning of the 19th century to the present)

BD (GE,162;NI,56,57)

- Knows ways in which communities reflect the cultural background of their inhabitants (e.g., distinctive building styles, billboards in Spanish, foreign-language advertisements in newspapers)

BD (GE,162-163;NI,57)

- Understands the significance in patterns of cultural diffusion (e.g., the use of terraced rice fields in China, Japan, Indonesia, and the Philippines; the use of satellite television dishes in the United States, England, Canada, and Saudi Arabia)

Level IV (Grades 9-12)

BD (GE,203;NI,56-57)

- Knows how cultures influence the characteristics of regions (e.g., level of technological achievement, cultural traditions, social institutions)

BD (GE,204)

- Understands how human characteristics make specific regions of the world distinctive (e.g., the effects of early Spanish settlement in the southwestern United States, the impact of Buddhism in shaping social attitudes in Southeast Asia, the specific qualities of Canada's culture regions resulting from the patterns of migration and settlement over four centuries)

BD (GE,205;NI,75)

- Understands how evolving political and economic alliances may affect the traditional

---

Codes (right side of page):   BD = Benchmark, Declarative; BP = Benchmark, Procedural; BC = Benchmark, Contextual

1st letter of each code in parentheses   *2nd letter of code*   *Number*
G = GESP: National Geography Standards   E = Explicitly stated in document   Page number of cited document
E = JCGE: Guidelines for Geographic Education   I = Implied in document   *or, for duplicates,*
N = NAEP: Item Specifications in Geography   Standard number & level of duplicate
T = GENIP: K-6 Geography: Themes, Key Ideas
D = Duplicated in another standard   378   MREL

cohesiveness of world culture regions (e.g., post-reunification Germany and its economic effect on the European Union, NAFTA's effect on trade relations among the United States, Canada, and Mexico)

- BD (GE,203;NI,67)
  Knows the role culture plays in incidents of cooperation and conflict in the present-day world (e.g., conflicts in sub-Saharan Africa in the 1960s, Central Europe in the 1980s and 1990s, states within the former Soviet Union in the 1990s; cooperation such as the religious and linguistic ties between Spain and parts of Latin America, ethnic ties among the Kurds living in Iran, Iraq, and Turkey)

- BD (GE,205;NI,75)
  Understands how communication and transportation technologies contribute to cultural convergence or divergence (e.g., convergence created by electronic media, computers, and jet aircraft; divergence created by technologies used to reinforce nationalistic or ethnic elitism or cultural separateness and independence)

(GE,126)
11. Understands the patterns and networks of economic interdependence on Earth's surface

Level I (Grades K-2)

- BD (GE,127;EI,12;NI,43;TI,10,18)
  Knows the modes of transportation used to move people, products, and ideas from place to place (e.g., barges, airplanes, automobiles, pipelines, ships, railroads), their importance, and their advantages and disadvantages

Level II (Grades 3-5)

- BD (GE,127;EI,15;NE,46;TE,28)
  Knows the factors that are important in the location of economic activities (e.g., warehouses and industries near major transportation routes; fast-food restaurants in highly accessible locations close to population concentrations; production sites near the sources of their raw materials or close to the consumers who buy their products)

- BD (GE,127;EI,15;NI,39;TI,29,33)
  Knows economic activities that use natural resources in the local region, state, and nation (e.g., agriculture, mining, fishing, forestry) and the importance of the activities to these areas

- BD (GE,127;EI,14;NI,47-48;TE,31,32;DI,3.2.3)
  Knows how transportation and communication have changed and how they have affected trade and economic activities (e.g., regions can specialize economically; with improved roads and refrigerated trucking, more fresh fruits and vegetables are available out of season;

Codes (right side of page): BD = Benchmark, Declarative; BP = Benchmark, Procedural; BC = Benchmark, Contextual
1st letter of each code in parentheses *2nd letter of code* *Number*
G = GESP: National Geography Standards E = Explicitly stated in document Page number of cited document
E = JCGE: Guidelines for Geographic Education I = Implied in document *or, for duplicates,*
N = NAEP: Item Specifications in Geography Standard number & level of duplicate
T = GENIP: K-6 Geography: Themes, Key Ideas
D = Duplicated in another standard 379 MᴄREL

regional, national, and global markets expand as transportation and communication systems improve)

BD (GE,126;NI,50-51)

- Knows the various ways in which people satisfy their basic needs and wants through the production of goods and services in different regions of the world (e.g., growing food and shopping for food in a developing vs. a developed society; economic activities in a rural region vs. those in an urban region in the same U.S. state)

BD (GE,126;NI,50)

- Knows how regions are linked economically and how trade affects the way people earn their living in each region (e.g., the flow of fuels from Southwest Asia to industrialized, energy-poor regions of the world; the flow of electronic goods from Pacific Rim nations to the United States)

Level III (Grades 6-8)

BD (GE,164;EI,15;NI,38,40,46;TI,31)

- Understands the spatial aspects of systems designed to deliver goods and services (e.g., the movement of a product from point of manufacture to point of use; imports, exports, and trading patterns of various countries; interruptions in world trade such as war, crop failures, and labor strikes)

BD (GE,165;EI,15;NI,38,41,46,48;TI,37)

- Understands issues related to the spatial distribution of economic activities (e.g., the impact of economic activities in a community on the surrounding areas; the effects of the gradual disappearance of small-scale retail facilities such as corner general stores and gas stations; the economic and social impacts on a community when a large factory or other economic activity leaves and moves to another place)

BD (GE,166;NI,66-67,70)

- Understands the factors that influence the location of industries in the United States (e.g., geographical factors, factors of production, changing spatial patterns)

BD (GE,165)

- Understands the primary geographic causes for world trade (e.g., the theory of comparative advantage that explains trade advantages associated with Hong Kong-made consumer goods, Chinese textiles, or Jamaican sugar; countries that export mostly raw materials and import mostly fuels and manufactured goods)

BD (GE,166;NI,57)

- Understands historic and contemporary economic trade networks (e.g., the triangular trade routes of the 16th and 17th centuries; national and global patterns of migrant workers; economic relationships under imperialism such as American colonies and England in the 18th and 19th centuries, or Belgium and the Congo in the 20th century)

Codes (right side of page): BD = Benchmark, Declarative; BP = Benchmark, Procedural; BC = Benchmark, Contextual
1st letter of each code in parentheses *2nd letter of code* *Number*
G = GESP: National Geography Standards E = Explicitly stated in document Page number of cited document
E = JCGE: Guidelines for Geographic Education I = Implied in document *or, for duplicates,*
N = NAEP: Item Specifications in Geography Standard number & level of duplicate
T = GENIP: K-6 Geography: Themes, Key Ideas
D = Duplicated in another standard 380 MREL

- Understands historic and contemporary systems of transportation and communication in the development of economic activities (e.g., the effect of refrigerated railroad cars, air-freight services, pipelines, telephone services, facsimile transmission services, satellite-based communications systems) BD (GE,166;NI,66)

- Knows primary, secondary, and tertiary activities in a geographic context (e.g., primary economic activities such as coal mining and salmon fishing; secondary economic activities such as the manufacture of shoes and the associated worldwide trade in raw materials; tertiary economic activity such as restaurants, theaters, and hotels) BD (GE,164)

Level IV (Grades 9-12)

- Knows the spatial distribution of major economic systems and their relative merits in terms of productivity and the social welfare of workers (e.g., North Korea as a command economy, Burkina Faso as a traditional economy in the hinterlands beyond its cities, Singapore as a market economy) BD (GE,206;NI,74)

- Understands the historical movement patterns of people and goods and their relationships to economic activity (e.g., spatial patterns of early trade routes in the era of sailing ships, land-use patterns that resulted in a system of monoculture) BD (GE,207;NI,75)

- Understands the relationships between various settlement patterns, their associated economic activities, and the relative land values (e.g., land values and prominent urban features; the zoned uses of land and the value of that land; economic factors and location of particular types of industries and businesses) BD (GE,207;NI,75)

- Understands the advantages and disadvantages of international economic patterns (e.g., how land values in an area may change due to the investment of foreign capital; the causes and geographic consequences of an international debt crisis; the advantages and disadvantages of allowing foreign-owned businesses to purchase land, open factories, or conduct other kinds of business in a country) BD (GE,207;NI,83)

12. Understands the patterns of human settlement and their causes (GE,128)

Level I (Grades K-2)

- Understands why people choose to settle in different places (e.g., job opportunities, available BD (GE,129;EI,13;NI,38-39;TE,21)

Codes (right side of page):   BD = Benchmark, Declarative; BP = Benchmark, Procedural; BC = Benchmark, Contextual
1st letter of each code in parentheses   *2nd letter of code*   *Number*
G = GESP: National Geography Standards   E = Explicitly stated in document   Page number of cited document
E = JCGE: Guidelines for Geographic Education   I = Implied in document   *or, for duplicates,*
N = NAEP: Item Specifications in Geography   Standard number & level of duplicate
T = GENIP: K-6 Geography: Themes, Key Ideas
D = Duplicated in another standard   381   MCREL

land, climate)

BD (GE,128;EI,12;NI,46;TI,18)

- Knows the similarities and differences in housing and land use in urban and suburban areas (e.g., where people live, where services are provided, where products are made, types of housing, yard size, population density, transportation facilities, presence of infrastructure elements such as sidewalks and street lights)

Level II (Grades 3-5)

BD (GE,128;EI,14;NI,38,48;TI,29)

- Knows areas of dense human settlement and why they are densely populated (e.g., fertile soil, good transportation, and availability of water in the Ganges River Valley; availability of coal, iron, and other natural resources and river transportation in the Ruhr)

BD (GE,129;EI,14;NI,38,48;TI,29,32)

- Knows reasons for similarities and differences in the population size and density of different regions (e.g., length of settlement, environment and resources, cultural traditions, historic events, accessibility)

BD (GE,129;NI,39)

- Knows the settlement patterns that characterize the development of a community or state (e.g., from the movement of people into an area previously unoccupied to the competition among villages for economic dominance and growth; from a small number of dispersed settlers with few services to the modern pattern of suburbanization and decentralization)

BD (GE,129;NI,39;TE,28,29)

- Knows reasons for the growth and decline of settlements (e.g., boomtowns to ghost towns in mining areas; the rise or decline of towns linked or not linked by highways or railroads; the history of company or single-industry towns in periods of prosperity or recession)

BD (GE,129;TE,37)

- Knows the characteristics and locations of cities (e.g., location along transportation routes, availability of resources, continued access to other cities and resources) and how they have changed over time (e.g., the movement of industry from downtown to the edge of cities; suburban growth; changes in the shapes of urban areas)

BD (GE,129;NI,38)

- Knows the similarities and differences among the world's culture hearths (culture groups' places of origin), why humans settled in those places, and why these settlements persist today (e.g., as centers of innovation and cultural, social, economic, and political development that attract people from other places)

Codes (right side of page):   BD = Benchmark, Declarative; BP = Benchmark, Procedural; BC = Benchmark, Contextual
1st letter of each code in parentheses   *2nd letter of code*   *Number*
G = GESP: National Geography Standards   E = Explicitly stated in document   Page number of cited document
E = JCGE: Guidelines for Geographic Education   I = Implied in document   *or, for duplicates,*
N = NAEP: Item Specifications in Geography   Standard number & level of duplicate
T = GENIP: K-6 Geography: Themes, Key Ideas   382
D = Duplicated in another standard

MREL

Level III (Grades 6-8)

- Knows the causes and consequences of urbanization (e.g., industrial development; cultural activities such as entertainment, religious facilities, higher education; economic attractions such as business and entrepreneurial opportunities, access to information and other resources) BD (GE,168;NI,57)

- Knows the similarities and differences in various settlement patterns of the world (e.g., agricultural settlement types such as plantations, subsistence farming, truck-farming communities; urban settlement types such as port cities, governmental centers, single-industry cities, planned cities) BD (GE,167;NI,52,57,65)

- Knows ways in which both the landscape and society change as a consequence of shifting from a dispersed to a concentrated settlement form (e.g., a larger marketplace; the need for an agricultural surplus to provide for the urban population; the loss of some rural workers as people decide to move into the city; changes in the transportation system) BD (GE,167-168;NI,64)

- Knows the factors involved in the development of cities (e.g., geographic factors for location such as transportation and food supply; the need for a marketplace; religious needs; military protection) BD (GE,167;NE,56,57)

- Knows the internal spatial structures of cities (e.g., the concentric zone model and the sector model of cities; the impact of different transportation systems on the spatial arrangement of business, industry, and residence in a city) BD (GE,168;NI,66-67)

Level IV (Grades 9-12)

- Understands how the functions of cities today differ from those of towns and villages and cities in earlier times (e.g., more specialized economic and social activities, greater concentration of services, greater availability of the same services) BD (GE,208;NI,66)

- Knows the shape of cities in the United States and factors that influence urban morphology (e.g., transportation routes, physical barriers, zoning regulations) BD (GE,208;NI,75)

- Knows the similarities and differences in settlement characteristics of economically developing and developed nations (characteristics of cities; residential and transportation patterns; travel distance to schools, shopping areas, and health care facilities) BD (GE,209;NI,75)

- Knows the consequences of factors such as population changes or the arrival/departure of BD (GE,209;NI,75)

Codes (right side of page):   BD = Benchmark, Declarative; BP = Benchmark, Procedural; BC = Benchmark, Contextual
1st letter of each code in parentheses   *2nd letter of code*   *Number*
G = GESP: National Geography Standards   E = Explicitly stated in document   Page number of cited document
E = JCGE: Guidelines for Geographic Education   I = Implied in document   *or, for duplicates,*
N = NAEP: Item Specifications in Geography   Standard number & level of duplicate
T = GENIP: K-6 Geography: Themes, Key Ideas
D = Duplicated in another standard   383   McREL

a major industry or business on the settlement patterns of an area (e.g., stress on infrastructure, problems of public safety and fire protection, crisis in delivering school and medical services)

BD (GE,209)

- Understands the physical and human impact of emerging urban forms in the present-day world (e.g., the rise of megalopoli, edge cities, and metropolitan corridors; increasing numbers of ethnic enclaves in urban areas and the development of legislation to protect the rights of ethnic and racial minorities; improved light-rail systems within cities providing ease of access to ex-urban areas)

(GE,130)

13. Understands the forces of cooperation and conflict that shape the divisions of Earth's surface

Level I (Grades K-2)

BD (GE,131;EI,13;NI,48-49;TI,18)

- Knows ways that people solve common problems by cooperating (e.g., working in groups to pick up trash along a road, participating in a neighborhood crime-watch group, participating in community house-building projects)

BD (GE,131;EI,14;NI,48-49;TI,31)

- Knows examples of world conflict or cooperation (e.g., countries in trade pacts, areas of the world with refugee problems)

Level II (Grades 3-5)

BD (GE,130,131;EI,14;NI,48;TI,27)

- Knows the functions of political units (e.g., law-making, law enforcement, provision of services, powers of taxation) and how they differ on the basis of scale (e.g., precinct, census district, school attendance zone, township, metropolitan area, county, state, nation)

BD (GE,130;EI,13;NI,38;TI,27)

- Knows the processes people use to divide Earth's surface into political and/or economic units (e.g., states in the United States and Mexico; provinces in Canada; countries in North and South America; countries linked in cooperative relationships, such as the European Union)

BD (GE,131;NI,48)

- Knows how and why people compete for control of Earth's surface (e.g., ethnic or national differences, desire for political control, economic inequalities)

Codes (right side of page):	BD = Benchmark, Declarative; BP = Benchmark, Procedural; BC = Benchmark, Contextual	
1st letter of each code in parentheses	*2nd letter of code*	*Number*
G = GESP: National Geography Standards	E = Explicitly stated in document	Page number of cited document
E = JCGE: Guidelines for Geographic Education	I = Implied in document	*or, for duplicates,*
N = NAEP: Item Specifications in Geography		Standard number & level of duplicate
T = GENIP: K-6 Geography: Themes, Key Ideas		
D = Duplicated in another standard	384	MREL

Level III (Grades 6-8)

- Understands factors that contribute to cooperation (e.g., similarities in religion, language, political beliefs) or conflict (e.g., economic competition for scarce resources, boundary disputes, cultural differences, control of strategic locations) within and between regions and countries ^{BD (GE,169;NE,67)}

- Knows the social, political and economic divisions on Earth's surface at the local, state, national and international levels (e.g., transnational corporations, political alliances, economic groupings, world religions) ^{BD (GE,170;NI,52,67)}

- Understands the various factors involved in the development of nation-states (e.g., competition for territory and resources, desire for self-rule, nationalism, history of domination by powerful countries) ^{BD (GE,170)}

- Understands the reasons for multiple and overlapping spatial divisions in society (e.g., postal zones, school districts, telephone area codes, voting wards) ^{BD (GE,169)}

- Understands the factors that affect the cohesiveness and integration of countries (e.g., language and religion in Belgium, the religious differences between Hindus and Moslems in India, the ethnic differences in some African countries that have been independent for only a few decades, the elongated shapes of Italy and Chile) ^{BD (GE,170;NE,67)}

- Understands the symbolic importance of capital cities (e.g., Canberra, a planned city, as the capital of Australia; The Hague as both a national capital of the Netherlands and a center for such global agencies as the World Court) ^{BD (GE,170)}

Level IV (Grades 9-12)

- Understands how cooperation and/or conflict can lead to the allocation of control of Earth's surface (e.g., formation and delineation of regional planning districts, regional school districts, countries, free-trade zones) ^{BD (GE,210;NI,85-86)}

- Knows the causes of boundary conflicts and internal disputes between culture groups (e.g., the conflict between North Korea and South Korea, friction between the Spanish majority and Basque minority in Spain, the civil war between the Hutus and the Tutsis in Rwanda) ^{BD (GE,210;NE,86)}

- Understands why the boundaries of congressional districts change in the United States (e.g., the effects of statutory requirements, population shifts, ethnic and racial considerations, ^{BD (GE,210;NI,85-86)}

Codes (right side of page):   BD = Benchmark, Declarative;   BP = Benchmark, Procedural;   BC = Benchmark, Contextual
1st letter of each code in parentheses   *2nd letter of code*   *Number*
G = GESP: National Geography Standards   E = Explicitly stated in document   Page number of cited document
E = JCGE: Guidelines for Geographic Education   I = Implied in document   *or, for duplicates,*
N = NAEP: Item Specifications in Geography   Standard number & level of duplicate
T = GENIP: K-6 Geography: Themes, Key Ideas
D = Duplicated in another standard

385

McREL

shifts in political power)

BD (GE,210;NI,85-86)

- Understands the changes that occur in the extent and organization of social, political, and economic entities on Earth's surface (e.g., imperial powers such as the Roman Empire, Han Dynasty, Carolingian Empire, British Empire)

BD (GE,211;NI,85-86)

- Understands why some countries are land-locked (e.g., wars between rival countries, isolation due to the size of landmasses and due to racial and cultural divisions)

BD (GE,211)

- Understands how external forces can conflict economically and politically with internal interests in a region (e.g., how the Pampas in Argentina underwent a significant socioeconomic transformation in the 19th and early 20th centuries as a consequence of European demands for grain and beef; the consequences of the French colonization of IndoChina in the 19th century to procure tin, tungsten, and rubber; the friction between Hindus and Moslems in the Indian subcontinent in the 1940s which led to the formation of India and Pakistan)

(GE,132)

14. Understands how human actions modify the physical environment

Level I (Grades K-2)

BD (GE,132;TE,17)

- Knows ways in which people depend on the physical environment (e.g., food, clean air, water, mineral resources)

Level II (Grades 3-5)

BD (GE,132-133;EE,14;NI,42-43;TE,29-30;DI,8.2.2)

- Knows the ways people alter the physical environment (e.g., by creating irrigation projects; clearing the land to make room for houses and shopping centers; planting crops; building roads)

BD (GE,133;NI,42-43;TE,31)

- Knows the ways in which the physical environment is stressed by human activities (e.g., changes in climate, air pollution, water pollution, expanding human settlement)

BD (GE,133;NE,43;TI,42)

- Knows how human activities have increased the ability of the physical environment to support human life in the local community, state, United States, and other countries (e.g., use of irrigation and dry-land farming techniques to improve crop yields, reforestation to prevent erosion, flood-control projects to make land habitable)

Codes (right side of page):   BD = Benchmark, Declarative; BP = Benchmark, Procedural; BC = Benchmark, Contextual
1st letter of each code in parentheses   *2nd letter of code*   *Number*
G = GESP: National Geography Standards   E = Explicitly stated in document   Page number of cited document
E = JCGE: Guidelines for Geographic Education   I = Implied in document   *or, for duplicates,*
N = NAEP: Item Specifications in Geography   Standard number & level of duplicate
T = GENIP: K-6 Geography: Themes, Key Ideas
D = Duplicated in another standard   386   MREL

Level III (Grades 6-8)

- Understands the environmental consequences of people changing the physical environment ^{BD (GE,171;NE,61)} (e.g., the effects of ozone depletion, climate change, deforestation, land degradation, soil salinization and acidification, ocean pollution, groundwater-quality decline, using natural wetlands for recreational and housing development)

- Understands the ways in which human-induced changes in the physical environment in one ^{BD (GE,171)} place can cause changes in other places (e.g., the effects of a factory's airborne emissions on air quality in communities located downwind and, because of acid rain, on ecosystems located downwind; the effects of pesticides washed into river systems on water quality in communities located downstream; the effects of the construction of dams and levees on river systems in one region on places downstream)

- Understands the ways in which technology influences the human capacity to modify the ^{BD (GE,172)} physical environment (e.g., effects of the introduction of fire, steam power, diesel machinery, electricity, work animals, explosives, chemical fertilizers and pesticides, hybridization of crops)

- Understands the environmental consequences of both the unintended and intended outcomes ^{BD (GE,172;NI,61-62)} of major technological changes in human history (e.g., the effects of automobiles using fossil fuels, nuclear power plants creating the problem of nuclear waste storage, the use of steel-tipped plows or the expansion of the amount of land brought into agriculture)

Level IV (Grades 9-12)

- Understands how the concepts of synergy, feedback loops, carrying capacity, and thresholds ^{BD (GE,212,214;NI,77)} relate to the limitations of the physical environment to absorb the impacts of human activity (e.g., levee construction on a flood plain, logging in an old-growth forest, construction of golf courses in arid areas)

- Understands the role of humans in decreasing the diversity of flora and fauna in a region ^{BD (GE,212;NE,77)} (e.g., the impact of acid rain on rivers and forests in southern Ontario, the effects of toxic dumping on ocean ecosystems, the effects of overfishing along the coast of northeastern North America or the Philippine archipelago)

- Understands the global impacts of human changes in the physical environment (e.g., ^{BD (GE,212-213;NI,77-78)} increases in runoff and sediment, tropical soil degradation, habitat destruction, air pollution; alterations in the hydrologic cycle; increases in world temperatures; groundwater reduction)

Codes (right side of page):   BD = Benchmark, Declarative;   BP = Benchmark, Procedural;   BC = Benchmark, Contextual
1st letter of each code in parentheses   *2nd letter of code*   *Number*
G = GESP: National Geography Standards   E = Explicitly stated in document   Page number of cited document
E = JCGE: Guidelines for Geographic Education   I = Implied in document   *or, for duplicates,*
N = NAEP: Item Specifications in Geography   Standard number & level of duplicate
T = GENIP: K-6 Geography: Themes, Key Ideas
D = Duplicated in another standard

MREL

BD (GE,213;NI,80)

- Knows how people's changing attitudes toward the environment have led to landscape changes (e.g., pressure to replace farmlands with wetlands in flood plain areas, interest in preserving wilderness areas, support for the concept of historic preservation)

(GE,134)

15. Understands how physical systems affect human systems

Level I (Grades K-2)

BD (GE,134)

- Not appropriate for this level

Level II (Grades 3-5)

BD (GE,134;EE,14;NE,42;TE,30)

- Knows how humans adapt to variations in the physical environment (e.g., choices of clothing, housing styles, agricultural practices, recreational activities, food, daily and seasonal patterns of life)

BD (GE,134-135;TE,23)

- Knows how communities benefit from the physical environment (e.g., people make their living by farming on fertile land, fishing in local water, working in mines; the community is a port located on a natural harbor, a tourist center located in a scenic or historic area, an industrial center with good access to natural resources)

BD (GE,135;NI,41-42;TE,23,30)

- Knows the ways in which human activities are constrained by the physical environment (e.g., effects of weather, climate, and landforms on agriculture, recreational activities, availability of water, expansion of settlement)

BD (GE,135;NE,43)

- Knows natural hazards that occur in the physical environment (e.g., floods, wind storms, tornadoes, earthquakes)

Level III (Grades 6-8)

BD (GE,173)

- Knows the ways in which human systems develop in response to conditions in the physical environment (e.g., patterns of land use, economic livelihoods, architectural styles of buildings, building materials, flows of traffic, recreation activities)

BD (GE,173;NE,61)

- Knows how the physical environment affects life in different regions (e.g., how people in Siberia, Alaska, and other high-latitude places deal with the characteristics of tundra environments; limitations to coastline settlements as a result of tidal, storm, and erosional

Codes (right side of page):　　　　　　　　BD = Benchmark, Declarative; BP = Benchmark, Procedural; BC = Benchmark, Contextual
1st letter of each code in parentheses　　　*2nd letter of code*　　　　　　　　*Number*
G = GESP: National Geography Standards　　E = Explicitly stated in document　　Page number of cited document
E = JCGE: Guidelines for Geographic Education　　I = Implied in document　　　*or, for duplicates,*
N = NAEP: Item Specifications in Geography　　　　　　　　　　　　　　　Standard number & level of duplicate
T = GENIP: K-6 Geography: Themes, Key Ideas
D = Duplicated in another standard　　　　　　　　　388　　　　　　　　　　　　　MREL

processes)

- Knows the ways people take aspects of the environment into account when deciding on locations for human activities (e.g., early American industrial development along streams and rivers at the fall line to take advantage of water-generated power) ^{BD (GE,174)}

- Knows the associations between population density and environmental quality (e.g., resource distribution, rainfall, temperature, soil fertility, landform relief, carrying capacity) ^{BD (GE,174;NI,60)}

- Knows the effects of natural hazards on human systems in different regions of the United States and the world (e.g., how the level of economic development and technology influences the effect of drought on populations in Ethiopia compared with populations in Australia or the southern part of the United States) ^{BD (GE,174-175)}

- Knows the ways in which humans prepare for natural hazards (e.g., earthquake preparedness, constructing houses on stilts in flood-prone areas, designation of hurricane shelters and evacuation routes in hurricane-prone areas) ^{BD (GE,175)}

Level IV (Grades 9-12)

- Knows changes in the physical environment that have reduced the capacity of the environment to support human activity (e.g., the drought-plagued Sahel; the depleted rain forests of central Africa; the Great Plains Dust Bowl; the impact of the economic exploitation of Siberia's resources on a fragile sub-Arctic environment) ^{BD (GE,214)}

- Knows how humans overcome "limits to growth" imposed by physical systems (e.g., technology, human adaptation) ^{BD (GE,214)}

- Knows conditions and locations that place limits on plant growth and therefore on the expansion of human settlement (e.g., soils with limited nutrients, high salt content, shallow depth; extremely cold, arid, or humid tropical climates; mountainous and coastal environments) ^{BD (GE,214-215;NI,78)}

- Understands how people who live in naturally hazardous regions adapt to their environments (e.g., the use of sea walls to protect coastal areas subject to severe storms, the use of earthquake-resistant construction techniques in different regions within the Ring of Fire) ^{BD (GE,215;NE,78)}

- Knows factors that affect people's attitudes, perceptions, and responses toward natural hazards (e.g., religious beliefs, socioeconomic status, previous experiences) ^{BD (GE,215;NI,79-80)}

Codes (right side of page): BD = Benchmark, Declarative; BP = Benchmark, Procedural; BC = Benchmark, Contextual
1st letter of each code in parentheses *2nd letter of code* *Number*
G = GESP: National Geography Standards E = Explicitly stated in document Page number of cited document
E = JCGE: Guidelines for Geographic Education I = Implied in document *or, for duplicates,*
N = NAEP: Item Specifications in Geography Standard number & level of duplicate
T = GENIP: K-6 Geography: Themes, Key Ideas
D = Duplicated in another standard

McREL

(GE,136)

16. Understands the changes that occur in the meaning, use, distribution, and importance of resources

Level I (Grades K-2)

BD (GE,137;EI,15;NI,51;TI,13)

- Knows the role that resources play in our daily lives (resources used to generate electricity; resources used to produce automobiles, medicines, clothing, and food)

Level II (Grades 3-5)

BD (GE,136;EI,15;NE,50;TI,23,37)

- Knows the characteristics, location, and use of renewable resources (e.g., timber), flow resources (e.g., running water or wind), and nonrenewable resources (e.g., fossil fuels, minerals)

BD (GE,136;EI,17;TI,42)

- Knows how settlement patterns are influenced by the discovery and use of resources (e.g., Colorado mining towns as centers of settlement in the late 19th century, the growth of industry and cities along the fall line of the Appalachians starting in the 18th century)

BD (GE,136;EE,17;NE,50;TE,37)

- Knows the relationships between economic activities and resources (e.g., the relationship of major industrial districts to the location of iron ore, coal, and other resources)

BD (GE,136;NI,39;TI,31)

- Knows the major transportation routes that link resources with consumers and the transportation modes used (e.g., ships, pipelines barges, railroads)

BD (GE,137;EI,14;NE,43;TI,37)

- Knows advantages and disadvantages of recycling and reusing different types of materials

BD (GE,137;NI,44;TI,29-30)

- Knows the different ways in which resources are used and valued in different regions of the world (e.g., the use of wood in the United States for construction compared to the use of wood in the Dominican Republic for fuel)

Level III (Grades 6-8)

BD (GE,177-178;NE,67)

- Understands the reasons for conflicting viewpoints regarding how resources should be used (e.g., attitudes toward electric cars, water rationing, urban public transportation, use of fossil fuels, excessive timber cutting in old-growth forests, buffalo in the western United States, soil conservation in semiarid areas)

BD (GE,178;NI,61;DI,18.2.2)

- Knows strategies for wise management and use of renewable, flow, and nonrenewable

---

Codes (right side of page):   BD = Benchmark, Declarative; BP = Benchmark, Procedural; BC = Benchmark, Contextual
1st letter of each code in parentheses   *2nd letter of code*   *Number*
G = GESP: National Geography Standards   E = Explicitly stated in document   Page number of cited document
E = JCGE: Guidelines for Geographic Education   I = Implied in document   *or, for duplicates,*
N = NAEP: Item Specifications in Geography   Standard number & level of duplicate
T = GENIP: K-6 Geography: Themes, Key Ideas
D = Duplicated in another standard   390   McREL

resources (e.g., wise management of agricultural soils, fossil fuels, and alternative energy sources; community programs for recycling or reusing materials)

- Knows world patterns of resource distribution and utilization (e.g., petroleum, coal, iron ore, diamonds, silver, gold, molybdenum) BD (GE,176;NE,69)

- Understands the consequences of the use of resources in the contemporary world (e.g., the relationship between a country's standard of living and its accessibility to resources; the competition for resources demonstrated by events such as the Japanese occupation of Manchuria in the 1930s or the Iraqi invasion of Kuwait in 1991) BD (GE,176-177;NI,67,70)

- Understands the role of technology in resource acquisition and use, and its impact on the environment (e.g., the use of giant earth-moving machinery in strip-mining; the use of satellite imagery technology in the search for petroleum; rates of resource consumption among countries of high or low levels of technological development) BD (GE,178;NI,62)

- Understands how energy resources contribute to the development and functioning of human societies (e.g., by providing power for transportation, manufacturing, the heating and cooling of buildings) BD (GE,178;NI,59)

- Understands how the development and widespread use of alternative energy sources (e.g., solar, wind, thermal) might have an impact on societies (in terms of, e.g., air and water quality, existing energy industries, and current manufacturing practices) BD (GE,178)

Level IV (Grades 9-12)

- Understands the relationships between resources and exploration, colonization, and settlement of different regions of the world (e.g., the development of mercantilism and imperialism and the consequent settlement of Latin America and other regions of the world by the Spanish and Portuguese; the abundance of fur, fish, timber, and gold in Siberia, Alaska, and California and the settlement of these areas by the Russians) BD (GE,216-217;NI,75)

- Understands programs and positions related to the use of resources on a local to global scale (e.g., community regulations for water usage during drought periods; local recycling programs for glass, metal, plastic, and paper products; different points of view regarding uses of the Malaysian rain forests) BD (GE,218;NI,80)

- Understands the impact of policy decisions regarding the use of resources in different regions of the world (e.g., the long-term impact on the economy of Nauru when its phosphate BD (GE,217;NI,88)

Codes (right side of page):   BD = Benchmark, Declarative; BP = Benchmark, Procedural; BC = Benchmark, Contextual

1st letter of each code in parentheses	*2nd letter of code*	*Number*
G = GESP: National Geography Standards	E = Explicitly stated in document	Page number of cited document
E = JCGE: Guidelines for Geographic Education	I = Implied in document	*or, for duplicates,*
N = NAEP: Item Specifications in Geography		Standard number & level of duplicate
T = GENIP: K-6 Geography: Themes, Key Ideas		
D = Duplicated in another standard	391	McREL

reserves are exhausted; the economic and social problems related to the overcutting of pine forests in Nova Scotia; the impact of petroleum consumption in the United States and Japan)

BD (GE,218;NI,80,88)
- Knows issues related to the reuse and recycling of resources (e.g., changing relocation strategies of industries seeking access to recyclable material, such as paper factories, container and can companies, glass, plastic, and bottle manufacturers; issues involved with the movement, handling, processing, and storing of toxic and hazardous waste materials; fully enforced vs. consistently neglected approaches to resource management)

(GE,138)

17.   Understands how geography is used to interpret the past

Level I (Grades K-2)

BD (GE,138;EE,14;NE,38;TE,16,20)
- Knows how areas of a community have changed over time (in terms of, e.g., size and style of homes; how people earn their living; changes in the plant and animal population)

Level II (Grades 3-5)

BD (GE,138;TI,23-24)
- Knows the factors that have contributed to changing land use in a community (e.g., street and road development, population shifts, regulations governing land use)

BD (GE,139)
- Knows the ways in which changes in people's perceptions of environments have influenced human migration and settlement over time (e.g., the history of oil discovery and its effect on migration in different United States regions such as Pennsylvania, Louisiana, or Texas)

BD (GE,139)
- Knows the geographic factors that have influenced people and events in the past (e.g., the effects of the site of a Civil War battle on the course of the conflict; how trade routes followed by early European colonists were linked to the trade winds; how Muslim trading vessels used monsoon winds to cross the Indian Ocean in the 8th century)

Level III (Grades 6-8)

BD (GE,180;NI,68-69)
- Knows how physical and human geographic factors have influenced major historic events and movements (e.g., the course and outcome of battles and wars; the forced transport of Africans to North and South America because of the need for cheap labor; the profitability of the triangle trade and the locations of prevailing wind and ocean currents; the effects of different land survey systems used in the U.S.)

Codes (right side of page):	BD = Benchmark, Declarative; BP = Benchmark, Procedural; BC = Benchmark, Contextual	
1st letter of each code in parentheses	*2nd letter of code*	*Number*
G = GESP: National Geography Standards	E = Explicitly stated in document	Page number of cited document
E = JCGE: Guidelines for Geographic Education	I = Implied in document	*or, for duplicates,*
N = NAEP: Item Specifications in Geography		Standard number & level of duplicate
T = GENIP: K-6 Geography: Themes, Key Ideas		
D = Duplicated in another standard	392	McREL

- Knows historic and current conflicts and competition regarding the use and allocation of ^{BD (GE,179;NI,67)} resources (e.g., the conflicts between Native Americans and colonists, between the Inuit and migrants to Alaska since 1950)

- Knows the ways in which the spatial organization of society changes over time (e.g., process ^{BD (GE,179;NI,56-57)} of urban growth in the United States; changes in the internal structure, form, and function of urban areas in different regions of the world at different times)

- Knows significant physical features that have influenced historical events (e.g., mountain ^{BD (GE,180)} passes that have affected military campaigns—such as the Khyber Pass, Burma Pass, or Brenner Pass; major water crossings that have affected U.S. history—such as the Tacoma Strait in Washington or the Delaware River near Trenton, New Jersey; major water gaps, springs, and other hydrologic features that have affected settlement in the U.S.—such as the Cumberland Gap, the Ogallala Aquifer, or the artesian wells of the Great Plains)

Level IV (Grades 9-12)

- Understands how the processes of spatial change have affected history (e.g., the diffusion ^{BD (GE,219)} of a phenomenon through regions of contact, such as the spread of bubonic plague, or the diffusion of tobacco smoking from North America to Europe, Africa, and Asia; the development of the national transportation systems in the U.S.; effects of migration streams and counterstreams)

- Understands how people's changing perceptions of geographic features have led to changes ^{BD (GE,219-220;NI,79-80)} in human societies (e.g., the effects of religion on world economic development patterns, cultural conflict, social integration, resource use; the effects of technology on human control over nature, such as large-scale agriculture in Ukraine and northern China, strip mining in Russia, and center-pivot irrigation in the southwestern United States)

- Understands the ways in which physical and human features have influenced the evolution ^{BD (GE,220)} of significant historic events and movements (e.g., the effects of imperialism, colonization, and decolonization on the economic and political developments of the 19th and 20th centuries; the geographical forces responsible for the industrial revolution in England in the late 18th and early 19th centuries; physical and human factors that have led to famines and large-scale refugee movements)

Codes (right side of page):   BD = Benchmark, Declarative; BP = Benchmark, Procedural; BC = Benchmark, Contextual
1st letter of each code in parentheses   *2nd letter of code*   *Number*
G = GESP: National Geography Standards   E = Explicitly stated in document   Page number of cited document
E = JCGE: Guidelines for Geographic Education   I = Implied in document   *or, for duplicates,*
N = NAEP: Item Specifications in Geography   Standard number & level of duplicate
T = GENIP: K-6 Geography: Themes, Key Ideas
D = Duplicated in another standard   393   *McREL*

(GI,140)

18. Understands global development and environmental issues

Level I (Grades K-2)

BD (GE,140)

- No material specifically designated for this grade level

Level II (Grades 3-5)

BD (GE,140;EI,17)

- Knows the relationship between population growth and resource use

BD (GE,140;NI,43;TI,30;DI,16.3.2)

- Knows the ways in which resources can be managed and why it is important to do so (e.g., soil conservation practices, recycling nonrenewable resources)

BD (GE,140;NE,44)

- Knows how differences in perception affect people's views of the world (e.g., how different groups of people perceive the same place, environment, or event; how children raised in different societies have different views regarding personal life, education, and aspirations)

BD (GE,141;NI,44)

- Knows human-induced changes that are taking place in different regions and the possible future impacts of these changes (e.g., development and conservation issues in terms of the wetland of coastal New Jersey)

Level III (Grades 6-8)

BD (GE,181;NI,60)

- Understands how the interaction between physical and human systems affects current conditions on Earth (e.g., the relationships involved in economic, political, social, and environmental changes; the geographic impact of using petroleum, coal, nuclear power, and solar power as major energy sources)

BD (GE,182;NI,60)

- Understands the possible impact that present conditions and patterns of consumption, production, and population growth might have on the future spatial organization of Earth

BD (GE,182)

- Knows how the quality of environments in large cities can be improved (e.g., greenways, transportation corridors, pedestrian walkways, bicycle lanes)

BD (GE,181-182;NI,62-63)

- Understands why different points of view exist regarding contemporary geographic issues (e.g., a forester and a conservationist debating the use of a national forest, a man and a woman discussing gender-based divisions of labor in a developing nation)

Codes (right side of page):   BD = Benchmark, Declarative; BP = Benchmark, Procedural; BC = Benchmark, Contextual
1st letter of each code in parentheses   *2nd letter of code*   *Number*
G = GESP: National Geography Standards   E = Explicitly stated in document   Page number of cited document
E = JCGE: Guidelines for Geographic Education   I = Implied in document   *or, for duplicates,*
N = NAEP: Item Specifications in Geography   Standard number & level of duplicate
T = GENIP: K-6 Geography: Themes, Key Ideas
D = Duplicated in another standard   394   MREL

Level IV (Grades 9-12)

BD (GE,221;NI,79-80)

- Understands the concept of sustainable development and its effects in a variety of situations (e.g., cutting the rain forests in Indonesia in response to a demand for lumber in foreign markets, or mining the rutile sands along the coast of eastern Australia near the Great Barrier Reef)

BD (GE,221;NI,79)

- Understands why policies should be designed to guide the use and management of Earth's resources and to reflect multiple points of view (e.g., the inequities of access to resources, or to political and economic power in developing countries; the impact of a natural disaster on a developed country vs. a developing country)

BD (GE,222;NI,76)

- Understands contemporary issues in terms of Earth's physical and human systems (e.g., the processes of land degradation and desertification; the consequences of population growth or decline in a developed economy; the consequences of a world temperature increase)

Codes (right side of page):   BD = Benchmark, Declarative;   BP = Benchmark, Procedural;   BC = Benchmark, Contextual

1st letter of each code in parentheses	*2nd letter of code*	*Number*
G = GESP: National Geography Standards	E = Explicitly stated in document	Page number of cited document
E = JCGE: Guidelines for Geographic Education	I = Implied in document	*or, for duplicates,*
N = NAEP: Item Specifications in Geography		Standard number & level of duplicate
T = GENIP: K-6 Geography: Themes, Key Ideas		
D = Duplicated in another standard	395	MREL

12. The Arts

The following process was used to identify standards and benchmarks for the arts:

Identification of National Reports

Four reports were identified as important for representing current thinking on knowledge and skills in the arts: *The National Standards for Arts Education* (1994) developed by the Consortium of National Arts Education Associations, the *NAEP Arts Education Assessment Framework* (NAEP, 1994), the *Visual and Performing Arts Framework for California Public Schools: K–12* (California Department of Education, 1989), and *The School Program: Description and Standards* (1986) from the Music Educators National Conference.

Selection of the Reference Document

The *National Standards for Arts Education* was selected as the reference document for constructing standards in the arts. The developers of the document represented a consortium of arts educators in music, theatre, the visual arts, and dance. The work provides content standards in each arts area, with "achievement standards" described for three levels: K–4, 5–8, and 9–12.

Identification of Standards and Benchmarks

At the standard level, most statements in the national document were retained with some revision to reflect the more content-oriented focus of this model. Additionally, one standard, Art Connections, was formed by combining very similar ideas from across the arts areas, namely, content that addressed the connections among various art forms and other disciplines.

At the benchmark level, there were some aspects in which the material for the arts standards was consistently revised and adapted to fit the model used in this study. This was the case when "achievement standards" in the national document were rewritten to describe specific knowledge and/or skill. For example, under the visual arts content standard "Using knowledge of structures and functions," one 8th-grade achievement standard is:

> a. [Students] generalize about the effects of visual structures and functions and reflect upon these effects in their own works (p. 50)

Because content standards are the focus of this study, material such as the example above was rewritten to describe the knowledge a student should have, rather than to describe an activity that might be used to demonstrate achievement of that knowledge. Additionally, detailed information was added to the benchmark when it was available; primary sources were the NAEP arts framework and a glossary provided in the *National Standards*. Thus, the benchmark was rewritten as:

(AE,50;CI,95-96;NE,101)

- Knows the effects of various visual structures (e.g., design elements such as line, color, shape; principles such as repetition, rhythm, balance) and functions of art

For the example analyzed here, it should be noted that another standard in the visual arts, "Understands the characteristics and merits of one's own artwork and the artwork of others," separately addresses that aspect of the activity that concerns the students' review of their own works.

Integration of Information from Other Documents

As demonstrated above, supplementary documents were used to provide detail (which was the primary use of the NAEP framework) and to provide page references to a well-known curriculum framework, in this case, the California Visual and Performing Arts Framework. Additionally, material from *The School Program,* produced by the Music Educators National Conference, was used to provide benchmarks at K–2 in the section on music. In the other arts areas, no documents were found suitable to address this need; consequently, areas other than music are presented at levels found in the arts standards document: K–4, 5–8, and 9–12.

Summary of Standards for the Arts

Art Connections
1.   Understands connections among the various art forms and other disciplines

Dance
1.   Identifies and demonstrates movement elements and skills in performing dance
2.   Understands choreographic principles, processes, and structures
3.   Understands dance as a way to create and communicate meaning
4.   Applies critical and creative thinking skills in dance
5.   Understands dance in various cultures and historical periods
6.   Understands connections between dance and healthful living

Music
1.   Sings, alone and with others, a varied repertoire of music
2.   Performs on instruments, alone and with others, a varied repertoire of music
3.   Improvises melodies, variations, and accompaniments
4.   Composes and arranges music within specified guidelines
5.   Reads and notates music
6.   Knows and applies appropriate criteria to music and music performances
7.   Understands the relationship between music and history and culture

Theatre
1.   Demonstrates competence in writing scripts
2.   Uses acting skills
3.   Designs and produces informal and formal productions
4.   Directs scenes and productions
5.   Understands how informal and formal theatre, film, television, and electronic media productions create and communicate meaning
6.   Understands the context in which theatre, film, television, and electronic media are performed today as well as in the past

Visual Arts
1.   Understands and applies media, techniques, and processes related to the visual arts
2.   Knows how to use the structures (e.g., sensory qualities, organizational principles, expressive features) and functions of art
3.   Knows a range of subject matter, symbols, and potential ideas in the visual arts
4.   Understands the visual arts in relation to history and cultures
5.   Understands the characteristics and merits of one's own artwork and the artwork of others

Art Connections

1. **Understands connections among the various art forms and other disciplines** (AE,25,28,31,35)

Level II (Grades K-4)

- Knows how visual, aural, oral, and kinetic elements are used in the various art forms BD (AE,31;NI,93)

- Knows how ideas (e.g., sibling rivalry, respect) and emotions (e.g., sadness, anger) are expressed in the various art forms BD (AE,31;NE,93)

- Knows the similarities and differences in the meanings of common terms used in the various arts (e.g., form, line, contrast) BD (AE,28)

- Knows ways in which the principles and subject matter of other disciplines taught in the school are interrelated with those of the arts (e.g., pattern in the arts and in science) BD (AI,25,28,35)

Level III (Grades 5-8)

- Understands how the characteristic materials of various arts (e.g., sound in music, visual stimuli in visual arts, movement in dance, human interrelationships in theatre) are used to transform similar events, scenes, emotions, or ideas into distinct works of art BD (AE,45)

- Understands characteristics of works in various art forms that share similar subject matter, historical periods, or cultural context BD (AE,51;NE,102,103)

- Understands the characteristics and presentation of characters, environments, and actions in the various art forms BD (NE,95;AE,47)

- Knows how various concepts and principles are used in the arts and disciplines outside the arts (e.g., balance, shape, pattern) BD (AE,41)

- Knows the aesthetic impact of arts performances seen live versus those recorded on audio or video BD (AE,41)

- Understands the functions and interaction between performing and visual artists and audience members in theatre, dance, music, and visual arts BD (AE,48)

Codes (right side of page):   BD = Benchmark, Declarative; BP = Benchmark, Procedural; BC = Benchmark, Contextual
1st letter of each code in parentheses   *2nd letter of code*   *Number*
A = CNAEA: National Standards for Arts Education   E = Explicitly stated in document   Page number of cited document
C = California Visual/Performing Arts Framework   I = Implied in document
N = NAEP: Arts Education Assessment Framework

Level IV (Grades 9-12)

BD (AE,66;CI,51)
- Knows ways in which various arts media can be integrated

BD (AE,62,72;NE,106)
- Knows how characteristics of the arts vary within a particular historical period or style and how these characteristics relate to ideas, issues, or themes in other disciplines

BD (AE,58,62,72;NE,106)
- Understands how elements, materials, technologies, artistic processes (e.g., imagination, craftsmanship), and organizational principles (e.g., unity and variety, repetition and contrast) are used in similar and distinctive ways in the various art forms

Codes (right side of page):   BD = Benchmark, Declarative; BP = Benchmark, Procedural; BC = Benchmark, Contextual
1st letter of each code in parentheses   *2nd letter of code*   *Number*
A = CNAEA: National Standards for Arts Education   E = Explicitly stated in document   Page number of cited document
C = California Visual/Performing Arts Framework   I = Implied in document
N = NAEP: Arts Education Assessment Framework

401   MREL

Dance

(AE,23)

1.   Identifies and demonstrates movement elements and skills in performing dance

Level II (Grades K-4)

- Knows basic nonlocomotor/axial movements (e.g., bend, twist, stretch, swing) _{BD (AE,23;CI,16;NE,75)}

BD (AE,23;CI,16;NE,75)
- Knows basic locomotor movements (e.g., walk, hop, leap, gallop, slide, skip) and different directions in which they can be performed (e.g., forward, backward, sideward, diagonally, turning)

BP (AE,23;CE,17)
- Creates shapes (e.g., body shapes, lines, angles, curves) at low, middle, and high levels (different heights from the floor)

BP (AE,23;CE,16;NE,76)
- Defines and maintains personal space (e.g., form, distance from others when moving through space as part of a group)

BP (AE,23;CI,17;NE,75)
- Uses movements in straight and curved pathways

BP (AE,23;CI,17;NE,75)
- Moves to a rhythmic accompaniment (e.g., drumbeat) and responds to changes in tempo

BP (AE,23;CE,22)
- Uses kinesthetic awareness, concentration, and focus in performing movement skills

BD (AE,23;CI,15;NE,76)
- Knows basic actions (e.g., skip, gallop) and movement elements (e.g., height of the dancer in relation to the floor, directions) and how they communicate ideas

Level III (Grades 5-8)

BD (AE,39;CI,17;NE,78)
- Understands various movements and their underlying principles (e.g., alignment, balance, initiation of movement, articulation of isolated body parts, weight shift, elevation and landing, fall and recovery)

BD (AE,39;CE,24;NE,77)
- Knows basic dance steps, body positions and spatial patterns for dances from various styles or traditions (e.g., ballet, square, Ghanaian, Middle Eastern, modern)

Codes (right side of page):   BD = Benchmark, Declarative; BP = Benchmark, Procedural; BC = Benchmark, Contextual
1st letter of each code in parentheses   *2nd letter of code*   *Number*
A = CNAEA: National Standards for Arts Education   E = Explicitly stated in document   Page number of cited document
C = California Visual/Performing Arts Framework   I = Implied in document
N = NAEP: Arts Education Assessment Framework

McREL

- BP (AE,39;CI,15;NE,77)
  Transfers a spatial pattern from the visual to the kinesthetic (e.g., reproduces a pattern drawn on paper by traveling through space)

- BP (AE,39;CI,15;NE,77)
  Transfers a rhythmic pattern from the aural to the kinesthetic (e.g., reproduces a rhythmic pattern beat on a drum by using movement)

- BD (AE,39;CE,17;NE,77)
  Knows a range of dynamics/movement qualities (e.g., sustained, swing, percussive, collapse; vibratory and effort combinations such as a float, dab, punch, and glide)

- BP (AE,39;CE,22;NE,77)
  Memorizes and reproduces movement sequences

- BD (AE,39;CI,23;NE,78)
  Understands the action and movement elements observed in dance, and knows appropriate movement/dance vocabulary (e.g., level, direction)

Level IV (Grades 9-12)

- BP (AE,55;CI,16;NE,79)
  Uses appropriate skeletal alignment (e.g., relationship of the skeleton to the line of gravity and the base of support), body-part articulation, strength, flexibility, agility, and coordination in locomotor and nonlocomotor/axial movements

- BD (AE,55;CI,24)
  Knows complex steps and patterns from various dance styles (e.g., dances of a particular performer, choreographer, period) and traditions (e.g., dances of bharata natyam, noh; folk dances of indigenous peoples of Europe or other areas)

- BD (AE,55;CE,17)
  Understands various complex time elements (e.g., duple and triple meters and tempo varied in relation to a basic pulse)

- BP (AE,55;CI,17;NI,78)
  Creates and performs combinations and variations in a broad dynamic range (e.g., sustained, percussive, vibratory, swing)

- BP (AE,55;CI,17)
  Uses projection in dance (e.g., confident presentation of one's body and energy to communicate movement and meaning to an audience, performance quality, positive sense of involvement)

- BP (AE,55;CE,22;NE,79)
  Memorizes and reproduces extended movement sequences and rhythmic patterns

---

Codes (right side of page):   BD = Benchmark, Declarative; BP = Benchmark, Procedural; BC = Benchmark, Contextual
1st letter of each code in parentheses   *2nd letter of code*   *Number*
A = CNAEA: National Standards for Arts Education   E = Explicitly stated in document   Page number of cited document
C = California Visual/Performing Arts Framework   I = Implied in document
N = NAEP: Arts Education Assessment Framework

(AE,24)

2. Understands choreographic principles, processes, and structures

Level II (Grades K-4)

- Creates a sequence with a beginning, middle, and ending

  BP (AE,24;CE,19;NE,75)

- Improvises, creates, and performs dances based on personal ideas and concepts from other sources

  BP (AE,24;CI,23;NI,75)

- Knows how improvisation is used to discover and invent movement and to solve movement problems

  BD (AE,24;CI,18)

- Creates a dance phrase (e.g., a brief sequence of related movements that has a sense of rhythmic completion), repeats it, and varies it (e.g., makes changes in the time, space, force/energy)

  BP (AE,24;CE,19;NE,75)

- Uses partner skills such as copying, leading, and following and mirroring

  BP (AE,24;NI,75)

Level III (Grades 5-8)

- Understands the principles of contrast and transition

  BD (AE,40;CE,19;NE,77)

- Understands the processes of reordering (e.g., elements such as specific movements or movement phrases are separated from their original relationship and restructured in a different pattern) and chance (e.g., elements are specifically chosen and defined but randomly structured to create a dance or movement phrase)

  BD (AE,40;NI,77)

- Understands structures or forms such as AB, ABA, canon, call and response, and narrative

  BD (AE,40;CE,19;NE,77)

- Uses partner skills such as creating complementary and contrasting shapes and taking and supporting weight

  BP (AE,40;NE,77)

Level IV (Grades 9-12)

- Knows how improvisation is used to generate movement for choreography

  BD (AE,56;NE,78)

Codes (right side of page):　　　BD = Benchmark, Declarative;　BP = Benchmark, Procedural;　BC = Benchmark, Contextual
1st letter of each code in parentheses　　　*2nd letter of code*　　　*Number*
A = CNAEA: National Standards for Arts Education　　　E = Explicitly stated in document　　　Page number of cited document
C = California Visual/Performing Arts Framework　　　I = Implied in document
N = NAEP: Arts Education Assessment Framework

McREL

- Understands structures or forms such as palindrome, theme and variation, rondo, round, and contemporary forms
  BD (AE,56;CE,19;NE,79)

- Identifies choreographic principles, processes, and structures used in dance
  BP (AI,56;CI,23;NE,79)

(AE,24)

3. Understands dance as a way to create and communicate meaning

Level II (Grades K-4)

- Knows how dance is different from other forms of human movement (e.g., sports, everyday gestures)
  BD (AE,24;NE,76)

- Knows how a dance may elicit various interpretations and reactions that differ from the meaning intended by the dancer
  BD (AE,24;CI,23;NI,76)

Level III (Grades 5-8)

- Understands the difference between pantomiming and abstracting a gesture
  BD (AE,40;CI,18)

- Understands how different accompaniments (e.g., sound, music, spoken text) can affect the meaning of a dance
  BD (AE,40)

- Understands how lighting and costuming can contribute to the meaning of a dance
  BD (AE,40)

- Creates dance that communicates topics/ideas of personal significance
  BP (AE,40;CE,18;NE,78)

Level IV (Grades 9-12)

- Understands how movement choices are used to communicate abstract ideas and themes in dance (e.g., isolation, relationships, poverty, the environment)
  BD (AE,56;CI,18;NE,79,80)

- Understands how interpretation of dance can be influenced by personal experience
  BD (AE,56)

Codes (right side of page):   BD = Benchmark, Declarative; BP = Benchmark, Procedural; BC = Benchmark, Contextual
1st letter of each code in parentheses   *2nd letter of code*   *Number*
A = CNAEA: National Standards for Arts Education   E = Explicitly stated in document   Page number of cited document
C = California Visual/Performing Arts Framework   I = Implied in document
N = NAEP: Arts Education Assessment Framework

McREL

(AE,24)

4. Applies critical and creative thinking skills in dance

Level II (Grades K-4)

BD (AE,24;NE,75)
- Knows how a variety of solutions can be used to solve a given movement problem

BD (AE,24;NE,76)
- Knows technical and artistic components of various forms of dance (e.g., body shapes, space, levels, pathways)

Level III (Grades 5-8)

BD (AE,40)
- Knows appropriate audience response to dance performances

BD (AE,40;NE,78)
- Knows the critical elements that contribute to a dance in terms of space (e.g., shape, pathways) time (e.g., rhythm, tempo), and force/energy (e.g., movement qualities)

BD (AE,40;CI,23;NE,78)
- Knows possible aesthetic criteria that could be used to evaluate dance (e.g., skill of performers, originality, visual and/or emotional impact, variety and contrast)

Level IV (Grades 9-12)

BP (AE,57;CI,19;NE,80)
- Establishes a set of aesthetic criteria and applies it in evaluating one's own work and that of others

BP (AE,57)
- Formulates and answers aesthetic questions (e.g., knows what makes a particular dance unique, how much one can change a dance before it becomes a different dance)

(AE,24)

5. Understands dance in various cultures and historical periods

Level II (Grades K-4)

BD (AE,24;CI,20,24;NE,76)
- Knows folk dances from various cultures

Codes (right side of page):   BD = Benchmark, Declarative; BP = Benchmark, Procedural; BC = Benchmark, Contextual
1st letter of each code in parentheses   *2nd letter of code*   *Number*
A = CNAEA: National Standards for Arts Education   E = Explicitly stated in document   Page number of cited document
C = California Visual/Performing Arts Framework   I = Implied in document
N = NAEP: Arts Education Assessment Framework

BD (AE,25;CE,21,24;NE,76)

- Knows the cultural and/or historical context of various dances (e.g., colonial America, dances within one's community)

Level III (Grades 5-8)

BD (AE,41;CI,20,24;NI,77)

- Knows the similarities and differences in steps and movement styles among folk dances and classical dances from various cultures

BD (AE,41;CI,21,24)

- Knows folk, social, and theatrical (e.g., jazz, tap) dances from a broad spectrum of 20th-century America

BD (AE,41;CI,21,24;NE,78)

- Knows the role of dance in various cultures and time periods

Level IV (Grades 9-12)

BD (AE,57;CI,24;NE,80)

- Knows the similarities and differences among various contemporary theatrical forms of dance (e.g., jazz, tap)

BD (AE,57;CI,24;NE,80)

- Knows the traditions and techniques of classical dance forms (e.g., Balinese, ballet)

BD (AE,57;CI,21;NE,80)

- Understands how dance and dancers are portrayed in contemporary media

(AE,25)

6.   Understands connections between dance and healthful living

Level II (Grades K-4)

BD (AE,25)

- Knows how healthy practices (e.g., nutrition, safety) enhance the ability to dance

Level III (Grades 5-8)

BD (AE,41;CE,16)

- Knows strategies to prevent dance injuries

BP (AE,41;CI,16;NE,77)

- Creates personal dance warm-up techniques

Codes (right side of page):   BD = Benchmark, Declarative; BP = Benchmark, Procedural; BC = Benchmark, Contextual
1st letter of each code in parentheses   *2nd letter of code*   *Number*
A = CNAEA: National Standards for Arts Education   E = Explicitly stated in document   Page number of cited document
C = California Visual/Performing Arts Framework   I = Implied in document
N = NAEP: Arts Education Assessment Framework

McREL

- Creates goals to improve as a dancer BP (AE,41)

Level IV (Grades 9-12)

- Knows how lifestyle choices affect the dancer as a professional performer BD (AE,58)

- Understands contemporary images of the body in dance and how images of the body vary across cultures and through history BD (AE,58)

Codes (right side of page):   BD = Benchmark, Declarative; BP = Benchmark, Procedural; BC = Benchmark, Contextual
1st letter of each code in parentheses   *2nd letter of code*   *Number*
A = CNAEA: National Standards for Arts Education   E = Explicitly stated in document   Page number of cited document
C = California Visual/Performing Arts Framework   I = Implied in document
N = NAEP: Arts Education Assessment Framework

408

MREL

Music

(AE,26)

1. Sings, alone and with others, a varied repertoire of music

Level I (Grades K-2)

BP (AE,26;CE,76;ME,22;NE,82)
● Sings ostinatos (repetitions of a short musical pattern), partner songs, and rounds

Level II (Grades 3-5)

BP (AE,26;CI,76;MI,23;NE,82)
● Sings on pitch and in rhythm, with appropriate timbre, diction, and posture, and maintains a steady tempo

BP (AE,26;CI,75;MI,23;NE,82)
● Sings expressively, with appropriate dynamics, phrasing, and interpretation

BP (AE,26;CI,76;ME,24;NE,82)
● Blends vocal timbres, matches dynamic levels, and responds to the cues of a conductor when singing as part of a group

BD (AE,26;CI,78;MI,23)
● Knows songs representing genres (e.g., march, work song, lullaby, Dixieland) and styles (e.g., of various composers, nations) from diverse cultures

Level III (Grades 6-8)

BP (AE,42;CI,76;ME,33;NI,85)
● Sings with good breath control, expression, and technical accuracy (e.g., appropriate timbre, intonation and diction; correct pitches and rhythms) at a level that includes modest ranges and changes of tempo, key, and meter

BP (AE,42;CE,76;ME,32;NE,85)
● Sings music written in two and three parts

BD (AE,42;CE,78;ME,32)
● Knows music that represents diverse genres (e.g., sonata, madrigal, jazz, barbershop) and cultures

---

Codes (right side of page):   BD = Benchmark, Declarative; BP = Benchmark, Procedural; BC = Benchmark, Contextual
1st letter of each code in parentheses   *2nd letter of code*   *Number*
A = CNAEA: National Standards for Arts Education   E = Explicitly stated in document   Page number of cited document
C = California Visual/Performing Arts Framework   I = Implied in document
M = MENC: The School Music Program
N = NAEP: Arts Education Assessment Framework

MREL

Level IV (Grades 9-12)

- Sings a varied repertoire of vocal literature with expression and technical accuracy at a moderate level of difficulty (e.g., attention to phrasing and interpretation, various meters and rhythms in a variety of keys) BP (AE,59;CI,76;ME,43;NI,88)

- Sings music written in four parts, with and without accompaniment BP (AE,59;CI,76;ME,43;NE,89)

- Uses ensemble skills (e.g., balance, intonation, rhythmic unity) BP (AE,49;MI,43;NE,89)

(AE,26)

2. Performs on instruments, alone and with others, a varied repertoire of music

Level I (Grades K-2)

- Echoes short rhythms (2-4 measure) and melodic patterns BP (AE,26;CE,74;MI,23;NE,82)

Level II (Grades 3-5)

- Performs on pitch, in rhythm, with appropriate dynamics and timbre, and maintains a steady tempo BP (AE,26;CD,76;MI,23;NE,82)

- Performs simple rhythmic, melodic, and chordal patterns accurately and independently on rhythmic, melodic, and harmonic classroom instruments (e.g., recorder-type instruments, percussion instruments, keyboard instruments, electronic instruments, fretted instruments such as a guitar or ukulele) BP (AE,26;CE,76;MI,23;NE,82,83)

- Knows a varied repertoire of music representing diverse genres and styles BD (AE,26;CI,78;MI,23;NI,82)

- Performs in groups (e.g., blends instrumental timbres, matches dynamic levels, and responds to the cues of a conductor) BP (AE,26;CI,76;ME,24;NE,82)

- Performs independent instrumental parts (e.g., simple rhythmic or melodic ostinatos, contrasting rhythmic lines, harmonic progressions and chords) while others sing or play contrasting parts BP (AE,26;CE,76;ME,23;NE,83)

Codes (right side of page):   BD = Benchmark, Declarative; BP = Benchmark, Procedural; BC = Benchmark, Contextual
1st letter of each code in parentheses   *2nd letter of code*   *Number*
A = CNAEA: National Standards for Arts Education   E = Explicitly stated in document   Page number of cited document
C = California Visual/Performing Arts Framework   I = Implied in document
M = MENC: The School Music Program
N = NAEP: Arts Education Assessment Framework

410   MꟼEL

Level III (Grades 6-8)

- Performs on an instrument (e.g., band or orchestra instrument, keyboard instrument, fretted instrument such as guitar, electronic instrument) accurately and independently, alone and in small and large ensembles, with good posture, good playing position, and good breath, bow, or stick control
  BP (AE,42;CI,76;MI,33;NE,86)

- Performs with expression and technical accuracy (on a string, wind, percussion, or other classroom instrument) a repertoire of instrumental literature that may include modest ranges and changes of tempo, key, and meter
  BP (AE,43;MI,33)

- Performs music representing diverse genres and cultures with expression appropriate for the work being performed
  BP (AE,43;CE,78;MI,33;NE,86)

- Plays by ear simple melodies (e.g., folk songs) on a melodic instrument and simple accompaniments (e.g., strummed, I, IV, V, vi, ii chords) on a harmonic instrument
  BP (AE,43;CE,76;MI,32;NE,86)

Level IV (Grades 9-12)

- Performs with expression (e.g., appropriate dynamics, phrasing, rubato) and technical accuracy a large and varied repertoire of instrumental literature at a moderate level of difficulty (e.g., attends to phrasing and interpretation, performs various meters and rhythms in a variety of keys)
  BP (AE,59;ME,44;NE,89)

- Uses ensemble skills (e.g., balance, intonation, rhythmic unity) when performing as part of a group
  BP (AE,60;MI,44;NE,89)

(AE,27)

3. Improvises melodies, variations, and accompaniments

Level I (Grades K-2)

- Improvises "answers" in the same style to given rhythmic and melodic phrases
  BP (AE,27;ME,22;NE,81)

Codes (right side of page):   BD = Benchmark, Declarative; BP = Benchmark, Procedural; BC = Benchmark, Contextual
1st letter of each code in parentheses   *2nd letter of code*   *Number*
A = CNAEA: National Standards for Arts Education   E = Explicitly stated in document   Page number of cited document
C = California Visual/Performing Arts Framework   I = Implied in document
M = MENC: The School Music Program
N = NAEP: Arts Education Assessment Framework

Level II (Grades 3-5)

- Improvises simple rhythmic and melodic ostinato (repetition of a short musical pattern) accompaniments
  BP (AE,27;CE,77;ME,23;NE,81)

- Improvises simple rhythmic variations and simple melodic embellishments on familiar melodies
  BP (AE,27;MI,23;NE,81)

- Improvises short songs and instrumental pieces using a variety of sound sources, including traditional sounds (e.g., voices, instruments), nontraditional sounds (e.g., paper tearing, pencil tapping), body sounds (e.g., hands clapping, fingers snapping), and sounds produced by electronic means (e.g., personal computers and basic MIDI devices such as keyboards, sequencers, synthesizers, and drum machines)
  BP (AE,27;CE,77;ME,23;NE,81)

Level III (Grades 6-8)

- Improvises simple harmonic accompaniments
  BP (AE,43;ME,32;NE,85)

- Improvises melodic embellishments and simple rhythmic and melodic variations on given pentatonic melodies and melodies in major keys
  BP (AE,43;CI,77;NE,85)

- Improvises short melodies, unaccompanied and over given rhythmic accompaniments, in a consistent style (e.g., classical, blues, folk, gospel), meter (e.g., duple, triple), and tonality (e.g., major, pentatonic)
  BP (AE,43;MI,32;NE,85)

Level IV (Grades 9-12)

- Improvises stylistically appropriate harmonizing parts
  BP (AE,60;NI,88)

- Improvises rhythmic and melodic variations on given pentatonic melodies and melodies in major and minor keys (e.g., folk songs, standard pop songs, hymn tunes)
  BP (AE,60;NE,88)

- Improvises original melodies over given chord progressions in a consistent style, meter, and tonality
  BP (AE,60;CI,77;NI,88)

Codes (right side of page):   BD = Benchmark, Declarative;   BP = Benchmark, Procedural;   BC = Benchmark, Contextual
1st letter of each code in parentheses   *2nd letter of code*   *Number*
A = CNAEA: National Standards for Arts Education   E = Explicitly stated in document   Page number of cited document
C = California Visual/Performing Arts Framework   I = Implied in document
M = MENC: The School Music Program
N = NAEP: Arts Education Assessment Framework

412

MᴦREL

(AE,27)

4. Composes and arranges music within specified guidelines

Level I (Grades K-2)

BP (AE,27;MI,22;NE,81)
- Uses a variety of sound sources when composing (e.g., classroom instruments, electronic sounds, body sounds)

Level II (Grades 3-5)

BP (AE,27;MI,23;NE,81)
- Creates and arranges music to accompany readings or dramatizations (e.g., manipulates dimensions such as the variety of sounds, tempo, loudness, mood)

BP (AE,27;CI,77;MI,22;NE,81)
- Creates and arranges short songs and instrumental pieces within specified guidelines (e.g., a particular style, form, instrumentation, compositional technique)

Level III (Grades 6-8)

BD (AE,43;MI,32;NE,84)
- Knows how the elements of music are used to achieve unity and variety, tension and release, and balance in musical compositions

BP (AE,43;CI,77;NE,84)
- Composes short pieces within specified guidelines (e.g., ABA form, limited range, and simple rhythms)

BP (AE,43;NE,84)
- Arranges simple pieces for voices or instruments other than those for which the pieces originally were written (e.g., a guitar accompaniment for a folk song)

BP (AE,43;MI,32;NE,84)
- Uses a variety of traditional and nontraditional sound sources and electronic media (e.g., synthesizer, sequencer) when composing and arranging

Level IV (Grades 9-12)

BP (AE,60;NE,87)
- Composes music in a variety of distinct styles (e.g., classical, folk, pop, jazz, rock)

BP (AE,60;CI,74-75;MI,44;NE,87)
- Uses the elements of music for expressive effect (e.g., pitch, rhythm, harmony, dynamics,

---

Codes (right side of page):   BD = Benchmark, Declarative; BP = Benchmark, Procedural; BC = Benchmark, Contextual
1st letter of each code in parentheses   *2nd letter of code*   *Number*
A = CNAEA: National Standards for Arts Education   E = Explicitly stated in document   Page number of cited document
C = California Visual/Performing Arts Framework   I = Implied in document
M = MENC: The School Music Program
N = NAEP: Arts Education Assessment Framework

McREL

timbre, texture, form)

- Arranges pieces for voices or instruments other than those for which the pieces originally were written in ways that preserve or enhance the expressive effect of the music (e.g., piano music, 4-part hymns, duets, trios, quartets) BP (AE,60;NE,88)

- Composes and arranges music for voices and various acoustic and electronic instruments BP (AE,60;CE,77;MI,45;NE,88)

- Understands the ranges and traditional uses of various sound sources (e.g., voices, acoustic instruments, electronic instruments) BD (AE,60;MI,43;NE,88)

(AE,27)

5.   Reads and notates music

Level I (Grades K-2)

- Knows standard symbols used to notate meter (e.g., 2/4, 3/4, 4/4 time signatures), rhythm (e.g., whole, half, dotted half, quarter, eighth notes), pitch (e.g., notes in treble clef), and dynamics (e.g., p, f, <, >) in simple patterns BD (AE,27;ME,22;NE,83)

- Uses a system (e.g., syllables, numbers, letters) to read simple pitch notation in the treble clef in major keys BP (AE,27;CE,77;ME,22;NI,82,83)

Level II (Grades 3-5)

- Reads whole, half, dotted half, quarter, and eighth notes and rests in 2/4, 3/4, and 4/4 meter signatures BP (AE,27;ME,23;NE,82,83)

- Knows symbols and traditional terms referring to dynamics (e.g., piano, forte, crescendo, diminuendo), tempo (e.g., presto, ritardando, accelerando), and articulation (e.g., staccato, legato, marcato, accent) BD (AE,27;MI,22;NE,83)

Level III (Grades 6-8)

- Reads sixteenth and dotted notes and rests in 6/8, 3/8, and alla breve (2/2) meter signatures BP (AE,44;NE,85,86,87)

Codes (right side of page):   BD = Benchmark, Declarative; BP = Benchmark, Procedural; BC = Benchmark, Contextual
1st letter of each code in parentheses   *2nd letter of code*   *Number*
A = CNAEA: National Standards for Arts Education   E = Explicitly stated in document   Page number of cited document
C = California Visual/Performing Arts Framework   I = Implied in document
M = MENC: The School Music Program
N = NAEP: Arts Education Assessment Framework

- Sight reads simple melodies in both the treble and bass clefs   BP (AE,44;ME,32;NE,85,86)

- Knows standard notation symbols for pitch, rhythm, dynamics (e.g., piano, forte, crescendo, diminuendo), tempo, articulation (e.g., accents, legato, staccato, marcato), and expression (e.g., phrasing)   BD (AE,44;CI,77;ME,32;NE,87)

- Uses standard notation to record musical ideas   BP (AE,44;ME,32;NE,85,87-88)

Level IV (Grades 9-12)

- Reads an instrumental or vocal score of up to four staves   BP (AE,61;NE,90)

- Reads music that contains moderate technical demands, expanded ranges, and varied interpretive requirements   BP (AE,61;CI,77;MI,43-44;NI,89)

(AI,28)

6.   Knows and applies appropriate criteria to music and musical performances

Level I (Grades K-2)

- Knows personal preferences for specific musical works and styles   BD (AE,28;CE,79;MI,22;NE,81-84)

- Identifies simple musical forms (e.g., AB, ABA, call and response) when presented aurally   BP (AE,28;ME,22;NE,83)

- Responds through purposeful movement (e.g., swaying, skipping, dramatic play) to selected prominent music characteristics or to specific music events (e.g., meter changes, dynamic changes, same/different sections)   BP (AE,28;CI,77;MI,22;NE,83)

Level II (Grades 3-5)

- Knows music of various styles representing diverse cultures   BD (AE,28;CI,79;MI,23;NE,83)

- Knows appropriate terminology used to explain music, music notation, musical instruments and voices, and musical performances   BD (AE,28;ME,23;NE,83)

Codes (right side of page):   BD = Benchmark, Declarative; BP = Benchmark, Procedural; BC = Benchmark, Contextual
1st letter of each code in parentheses   *2nd letter of code*   *Number*
A = CNAEA: National Standards for Arts Education   E = Explicitly stated in document   Page number of cited document
C = California Visual/Performing Arts Framework   I = Implied in document
M = MENC: The School Music Program
N = NAEP: Arts Education Assessment Framework

415

McREL

- BP (AE,28;CI,74;ME,23;NE,83)

  Identifies the sounds of a variety of instruments (e.g., orchestral, band, instruments from various cultures) and voices (e.g., male, female, children's voices)

Level III (Grades 6-8)

- BD (AE,44;CI,77;NE,86)

  Identifies specific musical events (e.g., entry of oboe, change of meter, return of refrain) when listening to music

- BD (AE,44;CI,77;MI,32;NE,86)

  Understands how the elements of music are used in various genres and cultures

- BD (AE,44;CI,74-75;MI,32;NE,86)

  Understands the basic principles of meter, rhythm, tonality, intervals, chords, and harmonic progressions

- BD (AE,44;CI,79;MI,32;NE,84,86)

  Knows criteria that affect the quality (e.g., use of elements to create unity, variety, tension/release, balance) and effectiveness (e.g., expressive impact) of musical performances and compositions

Level IV (Grades 9-12)

- BD (AE,61;CI,78;NE,90)

  Understands how the elements of music and expressive devices are used in music from diverse genres and cultures

- BD (AE,61;MI,46;NE,90)

  Understands the technical vocabulary of music (e.g., Italian terms, form, harmony, tempo markings)

- BD (AE,61;MI,45;NE,90)

  Understands compositional devices and techniques that are used to provide unity and variety and tension and release in a musical work (e.g., motives, imitation, retrograde, inversion)

- BD (AE,62;CI,79;NE,88-91)

  Knows specific criteria that affect the quality and effectiveness of musical performances, compositions, arrangements, and improvisations (e.g., considers questions of unity or variety, consistency, appropriate use of resources)

Codes (right side of page): BD = Benchmark, Declarative; BP = Benchmark, Procedural; BC = Benchmark, Contextual

1st letter of each code in parentheses   *2nd letter of code*   *Number*
A = CNAEA: National Standards for Arts Education   E = Explicitly stated in document   Page number of cited document
C = California Visual/Performing Arts Framework   I = Implied in document
M = MENC: The School Music Program
N = NAEP: Arts Education Assessment Framework

416

McREL

(AE,28)

7. Understands the relationship between music and history and culture

Level I (Grades K-2)

BD (AE,29;CE,78;MI,22;NE,84)
- Knows characteristics that make certain music suitable for specific uses

BD (AE,29;MI,22)
- Knows appropriate audience behavior for the context and style of music performed

Level II (Grades 3-5)

BP (AE,29;MI,23;NE,84)
- Identifies (by genre or style) music from various historical periods and cultures

BD (AE,29;MI,24;NE,84)
- Knows how basic elements of music are used in music from various cultures of the world

BD (AE,29;MI,24;NE,84)
- Understands the roles of musicians (e.g., orchestra conductor, folksinger, church organist) in various music settings and cultures

Level III (Grades 6-8)

BD (AE,45;CI,78;MI,32;NE,87)
- Understands distinguishing characteristics (e.g., relating to instrumentation, texture, rhythmic qualities, melodic lines, form) of representative music genres and styles from a variety of cultures

BD (AE,45;MI,46;NE,87)
- Understands characteristics that cause various musical works (e.g., from different genres, styles, historical periods, composers) to be considered exemplary

BD (AE,45;CI,78;NE,87)
- Understands the functions music serves, the roles of musicians (e.g., lead guitarist in a rock band, composer of jingles for commercials, singer in Peking opera), and conditions under which music is typically performed in various cultures of the world

Level IV (Grades 9-12)

BC (AE,63;CI,78,79;MI,46;NE,91)
- Classifies unfamiliar but representative aural examples of music (e.g., by genre, style, historical period, culture)

Codes (right side of page):   BD = Benchmark, Declarative;   BP = Benchmark, Procedural;   BC = Benchmark, Contextual
1st letter of each code in parentheses   *2nd letter of code*   *Number*
A = CNAEA: National Standards for Arts Education   E = Explicitly stated in document   Page number of cited document
C = California Visual/Performing Arts Framework   I = Implied in document
M = MENC: The School Music Program
N = NAEP: Arts Education Assessment Framework

- Knows sources of American music genres (e.g., swing, Broadway musical, blues), the evolution of these genres, and musicians associated with them $^{BD\,(AE,63;MI,46;NE,91)}$

- Knows various roles that musicians perform (e.g., entertainer, teacher, transmitter of cultural tradition) and representative individuals who have functioned in these roles $^{BD\,(AE,63;NE,91)}$

Codes (right side of page):   BD = Benchmark, Declarative; BP = Benchmark, Procedural; BC = Benchmark, Contextual
1st letter of each code in parentheses   *2nd letter of code*   *Number*
A = CNAEA: National Standards for Arts Education   E = Explicitly stated in document   Page number of cited document
C = California Visual/Performing Arts Framework   I = Implied in document
M = MENC: The School Music Program
N = NAEP: Arts Education Assessment Framework

418

McREL

Theatre

(AE,30)

1.   Demonstrates competence in writing scripts

Level II (Grades K-4)

BP (AE,30;NE,92)
- Selects interrelated characters, environments, and situations for simple dramatizations

BP (AE,30;NE,92)
- Improvises dialogue to tell stories

BP (AE,30)
- Writes or records dialogue

BP (AE,30)
- Plans and records improvisations based on personal experience and heritage, imagination, literature, and history

Level III (Grades 5-8)

BP (AE,46;CI,45;NE,94)
- Creates characters, environments (e.g., place, time, atmosphere/mood), and actions that create tension and suspense

BP (AE,46;NE,94)
- Refines and records dialogue and action

BP (AE,46)
- Creates improvisations and scripted scenes based on personal experience and heritage, imagination, literature, and history

Level IV (Grades 9-12)

BP (AE,64;CI,45;NE,95)
- Constructs imaginative scripts that convey story and meaning to an audience

BP (AE,64)
- Improvises, writes, and refines scripts based on personal experience and heritage, imagination, literature, and history

---

Codes (right side of page):   BD = Benchmark, Declarative; BP = Benchmark, Procedural; BC = Benchmark, Contextual
1st letter of each code in parentheses   *2nd letter of code*   *Number*
A = CNAEA: National Standards for Arts Education   E = Explicitly stated in document   Page number of cited document
C = California Visual/Performing Arts Framework   I = Implied in document
N = NAEP: Arts Education Assessment Framework

MREL

(AE,30)

2. Uses acting skills

Level II (Grades K-4)

BD (AE,30;NE,92)
- Knows characters in dramatizations, their relationships, and their environments

BP (AE,30;CI,44,47;NE,92)
- Uses variations of locomotor and nonlocomotor movement and vocal pitch, tempo, and tone for different characters

BP (AE,30;NE,92)
- Assumes roles that exhibit concentration and contribute to the action of dramatizations based on personal experience and heritage, imagination, literature, and history

BP (AE,30)
- Knows how to interact in improvisations

Level III (Grades 5-8)

BD (AE,46;NE,94)
- Understands how descriptions, dialogue, and actions are used to discover, articulate, and justify character motivation

BP (AE,46;CE,46;NE,94)
- Uses basic acting skills (e.g., sensory recall, concentration, breath control, diction, body alignment, control of isolated body parts) to develop characterizations that suggest artistic choices

BP (AE,46;CI,45;NE,94)
- Invents character behaviors based on observation of the interactions, ethical choices, and emotional responses of people

BP (AE,46;CI,45)
- Interacts as an invented character in improvised and scripted scenes

Level IV (Grades 9-12)

BD (AE,64;NE,96)
- Understands the physical, emotional, and social dimensions of characters found in dramatic texts from various genres and media

BD (AE,64;CE,53)
- Knows various classical and contemporary acting techniques and methods

---

Codes (right side of page):   BD = Benchmark, Declarative; BP = Benchmark, Procedural; BC = Benchmark, Contextual
1st letter of each code in parentheses   *2nd letter of code*   *Number*
A = CNAEA: National Standards for Arts Education   E = Explicitly stated in document   Page number of cited document
C = California Visual/Performing Arts Framework   I = Implied in document
N = NAEP: Arts Education Assessment Framework

420

McREL

- Develops, communicates, and sustains characters that communicate with audiences in improvisations and informal or formal productions
  BP (AE,64;NE,96)

(AE,31)

3. Designs and produces informal and formal productions

Level II (Grades K-4)

- Knows how visual elements (e.g., space, color, line, shape, texture) and aural aspects are used to communicate locale and mood
  BD (AE,31;CI,49;NE,92)

- Selects and organizes available materials that suggest scenery, properties, lighting, sound, costumes, and makeup
  BP (AE,31;CI,50;NE,92)

- Visualizes and arranges environments for classroom dramatizations
  BP (AE,31)

Level III (Grades 5-8)

- Understands the functions and interrelated nature of scenery, properties, lighting, sound, costumes, and makeup in creating an environment appropriate for the drama
  BD (AE,47;CI,50;NE,94)

- Understands technical requirements for various improvised and scripted scenes
  BD (AE,47;NE,94)

- Develops focused ideas for the environment using visual elements (e.g., line, texture, color, space), visual principles (e.g., repetition, balance, emphasis, contrast, unity), and aural qualities (e.g., pitch, rhythm, dynamics, tempo, expression) from traditional and nontraditional sources
  BP (AE,47)

- Selects and creates elements of scenery, properties, lighting, and sound to signify environments, and costumes and makeup to suggest character
  BP (AE,47;CI,50-51;NE,94)

Level IV (Grades 9-12)

- Understands the basic physical and chemical properties of the technical aspects of theatre (e.g., light, color, electricity, paint, makeup)
  BD (AE,65;CI,50)

Codes (right side of page):   BD = Benchmark, Declarative; BP = Benchmark, Procedural; BC = Benchmark, Contextual
1st letter of each code in parentheses   *2nd letter of code*   *Number*
A = CNAEA: National Standards for Arts Education   E = Explicitly stated in document   Page number of cited document
C = California Visual/Performing Arts Framework   I = Implied in document
N = NAEP: Arts Education Assessment Framework

- Understands production requirements for a variety of dramatic texts from cultural and historical perspectives _{BD (AE,65;NI,96)}

- Develops designs that use visual and aural elements to convey environments (e.g., place, time, atmosphere/mood) that clearly support the text _{BP (AE,65;CI,51;NE,96)3}

- Creates functional scenery, properties, lighting, sound, costumes, and makeup _{BP (AE,65;NI,96)}

- Conceptualizes and realizes artistic interpretations for informal or formal productions _{BP (AE,65)}

- Designs coherent stage management, promotional, and business plans _{BP (AE,65;CE,49;NE,96)}

4.   Directs scenes and productions _(AE,31)

Level II (Grades K-4)

- Knows various ways of staging classroom dramatizations _{BD (AE,31;CI,48;NE,92)}

- Plans and prepares improvisations _{BP (AE,31;NI,92)}

Level III (Grades 5-8)

- Plans visual and aural elements for improvised and scripted scenes _{BP (AE,47;NI,92)}

- Organizes rehearsals for improvised and scripted scenes _{BP (AE,47)}

Level IV (Grades 9-12)

- Develops multiple interpretations and visual and aural production choices for scripts and production ideas _{BP (AE,65;CI,48)}

- Justifies selections of text, interpretations, and visual and aural artistic choices (e.g., situation, action, direction, design) _{BP (AE,65;CI,48)}

Codes (right side of page):   BD = Benchmark, Declarative; BP = Benchmark, Procedural; BC = Benchmark, Contextual
1st letter of each code in parentheses   *2nd letter of code*   *Number*
A = CNAEA: National Standards for Arts Education   E = Explicitly stated in document   Page number of cited document
C = California Visual/Performing Arts Framework   I = Implied in document
N = NAEP: Arts Education Assessment Framework

422   MREL

BP (AE,65;CI,48;NE,96)

- Communicates directorial choices for improvised or scripted scenes

BP (AE,65)

- Organizes and conducts rehearsals for informal or formal productions

(AE,32)

5. Understands how informal and formal theatre, film, television, and electronic media productions create and communicate meaning

Level II (Grades K-4)

BD (AE,32;NE,93)

- Understands the visual, aural, oral, and kinetic elements of dramatic performances

BD (AE,32;NI,93)

- Understands how the wants and needs of characters are similar to and different from one's own wants and needs

BP (AE,32;NE,93)

- Provides rationales for personal preferences about the whole as well as the parts of dramatic performances

BD (AE,32;NE,93)

- Knows how alternative ideas can be used to enhance character roles, environments, and situations

BD (AE,32;CE,54)

- Knows appropriate terminology used in analyzing dramatizations (e.g., intent, structure, effectiveness, worth)

BP (AE,31)

- Identifies people, events, time, and place in classroom dramatizations

Level III (Grades 5-8)

BD (AE,48;NE,95)

- Understands the effect of publicity, study guides, programs, and physical environments on audience response and appreciation of dramatic performances

BP (AE,48;NE,95)

- Articulates the meanings constructed from one's own and others' dramatic performances

BP (AE,48;NE,95)

- Understands the perceived effectiveness of artistic choices found in dramatic performances

---

Codes (right side of page):   BD = Benchmark, Declarative; BP = Benchmark, Procedural; BC = Benchmark, Contextual
1st letter of each code in parentheses   *2nd letter of code*   *Number*
A = CNAEA: National Standards for Arts Education   E = Explicitly stated in document   Page number of cited document
C = California Visual/Performing Arts Framework   I = Implied in document
N = NAEP: Arts Education Assessment Framework

McREL

- Understands the perceived effectiveness of contributions to the collaborative process of developing improvised and scripted scenes (e.g., as playwrights, actors, designers, directors) ^{BD (AE,48;NE,95)}

- Applies research from print and nonprint sources to script writing, acting, design, and directing choices ^{BP (AE,47)}

Level IV (Grades 9-12)

- Knows how social meanings (aural, oral, and visual symbols with personal and/or social significance) communicated in informal productions, formal productions, and personal performances of different cultures and historical periods can relate to current personal, national, and international issues ^{BD (AE,67)}

- Articulates and justifies personal aesthetic criteria for critiquing dramatic texts and events that compare perceived artistic intent with the final aesthetic achievement ^{BP (AE,67;NE,97)}

- Understands how the context in which a dramatic performance is set can enhance or hinder its effectiveness ^{BD (AE,67;CI,55;NE,97)}

- Knows how varying collaborative efforts and artistic choices can affect the performance of informal and formal productions ^{BD (AE,67;NE,97)}

- Identifies and researches cultural, historical, and symbolic clues in dramatic texts ^{BP (AE,66;CE,52)}

- Understands the validity and practicality of cultural, historical, and symbolic information used in making artistic choices for informal and formal productions ^{BD (AE,66)}

^(AE,32)

6. **Understands the context in which theatre, film, television, and electronic media are performed today as well as in the past**

Level II (Grades K-4)

- Identifies and compares similar characters and situations in stories/dramas from and about various cultures ^{BC (AE,32;NE,93)}

Codes (right side of page):   BD = Benchmark, Declarative; BP = Benchmark, Procedural; BC = Benchmark, Contextual
1st letter of each code in parentheses   *2nd letter of code*   *Number*
A = CNAEA: National Standards for Arts Education   E = Explicitly stated in document   Page number of cited document
C = California Visual/Performing Arts Framework   I = Implied in document
N = NAEP: Arts Education Assessment Framework

424

McREL

BD (AE,32)

- Understands the various settings and reasons for creating dramas and attending theatre, film, television, and electronic media productions

BD (AE,32;NE,93)

- Knows ways in which theatre reflects life

Level III (Grades 5-8)

BC (AE,48;CI,53;NE,95)

- Understands the similarities and differences among archetypal characters (e.g., the trickster, the villain, the warrior, the superhero) and situations in dramas from and about various cultures and historical periods

BD (AE,48;NE,95)

- Understands the knowledge, skills, and discipline needed to pursue careers and avocational opportunities in theatre, film, television, and electronic media

BD (AE,48;CE,53;NE,95)

- Understands the emotional and social impact of dramatic performances in one's own life, in the community, and in other cultures

BD (AE,48)

- Knows ways in which theatre reflects a culture

BD (AE,48;NE,95)

- Knows how culture affects the content and production values of dramatic performances

BD (AE,48;NE,95)

- Understands how social concepts such as cooperation, communication, collaboration, consensus, self-esteem, risk taking, sympathy, and empathy apply in theatre

Level IV (Grades 9-12)

BD (AE,67;CI,53;NE,97)

- Understands how similar themes are treated in drama from various cultures and historical periods

BD (AE,67;NE,97)

- Understands ways in which theatre can reveal universal concepts

BD (AE,67;NE,97)

- Understands similarities and differences among the lives, works, and influence of representative theatre artists in various cultures and historical periods

BD (AE,67;NE,97)

- Knows cultural and historical influences on American theatre and musical theatre

BD (AE,67;NE,97)

- Understands ways in which personal and cultural experiences can affect an artist's dramatic work

---

Codes (right side of page):   BD = Benchmark, Declarative;   BP = Benchmark, Procedural;   BC = Benchmark, Contextual
1st letter of each code in parentheses   *2nd letter of code*   *Number*
A = CNAEA: National Standards for Arts Education   E = Explicitly stated in document   Page number of cited document
C = California Visual/Performing Arts Framework   I = Implied in document
N = NAEP: Arts Education Assessment Framework

McREL

Visual Arts

1. **Understands and applies media, techniques, and processes related to the visual arts** (AE,33)

Level II (Grades K-4)

- Knows the differences between art materials (e.g., paint, clay, wood, videotape), techniques (e.g., overlapping, shading, varying size or color), and processes (e.g., addition and subtraction in sculpture, casting and constructing in making jewelry) BD (AE,33;CI,98-99;NE,98)

- Knows how different materials, techniques, and processes cause different responses from the viewer BD (AE,33;NE,99)

- Knows how different media (e.g., oil, watercolor, stone, metal), techniques, and processes are used to communicate ideas, experiences, and stories BD (AE,34;CE,98-99;NE,98,99)

- Uses art materials and tools in a safe and responsible manner BP (AE,34;NE,98)

Level III (Grades 5-8)

- Understands what makes different art media, techniques, and processes effective (or ineffective) in communicating various ideas BD (AE,50;NE,101,102)

- Knows how the qualities and characteristics of art media, techniques, and processes can be used to enhance communication of experiences and ideas BD (AE,50)

Level IV (Grades 9-12)

- Applies media, techniques, and processes with sufficient skill, confidence, and sensitivity that one's intentions are carried out in artworks BP (AE,69;CE,98-99;NE,105)

- Understands how the communication of ideas relates to the media, techniques, and processes used BD (AE,69;CI,105;NE,104)

2. **Knows how to use the structures (e.g., sensory qualities, organizational principles, expressive features) and functions of art** (AE,34)

Level II (Grades K-4)

- Knows the differences among the visual characteristics (e.g., color, texture) and purposes of art (e.g., to convey ideas) BD (AE,34;NE,98)

- Understands how different expressive features and compositional and organizational BD (AE,34;CI,96;NE,99)

Codes (right side of page): BD = Benchmark, Declarative; BP = Benchmark, Procedural; BC = Benchmark, Contextual
1st letter of each code in parentheses *2nd letter of code* *Number*
A = CNAEA: National Standards for Arts Education E = Explicitly stated in document Page number of cited document
C = California Visual/Performing Arts Framework I = Implied in document
N = NAEP: Arts Education Assessment Framework

MREL

principles (e.g., repetition, balance, emphasis, contrast, unity) cause different responses (e.g., evoking joy, sadness, anger)

BP (AE,34)

- Uses the visual structures and functions of art to communicate ideas

Level III (Grades 5-8)

BD (AE,50;CI,95-96;NE,101)

- Knows the effects of various visual structures (e.g., design elements such as line, color, shape; principles such as repetition, rhythm, balance) and functions of art

BD (AE,50;NE,102)

- Understands what makes various organizational structures effective or ineffective in the communication of ideas

BD (AE,50;CI,96)

- Knows how the qualities of the structures and functions of art are used to improve communication of ideas

Level IV (Grades 9-12)

BD (AE,70;NE,104)

- Understands how the characteristics and structures of art are used to accomplish commercial, personal, communal, or other artistic intentions

BD (AE,70)

- Understands the effectiveness of various artworks in terms of organizational structures and functions

BD (AE,70;NE,104)

- Knows how organizational principles and functions can be used to solve specific visual arts problems

(AE,34)

3. Knows a range of subject matter, symbols, and potential ideas in the visual arts

Level II (Grades K-4)

BP (AE,34;CI,98;NE,99)

- Selects prospective ideas (e.g., formulated thoughts, opinions, concepts) for works of art

BD (AE,34)

- Knows how subject matter, symbols, and ideas are used to communicate meaning

Level III (Grades 5-8)

BD (AE,50;NE,102)

- Knows how visual, spatial, and temporal concepts integrate with content to communicate intended meaning in one's artworks

BD (AE,50;CI,105;NE,102)

- Knows different subjects, themes, and symbols (through context, value, and aesthetics) that convey intended meaning in artworks

Codes (right side of page):   BD = Benchmark, Declarative; BP = Benchmark, Procedural; BC = Benchmark, Contextual
1st letter of each code in parentheses   *2nd letter of code*   *Number*
A = CNAEA: National Standards for Arts Education   E = Explicitly stated in document   Page number of cited document
C = California Visual/Performing Arts Framework   I = Implied in document
N = NAEP: Arts Education Assessment Framework

427

MCREL

Level IV (Grades 9-12)

BD (AE,70;CI,103)

- Understands how visual, spatial, temporal, and functional values of artworks are tempered by culture and history

BP (AE,70)

- Applies various subjects, symbols, and ideas in one's artworks

(AE,34)

4. Understands the visual arts in relation to history and cultures

Level II (Grades K-4)

BD (AE,34;NE,98)

- Knows that the visual arts have a history and a specific relationship to various cultures

BC (AE,34;CE,103,103;NE,99)

- Identifies specific works of art as belonging to particular cultures, times, and places

BD (AE,34;NE,98)

- Knows how history, culture, and the visual arts can influence each other

Level III (Grades 5-8)

BD (AE,50;CI,106;NE,102,103)

- Understands the similarities and differences among the characteristics of artworks from various eras and cultures (e.g., materials; visual, spatial, and temporal structures)

BD (AE,50;NE,102,103)

- Understands the historical and cultural contexts of a variety of art objects

BD (AE,50;CI,102;NE,101,103)

- Understands how factors of time and place (e.g., climate, resources, ideas, technology) influence the visual, spatial, or temporal characteristics that give meaning or function to a work of art

Level IV (Grades 9-12)

BD (AE,71;NE,106)

- Knows a variety of historical and cultural contexts regarding the characteristics and purposes of works of art

BD (AE,71;CI,101;NE,106)

- Knows the function and meaning of specific art objects within varied cultures, times, and places

BD (AE,71;NE,106)

- Understands relationships among works of art in terms of history, aesthetics, and culture

---

Codes (right side of page):   BD = Benchmark, Declarative; BP = Benchmark, Procedural; BC = Benchmark, Contextual
1st letter of each code in parentheses   *2nd letter of code*   *Number*
A = CNAEA: National Standards for Arts Education   E = Explicitly stated in document   Page number of cited document
C = California Visual/Performing Arts Framework   I = Implied in document
N = NAEP: Arts Education Assessment Framework

(AE,34)

5. Understands the characteristics and merits of one's own artwork and the artwork of others

Level II (Grades K-4)

BD (AE,34;CI,102;NE,99,100)
- Knows various purposes for creating works of visual art

BD (AE,34;NE,99,100)
- Knows how people's experiences (e.g., cultural background, human needs) can influence the development of specific artworks

BD (AE,34)
- Understands that specific artworks can elicit different responses

Level III (Grades 5-8)

BC (AE,51;CI,102;NE,102)
- Distinguishes among multiple purposes for creating works of art

BD (AE,51;CI,101;NE,103)
- Understands the possible contemporary and historic meanings in specific artworks

BD (AE,51;NE,103)
- Understands how one's own artworks, as well as artworks from various eras and cultures, may elicit a variety of responses

Level IV (Grades 9-12)

BP (AE,71;CI,102;NE,105,107)
- Identifies the intentions of those creating artworks

BD (AE,71;NE,105,107)
- Understands some of the implications of intention and purpose in particular works of art

BD (AE,71;CI,103;NE,105)
- Knows how specific works are created and how they relate to historical and cultural contexts

BD (AE,71;NE,106,107)
- Understands how various interpretations can be used to understand and evaluate works of visual art

---

Codes (right side of page):   BD = Benchmark, Declarative; BP = Benchmark, Procedural; BC = Benchmark, Contextual
1st letter of each code in parentheses   *2nd letter of code*   *Number*
A = CNAEA: National Standards for Arts Education   E = Explicitly stated in document   Page number of cited document
C = California Visual/Performing Arts Framework   I = Implied in document
N = NAEP: Arts Education Assessment Framework

429   M∂REL

13. Civics

The following process was used to identify standards and benchmarks in civics:

Identification of National Reports

Two reports and a set of teacher's guides were selected for identifying standards in civics: *National Standards for Civics and Government* (1994) from the Center for Civic Education, *Civitas: A Framework for Civic Education* (Quigley & Bahmmeller, 1991), and a series of civics units authored and published by Law in a Free Society.

Selection of the Reference Document

The Center for Civic Education's *National Standards for Civics and Government* (1994) was selected as the reference report. The report was developed over two years, using a process that enlisted the participation of more than a thousand teachers and other educators as well as scholars, parents, educators, and representatives of public and private organizations.

Identification of Standards and Benchmarks

For the most part, the *Standards* document fits well with our model for the identification of standards. Essential ideas in civics are organized under some 70-plus content standards. Each content standard has associated with it a set of key concepts that students should know in order to meet the standard.

In three areas, however, the *Standards* document is not directly compatible with our approach. First, the content standards are often stated and elaborated upon through performance descriptions, that is, tasks that describe a specific demonstration of achievement. These tasks are prefaced with the statement, "To achieve this standard, students should be able to...." What follows are activities that may require the student to identify, describe, or explain an idea, or to take, defend, or evaluate a particular position. The activities also provide important information about the content standard. Since our approach seeks to provide content knowledge that is either declarative, procedural, or contextual (see Section 3), we translated such tasks to benchmark statements of knowledge and skills specifically related to content in civics.

The second area in which the approach used in *National Standards for Civics and Government* differs from our model has to do with the articulation of standards across K–12. While standards appear at levels K–4, 6–8, and 9–12, and many similar ideas are organized beneath each level, there is no articulation across K–12 by standard level. While we believe content information from the reference document should be minimally revised in the process of identifying benchmarks, we consider the standards under which they are found to be more arbitrary in composition (see Section 3). Thus, in order to accomplish the articulation of standards across grade levels, we revised and combined a number of standards and reorganized the benchmarks beneath them.

Finally, our model and the reference document differ concerning the range and number of benchmark levels. The *Standards* document specifies three benchmark levels: K–4, 5–8, and 9–12. Our model recommends four, corresponding to primary, upper elementary, middle, and high school.

431

In this case, then, completion of our benchmark levels depended upon an analysis of supplementary materials that could provide us with further benchmark information, especially at the primary grades (discussed below).

Integration of Information from Other Documents

The *Standards* document is unique in providing civics standards information from a national organization; in other words, supplementary documents were not available for the integration of other perspectives or for the verification of our content analysis. Supplementary material was instead used to provide the user with reference material keyed to the benchmark and to provide us a means for identifying knowledge and skills at the primary level. The Center for Civic Education's source book, *Civitas*, was cited at the benchmark level wherever possible. This was done to assist teachers and curriculum developers with a pointer to supporting material and information on a given topic. As noted above, the reference document does not isolate the knowledge and skills that might be especially suitable for the early (K–2) grades. In order to remedy this, we consulted a series of teacher guides available from Law and a Free Society. These books, which focus on the concepts of authority, privacy, justice, and responsibility, allowed us to distinguish information from the standards K–4 level that would be suitable for the primary grades.

Summary of Standards for Civics

What is Government and What Should it Do?

1. Understands ideas about civic life, politics, and government
2. Understands the essential characteristics of limited and unlimited governments
3. Understands the sources, purposes, and functions of law and the importance of the rule of law for the protection of individual rights and the common good
4. Understands the concept of a constitution, the various purposes that constitutions serve, and the conditions that contribute to the establishment and maintenance of constitutional government
5. Understands the major characteristics of systems of shared powers and of parliamentary systems
6. Understands the advantages and disadvantages of federal, confederal, and unitary systems of government
7. Understands alternative forms of representation and how they serve the purposes of constitutional government

What are the Basic Values and Principals of American Democracy?

8. Understands the central ideas of American constitutional government and how this form of government has shaped the character of American society
9. Understands the importance of Americans sharing and supporting certain values, beliefs, and principles of American constitutional democracy
10. Understands the roles of voluntarism and organized groups in American social and political life
11. Understands the role of diversity in American life and the importance of shared values, political beliefs, and civic beliefs in an increasingly diverse American society
12. Understands the relationships among liberalism, republicanism, and American constitutional democracy
13. Understands the character of American political and social conflict and factors that tend to prevent or lower its intensity
14. Understands issues concerning the disparities between ideals and reality in American political and social life

How Does the Government Established by the Constitution Embody the Purposes, Values, and Principles of American Democracy?

15. Understands how the United States Constitution grants and distributes power and responsibilities to national and state government and how it seeks to prevent the abuse of power

16. Understands the major responsibilities of the national government for domestic and foreign policy, and understands how government is financed through taxation

17. Understands issues concerning the relationship between state and local governments and the national government and issues pertaining to representation at all three levels of government

18. Understands the role and importance of law in the American constitutional system and issues regarding the judicial protection of individual rights

19. Understands what is meant by "the public agenda," how it is set, and how it is influenced by public opinion and the media

20. Understands the roles of political parties, campaigns, elections, and associations and groups in American politics

21. Understands the formation and implementation of public policy

What is the Relationship of the United States to Other Nations and to World Affairs?

22. Understands how the world is organized politically into nation-states, how nation-states interact with one another, and issues surrounding U.S. foreign policy

23. Understands the impact of significant political and nonpolitical developments on the United States and other nations

What are the Roles of the Citizen in American Democracy?

24. Understands the meaning of citizenship in the United States, and knows the requirements for citizenship and naturalization

25. Understands issues regarding personal, political, and economic rights

26. Understands issues regarding the proper scope and limits of rights and the relationships among personal, political, and economic rights

27. Understands how certain character traits enhance citizens' ability to fulfill personal and civic responsibilities

28. Understands how participation in civic and political life can help citizens attain individual and public goals

29. Understands the importance of political leadership, public service, and a knowledgeable citizenry in American constitutional democracy

(CE,89)

1. Understands ideas about civic life, politics, and government

Level I (Grades K-2)

BD (A1E,10-11)
- Knows examples of situations in which individuals are acting on their own (e.g., two friends decide to do something) and situations in which individuals' actions are directed by others (e.g., parents tell their children to do something)

BD (A1E,14-15;QI,95)
- Knows examples of authority (e.g., a teacher tells a group of students to do something) and power without authority (e.g., an older, larger student tells a group of younger students to do something)

BD (A1E,22)
- Knows some of the problems that might result from lack of effective authority (e.g., inability to settle disputes or accomplish necessary tasks)

Level II (Grades 3-4)

BD (CE,15;QI,331)
- Knows various people and groups who make, apply, and enforce rules and laws for others (e.g., adult family members, teachers, city councils, governors, tribal governments, national governments) and who manage disputes about rules and laws (e.g., courts at all levels)

BD (CE,16;QE,95)
- Knows the difference between power (e.g., the capacity to direct or control something or someone) and authority (e.g., power that people have the right to use because of custom, law, or the consent of the governed)

BD (CE,16;QI,102)
- Knows ways in which authority is used (e.g., parents have authority to direct and control their children, governors of states have the authority to carry out and enforce laws) and ways in which power can be used without authority (e.g., a bully forcing smaller children to give up their lunch money, a robber holding up a bank)

BD (CE,17)
- Knows possible consequences of the absence of government and rules and laws (e.g., the strong may take advantage of the weak, people may become disorderly or violent, people may feel insecure or be unable to plan for the future)

BD (CE,17;QE,14-15)
- Knows the basic purposes of government in the United States (e.g., to protect the rights of individuals, to promote the common good)

BD (CE,18)
- Knows the major things governments do in one's school, community, state, and nation (e.g.,

---

Codes (right side of page): BD = Benchmark, Declarative; BP = Benchmark, Procedural; BC = Benchmark, Contextual
1st letter of each code in parentheses *2nd letter of code* *Number*
C = CCE: National Standards for Civics E = Explicitly stated in document Page number of cited document
A1 = LFS: Authority, I (elementary) I = Implied in document *or, for duplicates,*
J1 = LFS: Justice, I (elementary) Standard number & level of duplicate
P1, P2 = LFS: Privacy, I & II (elementary)
Q = Quigley: Civitas
R1 = LFS: Responsibility, I (elementary) 435 MREL

make, carry out, and enforce laws; manage conflicts; provide national security)

- Knows how government makes it possible for people to work together to accomplish goals _{BD (CE,18)} they could not achieve individually

Level III (Grades 5-8)

- Distinguishes between private life and civic life (e.g., private life concerns the personal life _{BC (CE,45;QE,15-17)} of the individual such as being with family and friends or practicing one's religious beliefs, civic life concerns taking part in government such as helping to find solutions to problems or helping to make rules and laws)

- Understands how politics enables people with differing ideas to reach binding agreements _{BD (CE,45)} (e.g., presenting information and evidence, stating arguments, negotiating, compromising, voting)

- Knows institutions that have the authority to direct or control the behavior of members of _{BD (CE,45)} a society (e.g., a school board, state legislature, courts, Congress)

- Understands major ideas about why government is necessary (e.g., people's lives, liberty, _{BD (CE,46)} and property would be insecure without government; individuals by themselves cannot do many of the things they can do collectively such as create a highway system, provide armed forces for the security of the nation, or make and enforce laws)

- Understands competing ideas about the purposes government should serve (e.g., whether _{BD (CE,46)} government should protect individual rights, promote the common good, provide economic security, mold the character of citizens, promote a particular religion)

Level IV (Grades 9-12)

- Understands how politics enables a group of people with varying opinions and/or interests _{BD (CE,90)} to reach collective decisions, influence decisions, and accomplish goals that they could not reach as individuals (e.g., managing the distribution of resources, allocating benefits and burdens, managing conflicts)

- Knows formal institutions that have the authority to make and implement binding decisions _{BD (CE,90)} (e.g., tribal councils, courts, monarchies, democratic legislatures)

Codes (right side of page):   BD = Benchmark, Declarative; BP = Benchmark, Procedural; BC = Benchmark, Contextual
1st letter of each code in parentheses   *2nd letter of code*   *Number*
C = CCE: National Standards for Civics   E = Explicitly stated in document   Page number of cited document
A1 = LFS: Authority, I (elementary)   I = Implied in document   *or, for duplicates,*
J1 = LFS: Justice, I (elementary)   Standard number & level of duplicate
P1, P2 = LFS: Privacy, I & II (elementary)
Q = Quigley: Civitas
R1 = LFS: Responsibility, I (elementary)   436   M REL

- Understands the nature of political authority (e.g., characteristics such as legitimacy, stability, limitations) ^{BD (CE,90;QE,95)}

- Understands the sources of political theory (e.g., consent of the governed, birth, knowledge) and its functions (e.g., create and enforce laws) ^{BD (CE,90;QE,95)}

- Understands why politics is found wherever people gather as a group (e.g., it enables groups to reach collective, binding decisions that can be enforced) ^{BD (CE,90)}

- Understands major arguments for the necessity of politics and government (e.g., people cannot fulfill their potential without politics and government, people would be insecure or endangered without government, people working collectively can accomplish goals and solve problems they could not achieve alone) ^{BD (CE,90)}

- Understands some of the major competing ideas about the purposes of politics and government (e.g., achieving a religious vision, glorifying the state, enhancing economic prosperity, providing for a nation's security), and knows examples of past and present governments that serve these purposes ^{BD (CE,90-91)}

- Understands how the purposes served by a government affect relationships between the individual and government and between government and society as a whole (e.g., the purpose of promoting a religious vision of what society should be like may require a government to restrict individual thought and actions, and place strict controls on the whole of the society) ^{BD (CE,91)}

2. Understands the essential characteristics of limited and unlimited governments ^(CE,47)

Level I (Grades K-2)

- Knows that people in positions of authority have limits on their authority (e.g., a crossing guard cannot act as an umpire at a baseball game) ^{BD (A1,48-50;QE,332)}

Level II (Grades 3-4)

- Knows the basic conditions necessary to support a limited government (e.g., everyone, including all the people in positions of authority, must obey the laws) ^{BD (CE,20;QI,330-332)}

Codes (right side of page):	BD = Benchmark, Declarative; BP = Benchmark, Procedural; BC = Benchmark, Contextual

1st letter of each code in parentheses   *2nd letter of code*   *Number*

C = CCE: National Standards for Civics   E = Explicitly stated in document   Page number of cited document

A1 = LFS: Authority, I (elementary)   I = Implied in document   *or, for duplicates,*

J1 = LFS: Justice, I (elementary)   Standard number & level of duplicate

P1, P2 = LFS: Privacy, I & II (elementary)

Q = Quigley: Civitas

R1 = LFS: Responsibility, I (elementary)   437   MREL

- Knows how laws can limit the power of people in government (e.g., laws that prohibit a teacher from releasing personal information about students to people other than the students' parents or guardians; laws that prohibit governments from discriminating against people because of their religious or political beliefs) *BD (CE,20;QI,330-332)*

- Knows the general characteristics of unlimited government (e.g., a dictatorship in which there are no effective controls over the powers of its rulers; the rulers cannot be easily removed from office by peaceful, legal means) *BD (CE,20;QE,170-171)*

- Understands how limited government helps to protect personal rights (e.g., to choose friends, to practice the religion of one's choice), political rights (e.g., to express opinions, to vote), and economic rights (e.g., to own property, to choose the kind of work one pleases) *BD (CE,21;QE,170)*

Level III (Grades 5-8)

- Knows some of the restraints placed on a limited government's power (e.g., the legal limits placed on the political power of constitutional government) *BD (CE,47;QE,169)*

- Understands the basic structure of authoritarian systems and totalitarian systems, and how these systems are considered unlimited governments *BD (CE,47;QE,170-171)*

Level IV (Grades 9-12)

- Understands what "civil society" is and how it provides opportunities for individuals to associate for social, cultural, religious, economic, and political purposes (e.g., family, friendships, membership in organizations, participation in unions and business enterprises) *BD (CE,93)*

- Understands how civil society allows for individuals or groups to influence government in ways other than voting and elections *BD (CE,93)*

- Understands how the individual, social, and economic relationships that make up civil society have been used to maintain limited government *BD (CE,93)*

- Understands how relationships between government and civil society in constitutional democracies differ from those in authoritarian and totalitarian regimes *BD (CE,93;QI,169-171)*

- Knows essential political freedoms (e.g., freedom of religion, speech) and economic freedoms (e.g., freedom to enter into contracts, to choose one's own employment), and *BD (CE,93)*

Codes (right side of page):
1st letter of each code in parentheses
C = CCE: National Standards for Civics
A1 = LFS: Authority, I (elementary)
J1 = LFS: Justice, I (elementary)
P1, P2 = LFS: Privacy, I & II (elementary)
Q = Quigley: Civitas
R1 = LFS: Responsibility, I (elementary)

BD = Benchmark, Declarative; BP = Benchmark, Procedural; BC = Benchmark, Contextual
2nd letter of code
E = Explicitly stated in document
I = Implied in document

Number
Page number of cited document
or, for duplicates,
Standard number & level of duplicate

438

MᴄREL

understands competing ideas about the relationships between the two (e.g., that political freedom is more important than economic freedom, that political and economic freedom are inseparable)

BD (CE,94)

- Understands how political and economic freedoms serve to limit governmental power

(CE,48,92)

3. Understands the sources, purposes, and functions of law, and the importance of the rule of law for the protection of individual rights and the common good

Level I (Grades K-2)

BD (J1E,1;QE,374-375)

- Knows that promoting justice is one of the fundamental purposes of law in American society

BD (J1E,7;QE,374-375)

- Knows that justice means essentially the same thing as fairness

BD (J1E,5,13-16;QE,374-375)

- Knows that distributive justice refers to problems of fairness arising over "who gets what" based on the criteria of need, ability, and desert; and knows examples of situations that involve distributive justice (e.g., how much food should different members of a family receive at dinner time)

BD (J1E,37,41-43;QE,374-375)

- Knows that corrective justice deals with problems arising over how to make things right when a wrong or injury has occurred, and knows examples of situations involving corrective justice (e.g., how to deal justly with a child who has stolen something from a classmate)

BD (J1E,55,63;QE,374-375)

- Knows that procedural justice refers to problems arising over fair ways to gather information and make just decisions, and knows examples of situations involving procedural justice (e.g., how should a class president go about deciding which games the class will play)

BD (A1E,33-34)

- Knows that a good rule or law solves a specific problem, is fair, and "does not go too far"

Level II (Grades 3-4)

BD (CE,18;QE,331-332)

- Knows common ways in which rules and laws can be used (e.g., to describe how people should behave; to provide order, predictability, and security; to protect rights; to provide benefits; to assign burdens or responsibilities; to limit the power of people in authority)

BD (CE,18)

- Knows the characteristics of an effective rule or law (e.g., well designed to achieve its

Codes (right side of page):	BD = Benchmark, Declarative; BP = Benchmark, Procedural; BC = Benchmark, Contextual	
1st letter of each code in parentheses	*2nd letter of code*	*Number*
C = CCE: National Standards for Civics	E = Explicitly stated in document	Page number of cited document
A1 = LFS: Authority, I (elementary)	I = Implied in document	*or, for duplicates,*
J1 = LFS: Justice, I (elementary)		Standard number & level of duplicate
P1, P2 = LFS: Privacy, I & II (elementary)		
Q = Quigley: Civitas		
R1 = LFS: Responsibility, I (elementary)	439	M<REL

purposes, understandable, possible to follow, fair, designed to protect individual rights and promote the common good)

Level III (Grades 5-8)

- Understands the difference between the "rule of law" and the "rule of men" (e.g., government decisions and actions made according to established laws vs. arbitrary action or decree)
  BD (CE,48;QI,15)

- Understands how and why the rule of law can be used to restrict the actions of private citizens and government officials
  BD (CE,48;QI,15)

- Understands the possible consequences of the absence of a rule of law (e.g., anarchy, arbitrary and capricious rule, absence of predictability, disregard for established and fair procedures)
  BD (CE,48)

Level IV (Grades 9-12)

- Knows alternative ideas about the sources of law (e.g., custom, Supreme Being, sovereigns, legislatures) and different varieties of law (e.g., divine law, natural law, common law, statute law, international law)
  BD (CE,92;QE,335-339)

- Knows alternative ideas about the purposes and functions of law (e.g., regulating relationships among people and between people and their government; providing order, predictability, security, and established procedures for the management of conflict; regulating social and economic relationships in civil society)
  BD (CE,92;QE,330-331)

(CE,95)

4.   Understands the concept of a constitution, the various purposes that constitutions serve, and the conditions that contribute to the establishment and maintenance of constitutional government

Level I (Grades K-2)

BD (CE,49)

- Not appropriate for this level

Codes (right side of page):
1st letter of each code in parentheses
C = CCE: National Standards for Civics
A1 = LFS: Authority, I (elementary)
J1 = LFS: Justice, I (elementary)
P1, P2 = LFS: Privacy, I & II (elementary)
Q = Quigley: Civitas
R1 = LFS: Responsibility, I (elementary)

BD = Benchmark, Declarative; BP = Benchmark, Procedural; BC = Benchmark, Contextual
2nd letter of code
E = Explicitly stated in document
I = Implied in document

Number
Page number of cited document
or, for duplicates,
Standard number & level of duplicate

440

MREL

CIVICS

Level II (Grades 3-4)

BD (CE,49)

- Not appropriate for this level

Level III (Grades 5-8)

BD (CE,49;QI,169)
- Knows various uses of the term "constitution" (e.g., as a description of a form of government; as a document; as a higher law limiting the powers of government)

BD (CE,49;QE,169)
- Understands how a government with a constitution but without effective ways to enforce it may still have unlimited power (e.g., former Soviet Union, Nazi Germany, Iraq under Saddam Hussein)

BD (CE,49;QE,170)
- Knows past and present examples of countries with constitutions that actually did limit the power of government (e.g., United States, United Kingdom, Germany, Japan, Botswana, Chile)

BD (CE,49;QE,169)
- Knows some basic uses of constitutions (e.g., to set forth the purposes of government, to describe the way a government is organized and how power is allocated, to define the relationship between a people and their government)

BD (CE,49)
- Knows how constitutions have been used to promote the interests of a particular group, class, religion, or political party (e.g., the People's Republic of China, Kenya, Mexico)

BD (CE,49;QE,169)
- Knows how constitutions have been used to protect individual rights and promote the common good (e.g., First Amendment, Nineteenth Amendment in the United States Constitution)

BD (CE,50)
- Knows the type of citizenry needed to establish and maintain constitutional government (e.g., citizens should be educated and enjoy a reasonable standard of living, understand and support the constitution and its values and principles, willingly assume the responsibilities of citizenship, insist that government officials respect limitations the constitution places on their authority)

BD (CE,50)
- Knows the type of public servants needed to help establish and maintain constitutional government (e.g., persons serving in government should understand and support the constitution and its values and principles, respect limitations the constitution places on their authority)

Codes (right side of page): BD = Benchmark, Declarative; BP = Benchmark, Procedural; BC = Benchmark, Contextual
1st letter of each code in parentheses / *2nd letter of code* / *Number*
C = CCE: National Standards for Civics / E = Explicitly stated in document / Page number of cited document
A1 = LFS: Authority, I (elementary) / I = Implied in document / *or, for duplicates,*
J1 = LFS: Justice, I (elementary) / Standard number & level of duplicate
P1, P2 = LFS: Privacy, I & II (elementary)
Q = Quigley: Civitas
R1 = LFS: Responsibility, I (elementary)
MREL

Level IV (Grades 9-12)

- Distinguishes between governments with a constitution and constitutional (limited) government
  BD (CE,94;QI,169)

- Understands how constitutions set forth the structure of government, give the government power, and establish the relationship between the people and their government
  BD (CE,95;QE,169)

- Understands how constitutions may limit government's power in order to protect individual rights and promote the common good
  BD (CE,95;QE,169)

- Understands how constitutions, in the past as well as in the present, have been disregarded or used to promote the interests of a particular group, class, faction, or a government (e.g., slavery, exclusion of women from the body politic, prohibition of competing political parties)
  BD (CE,95)

- Understands how constitutions can be vehicles for change and for resolving social issues (e.g., use of the Fourteenth Amendment to the United States Constitution in the civil rights movement of the 1950s and 1960s; establishment of the Japanese Constitution after World War II, which provided women the right to vote)
  BD (CE,95)

- Understands how constitutions may be used to preserve core values and principles of a political system or society (e.g., prohibition of religious tests for public office, protection of private property by the United States Constitution)
  BD (CE,95;QI,169)

- Knows the social, economic, and political conditions that foster constitutional government
  BD (CE,95;QI,130-131)

- Understands reasons why some nations have been successful in establishing constitutional government (e.g., post-World War II Germany, Japan) whereas others have not (e.g., Nigeria, Kenya, Argentina under Peron)
  BD (CE,95)

- Knows responsibilities individual citizens and people serving in government should assume to insure the preservation and improvement of constitutional government
  BD (CE,95;QI,13)

Codes (right side of page):	BD = Benchmark, Declarative; BP = Benchmark, Procedural; BC = Benchmark, Contextual	
1st letter of each code in parentheses	*2nd letter of code*	*Number*
C = CCE: National Standards for Civics	E = Explicitly stated in document	Page number of cited document
A1 = LFS: Authority, I (elementary)	I = Implied in document	*or, for duplicates,*
J1 = LFS: Justice, I (elementary)		Standard number & level of duplicate
P1, P2 = LFS: Privacy, I & II (elementary)		
Q = Quigley: Civitas		
R1 = LFS: Responsibility, I (elementary)	442	MREL

(CE,97)

5. Understands the major characteristics of systems of shared powers and of parliamentary systems

Level I (Grades K-2)

BD (CE,51)

- Not appropriate for this level

Level II (Grades 3-4)

BD (CE,51)

- Not appropriate for this level

Level III (Grades 5-8)

BD (CE,51)

- Understands the primary responsibilities of each branch of government in a system of shared powers (e.g., legislative, executive, judicial) and ways in which each branch shares the powers and functions of the other branches

BD (CE,51;QI,170)

- Understands characteristics of systems of shared powers (e.g., in the United States the president and members of the president's Cabinet cannot be members of Congress)

BD (CE,51;QI,170)

- Understands characteristics of parliamentary systems (e.g., in the United Kingdom a legislature called Parliament assumes authority, the political party or parties that can form a majority in Parliament select the prime minister, and the prime minister selects cabinet members; the prime minister and members of the cabinet must all be members of Parliament)

BD (CE,51;QI,170)

- Understands that in parliamentary systems the prime minster and cabinet direct the administration of the government, but the prime minister and cabinet may be replaced by Parliament if a majority votes "no confidence" in the government

Level IV (Grades 9-12)

BD (CE,97;QE,15)

- Understands the major characteristics of systems of shared powers (e.g., in the United States and Brazil the executive, legislative, and judicial branches each have primary responsibility for certain functions and share some of the powers and functions of the other branches)

BD (CE,97;QI,170)

- Understands the major characteristics of parliamentary systems (e.g., in the United Kingdom and Israel authority is held by Parliament and the party or parties that form the majority

---

Codes (right side of page):	BD = Benchmark, Declarative; BP = Benchmark, Procedural; BC = Benchmark, Contextual	
1st letter of each code in parentheses	*2nd letter of code*	*Number*
C = CCE: National Standards for Civics	E = Explicitly stated in document	Page number of cited document
A1 = LFS: Authority, I (elementary)	I = Implied in document	*or, for duplicates,*
J1 = LFS: Justice, I (elementary)		Standard number & level of duplicate
P1, P2 = LFS: Privacy, I & II (elementary)		
Q = Quigley: Civitas		
R1 = LFS: Responsibility, I (elementary)	443	

MREL

select the prime minister)

- Understands the relative advantages and disadvantages of the various ways power is distributed, shared, and limited in systems of shared powers and parliamentary systems (e.g., in terms of effectiveness, prevention of the abuse of power, responsiveness to popular will, stability, ability to serve the purposes of constitutional government) BD (CE,97;QI,169-170)

6. Understands the advantages and disadvantages of federal, confederal, and unitary systems of government (CE,97)

Level I (Grades K-2)

- Not appropriate for this level BD (CE,52)

Level II (Grades 3-4)

- Not appropriate for this level BD (CE,52)

Level III (Grades 5-8)

- Knows the basic characteristics of a confederal system of government (e.g., sovereign states delegate powers to a national government for specific purposes), and knows examples of this system of government (e.g., the United States under the Articles of Confederation and the Confederate States of America) BD (CE,52)

- Knows the basic characteristics of a federal system of government (e.g., power is divided and shared between national and state governments), and knows examples of this system of government (e.g., the government of the United States) BD (CE,52;QE,170)

- Knows the basic characteristics of a unitary system of government (e.g., power is concentrated in a central government; state and local governments can exercise only those powers given to them by the central government), and knows examples of this system of government (e.g., state governments of the United States) BD (CE,52;QE,170)

Codes (right side of page):   BD = Benchmark, Declarative; BP = Benchmark, Procedural; BC = Benchmark, Contextual
1st letter of each code in parentheses   *2nd letter of code*   *Number*
C = CCE: National Standards for Civics   E = Explicitly stated in document   Page number of cited document
A1 = LFS: Authority, I (elementary)   I = Implied in document   *or, for duplicates,*
J1 = LFS: Justice, I (elementary)   Standard number & level of duplicate
P1, P2 = LFS: Privacy, I & II (elementary)
Q = Quigley: Civitas
R1 = LFS: Responsibility, I (elementary)   444   McREL

Level IV (Grades 9-12)

- Understands how power is distributed, shared, and limited in confederal, federal, and unitary systems of government (e.g., in terms of effectiveness, prevention of the abuse of power, responsiveness to popular will, stability) _{BD (CE,98;QI,170)}

- Knows the advantages and disadvantages of confederal, federal, and unitary systems in fulfilling the purposes of constitutional government _{BD (CE,98)}

7. **Understands alternative forms of representation and how they serve the purposes of constitutional government** _(CE,98)

Level I (Grades K-2)

- Not appropriate for this level _{BD (CE,98)}

Level II (Grades 3-4)

- Not appropriate for this level _{BD (CE,98)}

Level III (Grades 5-8)

- Not appropriate for this level _{BD (CE,98)}

Level IV (Grades 9-12)

- Understands the major arguments for and against representative government as distinguished from direct popular rule _{BD (CE,98)}

- Knows common bases upon which representation is or has been established (e.g., geographic areas; citizenship; social class or caste; age, sex, or property; religion, race, and ethnicity) _{BD (CE,98;QI,422-423)}

- Understands differing bases of electoral systems (e.g., winner-take-all systems, proportional systems) _{BD (CE,98;QI,488)}

- Understands differing theories of representation (e.g., obligation of a representative to _{BD (CE,98;QI,422-423)}

Codes (right side of page):   BD = Benchmark, Declarative; BP = Benchmark, Procedural; BC = Benchmark, Contextual
1st letter of each code in parentheses   *2nd letter of code*   *Number*
C = CCE: National Standards for Civics   E = Explicitly stated in document   Page number of cited document
A1 = LFS: Authority, I (elementary)   I = Implied in document   *or, for duplicates,*
J1 = LFS: Justice, I (elementary)   Standard number & level of duplicate
P1, P2 = LFS: Privacy, I & II (elementary)
Q = Quigley: Civitas
R1 = LFS: Responsibility, I (elementary)   445   MREL

promote the interests of a particular constituency vs. obligation to promote the interests of the society as a whole)

8. **Understands the central ideas of American constitutional government and how this** (CE,53,100) **form of government has shaped the character of American society**

Level I (Grades K-2)

- Knows that America has had a historical commitment to the pursuit of justice BD (JE1,1;QE,21;DE,4.1.1)

Level II (Grades 3-4)

- Knows the fundamental values of American democracy (e.g., individual rights to life, liberty, property, and the pursuit of happiness; the public or common good; justice; equality of opportunity; diversity; truth; patriotism) BD (CE,22;QE,361;DI,9.2.2)

- Knows the fundamental principles of American democracy (e.g., the people are sovereign; the power of government is limited by law; people exercise their authority directly through voting; people exercise their authority indirectly through elected representatives) BD (CE,22-23;QE,361,378-380;DI,9.2.2)

- Knows how fundamental values and principles of American democracy are expressed in documents such as the Declaration of Independence, the Preamble to the United States Constitution, and the Bill of Rights, as well as in American songs, stories, and speeches BD (CE,23;QE,416-419;DE,9.2.3)

- Understands the focus on "the individual" in American society (e.g., a primary purpose of government is to protect the rights of the individual to life, liberty, property, and the pursuit of happiness; individuals have the right to differ about politics, religion, or any other matter; the vote of one individual should count as much as another's) BD (CE,23;FE,131,362-363)

- Understands the focus on the school, community, state, and nation in American society (e.g., people should try to improve the quality of life in their schools, communities, states, and nation; people should help others who are less fortunate than they and assist them in times of need, emergency, or natural disaster) BD (CE,23-24;QI,132)

- Understands the importance of equality of opportunity and equal protection of the law as a characteristic of American society (e.g., all people have a right to equal opportunity in education, employment, housing, and to equal access to public facilities; all people have a BD (CE,24;QE,24-25)

Codes (right side of page):   BD = Benchmark, Declarative; BP = Benchmark, Procedural; BC = Benchmark, Contextual
1st letter of each code in parentheses   *2nd letter of code*   *Number*
C = CCE: National Standards for Civics   E = Explicitly stated in document   Page number of cited document
A1 = LFS: Authority, I (elementary)   I = Implied in document   *or, for duplicates,*
J1 = LFS: Justice, I (elementary)   Standard number & level of duplicate
P1, P2 = LFS: Privacy, I & II (elementary)
Q = Quigley: Civitas
R1 = LFS: Responsibility, I (elementary)   446

MREL

right to participate in political life by expressing their opinions and trying to persuade others; everyone has the right to be treated equally in the eyes of the law)

BD (CE,24;QE,15,379)
- Understands the importance of respect for the law as a characteristic of American society (e.g., everyone, including government officials, must obey the law; people have the right to work together to see that laws they consider unfair or unwise are changed by peaceful means)

BD (CE,24;QE,132)
- Understands the importance of education as a characteristic of American society (e.g., education is essential for informed and effective citizenship; education is important for earning a living; everyone has a right to public education; people with special needs should be provided with appropriate educational opportunities)

BD (CE,24)
- Understands the importance of work as a characteristic of American society (e.g., work is important to a person's independence and self-esteem; work is important to the well-being of the family, community, state, and nation; all honest work is worthy of respect)

Level III (Grades 5-8)

BD (CE,53;QE,378-380)
- Knows the essential ideas of American constitutional government that are expressed in the Declaration of Independence, the Constitution, and other writings (e.g., the Constitution is a higher law that authorizes a government of limited powers; the Preamble to the Constitution states the purposes of government such as to form a more perfect union, establish justice, provide for the common defense, and promote the general welfare)

BD (CE,54;QE,380)
- Knows how certain provisions of the United States Constitution give government the necessary power to fulfill its purposes (e.g., delegated or enumerated powers as stated in Articles I, II, and III; the general welfare provision as stated in Article I, Section 8; the necessary and proper clause as stated in Article I, Section 8, Clause 18)

BD (CE,54;QE,379)
- Understands how the United States Constitution serves to limit the powers of government (e.g., separation and sharing of powers, checks and balances, Bill of Rights)

BD (CE,54;QI,169)
- Understands how specific provisions of the United States Constitution (including the Bill of Rights) limit the powers of government in order to protect the rights of individuals (e.g., habeas corpus; trial by jury; ex post facto; freedom of religion, speech, press, and assembly; equal protection of the law; due process of law; right to counsel)

Codes (right side of page):	BD = Benchmark, Declarative; BP = Benchmark, Procedural; BC = Benchmark, Contextual	
1st letter of each code in parentheses	*2nd letter of code*	*Number*
C = CCE: National Standards for Civics	E = Explicitly stated in document	Page number of cited document
A1 = LFS: Authority, I (elementary)	I = Implied in document	*or, for duplicates,*
J1 = LFS: Justice, I (elementary)		Standard number & level of duplicate
P1, P2 = LFS: Privacy, I & II (elementary)		
Q = Quigley: Civitas		
R1 = LFS: Responsibility, I (elementary)	447	*MREL*

- BD (CE,54)

  Knows opposing positions on current issues involving constitutional protection of individual rights such as limits on speech (e.g., "hate speech," advertising), separation of church and state (e.g., school vouchers, prayer in public schools), cruel and unusual punishment (e.g., death penalty), search and seizure (e.g., warrantless searches), and privacy (e.g., national identification cards, wiretapping)

- BD (CE,55)

  Understands important factors that have helped shape American society (e.g., absence of a nobility or an inherited caste system; religious freedom; abundance of land and widespread ownership of property; large scale immigration; diversity of the population; market economy; relative social equality; universal public education)

Level IV (Grades 9-12)

- BD (CE,99;QI,330-331)

  Knows major historical events that led to the creation of limited government in the United States (e.g., Magna Carta (1215), common law, and the Bill of Rights (1689) in England; colonial experience, Declaration of Independence (1776), Articles of Confederation (1781), state constitutions and charters, United States Constitution (1787), Bill of Rights (1791) in the United States)

- BD (CE,99;QI,612)

  Knows how the creation of American constitutional government was influenced by the central ideas of the natural rights philosophy (e.g., all persons have the right to life, liberty, property, and the pursuit of happiness; the major purpose of government is to protect those rights)

- BD (CE,100,FE,12)

  Knows the major ideas about republican government that influenced the development of the United States Constitution (e.g., the concept of representative government, the importance of civic virtue or concern for the common good)

- BD (CE,100;QE,14,378)

  Understands the concept of popular sovereignty as a central idea of American constitutional government (e.g., the people as the ultimate source of the power to create, alter, or abolish governments)

- BD (CE,100;QI,169-170,378-380)

  Understands the necessity for a written Constitution to set forth the organization of government and to grant and distribute its powers (e.g., among different branches of the national government, between the national government and the states, between the people and the government)

Codes (right side of page):   BD = Benchmark, Declarative; BP = Benchmark, Procedural; BC = Benchmark, Contextual
1st letter of each code in parentheses   *2nd letter of code*   *Number*
C = CCE: National Standards for Civics   E = Explicitly stated in document   Page number of cited document
A1 = LFS: Authority, I (elementary)   I = Implied in document   *or, for duplicates,*
J1 = LFS: Justice, I (elementary)   Standard number & level of duplicate
P1, P2 = LFS: Privacy, I & II (elementary)
Q = Quigley: Civitas
R1 = LFS: Responsibility, I (elementary)   448   MREL

- Understands how various provisions of the Constitution and principles of the constitutional system help to insure an effective government that will not exceed its limits BD (CE,100;QE,169,378-380)

- Understands how the design of the institutions of government and the federal system works to channel and limit governmental power in order to serve the purposes of American constitutional government BD (CE,100;QE,379-380)

- Understands how the belief in limited government and the values and principles of the Constitution have influenced American society (e.g., the Constitution has encouraged Americans to engage in commercial and other productive activities) BD (CE,100;QE,378-380)

- Knows ways in which Americans have attempted to make the values and principles of the Constitution a reality BD (CE,100)

- Knows how the distinctive characteristics of American society are similar to and different from the characteristics of other societies BD (CE,102)

(CE,107)
9. Understands the importance of Americans sharing and supporting certain values, beliefs, and principles of American constitutional democracy

Level I (Grades K-2)

BD (CE,25)
- No material specifically designated for this level

Level II (Grades K-4)

- Understands how Americans are united by the values, principles, and beliefs they share rather than by ethnicity, race, religion, class, language, gender, or national origin BD (CE,25;QI,25-27,361;DI,11.3.5)

- Understands how shared values, principles, and beliefs contribute to the continuation and improvement of American democracy BD (CE,25;QE,361;DI,8.2.1,8.2.2)

- Knows how specific documents in American history set forth shared values, principles, and beliefs (e.g., Declaration of Independence, United States Constitution and Bill of Rights, Pledge of Allegiance) BD (CE,25;QE,416-419;DE,8.2.3)

- Knows how various symbols are used to depict Americans' shared values, principles, and BD (CE,25)

Codes (right side of page): BD = Benchmark, Declarative; BP = Benchmark, Procedural; BC = Benchmark, Contextual
1st letter of each code in parentheses *2nd letter of code* *Number*
C = CCE: National Standards for Civics E = Explicitly stated in document Page number of cited document
A1 = LFS: Authority, I (elementary) I = Implied in document *or, for duplicates,*
J1 = LFS: Justice, I (elementary) Standard number & level of duplicate
P1, P2 = LFS: Privacy, I & II (elementary)
Q = Quigley: Civitas
R1 = LFS: Responsibility, I (elementary) 449 MᴄREL

beliefs and explain their meaning (e.g., the flag, Statue of Liberty, Statue of Justice, Uncle Sam, great seal, national anthem, oaths of office, mottoes such as *E Pluribus Unum*)

BD (CE,25)
- Knows how various American holidays reflect the shared values, principles, and beliefs of Americans (e.g., Fourth of July; Labor Day; Memorial Day; Presidents' Day; Columbus Day; Thanksgiving; Veterans Day; Martin Luther King, Jr.'s Birthday)

BD (CE,27;QE,13)
- Knows how the values and principles of American democracy can be promoted through respecting the rights of others (e.g., being open to opposing views, not invading others' privacy, not discriminating unfairly against others)

BD (CE,27;QE,361-363)
- Knows how the values and principles of American democracy can be fostered through helping to promote the common good (e.g., volunteer work)

BD (CE,27;QE,39)
- Knows how the values and principles of American democracy can be promoted through participating in government (e.g., voting, keeping informed about public issues, writing to legislators, serving on juries)

Level III (Grades 5-8)

BD (CE,58;QI,378-380)
- Identifies fundamental values and principles that are expressed in basic documents (e.g., Declaration of Independence, United States Constitution), significant political speeches and writings (e.g., *The Federalist*, King's "I Have a Dream" speech), and individual and group actions that embody fundamental values and principles (e.g., suffrage and civil rights movements)

BD (CE,59;QE,361)
- Understands how certain values (e.g., individual rights, the common good, self government, justice, equality, diversity, openness and free inquiry, truth, patriotism) are fundamental to American public life

BD (CE,59;QE,131;378)
- Knows that popular sovereignty is a fundamental principle of American constitutional democracy (e.g., ultimate political authority rests with the people who create and can alter or abolish governments)

BD (CE,59;QE,131,378-379)
- Knows that constitutional government is a fundamental principle of American democracy (e.g., the rule of law, representative institutions, shared powers, checks and balances, individual rights, separation of church and state, federalism, civilian control of the military)

Codes (right side of page):   BD = Benchmark, Declarative; BP = Benchmark, Procedural; BC = Benchmark, Contextual
1st letter of each code in parentheses   *2nd letter of code*   *Number*
C = CCE: National Standards for Civics   E = Explicitly stated in document   Page number of cited document
A1 = LFS: Authority, I (elementary)   I = Implied in document   *or, for duplicates,*
J1 = LFS: Justice, I (elementary)   Standard number & level of duplicate
P1, P2 = LFS: Privacy, I & II (elementary)
Q = Quigley: Civitas
R1 = LFS: Responsibility, I (elementary)

McREL

Level IV (Grades 9-12)

- Understands how the institutions of government reflect fundamental values and principles (e.g., justice, equality, the common good, popular sovereignty, checks and balances) ^{BD (CE,108;QE,380)}

- Understands the interdependence among certain values and principles (e.g., individual liberty and diversity) ^{BD (CE,108;QI,378-80)}

- Understands the significance of fundamental values and principles for the individual and society ^{BD (CE,108;QE,361)}

10. Understands the roles of voluntarism and organized groups in American social and political life ^(CE,102)

Level I (Grades K-2)

- No material specifically designated for this level ^{BD (CE,55)}

Level II (Grades K-4)

- Understands the importance of voluntarism as a characteristic of American society (e.g., people should volunteer to help others in their family, schools, communities, state, nation, and the world; volunteering is a source of individual satisfaction and fulfillment) ^{BD (CE,24;QE,16,363)}

Level III (Grades 5-8)

- Knows factors that have influenced American voluntarism (e.g., colonial conditions, frontier traditions, religious beliefs) ^{BD (CE,55;QI,16,363)}

- Knows services that are provided by charitable, religious, and civic groups in the community (e.g., health, child, and elderly care; disaster relief; counseling; tutoring; basic needs such as food, clothing, shelter) ^{BD (CE,56;QI,16,363)}

- Knows volunteer opportunities that exist in one's own school and community ^{BD (CE,56)}

Codes (right side of page):   BD = Benchmark, Declarative; BP = Benchmark, Procedural; BC = Benchmark, Contextual
1st letter of each code in parentheses   *2nd letter of code*   *Number*
C = CCE: National Standards for Civics   E = Explicitly stated in document   Page number of cited document
A1 = LFS: Authority, I (elementary)   I = Implied in document   *or, for duplicates,*
J1 = LFS: Justice, I (elementary)   Standard number & level of duplicate
P1, P2 = LFS: Privacy, I & II (elementary)
Q = Quigley: Civitas
R1 = LFS: Responsibility, I (elementary)   451   M REL

Level IV (Grades 9-12)

- Knows how the Puritan ethic encouraged American voluntarism

  BD (CE,102)

- Knows how voluntary associations and other organized groups have been involved in functions usually associated with government (e.g., social welfare, education)

  BD (CE,102)

- Knows the extent of voluntarism in American society compared to other countries

  BD (CE,102;QI,16,363)

- Understands the relationship between American voluntarism and Americans' ideas about limited government

  BD (CE,102;QE,16-17,363)

- Understands issues that arise regarding what responsibilities belong to individuals and groups and the private sector, what responsibilities belong to the government, and how these responsibilities should be shared by the private sector and the government

  BD (CE,102;QE,16-17)

- Knows the historical and contemporary role of various organized groups in local, state, and national politics (e.g., unions; professional organizations; religious, charitable, service, and civic groups)

  BD (CE,102)

11. Understands the role of diversity in American life and the importance of shared values, political beliefs, and civic beliefs in an increasingly diverse American society

  (CE,103)

Level I (Grades K-2)

- No material specifically designated for this level

  BD (CE,26)

Level II (Grades K-4)

- Understands the concept of diversity

  BD (CE,26)

- Knows some common forms of diversity in the United States (e.g., ethnic, racial, religious, class, linguistic, gender, national origin)

  BD (CE,26;QE,25-27)

- Knows reasons why diversity is so prevalent in the United States

  BD (CE,26;QE,25-27)

- Knows some of the benefits of diversity (e.g., it fosters a variety of viewpoints, new ideas, and fresh ways of looking at and solving problems; it provides people with choices in the

  BD (CE,26;QE,25-27)

Codes (right side of page):   BD = Benchmark, Declarative; BP = Benchmark, Procedural; BC = Benchmark, Contextual
1st letter of each code in parentheses   *2nd letter of code*   *Number*
C = CCE: National Standards for Civics   E = Explicitly stated in document   Page number of cited document
A1 = LFS: Authority, I (elementary)   I = Implied in document   *or, for duplicates,*
J1 = LFS: Justice, I (elementary)   Standard number & level of duplicate
P1, P2 = LFS: Privacy, I & II (elementary)
Q = Quigley: Civitas
R1 = LFS: Responsibility, I (elementary)   452   MREL

arts, music, literature, and sports; it helps people appreciate cultural traditions and practices other than their own)

BD (CE,26;QE,25-27)
- Knows some of the costs of diversity (e.g., people sometimes discriminate unfairly against others on the basis of age, religious beliefs, race, or disability; members of different groups sometimes misunderstand each other and conflicts subsequently arise)

BD (CE,26;QE,25-27)
- Knows conflicts that are caused by diversity (e.g., unfair discrimination on the basis of race, ethnicity, religion, language, and gender; alienation of one group from another; efforts to impose beliefs and customs on others)

BD (CE,26-27;QE,25-27)
- Knows ways in which conflicts about diversity can be prevented (e.g., encouraging communication among different groups; identifying common beliefs, interests, and goals; learning about others' customs, beliefs, history, and problems; listening to different points of view; adhering to the values and principles of American democracy)

BD (CE,27;QE,25-27)
- Knows ways in which conflicts about diversity can be managed fairly when they occur (e.g., provide opportunities for people to present their points of view; arrange for an impartial individual or group to listen to all sides of a conflict and suggest solutions to problems)

Level III (Grades 5-8)

BD (CE,56;QE,25-27)
- Knows a variety of forms of diversity in American society (e.g., regional, linguistic, socioeconomic)

BD (CE,56;QE,25-27)
- Knows how diversity encourages cultural creativity

BD (CE,56FE,227-231)
- Knows major conflicts in American society that have arisen from diversity (e.g., North/South conflict; conflict about land, suffrage, and other rights of Native Americans; Catholic/Protestant conflicts in the nineteenth century; conflict about civil rights of minorities and women; present day ethnic conflict in urban settings)

BD (CE,56;QE,25-27)
- Knows ways in which conflicts about diversity can be resolved in a peaceful manner that respects individual rights and promotes the common good

BD (CE,57;QE,25-27,361;DI,9.2.1)
- Knows how an American's identity stems from belief in and allegiance to shared political values and principles, and how this identity differs from that of most other nations, which often base their identity on such things as ethnicity, race, religion, class, language, gender,

---

Codes (right side of page):   BD = Benchmark, Declarative; BP = Benchmark, Procedural; BC = Benchmark, Contextual
1st letter of each code in parentheses   *2nd letter of code*   *Number*
C = CCE: National Standards for Civics   E = Explicitly stated in document   Page number of cited document
A1 = LFS: Authority, I (elementary)   I = Implied in document   *or, for duplicates,*
J1 = LFS: Justice, I (elementary)   Standard number & level of duplicate
P1, P2 = LFS: Privacy, I & II (elementary)
Q = Quigley: Civitas
R1 = LFS: Responsibility, I (elementary)   453   McREL

or national origin

- Knows basic values and principles that Americans share (e.g., as set forth in documents such as the Declaration of Independence, the United States Constitution, the Gettysburg Address) BD (CE,57;QE,361)

- Knows why it is important to the individual and society that Americans understand and act on their shared political values and principles BD (CE,57;QE,361)

Level IV (Grades 9-12)

- Knows how the racial, religious, socioeconomic, regional, ethnic, and linguistic diversity of American society has influenced American politics through time BD (CE,103;QE,25-27)

- Knows different viewpoints regarding the role and value of diversity in American life BD (CE,103;QE,25-27)

- Knows examples of conflicts stemming from diversity, and understands how some conflicts have been managed and why some of them have not yet been successfully resolved BD (CE,103;QE,27-231)

- Knows why constitutional values and principles must be adhered to when managing conflicts over diversity BD (CE,103;QI,25-27)

- Knows beliefs that are common to American political culture (e.g., belief in equality of opportunity; mistrust of power, as well as high expectations of what elected officials and government should do; the need to admit to faults or shortcomings in the society; the belief that social, economic, or political problems can be alleviated through collective effort) BD (CE,104;QE,131)

- Knows how shared ideas and values of American political culture are reflected in various sources and documents (e.g., the Bill of Rights, *The Federalist* and Anti-federalist writings, Woodrow Wilson's "Fourteen Points," Martin Luther King, Jr.'s "Letter from the Birmingham Jail," landmark decisions of the Supreme Court of the United States) BD (CE,104;QI,416-419)

12.   Understands the relationships among liberalism, republicanism, and American constitutional democracy (CE,106,107)

Level I (Grades K-2)

- Not appropriate for this level BD (CE,106)

Codes (right side of page):	BD = Benchmark, Declarative; BP = Benchmark, Procedural; BC = Benchmark, Contextual
1st letter of each code in parentheses	*2nd letter of code*

Codes (right side of page):   BD = Benchmark, Declarative; BP = Benchmark, Procedural; BC = Benchmark, Contextual
1st letter of each code in parentheses   *2nd letter of code*   *Number*
C = CCE: National Standards for Civics   E = Explicitly stated in document   Page number of cited document
A1 = LFS: Authority, I (elementary)   I = Implied in document   *or, for duplicates,*
J1 = LFS: Justice, I (elementary)   Standard number & level of duplicate
P1, P2 = LFS: Privacy, I & II (elementary)
Q = Quigley: Civitas
R1 = LFS: Responsibility, I (elementary)   454   MⳭREL

Level II (Grades 3-4)

BD (CE,106)

- Not appropriate for this level

Level III (Grades 5-8)

BD (CE,106)

- Not appropriate for this level

Level IV (Grades 9-12)

BD (CE,106;QE,12)

- Understands that the central idea of liberalism is the belief that the individual has rights that exist independently of government and that ought to be protected by and against government

BD (CE,106;QE,12)

- Knows the general history of liberalism (e.g., ideas of liberalism that emerged in the seventeenth century and developed during the eighteenth-century Enlightenment; relationship between liberalism and the Protestant Reformation and the rise of market economies and free enterprise)

BD (CE,106)

- Knows the difference between the use of the term "liberal" in referring to the American form of government and the use of the terms "liberal" and "conservative" in referring to positions on the spectrum of American politics

BD (CE,106;QI,112)

- Understands that the term "democracy" is derived from the Greek word for "rule by the people," and that the central focus of democracy is the idea that the people are the source of authority for government

BD (CE,106)

- Knows the difference between the use of the term "democratic" to refer to the American form of government and the use of the term to refer to the Democratic Party in the United States

BD (CE,106-107;QE,133)

- Understands how the basic premises of liberalism and democracy are joined in the Declaration of Independence, where they are stated as "self-evident Truths" (e.g., "all men are created equal," authority is derived from consent of the governed, people have the right to alter or abolish government when it fails to fulfill its purposes)

BD (CE,107;QE,362)

- Understands that a "republic" is a state in which the citizenry as a whole is considered sovereign but which is governed by elected representatives rather than directly by the people as in direct democracy

---

Codes (right side of page):	BD = Benchmark, Declarative; BP = Benchmark, Procedural; BC = Benchmark, Contextual	
1st letter of each code in parentheses	*2nd letter of code*	*Number*
C = CCE: National Standards for Civics	E = Explicitly stated in document	Page number of cited document
A1 = LFS: Authority, I (elementary)	I = Implied in document	*or, for duplicates,*
J1 = LFS: Justice, I (elementary)		Standard number & level of duplicate
P1, P2 = LFS: Privacy, I & II (elementary)		
Q = Quigley: Civitas		
R1 = LFS: Responsibility, I (elementary)		

MREL

- Knows the major ideas of republicanism (e.g., government of a republic seeks the public or common good rather than the good of a particular group or class of society; "civic virtue" of citizens is essential, in which citizens put the public or common good above their private interests) BD (CE,107;QE,12,362)

- Knows how ideas of classical republicanism are reflected in the United States Constitution (e.g., the guarantee to the states of a "republican form of government" in Article IV, Section 4; provisions for the election of representatives to the Congress in Article I, Section 2 and the Seventeenth Amendment) BD (CE,107;QI,12)

- Knows how the use of the term "republican" to refer to the American form of government differs from the use of the term to refer to the Republican Party in the United States BD (CE,107)

- Understands reasons why classical republicanism and liberalism are potentially in conflict (e.g., on the primary purpose of government as the promotion of the public good or as the promotion of the protection of individual rights) BD (CE,107;QE,12)

- Knows various viewpoints regarding the importance of civic virtue for American democracy today BD (CE,107;QE,12)

13.   Understands the character of American political and social conflict and factors that tend to prevent or lower its intensity (CE,104)

Level I (Grades K-2)

- Not appropriate for this level BD (CE,59)

Level II (Grades 3-4)

- Not appropriate for this level BD (CE,59)

Level III (Grades 5-8)

- Knows conflicts that have arisen regarding fundamental values and principles (e.g., conflicts between liberty and equality, conflicts between individual rights and the common good) BD (CE,59;QE,361,416-419)

Codes (right side of page):
1st letter of each code in parentheses
C = CCE: National Standards for Civics
A1 = LFS: Authority, I (elementary)
J1 = LFS: Justice, I (elementary)
P1, P2 = LFS: Privacy, I & II (elementary)
Q = Quigley: Civitas
R1 = LFS: Responsibility, I (elementary)

BD = Benchmark, Declarative; BP = Benchmark, Procedural; BC = Benchmark, Contextual
2nd letter of code
E = Explicitly stated in document
I = Implied in document

Number
Page number of cited document
or, for duplicates,
Standard number & level of duplicate

456

McREL

- Knows how disagreements regarding specific issues may arise between people even though the people agree on values or principles in the abstract (e.g., people may agree on the value of freedom of expression but disagree about the extent to which expression of unpopular and offensive views should be tolerated; people may agree on the value of equality but disagree about affirmative action programs)

  BD (CE,59-60)

- Knows sources of political conflict that have arisen in the United States historically as well as in the present (e.g., geographic and sectional interests, slavery and indentured servitude, national origins, extending the franchise, extending civil rights to all Americans, the role of religion in American public life, engaging in wars)

  BD (CE,57;QE,227-234)

- Knows reasons why most political conflict in the United States has generally been less divisive than in many other nations (e.g., a shared respect for the Constitution and its principles, a sense of unity within diversity, willingness to relinquish power when voted out of office, willingness to use the legal system to manage conflicts, opportunities to improve one's economic condition)

  BD (CE,57)

- Knows instances in which political conflict in the United States has been divisive and reasons for this division (e.g., the Civil War, labor unrest, civil rights struggles, opposition to the war in Vietnam)

  BD (CE,57;QE,227-231)

Level IV (Grades 9-12)

- Understands issues that involve conflicts among fundamental values and principles such as the conflict between liberty and authority

  BD (CE,108;QE,416-419)

- Knows why people may agree on values or principles in the abstract but disagree when they are applied to specific issues such as the right to life and capital punishment

  BD (CE,109)

- Knows how the rights of organized labor and the role of government in regulating business have created political conflict

  BD (CE,104)

- Knows how the concept of a loyal opposition and recourse to the legal system to manage conflicts have helped to lessen the divisiveness of political conflict in the United States

  BD (CE,104)

- Knows how universal public education and the existence of a popular culture that crosses class boundaries have tended to reduce the intensity of political conflict (e.g., by creating common ground among diverse groups)

  BD (CE,104;QI,25-27)

Codes (right side of page):	BD = Benchmark, Declarative; BP = Benchmark, Procedural; BC = Benchmark, Contextual	
1st letter of each code in parentheses	*2nd letter of code*	*Number*
C = CCE: National Standards for Civics	E = Explicitly stated in document	Page number of cited document
A1 = LFS: Authority, I (elementary)	I = Implied in document	*or, for duplicates,*
J1 = LFS: Justice, I (elementary)		Standard number & level of duplicate
P1, P2 = LFS: Privacy, I & II (elementary)		
Q = Quigley: Civitas		
R1 = LFS: Responsibility, I (elementary)	457	MREL

14. **Understands issues concerning the disparities between ideals and reality in American political and social life** (CE,109)

Level I (Grades K-2)

- Not appropriate for this level BD (CE,60)

Level II (Grades 3-4)

- Not appropriate for this level BD (CE,60)

Level III (Grades 5-8)

- Knows some important American ideals (e.g., liberty and justice for all, an informed citizenry, civic virtue or concern for the common good, respect for the rights of others) BD (CE,60;QE,131,361)

- Knows why political and social ideals are important, even if they cannot be fully achieved BD (CE,60;QE,361)

- Knows some of the discrepancies that have arisen between American ideals and the realities of political and social life in the United States (e.g., the ideal of equal justice for all and the reality that the poor may not have equal access to the judicial system) BD (CE,60)

- Knows some of the efforts that have been put forth to reduce discrepancies between ideals and the reality of American public life (e.g., abolition, suffrage, civil rights, environmental protection movements) BD (CE,60)

- Knows how various individual actions, social actions, and political actions can help to reduce discrepancies between reality and the ideals of American constitutional democracy BD (CE,60;QI,361)

Level IV (Grades 9-12)

- Understands the importance of established ideals in political life and why Americans should insist that current practices constantly be compared with these ideals BD (CE,109;QE,361)

- Knows discrepancies between American ideals and the realities of American social and political life (e.g., the ideal of equal opportunity and the reality of unfair discrimination) BD (CE,109)

Codes (right side of page):
1st letter of each code in parentheses
C = CCE: National Standards for Civics
A1 = LFS: Authority, I (elementary)
J1 = LFS: Justice, I (elementary)
P1, P2 = LFS: Privacy, I & II (elementary)
Q = Quigley: Civitas
R1 = LFS: Responsibility, I (elementary)

BD = Benchmark, Declarative; BP = Benchmark, Procedural; BC = Benchmark, Contextual
2nd letter of code
E = Explicitly stated in document
I = Implied in document

Number
Page number of cited document
or, for duplicates,
Standard number & level of duplicate

458

MREL

- Knows historical and contemporary efforts to reduce discrepancies between ideals and reality in American public life (e.g., union movements, government programs such as Head Start, civil rights legislation and enforcement)

BD (CE,109)

15. Understands how the United States Constitution grants and distributes power and responsibilities to national and state government and how it seeks to prevent the abuse of power

(CE, 110)

Level I (Grades K-2)

- No material specifically designated for this level

BD (CE,28)

Level II (Grades K-4)

- Understands that the Constitution is a written document which states that the fundamental purposes of American government are to protect individual rights and promote the common good

BD (CE,28;QE,15)

- Knows that the Constitution describes how the government is organized, defines and limits the powers of government, and is the highest law in the land

BD (CE,28;QE,378-379)

- Knows that the government was created by people who had the following beliefs: the government is established by and for the people, the people have the right to choose their representatives, and the people have the right to change their government and the Constitution

BD (CE,28;QE,378-379)

- Knows that Congress passes laws to protect individual rights (e.g., laws protecting freedom of religion and expression, and preventing unfair discrimination) and promote the common good (e.g., laws providing for clean air, national parks, and the defense of the nation)

BD (CE,29;QI,380)

- Knows that the executive branch carries out and enforces laws to protect individual rights (e.g., voting rights, equal opportunities to attain an education) and promote the common good (e.g., enforcement of pure food and drug laws, enforcement of clean air laws)

BD (CE,29;QI,380)

- Knows that the judicial branch, headed by the Supreme Court, makes decisions concerning the law that aim to protect individual rights (e.g., the right to a fair trial, to vote, to practice

BD (CE,29;QI,380;DE,18,2.1)

Codes (right side of page): BD = Benchmark, Declarative; BP = Benchmark, Procedural; BC = Benchmark, Contextual

1st letter of each code in parentheses	*2nd letter of code*	*Number*
C = CCE: National Standards for Civics	E = Explicitly stated in document	Page number of cited document
A1 = LFS: Authority, I (elementary)	I = Implied in document	*or, for duplicates,*
J1 = LFS: Justice, I (elementary)		Standard number & level of duplicate
P1, P2 = LFS: Privacy, I & II (elementary)		
Q = Quigley: Civitas		
R1 = LFS: Responsibility, I (elementary)	459	MREL

one's religious beliefs) and promote the common good (e.g., upholding laws that protect the rights of all people to equal opportunity)

Level III (Grades 5-8)

- Understands how the first three words of the Preamble to the Constitution, "We the People...," embodies the principle of the people as the ultimate source of sovereignty BD (CE,61;QE,378)

- Understands how the legislative, executive, and judicial branches share power and responsibilities (e.g., each branch has varying degrees of legislative, executive, and judicial powers and responsibilities) BD (CE,61-62;QE,380)

- Understands how the legislative branch can check the powers of the executive and judicial branches by establishing committees to oversee the executive branch's activities; impeaching the president, other members of the executive branch, and federal judges; overriding presidential vetoes; disapproving presidential appointments; and proposing amendments to the Constitution BD (CE,62;QE,380)

- Understands how the executive branch can check the powers of the legislative and judicial branches by vetoing laws passed by Congress and nominating members of the federal judiciary BD (CE,62;QE,380)

- Understands how the judicial branch can check the powers of the executive and legislative branches by overruling decisions made by lower courts and ruling on the constitutionality of laws made by Congress and the actions of the executive branch BD (CE,62;QE,380)

- Knows the major parts of the federal system including the national government, state governments, and other governmental units (e.g., District of Columbia, American tribal governments, Virgin Islands) BD (CE,62;QE,392)

- Knows which powers are primarily exercised by the state governments (e.g., education, law enforcement, roads), which powers are prohibited to state governments (e.g., coining money, conducting foreign relations, interfering with interstate commerce), and which powers are shared by state and national governments (e.g., power to tax, borrow money, regulate voting) BD (CE,62;QI,466)

- Understands how the distribution and sharing of power between the national and state governments increases opportunities for citizens to participate and hold their governments accountable BD (CE,63;QI,392)

Codes (right side of page):   BD = Benchmark, Declarative; BP = Benchmark, Procedural; BC = Benchmark, Contextual
1st letter of each code in parentheses   *2nd letter of code*   *Number*
C = CCE: National Standards for Civics   E = Explicitly stated in document   Page number of cited document
A1 = LFS: Authority, I (elementary)   I = Implied in document   *or, for duplicates,*
J1 = LFS: Justice, I (elementary)   Standard number & level of duplicate
P1, P2 = LFS: Privacy, I & II (elementary)
Q = Quigley: Civitas
R1 = LFS: Responsibility, I (elementary)   460   MREL

Level IV (Grades 9-12)

- BD (CE,110;QI,378-380)

  Understands how the overall design and specific features of the Constitution prevent the abuse of power by aggregating power at the national, state, and local levels to allow government to be responsive; dispersing power among different levels of government to protect individual rights, promote the common good, and encourage citizen participation; and using a system of checks and balances (e.g., separated institutions with shared powers, provisions for veto and impeachment, federalism, judicial review, the Bill of Rights)

- BD (CE,111;QI,378-379)

  Knows why the framers adopted a federal system in which power and responsibility are divided and shared between a national government and state governments

- BD (CE,111;QI,467)

  Understands ways in which federalism is designed to protect individual rights to life, liberty, and property and how it has at times made it possible for states to deny the rights of certain groups, (e.g. states' rights and slavery, denial of suffrage to women and minority groups)

- BD (CE,111;QI,466)

  Understands both the historical and contemporary roles of national and state governments in the federal system and the importance of the Tenth Amendment

- BD (CE,112;QE,380)

  Understands the purposes, organization, and functions of the legislative, executive, and judicial branches and the independent regulatory agencies (e.g., agencies such as the Federal Reserve, Food and Drug Administration, Federal Communications Commission)

- BD (CE,112;QI,378-380)

  Understands the extent to which each branch of the government reflects the people's sovereignty (e.g., Congress legislates on behalf of the people, the president represents the nation as a whole, the Supreme Court interprets the Constitution on behalf of the people)

- BD (CE,112;QI,380)

  Understands how specific features and the overall design of the Constitution results in tensions among the three branches (e.g., the power of the purse, the power of impeachment, advice and consent, veto power, judicial review), and comprehends the argument that the tensions resulting from separation of powers, checks and balances, and judicial review tend to slow down the process of making and enforcing laws, thus insuring better outcomes

- BD (CE,112)

  Knows current issues concerning representation (e.g., term limitations, legislative districting, geographical and group representation)

- BD (CE,112)

  Understands how and why beliefs about the purposes and functions of the national government have changed over time

Codes (right side of page):	BD = Benchmark, Declarative; BP = Benchmark, Procedural; BC = Benchmark, Contextual	
1st letter of each code in parentheses	*2nd letter of code*	*Number*
C = CCE: National Standards for Civics	E = Explicitly stated in document	Page number of cited document
A1 = LFS: Authority, I (elementary)	I = Implied in document	*or, for duplicates,*
J1 = LFS: Justice, I (elementary)		Standard number & level of duplicate
P1, P2 = LFS: Privacy, I & II (elementary)		
Q = Quigley: Civitas		
R1 = LFS: Responsibility, I (elementary)	461	McREL

16. Understands the major responsibilities of the national government for domestic and foreign policy, and understands how government is financed through taxation

(CE,112-113)

Level I (Grades K-2)

- Not appropriate for this level

BD (CE,63)

Level II (Grades 3-4)

- Not appropriate for this level

BD (CE,63)

Level III (Grades 5-8)

- Understands how and why domestic policies affect American citizens' lives, and knows historical and contemporary examples of important domestic policies (e.g., Pure Food and Drug Act, Environmental Protection Act, civil rights laws, minimum wage laws, Social Security)

BD (CE,63;QI,638)

- Understands how and why foreign policies affect the lives of American citizens, and knows historical and contemporary examples of important foreign policies (e.g., Monroe Doctrine, Marshall Plan, immigration acts, arms control, promoting democracy and human rights throughout the world)

BD (CE,63;QI,328-330)

- Understands why taxation is necessary to pay for government, and knows which provisions of the United States Constitution give the national government the right to collect taxes (i.e., Article One, Sections 7 and 8; Sixteenth Amendment)

BD (CE,63)

- Knows major sources of revenue for the national government (e.g., individual income taxes, social insurance receipts such as Social Security and Medicare, borrowing, taxes on corporations and businesses, estate and excise taxes, tariffs on foreign goods)

BD (CE,64)

- Knows major uses of tax revenues received by the national government (e.g. direct payments to individuals such as Social Security, Medicaid, Medicare, and Aid to Families with Dependent Children; national defense; interest on the federal debt; interstate highways)

BD (CE,64;QI,482-483)

Codes (right side of page):
1st letter of each code in parentheses
C = CCE: National Standards for Civics
A1 = LFS: Authority, I (elementary)
J1 = LFS: Justice, I (elementary)
P1, P2 = LFS: Privacy, I & II (elementary)
Q = Quigley: Civitas
R1 = LFS: Responsibility, I (elementary)

BD = Benchmark, Declarative; BP = Benchmark, Procedural; BC = Benchmark, Contextual
2nd letter of code
E = Explicitly stated in document
I = Implied in document

Number
Page number of cited document
or, for duplicates,
Standard number & level of duplicate

462

MCREL

Level IV (Grades 9-12)

- BD (CE,113;QI,328-330)

  Understands how specific foreign policies such as national security and trade policy affect the everyday lives of American citizens and their communities

- BD (CE,113;QI,328-330,638)

  Understands competing arguments concerning the role of government in major areas of domestic and foreign policy (e.g., health care, education, child care, regulation of business and industry, foreign aid, intervention abroad)

- BD (CE,113;QI,482-483)

  Understands the tensions that results from citizens' desire for government services and benefits and their unwillingness to pay taxes for them

- BD (CE,113)

  Knows the history of taxation in the United States

- BD (CE,113)

  Understands the equity of various kinds of taxes

(CE,65,114)

17. Understands issues concerning the relationship between state and local governments and the national government and issues pertaining to representation at all three levels of government

Level I (Grades K-2)

- BD (CE,30)

  No material specifically designated for this level

Level II (Grades K-4)

- BD (CE,30-31)

  Knows how to distinguish among national, state, and local governments

- BD (CE,30;QE,470-473)

  Knows the major responsibilities of the legislative, executive, and judicial branches of his/her state government

- BD (CE,30-31;QE,466-467)

  Knows major services provided by state and local governments (e.g., state services such as education and health services and local services such as transportation, education, recreation, public safety, public utilities), and knows how these services are paid for (e.g., taxes, fees, licenses)

- BD (CE,30-31)

  Knows how state and local government officials are chosen (i.e., by election or appointment)

Codes (right side of page):   BD = Benchmark, Declarative; BP = Benchmark, Procedural; BC = Benchmark, Contextual
1st letter of each code in parentheses   *2nd letter of code*   *Number*
C = CCE: National Standards for Civics   E = Explicitly stated in document   Page number of cited document
A1 = LFS: Authority, I (elementary)   I = Implied in document   *or, for duplicates,*
J1 = LFS: Justice, I (elementary)   Standard number & level of duplicate
P1, P2 = LFS: Privacy, I & II (elementary)
Q = Quigley: Civitas
R1 = LFS: Responsibility, I (elementary)   463   MREL

- Knows how people can participate in their state and local government (e.g., being informed, taking part in discussing issues, voting, volunteering their time), and understands why it is important that people participate in their state and local government (e.g., improve the quality of life in their community, gain personal satisfaction, prevent officials from abusing power)
  BD (CE,30-31;QI,39-40)

- Knows the names of his/her legislators at the state and national levels (e.g., representatives and senators in his/her state legislature and in Congress) and the names of his/her representatives in the executive branches of government at the national, state, and local levels (e.g., mayor, governor, president)
  BD (CE,32)

- Knows how to contact his/her representatives and which levels of government he/she should contact to express his/her opinions or get help on a specific problem (e.g., the environment, crime, stray or wild animals)
  BD (CE,32)

Level III (Grades 5-8)

- Understands that his/her state has a constitution because the United States is a federal system
  BD (CE,64;QE,466)

- Knows the major purposes of his/her state constitution, the process by which citizens can change their state constitution, and the basic similarities and differences between his/her state constitution and the United States Constitution
  BD (CE,64)

- Understands why the United States Constitution cannot be violated by state constitutions and state governments
  BD (CE,64)

- Understands the process by which citizens can change their state constitution and cite examples of changes
  BD (CE,64)

- Knows the major responsibilities of his/her state and local governments (e.g., education, welfare, streets and roads, parks, recreation, law enforcement), and understands the organization of his/her state and local governments (e.g., legislative, executive, and judicial functions at state and local levels)
  BD (CE,65)

- Knows major sources of revenue for state and local governments (e.g., property, sales, and income taxes; fees and licenses; taxes on corporations and businesses; borrowing)
  BD (CE,65;QE,475-476)

- Understands how he/she can contact his/her representatives and why it is important to do so,
  BD (CE,65)

Codes (right side of page): BD = Benchmark, Declarative; BP = Benchmark, Procedural; BC = Benchmark, Contextual
1st letter of each code in parentheses   *2nd letter of code*   *Number*
C = CCE: National Standards for Civics   E = Explicitly stated in document   Page number of cited document
A1 = LFS: Authority, I (elementary)   I = Implied in document   *or, for duplicates,*
J1 = LFS: Justice, I (elementary)   Standard number & level of duplicate
P1, P2 = LFS: Privacy, I & II (elementary)
Q = Quigley: Civitas
R1 = LFS: Responsibility, I (elementary)   464   MREL

and knows which level of government he/she should contact to express his/her opinions or to get help on a specific problem (e.g., opinions about a curfew for juveniles, an increase in state sales tax, aid to another country; problems with street lights, driver's license, federal income taxes)

Level IV (Grades 9-12)

- BD (CE,114;QI,466-467)
  Knows the limits the United States Constitution places on the powers of the states (e.g., prohibitions against impairing interstate commerce, restrictions imposed by the Fourteenth Amendment and the Bill of Rights through the process of incorporation) and the limits the Constitution places on the powers of the national government over state governments (e.g., the national government cannot abolish a state, the Tenth Amendment to the Constitution reserves certain powers to the states)

- BD (CE,114;QE,466)
  Understands that the two kinds of power most commonly associated with state governments are reserved powers, which are powers not delegated to the national government or prohibited to states by the United States Constitution (e.g., legislation regarding public safety, marriage, and divorce; education; the conduct of elections; chartering regional and local governments; licensing drivers, businesses, and professions) and concurrent powers, which are powers jointly held with the national government (e.g., legislating taxation, regulating trade and industry, borrowing money, maintaining courts, protecting the environment)

- BD (CE,114)
  Understands criteria for evaluating how the relationship between state and local governments and the national government has changed over time

- BD (CE,114;QI,480)
  Understands criteria for evaluating the argument that state and local governments provide significant opportunities for experimentation and innovation

- BD (CE,115)
  Understands criteria for evaluating the relationship between his/her state and local governments

- BD (CE,115)
  Understands how the policies of state and local governments provide citizens with ways to monitor and influence the actions of members of government and hold them responsible for their actions (e.g., requirements of fair and public notice of meetings, meetings of government agencies must be open to the public, public trials, provision of opportunities for citizens to be heard)

Codes (right side of page):   BD = Benchmark, Declarative; BP = Benchmark, Procedural; BC = Benchmark, Contextual
1st letter of each code in parentheses   *2nd letter of code*   *Number*
C = CCE: National Standards for Civics   E = Explicitly stated in document   Page number of cited document
A1 = LFS: Authority, I (elementary)   I = Implied in document   *or, for duplicates,*
J1 = LFS: Justice, I (elementary)   Standard number & level of duplicate
P1, P2 = LFS: Privacy, I & II (elementary)
Q = Quigley: Civitas
R1 = LFS: Responsibility, I (elementary)

McREL

18. **Understands the role and importance of law in the American constitutional system and issues regarding the judicial protection of individual rights** (CE,116,117)

Level I (Grades K-2)

- No material specifically designated for this level
BD (CE,29)

Level II (Grades K-4)

BD (CE,29;QI,380;DE,15.2.6)
- Knows that the judicial branch, headed by the Supreme Court, makes decisions concerning the law that aim to protect individual rights (e.g., the right to a fair trial, to vote, to practice one's religious beliefs) and promote the common good (e.g., upholding laws that protect the rights of all people to equal opportunity)

Level III (Grades 5-8)

BD (CE,66;QE,15,379)
- Understands the importance of the rule of law in establishing limits on both those who govern and the governed, protecting individual rights, and promoting the common good

BD (CE,66)
- Knows historical and contemporary examples of the rule of law (e.g., *Marbury* v. *Madison, Brown* v. *Board of Education, U.S.* v. *Nixon)*

BD (CE,66;QI,332-333)
- Knows principle varieties of law (e.g., constitutional, criminal, civil), and understands how the principal varieties of law protect individual rights and promote the common good

BD (CE,67)
- Understands criteria for evaluating the strengths and weaknesses of a rule or law by determining if it is understandable (i.e., clearly written with explicit requirements), possible to follow (i.e., does not demand the impossible), fair, well designed to achieve its purposes, and designed to protect individual rights and to promote the common good

BD (CE,67)
- Understands the process necessary for drafting rules in his/her school or community that meets the criteria for a well-constructed rule or law

BD (CE,67;FE;619-620)
- Understands the basic concept of due process of law (i.e., government must use fair procedures to gather information and make decisions in order to protect the rights of individuals and the interests of society)

Codes (right side of page):
1st letter of each code in parentheses
C = CCE: National Standards for Civics
A1 = LFS: Authority, I (elementary)
J1 = LFS: Justice, I (elementary)
P1, P2 = LFS: Privacy, I & II (elementary)
Q = Quigley: Civitas
R1 = LFS: Responsibility, I (elementary)

BD = Benchmark, Declarative; BP = Benchmark, Procedural; BC = Benchmark, Contextual
2nd letter of code
E = Explicitly stated in document
I = Implied in document

Number
Page number of cited document
or, for duplicates,
Standard number & level of duplicate

MREL

- Understands the importance to individuals and to society of major due process protections such as habeas corpus, presumption of innocence, fair notice, impartial tribunal, speedy and public trials, right to counsel, trail by jury, right against self incrimination, protection against double jeopardy, right of appeal *BD (CE,67;QE,619-620)*

- Understands why due process rights in administrative and legislative procedures are essential for the protection of individual rights and the maintenance of limited government (e.g., the right to adequate notice of a hearing that may affect one's interests, the right to counsel in legislative hearings) *BD (CE,67;QE,619-622)*

- Understands the advantages and disadvantages of the adversary system and the advantages and disadvantages of alternative means of conflict management (e.g., negotiation, mediation, arbitration, and litigation) *BD (CE,67-68)*

- Knows the basic principles of the juvenile system and the major differences between the due process rights of juveniles and adults *BD (CE,67)*

- Understands current issues regarding judicial protection of the rights of individuals *BD (CE,68)*

Level IV (Grades 9-12)

- Understands how the rule of law makes possible a system of ordered liberty that protects the basic rights of citizens *BD (CE,116;QE,15,379)*

- Knows historical and contemporary practices that illustrate the central place of the rule of law (e.g., submitting bills to legal counsel to insure congressional compliance with constitutional limitations, higher court review of lower court compliance with the law, executive branch compliance with laws enacted by Congress) *BD (CE,116)*

- Knows historical and contemporary events and practices that illustrate the absence or breakdown of the rule of law (e.g., events such as vigilantism in the early West, Ku Klux Klan attacks, urban riots, corruption in government and business, police corruption, organized crime; practices such as illegal searches and seizures, bribery, interfering with the right to vote, perjury) *BD (CE,116)*

- Knows historical and contemporary illustrations of the idea of equal protection of the laws for all persons (e.g., the Fourteenth Amendment, Americans with Disabilities Act, equal opportunity legislation) *BD (CE,116;QE,619-620)*

Codes (right side of page): BD = Benchmark, Declarative; BP = Benchmark, Procedural; BC = Benchmark, Contextual
1st letter of each code in parentheses *2nd letter of code* *Number*
C = CCE: National Standards for Civics E = Explicitly stated in document Page number of cited document
A1 = LFS: Authority, I (elementary) I = Implied in document *or, for duplicates,*
J1 = LFS: Justice, I (elementary) Standard number & level of duplicate
P1, P2 = LFS: Privacy, I & II (elementary)
Q = Quigley: Civitas
R1 = LFS: Responsibility, I (elementary)

McREL

BD (CE,116;QI,332-333)

- Understands how the individual's rights to life, liberty, and property are protected by the trial and appellate levels of the judicial process and by the principal varieties of law (e.g., constitutional, criminal, and civil law)

BD (CE,116)

- Understands the effects of Americans relying on the legal system to solve social, economic, and political problems rather than using other means, such as private negotiations, mediation, and participation in the political process

BD (CE,117)

- Understands the importance of an independent judiciary in a constitutional democracy

BD (CE,117)

- Knows historical and contemporary instances in which judicial protections have not been extended to all persons and instances in which judicial protections have been extended to those deprived of them in the past

BD (CE,117;QI,619-622)

- Understands why due process rights in administrative and legislative procedures are essential for protecting individual rights and maintaining limited government

BD (CE,117;QI,615)

- Knows how state and federal courts' power of judicial reflects the American idea of constitutional government (i.e., limited government) and understands the merits of arguments for and against judicial review

(CE,118)

19. Understands what is meant by "the public agenda," how it is set, and how it is influenced by public opinion and the media

Level I (Grades K-2)

BD (CE,68)

- Not appropriate for this level

Level II (Grades 3-4)

BD (CE,68)

- Not appropriate for this level

Level III (Grades 5-8)

BD (CE,68;QE,641)

- Knows that the public agenda consists of those matters that occupy public attention at any particular time (e.g., crime, health care education, child care, environmental protection, drug

---

Codes (right side of page):   BD = Benchmark, Declarative; BP = Benchmark, Procedural; BC = Benchmark, Contextual
1st letter of each code in parentheses   *2nd letter of code*   *Number*
C = CCE: National Standards for Civics   E = Explicitly stated in document   Page number of cited document
A1 = LFS: Authority, I (elementary)   I = Implied in document   *or, for duplicates,*
J1 = LFS: Justice, I (elementary)   Standard number & level of duplicate
P1, P2 = LFS: Privacy, I & II (elementary)
Q = Quigley: Civitas
R1 = LFS: Responsibility, I (elementary)   468   McREL

abuse)

- Knows how the public agenda is shaped by political leaders, interest groups, and state and federal courts; and understands how individual citizens can help shape the public agenda (e.g., by joining interest groups or political parties, making presentations at public meetings, writing letters to government officials and to newspapers) ^{BD (CE,68;QI,641)}

- Understands the importance of freedom of the press to informed participation in the political system; and understands the influence of television, radio, the press, newsletters, and emerging means of electronic communication on American politics ^{BD (CE,69;QE,539)}

- Knows how Congress, the president, the Supreme Court, and state and local public officials use the media to communicate with the citizenry ^{BD (CE,69;QI,544-545)}

- Understands how citizens can evaluate information and arguments received from various sources so that they can make reasonable choices on public issues and among candidates for political office ^{BD (CE,69)}

- Understands the opportunities that the media provides for individuals to monitor the actions of their government (e.g., televised broadcasts of proceedings of governmental agencies such as Congress and the courts, public officials' press conferences) and communicate their concerns and positions on current issues (e.g., letters to the editor, talk shows, "op-ed pages," public opinion polls) ^{BD (CE,69;QI,538-539)}

Level IV (Grades 9-12)

- Understands how political institutions and political parties shape the public agenda ^{BD (CE,118)}

- Understands why issues important to some groups and the nation do not become part of the public agenda ^{BD (CE,118;QI,641)}

- Understands the concept of public opinion, and knows alternative views of the proper role of public opinion in a democracy ^{BD (CE,118;QE,569)}

- Understands how public opinion is measured, used in public debate, and how it can be influenced by the government and the media ^{BD (CE,118;QI,570-571)}

- Understands the influence that public opinion has on public policy and the behavior of public ^{BD (CE,118;QE,568-570)}

Codes (right side of page):	BD = Benchmark, Declarative; BP = Benchmark, Procedural; BC = Benchmark, Contextual	
1st letter of each code in parentheses	*2nd letter of code*	*Number*
C = CCE: National Standards for Civics	E = Explicitly stated in document	Page number of cited document
A1 = LFS: Authority, I (elementary)	I = Implied in document	*or, for duplicates,*
J1 = LFS: Justice, I (elementary)		Standard number & level of duplicate
P1, P2 = LFS: Privacy, I & II (elementary)		
Q = Quigley: Civitas		
R1 = LFS: Responsibility, I (elementary)	469	

MREL

officials

BD (CE,118;QE,645-646)
- Understands the ways in which television, radio, the press, newsletters, and emerging means of communication influence American politics; and understands the extent to which various traditional forms of political persuasion have been replaced by electronic media

BD (CE,119)
- Knows how to use criteria such as logical validity, factual accuracy, emotional appeal, distorted evidence, and appeals to bias or prejudice in order to evaluate various forms of historical and contemporary political communication (e.g., Lincoln's "House Divided," Sojourner Truth's "Ain't I a Woman?," Chief Joseph's "I Shall Fight No More Forever," Martin Luther King, Jr.'s "I Have a Dream," campaign advertisements, political cartoons)

(CE,119)
20. Understands the roles of political parties, campaigns, elections, and associations and groups in American politics

Level I (Grades K-2)

BD (CE,69)
- Not appropriate for this level

Level II (Grades 3-4)

BD (CE,69)
- Not appropriate for this level

Level III (Grades 5-8)

BD (CE,69;QE,486-487,502)
- Understands the role of political parties

BD (CE,69;QI,486-487)
- Knows the various kinds of elections (e.g., primary and general, local and state, congressional, presidential, recall)

BD (CE,69;QE,486-487)
- Understands the ways in which individuals can participate in political parties, campaigns, and elections

BD (CE,69;QI,503)
- Understands the historical and contemporary roles of prominent associations and groups in local, state, and national politics (e.g., historical associations such as abolitionists, suffragists, labor unions, civil rights groups; religious organizations and contemporary

Codes (right side of page): BD = Benchmark, Declarative; BP = Benchmark, Procedural; BC = Benchmark, Contextual
1st letter of each code in parentheses *2nd letter of code* *Number*
C = CCE: National Standards for Civics E = Explicitly stated in document Page number of cited document
A1 = LFS: Authority, I (elementary) I = Implied in document *or, for duplicates,*
J1 = LFS: Justice, I (elementary) Standard number & level of duplicate
P1, P2 = LFS: Privacy, I & II (elementary)
Q = Quigley: Civitas
R1 = LFS: Responsibility, I (elementary) 470 McREL

associations such as AFL-CIO, National Education Association, Common Cause, League of Women Voters, Greenpeace, National Association for the Advancement of Colored People)

BD (CE,69;QE,503)
- Knows how and why Americans become members of associations and groups, and understands how membership in these associations provides individuals with opportunities to participate in the political process.

Level IV (Grades 9-12)

BD (CE,119;QI,488-489,496-497)
- Knows the origins and development of the two party system in the United States, and understands the role of third parties

BD (CE,119)
- Understands how and why American political parties differ from ideological parties in other countries

BD (CE,119;QI,487)
- Knows the major characteristics of American political parties, how they vary by locality, how they reflect the dispersion of power, and how they provide citizens with numerous opportunities for participation

BD (CE,119;QE,487,497-498)
- Understands how political parties are involved in channeling public opinion, allowing people to act jointly, nominating candidates, conducting campaigns, and training future leaders; and understands why political parties in the United States are weaker today than they have been at times in the past

BD (CE,119)
- Knows the characteristics of initiatives and referendums

BD (CE,119;QE,486-487)
- Understands the significance of campaigns and elections in the American political system, and knows current criticisms of campaigns and proposals for their reform

BD (CE,120)
- Knows historical and contemporary examples of associations and groups performing functions otherwise performed by the government such as social welfare and education

BD (CE,120;QE,503)
- Understands the extent to which associations and groups enhance citizen participation in American political life

---

Codes (right side of page):   BD = Benchmark, Declarative; BP = Benchmark, Procedural; BC = Benchmark, Contextual
1st letter of each code in parentheses   *2nd letter of code*   *Number*
C = CCE: National Standards for Civics   E = Explicitly stated in document   Page number of cited document
A1 = LFS: Authority, I (elementary)   I = Implied in document   *or, for duplicates,*
J1 = LFS: Justice, I (elementary)   Standard number & level of duplicate
P1, P2 = LFS: Privacy, I & II (elementary)
Q = Quigley: Civitas
R1 = LFS: Responsibility, I (elementary)   471   McREL

21. Understands the formation and implementation of public policy

(CE,120)

Level I (Grades K-2)

- Not appropriate for this level

BD (CE,70)

Level II (Grades 3-4)

- Not appropriate for this level

BD (CE,70)

Level III (Grades 5-8)

BD (CE,70;QE,638-639)
- Understands what public policy is and knows examples at local, state, and national levels

BD (CE,70;QE,638-639)
- Knows how public policies are formed and implemented, and understands how citizens can monitor and influence policies

BD (CE,70;QE,640-641)
- Understands why conflicts about values, principles, and interests may make agreement difficult or impossible on certain issues of public policy (e.g., affirmative action, gun control, environmental protection, capital punishment, equal rights)

Level IV (Grades 9-12)

BD (CE,120)
- Knows a public policy issue at the local, state, or national level well enough to identify the major groups interested in that issue and explain their respective positions

BD (CE,120;QE,638-639)
- Understands the processes by which public policy concerning a local, state, or national issue is formed and carried out

BD (CE,120;QE,638-639)
- Knows the points at which citizens can monitor or influence the process of public policy formation

BD (CE,120;QI,640-641)
- Understands why agreement may be difficult or impossible on issues such as abortion because of conflicts about values, principles, and interests

Codes (right side of page):   BD = Benchmark, Declarative; BP = Benchmark, Procedural; BC = Benchmark, Contextual
1st letter of each code in parentheses   *2nd letter of code*   *Number*
C = CCE: National Standards for Civics   E = Explicitly stated in document   Page number of cited document
A1 = LFS: Authority, I (elementary)   I = Implied in document   *or, for duplicates,*
J1 = LFS: Justice, I (elementary)   Standard number & level of duplicate
P1, P2 = LFS: Privacy, I & II (elementary)
Q = Quigley: Civitas
R1 = LFS: Responsibility, I (elementary)   472   MREL

22. Understands how the world is organized politically into nation-states, how nation-states interact with one another, and issues surrounding U.S. foreign policy

(CE,121-123)

Level I (Grades K-2)

- No material specifically designated for this level

BD (CE,33)

Level II (Grades K-4)

- Knows that the world is divided into many different nations with each one having its own government, and knows that a nation consists of its territory, people, laws, and government

BD (CE,33;QE,279-280)

- Knows that the United States is one nation and that it interacts with every other nation in the world

BD (CE,33;QE,278-279)

- Knows the major ways nations interact with each other such as trade, diplomacy, cultural contacts, treaties or agreements, and use of military force

BD (CE,34;QI,280-282)

- Understands why it is important for nations to try to resolve problems peacefully (e.g., people's standard of living will improve due to increased trade, people's health will improve due to the exchange of medical and scientific knowledge)

BD (CE,34)

Level III (Grades 5-8)

- Knows that the world is divided into nation-states that claim sovereignty over a defined territory and jurisdiction over everyone within it, and understands why the nation-state is the most powerful form of political organization at the international level

BD (CE,71;QE,279-280)

- Knows the most important means used by nation-states to interact with one another (e.g., trade, diplomacy, treaties and agreements, humanitarian aid, economic incentives and sanctions, military force and the threat of force)

BD (CE,71;QI,280-282)

- Knows reasons for the breakdown of order among nation-states (e.g., conflicts about national interests, ethnicity, and religion; competition for resources and territory; absence of effective means to enforce international law), and understands the consequences of the breakdown of order among nation-states

BD (CE,72;QI,280-282)

Codes (right side of page):   BD = Benchmark, Declarative; BP = Benchmark, Procedural; BC = Benchmark, Contextual
1st letter of each code in parentheses   *2nd letter of code*   *Number*
C = CCE: National Standards for Civics   E = Explicitly stated in document   Page number of cited document
A1 = LFS: Authority, I (elementary)   I = Implied in document   *or, for duplicates,*
J1 = LFS: Justice, I (elementary)   Standard number & level of duplicate
P1, P2 = LFS: Privacy, I & II (elementary)
Q = Quigley: Civitas
R1 = LFS: Responsibility, I (elementary)   473   MREL

- Knows the most important powers the United States Constitution gives to the Congress, president, and federal judiciary in foreign affairs (e.g., Congress can declare war, raise and support armies, provide a navy [Article I, Section 8] and the Senate can approve treaties; the president is Commander in Chief and can make treaties and appoint ambassadors [Article II]; the federal judiciary can decide cases affecting treaties and ambassadors, and those involving treason [Article III]) ^BD (CE,72;QE,328)

- Knows various means used to attain the ends of United States foreign policy (e.g., diplomacy; economic, military, and humanitarian aid; treaties; trade agreements; incentives; sanctions; military intervention; covert action) ^BD (CE,72;QI,280-282)

- Knows examples of important current foreign policy issues and the means the United States is using to deal with them ^BD (CE,72)

- Knows the purposes and functions of major governmental international organizations (e.g., UN, NATO, OAS, World Court) and nongovernmental international organizations (e.g., International Red Cross, World Council of Churches, Amnesty International) ^BD (CE,72;QI,300)

Level IV (Grades 9-12)

- Understands the significance of principal foreign policies and events in the United States' relations with the world (e.g., Monroe Doctrine, World Wars I and II, formation of the United Nations, Marshall Plan, NATO, Korean and Vietnam Wars, end of the Cold War) ^BD (CE,122;QI,300)

- Understands how and why the United States assumed the role of world leader after World War II and what its current leadership role is in the world ^BD (CE,123)

- Understands the major foreign policy positions that have characterized the United States' relations with the world (e.g., isolated nation, imperial power, and world leader) ^BD (CE,123;QE,278-279)

- Knows how the powers over foreign affairs that the Constitution gives to the president, Congress, and the federal judiciary have been used over time; and understands the tension between constitutional provisions and the requirements of foreign policy (e.g., the power of Congress to declare war and the need of the president to make expeditious decisions in times of international emergency, the power of the president to make treaties and the need for the Senate to approve them) ^BD (CE,123;QI,328)

- Understands the process by which United States foreign policy is made, including the roles ^BD (CE,123;QE,328-330)

Codes (right side of page):
1st letter of each code in parentheses
C = CCE: National Standards for Civics
A1 = LFS: Authority, I (elementary)
J1 = LFS: Justice, I (elementary)
P1, P2 = LFS: Privacy, I & II (elementary)
Q = Quigley: Civitas
R1 = LFS: Responsibility, I (elementary)

BD = Benchmark, Declarative; BP = Benchmark, Procedural; BC = Benchmark, Contextual
2nd letter of code
E = Explicitly stated in document
I = Implied in document

Number
Page number of cited document
or, for duplicates,
Standard number & level of duplicate

474

M⁄REL

of federal agencies, domestic interest groups, the media, and the public; and knows the ways in which Americans can influence foreign policy

BD (CE,123)

- Understands how and why domestic politics may impose constraints or obligations on the ways in which the United States acts in the world (e.g., long-standing commitments to certain nations, lobbying efforts of domestic groups, economic needs)

BD (CE,123;QI,278-279)

- Understands the idea of the national interest and how it is used as a criterion for shaping American foreign policy

BD (CE,123)

- Understands the influence of American constitutional values and principles on American foreign policy (e.g., a commitment to the self-determination of nations), and understands the tensions that might arise among American values, principles, and interests as the nation deals with the practical requirements of international politics (e.g., a commitment to human rights and the requirements of national security)

BD (CE,123;QI,288)

- Understands the current role of the United States in peacemaking and peacekeeping

BD (CE,122)

- Understands the purposes and functions of major governmental international organizations such as the Organization of American States and major nongovernmental international organizations such as the Roman Catholic Church and multinational corporations

BD (CE,126;QI,300)

- Understands the role of the United States in establishing and maintaining principal international organizations (e.g., UN, UNICEF, GATT, NATO, OAS, World Bank, International Monetary Fund)

BD (CE,126)

- Knows some important bilateral and multilateral agreements to which the United States is signatory (e.g., NAFTA, Helsinki Accord, Antarctic Treaty, Most Favored Nation Agreements)

(CE,123-125)

23. Understands the impact of significant political and nonpolitical developments on the United States and other nations

Level I (Grades K-2)

BD (CE,73)

- Not appropriate for this level

Codes (right side of page):	BD = Benchmark, Declarative; BP = Benchmark, Procedural; BC = Benchmark, Contextual	
1st letter of each code in parentheses	*2nd letter of code*	*Number*
C = CCE: National Standards for Civics	E = Explicitly stated in document	Page number of cited document
A1 = LFS: Authority, I (elementary)	I = Implied in document	*or, for duplicates,*
J1 = LFS: Justice, I (elementary)		Standard number & level of duplicate
P1, P2 = LFS: Privacy, I & II (elementary)		
Q = Quigley: Civitas		
R1 = LFS: Responsibility, I (elementary)	475	MREL

Level II (Grades 3-4)

BD (CE,73)

- Not appropriate for this level

Level III (Grades 5-8)

BD (CE,73;QI,133-134)

- Understands the impact that the American Revolution and the values and principles expressed in the Declaration of Independence, the United States Constitution, and the Bill of Rights has had on other nations

BD (CE,73;QI,134)

- Understands the influence that American ideas about rights have had on other nations and international organizations (e.g., French Revolution; democracy movements in Eastern Europe, People's Republic of China, Latin America, South Africa; United Nations Charter; Universal Declaration of Human Rights)

BD (CE,73;QI,612)

- Understands the impact that other nations' ideas about rights have had on the United States (e.g., natural rights in the seventeenth and eighteenth centuries, social and economic rights in the twentieth century)

BD (CE,73)

- Understands the impact that current political developments around the world have on the United States (e.g., conflicts within and among other nations, efforts to establish democratic governments)

BD (CE,73;QI,251-252)

- Understands the impact of major demographic trends on the United States (e.g., population growth, increase in immigration and refugees)

BD (CE,73;QI,520)

- Knows examples of environmental conditions that affect the United States' domestic and foreign policies (e.g., destruction of rain forests and animal habitats, depletion of fishing grounds, air and water pollution)

Level IV (Grades 9-12)

BD (CE,124)

- Understands the influence that American ideas about rights have had abroad and how other peoples' ideas about rights have influenced Americans

BD (CE,125)

- Understands the effects that significant world political developments have on the United States (e.g., the French, Russian, and Chinese Revolutions; rise of nationalism; World Wars I and II; decline of colonialism; terrorism; multiplication of nation-states and the

Codes (right side of page): BD = Benchmark, Declarative; BP = Benchmark, Procedural; BC = Benchmark, Contextual
1st letter of each code in parentheses *2nd letter of code* *Number*
C = CCE: National Standards for Civics E = Explicitly stated in document Page number of cited document
A1 = LFS: Authority, I (elementary) I = Implied in document *or, for duplicates,*
J1 = LFS: Justice, I (elementary) Standard number & level of duplicate
P1, P2 = LFS: Privacy, I & II (elementary)
Q = Quigley: Civitas
R1 = LFS: Responsibility, I (elementary) 476 MREL

Level IV (Grades 9-12)

- Knows various ways students can exercise leadership in public affairs, and knows ^{BD (CE,136)} opportunities for citizens to engage in careers in public service

- Understands why becoming knowledgeable about public affairs and the values and principles ^{BD (CE,137;QE,43;DE,28.3.6,29.3.7)} of American constitutional democracy, and communicating that knowledge to others are important forms of participation, and understands the argument that constitutional democracy requires the participation of an attentive, knowledgeable, and competent citizenry

- Understands how awareness of the nature of American constitutional change gives citizens ^{BD (CE,137;DE,29.3.8.)} the ability to reaffirm or change fundamental constitutional values

Codes (right side of page):   BD = Benchmark, Declarative; BP = Benchmark, Procedural; BC = Benchmark, Contextual
1st letter of each code in parentheses   *2nd letter of code*   *Number*
C = CCE: National Standards for Civics   E = Explicitly stated in document   Page number of cited document
A1 = LFS: Authority, I (elementary)   I = Implied in document   *or, for duplicates,*
J1 = LFS: Justice, I (elementary)   Standard number & level of duplicate
P1, P2 = LFS: Privacy, I & II (elementary)
Q = Quigley: Civitas
R1 = LFS: Responsibility, I (elementary)   489   MREL

14. Economics

The following process was used to identify standards and benchmarks in the field of economics:

Identification of National Reports

Four reports were selected to assist in the identification of standards and benchmarks in economics. Two of the reports consulted were published by the National Council on Economic Education (NCEE): *Economics, What and When: Scope and Sequence Guidelines, K–12* (Gilliard et al., 1989); and *A Framework for Teaching Basic Economic Concepts with Scope and Sequence Guidelines, K–12* (Saunders & Gilliard, 1995); one report was authored by the Colorado Council on Economic Education, *Conceptual Content Standards: Grades K–12* (1994); another by the National Council for the Social Studies' *Expectations of Excellence: Curriculum Standards for Social Studies* (1994).

Selection of the Reference Document

While there are economic standards in draft from the National Council on Economic Education (see Section 2), the material currently available does not present information organized by grade level. In addition, the content of the drafts appears to be very close, if not otherwise identical, to related curriculum material from the Council on Economic Education. For this reason, the document selected as the principle reference for the identification of standards was *A Framework for Teaching Basic Economic Concepts*. This recently published work is written "to enable students, by the time they graduate from high school, to understand enough economics to make reasoned judgements about both personal economic questions and broader questions of economic policy in a complex and changing world" (p. 3).

Identification of Standards and Benchmarks

We found the *Framework* useful for identifying benchmarks. Important concepts and generalizations in economics are organized by the grade levels at which they should be introduced and developed within the curriculum. The source material is written such that the smallest organizational unit, the content statement, is written at a level of generality that is equivalent to our benchmark. Thus, it was not difficult to determine what information should comprise a benchmark.

In some respects the reference document was not entirely compatible with our model for standards identification. First, the document includes challenging material designed for a capstone course in economics. Since our model calls for literacy rather than expertise in the subject areas, such standards material was not included in our analysis. Next, there were differences in organization. The reference document arranges content statements under 21 topic areas, which we found somewhat too narrow in scope to be useful as standards for organizing benchmark information articulated across grades K–12. Inasmuch as we consider the benchmark (as well as the grade sequence of benchmarks) to provide critical subject information, but view the organization of benchmarks into standards as arbitrary to some degree (see Section 3), we elected to consolidate some material under slightly larger ideas in order to provide a more even distribution of benchmarks across standards. This reorganization was done through consulting the supplementary documents (see below). Finally, there were differences between the reference document and our model in the grade ranges provided. The reference document provides content information at three levels of schooling, K–4, 5–8, and 9–12; we prefer four: primary, upper elementary, middle, and high school. We were able to provide benchmarks at all four levels through the use of the supplementary material discussed below.

Integration of Information from Other Documents

Material from NCEE, *Economics, What and When: Scope and Sequence Guidelines, K–12*, was useful for constructing benchmarks at the four levels our model adopts (primary, elementary, middle, and high school), since the document presents content material at two-grade increments from K–1 through grades 11–12. The document also was found useful for the examples it provided to help clarify content statements. Additionally, each statement of content in *Scope and Sequence* is accompanied by "student language" — a version of the concept or generalization written in terms more accessible to students at the targeted grade levels. This language provided us with the means for composing benchmarks that were still accurate if somewhat less technical. Draft material from the Colorado Council for Economic Education (CCE) also provided guidance in writing benchmark statements. The CCE draft was found useful for the organization of benchmark statements into standards as well; some seven of our ten standards are closely modeled on that document. As is the case with all our supplementary documents, benchmarks include page number citations to the CCE document wherever similar content material has been identified.

In order to provide users of the National Council for the Social Studies' *Expectations of Excellence: Curriculum Standards for Social Studies* with a pointer to content information in economics, that document is cited at the benchmark level wherever appropriate. Additionally, these citations, along with those from the CCE draft might prove useful to those who desire some additional criteria for selecting a subset of benchmarks from the economics standards.

Summary of Standards for Economics

1. Understands that scarcity of productive resources requires choices which generate opportunity costs
2. Understands characteristics of different economic systems, economic institutions, and economic incentives
3. Understands the concept of prices and the interaction of supply and demand in a market economy
4. Understands basic features of market structures and exchanges
5. Understands unemployment and income distribution in a market economy
6. Understands the roles government plays in the United States economy
7. Understands aggregate supply and aggregate demand
8. Understands basic concepts of United States fiscal policy and monetary policy
9. Understands how Gross Domestic Product and inflation and deflation provide indications of the state of the economy
10. Understands basic concepts about international economics

1. Understands that scarcity of productive resources requires choices that generate opportunity costs

Level I (Grades K-2)

- Knows that goods are objects that can satisfy people's wants, and services are activities that can satisfy people's wants
BD (EE,78;CE,3;JE,15;SI,41)

- Understands that since people cannot have everything they want, they must make choices about using goods and services to satisfy wants
BD (EE,78;CE,3;JE,15;SE,41)

- Knows that people who use goods and services are called consumers, and people who make goods or provide services are called producers
BD (EE,78;CE,4;JE,15;SI,41)

- Knows that natural resources are "gifts of nature" because they are present without human intervention
BD (EE,78;CE,3;JE,15;SI,41)

- Knows that capital resources are things made by people that are used to make other goods or to provide services
BD (EE,78;CE,3;JE,15;SI,41)

- Knows that human resources (i.e., labor or human capital) are the efforts of people who work to produce goods and to provide services
BD (EE,78;CE,3;JE,15;SI,41)

- Understands that most people work in jobs where they produce a few special goods or services
BD (EE,78;JE,17;SE,41)

- Knows that opportunity cost is what someone gives up in order to get something, and that when someone chooses to buy a good or service, there is always an opportunity cost
BD (EE,78;CE,3;JE,18;SE,41)

Level II (Grades 3-5)

- Knows that productive resources are all natural resources, human resources, and capital resources used to produce goods and to provide services
BD (EE,78;CI,3;JE,15;SI,41)

- Understands that goods and services are scarce because there are not enough productive resources to satisfy all of the wants of individuals, governments, and societies
BD (EE,92;CI,3;JE,16;SE,41)

- Understands that federal, state, and local governments have problems of scarcity also; because they have limited budgets, they must compare their revenues to the costs of public
BD (EE,92;CI,3,4;JE,16;SI,41)

Codes (right side of page): BD = Benchmark, Declarative; BP = Benchmark, Procedural; BC = Benchmark, Contextual
1st letter of each code in parentheses *2nd letter of code* *Number*
E = NCEE: Framework for Economics E = Explicitly stated in document Page number of cited document
C = Colorado Council on Economic Education I = Implied in document
J = JCEE: Economics, What and When
S = NCSS: Curriculum Standards for Social Studies 494 MREL

projects their citizens want

- Knows that entrepreneurs are people who use resources to produce goods and services they hope people will buy
  BD (EE,92;CE,3;JE,16;SI,41)

- Understands that entrepreneurs take the risk that people won't buy their products or won't pay enough for them to cover the entrepreneurs' costs
  BD (EE,92;CE,3;JE,16;SI,41)

- Understands that when productive resources are used to produce one good or service, the opportunity cost is other goods and services that would have been made with the same resources if the chosen good or service had not been made
  BD (EE,78;CE,3;JE,17;SI,41)

- Understands that choices usually involve trade-offs; people can give up buying or doing a little of one thing in order to buy or do a little of something else
  BD (EE,92;CE,3;JE,17;SI,41)

- Knows that economic specialization occurs when people produce a narrower range of goods and services than they consume
  BD (EE,78;JE,18;SI,41)

- Understands that specialization usually lowers costs and increases the amount of goods and services produced
  BD (EE,78;JE,18;SE,41)

Level III (Grades 6-8)

- Understands that scarcity of resources necessitates choice at both the personal and the societal levels
  BD (EE,92;CE,3;JE,16;SE,41)

- Knows that all decisions involve opportunity costs and that effective economic decision making involves weighing the costs and benefits associated with alternative choices
  BD (EE,92;CE,4;JE,17;SI,41)

- Knows that productivity can be measured as output per worker, per hour, per machine, or per unit of land
  BD (EE,92;CE,4;JE,18;SI,41)

- Understands how specialization, division of labor, and more capital goods such as tools and machines usually increase labor productivity
  BD (EE,92;CE,4;JE,18;SI,41)

Level IV (Grades 9-12)

- Understands that the quality of labor resources (i.e., human capital) can be improved through investments in education, training, and health care
  BD (EE,92;CE,4;JE,16;SI,41)

Codes (right side of page):   BD = Benchmark, Declarative; BP = Benchmark, Procedural; BC = Benchmark, Contextual
1st letter of each code in parentheses   *2nd letter of code*   *Number*
E = NCEE: Framework for Economics   E = Explicitly stated in document   Page number of cited document
C = Colorado Council on Economic Education   I = Implied in document
J = JCEE: Economics, What and When
S = NCSS: Curriculum Standards for Social Studies   McREL

- Understands that technological change depends heavily on incentives to reward innovation and on investments in capital, research, and development

  BD (EE,121;JE,19;SI,41)

- Understands that productive resources used to produce capital cannot be used to make consumer goods and services, and that this is the trade-off for higher expected productivity in the future

  BD (EE,92;CI,4;JE,18;SI,41)

- Understands that technological change and investments in capital goods and human capital may increase labor productivity but have significant opportunity costs and economic risks

  BD (EE,92,121;CE,4;JE,19;SI,41)

- Understands that increasing labor productivity is the major way in which a nation can improve the standard of living of its people

  BD (EE,121;CI,4;JE,19;SI,41)

(EE,14-17)

2. Understands characteristics of different economic systems, economic institutions, and economic incentives

Level I (Grades K-2)

- Not appropriate for this level

  BD (EE,62)

Level II (Grades 3-5)

- Knows that the United States economy is organized around a system in which prices for most goods and services are established by buyers and sellers making exchanges in private markets

  BD (EE,78;JE,19;SI,41)

- Understands that the hope of earning profit (i.e., the difference between revenues and the costs of producing or selling a good or service) is the incentive that persuades entrepreneurs and business firms to take the risks of producing goods and services to sell

  BD (EE,79,93;CI,6;JE,21;SI,41)

- Knows that profit-seeking firms are the basic production units in a market economy; successful business firms earn profits, while unsuccessful firms suffer losses

  BD (EE,79,93;CE,5;JE,21;SI,41)

- Knows that households (i.e., individuals or family units), as consumers, buy goods and services from business firms

  BD (EE,79,93;CE,5;JE,21;SI,41)

- Knows that households, as resource owners, sell productive resources (e.g., labor, natural resources, capital resources, entrepreneurial resources) to firms in order to earn income

  BD (EE,79,93;CE,5;JE,21;SI,41)

Codes (right side of page): BD = Benchmark, Declarative; BP = Benchmark, Procedural; BC = Benchmark, Contextual
1st letter of each code in parentheses *2nd letter of code* *Number*
E = NCEE: Framework for Economics E = Explicitly stated in document Page number of cited document
C = Colorado Council on Economic Education I = Implied in document
J = JCEE: Economics, What and When
S = NCSS: Curriculum Standards for Social Studies

McREL

BD (EE,94;CE,6;JE,26;SE,41)

- Understands that relative prices and how they affect people's decisions are the means by which a market system provides answers to the basic economic questions: What goods and services will be produced? How will they be produced? Who will buy them?

BD (EE,94;CE,6-7;JE,26)

- Understands that the circular flow model shows that businesses get money from households in exchange for goods and services and return that money to households by paying for the factors of production that households have to sell

BD (EE,94;CI,6;JE,27;SE,41)

- Understands that market prices are set by forces of supply and demand and are measures of the relative scarcity of different products

BD (EE,94;JE,28;SI,41)

- Understands that the price of any one product is influenced by and also influences the prices of many other products

BD (EE,94;JE,27,28;SI,41)

- Knows that demand shows the relationship between different prices for a product and how much of it people will be willing to buy at each price, and that supply shows the relationship between different prices for a product and how much of it producers will offer for sale at each price

BD (EE,94;JE,28)

- Knows that market demand reflects the demand of all individual consumers in a market, and market supply reflects the supply of all individual producers in a market

Level IV (Grades 9-12)

BD (EE,122;CI,6;JE,27;SI,41)

- Understands that in a market system prices provide information to consumers and producers, which encourages the efficient production and allocation of the goods and services consumers demand

BD (EE,122;JE,28;SI,41)

- Understands that the demand curve shows an inverse, or negative, relationship between price and quantity demanded because of the income and substitution effects (i.e., when the prices of goods and services go up and income does not, in real terms the consumers are poorer and buy less; consumers also buy less when prices rise because they are able to use other goods and services that have become relatively cheaper to satisfy the same general wants)

BD (EE,122;CE,6;JE,28;SI,41)

- Understands that the demand for a product will normally change (i.e., the demand curve will shift) if there is a change in consumers' incomes, tastes, and preferences, or a change in the prices of related (i.e., complementary or substitute) products

BD (EE,122;JE,29;SI,41)

- Understands that the law of diminishing returns states that when more variable factors of

---

Codes (right side of page):   BD = Benchmark, Declarative;   BP = Benchmark, Procedural;   BC = Benchmark, Contextual
1st letter of each code in parentheses   *2nd letter of code*   *Number*
E = NCEE: Framework for Economics   E = Explicitly stated in document   Page number of cited document
C = Colorado Council on Economic Education   I = Implied in document
J = JCEE: Economics, What and When
S = NCSS: Curriculum Standards for Social Studies   499   MCREL

production are added to a fixed factor of production, at some point the number of additional products resulting from each added variable factor will begin to decrease, thus increasing the average cost of all units of the product

- Understands that the supply curve shows a direct, or positive, relationship between price and quantity supplied in the short run (i.e., a period of time in which at least one factor of production, usually capital or land, cannot be changed, although the amount of other, variable factors of production can be changed), but that this relationship is limited by the law of diminishing returns
BD (EE,122;JE,29;SI,41)

- Understands that the supply of a product will normally change (i.e., the supply curve will shift) if there is a change in technology, in prices of inputs, or in the prices of other products that could be made and sold by producers
BD (EE,122;CE,6;JE,29;SI,41)

- Understands that shortages or surpluses usually result in price changes for products in a market economy
BD (EE,122;JE,30;SI,41)

- Understands that when price controls are enforced, shortages and surpluses occur and create long-run allocation problems in the economy
BD (EE,122;JE,30;SI,41)

- Understands that in the long run all inputs (i.e., factors of production), including those that are fixed in the short run, can be changed
BD (EE,122;JE,29;SI,41)

4. Understands basic features of market structures and exchanges   (EE,22-23,24-26)

Level I (Grades K-2)

- Knows that markets are where buyers and sellers establish prices for identical or very similar products
BD (EE,79;CE,5;JE,31;SI,41-42)

- Understands that in an exchange people trade goods and services for other goods and services or for money
BD (EE,79;CI,6;JE,23;SI,41)

- Knows that money is a good that can be used to buy all other goods and services
BD (EE,79;CE,6;JE,23;SE,41)

- Understands that when two people trade because they want to, they expect to be better off after the exchange
BD (EE,79;CE,6;JE,24;SI,42)

- Knows that barter is trading goods and services for other goods and services without using
BD (EE,79;CE,6;JE,24;SI,42)

Codes (right side of page):   BD = Benchmark, Declarative; BP = Benchmark, Procedural; BC = Benchmark, Contextual
1st letter of each code in parentheses   *2nd letter of code*   *Number*
E = NCEE: Framework for Economics   E = Explicitly stated in document   Page number of cited document
C = Colorado Council on Economic Education   I = Implied in document
J = JCEE: Economics, What and When
S = NCSS: Curriculum Standards for Social Studies   500

MᴙREL

money

Level II (Grades 3-5)

- BD (EE,94;CI,5,6;JE,31;SI,41-42)

  Knows that competitive markets are those with many buyers and sellers, where no one person or firm controls prices or the number of products for sale

- BD (EE,79;CI,6;JE,24;SI,41)

  Understands that exchanges made through barter face problems of divisibility, portability, storage, and the "double coincidence of wants" (i.e., a person who wants to trade a good or service must find another person who wants that good or service and also has something to trade that the first person wants)

- BD (EE,79;CI,6;JE,24;SE,41)

  Understands that money reduces the problems barter faces because money is easy to divide, carry, and store

- BD (EE,79;CE,6;JE,25;SE,41)

  Knows that banks play a key role in providing currency and other forms of money to consumers, and that banks serve as intermediaries between savers and borrowers

- BD (EE,79;CE,9;JE,25;SE,41)

  Understands that when people and nations specialize, they become more interdependent (i.e., less self-sufficient and more dependent on exchange)

- BD (EE,93;CI,6;JE,24;SE,41)

  Understands that money makes it easier to compare the value of different kinds of goods and services and allows people to save purchasing power for a later time because it can easily be traded for goods and services at any time

- BD (EE,93;CE,6;JE,24;SI,41)

  Knows that the basic money supply is usually measured as the total value of coins, currency, and checks held by the public

Level III (Grades 6-8)

- BD (EE,94;CE,6;JE,31;SI,41)

  Knows that an industry is made up of all the producers of identical or very similar products in a market area, and that a monopoly exists when only one producer sells a product that has no close substitutes

- BD (EE,94;CI,6;JE,31;SI,41)

  Understands how active competition among sellers results in lower prices and profit levels

- BD (EE,94;CI,6;JE,32;SI,41)

  Understands that not all competition is on the basis of price for identical products and that nonprice competition includes style and quality differences, advertising, customer services, and credit policies

---

Codes (right side of page):	BD = Benchmark, Declarative; BP = Benchmark, Procedural; BC = Benchmark, Contextual	
1st letter of each code in parentheses	*2nd letter of code*	*Number*
E = NCEE: Framework for Economics	E = Explicitly stated in document	Page number of cited document
C = Colorado Council on Economic Education	I = Implied in document	
J = JCEE: Economics, What and When		
S = NCSS: Curriculum Standards for Social Studies	501	MREL

- Understands how competition among buyers of a product results in higher prices for the product
  BD (EE,94;CI,6;JE,31;SI,41)

- Understands that money encourages people to specialize because they can operate more efficiently in an exchange (i.e., sell what they produce to anyone, not just to someone who has something they want)
  BD (EE,93;CE,6;JE,25;SE,41)

- Understands that the extent of the market for different goods and services limits the degree to which workers and producers can specialize
  BD (EE,93;JE,25;SE,41)

- Understands that in a situation of interdependence, decisions or events in one part of the world or in one part of the economy also affect the trading partners of those areas
  BD (EE,93;CI,9;JE,25;SI,42)

Level IV (Grades 9-12)

- Knows that collusion among buyers or sellers reduces the level of competition in a market and is more difficult in markets with large numbers of buyers and sellers
  BD (EE,123;CI,6;JE,32;SI,41)

- Knows that cartels are explicit forms of collusion concerned with product price, output, service, or sales
  BD (EE,123;CI,6;JE,32;SI,41)

- Understands that the United States government uses laws and regulations to maintain competition, but sometimes the government reduces competition unintentionally or in response to special interest groups
  BD (EE,123;CE,8;JE,32;SE,41)

- Understands that in the long run the level of competition in an industry is determined largely by how difficult and expensive it is for new firms to enter the market
  BD (EE,123;JE,32;SI,41)

- Understands that externalities are unintended positive or negative side effects that result when the production or consumption of a good or service affects the welfare of people who are not the parties directly involved in the market exchange (e.g., a negative externality in consumption occurs when cigarette smoking by one individual has harmful or undesirable effects on nonsmokers, a positive externality in production occurs when a neighbor's home improvements increase the value of nearby properties)
  BD (EE,95;JE,35;SI,41)

- Understands that a natural monopoly exists when it is cheaper for one supplier to produce all of the output in a market than for two or more producers to share the output (e.g., electric companies)
  BD (EE,95;CI,6;JE,36;SI,41)

Codes (right side of page):	BD = Benchmark, Declarative; BP = Benchmark, Procedural; BC = Benchmark, Contextual	
1st letter of each code in parentheses	*2nd letter of code*	*Number*
E = NCEE: Framework for Economics	E = Explicitly stated in document	Page number of cited document
C = Colorado Council on Economic Education	I = Implied in document	
J = JCEE: Economics, What and When		
S = NCSS: Curriculum Standards for Social Studies	502	

MREL

- Understands how relationships between aggregate demand and potential aggregate supply affect unemployment or inflation

  BD (EE,125;JE,41)

- Knows that when aggregate demand is equal to aggregate supply at a level that just employs all available productive resources with no change in the overall price level, the economy is at a full-employment, noninflationary equilibrium

  BD (EE,125;JE,42)

- Understands that when aggregate demand is not enough to buy all good and services that are produced (i.e., when aggregate demand falls below the full-employment level of aggregate supply), business firms will reduce production, aggregate supply will decline, and workers will become unemployed in the short run (i.e., cyclical unemployment)

  BD (EE,125;JE,42)

- Understands that when aggregate demand is greater than the amount of goods and services that the economy is capable of producing (i.e., aggregate demand rises above the full-employment level of aggregate supply), costs rise as business firms compete for productive resources, and prices rise in the short run (i.e., demand-pull inflation)

  BD (EE,125;JE,42)

- Understands how changes in taxing and government spending affect aggregate demand and income

  BD (EE,127;JE,53)

8. Understands basic concepts of United States fiscal policy and monetary policy

(EE,34-35)

Level I (Grades K-2)

- Not appropriate for this level

  BD (EE,62)

Level II (Grades 3-5)

- Not appropriate for this level

  BD (EE,62)

Level III (Grades 6-8)

- Knows that fiscal policy involves the use of national government spending and taxation programs to affect the level of economic activity in order to promote price stability, maximum employment, and reasonable economic growth

  BD (EE,96;CI,8;JE,53)

- Understands the concepts of balanced budget, budget deficit, and budget surplus

  BD (EE,127;CI,8;JE,53)

Codes (right side of page):   BD = Benchmark, Declarative; BP = Benchmark, Procedural; BC = Benchmark, Contextual

1st letter of each code in parentheses   *2nd letter of code*   *Number*

E = NCEE: Framework for Economics   E = Explicitly stated in document   Page number of cited document

C = Colorado Council on Economic Education   I = Implied in document

J = JCEE: Economics, What and When

S = NCSS: Curriculum Standards for Social Studies

MREL

- Understands that when the government runs a budget deficit, it must borrow from individuals, corporations, or financial institutions to finance the excess of expenditures over tax revenues BD (EE,127;JE,53)

- Knows that the national debt is the total amount of money that the government has borrowed over all the years it ran deficits that have not been repaid BD (EE,127;JE,54)

- Knows that the Federal Reserve System is the principal organization that regulates money and banking in the United States BD (EE,127;CE,7;JE,50)

- Knows that monetary policy refers to actions by the Federal Reserve System that lead to changes in the amount of money in circulation and the availability of credit in the financial system BD (EE,127;CE,7;JE,50)

Level IV (Grades 9-12)

- Knows that the United States government may borrow from foreigners and foreign governments to finance its deficits, and that when the United States repays such loans, income is transferred from United States citizens to foreign economies BD (EE,127;JE,54)

- Understands that fiscal policies and monetary policies are often a result of political factors as well as economic factors BD (EE,127;JE,52,54)

- Understands that fiscal policies take time to affect the economy and that they may be reinforced or offset by monetary policies BD (EE,127;JE,54)

- Understands that when banks make loans, the money supply increases, and when loans are paid back, the country's money supply shrinks BD (EE,126;CE,7;JE,50)

- Knows that banks may lend a certain percentage of the money that is deposited with them, but they may not lend over the amount of reserves they are required to keep by the Federal Reserve System BD (EE,126;JE,50)

- Understands that changes in the money supply lead to changes in interest rates and in individual and corporate spending which may influence the levels of spending, employment, prices, and economic growth in the economy BD (EE,126;CE,7;JE,51)

- Understands that monetary policy can cause serious economic problems if it follows an inconsistent pattern in terms of changes in the rate of growth of the money supply BD (EE,127;CE,7;JE,52)

Codes (right side of page):   BD = Benchmark, Declarative; BP = Benchmark, Procedural; BC = Benchmark, Contextual
1st letter of each code in parentheses   *2nd letter of code*   *Number*
E = NCEE: Framework for Economics   E = Explicitly stated in document   Page number of cited document
C = Colorado Council on Economic Education   I = Implied in document
J = JCEE: Economics, What and When
S = NCSS: Curriculum Standards for Social Studies

MCREL

9. **Understands how Gross Domestic Product and inflation and deflation provide indications of the state of the economy**

(EE,29,32-33)

Level I (Grades K-2)

- Not appropriate for this level

BD (EE,62)

Level II (Grades 3-5)

- Not appropriate for this level

BD (EE,62)

Level III (Grades 6-8)

- Knows that inflation refers to a sustained increase in the average price level of the entire economy

BD (EE,96;CE,7;JE,47)

- Knows that deflation refers to a sustained decrease in the average price level of the entire economy

BD (EE,96;CE,7;JE,47)

- Knows that inflation is usually measured by the Consumer Price Index (CPI) which shows the increases or decreases in price level from one year to another

BD (EE,96;CE,7;JE,47)

Level IV (Grades 9-12)

- Knows that Gross Domestic Product (GDP) is the total market value, expressed in dollars, of all final goods and services produced in the economy in a given year and is used as an indicator of the state of the economy

BD (EE,124;CE,4;JE,39)

- Knows the difference between "nominal" GDP (i.e., GDP stated in current dollars where an increase in GDP may reflect not only increases in the production of goods and services, but also increases in general prices) and "real" GDP (i.e., GDP which has been adjusted for price level changes)

BD (EE,124;JE,40)

- Knows the factors upon which a country's GDP depends (e.g., quantity and quality of natural resources, size and skills of labor force, size and quality of capital stock)

BD (EE,124;JE,40)

- Understands that real GDP in the United States and other industrialized nations has grown fairly steadily in modern times, but short-run fluctuations in business activity (i.e., business

BD (EE,124;JE,40)

Codes (right side of page):   BD = Benchmark, Declarative; BP = Benchmark, Procedural; BC = Benchmark, Contextual
1st letter of each code in parentheses   *2nd letter of code*   *Number*
E = NCEE: Framework for Economics   E = Explicitly stated in document   Page number of cited document
C = Colorado Council on Economic Education   I = Implied in document
J = JCEE: Economics, What and When
S = NCSS: Curriculum Standards for Social Studies   509   MREL

cycles) are not smooth or completely predictable

- Understands that a recession occurs when real GDP declines for at least six months
  BD (EE,124;JE,40)

- Understands that governments sometimes attempt to smooth out business cycles by using policies to moderate fluctuations in the growth of real GDP, thus reducing unemployment or inflation
  BD (EE,125;JE,41)

- Understands that the Consumer Price Index (CPI) does not perfectly measure the effects of inflation on individual households
  BD (EE,126;JE,47)

- Understands that inflation creates uncertainty because it affects different groups differently
  BD (EE,126;CE,7;JE,48)

- Knows that demand-pull inflation occurs when total spending rises faster than total production, and may result from expansive monetary or fiscal policies, or from expectations of businesses and consumers that prices will rise in the future
  BD (EE,126;CI,7;JE,48)

- Knows that cost-push inflation occurs when increases in the overall costs of making and selling goods and services raise the price level, and may result from the effects of monopolization in product or factor markets, or from a sudden reduction in the supply of an important product or factor of production
  BD (EE,126;JE,48)

- Knows that there are various policy options available to combat inflation (e.g., monetary and fiscal policies, wage and price controls, antitrust actions, tax incentives, automatic adjustment mechanisms)
  BD (EE,126;JE,48)

- Knows that a country experiencing "stagflation" has both a high unemployment rate and a high inflation rate at the same time
  BD (EE,126;JE,49)

- Understands that government policies designed to reduce unemployment may increase inflation, and vice versa
  BD (EE,126;JE,49)

10. Understands basic concepts about international economics
(EE,35-40)

Level I (Grades K-2)

- Not appropriate for this level
  BD (EE,62)

Codes (right side of page):   BD = Benchmark, Declarative; BP = Benchmark, Procedural; BC = Benchmark, Contextual
1st letter of each code in parentheses   *2nd letter of code*   *Number*
E = NCEE: Framework for Economics   E = Explicitly stated in document   Page number of cited document
C = Colorado Council on Economic Education   I = Implied in document
J = JCEE: Economics, What and When
S = NCSS: Curriculum Standards for Social Studies   510   MREL

Level II (Grades 3-5)

BD (EE,96;CE,3;JE,55;SI,42)
- Understands that nations have different kinds of productive resources, and that some nations have more or higher quality resources than others

Level III (Grades 6-8)

BD (EE,96;CE,8;JE,55;SI,42)
- Knows that international trade is the exchange of goods and services between people and institutions in different nations

BD (EE,96;CE,9;JE,55;SI,42)
- Knows that exports are goods and services produced in one nation but sold to buyers in another nation

BD (EE,96;CE,9;JE,55;SI,42)
- Knows that imports are goods or services bought from sellers in another nation

BD (EE,96;CE,9;JE,56;SI,42)
- Understands that international trade promotes greater specialization, which increases total world output

BD (EE,96,128;CE,9;JE,57;SI,42)
- Knows that different currencies are used in different countries

BD (EE,128;CE,9;JE,57;SI,42)
- Knows that an exchange rate is the price of one nation's currency in terms of another nation's currency

Level IV (Grades 9-12)

BD (EE,128;CE,9;JE,56;SI,42)
- Understands that trade between nations would not occur if nations had the same kinds of productive resources and could produce all goods and services at the same real costs

BD (EE,128;CI,9;JE,56;SI,42)
- Knows that a nation has an absolute advantage if it can produce more of a product with the same amount of resources than another nation, and it has a comparative advantage when it can produce a product at a lower opportunity cost than another nation

BD (EE,128;CE,9;JE,56,57;SI,42)
- Knows that despite the advantages of international trade, many nations restrict the free flow of goods and services through a variety of devices known as "barriers to trade" (e.g., tariffs, quotas)

BD (EE,128;CE,9;JE,57;SI,42)
- Understands that a change in exchange rates changes the relative price of goods and services traded by the two countries and can have a significant effect on the flow of trade between nations and on a nation's domestic economy

Codes (right side of page):   BD = Benchmark, Declarative; BP = Benchmark, Procedural; BC = Benchmark, Contextual
1st letter of each code in parentheses   *2nd letter of code*   *Number*
E = NCEE: Framework for Economics   E = Explicitly stated in document   Page number of cited document
C = Colorado Council on Economic Education   I = Implied in document
J = JCEE: Economics, What and When
S = NCSS: Curriculum Standards for Social Studies   511

MREL

- Understands that extensive international trade requires an organized system for exchanging money between nations (i.e., a foreign exchange market)

  BD (EE,128;JE,57;SI,42)

- Understands that countries that engage in foreign trade maintain a "balance sheet" to measure the value of goods and services exchanged and the flow of financial reserves used to keep total payments between the countries in balance

  BD (EE,128;JE,58)

- Knows how the level of real GDP per capita is used to compare the level of economic development in different nations

  BD (EE,129;JE,60)

- Knows the factors that have led to increased interdependence among nations (e.g., transfer of technology, exchange of productive resources, trade of finished goods and services)

  BD (EE,129;JE,60;SI,42)

- Understands that increasing international interdependence causes economic conditions and policies in one nation to affect economic conditions in many other nations

  BD (EE,129;JE,60;SI,42)

- Understands that public policies affecting foreign trade impose costs and benefits on different groups of people and that decisions on these policies reflect economic and political interests and forces

  BD (EE,129;CI,8;JE,60;SI,42)

Codes (right side of page):   BD = Benchmark, Declarative; BP = Benchmark, Procedural; BC = Benchmark, Contextual
1st letter of each code in parentheses   *2nd letter of code*   *Number*
E = NCEE: Framework for Economics   E = Explicitly stated in document   Page number of cited document
C = Colorado Council on Economic Education   I = Implied in document
J = JCEE: Economics, What and When
S = NCSS: Curriculum Standards for Social Studies   512   McREL

Summary of Standards for Foreign Language

1. Uses the target language to engage in conversations, express feelings and emotions, and exchange opinions and information
2. Comprehends and interprets written and spoken language on diverse topics from diverse media
3. Presents information, concepts, and ideas to an audience of listeners or readers on a variety of topics
4. Demonstrates knowledge and understanding of traditional ideas and perspectives, institutions, professions, literary and artistic expressions, and other components of target culture
5. Recognizes that different languages use different patterns to communicate and applies this knowledge to the native language

(AE,17)

1. Uses the target language to engage in conversations, express feelings and emotions, and exchange opinions and information

Level II (Grades 3-5)

- Knows how to express likes, dislikes, and simple preferences in everyday situations (e.g., objects, categories, people, events)
  BP (AE,18;CE,8)

- Uses basic vocabulary to describe assorted objects in everyday environments
  BP (AE,18;CE,8)

- Knows how to give and follow simple instructions in the target language (e.g., in games, with partners or groups, giving commands suggested by a picture)
  BP (AE,18;CI,8)

- Knows how to exchange information with peers about preferences (e.g., favorite activities)
  BP (AE,18)

- Knows how to use non-verbal language (e.g., gestures) to clarify a verbal message when vocabulary is limited
  BP (AE,18)

- Knows how to exchange information about general events (e.g., classes, meetings, concerts, meals) and transportation (e.g., place, date, time)
  BP (AE,18)

- Uses appropriate vocabulary, gestures, and oral expressions for greetings, introductions, leave takings, and other common or familiar interactions (e.g., name, address, phone number, place of origin, general health/state of being)
  BP (AE,18,27;CI,14)

Level III (Grades 5-8)

- Uses verbal and written exchanges to gather and share personal data, information, and opinions (e.g., events in one's life, past experiences, significant details related to topics that are of common interest, opinions about topics of personal or community interest)
  BP (AE,18,19;CI,9)

- Uses the target language to plan events and activities with others (e.g., using authentic schedules, budgets)
  BC (AE,18)

- Uses vocabulary and cultural expressions to express the failure to understand the message or to request additional information (e.g., request that the speaker restate the message, ask appropriate questions for clarification)
  BP (AE,18,19)

- Uses repetition, rephrasing, and gestures to assist in communicating spoken messages
  BP (AE,18;CI,14)

Codes (right side of page):   BD = Benchmark, Declarative; BP = Benchmark, Procedural; BC = Benchmark, Contextual
1st letter of each code in parentheses   *2nd letter of code*   *Number*
A = National Standards in Foreign Language   E = Explicitly stated in document   Page number of cited document
C = Colorado Foreign Language Standards   I = Implied in document

MREL

historical interest to members of the target culture

BP (AI,23)
- Presents cultural and literary works in the target language that are appropriate at this developmental level (e.g., performs scenes from plays, recites poems or excerpts from short stories)

BP (AI,23;CE,11)
- Presents information orally or in writing on literary and cultural topics that are appropriate at this developmental level (e.g., presents the plot, character descriptions and development, and themes found in authentic literary works; expresses opinions and appreciation for various forms of literature, radio programs, songs, films, visual works)

(AE,27)
4. Demonstrates knowledge and understanding of traditional ideas and perspectives, institutions, professions, literary and artistic expressions, and other components of target culture

Level II (Grades K-4)

BD (AE,27,37;CI,14)
- Knows various age-appropriate cultural activities practiced in the target culture (e.g., games, songs, birthday celebrations, story telling, dramatizations, role playing)

BD (AE,27,37;CI,14)
- Knows simple patterns of behavior and interaction in various settings in the target culture (e.g., school, family, community) and how these patterns compare to those in one's native culture

BD (AE,27,37)
- Knows familiar utilitarian forms of the culture (e.g., toys, dress, types of dwellings, typical foods) and how they compare to those in one's native culture

BD (AE,27,37;CE,14)
- Knows some basic expressive forms of the target culture (e.g., children's songs, simple selections from authentic children's literature, types of artwork or graphic representations enjoyed or produced by the peer group in the culture studied)

BD (AE,28,37)
- Knows basic cultural beliefs and perspectives of people in both native and target cultures relating to family, school, work, and play

BP (AE,40)
- Identifies professions that require proficiency in the target language

Level III (Grades 5-8)

BD (AE,28;CI,14)
- Knows various age-appropriate cultural activities practiced in the target culture (e.g.,

---

Codes (right side of page):   BD = Benchmark, Declarative; BP = Benchmark, Procedural; BC = Benchmark, Contextual

1st letter of each code in parentheses   *2nd letter of code*   *Number*

A = National Standards in Foreign Language   E = Explicitly stated in document   Page number of cited document

C = Colorado Foreign Language Standards   I = Implied in document

adolescents' games such as card games, board games, and outdoor games; sports-related activities; music; television)

- Knows cultural traditions and celebrations that exist in the target culture and how these traditions and celebrations compare with those of the native culture (e.g., holidays, birthdays, "coming of age" celebrations, seasonal festivals, religious ceremonies, recreational gatherings) ^{BD (AE,37)}

- Knows and recognizes patterns of behavior or interaction typical of one's age group in various settings in the target culture (e.g., dating, telephone usage, etiquette) ^{BD (AE,28;CE,17)}

- Knows a variety of age-appropriate utilitarian forms of the target culture (e.g., educational institutions or systems, means of transportation, various rules as they apply to the peer group in the culture being studied), their significance, and how these forms have influenced the larger community ^{BD (AE,28)}

- Knows a variety of age-appropriate expressive forms of the culture (e.g., popular music and dance; appropriate authentic texts, such as children's magazines, comic books, children's literature; the use of color; common or everyday artwork such as designs typical of the culture's clothing, pottery, ceramics, paintings, architectural structures) and how these expressive forms compare with those of the native culture ^{BD (AE,28,37;CE,14)}

- Knows how "local" opinions of various aspects of the native culture compare with the views of peers from the target culture ^{BD (AE,37)}

- Knows how various community members use the target language in their work ^{BD (AI,40)}

Level IV (Grades 9-12)

- Understands various patterns of behavior or interaction that are typical of one's age group (e.g., extra-curricular activities, social engagements) ^{BD (AE,28;CI,15)}

- Knows age-appropriate utilitarian forms of the target culture (e.g., social, economic, and political institutions; laws), how they are reflected in American culture, and their significance ^{BD (AE,28,37;CE,15)}

- Understands age-appropriate expressive forms of the target culture (e.g., literature; popular books; periodicals; videos; commercials; fine arts such as music, dance, design, painting) and their significance in the wider community ^{BD (AE,28-29)}

Codes (right side of page):   BD = Benchmark, Declarative; BP = Benchmark, Procedural; BC = Benchmark, Contextual
1st letter of each code in parentheses   *2nd letter of code*   *Number*
A = National Standards in Foreign Language   E = Explicitly stated in document   Page number of cited document
C = Colorado Foreign Language Standards   I = Implied in document

- Understands contrasting ways in which information about national and international events is reported in the target culture and the native culture
  BD (AE,19)

- Understands contrasting ways in which familial, economic, environmental, and political issues are reflected through oral, written, and artistic expression in the native and target cultures
  BD (AE,37;CI,15)

- Understands how other cultures view the role of the native culture in the world arena
  BP (AI,37)

- Identifies career options that require knowledge of the target culture and proficiency in the target language
  BP (AI,40)

5. Recognizes that different languages use different patterns to communicate and applies this knowledge to the native language
(AE,36)

Level II (Grades K-4)

- Knows words that have been borrowed from one language to another and how these word borrowings may have developed
  BD (AE,36)

- Knows basic elements of the sound and writing systems of the target language and how these elements differ from the same elements of one's native language
  BD (AE,36)

- Understands that an idea may be expressed in multiple ways in the target language
  BD (AE,18)

Level III (Grades 5-8)

- Understands how idiomatic expressions have an impact on communication and reflect culture (e.g., anticipates larger units of meaning rather than individual word equivalencies)
  BD (AE,36)

- Uses a variety of sources in the target language to obtain information on topics of personal interest
  BP (AE,41)

- Uses various media from the target language and culture for entertainment
  BP (AE,41)

Level IV (Grades 9-12)

- Knows various linguistic elements of the target language (e.g., time, tense) and how these
  BD (AE,36)

Codes (right side of page):   BD = Benchmark, Declarative;   BP = Benchmark, Procedural;   BC = Benchmark, Contextual
1st letter of each code in parentheses   *2nd letter of code*   *Number*
A = National Standards in Foreign Language   E = Explicitly stated in document   Page number of cited document
C = Colorado Foreign Language Standards   I = Implied in document

523

McREL

elements compare to linguistic elements in one's native language

- Understands that the ability to comprehend language surpasses the ability to produce language ^BD (AE,19)

- Uses a dictionary or thesaurus written entirely in the target language to select appropriate words for use in preparing written and oral reports ^BP (AE,23)

Codes (right side of page):   BD = Benchmark, Declarative; BP = Benchmark, Procedural; BC = Benchmark, Contextual
1st letter of each code in parentheses   *2nd letter of code*   *Number*
A = National Standards in Foreign Language   E = Explicitly stated in document   Page number of cited document
C = Colorado Foreign Language Standards   I = Implied in document

524

McREL

16. Health

The following describes the process used to identify standards for health:

Identification of National Reports

Six reports were identified as providing useful information on health education standards in the schools: *National Health Education Standards: Achieving Health Literacy* (1995) from the Joint Committee on National Health Education Standards; *Benchmarks for Science Literacy* (1993) from Project 2061, American Association for the Advancement of Science; *Health Framework for California Public Schools* from the California Department of Education (1994); the *Report of the 1990 Joint Committee on Health Education Terminology*, from JCHET (1990); the *Michigan Essential Goals/Objectives for Health Education* (1988) from the Michigan State Board of Education; and the *National Science Education Standards* (draft 1994) from the National Committee on Science Education Standards and Assessment.

Selection of the Reference Document

National Health Education Standards: Achieving Health Literacy was used as a reference document. However, some basic content information was also drawn from the Michigan and California documents identified above, and supporting material (as well as some primary material) came from the two science documents, *National Science Education Standards* and Project 2061's *Benchmarks*.

Identification of Standards and Benchmarks

At the benchmark level, information was derived from *National Health Education Standards* and from all other reports cited above. These reports, except for the California framework, which was more curricular in scope, provided relatively straightforward descriptions of knowledge and skills recommended for health education. Consequently, most of the effort in the identification of benchmarks for health education centered on the synthesis and citation of information from multiple sources.

After the content review, those benchmark items that arose in all the reports were analyzed and grouped. Thus, the standards were developed working up from the benchmark level. However, for the most part, it was found that the resulting standards were similar to the topic level recommendations found in the *Report of the 1990 Joint Committee on Health Education Terminology*. In addition to these topic areas, a standard on Growth and Development was added, derived largely from information in the two science documents, *Science Standards* and Project 2061's *Benchmarks for Science Literacy*.

Integration of Information from Other Documents

As mentioned above, material from the other documents was not only integrated with the reference material, but new material was added from them as well. This was done when information was found to be present in more than one of the selected reports. It should be noted, however, that all benchmark information from the reference document, the *National Health Education Standards*, will be found in this report.

Summary of Standards for Health

1. Knows the availability and effective use of health services, products, and information
2. Knows environmental and external factors that affect individual and community health
3. Understands the relationship of family health to individual health
4. Knows how to maintain mental and emotional health
5. Knows essential concepts and practices concerning injury prevention and safety
6. Understands essential concepts about nutrition and diet
7. Knows how to maintain and promote personal health
8. Knows essential concepts about the prevention and control of disease
9. Understands aspects of substance use and abuse
10. Understands the fundamental concepts of growth and development

Level IV (Grades 9-12)

- Understands methods to facilitate the transition from the role of a child to the role of an independent adult in the family

  <small>BD (CE,135;MI,18)</small>

- Knows the effects of teenage pregnancy on teenagers, their children, their parents, and society

  <small>BD (CE,146;ME,17,18;SI,V161)</small>

- Understands the responsibilities inherent in dating relationships, marriage, and parenthood

  <small>BD (CE,137-138;ME,18)</small>

4. Knows how to maintain mental and emotional health

<small>(JE,106)</small>

Level I (Grades K-2)

- Identifies and shares feelings in appropriate ways

  <small>BP (2E,148;CE,59,67;ME,19)</small>

Level II (Grades 3-5)

- Knows the relationships between physical health and mental health

  <small>BD (2E,148;CE,75;ME,19)</small>

- Knows common sources of stress for children and ways to manage stress

  <small>BD (HE,19;CE,76;ME,19)</small>

- Knows how mood changes and strong feelings affect thoughts and behavior, and how they can be managed successfully

  <small>BD (HI,21;2E,148;CE,86;ME,19,20)</small>

- Knows behaviors that communicate care, consideration, and respect of self and others (including those with disabilities or handicapping conditions)

  <small>BP (HE,21;CE,59,84;ME,20)</small>

- Understands how one responds to the behavior of others and how one's behavior may evoke responses in others

  <small>BD (2I,148;CI,84;ME,20)</small>

- Knows strategies for resisting negative peer pressure

  <small>BD (CE,76,84;ME,20)</small>

- Knows how attentive listening skills can be used to build and maintain healthy relationships

  <small>BD (HE,21;CE,67)</small>

Codes (right side of page):   BD = Benchmark, Declarative;   BP = Benchmark, Procedural;   BC = Benchmark, Contextual
1st letter of each code in parentheses   *2nd letter of code*   *Number*
H = JHESC: National Health Education Standards   E = Explicitly stated in document   Page number of cited document
2 = Project 2061: Benchmarks for Science Literacy   I = Implied in document   *or, for duplicates:*
C = CDE: Health Framework for Calif. Public Schools   Standard number & level of duplicate
J = Joint Committee on Health Ed. Terminology
M = MSBE: Michigan Essential Goals/Obj. for Health
S = NCSESA: National Science Education Standards
D = Duplicated in another standard   531   MREL

Level III (Grades 6-8)

BD (HE,19,21;2E,149;CE,96,112)
- Knows strategies to manage stress and feelings caused by disappointment, separation, or loss (e.g., talking over problems with others, understanding that feelings of isolation and depression will pass, examining the situation leading to the feelings)

BD (CE,95;ME,19)
- Knows characteristics and conditions associated with positive self-esteem

BD (HE,21;CE,96,108;MI,20)
- Knows appropriate ways to build and maintain healthy relationships with peers, parents, and other adults (e.g., interpersonal communication)

BD (HE,19;CE,108-109;MI,20)
- Understands the difference between safe and risky or harmful behaviors in relationships

BD (2I,149;CE,96;ME,21)
- Knows techniques for seeking help and support through appropriate resources

Level IV (Grades 9-12)

BD (HE,21;CE,125;DI,3.3.3)
- Knows skills used to communicate effectively with family, friends, and others, and the effects of open and honest communication

BD (HE,19,21;CE,124-125;MI,20-21)
- Knows strategies for coping with and overcoming feelings of rejection, social isolation, and other forms of stress

BD (CE,125;MI,20-21)
- Understands the role of denial as a negative influence on mental and emotional health, and ways to overcome denial and seek assistance when needed

(JE,106)
5. Knows essential concepts and practices concerning injury prevention and safety

Level I (Grades K-2)

BD (CE,62;ME,27)
- Knows basic fire, traffic, water, and recreation safety practices

BD (CE,62;ME,27)
- Knows precautions that should be taken in special conditions (e.g., bad weather, Halloween, darkness, staying home alone, being approached by strangers, avoiding conflicts)

BP (CE,62,64;ME,28)
- Knows how to recognize emergencies and respond appropriately (e.g., uses a telephone appropriately to obtain help; identifies and obtains help from police officers, fire fighters,

---

Codes (right side of page):   BD = Benchmark, Declarative;   BP = Benchmark, Procedural;   BC = Benchmark, Contextual
1st letter of each code in parentheses   *2nd letter of code*   *Number*
H = JHESC: National Health Education Standards   E = Explicitly stated in document   Page number of cited document
2 = Project 2061: Benchmarks for Science Literacy   I = Implied in document   *or, for duplicates:*
C = CDE: Health Framework for Calif. Public Schools   Standard number & level of duplicate
J = Joint Committee on Health Ed. Terminology
M = MSBE: Michigan Essential Goals/Obj. for Health
S = NCSESA: National Science Education Standards
D = Duplicated in another standard   532   MREL

and medical personnel; treats simple injuries such as scratches, cuts, bruises, and first-degree burns)

BD (CE,63;ME,27;SE,V42)
- Knows ways to seek assistance if worried, abused, or threatened (e.g., physically, emotionally, sexually)

Level II (Grades 3-5)

BD (HI,19;CE,57;ME,27;SE,V42)
- Knows safety rules and practices to be used in home, school, and community settings (e.g., using a seat belt or helmet, protecting ears from exposure to excessive noise, wearing appropriate clothing and protective equipment for sports, using sunscreen or a hat in bright sunlight)

BD (HE,19;CE,79,81)
- Knows methods used to recognize and avoid threatening situations (e.g., not leaning into a car when giving directions to a stranger) and ways to get assistance

BD (HI,17;CE,81;ME,28)
- Knows basic first aid procedures appropriate to common emergencies in home, school, and community (e.g., proper responses to breathing and choking problems, bleeding, shock, poisonings, minor burns; universal precautions to be taken when dealing with other people's blood)

BD (HE,21;CI,79;MI,19,20)
- Knows the difference between positive and negative behaviors used in conflict situations

BD (HE,21;CE,79;ME,20)
- Knows some non-violent strategies to resolve conflicts

Level III (Grades 6-8)

BD (HE,19;CE,104;SI,V98)
- Knows injury prevention strategies for family health (e.g., having a personal and family emergency plan, including maintaining supplies ready for emergencies; identifying and removing safety hazards in the home)

BP (HE,19;CE,104;ME,28)
- Knows strategies for managing a range of situations involving injury (e.g., first aid procedures, abdominal thrust maneuver, cardiopulmonary resuscitation)

BD (HI,19;ME,20)
- Knows potential signs of self- and other-directed violence

BD (HE,21;CE,109)
- Knows the various possible causes of conflict among youth in schools and communities, and

---

Codes (right side of page): BD = Benchmark, Declarative; BP = Benchmark, Procedural; BC = Benchmark, Contextual

1st letter of each code in parentheses	*2nd letter of code*	*Number*
H = JHESC: National Health Education Standards	E = Explicitly stated in document	Page number of cited document
2 = Project 2061: Benchmarks for Science Literacy	I = Implied in document	*or, for duplicates:*
C = CDE: Health Framework for Calif. Public Schools		Standard number & level of duplicate
J = Joint Committee on Health Ed. Terminology		
M = MSBE: Michigan Essential Goals/Obj. for Health		
S = NCSESA: National Science Education Standards		
D = Duplicated in another standard		

McREL

strategies to manage conflict

- Knows how refusal and negotiation skills can be used to enhance health ^BD (HE,21;CE,96;ME,17,20)

Level IV (Grades 9-12)

- Knows injury prevention and management strategies for community health (e.g., neighborhood safety, traffic safety, safe driving) ^BD (HE,19;SI,V160)

- Knows possible causes of conflicts in schools, families, and communities, and strategies to prevent conflict in these situations ^BD (HE,21)

- Knows strategies for solving interpersonal conflicts without harming self or others ^BD (HE,21;CE,129)

- Knows how refusal, negotiation, and collaboration skills can be used to avoid potentially harmful situations ^BD (HE,21;CE,129)

6. Understands essential concepts about nutrition and diet (JE,106)

Level I (Grades K-2)

- Classifies foods and food combinations according to the food groups ^BP (CE,58;ME,14)

Level II (Grades 3-5)

- Knows the nutritional value of different foods ^BD (CE,75,90;ME,14;SI,V42)

- Knows healthy eating practices (e.g., eating a nutritious breakfast, eating a variety of foods, eating nutritious meals and snacks at regular intervals to satisfy individual energy and growth needs) ^BD (CE,75;ME,14;SE,V42)

- Knows factors that influence food choices (e.g., activity level, peers, culture, religion, advertising, time, age, health, money/economics, convenience, environment, status, personal experience) ^BD (CE,75;ME,14)

- Knows how food-preparation methods and food-handling practices affect the safety and ^BD (CE,75;MI,15)

Codes (right side of page):	BD = Benchmark, Declarative; BP = Benchmark, Procedural; BC = Benchmark, Contextual

1st letter of each code in parentheses — *2nd letter of code* — *Number*

H = JHESC: National Health Education Standards — E = Explicitly stated in document — Page number of cited document
2 = Project 2061: Benchmarks for Science Literacy — I = Implied in document — *or, for duplicates:*
C = CDE: Health Framework for Calif. Public Schools — Standard number & level of duplicate
J = Joint Committee on Health Ed. Terminology
M = MSBE: Michigan Essential Goals/Obj. for Health
S = NCSESA: National Science Education Standards
D = Duplicated in another standard

534

MREL

nutrient quality of foods

Level III (Grades 6-8)

- Understands how eating properly can help to reduce health risks (in terms of anemia, dental health, osteoporosis, heart disease, cancer, malnutrition)

  BD (CE,94;ME,14,15)

- Knows appropriate methods to maintain, lose, or gain weight according to individual needs and scientific research

  BD (CE,94,119;MI,15;SI,V98)

- Knows eating disorders that affect health adversely (e.g., anorexia, overeating, bulimia)

  BD (CI,118;ME,15)

- Knows the principles of food safety involved with food storage and preparation (e.g., proper refrigeration, hand washing, proper cooking and storage temperatures)

  BD (CE,94;ME,15)

Level IV (Grades 9-12)

- Understands how nutrient and energy needs vary in relation to gender, activity level, and stage of life cycle

  BD (CE,122;ME,14;SI,V160-V161)

- Understands the reliability and validity of various sources of food and nutrition information (e.g., dietary supplements, diet aids, fad diets, food labels)

  BP (CE,149-150;ME,15;SI,V160-V161)

- Understands the role of food additives and their relationship to health

  BD (CI,150;ME,15)

(JE,106)

7. Knows how to maintain and promote personal health

Level I (Grades K-2)

- Knows basic personal hygiene habits required to maintain health (e.g., caring for teeth, gums, eyes, ears, nose, skin, hair, nails)

  BD (HI,19;CE,58;ME,13;SE,V42)

Codes (right side of page):   BD = Benchmark, Declarative; BP = Benchmark, Procedural; BC = Benchmark, Contextual
1st letter of each code in parentheses   *2nd letter of code*   *Number*
H = JHESC: National Health Education Standards   E = Explicitly stated in document   Page number of cited document
2 = Project 2061: Benchmarks for Science Literacy   I = Implied in document   *or, for duplicates:*
C = CDE: Health Framework for Calif. Public Schools   Standard number & level of duplicate
J = Joint Committee on Health Ed. Terminology
M = MSBE: Michigan Essential Goals/Obj. for Health
S = NCSESA: National Science Education Standards
D = Duplicated in another standard

McREL

Level II (Grades 3-5)

- Understands the influence of rest, food choices, exercise, sleep, and recreation on a person's well-being
  BD (HE,17,19;CE,75,86;ME,13;SI,V42)

- Knows common health problems that should be detected and treated early
  BD (HE,17;CE,78;MI,11)

- Knows behaviors that are safe, risky, or harmful to self and others
  BD (HE,19;MI,13)

- Sets a personal health goal and makes progress toward its achievement
  BP (HE,22)

- Knows that making health-related decisions and setting health goals sometimes requires asking for assistance
  BD (HE,22)

- Knows the basic structure and functions of the human body systems (e.g., how they are interrelated; how they function to fight disease)
  BD (HE,17;CE,74;ME,16)

Level III (Grades 6-8)

- Knows personal health strengths and risks (e.g., results of a personal health assessment)
  BD (HE,17;MI,13)

- Knows how positive health practices and appropriate health care can help to reduce health risks (e.g., good personal hygiene, health screenings, self-examinations)
  BD (HE,17,19;CE,93,97,98;ME,13)

- Knows strategies and skills that are used to attain personal health goals (e.g., maintaining an exercise program, making healthy food choices)
  BD (HE,22;CE,94,95;MI,13;SE,V98)

- Understands how changing information, abilities, priorities, and responsibilities influence personal health goals
  BD (HE,22)

- Knows how health is influenced by the interaction of body systems
  BD (HE,17;CI,93)

Level IV (Grades 9-12)

- Knows how personal behaviors relate to health and well-being and how these behaviors can be modified if necessary to promote achievement of health goals throughout life (e.g., following a personal nutrition plan to reduce the risk of disease, periodically self-assessing physical fitness)
  BP (HE,17,19,22;CE,122-123;MI,13;SI,V160)

Codes (right side of page):	BD = Benchmark, Declarative; BP = Benchmark, Procedural; BC = Benchmark, Contextual	
1st letter of each code in parentheses	*2nd letter of code*	*Number*
H = JHESC: National Health Education Standards	E = Explicitly stated in document	Page number of cited document
2 = Project 2061: Benchmarks for Science Literacy	I = Implied in document	*or, for duplicates:*
C = CDE: Health Framework for Calif. Public Schools		Standard number & level of duplicate
J = Joint Committee on Health Ed. Terminology		
M = MSBE: Michigan Essential Goals/Obj. for Health		
S = NCSESA: National Science Education Standards		
D = Duplicated in another standard	536	McREL

- Understands the short- and long-term consequences of safe, risky, and harmful behaviors BD (HE,3;CI,128-129)

- Understands how personal health needs change during the life cycle BD (HI,17;CE,121)

- Understands the impact of personal health behaviors on the functioning of body systems BD (HE,17)

8. Knows essential concepts about the prevention and control of disease (JE,106)

Level I (Grades K-2)

- Knows the signs and symptoms of common illnesses (e.g., fever, rashes, coughs, congestion, wheezing) BD (CE,61;ME,11;SI,V42)

Level II (Grades 3-5)

- Knows ways in which a person can prevent or reduce the risk of disease and disability (e.g., practicing good personal hygiene, making healthy food choices, acknowledging the importance of immunizations, cooperating in regular health screenings) BD (HE,17;2E,144;CE,60,77;ME,11,12;SE,V42)

- Knows the benefits of early detection and treatment of disease BD (CI,77;ME,11)

- Knows ways to maintain a functional level of health in the presence of disease or disability (e.g., cooperating with parents and health care providers, taking prescription or over-the-counter medicines properly, correctly interpreting instructions for taking medicine) BD (CE,78,89;ME,12)

Level III (Grades 6-8)

- Understands how lifestyle, pathogens, family history, and other risk factors are related to the cause or prevention of disease and other health problems BD (HE,17;CE,97;ME,11)

- Knows communicable, chronic, and degenerative disease processes and the differences between them BD (CE,97-98;ME,11;SI,V98)

- Understands personal rights and responsibilities involved in the treatment of disease (e.g., proper use of medication, the influence of family and culture on the treatment of disease) BD (HI,17;CE,99)

Codes (right side of page):   BD = Benchmark, Declarative; BP = Benchmark, Procedural; BC = Benchmark, Contextual
1st letter of each code in parentheses   *2nd letter of code*   *Number*
H = JHESC: National Health Education Standards   E = Explicitly stated in document   Page number of cited document
2 = Project 2061: Benchmarks for Science Literacy   I = Implied in document   *or, for duplicates:*
C = CDE: Health Framework for Calif. Public Schools   Standard number & level of duplicate
J = Joint Committee on Health Ed. Terminology
M = MSBE: Michigan Essential Goals/Obj. for Health
S = NCSESA: National Science Education Standards
D = Duplicated in another standard

MREL

Level IV (Grades 9-12)

BD (2E,145;CE,125-126;MI,11;SI,V160)
- Understands how the immune system functions to prevent or combat disease

BD (HI,17;CE,126;MI,12)
- Understands the importance of regular examinations (including self-examination of the breasts or testicles) in detecting and treating diseases early

BD (CE,126;ME,17;DI,10.4.3)
- Understands the importance of prenatal and perinatal care to both the.mother and the child

BD (CE,125;ME,11)
- Understands the social, economic, and political effects of disease on individuals, families, and communities

(JE,106)
9. Understands aspects of substance use and abuse

Level I (Grades K-2)

BD (CE,63;MI,22;SI,V42)
- Knows how to distinguish between helpful and harmful substances

Level II (Grades 3-5)

BP (CE,80;MI,22;SI,V42)
- Differentiates between the use and misuse of prescription and nonprescription drugs

BD (CE,80;ME,23)
- Knows influences that promote alcohol, tobacco, and other drug use (e.g., peer pressure, peer and adult modeling, advertising, overall availability, cost)

BP (CE,80;ME,23)
- Recognizes high-risk substance abuse situations that pose an immediate threat to oneself or one's friends or family (e.g., drunk and drugged driving, violent arguments) as well as how and where to obtain help

BD (HE,21;CE,80;ME,24)
- Knows ways to avoid, recognize, and respond to negative social influences and pressures to use alcohol, tobacco, or other drugs (e.g., refusal skills, self-control)

Level III (Grades 6-8)

BD (CE,102;ME,22;SI,V98)
- Knows conditions that may put people at higher risk for substance abuse problems (e.g., genetic inheritability, substance abuse in family, low frustration tolerance)

Codes (right side of page):   BD = Benchmark, Declarative; BP = Benchmark, Procedural; BC = Benchmark, Contextual
1st letter of each code in parentheses   *2nd letter of code*   *Number*
H = JHESC: National Health Education Standards   E = Explicitly stated in document   Page number of cited document
2 = Project 2061: Benchmarks for Science Literacy   I = Implied in document   *or, for duplicates:*
C = CDE: Health Framework for Calif. Public Schools   Standard number & level of duplicate
J = Joint Committee on Health Ed. Terminology
M = MSBE: Michigan Essential Goals/Obj. for Health
S = NCSESA: National Science Education Standards
D = Duplicated in another standard   538   MREL

- Knows factors involved in the development of a drug dependency and the early, observable signs and symptoms (e.g., tolerance level, drug-seeking behavior, loss of control, denial)
  BD (CI,102;ME,23;SE,V98)

- Knows the short- and long-term consequences of the use of tobacco, alcohol, and other drugs (e.g., physical consequences such as shortness of breath, cirrhosis, lung cancer, emphysema; psychological consequences such as low self-esteem, paranoia, depression, apathy; social consequences such as crime, domestic violence, loss of friends)
  BD (CE,101-102;ME,22,23;SE,V98)

- Knows public policy approaches to substance abuse control and prevention (e.g., pricing and taxation, warning labels, regulation of advertising, restriction of alcohol consumption at sporting events)
  BD (CE,102;ME,24)

- Knows community resources that are available to assist people with alcohol, tobacco, and other drug problems
  BD (HI,18;CE,102;ME,24)

Level IV (Grades 9-12)

- Knows the short- and long-term effects associated with the use of alcohol, tobacco, and other drugs on reproduction, pregnancy, and the health of children
  BD (CE,129-130;MI,23;SI,V160)

- Knows how the abuse of alcohol, tobacco, and other drugs often plays a role in dangerous behavior and can have adverse consequences on the community (e.g., house fires, motor vehicle crashes, domestic violence, date rape, transmission of diseases through needle sharing or sexual activity)
  BD (CE,130;ME,22;SE,V160)

- Understands that alcohol, tobacco, and other drug dependencies are treatable diseases/conditions
  BD (CE,131;ME,24)

10. Understands the fundamental concepts of growth and development
(2E,131;CE,52;ME,16)

Level I (Grades K-2)

- Understands individual differences (in terms of appearance, behavior)
  BD (CE,70;MI,16)

- Knows the cycle of growth and development in humans from infancy to old age
  BD (2E,132;CE,69;ME,16)

Codes (right side of page):   BD = Benchmark, Declarative; BP = Benchmark, Procedural; BC = Benchmark, Contextual
1st letter of each code in parentheses   *2nd letter of code*   *Number*
H = JHESC: National Health Education Standards   E = Explicitly stated in document   Page number of cited document
2 = Project 2061: Benchmarks for Science Literacy   I = Implied in document   *or, for duplicates:*
C = CDE: Health Framework for Calif. Public Schools   Standard number & level of duplicate
J = Joint Committee on Health Ed. Terminology
M = MSBE: Michigan Essential Goals/Obj. for Health
S = NCSESA: National Science Education Standards
D = Duplicated in another standard

McREL

Level II (Grades 3-5)

- BD (2E,132;CE,86-87;ME,17)

  Knows the changes that occur during puberty (e.g., physical changes such as sexual maturation, changes in voice, acne; emotional and social changes such as a growing sensitivity to peer influence, family tensions, mood swings; cognitive and intellectual development)

- BD (2I,132;CE,87-88;ME,16)

  Knows that the rate of change during puberty varies with each individual and that people vary widely in size, height, shape, and rate of maturation

Level III (Grades 6-8)

- BD (2E,133;CI,140)

  Understands how the human body changes as people age (e.g., muscles and joints become less flexible, bones and muscles lose mass, energy levels diminish, senses become less acute)

- BD (CE,114;MI,16,17)

  Knows the similarities and differences between male and female sexuality

- BD (2E,133;CE,141;ME,17)

  Understands the processes of conception, prenatal development, and birth

- BD (CE,112;MI,16)

  Knows strategies for coping with concerns and stress related to the changes that occur during adolescence

Level IV (Grades 9-12)

- BD (CE,140-141;MI,16-17)

  Understands a variety of physical, mental, emotional, and social changes that occur throughout life, and how these changes differ among individuals (e.g., young adulthood, pregnancy, middle age, old age)

- BD (2I,134;CE,147;MI,16-17;SE,V161)

  Understands how physical, mental, social, and cultural factors influence attitudes and behaviors regarding sexuality

- BD (2I,133;CE,141-142;ME,17;DI,8.4.3)

  Knows sound health practices in the prenatal period that are important to the health of the fetus and young child (e.g., diet, refraining from cigarette smoking or use of alcohol or other drugs)

Codes (right side of page):	BD = Benchmark, Declarative; BP = Benchmark, Procedural; BC = Benchmark, Contextual

1st letter of each code in parentheses   *2nd letter of code*   *Number*

H = JHESC: National Health Education Standards   E = Explicitly stated in document   Page number of cited document

2 = Project 2061: Benchmarks for Science Literacy   I = Implied in document   *or, for duplicates:*

C = CDE: Health Framework for Calif. Public Schools   Standard number & level of duplicate

J = Joint Committee on Health Ed. Terminology

M = MSBE: Michigan Essential Goals/Obj. for Health

S = NCSESA: National Science Education Standards

D = Duplicated in another standard   540   MREL

17. Physical Education

The following process was used to identify standards and benchmarks in the field of physical education:

Identification of National Reports

Three reports were identified as useful documents for identifying physical education standards: *Moving into the Future: National Standards for Physical Education: A Guide to Content and Assessment* (1995) and *Outcomes of Quality Physical Education Programs* (1992), both from the National Association for Sport and Physical Education (NASPE); and *Physical Education: Working Draft Content Standards and Benchmarks* (1995) from the state of Michigan's department of education.

Selection of the Reference Document

The NASPE's *Moving into the Future: National Standards for Physical Education: A Guide to Content and Assessment* (1995) was selected as reference document for identifying standards and benchmarks. The *Standards* were developed with the input of physical education professionals across the country. The work was also based on the *Outcomes of Quality Physical Education Programs* (1992) from NASPE.

Identification of Standards and Benchmarks

The *Standards* work shares a number of features with our model for the identification of benchmarks and standards. First, the standards statements in the document are expressed at an appropriate level of generality, since they are stated broadly enough to allow for benchmark statements to be articulated across K–12. In addition, beneath each standard, the document provides various descriptions of the knowledge and skills that students should acquire from K–12, stated for selected developmental levels.

There were a few areas, however, in which the document was not directly compatible with our approach. Beneath each standard, student knowledge and skill is described in several sections: a paragraph summarizing the knowledge and abilities expected for the grade range under discussion; a more specific list of those skills that should receive particular emphasis; and sample "performance benchmarks," assessment examples, and criteria for assessment. Frequently, it was necessary to take information from several of these sections in order to construct each benchmark. This was done, for example, when the assessment criteria section could provide additional information on the knowledge or skills identified, or when material from still another section helped to make a benchmark less narrow in scope, or when specific examples of the kind of knowledge and skills required was found to be useful. In addition to this modification in the content, some changes for the grade range of the material were necessary. The reference work has six levels: kindergarten, and grades 2, 4, 6, 8, 10, and 12. Because our benchmarks are at primary, upper elementary, middle, and high school, we adopted the following method for aligning the grade levels between the two documents in order to maintain as much grade-specific information as possible. For the primary grades (level I), the information from grade 2 of the reference material was our primary source, but it was supplemented with information from kindergarten for any descriptions of knowledge or skill that weren't encompassed by the material at grade 2. Similarly, for our level II, we identified grade 6 as the primary source of information, using grade 4 material from the reference document wherever material was found that was not presented at grade 6. Middle school (level III) was defined as grades 7–8 and was taken solely from grades 7–8 in the reference work; high school (level IV) was identified from the material at grades 10 and 12, again using the material from the earlier grade to supplement information taken primarily from the later grade.

Integration of Information from Other Documents

Additional material from NASPE was also used and cited in many benchmarks. Their 1992 *Outcomes* document provided us numerous examples or elaborations on material found in the *Standards* document. Also useful was a working draft on physical education from Michigan's department of education. This draft was found to provide some explanatory detail we found useful in identifying benchmarks from the NASPE material. The Michigan document was cited not only in those instances where supplemental material was gained, but also wherever similar benchmark information was found in the document.

Summary of Standards for Physical Education

1. Uses a variety of basic and advanced movement forms
2. Uses movement concepts and principles in the development of motor skills
3. Understands the benefits and costs associated with participation in physical activity
4. Understands how to monitor and maintain a health-enhancing level of physical fitness
5. Understands the social and personal responsibility associated with participation in physical activity

1. Uses a variety of basic and advanced movement forms

(PE,6;MI,1-5;OE,7)

Level I (Grades K-2)

- Uses a variety of basic locomotor movements (e.g., running, skipping, hopping, galloping, sliding)
  BP (PE,18;ME,1;OE,7,11)

- Uses a variety of basic non-locomotor skills (e.g., bending, twisting, stretching, turning, lifting)
  BP (PE,6;ME,2;OE,7)

- Uses a variety of basic object control skills (e.g., underhand and overhand throw, catch, hand dribble, foot dribble, kick and strike)
  BP (PI,18;ME,1;OE,10,11)

- Uses simple combinations of fundamental movement skills (e.g., locomotor, non-locomotor, object control, body control, and rhythmical skills)
  BP (PE,18;ME,4;OI,11)

- Uses control in weight-bearing activities on a variety of body parts (e.g., jumping and landing using combinations of one and two foot take-offs and landings)
  BP (PE,18;OI,11)

- Uses control in balance activities on a variety of body parts (e.g., one foot, one hand and one foot, hands and knees, headstands)
  BP (PE,18,19;ME,2;OE,10,11)

- Uses control in travel activities on a variety of body parts (e.g., travels in backward direction and changes direction quickly and safely, without falling; changes speeds and directions in response to various rhythms; combines traveling patterns to music)
  BP (PE,18;ME,4;OE,11)

- Uses smooth transitions between sequential motor skills (e.g., running into a jump)
  BP (PE,18;ME,4;OI,11)

- Uses locomotor skills in rhythmical patterns (e.g., even, uneven, fast, and slow)
  BP (PE,18;ME,3;OI,11)

Level II (Grades 3-6)

- Uses mature form in object control skills (e.g., underhand and overhand throw, catch, hand dribble, foot dribble, kick and strike, batting, punt, pass)
  BP (PE,46;ME,1;OE,12,13)

- Uses basic sport-specific skills for a variety of physical activities (e.g., basketball chest pass, soccer dribble, fielding a softball with a glove)
  BP (PE,32,46;ME,5;OI,13)

- Uses mature form and appropriate sequence in combinations of fundamental locomotor,
  BP (PI,46;ME,4;OI,13)

Codes (right side of page):   BD = Benchmark, Declarative; BP = Benchmark, Procedural; BC = Benchmark, Contextual
1st letter of each code in parentheses   *2nd letter of code*   *Number*
P = NASPE: Standards for Physical Education   E = Explicitly stated in document   Page number of cited document
M = MDOE: Physical Education Working Draft   I = Implied in document
O = NASPE: Outcomes of Physical Education

McREL

object control, and rhythmical skills that are components of selected modified games, sports, and dances (e.g., combining steps to perform certain dances; combining running, stopping, throwing, shooting, kicking for sideline soccer)

BP (PE,32;ME,2;OE,12)
- Uses mature form in balance activities on a variety of apparatuses (e.g., balance board, large apparatus, skates)

BP (PE,46;MI,9;OE,13)
- Uses beginning strategies for net and invasion games (e.g., keeping object going with partner using striking pattern, placing ball away from opponent in a racket sport, hand and foot dribble while preventing an opponent from stealing the ball in basketball)

Level III (Grades 7-8)

BP (PI,63-64;ME,5;OE,14)
- Uses intermediate sport-specific skills for individual, dual, and team sports

BP (PI,63-63;ME,5;OE,14)
- Uses intermediate sport-specific skills for dance and rhythmical activities

BP (PI,63-64;ME,5;OE,14)
- Uses intermediate sport-specific skills for outdoor activities

Level IV (Grades 9-12)

BP (PI,90;MI,5;OE,16)
- Uses advanced sport-specific skills in selected physical activities (e.g., aquatics, dance, outdoor pursuits, individual, dual, and team sports and activities)

BP (PE,2,76,90)
- Uses skills in complex rather than modified versions of physical activities (e.g., more players or participants, rules and strategies)

(PE,7;MI,8;OE,7)
2. Uses movement concepts and principles in the development of motor skills

Level I (Grades K-2)

BD (PE,8;MI,7-8;OI,10)
- Understands a vocabulary of basic movement concepts (e.g., personal space, high/low levels, fast/slow speeds, light/heavy weights, balance, twist)

BD (PE,8;ME,8;OE,10)
- Understands terms that describe a variety of relationships with objects (e.g., over/under, behind, alongside, through)

BC (PE,20;MI,7;OI,10,11)
- Uses concepts of space awareness and movement control with a variety of basic skills (e.g.,

---

Codes (right side of page):   BD = Benchmark, Declarative; BP = Benchmark, Procedural; BC = Benchmark, Contextual
1st letter of each code in parentheses   *2nd letter of code*   *Number*
P = NASPE: Standards for Physical Education   E = Explicitly stated in document   Page number of cited document
M = MDOE: Physical Education Working Draft   I = Implied in document
O = NASPE: Outcomes of Physical Education

running, hopping, skipping) while interacting with others

- Understands the critical elements of a variety of basic movement patterns such as throwing (e.g., the ready position, arm preparation, step with leg opposite the throwing arm, follow-through, accuracy of throw)

  BC (PE,20;ME,8;OI,11)

- Uses feedback to improve performance (e.g., peer/coach review)

  BC (PE,20-21;MI,9)

- Understands the importance of practice in learning skills

  BC (OE,10;ME,9)

Level II (Grades 3-6)

- Uses information from a variety of internal and external sources to improve performance (e.g., group projects, student journal, self-assessment, peer and coach review)

  BC (PE,48;ME,9;OE,13)

- Understands principles of practice and conditioning that improve performance

  BC (PE,48;OI,13)

- Understands proper warm-up and cool-down techniques and reasons for using them

  BC (PE,48;OE,13)

- Uses basic offensive and defensive strategies in unstructured game environments (e.g., limited rules, modified equipment, small numbers of participants)

  BC (PE,48;MI,9;OI,13)

Level III (Grades 7-8)

- Understands principles of training and conditioning for specific physical activities

  BC (PE,64;MI,9;OE,14)

- Understands the critical elements of advanced movement skills (e.g., such as a racing start in freestyle swimming)

  BD (PE,63-64;MI,9)

- Uses basic offensive and defensive strategies in a modified version of a team and individual sport

  BC (PE,62;MI,9;OE,14)

- Understands movement forms associated with highly skilled physical activities (e.g., moves that lead to successful serves, passes, and spikes in an elite volleyball game)

  BD (PE,63-64;MI,9)

Level IV (Grades 9-12)

- Understands biomechanical concepts that govern different types of movement (e.g.,

  BD (PE,77,92;OE,15)

Codes (right side of page):   BD = Benchmark, Declarative; BP = Benchmark, Procedural; BC = Benchmark, Contextual
1st letter of each code in parentheses   *2nd letter of code*   *Number*
P = NASPE: Standards for Physical Education   E = Explicitly stated in document   Page number of cited document
M = MDOE: Physical Education Working Draft   I = Implied in document
O = NASPE: Outcomes of Physical Education

546

MREL

in physical activities that reflect personal interests)

BP (PE,95;MI,6-7;OI,16)
- Designs a personal fitness program that is based on the basic principles of training and encompasses all components of fitness (e.g., cardiovascular and respiratory efficiency, muscular strength and endurance, flexibility, and body composition)

(PI,11,13,14;ME,12;OI,7)
5. Understands the social and personal responsibility associated with participation in physical activity

Level I (Grades K-2)

BP (PE,12-13,25;ME,9;OI,11)
- Follows rules and procedures (e.g., playground, classroom, and gymnasium rules) with little reinforcement

BP (PE,12,25;ME,9;OE,10)
- Uses equipment and space safely and properly (e.g., takes turns using equipment, puts equipment away when not in use)

BD (PE,25;ME,9;OI,11)
- Understands the purpose of rules in games

BP (PE,21,23;ME,13;OI,11)
- Understands the social contributions of physical activity (e.g., learning to cooperate and interact with others, having a role in team sports)

BP (PE,25;ME,13;OI,11)
- Works cooperatively (e.g., takes turns, is supportive, assists partner) with another to complete an assigned task

BD (PE,27;MI,13;OI,11)
- Understands the elements of socially acceptable conflict resolution in physical activity settings (e.g., cooperation, sharing, consideration)

BD (PE,27;MI,13;OI,11)
- Understands the importance of playing, cooperating, and respecting others regardless of personal differences (e.g., gender, ethnicity, disability) during physical activity

Level II (Grades 3-6)

BC (PE,54;MI,9)
- Knows how to develop rules, procedures, and etiquette that are safe and effective for specific activity situations

BP (PE,54;MI,13;OI,13)
- Works in a group to accomplish a set goal in both cooperative and competitive activities

---

Codes (right side of page): BD = Benchmark, Declarative; BP = Benchmark, Procedural; BC = Benchmark, Contextual
1st letter of each code in parentheses *2nd letter of code* *Number*
P = NASPE: Standards for Physical Education E = Explicitly stated in document Page number of cited document
M = MDOE: Physical Education Working Draft I = Implied in document
O = NASPE: Outcomes of Physical Education

MREL

- Understands the role of physical activities in learning more about others of like and different backgrounds (e.g., gender, culture, ethnicity, and disability) ^{BD (PI,56;ME,13;OE,13)}

- Understands the physical challenges faced by people with disabilities (e.g., wheelchair basketball, dancing with a hearing disability) ^{BD (PE,57;MI,13;OI,13)}

- Understands the origins of different sports and how they have evolved ^{BD (PE,56)}

Level III (Grades 7-8)

- Understands the importance of rules, procedures, and safe practice in physical activity settings ^{BD (PE,69;MI,9;OE,14)}

- Understands proper attitudes toward both winning and losing ^{BD (PE,70;ME,13)}

- Knows the difference between inclusive (e.g., changing rules of activity to include less skilled players) and exclusionary (e.g., failing to pass ball to less skilled players) behaviors in physical activity settings ^{BD (PE,71;MI,13;OI,14)}

- Understands physical activity as a vehicle for self-expression (e.g., dance, gymnastics, and various sport activities) ^{BD (PE,73;MI,13;OE,14)}

- Understands the concept that physical activity (e.g., sport, games, dance) is a microcosm of modern culture and society ^{BD (PE,71-72)}

Level IV (Grades 9-12)

- Uses leadership and follower roles, when appropriate, in accomplishing group goals in physical activities ^{BP (PI,97;MI,12)}

- Works with others in a sport activity to achieve a common goal (e.g., winning a team championship) ^{BP (PE,87;MI,12,13)}

- Understands how participation in physical activity fosters awareness of diversity (e.g., cultural, ethnic, gender, physical) ^{BD (PE,99;ME,10;OI,16)}

- Includes persons of diverse backgrounds and abilities in physical activity ^{BP (PE,99;MI,10;OI,16)}

Codes (right side of page): BD = Benchmark, Declarative; BP = Benchmark, Procedural; BC = Benchmark, Contextual
1st letter of each code in parentheses   *2nd letter of code*   *Number*
P = NASPE: Standards for Physical Education   E = Explicitly stated in document   Page number of cited document
M = MDOE: Physical Education Working Draft   I = Implied in document
O = NASPE: Outcomes of Physical Education

552   MREL

- Understands the history and purpose of international competitions (e.g., Olympics, Special Olympics, Pan American Games, World Cup Soccer) ^{BD (PE,85;MI,13;OE,15)}

- Understands the role of sport in a diverse world (e.g., the influence of professional sport in society, the usefulness of dance as an expression of multiculturalism, the affect of age and gender on sport participation patterns) ^{BD (PE,85;MI,13;OI,16)}

- Understands the concept of "sportsmanship" and the importance of responsible behavior while participating in physical activities ^{BD (PI,97-98;ME,13)}

Codes (right side of page):   BD = Benchmark, Declarative; BP = Benchmark, Procedural; BC = Benchmark, Contextual
1st letter of each code in parentheses   *2nd letter of code*   *Number*
P = NASPE: Standards for Physical Education   E = Explicitly stated in document   Page number of cited document
M = MDOE: Physical Education Working Draft   I = Implied in document
O = NASPE: Outcomes of Physical Education

McREL

BD (SE,33,79)
- Understands how language, literature, the arts, architecture, other artifacts, traditions, beliefs, values, and behaviors contribute to the development and transmission of culture

BD (2I,159;SE,33)
- Understands that there are similarities and differences within groups as well as among groups

BD (2E,155;SI,37)
- Understands that a large society may be made up of many groups, and these groups may contain many distinctly different subcultures (e.g., associated with region, ethnic origin, social class, interests, values)

Level IV (Grades 9-12)

BD (2E,160;SI,33)
- Understands that while a group may act, hold beliefs, and/or present itself as a cohesive whole, individual members may hold widely varying beliefs, so the behavior of a group may not be predictable from an understanding of each of its members

BD (2E,160;SI,33)
- Understands that social organizations may serve business, political, or social purposes beyond those for which they officially exist, including unstated ones such as excluding certain categories of people from activities

BD (SE,33)
- Understands how the diverse elements that contribute to the development and transmission of culture (e.g., language, literature, the arts, traditions, beliefs, values, behavior patterns) function as an integrated whole

BD (2I,163;SE,33)
- Understands that groups have patterns for preserving and transmitting culture even as they adapt to environmental and/or social change

BD (2I,160;SE,33)
- Understands that social groups may have patterns of behavior, values, beliefs, and attitudes that can help or hinder cross-cultural understanding

(2E,139;SE,37)
3. Understands that interactions among learning, inheritance, and physical development affect human behavior

Level I (Grades K-2)

BD (2E,140;SI,37)
- Knows that people use their senses to find out about their surroundings and themselves and that different senses provide different information

---

Codes (right side of page):   BD = Benchmark, Declarative; BP = Benchmark, Procedural; BC = Benchmark, Contextual
1st letter of each code in parentheses   *2nd letter of code*   *Number*
2 = Project 2061: Benchmarks for Science Literacy   E = Explicitly stated in document   Page number of cited document
S = NCSS: Curriculum Standards for Social Studies   I = Implied in document

- Understands that sometimes a person can get different information about the same thing by moving closer to it or further away from it _{BD (2E,140;SI,37)}

- Understands that some of the things people do (e.g., playing soccer, reading, writing) must be deliberately learned _{BD (2E,140;SI,37)}

- Understands that practice helps people to improve, and that how well a person learns sometimes depends on how she or he does it as well as how often and how hard she or he tries to learn _{BD (2E,140;SI,37)}

- Knows that people can learn from each other in many ways (e.g., telling and listening, showing and watching, imitating) _{BD (2E,140;SI,37)}

Level II (Grades 3-5)

- Knows that human beings have different interests, motivations, skills, and talents _{BD (2E,140;SE,37)}

- Understands that human beings can use the memory of their past experiences to make judgements about new situations _{BD (2E,140;SI,37)}

- Understands that many skills can be practiced until they become automatic, and that if the right skills are practiced, performance may improve _{BD (2E,140;SI,37)}

- Understands that human beings tend to repeat behaviors that feel good or have pleasant consequences and to avoid behaviors that feel bad or have unpleasant consequences _{BD (2E,140;SI,37)}

- Knows that learning means using what one already knows to make sense out of new experiences or information, not just storing the new information in one's head _{BD (2E,140;SI,37)}

- Understands roles as learned behavior patterns in group situations (e.g., student, family member, team member) _{BD (2I,140;SE,38)}

- Understands that as roles vary depending on expectations and changing conditions (e.g., worker, parent, volunteer, student), behavior, attitudes, and goals change _{BD (2I,140;SE,38,61)}

Level III (Grades 6-8)

- Understands that all behavior is affected by both inheritance and experience _{BD (2E,141;SI,37)}

Codes (right side of page):   BD = Benchmark, Declarative;   BP = Benchmark, Procedural;   BC = Benchmark, Contextual
1st letter of each code in parentheses   *2nd letter of code*   *Number*
2 = Project 2061: Benchmarks for Science Literacy   E = Explicitly stated in document   Page number of cited document
S = NCSS: Curriculum Standards for Social Studies   I = Implied in document

MREL

- Knows that some animal species are limited to a repertoire of genetically determined behaviors and others have more complex brains and can learn a wide variety of behaviors BD (2E,141;SI,37)

- Understands that the level of skill a person can reach in any particular activity depends on a variety of factors (e.g., innate abilities, amount of practice, the use of appropriate learning technologies) BD (2E,141;SI,37)

- Knows that human beings can detect a tremendous range of visual and olfactory stimuli and that the strongest stimulus they can tolerate may be more than a trillion times as intense as the weakest they can detect, but there are many kinds of signals in the world that people cannot detect directly BD (2E,141;SI,37)

- Understands that paying attention to any one input of information usually reduces the ability to attend to others at the same time BD (2E,141;SI,37)

- Understands that learning often results from two perceptions or actions occurring at about the same time, and the more often the same combination occurs, the stronger the mental connection between them is likely to be BD (2E,142;SI,37)

- Understands that occasionally a single vivid experience will connect two things permanently in people's minds BD (2E,142;SI,37)

- Understands that language and tools enable human beings to learn complicated and varied things from others BD (2E,142;SI,37)

Level IV (Grades 9-12)

- Understands that differences in the behavior of individuals arise from the interaction of heredity and experience BD (2E,142;SI,37)

- Understands that even instinctive behavior may not develop well if a person is exposed to abnormal conditions BD (2E,142;SI,37)

- Understands that expectations, moods, and prior experiences of human beings can affect how they interpret new perceptions or ideas BD (2E,142;SI,37)

- Understands that people might ignore evidence that challenges their beliefs and more readily accept evidence that supports them BD (2E,142;SI,37)

Codes (right side of page):   BD = Benchmark, Declarative; BP = Benchmark, Procedural; BC = Benchmark, Contextual
1st letter of each code in parentheses   *2nd letter of code*   *Number*
2 = Project 2061: Benchmarks for Science Literacy   E = Explicitly stated in document   Page number of cited document
S = NCSS: Curriculum Standards for Social Studies   I = Implied in document

MREL

- Understands that the context in which something is learned may limit the contexts in which the learning can be used
BD (2E,142;SI,37)

- Knows that human thinking involves the interaction of ideas, and ideas about ideas
BD (2E,142;SI,37)

- Knows that people can produce many associations internally without receiving information from their senses
BD (2E,142;SI,37)

(2E,171;SE,38)

4. Understands conflict, cooperation, and interdependence among individuals, groups, and institutions

Level I (Grades K-2)

- Knows that disagreements are common, even between family members or friends
BD (2E,172;SI,38,44)

- Understands that some ways of dealing with disagreements work better than others, and that people who are not involved in an argument may be helpful in solving it
BD (2E,172;SI,38,44)

- Understands that rules at home, at school, and in the community let individuals know what to expect and so can reduce the number of disputes
BD (2E,172;SI,38)

Level II (Grades 3-5)

- Knows that communicating different points of view in a dispute can often help people to find a satisfactory compromise
BD (2E,172;SI,38,44)

- Understands that resolving a conflict by force rather than compromise can lead to more problems
BD (2E,172;SI,38,44)

- Understands that one person's exercise of freedom may conflict with the freedom of others and that rules can help to resolve conflicting freedoms
BD (2E,172;SI,38)

- Understands that if a conflict cannot be settled by compromise, it may be decided by a vote—if everyone agrees to accept the results
BD (2E,172;SI,38)

- Understands that beliefs and customs held by certain groups can help or hinder people as they strive to use their talents and that sometimes individuals can change those beliefs and customs in ways that will help people to succeed more easily in the future
BD (2I,172;SE,38,61-62)

Codes (right side of page):   BD = Benchmark, Declarative; BP = Benchmark, Procedural; BC = Benchmark, Contextual
1st letter of each code in parentheses   *2nd letter of code*   *Number*
2 = Project 2061: Benchmarks for Science Literacy   E = Explicitly stated in document   Page number of cited document
S = NCSS: Curriculum Standards for Social Studies   I = Implied in document

McREL

BD (SE,38)

- Knows various forms that institutions take (e.g., religious, social, political)

Level III (Grades 6-8)

BD (2E,159,173;SI,38)

- Understands that being a member of a group can increase an individual's social power and also can increase hostile actions toward or from other groups or individuals

BD (2E,173;SI,38,44)

- Understands that most groups have formal or informal procedures for arbitrating disputes among their members

BD (2I,173;SE,38)

- Understands how various institutions (e.g., banks, schools, hospitals, the military) influence people, events, and elements of culture and how people interact with different institutions

BD (2I,173;SE,38)

- Understands how role, status, and social class may affect interactions of individuals and social groups

BD (2I,173;SE,38)

- Understands how tensions might arise between expressions of individuality and group or institutional efforts to promote social conformity

Level IV (Grades 9-12)

BD (2E,173;SI,38,44)

- Understands that conflict between people or groups may arise from competition over ideas, resources, power, and/or status

BD (2E,173;SI,38)

- Understands that social change, or the prospect of it, promotes conflict because social, economic, and political changes usually benefit some groups more than others (which is also true of the status quo)

BD (2E,173;SI,38)

- Understands that conflicts are especially difficult to resolve in situations in which there are few choices and little room for compromise

BD (2E,173;SI,38)

- Understands that some informal ways of responding to conflict (e.g., pamphlets, demonstrations, cartoons) may reduce tensions and lead to compromise but may be inflammatory and make agreement more difficult to reach

BD (2E,174;SE,38)

- Understands that conflict within a group may be reduced by conflict between it and other groups

---

Codes (right side of page):	BD = Benchmark, Declarative; BP = Benchmark, Procedural; BC = Benchmark, Contextual	
1st letter of each code in parentheses	*2nd letter of code*	*Number*
2 = Project 2061: Benchmarks for Science Literacy	E = Explicitly stated in document	Page number of cited document
S = NCSS: Curriculum Standards for Social Studies	I = Implied in document	

McREL

- Understands that intergroup conflict does not necessarily end when one segment of society gets a decision in its favor because the "losers" then may work even harder to reverse, modify, or circumvent the change $^{BD\ (2E,174;SI,38,44)}$

- Understands that even when the majority of people in a society agree on a social decision, the minority who disagree must be protected from oppression, just as the majority may need protection against unfair retaliation from the minority $^{BD\ (2E,174;SI,38)}$

- Understands how various institutions (e.g., social, religious, political) develop and change over time (i.e., what is taught in school and school policies toward student behavior have changed over the years in response to family and community pressures), and how they further both continuity and change in societies $^{BD\ (2E,163;SE,38)}$

- Understands how changes in social and political institutions (e.g., church, schools, political party) both reflect and affect individuals' career choices, values, and significant actions $^{BD\ (2I,163;SE,38,124)}$

- Understands that the decisions of one generation both provide and limit the range of possibilities open to the next generation $^{BD\ (2E,163;SI,38)}$

- Understands that mass media, migrations, and conquest affect social change by exposing one culture to another, and that extensive borrowing among cultures has led to the virtual disappearance of some cultures but only modest change in others $^{BD\ (2E,163;SI,38)}$

Codes (right side of page):   BD = Benchmark, Declarative; BP = Benchmark, Procedural; BC = Benchmark, Contextual
1st letter of each code in parentheses   *2nd letter of code*   *Number*
2 = Project 2061: Benchmarks for Science Literacy   E = Explicitly stated in document   Page number of cited document
S = NCSS: Curriculum Standards for Social Studies   I = Implied in document

566

MREL

19. Life Skills

Life skills describes a category of knowledge that is useful across the content areas as well as important for the world of work. This category is comprised of four areas: Thinking and Reasoning, Working with Others, Self Regulation, and Life Work.

Thinking and Reasoning

The following process was used to identify standards and benchmarks in the category of thinking and reasoning:

Identification of Target Reports

No single document was used as the reference report for standards and benchmarks in the thinking and reasoning category. Rather, those statements that were judged to articulate thinking and reasoning processes that can be applied across content areas were extracted from the various documents reviewed. The following documents have been used to construct standards and benchmarks in the thinking and reasoning category:

* *Incomplete Work of the Task Force of the Standards Project for English Language Arts* (Standards Project for the English Language Arts, 1992).
* *Benchmarks for Science Literacy* (Project 2061, 1993).
* *What Work Requires of Schools: A SCANS Report for America 2000* (The Secretary's Commission on Achieving Necessary Skills, 1991).
* *Workplace Basics: The Essential Skills Employers Want* (Carnevale, Gainer & Meltzer, 1990).
* *Curriculum and Evaluation Standards for School Mathematics* (NCTM, 1989).
* *Mathematics Assessment Framework for the 1994 National Assessment of Educational Progress* (NAEP, 1992).
* *Building a history curriculum: Guidelines for teaching history in the schools* (Bradley Commission on History in the Schools, 1988).
* *Democracy through Language* (NCTE, 1989).
* *Geography for Life: National Geography Standards* (Geography Education Standards Project, 1994).
* *National Standards for History for Grades K–4: Expanding Children's World in Time and Space* (NCHS, 1994).
* *National Standards for United States History: Exploring the American Experience* (NCHS, 1994).
* *National Standards for World History: Exploring Paths to the Present* (NCHS, 1994).
* *Expectations of Excellence: Curriculum Standards for Social Studies* (NCSS, 1994).

Identification of Standards and Benchmarks from Target Reports

Explicit statements of thinking and reasoning were identified in all target reports. To illustrate, consider the following statements from NCTM's *Curriculum and Evaluation Standards for School Mathematics* (1989):

- make and test conjectures
- formulate counter examples
- follow logical arguments
- judge the validity of arguments
- construct simple valid arguments

Each of these statements represents a reasoning process or subprocess that could be used in a variety of subject areas. For example, one could judge the validity of arguments or construct simple valid arguments in mathematics, in science or in history. Statements such as these found in any document were extracted and used as the statement base from which the thinking and reasoning standards were constructed.

In addition to explicit statements of general reasoning processes like those above, implicit statements of general thinking and reasoning processes were also identified. For example, the NCTM document contains the following statement:

- formulate problems from everyday and mathematical situations (p.23)

In this case, the thinking and reasoning process was made explicit:

- formulate problems within a variety of situations

In summary, both implicit and explicit statements of general thinking and reasoning processes were used to construct the standards and benchmarks in the thinking and reasoning category. It is again important to emphasize that our listing of these processes is not meant to imply that thinking and reasoning can or should be addressed in isolation of domain-specific content. However, providing a listing of generalized processes allows a school or district to distribute thinking and reasoning processes systematically throughout the various content domains. Additionally, it is our hope that a listing such as ours will help schools and districts break the perceptual set regarding many thinking and reasoning processes. For example, it is usually assumed that problem solving should be assigned exclusively to the domain of mathematics and hypothesis testing exclusively to the domain of science. However, careful examination of the standard in this section entitled "applies basic trouble-shooting and problem-solving techniques" will show that it is applicable to many domains as is the standard "understands and applies basic principles of hypothesis testing and scientific inquiry."

Working with Others

The following process was used to identify standards and benchmarks in the category of working with others:

Identification of National Reports and Reference Documents

The category of standards entitled "working with others" deals with skills and abilities that are

Identification of Standards and Benchmarks and Integration of Information from Other Documents

Although both reference documents list skills and abilities at a high level of specificity that renders them quite compatible with the structure of standards used in this study, neither identifies the level at which these skills and abilities should be addressed. Consequently, with one exception, the elements listed under the standards in this section are all assigned to level IV (grades 9–12). The one exception is the standard entitled "Makes effective use of basic tools." All components for this standard were drawn from the document *Benchmarks for Science Literacy* (1993), which lists skills and abilities by grade level.

Summary of Standards for Life Skills

Thinking and Reasoning
1. Understands and applies basic principles of presenting an argument
2. Understands and applies basic principles of logic and reasoning
3. Effectively uses mental processes that are based on identifying similarities and dissimilarities (compares, contrasts, classifies)
4. Understands and applies basic principles of hypothesis testing and scientific inquiry
5. Applies basic trouble-shooting and problem-solving techniques
6. Applies decision-making techniques

Working with Others
1. Contributes to the overall effort of a group
2. Uses conflict-resolution techniques
3. Works well with diverse individuals and in diverse situations
4. Displays effective interpersonal communication skills
5. Demonstrates leadership skills

Self-Regulation
1. Sets and manages goals
2. Performs self-appraisal
3. Considers risks
4. Demonstrates perseverance
5. Maintains a healthy self-concept
6. Restrains impulsivity

Life Work
1. Makes effective use of basic tools
2. Understands the characteristics and uses of basic computer hardware, software, and operating systems
3. Uses basic word processing, spreadsheet, database, and communication programs
4. Manages money effectively
5. Pursues specific jobs
6. Makes general preparation for entering the work force
7. Makes effective use of basic life skills
8. Displays reliability and a basic work ethic
9. Operates effectively within organizations

Thinking and Reasoning

(EE,4,20;GE,55;WI,64)

1. Understands and applies the basic principles of presenting an argument

Level I (Grades K-2)

- BD (2E,232)

  Understands that people are more likely to believe a person's ideas if that person can give good reasons for them

- BP (2I,298;WI,64)

  Provides coherent (though not necessarily valid or convincing) answers when asked why one believes something to be true or how one knows something

- BP (2I,298)

  Asks "how do you know" in appropriate situations

Level II (Grades 3-5)

- BC (2I,299)

  Uses facts from books, articles, and databases to support an argument

- BP (2I,299;WI,64)

  Identifies basic informal fallacies, including appeals to authority, the use of statements such as "everybody knows," and vague references such as "leading doctors say"

- BD (2E,232)

  Understands that reasoning can be distorted by strong feelings

- BP (2I,299)

  Analyzes arguments to determine if they are supported by facts from books, articles, and databases

- BP (2E,299)

  Raises questions about arguments that are based on the assertion that "everybody knows" or "I just know"

- BP (2I,299)

  Seeks reasons for believing things other than the assertion that "everybody agrees"

- BP (2I,299)

  Recognizes when a comparison is not fair because important characteristics are not the same

---

Codes (right side of page): BD = Benchmark, Declarative; BP = Benchmark, Procedural; BC = Benchmark, Contextual
1st letter of each code in parentheses *2nd letter of code* *Number*
2 = Project 2061: Benchmarks for Science Literacy E = Explicitly stated in document Page number of cited document
B = Bradley Commission on History I = Implied in document
E = NCTE: Democracy Through Language
G =GESP: National Standards for Geography
H = NCHS: History for Grades K-4
M = NCTM: Curric. & Eval. Stan. for School Math.
N = NAEP: Mathematics Assessment Framework
SS = NCSS: Curriculum Standards for Social Studies
US = NCHS: National Standards for U.S. History
W = Carnevale: Workplace Basics
WH = NCHS: National Standards for World History

MREL

Level III (Grades 6-8)

- Evaluates arguments that are based on quantitative data and mathematical concepts ^{BP (MI,78;ME,105)}

- Questions claims that use vague references such as "leading experts say..." or are based on the statements of people speaking outside of their expertise (e.g., celebrities) ^{BP (2E,299;SSE,148)}

- Questions conclusions based on very small samples of data, biased samples, or samples for which there is no central sample ^{BP (2E,299)}

- Makes basic distinctions between information that is based on fact and information that is based on opinion ^{BP (2E,299;SSE,148)}

- Identifies and questions false analogies ^{BP (2E,299;SSE,148)}

- Identifies and questions arguments in which all members of a group are implied to possess nearly identical characteristics that are considered to be different from those of another group ^{BP (2E,299;SSE,148)}

- Compares and contrasts the credibility of differing accounts of the same event ^{BC (SSE,148)}

Level IV (Grades 9-12)

- Understands that when people try to prove a point, they may at times select only the information that supports it and ignore the information that contradicts it ^{BD (2I,300;SSE,148;WI,64)}

- Identifies techniques used to slant information in subtle ways ^{BP (SSE,148;WI,64)}

- Identifies the logic of arguments that are based on quantitative data ^{BC (MI,143)}

- Identifies or seeks out the critical assumptions behind a line of reasoning and uses that to judge the validity of an argument ^{BP (2I,300;SSE,148)}

- Understands that to be convincing, an argument must have both true statements and valid connections among them ^{BD (2E,234)}

Codes (right side of page):   BD = Benchmark, Declarative;   BP = Benchmark, Procedural;   BC = Benchmark, Contextual
1st letter of each code in parentheses   *2nd letter of code*   *Number*
2 = Project 2061: Benchmarks for Science Literacy   E = Explicitly stated in document   Page number of cited document
B = Bradley Commission on History   I = Implied in document
E = NCTE: Democracy Through Language
G =GESP: National Standards for Geography
H = NCHS: History for Grades K-4
M = NCTM: Curric. & Eval. Stan. for School Math.
N = NAEP: Mathematics Assessment Framework
SS = NCSS: Curriculum Standards for Social Studies
US = NCHS: National Standards for U.S. History
W = Carnevale: Workplace Basics
WH = NCHS: National Standards for World History   574   MREL

BP (2E,297)

- Uses tables, charts, and graphs in constructing arguments

BP (2E,299;SSE,148)

- Analyzes the effectiveness of arguments based on the extent to which they rely on facts versus opinions

(EE,22;SI,xviii;WI,64)

2. Understands and applies basic principles of logic and reasoning

Level III (Grades 6-8)

BP (MI,81;NI,34)

- Uses formal deductive connectors ("if...then," "not," "and," "or") in the construction of deductive arguments

BD (2E,233)

- Understands that some aspects of reasoning have very rigid rules but other aspects do not

BD (2E,233)

- Understands that when people have rules that always hold for a given situation and good information about the situation, then logic can help them figure out what is true about the situation

BD (2E,233)

- Understands that reasoning by similarities can suggest ideas but cannot be used to prove things

BD (2E,233)

- Understands that people are using incorrect logic when they make a statement such as "if x is true, then y is true; but x isn't true, therefore y isn't true"

BD (2E,233)

- Understands that a single example can never prove that something is true, but a single example can prove that something is not true

BD (2E,233)

- Understands that some people invent a general rule to explain how something works by summarizing observations

BD (2E,233)

- Understands that people overgeneralize by making up rules on the basis of only a few observations

BD (SSI,149)

- Understands that personal values influence the types of conclusions people make

---

Codes (right side of page):   BD = Benchmark, Declarative; BP = Benchmark, Procedural; BC = Benchmark, Contextual
1st letter of each code in parentheses   *2nd letter of code*   *Number*
2 = Project 2061: Benchmarks for Science Literacy   E = Explicitly stated in document   Page number of cited document
B = Bradley Commission on History   I = Implied in document
E = NCTE: Democracy Through Language
G =GESP: National Standards for Geography
H = NCHS: History for Grades K-4
M = NCTM: Curric. & Eval. Stan. for School Math.
N = NAEP: Mathematics Assessment Framework
SS = NCSS: Curriculum Standards for Social Studies
US = NCHS: National Standards for U.S. History
W = Carnevale: Workplace Basics
WH = NCHS: National Standards for World History

MREL

- Recognizes situations in which a variety of conclusions can be drawn from the same information ^BP (SSE,149)

Level IV (Grades 9-12)

- Understands the differences between the formal and informal uses (e.g., in everyday situations) of the logical connectors: "if...then," "not," "and," "or" ^BD (2I,297)

- Analyzes the deductive validity of arguments based on implicit or explicit assumptions ^BP (2I,300)

- Understands the difference between formal and informal uses (e.g., in everyday situations) of the terms "sufficient" and "necessary" ^BD (2I,297)

- Understands the formal meaning of the logical quantifiers: "some," "none," and "all" ^BD (2I,297)

- Understands that formal logic is mostly about connections between statements and that these connections can be considered without attention to whether the statements themselves are true or not ^BD (2E,234)

- Understands that people sometimes reach false conclusions either by applying faulty logic to true statements or by applying valid logic to false statements ^BD (2E,234)

- Understands that a reason may be *sufficient* to get a result but may not be the only way to get the result (i.e., may not be *necessary*), or a reason may be *necessary* to obtain a result but not *sufficient* (i.e., other things are also required; some reasons may be both *necessary* and *sufficient*) ^BD (2E,234,297)

- Understands that logic can be used to test how well any general rule works ^BD (2E,234)

- Understands that proving a general rule to be false can be done by finding just one exception; this is much easier than proving a general rule to be true for all possible cases ^BD (2E,234)

- Understands that logic may be of limited help in finding solutions to problems if the general rules upon which conclusions are based do not always hold true; most often, we have to deal ^BD (2E,234)

Codes (right side of page):   BD = Benchmark, Declarative;   BP = Benchmark, Procedural;   BC = Benchmark, Contextual

1st letter of each code in parentheses   *2nd letter of code*   *Number*

2 = Project 2061: Benchmarks for Science Literacy   E = Explicitly stated in document   Page number of cited document
B = Bradley Commission on History   I = Implied in document
E = NCTE: Democracy Through Language
G =GESP: National Standards for Geography
H = NCHS: History for Grades K-4
M = NCTM: Curric. & Eval. Stan. for School Math.
N = NAEP: Mathematics Assessment Framework
SS = NCSS: Curriculum Standards for Social Studies
US = NCHS: National Standards for U.S. History
W = Carnevale: Workplace Basics
WH = NCHS: National Standards for World History   576   MREL

with probabilities rather than certainties

BD (2E,234)

- Understands that once a person believes a general rule, he or she may be more likely to notice things that agree with that rule and not notice things that do not; to avoid this "confirmatory bias," scientific studies sometimes use observers who do not know what the results are supposed to be

BD (2E,234)

- Understands that very complex logical arguments can be formulated from a number of simpler logical arguments

BP (ME,143)

- Identifies counter examples to conclusions that have been developed

(WI,90,202)

3. Effectively uses mental processes that are based on identifying similarities and differences (compares, contrasts, classifies)

Level I (Grades K-2)

BC (WE,90)

- Classifies objects by size, color, or other significant characteristics

BC (MI,32,60)

- Identifies the similarities and differences between persons, places, things, and events using concrete criteria

BC (2E,296)

- Describes and compares things in terms of number, shape, texture, size, weight, color, and motion

BC (2I,217)

- Recognizes simple patterns in the surrounding events and objects

Level II (Grades 3-5)

BD (2E,232)

- Understands that one way to make sense of something is to think how it is like something more familiar

BP (2E,299)

- Recognizes when comparisons might not be fair because some characteristics are not the same

---

Codes (right side of page): BD = Benchmark, Declarative; BP = Benchmark, Procedural; BC = Benchmark, Contextual
1st letter of each code in parentheses *2nd letter of code* *Number*
2 = Project 2061: Benchmarks for Science Literacy E = Explicitly stated in document Page number of cited document
B = Bradley Commission on History I = Implied in document
E = NCTE: Democracy Through Language
G =GESP: National Standards for Geography
H = NCHS: History for Grades K-4
M = NCTM: Curric. & Eval. Stan. for School Math.
N = NAEP: Mathematics Assessment Framework
SS = NCSS: Curriculum Standards for Social Studies
US = NCHS: National Standards for U.S. History
W = Carnevale: Workplace Basics
WH = NCHS: National Standards for World History

McREL

- Compares people in terms of important ethnic, religious, and cultural characteristics ^{BC (HE,23;MI,32,60)}

- Makes comparisons between countries in terms of relatively concrete characteristics (e.g., size, population, products) ^{BC (GI,48;MI,32,60)}

Level III (Grades 6-8)

- Compares consumer products on the basis of features, performance, durability, and cost, and considers personal tradeoffs ^{BC (2E,299)}

- Understands that an analogy not only contains some likenesses but also some differences ^{BD (2E,233)}

- Selects criteria or rules for category membership that are relevant and important ^{BP (SSI,149)}

- Orders information or events based on frequency of occurrence ^{BC (SSI,149)}

- Orders information based on importance to a given criterion ^{BC (SSE,149)}

- Articulates abstract relationships between existing categories of information ^{BD (SSE,149)}

- Creates a table to compare specific abstract and concrete features of two items ^{BP (GE,50)}

- Compares different sources of information for the same topic in terms of basic similarities and differences ^{BC (HE,24;SSI,149;USI,21,27,28;WHI,21,27,28)}

- Identifies the abstract relationships that form the basis for analogies ^{BP (HI,23;SSI,149;USI,21,27,28;WHI,21,27,28)}

Level IV (Grades 9-12)

- Uses a comparison table to compare multiple items on multiple abstract characteristics ^{BP (GI,54)}

- Identifies abstract patterns of similarities and differences between information on the same topic but from different sources ^{BC (GE,55;SSI,149;USI,21,27,28;WHI,21,27,28)}

Codes (right side of page):   BD = Benchmark, Declarative; BP = Benchmark, Procedural; BC = Benchmark, Contextual

1st letter of each code in parentheses	2nd letter of code	Number
2 = Project 2061: Benchmarks for Science Literacy	E = Explicitly stated in document	Page number of cited document
B = Bradley Commission on History	I = Implied in document	
E = NCTE: Democracy Through Language		
G =GESP: National Standards for Geography		
H = NCHS: History for Grades K-4		
M = NCTM: Curric. & Eval. Stan. for School Math.		
N = NAEP: Mathematics Assessment Framework		
SS = NCSS: Curriculum Standards for Social Studies		
US = NCHS: National Standards for U.S. History		
W = Carnevale: Workplace Basics		
WH = NCHS: National Standards for World History		

578

MᴄREL

BP (ME,146;SSI,149;USI,21,27,28;WHI,21,27,28)
- Identifies abstract relationships between seemingly unrelated items

BP (SSE,149)
- Identifies the qualitative and quantitative traits (other than frequency and obvious importance) that can be used to order and classify items

(WI,64)
4. Understands and applies basic principles of hypothesis testing and scientific inquiry

Level I (Grades K-2)

BP (2E,298)
- Asks "how do you know" in appropriate situations and attempts to provide reasonable answers when others ask the same question

BD (2I,217)
- Understands that changing one thing sometimes causes changes in something else and that changing the same thing in the same way usually has the same result

Level II (Grades 3-5)

BP (2I,293)
- Keeps a notebook that describes observations made

BP (MI,23,36,75;NI,27)
- Attempts to verify the results of experiments done by others

BP (2E,293)
- Carefully distinguishes between actual observations and ideas or conclusions about what was observed

BC (GE,46)
- Makes records of observations regarding time and place to formulate hypotheses

BC (GE,47)
- Keeps systematic records of temperature, precipitation, cloud cover, and other weather information to formulate hypotheses

Level III (Grades 6-8)

BD (2I,233)
- Understands that there are a variety of ways people can form hypotheses, including basing them on many observations, basing them on very few observations, and constructing them

---

Codes (right side of page):   BD = Benchmark, Declarative; BP = Benchmark, Procedural; BC = Benchmark, Contextual
1st letter of each code in parentheses   *2nd letter of code*   *Number*
2 = Project 2061: Benchmarks for Science Literacy   E = Explicitly stated in document   Page number of cited document
B = Bradley Commission on History   I = Implied in document
E = NCTE: Democracy Through Language
G =GESP: National Standards for Geography
H = NCHS: History for Grades K-4
M = NCTM: Curric. & Eval. Stan. for School Math.
N = NAEP: Mathematics Assessment Framework
SS = NCSS: Curriculum Standards for Social Studies
US = NCHS: National Standards for U.S. History
W = Carnevale: Workplace Basics
WH = NCHS: National Standards for World History   579   *MREL*

on only one or two observations

- Accurately and effectively verifies results of experiments
  BP (MI,75;NI,27)

- Understands that there may be more than one valid way to interpret a set of findings
  BD (2E,299)

- Questions findings in which no mention is made of whether the control group is very similar to the experimental group
  BP (2E,299)

- Reformulates a new hypothesis for study after an old hypothesis has been eliminated
  BP (SSE,149)

- Makes and validates conjectures about outcomes of specific alternatives or events regarding an experiment
  BP (MI,78,81,143;NI,34)

Level IV (Grades 9-12)

- Identifies and critiques studies in which data, explanations, or conclusions are presented as the only ones worth considering
  BP (2E,300)

- Tests hypotheses statistically
  BP (ME,167)

- Presents alternative explanations and conclusions to one's own experiments
  BP (2E,300)

- Gathers and analyzes field data using spatial sampling (e.g., place a transparent grid of squares on maps to count whether two characteristics—such as corn production and hogs—that are hypothesized to be spatially related coexist within the grid cells)
  BP (GE,53)

5. Applies basic trouble-shooting and problem-solving techniques
(SI,xviii;WE,182;WI,64)

Level I (Grades K-2)

- No materials specifically designated for this level
  BP (HI,27)

Codes (right side of page):   BD = Benchmark, Declarative; BP = Benchmark, Procedural; BC = Benchmark, Contextual
1st letter of each code in parentheses   *2nd letter of code*   *Number*
2 = Project 2061: Benchmarks for Science Literacy   E = Explicitly stated in document   Page number of cited document
B = Bradley Commission on History   I = Implied in document
E = NCTE: Democracy Through Language
G =GESP: National Standards for Geography
H = NCHS: History for Grades K-4
M = NCTM: Curric. & Eval. Stan. for School Math.
N = NAEP: Mathematics Assessment Framework
SS = NCSS: Curriculum Standards for Social Studies
US = NCHS: National Standards for U.S. History
W = Carnevale: Workplace Basics
WH = NCHS: National Standards for World History

McREL

Level II (Grades 3-5)

- Identifies issues and problems in the school or community that one might help solve

  BP (HI,27)

- Studies problems in the community and how they were solved

  BP (HI,27)

- Analyzes the problems that have confronted people in the past in terms of the major goals and obstacles to those goals

  BP (HE,27)

Level III (Grades 6-8)

- Identifies alternative courses of action and predicts likely consequences of each

  BP (SSI,148)

- Selects the most appropriate strategy or alternative for solving a problem

  BP (SSE,148)

- Examines different alternatives for resolving local problems and compares the possible consequences of each alternative

  BC (USE,32;WHE,33)

Level IV (Grades 9-12)

- Applies trouble-shooting strategies to complex real-world situations

  BP (SI,xvii)

- Understands that trouble-shooting almost anything may require many-step branching logic

  BD (2E,233)

- Trouble-shoots common mechanical and electrical systems, checking for possible causes of malfunction, and decides on that basis whether to make a change or get advice from an expert before proceeding

  BP (2E,234)

- Engages in problem finding and framing for personal situations and situations in the community

  BP (SI,xviii;WI,64)

- Represents a problem accurately in terms of resources, constraints, and objectives

  BP (MI,23;WE,182;WE,329)

- Provides summation of the effectiveness of problem-solving techniques

  BP (WE,182)

Codes (right side of page):　　　　　BD = Benchmark, Declarative; BP = Benchmark, Procedural; BC = Benchmark, Contextual
1st letter of each code in parentheses　　　*2nd letter of code*　　　　*Number*
2 = Project 2061: Benchmarks for Science Literacy　　E = Explicitly stated in document　　Page number of cited document
B = Bradley Commission on History　　　　I = Implied in document
E = NCTE: Democracy Through Language
G =GESP: National Standards for Geography
H =NCHS: History for Grades K-4
M = NCTM: Curric. & Eval. Stan. for School Math.
N = NAEP: Mathematics Assessment Framework
SS = NCSS: Curriculum Standards for Social Studies
US = NCHS: National Standards for U.S. History
W = Carnevale: Workplace Basics
WH = NCHS: National Standards for World History

McREL

- Reframes problems when alternative solutions are exhausted

  BP (WE,182,202)

- Examines different options for solving problems of historical importance and determines why specific courses of action were taken

  BC (USI,33;WHE,34)

- Evaluates the feasibility of various solutions to problems; recommends and defends a solution

  BP (GE,55)

6. Applies decision-making techniques

(SSE,149)

Level I (Grades K-2)

- No materials specifically designated for this level

  BP (HI,27)

Level II (Grades 3-5)

- Studies decisions that were made in the community in terms of the alternatives that were considered

  BP (HI,27)

- Analyzes important decisions made by people in the past in terms of possible alternatives that were considered

  BP (HE,27)

Level III (Grades 6-8)

- Identifies situations in the community and in one's personal life in which a decision is required

  BP (SSE,149)

- Secures factual information needed to evaluate alternatives

  BP (SSE,149)

- Identifies the values underlying the alternatives that are considered and the criteria that will be used to make a selection among the alternatives

  BP (SSI,149)

- Predicts the consequences of selecting each alternative

  BP (SSI,148)

Codes (right side of page):　　　　BD = Benchmark, Declarative; BP = Benchmark, Procedural; BC = Benchmark, Contextual
1st letter of each code in parentheses　　　*2nd letter of code*　　　*Number*
2 = Project 2061: Benchmarks for Science Literacy　　　E = Explicitly stated in document　　　Page number of cited document
B = Bradley Commission on History　　　I = Implied in document
E = NCTE: Democracy Through Language
G =GESP: National Standards for Geography
H = NCHS: History for Grades K-4
M = NCTM: Curric. & Eval. Stan. for School Math.
N = NAEP: Mathematics Assessment Framework
SS = NCSS: Curriculum Standards for Social Studies
US = NCHS: National Standards for U.S. History
W = Carnevale: Workplace Basics
WH = NCHS: National Standards for World History

MREL

- Makes decisions based on the data obtained and the criteria identified BP (SSE,148)

- When appropriate, takes action to implement the decision BP (SSE,148)

- Makes effective decisions about consumer products based on important criteria, including external features, performance, durability, cost, and personal tradeoffs BP (2E,299)

- Analyzes personal decisions in terms of the options that were considered BP (USI,33;WHI,34)

- Uses a decision-making grid or matrix to make or study decisions involving a relatively limited number of alternatives and criteria BP (GI,51;SSI,149)

- Selects appropriate locations for specific service industries within the community BC (GE,52)

Level IV (Grades 9-12)

- Analyzes decisions that were major turning points in history and describes how things would have been different if other alternatives had been selected BP (USI,33;WHI,34)

- Analyzes current or pending decisions that can affect national or international policy and identifies the consequences of each alternative BP (USI,33;WHI,34)

- Uses a decision-making grid or matrix to make or study decisions involving a relatively large number of alternatives and criteria BP (GI,54;SSI,149)

- Uses a balance sheet to evaluate the costs and benefits of various alternatives within a decision BP (GE,55)

Codes (right side of page):   BD = Benchmark, Declarative;   BP = Benchmark, Procedural;   BC = Benchmark, Contextual

1st letter of each code in parentheses	*2nd letter of code*	*Number*
2 = Project 2061: Benchmarks for Science Literacy	E = Explicitly stated in document	Page number of cited document
B = Bradley Commission on History	I = Implied in document	
E = NCTE: Democracy Through Language		
G =GESP: National Standards for Geography		
H = NCHS: History for Grades K-4		
M = NCTM: Curric. & Eval. Stan. for School Math.		
N = NAEP: Mathematics Assessment Framework		
SS = NCSS: Curriculum Standards for Social Studies		
US = NCHS: National Standards for U.S. History		
W = Carnevale: Workplace Basics		
WH = NCHS: National Standards for World History		

McREL

Working with Others

1. Contributes to the overall effort of a group

(EI,3;WI,64;WE,307)

Level IV (K-12)

- Responsibly challenges practices in a group that are not working

  BP (SE,xvii)

- Demonstrates respect for others in the group

  BP (SI,xviii)

- Identifies and uses the strengths of others

  BP (WE,307)

- Takes initiative when needed

  BP (WE,307)

- Identifies and deals with causes of conflict in a group

  BP (WE,307)

- Helps the group establish goals

  BP (WE,397)

- Engages in active listening

  BP (WE,307-308)

- Takes the initiative in interacting with others

  BP (WE,307-308)

- Evaluates the overall progress of a group toward a goal

  BP (WE,329)

- Keeps requests simple

  BP (WE,231)

- Contributes to the development of a supportive climate in groups

  BP (SSE,149)

2. Uses conflict-resolution techniques

(WI,349)

Level IV (Grades K-12)

- Communicates ideas in a manner that does not irritate others

  BP (SE,xvii)

- Effectively resolves conflicts of interest

  BP (SE,xvii)

- Identifies goals and values important to opponents

  BD (WE,349)

- Understands the impact of criticism on psychological state, emotional state, habitual

  BD (WE,231)

Codes (right side of page):   BD = Benchmark, Declarative; BP = Benchmark, Procedural; BC = Benchmark, Contextual
1st letter of each code in parentheses   *2nd letter of code*   *Number*
E = NCTE: Democracy Through Lang.   E = Explicitly stated in document   Page number of cited document
S = SCANS: Report for America 2000   I = Implied in document
SS = NCSS: Curric. Standards for Social Studies
W = Carnevale: Workplace Basics   584   McREL

- Occasionally serves as a follower in groups

  BP (SSE,149)

- Enlists others in working toward a shared vision

  BP (WE,397)

- Plans small wins

  BP (WE,397)

- Celebrates accomplishments

  BP (WE,397)

- Recognizes the contributions of others

  BP (WE,397)

- Passes on authority when appropriate

  BP (WE,397)

Codes (right side of page):   BD = Benchmark, Declarative; BP = Benchmark, Procedural; BC = Benchmark, Contextual
1st letter of each code in parentheses   *2nd letter of code*   *Number*
E = NCTE: Democracy Through Lang.   E = Explicitly stated in document   Page number of cited document
S = SCANS: Report for America 2000   I = Implied in document
SS = NCSS: Curric. Standards for Social Studies
W = Carnevale: Workplace Basics   587   McREL

Self-Regulation

1. Sets and manages goals

(WE,284-285)

Level IV (Grades K-12)

- Sets explicit long-term goals

  BP (SI,xviii)

- Identifies and ranks relevant options in terms of accomplishing a goal

  BP (SE,xvii;WI,284-285)

- Prepares and follows a schedule for carrying out options

  BP (SE,xvii;WI,284-285)

- Understands personal wants versus needs

  BD (WE,231)

- Establishes personal milestones

  BP (WI,231)

- Identifies resources necessary to complete a goal

  BP (WI,231,241)

- Displays a sense of personal direction and purpose

  BP (WI,64)

- Maintains an awareness of proximity to goal

  BP (WI,241;WE,64)

- Makes a cumulative evaluation of goal

  BP (WE,182-184)

- Understands the differences between various types of goals

  BD (WE,241)

- Sets routine goals for improving daily life

  BP (WE,241)

- Identifies explicit criteria for evaluating goals

  BP (WE,241)

- Makes contingency plans

  BP (WE,284-285)

2. Performs self-appraisal

(WI,231;SE,xviii)

Level IV (Grades K-12)

- Distributes work according to perceived strengths

  BP (SE,xvii)

- Identifies personal styles

  BD (WI,64)

Codes (right side of page):   BD = Benchmark, Declarative; BP = Benchmark, Procedural; BC= Benchmark, Contextual
1st letter of each code in parentheses   *2nd letter of code*   *Number*
S = SCANS: Report for America 2000   E = Explicitly stated in document   Page number of cited document
W = Carnevale: Workplace Basics   I = Implied in document

- Identifies personal strengths and weaknesses   BD (WE,231)

- Utilizes techniques for overcoming weaknesses   BP (WE,231)

- Identifies basic values   BD (WE,231)

- Performs analysis of employability   BP (WE,284-285)

- Understands preferred working environments   BD (WE,284)

- Understands career goals   BD (WE,284)

- Identifies a compensating strength for each weakness   BP (WE,231)

- Develops an inventory of wants versus needs   BP (WI,231)

- Determines explicit behaviors that are used and should be adopted to obtain wants and/or needs   BD (WE,231)

- Identifies personal motivational patterns   BD (WE,284-285)

- Keeps a log documenting personal improvement   BP (WE,231)

- Summarizes personal educational background   BP (WE,284-285)

- Summarizes personal work experience   BP (WE,284-285)

- Identifies key accomplishments and successes in life   BD (WE,284-285)

- Identifies peak experiences and significant life experiences   BD (WE,284-285)

- Identifies desired future accomplishments   BD (WE,284-285)

- Identifies preferred lifestyle   BD (WE,284-285)

Codes (right side of page):   BD = Benchmark, Declarative; BP = Benchmark, Procedural; BC= Benchmark, Contextual

1st letter of each code in parentheses	*2nd letter of code*	*Number*
S = SCANS: Report for America 2000	E = Explicitly stated in document	Page number of cited document
W = Carnevale: Workplace Basics	I = Implied in document	

McREL

(SI,xviii;WI,90-91)

3.   Considers risks

Level IV (Grades K-12)

- Weighs risks in making decisions and solving problems BP (SI,xviii)

- Uses common knowledge to avoid hazard or injury BP (WE,90-91)

- Applies preventative measures prior to a task to minimize security or safety problems BP (WE,90-91)

- Selects an appropriate course of action in an emergency BP (WE,90-91)

- Identifies emergency and safety procedures before undertaking hazardous procedures BP (WE,281-283)

- Thinks clearly under stress BP (WE,349)

(SE,xviii;WE,202)

4.   Demonstrates perseverance

Level IV (Grades K-12)

- Demonstrates perseverance relative to personal goals BP (SE,xviii)

- Demonstrates a sense of purpose BP (WI,64)

- Maintains a high level of energy over a prolonged period of time when engaged in tasks BP (WE,202)

- Persists in the face of difficulty BP (WE,202)

- Concentrates mental and physical energies BP (WE,151-154)

(WE,231)

5.   Maintains a healthy self-concept

Level IV (Grades K-12)

- Has basic belief in ability to succeed BD (SI,xviii)

- Uses techniques to remind self of strengths BP (WE,231)

Codes (right side of page):   BD = Benchmark, Declarative; BP = Benchmark, Procedural; BC= Benchmark, Contextual
1st letter of each code in parentheses   *2nd letter of code*   *Number*
S = SCANS: Report for America 2000   E = Explicitly stated in document   Page number of cited document
W = Carnevale: Workplace Basics   I = Implied in document

McREL

- Uses techniques to offset the negative effects of mistakes   BP (WE,231)

- Avoids overreacting to criticism   BP (WE,231)

- Uses affirmations to improve sense of self   BP (WE,231)

- Analyzes self-statements for their positive and negative effects   BP (WE,231)

- Examines "shoulds" to determine their negative and positive effects   BP (WE,231)

- Revises "shoulds" to reflect the reality of personal needs   BP (WE,231)

- Understands that everyone makes mistakes   BD (WE,231)

- Understands that mistakes are a natural consequence of living and of limited resources   BD (WE,231)

- Takes criticism in a dispassionate manner   BP (WE,231)

- Analyzes criticisms to determine their accuracy and identifies useful lessons learned   BP (WE,231)

- Uses high self-esteem body language   BP (WE,231)

6.   Restrains impulsivity   (WI,202)

Level IV (Grades K-12)

- Keeps responses open as long as possible   BP (WE,202)

- Remains passive while assessing situation   BP (WE,151-154)

- Suspends judgment   BP (WE,202)

Codes (right side of page):   BD = Benchmark, Declarative; BP = Benchmark, Procedural; BC= Benchmark, Contextual
1st letter of each code in parentheses   *2nd letter of code*   *Number*
S = SCANS: Report for America 2000   E = Explicitly stated in document   Page number of cited document
W = Carnevale: Workplace Basics   I = Implied in document

McREL

Life Work

1. Makes effective use of basic tools

(2I,292)

Level I (Grades K-2)

- Uses hammers, screwdrivers, clamps, rulers, scissors, and hard lenses; operates ordinary audio equipment

  BP (2E,293)

- Assembles, describes, takes apart, and reassembles constructions using interlocking blocks, erector sets and the like

  BP (2E,293)

- Makes something out of paper, cardboard, wood, plastic, metal, or existing objects that can be used to perform a task

  BP (2E,293)

Level II (Grades 3-5)

- Chooses appropriate common materials for making simple mechanical constructions and controlling things

  BP (2E,293)

- Measures and mixes dry and liquid materials in prescribed amounts, exercising reasonable safety

  BP (2E,293)

Level III (Grades 6-8)

- Uses hand and power tools to shape, fasten, and unfasten such materials as wood, plastic, and soft metal, exercising reasonable safety

  BP (SI,xvii)

- Inspects, disassembles, and reassembles simple mechanical devices and describes the various parts

  BP (2E,294)

Level IV (Grades 9-12)

- Uses work space effectively

  BP (SE,xvii)

- Quickly learns the proper use of new instruments by following instructions in a manual or by taking instructions from an experienced user

  BP (2E,294)

- Uses power tools safely to shape, smooth, and join wood, plastic, and soft metal

  BP (2E,294)

Codes (right side of page): BD = Benchmark, Declarative; BP = Benchmark, Procedural; BC= Benchmark, Contextual
1st letter of each code in parentheses *2nd letter of code* *Number*
2 = Project 2061: Benchmarks for Science Literacy E = Explicitly stated in document Page number of cited document
H = CORD: Hazardous Materials Mgmt. Tech. I = Implied in document
S = SCANS: Report for America 2000
W = Carnevale: Workplace Basics

(HE,23)

2. Understands the characteristics and uses of basic computer hardware, software, and operating systems

Level IV (Grades K-12)

- Identifies common computer hardware (e.g., keyboard, monitor, mouse, CD-ROM, printer, various drives, casement housing the computer's electronics) BP (HE,23)

- Knows how to turn on a computer system (i.e., the computer, monitor, and printer) and how to reboot when necessary BP (HE,23)

- Knows various types of common data disks (e.g., 5.25" diskette, 3.5" diskette, hard diskette, CD-ROM), and the differences between them BD (HE,23)

- Knows basic characteristics and functions of an operating system (e.g., formatting diskettes; identifying a system prompt and basic dialog box, and recognizing the action required) BD (HE,23)

- Knows how to load various programs (e.g., word-processing programs, database programs, spreadsheet programs) BP (HE,23)

- Knows how to use menus, arrow keys, and/or a mouse to operate specified features of a program BP (HE,23)

- Knows how to manage various computer programs (e.g., load, copy, move, save, delete, print) BP (HE,23)

(HE,23)

3. Uses basic word processing, spreadsheet, database, and communication programs

Level IV (Grades K-12)

- Knows basic capabilities of a word-processing program BD (HE,23)

- Uses basic editing commands in a word-processing program (e.g., copying, moving, and deleting individual characters or blocks of data; using "search" and "replace" commands; using the "undo" command) BP (HE,23)

- Uses basic formatting techniques in a word-processing program (e.g., placing page breaks; using standard formatting guidelines for margins, tabs, and line spacing) BP (HE,23)

Codes (right side of page):   BD = Benchmark, Declarative; BP = Benchmark, Procedural; BC= Benchmark, Contextual
1st letter of each code in parentheses   *2nd letter of code*   *Number*
2 = Project 2061: Benchmarks for Science Literacy   E = Explicitly stated in document   Page number of cited document
H = CORD: Hazardous Materials Mgmt. Tech.   I = Implied in document
S = SCANS: Report for America 2000
W = Carnevale: Workplace Basics   593   MREL

- Knows how to use basic word processing tools (e.g., HELP screens, spell checker, thesaurus) BP (HE,23)

- Knows basic capabilities of spreadsheet and database programs BD (HE,24)

- Knows how to enter data into the appropriate rows and columns of a spreadsheet and/or into a database table BP (HE,24)

- Knows how to sum the data of a spreadsheet column or row BP (HE,24)

- Knows how to use simple formulas in spreadsheet cells to calculate desired values from data in other cells BP (HE,24)

- Knows how to use a spreadsheet program to make data displays (e.g., line chart, bar chart, circular or pie chart) BP (HE,24)

- Knows how to search for information in a (query) database table BP (HE,24)

- Knows how to set up and use a communications program (e.g., for the correct bit per second (bps) rate parity, databits and stop bit) to communicate with a computer at another location BP (HE,24)

- Knows how to connect to a dial-up, on-line service and search for programs or data and participate in discussion groups or forums BP (HE,24)

- Knows how to download file(s) from a remote computer to a local computer using a communications program BP (HE,24)

- Knows how to access available databases via the Internet BP (HE,24)

4. Manages money effectively (SI,xvii;WE,281)

Level IV (Grades 9-12)

- Prepares and follows a budget BP (SE,xvii;WE,281-283)

- Makes forecasts regarding future income and expenses BP (SE,xvii)

- Uses sound buying principles for purchasing goods and services BP (WE,281-283)

- Understands credit and uses it effectively BP (WE,281-283)

Codes (right side of page):   BD = Benchmark, Declarative; BP = Benchmark, Procedural; BC= Benchmark, Contextual
1st letter of each code in parentheses   *2nd letter of code*   *Number*
2 = Project 2061: Benchmarks for Science Literacy   E = Explicitly stated in document   Page number of cited document
H = CORD: Hazardous Materials Mgmt. Tech.   I = Implied in document
S = SCANS: Report for America 2000
W = Carnevale: Workplace Basics   594   McREL

(WI,281)

5. Pursues specific jobs

Level IV (Grades 9-12)

- Determines key contacts within a prospective employer's organization

  BP (WE,281)

- Determines specific procedures for applying for a specific job

  BP (WE,281)

- Identifies important benefits and procedures of prospective employers (salary, deductions, vacation)

  BD (WE,281)

- Identifies a prospective employer's products and services

  BD (WE,281-283)

- Identifies the procedures involved in applying for a job at a company's personnel office

  BD (WE,281-283)

- Accurately fills out a job application

  BP (WE,281-283)

- Prepares letters of inquiry or application

  BP (WE,281-283)

- Identifies and engages in necessary steps to prepare for a job interview

  BP (WE,281-283)

(WI,281)

6. Makes general preparation for entering the work force

Level IV (Grades 9-12)

- Understands basic market trends

  BD (WE,281)

- Determines the types of preparation and training needed for entry-level jobs

  BP (WE,281)

- Understands occupational apprenticeships and other training opportunities

  BD (WE,281)

- Understands available educational opportunities (e.g., college, junior college)

  BD (WE,281)

- Understands availability of child care

  BD (WE,281)

- Understands significant life decisions and their effect on the present

  BD (WE,284)

- Analyzes a current job and its future possibilities

  BP (WE,284)

Codes (right side of page):   BD = Benchmark, Declarative; BP = Benchmark, Procedural; BC= Benchmark, Contextual
1st letter of each code in parentheses   *2nd letter of code*   *Number*
2 = Project 2061: Benchmarks for Science Literacy   E = Explicitly stated in document   Page number of cited document
H = CORD: Hazardous Materials Mgmt. Tech.   I = Implied in document
S = SCANS: Report for America 2000
W = Carnevale: Workplace Basics

MREL

- Develops an employment profile $^{BP\,(WE,284)}$

- Uses multiple resources to obtain information about prospective jobs (e.g., classified, word of mouth, free services provided by state) $^{BP\,(WE,281)}$

- Determines how private employment agencies operate on a fee basis to help people find jobs $^{BP\,(WE,281-283)}$

- Prepares for common types of employment tests $^{BP\,(WE,281-283)}$

- Applies for a social security card, work permit, license $^{BP\,(WE,281-283)}$

- Prepares a resume summarizing experience, education, and job training $^{BP\,(WE,281-283)}$

- Establishes an explicit career action plan $^{BP\,(WE,284-285)}$

- Makes an accurate appraisal of prior work experience, career goals, personal character, job references, and personal aptitudes $^{BP\,(WE,281-283)}$

- Understands the nature and function of worker's compensation and unemployment insurance $^{BD\,(WE,281-283)}$

- Evaluates the chances of getting a job now and in the future in fields of work that are of interest $^{BP\,(WE,281-283)}$

- Makes an accurate appraisal of available work options $^{BP\,(WE,284-285)}$

- Makes an accurate appraisal of basic insurance needs $^{BP\,(WE,281-283)}$

7. Makes effective use of basic life skills $\qquad$ (WE,281)

Level IV (Grades 9-12)

- Uses a telephone effectively $^{BP\,(WE,281)}$

- Uses public transportation effectively $^{BP\,(WE,281)}$

- Understands the rules and regulations of the Internal Revenue Service $^{BD\,(WE,281)}$

- Understands the availability of health care and child care services $^{BD\,(WE,281)}$

Codes (right side of page):   BD = Benchmark, Declarative; BP = Benchmark, Procedural; BC= Benchmark, Contextual
1st letter of each code in parentheses   *2nd letter of code*   *Number*
2 = Project 2061: Benchmarks for Science Literacy   E = Explicitly stated in document   Page number of cited document
H = CORD: Hazardous Materials Mgmt. Tech.   I = Implied in document
S = SCANS: Report for America 2000
W = Carnevale: Workplace Basics   596   McREL

- Understands the basic nature of contracts

  BD (WE,281)

- Understands the basic process of renting an apartment

  BD (WE,281)

- Understands basic banking services (e.g., checking accounts, savings accounts)

  BD (WE,281)

- Understands the basic process of buying and maintaining a car

  BD (WE,281-283)

8. Displays reliability and a basic work ethic

(WI,281)

Level IV (Grades 9-12)

- Completes tasks on time

  BP (WE,281)

- Chooses ethical courses of action

  BP (SI,xviii)

- Establishes an acceptable attendance record

  BP (WE,281)

- Uses appropriate language in work situations

  BP (WE,281)

- Maintains a sense of congeniality at work

  BP (WE,281)

- Maintains an effective work station

  BP (WE,281)

- Is attentive to requests and preferences of supervisors

  BP (WE,281)

- Requests clarification when needed

  BP (WE,281)

- Accurately identifies important goals and priorities of employer

  BP (WE,375)

- Practices appropriate hygiene and dress at work

  BP (WE,281-283)

- Carries out assigned tasks

  BP (WE,281-283)

- Does not bring personal problems into work

  BP (WE,281-283)

- Prepares, plans, and organizes job responsibilities

  BP (WE,281-283)

- Recognizes and respects authority

  BP (WE,281-283)

Codes (right side of page): BD = Benchmark, Declarative; BP = Benchmark, Procedural; BC= Benchmark, Contextual
1st letter of each code in parentheses *2nd letter of code* *Number*
2 = Project 2061: Benchmarks for Science Literacy E = Explicitly stated in document Page number of cited document
H = CORD: Hazardous Materials Mgmt. Tech. I = Implied in document
S = SCANS: Report for America 2000
W = Carnevale: Workplace Basics

McREL

- Accepts guidance and constructive criticism

  BP (WE,281-283)

- Demonstrates loyalty to the organization

  BP (WE,281-283)

(WE,375)

9. Operates effectively within organizations

Level IV (Grades 9-12)

- Understands the organization's basic goals and values

  BD (WE,375)

- Understands the extent to which organizational values are compatible with personal values

  BD (WE,375)

- Develops an action plan that identifies how personal skills can be used to increase organizational effectiveness

  BP (WE,375)

- Develops and carries out strategies to make personal skills and abilities more visible to an organization

  BP (WE,375)

Codes (right side of page):   BD = Benchmark, Declarative;   BP = Benchmark, Procedural;   BC= Benchmark, Contextual
1st letter of each code in parentheses   *2nd letter of code*   *Number*
2 = Project 2061: Benchmarks for Science Literacy   E = Explicitly stated in document   Page number of cited document
H = CORD: Hazardous Materials Mgmt. Tech.   I = Implied in document
S = SCANS: Report for America 2000
W = Carnevale: Workplace Basics   598   MREL

Bibliography

Aldridge, B. G. (Ed). (1995). *Scope, sequence, and coordination of secondary school science: Vol. 3. A high school framework for national science education standards*. Arlington, VA: National Science Teachers Association.

Aldridge, B. G., & Strassenburg, A. A. (Eds.). (1995). *Scope, sequence, and coordination of national science education content standards: An addendum to the content core based on the 1994 draft national science education standards*. Arlington, VA: National Science Teachers Association.

American Council on the Teaching of Foreign Languages. (1995, April). *Standards for foreign language learning: Preparing for the 21st century*. (Draft). Yonkers, NY: Author.

American Federation of Teachers. (1985, September). Critical thinking: It's a basic. *American Teacher*, p. 21.

Assessment Standards Working Groups. (1993). *Assessment standards for school mathematics*. (Working draft). Reston, VA: National Council of Teachers of Mathematics.

Australian Education Council. (1994). *English: A curriculum profile for Australian schools*. Commonwealth of Australia: Curriculum Corporation.

Bradley Commission on History in the Schools. (1988). *Building a history curriculum: Guidelines for teaching history in the schools*. Washington, DC: Educational Excellence Network.

California Department of Education. (1989). *Recommended literature, grades nine through twelve*. Sacramento, CA: Author.

California Department of Education. (1989). *Visual and performing arts framework for California public schools: Kindergarten through grade twelve*. Sacramento, CA: Author.

California Department of Education. (1990). *Recommended readings in literature, kindergarten through grade eight*. Sacramento, CA: Author.

California Department of Education. (1990). *Science framework for California public schools: Kindergarten through grade 12*. Sacramento, CA: Author.

California Department of Education. (1991). *Model curriculum standards: Grades nine through twelve*. Sacramento, CA: Author.

California Department of Education (1993). *The writing assessment handbook: High School*. Sacramento, CA Author.

California Department of Education. (1994a). *Health framework for California public schools: Kindergarten through grade twelve*. Sacramento, CA: Author.

California Department of Education. (1994b). *1994 elementary performance assessments: Integrated English-language arts illustrative material, grade 4*. Sacramento, CA: Author.

California Department of Education. (1994c). *1994 middle grades performance assessments: Integrated English-language arts illustrative material, grade 8*. Sacramento, CA: Author.

Carnevale, A. P., Gainer, L. J., & Meltzer, A. S. (1990). *Workplace basics: The essential skills employers want*. San Francisco: Jossey-Bass.

Center for Civic Education. (1994). *National standards for civics and government*. Calabasas, CA: Author.

Center for Occupational Research and Development. (1995). *National voluntary skills standard: Hazardous materials management technology*. Waco, TX: Author.

College Board. (1983). *Academic preparation for college: What students need to know and be able to do*. New York: College Entrance Examination Board.

Colorado Council on Economic Education. (1994). *Economics: Conceptual content standards, grades K-12*. (Draft). Denver: Colorado Council on Economic Education.

Colorado Department of Education. (1995, August). *Content standards for foreign language*. (Draft). Denver, CO: Author

Committee on the Junior High and Middle School Booklist of the National Council of Teachers of English & Nilsen, A.P. (Ed.). (1991). *Your reading: A booklist for junior high and middle school students* (8th ed.). Urbana, IL: National Council of Teachers of English.

Committee on the Senior High School Booklist of the National Council of Teachers of English & Wurth, S. (Ed.). (1992). *Books for you: A booklist for senior high students* (11th ed.). Urbana, IL: National Council of Teachers of English.

Consortium of National Arts Education Associations. (1994). *National standards for arts education: What every young American should know and be able to do in the arts*. Reston, VA: Music Educators National Conference.

Council for Basic Education. (1995, October 11). Review panels find history standards worth revising. News release submitted for publication.

Crabtree, C., Nash, G. B., Gagnon, P., & Waugh, S. (Eds.). (1992). *Lessons from history: Essential understandings and historical perspectives students should acquire*. Los Angeles: National Center for History in the Schools.

Cross, C. (1993, April 21). Education standards: A question of time? *Education Week*, p. 30.

Dewey, J. (1916). *Democracy and education*. New York: Macmillan.

Draft standards tackle slippery subject: English (1995, October 25). *Education Daily*, pp. 1,3.

Economics group begins minting national standards. (1995, October 25). *Report on Education Research, 27*, 8.

Edison Project. (1994a). *Student standards for the elementary academy*. New York: Author.

Edison Project. (1994b). *Student standards for the junior academy*. New York: Author.

Edison Project. (1994c). *Student standards for the primary academy*. New York: Author.

Educational Policies Commission. (1961). *The central purpose of American education*. Washington, DC: National Education Association.

Futrell, M. H. (1987, December 9). A message long overdue. *Education Week*, p. 9.

Gagnon, P., & Bradley Commission on History in the Schools (Eds.). (1989). *Historical literacy: The case for history in American education*. Boston: Houghton Mifflin Company.

Geographic Education National Implementations Project. (1987). *K-6 geography: Themes, key ideas, and learning opportunities*. Washington, DC: Author.

Geography Education Standards Project. (1994). *Geography for life: National geography standards*. Washington, DC: National Geographic Research and Exploration.

Gillespie, John T. (Ed.) (1991a). *Best books for junior high readers*. New Providence, NJ: Bowker.

Gillespie, John T. (Ed.) (1991b). *Best books for senior high readers*. New Providence, NJ:Bowker.

Gilliard, J. V., Caldwell, J., Dalgaard, B. R., Highsmith, R. J., Reinke, R., & Watts, M. (with Leet, D. R., Malone, M. G., & Ellington, L.). (1989). *Economics, what and when: Scope and sequence guidelines, K-12.* New York: Joint Council on Economic Education.

Glaser, R. (1984). Education and thinking: The role of knowledge. *American Psychologist, 39,* 93-104.

Hazen, R. M., & Trefil, J. (1991). *Science matters: Achieving scientific literacy.* New York: Doubleday.

Hirsch, E. D., Jr. (1987). *Cultural literacy: What every American needs to know.* Boston: Houghton Mifflin Company.

Hirsch, E.D., Jr. (Ed.). (1993a). *What your 1st grader needs to know: Fundamentals of a good first-grade education. The core knowledge series: Resource books for grades one through six, book I.* New York: Delta.

Hirsch, E.D., Jr. (Ed.). (1993b). *What your 2nd grader needs to know: Fundamentals of a good second-grade education. The core knowledge series: Resource books for grades one through six, book II.* New York: Delta.

Hirsch, E.D., Jr. (Ed.). (1993c). *What your 3rd grader needs to know: Fundamentals of a good third-grade education. The core knowledge series: Resource books for grades one through six, book III.* New York: Delta.

Hirsch, E.D., Jr. (Ed.). (1993d). *What your 4th grader needs to know: Fundamentals of a good fourth-grade education. The core knowledge series: Resource books for grades one through six, book IV.* New York: Delta.

Hirsch, E.D., Jr. (Ed.). (1993e). *What your 5th grader needs to know: Fundamentals of a good fifth-grade education. The core knowledge series: Resource books for grades one through six, book V.* New York: Delta.

Hirsch, E.D., Jr. (Ed.). (1993f). What your 6th grader needs to know: Fundamentals of a good sixth-grade education. *The core knowledge series: Resource books for grades one through six, book VI.* New York: Delta.

History standards project opens door to revisions. (1995, January 17). *Education Daily, 28,* 1-2.

Joint Committee on Geographic Education. (1984). *Guidelines for geographic education: Elementary and secondary schools.* Washington, DC: Association of American Geographers.

Joint Committee on Health Education Terminology. (1991). Report of the 1990 Joint Committee on Health Education Terminology. *Journal of Health Education, 22,* (2), 97-107.

Joint Committee on National Health Education Standards. (1995). *National health education standards: Achieving health literacy.* Reston, VA: Association for the Advancement of Health Education.

Kendall, J. S., & Marzano, R. J. (1994). *The systematic identification and articulation of content standards and benchmarks: Update, January 1994.* Aurora, CO: Mid-continent Regional Education Laboratory.

Kendall, J. S., & Marzano, R. J. (1995). *The systematic identification and articulation of content standards and benchmarks: Update, March 1995.* Aurora, CO: Mid-continent Regional Education Laboratory.

Law in a Free Society. (1977). *Authority I (elementary): a civic education unit* (Teacher's ed.). Calabasas, CA: Author.

Law in a Free Society. (1977). *Privacy I (elementary): a civic education unit* (Teacher's ed.). Calabasas, CA: Author.

Law in a Free Society. (1977). *Privacy II (elementary): a civic education unit* (Teacher's ed.). Calabasas, CA: Author.

Law in a Free Society. (1979). *Justice I (elementary): a civic education unit* (Teacher's ed.). Calabasas, CA: Author.

Law in a Free Society. (1983). *Responsibility I (elementary): a civic educaton unit* (Teacher's ed.). Calabasas, CA: Author.

Levine, D.V., & Associates. (1985). *Improving student achievement through mastery learning programs*. San Francisco: Jossey-Bass.

Mager, Robert F. (1962). *Preparing instructional objectives*. Palo Alto, CA: Fearon Publishers.

Marzano, R. J., & Kendall, J. S. (1993). *The systematic identification and articulation of content standards and benchmarks: An illustration using mathematics*. Aurora, CO: Mid-continent Regional Education Laboratory.

Michigan Department of Education. (1995, September). *Physical Education: Working draft content standards and benchmarks*. (Draft). Lansing: Author.

Michigan State Board of Education. (1988). *Michigan essential goals and objectives for health education*. Lansing, MI: Author.

Music Educators National Conference. (1986). *The school music program: Description and standards*. Reston, VA: Author.

National Assessment of Educational Progress. (1989). *Science objectives: 1990 assessment*. Princeton, NJ: Educational Testing Service.

National Assessment of Educational Progress. (1992). *Description of writing achievement levels-setting process and proposed achievement level definitions*. Iowa City, IA: American College Testing Program.

National Assessment of Educational Progress. (n.d.). *Framework for the 1994 National Assessment of Educational Progress U.S. history assessment*. Washington, DC: Author.

National Assessment of Educational Progress. (1992). *Item specifications: 1994 national assessment of educational progress in geography*. Washington, DC: National Assessment Governing Board.

National Assessment of Educational Progress. (March 26, 1992). *Content specifications for the 1994 National Assessment of Educational Progress mathematics assessment*. Washington, DC: Author.

National Assessment of Educational Progress. (March 31, 1992). *Framework for the 1994 National Assessment of Educational Progress mathematics assessment*. Washington, DC: Author.

National Assessment of Educational Progress. (1992). *Provisional item specifications: 1994 national assessment of educational progress in U.S. history*. Washington, DC: National Assessment Governing Board.

National Assessment of Educational Progress Arts Education Consensus Project. (1994). *Arts education assessment framework*. Washington, DC: National Assessment Governing Board.

National Assessment of Educational Progress in U.S. History. (1994). *Provisional item specifications*. Washington, DC: Council of Chief State School Officers.

National Assessment of Educational Progress Geography Consensus Project. (1992). *Geography assessment framework for the 1994 National Assessment of Educational Progress.* (Draft). Washington, DC: National Assessment Governing Board.

National Assessment of Educational Progress Reading Consensus Project. (1990). *Assessment and exercise specifications: 1992 NAEP reading assessment.* Washington, DC: National Assessment Governing Board.

National Assessment of Educational Progress Reading Consensus Project. (1990). *Reading assessment framework for the 1992 National Assessment of Educational Progress.* Washington, DC: National Assessment Governing Board.

National Assessment of Educational Progress Science Consensus Project. (1993). *Science assessment and exercise specifications for the 1994 National Assessment of Educational Progress.* Washington, DC: National Assessment Governing Board.

National Association for Sport and Physical Education. (1995). *Moving into the future, national standards for physical education: A guide to content and assessment.* St. Louis: Mosby.

National Association for Sport and Physical Education. (1992). *Outcomes of quality physical education programs.* Reston, VA: Author.

National Center for History in the Schools. (1994). *National standards for history for Grades K-4: Expanding children's world in time and space.* Los Angeles: Author.

National Center for History in the Schools. (1994). *National standards for United States history: Exploring the American experience.* Los Angeles: Author.

National Center for History in the Schools. (1994). *National standards for world history: Exploring paths to the present.* Los Angeles: Author.

National Commission on Excellence in Education. (1983). *A nation at risk: The imperative for educational reform.* Washington, DC: Government Printing Office.

National Committee on Science Education Standards and Assessment. (1994, November). *National science education standards.* (Draft). Washington, DC: National Academy Press.

National Council for the Social Studies. (1994). *Expectations of excellence: Curriculum standards for social studies.* Washington, DC: Author.

National Council of Teachers of English. (1982). *Essentials of English: A document for reflection and dialogue.* Urbana, IL: Author.

National Council of Teachers of English. (1989). *The English coalition conference: Democracy through language.* Urbana, IL: Author.

National Council of Teachers of English and the International Reading Association (October, 1995). *Standards for the English Language Arts.* (Draft). Urbana, IL: National Council of Teachers of English.

National Council of Teachers of Mathematics. (1989). *Curriculum and evaluation standards for school mathematics.* Reston, VA: Author.

National Council on Education Standards and Testing. (1992). *Raising standards for American education: A report to Congress, the Secretary of Education, the National Education Goals Panel, and the American people.* Washington, DC: Government Printing Office.

National Education Standards and Improvement Council. (1993). *Promises to keep: Creating high standards for American students. Report on the review of educational standards from the Goals 3 and 4 Technical Planning Group to the National Education Goals Panel*. Washington, DC: National Goals Panel.

National History Standards Project. (1992, November). *Progress report and sample standards*. Los Angeles: National Center for History in the Schools.

National History Standards Project. (1993, March). *Progress report and sample standards*. Los Angeles: National Center for History in the Schools.

National Science Board Commission on Precollege Education in Mathematics, Science and Technology. (1983). *Educating Americans for the 21st century*. Washington, DC: National Science Board Commission.

National Science Teachers Association. (1993). *Scope, sequence, and coordination of secondary school science. Vol. 1. The content core: A guide for curriculum designers*. Washington, DC: Author.

NCTE/IRA say standards effort will continue. (1994, June). *The Council Chronicle, 3*, 1,4.

New Standards. (June, 1995). *Draft performance standards for English language arts*. Washington, DC: Author.

New Standards. (June, 1995). *Draft performance standards for mathematics*. Washington, DC: Author.

New York State Education Department. (1994) *Curriculum, instruction, and assessment: Preliminary draft framework for English language arts*. Albany: Author.

Pearsall, M. K. (Ed). (1993). *Scope, sequence, and coordination of secondary school science. Vol. 1. The content core: A guide for curriculum designers*. Washington, DC: National Science Teachers Association..

Project 2061, American Association for the Advancement of Science. (1992). *Science for all Americans*. Washington, DC:Author.

Project 2061, American Association for the Advancement of Science. (1993). *Benchmarks for science literacy*. New York: Oxford University Press.

Quigley, C. N., & Bahmmeller, C. F. (Eds.). (1991). *Civitas: A framework for civic education*. (National council for social studies, bulletin no. 86). Calabasas, CA: Center for Civic Education.

Ravitch, D. (1992, January 27). National Educational Standards. *Roll call: Education policy briefing*. pp. 24-25.

Ravitch, D. and Finn, C. E., Jr. (1987). *What do our 17-year-olds know?* New York: Harper & Row.

Resnick, L. B. (1987). *Education and learning to think*. Washington, DC: National Academy Press.

Saunders, P., & Gilliard, J. (Eds.). (1995). *A framework for teaching basic economic concepts with scope and sequence guidelines, K-12*. New York: National Council on Economic Education.

Secretary's Commission on Achieving Necessary Skills. (1991). *What work requires of schools: A SCANS report for America 2000*. Washington, DC: U.S. Department of Labor.

Shanker, A. (1992, June 17). Coming to terms on world-class standards. *Education Week: Special Report*. p. S11.

Shavelson, R., Baxter, G., & Pine, J. (1992). Performance assessment: Political rhetoric and measurement reality. *Educational Researcher, 21*, (4), 22-27.

Shepard, L. (1993). *Setting performance standards for student achievement: A report of the National Academy of Education Panel on the evaluation of the NAEP trial state assessment: An evaluation of the 1992 achievement levels.* Stanford, CA: The National Academy of Education, Stanford University.

Spady, W. G. (1988). Organizing for results: The basis of authentic restructuring and reform. *Education Leadership, 46,* (2), 4-8.

Standards Project for English Language Arts. (1994, February). *Incomplete work of the task forces of the standards project for English language arts.* (Draft). Urbana, IL: National Council of Teachers of English.

Stotsky, S., Anderson, P., & Beierl, D. (1989). *Variety and individualism in the English class: Teacher-recommended lists of reading for grades 7 - 12.* Boston, MA: New England Association of Teachers of English.

Tucker, M. (1992, June 17). A new social compact for mastery in education. *Education Week: Special Report.* p. S3.

Viadero, D. (1993, June 16). Standards deviation: Benchmark-setting is marked by diversity. *Education Week,* pp. 1, 14-17.

Yoon, B., Burstein, L., & Gold, K. (n.d.). *Assessing the content validity of teacher's reports of content coverage and its relationship to student achievement.* (CSE Report No. 328). Los Angeles: Center for Research on Evaluation, Standards and Student Testing, University of California, Los Angeles.

Wiggins, G. (1989). Teaching to the (authentic) test. *Educational Leadership, 46,* (7), 41-47.

Wiggins, G. (1993, November). Assessment: authenticity, context, and validity. *Phi Delta Kappan,* 200-214.

Appendix

For more information on national standards in specific fields of study, contact the following professional organizations:

THE ARTS
Music Educators National Conference
1902 Association Drive
Reston, VA 22091
703-860-4000

CIVICS AND GOVERNMENT
The Center for Civic Education
5146 Douglas Fir Road
Calabasas, CA 91203
818-591-9321

ECONOMICS
The National Council on Economic
  Education
1140 Avenue of the Americas
New York, NY 10036
212-730-7007

FOREIGN LANGUAGE
American Council on the Teaching of
  Foreign Languages
Six Executive Plaza
Yonkers, NY 10801-6801
914-963-8830

GEOGRAPHY
National Council for Geographic Education
1600 M Street, NW
Suite 2500
Washington, DC 20036
202-775-7832

GLOBAL EDUCATION
The American Forum
120 Wall Street
Suite 2600
New York, NY 10005
212-742-8232

HEALTH EDUCATION
Association for the Advancement of Health
  Education
1900 Association Drive
Reston, VA 22091
703-476-3437

HISTORY
National Center for History in the Schools
UCLA, 231 Noore Hall
Los Angeles, CA 90024
310-825-4702

LANGUAGE ARTS
National Standards for the English Language
  Arts Project
The International Reading Association
  Division of Research
800 Barksdale Road
P.O. Box 8139
Newark, DE 19714-8139
302-731-1600, ext. 226

MATHEMATICS
National Council of Teachers of Mathematics
1906 Association Drive
Reston, VA 22091
703-620-9840

PHYSICAL EDUCATION
National Association for Sport and Physical
  Education
1900 Association Drive
Reston, VA 22091
703-476-3410

SCIENCE
National Science Education Standards
2101 Constitution Ave., NW
HA 486
Washington, DC 20418
202-334-1399

SOCIAL STUDIES
National Council for the Social Studies
3501 Newark St., NW
Washington, DC 20016
202-966-7840

VOCATIONAL EDUCATION
National Center for Research in Vocational
  Education
University of California, Berkeley
2150 Shattuck Avenue, Suite 1250
Berkeley, CA 94704
510-642-4004